WITHDRAWN

Biblical Theological
Seminary Library
P.O. BOX 9 (200 N. MAIN)
HATFIELD, PA 19440

35068

Biblical Theological
Seminary Library
P.O. BOX 9 (200 N. MAIN)
HATFIELD, PA 19440

The
International Critical Commentary
on the Holy Scriptures of the Old and New Testaments.

UNDER THE EDITORSHIP OF

THE REV. SAMUEL ROLLES DRIVER, D.D.,
Regius Professor of Hebrew, Oxford;

THE REV. ALFRED PLUMMER, M.A., D.D.,
Master of University College, Durham;

AND

THE REV. CHARLES AUGUSTUS BRIGGS, D.D.,
*Edward Robinson Professor of Biblical Theology,
Union Theological Seminary, New York.*

Biblical Theological
Seminary Library
P.O. BOX 9 (200 N. MAIN)
HATFIELD, PA 19440

THE INTERNATIONAL CRITICAL COMMENTARY

A

CRITICAL AND EXEGETICAL
COMMENTARY

ON

THE BOOK OF ESTHER

BY

LEWIS BAYLES PATON, Ph.D., D.D.
PROFESSOR OF OLD TESTAMENT EXEGESIS AND CRITICISM
HARTFORD THEOLOGICAL SEMINARY, HARTFORD, CONN.

Biblical Theological
Seminary Library
P. O. BOX 9 (200 N. MAIN)
HATFIELD, PA 19440

EDINBURGH: T. & T. CLARK, 38 GEORGE STREET

35068

PRINTED IN SCOTLAND BY
MORRISON AND GIBB LIMITED
EDINBURGH AND LONDON
FOR
T. & T. CLARK LTD., EDINBURGH

0 567 05009 2

FIRST PRINTED . . . 1908
LATEST IMPRESSION . . 1976

All Rights Reserved. No part of this publication may be reproduced, stored in a retrieval system, or transmitted, in any form or by any means, electronic, mechanical, photocopying, recording or otherwise, without the prior permission of T. & T. Clark Ltd.

PREFACE

THE Book of Esther presents no complicated problems of documentary analysis, such as are found in most of the other historical books of the Old Testament. With the possible exception of the concluding verses in 9^{20}–10^3, its unity is recognized by all schools of criticism. It also presents no difficult problems of dating, such as are found in the prophetical books. There is general agreement that it belongs to the Greek period, and probably to the latter part of that period. Questions of composition and age, accordingly, can be dismissed in this case far more rapidly than in other commentaries of the series. On the other hand, the text of the book raises a number of problems that have no parallels in the criticism of the rest of the Old Testament. Beginning with the Greek translation, and continuing through the Old Latin, Vulgate, Josephus, and Peshitto down to the Talmud and Targums, the versions of Esther disclose a number of remarkable additions to the Massoretic text that have no analogies in the versions of other books. These are found in full in none of the commentaries and are not easily accessible to the student, yet they are important both for the history of the text and for the history of exegesis.

This being the case, it is proper that a critical commentary should present these variations completely, and should discuss their textual and exegetical value. In preparing my apparatus, I soon discovered that ordinary methods of recording readings were inadequate on account of the extraordinary number of the variants. After a number of experiments I found that the only practical way was to have a separate large card for every word in the Massoretic text, and on this to record the alternate readings of the versions and recensions. The numerous additions could then be inserted on other cards whenever they interrupted the

Massoretic text. By this method I have secured, I believe, both completeness and accuracy. I have taken the *textus receptus* of Van der Hooght (1705) as the standard of comparison, and all departures from it in recensions, MSS., printed editions, or ancient versions I have recorded in the critical notes. Only minor variations of vocalization or accentuation, which do not affect the interpretation, and which for the most part represent only the notions of particular punctuators or schools of punctuators, I have not thought it worth while to insert. Variants in the versions which represent the same Hebrew word I have not included. To have recorded all the cases of this sort would have been useless and would have swelled the volume to an enormous size.

How to treat the insertions of the versions has been a puzzling question. Substitutions of other readings for those of the Massoretic text should obviously be given in the original Greek, Latin, or Aramaic, in order that students may judge of their textual value; but the long additions of the versions are not translations from Hebrew, and, therefore, no good reason appears why they should be inserted in the original languages. For the ordinary reader a translation is more serviceable, and the specialist will have no difficulty in referring to the originals whenever this is necessary. Accordingly, I have given all the additions in English, making in each case a new translation from the best critical editions. Any one who is curious to see the originals and the textual variants in the Greek will find them in my article, "A Text-Critical Apparatus to the Book of Esther," in *Old Testament and Semitic Studies in Memory of W. R. Harper* (1908), ii. pp. 1-52. In the revision of this article I had the valuable help of Professor G. F. Moore of Harvard University, one of the editors of the Memorial Volume, and his suggestions in connection with this preliminary piece of work have been no small help in the preparation of the commentary. Many of the additions of the Midrashim are similar in character to those of the Targumim, and it would have been interesting to have included them also in this volume; but, with the limits of space imposed upon me, this was impossible. I hope presently to publish them in a volume entitled "The Story of Esther in the Bible and in Later Tradition."

Where to place the additions of the versions in the commentary has also been a problem. As textual amplifications, they seem to belong with the other textual apparatus in the critical notes. As secondary elements that interrupt the progress of the Hebrew text, they might conveniently be relegated to footnotes or appendixes; and, by using small type, much space might be saved for other matters. Practically, however, these additions are commentaries on the Hebrew text, and are interesting and valuable only as they are read in the same connection in which they were placed by the ancient versions. Accordingly, I have decided to insert them in square brackets in my translation of the Hebrew text at the same points where they are inserted in the originals. Thus they can be read in the way in which they were meant to be read by their authors. Let no one suppose that the matter in brackets is regarded as an integral part of the text. It is only the earliest extant commentary that I have interwoven with the text in the same manner as my own annotations. The Hebrew original is discriminated from the amplifications by the fact that its translation is given in italics. Ordinarily I have inserted the additions without note or comment, since a commentary on them would have carried the volume beyond the prescribed limits; but whenever the versions seem to preserve a reading that has been lost by the Hebrew, I have called attention to this fact.

In spite of the smallness of the Book of Esther its bibliography is exceedingly copious. Its quasi-legal character gave it a large place in the discussions of the doctors of the Talmud. It has two Targums and at least eight Midrashes, and all of these have been made the basis of numerous super-commentaries and discussions. More Jewish commentaries have been written upon it than upon any other book except the Law, and these in their turn have been explained by later scholars. The problem of its canonicity attracted much attention in the early Christian centuries, and the additions of the Greek text brought it into the discussion of the canonicity of the Apocrypha. In modern times its historical difficulties have called forth a host of treatises attacking or defending its credibility, and within the last few years the "Panbabylonisten" have deluged us with literature endeavouring to prove the Baby-

*

lonian origin of Purim. My bibliography contains upward of 700 titles of books and articles on Esther. The more important half of these I have found in the admirable library of Hartford Theological Seminary, and my hearty thanks are due to Dr. Charles S. Thayer, the librarian, and to Mr. M. H. Ananikian, the assistant librarian, for the great help that they have given me in hunting out these books and in putting them at my disposal for long periods of time. The remaining works, with the exception of about fifty, I have found in the libraries of Harvard, Yale, and Princeton Universities, and of Harvard, Princeton, Union, and the New York Jewish Theological Seminaries. The rich collection of the Jewish Theological Seminary in particular contains almost no gaps in the series of Jewish commentaries. To the librarians of all these institutions I wish to express my gratitude for the assistance they have given me and for the books they have so willingly put at my disposal. As a result of my search I have reached the conclusion that, with the exception of MSS., all the books that a student of the Old Testament needs can now be found in American libraries quite as well as in those of Europe, and that the conditions attached to their use are much less strict on this side of the Atlantic than on the other. In subsequent references it will be understood that I have had personal access to the literature mentioned except in cases where I indicate the contrary.

LEWIS BAYLES PATON.

HARTFORD THEOLOGICAL SEMINARY.

CONTENTS

	PAGE
ABBREVIATIONS	xi
INTRODUCTION TO THE BOOK OF ESTHER	1

I. PLACE OF ESTHER IN THE OLD TESTAMENT

§ 1. PLACE IN THE HEBREW BIBLE	1
§ 2. PLACE IN THE GREEK VERSION	3

II. THE TEXT OF ESTHER

a. DESCENDANTS OF THE TIBERIAN MASSORETIC TEXT

§ 3. MSS. WITH TIBERIAN VOCALIZATION	5
§ 4. THE PRINTED EDITIONS	10
§ 5. THE MASSORA	12
§ 6. CITATIONS IN JEWISH COMMENTARIES	13

b. OTHER DESCENDANTS OF THE TEXT OF THE SOPHERIM

§ 7. MSS. WITH BABYLONIAN VOCALIZATION	14
§ 8. THE SYRIAC PESHIṬṬO	16
§ 9. THE FIRST TARGUM	18
§ 10. THE SECOND TARGUM	21
§ 11. THE LATIN VERSION OF JEROME	24
§ 12. CITATIONS IN THE TALMUD	28

c. OTHER DESCENDANTS OF THE ORIGINAL TEXT

§ 13. THE GREEK VERSION	29
§ 14. THE UNREVISED GREEK TEXT	31
§ 15. THE RECENSION OF ORIGEN	34
§ 16. THE RECENSION OF HESYCHIUS	36
§ 17. THE RECENSION OF LUCIAN	37
§ 18. JOSEPHUS	39
§ 19. THE OLD LATIN VERSION	40
§ 20. ORIGIN OF THE ADDITIONS IN GREEK	41

CONTENTS

III. HIGHER CRITICISM

		PAGE
§ 21.	OUTLINE OF THE BOOK	47
§ 22.	IDENTITY OF AHASUERUS	51
§ 23.	PURPOSE OF THE BOOK	54
§ 24.	INDEPENDENCE OF $9^{20}-10^3$	57
§ 25.	AGE OF THE BOOK	60
§ 26.	AUTHORSHIP	63
§ 27.	HISTORICAL CHARACTER	64
§ 28.	ORIGIN OF THE FEAST OF PURIM	77

IV. CANONICITY

§ 29.	OMISSION OF THE NAME OF GOD	94
§ 30.	MORAL TEACHING OF THE BOOK	96
§ 31.	ESTIMATE OF THE CHURCH	96

V. INTERPRETATION

§ 32.	EARLIEST JEWISH EXEGESIS	97
§ 33.	EARLIEST CHRISTIAN EXEGESIS	101
§ 34.	THE TARGUMS AND MIDRASHES	101
§ 35.	OTHER MEDIÆVAL JEWISH COMMENTARIES	104
§ 36.	MEDIÆVAL CHRISTIAN INTERPRETATION	107
§ 37.	THE REFORMATION PERIOD	107
§ 38.	THE POST-REFORMATION PERIOD	110
§ 39.	THE MODERN CRITICAL PERIOD	111

COMMENTARY 119

INDEXES 309
    I. HEBREW 309
    II. NAMES OF AUTHORS AND BOOKS 312
    III. SUBJECTS 321
    IV. BIBLICAL PASSAGES 335

ABBREVIATIONS

I. TEXTS AND VERSIONS

ℵ	= Codex Sinaiticus.		M	= Michaelis, *Bib. Heb.*
A	= Codex Alexandrinus.		𝔐	= Massoretic Hebrew text.
Ald.	= The Aldine text of 𝔊.		Mas.	= Massora.
AV.	= Authorized Version.			
			N	= Codex Basiliano-Vaticanus.
B	= Codex Vaticanus.		N¹	= Hagiographa, Naples, 1486.
Ba.	= Baer, *Quinque Volumina*.		N²	= Bible, Naples, 1491–93.
Br.	= Edition, Brescia, 1492.		NT.	= New Testament.
B¹	= Bomberg Bible, 1516–17.			
B²	= Bomberg Bible, 1526.		O	= Origenic recension of 𝔊.
BT.	= Babylonian Talmud.		Oc.	= Occidental MSS.
			Or.	= Oriental MSS.
C	= Complutensian Polyglot.		OT.	= Old Testament.
𝔊	= Greek Version, except L.		Q	= *Qĕrê*, or variants of 𝔐.
G	= Ginsburg, *Heb. Bible*.			
			R	= De Rossi, *Var. Lect.*
H	= Hesychian recension of 𝔊.		RV.	= Revised Version.
𝔥	= Hebrew consonantal text.			
			S	= Bible, Soncino, 1488.
𝔍	= Latin version of Jerome.		𝔖	= Syriac version.
Jos.	= Josephus, *Ant.* xi.		𝔖ᴬ	= Syriac, Codex Ambrosianus.
JT.	= Jerusalem Talmud.		𝔖ᴸ	= Syriac, London Polyglot.
			𝔖ᴹ	= Syriac, Mosul edition.
K	= Kennicott, *Var. Lect.*		𝔖ᵁ	= Syriac, Urumia edition.
L	= Lucianic recension of 𝔊.			
𝔏	= Old Latin version.		𝔗¹	= First Targum.
𝔏ᶜ	= Latin, Codex Corbeiensis.		𝔗²	= Second Targum.
𝔏ᴾ	= Latin, Codex Pechianus.		Vrss.	= Ancient versions.

ABBREVIATIONS

CURSIVE MSS.

(ACCORDING TO HOLMES AND PARSONS)

19 = Rome, Chigi R vi. 38.	106 = Ferrara, Bibl. Comm. **Gr.** 187.
44 = Zittau, A 1. 1.	107 = Ferrara, Bibl. Comm. **Gr.** 188.
52 = Florence, Laur. Acq. 44.	108 = Rome, Vat. Gr. 330.
55 = Rome, Vat. Reg. Gr. 1.	120 = Venice, St. Mark's Gr. 4.
64 = Paris, Nat. Reg. Gr. 2.	236 = Rome, Vat. Gr. 331.
68 = Venice, St. Mark's Gr. 5.	243 = Venice, St. Mark's Gr. 16.
71 = Paris, Nat. Reg. Gr. 1.	248 = Rome, Vat. Gr. 346.
74 = Florence, Laur. Acq. 700 (49).	249 = Rome, Vat. Pius 1.
76 = Paris, Nat. Reg. Gr. 4.	
93 = London, B. M. Reg. i. D. 2.	

II. BOOKS OF THE OLD TESTAMENT AND APOCRYPHA

Ad. Est. = The Rest of the Book of Esther.
Am. = Amos.

1, 2 Ch. = 1, 2 Chronicles.
Ct. = Canticles = The Song of Songs.

Dn. = Daniel.
Dt. = Deuteronomy.

Ec. = Ecclesiastes.
Ecclus. = Ecclesiasticus.
Est. = Esther.
Ex. = Exodus.
Ez. = Ezekiel.
Ezr. = Ezra.

Gn. = Genesis.

Hb. = Habakkuk.
Hg. = Haggai.
Ho. = Hosea.

Is. = Isaiah.

Jb. = Job.
Je. = Jeremiah.
Jo. = Joel.

Jon. = Jonah.
Jos. = Joshua.
Ju. = Judges.
Jud. = Judith.

1, 2 K. = 1, 2 Kings.

La. = Lamentations.
Lv. = Leviticus.

Mal. = Malachi.
1, 2 Mac. = 1, 2 Maccabees.
Mi. = Micah.

Na. = Nahum.
Ne. = Nehemiah.
Nu. = Numbers.

Ob. = Obadiah.

Pr. = Proverbs.
Ps. = Psalms.

Ru. = Ruth.

1, 2 S. = 1, 2 Samuel.

Tob. = Tobit.

Zc. = Zechariah.
Zp. = Zephaniah.

ABBREVIATIONS

III. AUTHORS AND WRITINGS

Ad.	= W. F. Adeney.	ET.	= *Expository Times.*
AJSL.	= *American Journal of Semitic Languages.*	Ew.	= H. Ewald.
		Exp.	= *Expositor.*
And.	= L. E. T. André.	Frit.	= O. F. Fritzsche.
ÄZ.	= *Zeitschrift für Ägyptologie.*		
		Gem.	= The *Gemara.*
Bar.	= R. A. F. Barrett.	Ges.	= W. Gesenius.
Baud.	= W. W. Baudissin.	GGA.	= *Göttingsche Gelehrte Anzeigen.*
Bau.	= G. L. Bauer.	GGN.	= *Göttingsche Gelehrte Nachrichten.*
Baum.	= M. Baumgarten.		
BDB.	= Brown, Driver, Briggs, *Heb.-Eng. Lexicon.*	Gins.	= C. D. Ginsburg.
		Grot.	= H. Grotius.
Bell.	= R. Bellarmin.		
Bert.	= E. Bertheau.	Häv.	= H. C. A. Hävernick.
Biss.	= E. C. Bissell.	HDB.	= *Hastings' Dictionary of the Bible.*
Böt.	= F. Böttcher.		
Bon.	= O. Bonart.	Hen.	= M. Henry.
Bux.	= J. Buxtorf.	Her.	= Herodotus.
BW.	= *Biblical World.*	Hew.	= J. Hewlett.
		HM.	= *OT. and Semitic Studies in Memory of W. R. Harper.*
Caj.	= T. deV. Cajetan.		
Cal.	= A. Calovius.		
Calm.	= A. Calmet.	HP.	= Holmes and Parsons.
Calv.	= J. Calvin.		
Carp.	= J. G. Carpzov.	IE.	= Ibn Ezra.
Cas.	= P. Cassel.	IM.	= Ibn Melech.
Che.	= T. K. Cheyne.	JA.	= *Journal Asiatique.*
Cler.	= J. Clericus.	JAOS.	= *Journal of the American Oriental Society.*
Corn.	= C. H. Cornill.		
Crit. Sac.	= *Critici Sacri.*	JBL.	= *Journal of Biblical Literature.*
Dav.	= A. B. Davidson.		
Del.	= Friedrich Delitzsch.	JE.	= *Jewish Encyclopædia.*
Diest.	= L. Diestel.		
Dill.	= A. Dillmann.	Jer.	= Jerome.
Dri.	= S. R. Driver.	JLB.	= *Jüdisches Litteraturblatt.*
Drus.	= J. Drusius.		
		Jos.	= Josephus.
EB.	= *Encyclopædia Britannica*[9].	JPT.	= *Jahrbücher für protestantische Theologie.*
EBi.	= *Encyclopædia Biblica.*		
Eich.	= J. G. Eichhorn.	JQR.	= *Jewish Quarterly Review.*
Esti.	= G. Estius.		

ABBREVIATIONS

J. & T.	= Junius and Tremellius.	Nöld.	= T. Nöldeke.
		Now.	= W. Nowack.
Kamp.	= A. Kamphausen.	Oet.	= S. Oetli.
KAT.	= E. Schrader, *Die Keilinschriften und das Alte Testament*.	Ols.	= J. Olshausen, *Grammatik*.
		OLZ.	= *Orientalistische Litteratur-Zeitung*.
Kau.	= E. Kautzsch.		
KB.	= *Keilinschriftliche Bibliothek*.	Opp.	= J. Oppert.
		Osi.	= L. Osiander.
Kön.	= E. König, *Lehrgeb*.	Pag.	= S. Pagninus.
Kuen.	= A. Kuenen.	Par.	= D. Pareus.
Lag.	= P. de Lagarde.	Pat.	= S. Patrick.
Lap.	= C. à Lapide.	Paul.	= Paulus Burgensis.
Mal.	= T. Malvenda.	Pel.	= C. Pellican.
Mar.	= J. Mariana.	*Pirq. R. E.*	= *Pirqe Rabbi Eliezer*.
Maur.	= F. J. V. D. Maurer.	Pisc.	= J. Piscator.
May.	= J. Mayer.	PRE.	= *Real-Encyclopädie für protestantische Theologie u. Kirche*.
Meg.	= Tractate *Megilla* in BT. and JT.		
Men.	= J. S. Menochius.	PSBA.	= *Proceedings of the Society of Biblical Archæology*.
Mey.	= E. Meyer.		
MGWJ.	= *Magazin für die Geschichte u. Wissenschaft des Judenthums*.	RaLBaG	= Rabbi Levi ben Gershom.
		Ramb.	= J. J. Rambach.
Mich.	= J. D. Michaelis.	RaShBaM	= Rabbi Samuel ben Meir.
Mid.	= *Midrash Esther Rabba*		
Mid. A. G	= *Midrash Abba Goryon*	RaShI	= Rabbi Solomon ben Isaac.
Mid. L. T.	= *Midrash Leqah Ṭob.*		
Mid. M. E.	= *Midrash Megillath Esther.*	Raw.	= G. Rawlinson.
		RÉJ.	= *Revue des Études Juives*.
Mid. P. A.	= *Midrash Ponim Aḥerim.*	Reu.	= E. Reuss.
Mid. S. T.	= *Midrash Shoher Ṭob.*	Ri.	= E. Riehm, *Handwörterbuch*.
Mish.	= The *Mishna*.		
Mün.	= S. Münster.	Rys.	= V. Ryssel.
MVG.	= *Mitteilungen der Vorderasiatischen Gesellschaft*.	Sal.	= J. Salianus.
		Sanc.	= C. Sanctius.
		SBL.	= Schenkel's *Bibel-Lexicon*.
Net.	= B. Neteler.		
NHWB.	= Levy, *Neuhebr. Wörterbuch*.	Schr.	= E. Schrader.
		Schü.	= E. Schürer.

ABBREVIATIONS

Schu.	= F. W. Schultz.	Vat.	= F. Vatable.
SDB.	= Smith's *Dictionary of the Bible.*	Vit.	= C. Vitringa.
Ser.	= N. Serarius.	West.	= *Westminster Assembly's Annotations.*
Sieg.	= C. Siegfried.		
SK.	= *Theologische Studien u. Kritiken.*	Wild.	= G. Wildeboer.
		Will.	= H. Willrich.
Spieg.	= F. Spiegel.	Winck.	= H. Winckler.
SS.	= Siegfried u. Stade, *Heb. Wörterbuch.*	WZKM.	= *Wiener Zeitschrift für die Kunde des Morgenlandes.*
Sta.	= B. Stade, *Grammatik.*		
Str.	= H. Strack.		
Stre.	= A. W. Streane.	Yalq.	= *Yalquṭ Shimʻoni.*
Stri.	= V. Strigel.	Yos.	= Yosippon.
Tig.	= *Versio Tigurina.*		
Tir.	= J. Tirinus.	ZA.	= *Zeitschrift für Assyriologie.*
TLZ.	= *Theologische Literaturzeitung.*	ZATW.	= *Zeitschrift für die Alttestamentliche Wissenschaft.*
TS.	= *Theologische Studien.*		
TSBA.	= *Transactions of the Society of Biblical Archæology.*	ZDPV.	= *Zeitschrift des deutschen Palästina Vereins.*
TT.	= *Theologisch Tijdschrift.*		

IV. GENERAL, ESPECIALLY GRAMMATICAL

abr.	= abbreviation.	Ar.	= Arabic.
abs.	= absolute.	Aram.	= Aramaic.
abstr.	= abstract.	art.	= article.
acc.	= accusative.	As.	= Assyrian.
acc. cog.	= cognate acc.		
acc. pers.	= acc. of person.	Bab.	= Babylonian.
acc. rei	= acc. of thing.	B. Aram.	= Biblical Aramaic.
acc. to	= according to.		
act.	= active.	c.	= *circa*, about.
adj.	= adjective.	caus.	= causative.
adv.	= adverb.	cod., codd.	= codex, codices.
aft.	= after.	cf.	= *confer*, compare.
ἅ.λ.	= ἅπαξ λεγόμενον, word or phr. used once.	cog.	= cognate.
		coll.	= collective.
al.	= *et aliter*, and elsw.	comm.	= commentaries.
a. l.	= *ad locum.*	comp.	= compare.
alw.	= always.	concr.	= concrete.
apod.	= apodosis.	conj.	= conjunction.

ABBREVIATIONS

consec.	= consecutive.	n.	= noun.
contr.	= contract, contracted.	n. p.	= proper name.
cstr.	= construct.	n. pr. loc.	= proper noun of place.
d.f.	= *daghesh forte.*	n. unit.	= noun of unity.
def.	= defective.	NH.	= New Hebrew.
del.	= *dele*, strike out.	*Niph.*	= *Niphal* of verb.
dittog.	= dittography.	obj.	= object.
		om.	= omit.
e.g.	= *exempli gratia*, for instance.	opp.	= opposite, as opposed to or contrasted with.
elsw.	= elsewhere.		
esp.	= especially.	p.	= person.
emph.	= emphasis, emphatic.	part.	= particle.
Eth.	= Ethiopic.	pass.	= passive.
exc.	= except.	pf.	= perfect.
		Ph.	= Phœnician.
f.	= feminine.	ph.	= perhaps.
fpl.	= feminine plural.	phr.	= phrase.
fr.	= from.	*Pi.*	= *Piel* of verb.
freq.	= frequentative.	pl.	= plural.
fs.	= feminine singular.	post-B.	= post-Biblical.
Gr.	= Greek.	postex.	= postexilic.
		pr.	= preceded by.
haplog.	= haplography.	pred.	= predicate.
Heb.	= Hebrew.	preëx.	= preëxilic.
Hiph.	= *Hiphil* of verb.	preg.	= pregnant.
Hithp.	= *Hithpael* of verb.	prep.	= preposition.
Hithpalp.	= *Hithpalpel* of verb.	prob.	= probable.
impf.	= imperfect.	pron.	= pronoun.
imv.	= imperative.	ptc.	= participle.
indef.	= indefinite.	*Pu.*	= *Pual* of verb.
inf.	= infinitive.		
i.p.	= in pause.	q.v.	= *quod vide.*
i.q.	= *id quod*, the same with.	refl.	= reflexive.
intrans.	= intransitive.	rel.	= relative.
juss.	= jussive.	sf.	= suffix.
		sg.	= singular.
Lat.	= Latin.	*sq.*	= followed by.
l.c.	= last citation.	st.	= *status*, state, stative.
lit.	= literal, literally.	subj.	= subject.
loc.	= local, locality.	subst.	= substantive.
m.	= masculine.	*s.v.*	= *sub voce.*
mpl.	= masculine plural.	syn.	= synonymous.
ms.	= masculine singular.	Syr.	= Syriac.

t.	= times (following a number).	v.	= verse.
		v.	= *vide*, see.
tr.	= transpose.	vb.	= verb.
trans.	= transitive.		

V. REMARKS

Biblical passages are cited according to the verses of the Hebrew text.

Numerals raised above the line (1) after numerals designating chapters indicate verses (Gn. 6³); (2) after proper names refer to editions of books (Ges.[27]).

Proper names usually refer to works upon Esther given in the History of Interpretation.

INTRODUCTION.

I. PLACE OF ESTHER IN THE OLD TESTAMENT.

§ 1. PLACE IN THE HEBREW BIBLE.

In codices and printed editions of the Hebrew Bible the Book of Esther is one of the $K^e th\hat{u}bh\hat{\imath}m$ or 'Writings' that constitute the third division of the OT. canon. The various arrangements of the books that form this collection are exhibited in the following tables:

1	2	3	4
Ruth	Ruth	Ruth	Chr.
Psal.	Psal.	Psal.	Ruth
Job	Job	Job	Psal.
Prov.	Prov.	Prov.	Job
Eccl.	Song	Song	Prov.
Song	Eccl.	Eccl.	Song
Lam.	Lam.	Lam.	Eccl.
Dan.	Dan.	Esth.	Lam.
Esth	Esth.	Dan.	Esth.
Ezr.-Ne.	Ezr.-Ne.	Ezr.-Ne.	Dan.
Chr.	Chr.	Chr.	Ezr.-Ne.

The first of these arrangements is that of the Madrid codex of A.D. 1280, of five codices of the British Museum, namely Harley 1528, Add. 1525, Or. 2212, Or. 2375, Or. 4227, and of the Babylonian codex Berlin Or. Qu. 680. This order is the least logical and, therefore, probably the most primitive. The Babylonian Talmud, our earliest witness on the subject, declares it to be the correct arrangement (*Baba Bathra* 14*b*).

The second arrangement is found in one codex of the British Museum,

Add. 15252. It differs from the first merely in the inversion of the order of Ec. and Song. Ec. is placed last, possibly, because it is regarded as a product of Solomon's old age.

The third arrangement is that of the Paris Codex (A.D. 1286) and British Museum Or. 2091. It differs from the second in the transposition of Dan. and Est. This brings together the four little books, Song, Ec., Lam., Est., and is therefore a step in the direction of the formation of the sub-collection of the Five $M^eghillôth$ or "Rolls."

The fourth arrangement is found in the codex Arundel Orient. 16. It differs from the third only in the transposition of Ch. from the end to the beginning of the Hagiographa.

5	6	7	8
Psal.	Chr.	Chr.	Psal.
Job	Psal.	Psal.	Prov.
Prov.	Job	Prov.	Job
Ruth	Prov.	Job	Song
Song	Ruth	Dan.	Ruth
Eccl.	Song	Ruth	Lam.
Lam.	Eccl.	Song	Eccl.
Esth.	Lam.	Lam.	Esth.
Dan.	Esth.	Eccl.	Dan.
Ezr.-Ne.	Dan.	Esth.	Ezr.-Ne.
Chr.	Ezr.-Ne.	Ezr.-Ne.	Chr.

The fifth arrangement occurs in the codex British Museum Or. 2201 (A.D. 1246). It is derived from the third by the transposition of Ruth to a position before Song of Songs. Here for the first time the five little books, Ru., Song, Ec., Lam., Est., are grouped in the sub-collection of the Five $M^eghillôth$. There is no trace of this grouping in the Talmud or Midrashim, nor is the name Five $M^eghillôth$ known. It arose during the Middle Ages in consequence of the liturgical use of these books in the service of the Synagogue.

The sixth arrangement is that of the St. Petersburg Babylonian codex of A.D. 1207, British Museum codices, Harley 5710-11, Add. 15251, most Spanish codd., and most codd. with Massoretic apparatus. It differs from the fifth in the transposition of Ch. from the end of the Hagiographa to the beginning. The Massoretic treatise '$Ādhath$ $D^ebhārîm$ (A.D. 1207) declares this to be the orthodox Palestinian arrangement, and that which places Ch. at the end to be an innovation of "the men of Shinar" (cf. Strack, ZLT. xxxvi. 1875, p. 605). This is a mistake. Ch. was not taken into the canon early, because it was not needed alongside of Samuel and Kings; and when it was added, it was appended to the end of the collection. The transposition to the begin-

ning is a late alteration due to the fact that most of the history of Ch. belongs chronologically before the rest of the K*ethûbhîm*.
The seventh arrangement is that of the codex British Museum Or. 2626–28. It is derived from the sixth by the transposition of Jb. and Pr., the idea apparently being to place the writings of Solomon immediately after the writings of David.
The eighth arrangement is that of most German and French codd. and of all the printed editions, except the first three and the Bomberg quarto editions of 1521 and 1525, where the Five *Meghillôth* follow the Pentateuch. This order is derived from the fifth by the transposition of Jb. and Pr., Ru. and Song, Ec. and La. In this way the Five *Meghillôth* come to stand in the order in which they are read on the five great holy days of the year. Song is read at Passover in the first month, Ru. at Pentecost in the third month, La. on the anniversary of the destruction of the Temple in the fifth month, Ec. at the feast of Tabernacles in the seventh month, and Est. at the feast of Purim in the twelfth month. This arrangement is the latest of all, since this liturgical use of the Rolls did not grow up until the Middle Ages.
In the official synagogue-rolls the Book of Est. is frequently found immediately after the Law, less often with the other *Meghillôth*, and rarely with the *Meghillôth* and *Haftārôth*, or lessons from the Prophets. This arrangement is due to the desire to have these books in a convenient form for liturgical use, and is evidently the latest of all the groupings. The varying arrangements of the *Meghillôth* in the synagogue-rolls correspond to the arrangements in the Hagiographa given above. Orders 5 and 6 are represented by the codd. British Museum, Harley 5773 and Harley 15283. Order 7 is represented by Add. 15282; order 8, by Add. 9400, Add. 9403, Add. 19776, the printed editions of Soncino 1488, Naples 1491–3, Brescia 1492–4, and the Bomberg quarto editions of 1521 and 1525. The peculiar order, Est., Song, Ru., La., Ec., found in Add. 9404, Harley 5706 and Orient. 2786, but not found in any canons of the Hagiographa, has evidently arisen from the later addition of the remaining four *Meghillôth* to a roll which originally contained only the Pentateuch and Esther (see Ginsburg, *Introduction*, pp. 1–8; Ryle, *Canon*, p. 280).

§ 2. PLACE IN THE GREEK VERSION.

In Greek codd. and lists given by the Fathers, the books of the Hagiographa are scattered in various positions among the Former and Latter Prophets. Ru. always follows Ju. La. is appended to Je. and Dn. to the Major Prophets. The five poetical books, Jb., Ps., Pr., Ec. and Song, in varying orders, usually stand together. The Pentateuch, Prophetical Histories, Ch., Ez. and Ne. always stand first, except in the eccentric lists of Epiphanius (*Hær.* i. 1⁵; *De Mens.* 4; *ib.* 23), which give his own theories rather than the established order; accordingly, we may dismiss these books from further consideration. The remaining books of the OT. are grouped in the following ways:

1	2	3	4
Poetical	Poetical	Poetical	Esther
Minor Pr.	Major Pr.	Esther	Poetical
Major Pr.	Minor Pr.	Minor Pr.	Minor Pr.
Esther	Esther	Major Pr.	Major Pr.

5	6	7	8
Esther	Minor Pr.	Esther	Esther
Poetical	Major Pr.	Minor Pr.	Major Pr.
Major Pr.	Esther	Major Pr.	Minor Pr.
Minor Pr.	Poetical	Poetical	Poetical

The first of these is the order given by Origen (in Eusebius, *Hist. Eccl.* vi. 25), Athanasius (*Ep. Fest.* 39, in Migne, *Patr. Græc.* xxvi. 1437), the anonymous *Dialogue of Timothy and Aquila*, Epiphanius (*l. c.*), John of Damascus (*De Fide Orthodox.* iv. 17), Ebedjesu (*Catal. Libr. Eccl.* in Assemani, *Bibl. Orient.* iii. 5 *f.*), the list in the codices Barocc. 206, *Brit. Mus. Add.* 17469, Coisl. 120; Hilary (*Proleg. in Libr. Psalm.*), and the list in *Codex Claromontanus*. This order is most widely attested, and from it the other orders can be explained most readily; it is, therefore, probably the original arrangement of the Septuagint. The position of Est. at the end of the list is due to the fact that this book was written after the Alexandrian canon was practically completed, so that it had to be added as an appendix.

The second arrangement is found in Nicephorus (*Stichometria*) and Cassiodorus (*De Inst. Div. Lit.* 14). It differs from the first only in the inversion of the Minor and the Major Prophets, possibly through the influence of the Hebrew order.

The third arrangement is that of *Codex Vaticanus* (B). It is obtained from the first by placing Est. before the Minor and the Major Prophets. The aim of this transposition is doubtless to bring the Prophets immediately before the Gospels.

The fourth arrangement is found in *Codex Basiliano-Vaticanus* (N), Cyril of Jerusalem (*Catech.* iv. 35), a synopsis given by Lagarde (*Septuagintastudien*, ii. 60 *f.*), Pseudo-Athanasius (*Syn. Scr. Sacr.* in Migne, *Patr. Græc.* xxviii. 283 *ff.*), the *Canons of Laodicea* (lx), the *Apostolic*

Canons (lxxxiv), Augustine (*De Doctr. Christ.* ii. 13), *Canons of Carthage* (xlvii–xxxix). This order differs from the preceding in placing Est. before the Poetical Books. This has the advantage of bringing the Prophets immediately before the Gospels and also of associating Est. with the other historical books.

The fifth arrangement appears in a list discovered by Mommsen (*cf.* Zahn, *Gesch. d. N. T. Kanons*, ii. 143 *f.*, Sanday, *Studia Biblica*, iii. 222 *f.*; Preuschen, *Analecta*, 138). It is the order followed by Jerome in the Vulgate, from which it has passed into all the modern versions. It is derived from 2 by the transposition of Est. to a position after the Historical Books, and it differs from 4 only in the different order of the Major and the Minor Prophets.

The sixth arrangement is that of *Codex Alexandrinus* (A). It is apparently derived from 1 by the transposition of the Poetical Books to the end. What considerations led to this change it is impossible to say.

The seventh arrangement appears in Junilius (*De Instit. Reg. Div. Legis*, i. 3 *ff.*). It is derived from 3 by the transposition of the Poetical Books to the end of the list.

The eighth arrangement is that of *Codex Sinaiticus* (א), Ruffinus (*Comm. in Symb.* 36), Isiodorus (*De Ord. Libr. Sac. Scr.*), and the *Liber Sacramentorum* (Bobbio, 6th or 7th cent.). It differs from 7 only in the transposition of the Major and the Minor Prophets. None of these orders of 𝔊 can claim to be more primitive than the orders in 𝔐, all of which preserve the original threefold canon. The different arrangements in 𝔊 have arisen from the effort to group the books either chronologically or logically, and are all secondary. (See Swete, *Introduction*, pp. 197 *ff.*)

II. THE TEXT OF ESTHER.

a. DESCENDANTS OF THE TIBERIAN MASSORETIC TEXT.

§ 3. MANUSCRIPTS WITH TIBERIAN VOCALIZATION.

Manuscripts of the Book of Esther are more numerous than of any other portion of the Old Testament. It is found in all complete private Bible codices; also appended to the Law in most of the sacred, or synagogue, rolls, and, together with the other four M^eghillôth, in numerous liturgical scrolls. So high is the esteem which this book enjoys among the Jews that every family is anxious to own it in the manuscript form prescribed by the Talmud for reading at Purim, and this has led to the production of an immense number of separate Esther rolls that are often masterpieces of the writer's and illuminator's arts, and that are enclosed in gold and silver cases of exquisite workmanship (see *JE*. viii. pp. 429 *ff*.). No extant MS. of this book is earlier than the eleventh century of the Christian era. The oldest is the St. Petersburg Codex B 19 *a*, written in A.D. 1009.

Enumerations and descriptions of manuscripts containing Est. are given by Le Long, *Bibl. Sacra* (1723); Wolf, *Bibl. Hebr.* (1721 *f*.); Kennicott, *Dissertatio* (1780; ed. Bruns, 1783); De Rossi, *Apparatus* (1716); *Manuscripti* (1803); *Libri Stampati* (1812); Assemani, *Bibl. Vaticanus Catalogus*, I. i. (1756); Uri, *Bibl. Bodleianæ Catalogus*, i. (1787); *Catalogue des manuscrits hébreux*, Paris (1866); Kraft and Deutsch, *Die handschriftlichen hebräischen Werke* . . . *zu Wien* (1847); Steinschneider, *Hebr. Handschriften in Berlin* (1878, 1897); *Hebr. Handschriften in München* (1895); Harkavy and Strack, *Catalog der Hebr. Bibelhandschriften* . . . *zu St. Petersburg* (1875); Schiller-Szinessy, *Catalogue of the Hebr. MSS. Cambridge* (1876); Neubauer, *Catalogue of the Hebr. MSS. in the Bodleian Library* (1886); Derenbourg, *Catalogue des manuscrits judaïques entres au British Museum de 1867–1890*, *Rev. des Études Juives*, 1891. Ginsburg, *Introduction*, 1897. For additional catalogues see Strack, *Prolegomena Critica*, pp. 29–33, 119–121; *Einleitung in das A. T.*[5], p. 182.

All these MSS. exhibit the Tiberian or infralinear system of vocalization and accentuation that is found in our ordinary printed editions. This was introduced about 650 A.D. by the Massorites, or custodians of oral textual tradition, who had their headquarters at Tiberias in Palestine. Mss. of this recension are practically identical with one another. They have the same division of words and sentences. The Massora at the end of Est. says that there are 167 verses and that the middle verse is 5^7. With this all the MSS. agree. They agree also in dividing the text into 5 *sedhārîm* or triennial pericopes and into 15 smaller sections. In regard to the length of the space between the sections, which indicates whether they are open or closed, there is strict uniformity. In all MSS. the first word of 1^6 has an abnormally large initial letter. In all the names of the ten sons of Haman ($9^{7\cdot 9}$) are written in a vertical line on the right margin of the page, or the column, while the conjunctions and demonstrative particles that precede each name form another line on the left margin. The name of the first son, Parshandatha, is uniformly written with *th* smaller than the other letters. Parmashta (9⁹) is written with both *sh* and *t* small. Wayzatha (9⁹) has a large *w* and a small *z*. The first word of 9²⁹ is always written with a large initial *t*.

The few variants that exist in these MSS. have been laboriously collated by Jedidiah Solomon Norzi in his commentary on the Bible entitled *Gôdēr Pēreç* (completed in 1626, first printed in the Bible of Raphael Ḥayyim Basila under the title *Minḥath Shay*, Mantua, 1742–4; again in the Warsaw Rabbinic Bible; separate edition, Vienna, 1813); also by J. H. Michaelis, *Biblia Hebraica*, Halle, 1720; by Kennicott, *Vetus Testamentum Hebraicum cum variis lectionibus* (1776); and by De Rossi, *Variæ lectiones Veteris Testamenti* (1884–88). The number of variants that these elaborate studies have yielded is surprisingly small. As the result of a collation of many hundreds of MSS., Kennicott and De Rossi together record only 29 variants in the consonantal text of Est., and these all of a trivial character. They are as follows:

1¹, two MSS. omit "this is Ahasuerus"; 2¹¹, one MS. reads "in the court" instead of "before the court"; several MSS. read "to her" instead of "of her"; 3⁵, six MSS. after "then was Haman full of wrath" add "against Mordecai"; 4¹⁶, fifty-seven MSS. omit "and" before "neither eat"; seventy-two MSS. add "and" before "I also"; 4¹⁷, one MS. omits "according to"; 5⁴, six MSS. omit "this day"; 5¹¹, three MSS. add "all" before "the princes"; 6⁶, one MS. reads " to Haman" instead of "to him"; 6¹¹, three MSS. after "caused him to ride" add "on a horse"; 8², four MSS. after "his ring" add "from off his hand"; 8⁵, one MS. reads "and Esther said" instead of "and she said"; one hundred and fifteen MSS. add "all" before "the Jews"; 8⁶, two MSS. have the verb "shall come" in the feminine instead of the masculine; 8⁹, seven MSS. before "an hundred twenty and seven" add "unto"; 8¹¹, some MSS. omit "and" before "to slay"; 9², some MSS. read "no man could stand unto their faces," instead of "no man could stand in their faces"; 9¹², fifty-four MSS. omit "and" (RV. "now") before "what is thy petition"? 9¹⁴, three MSS. after "and they hanged Haman's ten sons" add "upon the gallows"; 9¹⁶, fifteen MSS add "all" after "in"; 9¹⁸, three MSS. omit the entire verse; one MS. reads the finite verb instead of the infinitive in "and made"; 9²⁰, two MSS. before "these things" add "all"; 9²², three MSS. read "in" instead of "as"; 9²³, twenty-nine MSS. read the finite verb instead of the infinitive "undertook"; nineteen MSS. read "upon them" instead of "unto them"; 9^{24}, four MSS. omit "all" before "the Jews"; 9^{27}, many MSS. read the finite verb instead of the infinitive "took." A number of these variants are found also in 𝔖, 𝔍, and 𝔊, which shows that they are survivals of ancient textual differences.

Six late codd., namely, Cod. Vat. Urbin. 1, fol. 869; Cod. Ambrosian. B. 35; Cod. Pii. VI.; Codd. De Rossi 7, 42, 737, append to the Book of Est. an Aramaic addition containing the dream and the prayers of Esther and Mordecai. This was published by Assemani, *Bibl. Vaticanæ Catalogus* (1756), pp. 452 *ff.*; by De Rossi, *Specimen variarum lectionum, sacri textus et Chaldaica Esteris additamenta cum Latine versione ac notis* (1782); also by Jellinek, *Beth ham-Midrash* (1873), v. pp. 1–81; Lagarde, *Hagiographa Chaldaice* (1873), pp. 362–365; Merx, *Chrestomathia Targumica*, pp. 154 *ff.* De Rossi attached great importance to these codd. as evidence that the additions of the Greek version were derived from an ancient Aramaic original, but it is now generally believed that these Aramaic additions are borrowed from the Hebrew translation of Josephus made by Joseph ben Goryon (Josephus Gorionides, or Yosippon) in the tenth century. They have, therefore, no text-critical value (see Zunz, *Gottesdienstliche Vorträge der Juden*, p. 121; Fritzsche, *Kurzgefasstes exegetisches Handbuch zu den Apokryphen*, i. 70; Dalman, *Grammatik des jüdisch-palästinischen Aramäisch*, p. 30; Ryssel, *Zusätze zum Buche Esther*, in Kautzsch's *Apokryphen und Pseudepigraphen des A. T.*, p. 195; Bissell, *The Apocrypha of the O. T.*, 1880, p. 202; Fuller in Wace's *Apocrypha*, p. 364).

Three MSS. contain acrostics of the divine name YHWH, formed by writing the initial or final letters of consecutive words larger than the other letters. In 1^{20} these are the initial letters of "it, all the wives shall give," read from left to right. In 5^4 they are the initial letters of "let the King come and Haman to-day," read from right to left. In 5^{13} they are the final letters of "this availeth me nothing," read from left to right; and in 7^7 they are the final letters of "that there was evil determined against him," read from right to left. These are mere rabbinic conceits devised to discover the name of God in the book. They have **no** text-critical value.

Variants in vocalization and accentuation are more numerous, but are of the most trivial character and do not affect the sense of a single passage. They are collected in the text-critical works named above (except Kennicott and De Rossi), and in the Massoretico-critical editions of Baer (1886) and Ginsburg (1894). There is seldom any doubt as to the correct Massoretic text. The rival editions of Baer and Ginsburg present only a few trifling differences of punctuation.

The extraordinary similarity of all the MSS. of the Tiberian family shows that they are descended from a single prototype. Elias Levita, *Massoreth Ham-Massoreth* (ed. Ginsburg, p. 114), quotes a passage from Maimonides to the effect that "the recension of our manuscripts is according to the well-known codex in Egypt, which contains the twenty-four sacred books, which had formerly been in Jerusalem for many years in order that other codices might be corrected by it; and that both he and all others followed it because Ben Asher corrected it and minutely elaborated it for many years and revised it many times, as it has been transmitted to us." To this Levita appends the remark: "The Occidentals in every land follow Ben Asher, but the Orientals follow the recension of Ben Naphtali." (*Cf.* Ginsburg, *Introduction*, p. 247.) Ben Asher flourished in the tenth century of our era, and was the last great representative of the Tiberian school of Massorites. He prepared a standard codex of the Old Testament in which the Palestinian or Occidental textual tradition received its final form. This codex has perished, but direct copies from it are preserved in the synagogues of Aleppo and Cairo. The statements of Maimonides and Levita, that all Occidental MSS.—that is, all MSS. of the common Tiberian type—are descendants of the Codex Ben Asher, is to be taken with some reserve, since they do not uniformly exhibit the readings which the official lists ascribe to Ben Asher; nevertheless, as a rule, they follow this text, and there can be no doubt that a systematic effort was made by the Occidental Jews to conform their codices to this standard.

Back of Ben Asher must have stood another standard codex of the seventh century in which the Tiberian Massorites first embodied their oral tradition as to the correct pronunciation of the

Old Testament. The trifling differences from Ben Asher which Occidental (Tiberian) MSS. contain, are corruptions that came into the text during the period that intervened between the standard codex of the seventh century and the Codex Ben Asher of the tenth century.

§ 4. THE PRINTED EDITIONS.

All printed editions of the Book of Esther are based upon MSS. with the Tiberian system of vocalization. The earlier editions rest upon a direct collation of MSS. and therefore have text-critical interest. The first edition of Est. is in the *editio princeps* of the Hagiographa, Naples, 1486-87, part iii. The editor was a certain Samuel of Rome.

The second edition is the *editio princeps* of the entire Bible, Soncino, 1488. It bears the name of R. Joshua ben Israel Nathan of Soncino and of Abraham ben Hayyim de Tintori of Bologna. It is based upon German and Franco-German codd., and, apart from errors, contains a number of interesting variants from the official Massoretic text.

The third edition is the complete Bible, Naples, 1491-93. This edition is more accurate than either of its predecessors. It seeks to conform closely to the Massora, and therefore its variants are of exceptional importance.

The fourth edition is the Pentateuch with the five *M^{e}ghillôth* and the *Haphṭārôth*, or lessons from the Prophets, Brescia, 1492. It is based upon the Soncino edition of 1488, but is carefully corrected from German and Franco-German codd. The phenomenal letters, *i.e.*, those larger or smaller than the ordinary, are ignored in this edition.

The fifth edition is the Complutensian Polyglot, published under the patronage of Cardinal Ximenes, at Alcalà (Complutum) in Spain, 1514-17. Est. is the fifth book in the third volume. The Hebrew text, with vowels, but without accents, occupies the outer column. The middle column contains the Latin version of Jerome, and the inner column contains the Greek version. Reverence for the Vulgate has led the editors to arrange the Heb. folios so as to read from left to right, to ignore the Massoretic division into pericopes and sections, and to adopt the Christian division of the text into chapters. According to Ginsburg (*Introduction*, p. 918), the Hebrew text of the Complutensian Polyglot is based upon the Spanish MS., Madrid University Library No. 1, with modifications derived from the Naples edition of 1491–93. The absence of accents is a serious defect in this edition, and the vowel points are not accurately printed.

The sixth edition is the Rabbinic Bible, edited by Felix Pratensis and issued from the Bomberg press in Venice in 1516–17, 4 vols. fol. The fourth volume contains Est. with the First Targum and the commentary of RaShI, and in an appendix, the Second Targum to Est. In this edition the Massoretic divisions of the text are carefully observed, but the distinction between open and closed sections is not preserved. The Christian division into chapters is indicated by Hebrew numeral letters placed in the margin. The $Q^e r\hat{e}$, or Massoretic variants, and numerous other variants are also given in the margin. This edition is based on a new collation, and therefore is of considerable text-critical importance.

The seventh independent edition is the great Rabbinic Bible, edited by Jacob ben Ḥayyim ibn Adonijah, and published by Bomberg, Venice, 1524–25, 4 vols. fol. Esther, with the other $M^e ghill\hat{o}th$, is found among the Hagiographa in the fourth volume. The Hebrew text and Targum occupy the middle of the page, and on either side are the commentaries of RaShI and Ibn Ezra. The textual annotations of the Massora Magna occupy the upper and lower margins, and those of the Massora Parva the space between the middle columns. This edition is based upon a careful collation of MSS., and presents for the first time an accurate reproduction of the standard text of the Tiberian school. The peculiarities of the best codices are faithfully reproduced with the Massoretic notes which guard them from alteration. The Massoretic sectional divisions are accurately followed, but no distinction is made between the open and the closed sections. The division into chapters is not introduced into the text, but in the preface the editor gives a list of the Christian chapters with their opening words in Hebrew. So well did Jacob ben Ḥayyim do his work that this edition has become the *textus receptus* of the Hebrew Bible down to the present day. All later printed editions are based upon this, either alone, or in combination with the earlier editions. None of these later editions, accordingly, have independent text-critical value.

Arias Montanus in his Hebrew Bible with interlinear Latin translation, Antwerp, Plantin, 1571, one vol. fol., first divided the Hebrew text into chapters, and inserted the Hebrew numeral letters in the text. He also added the Arabic verse numbers in the margin. From this edition and from the polyglots the practice of inserting chapter and verse numbers spread to all the later editions. Athias in his standard edition (1659-61) went so far as to invent enumerations in Massoretic style of the number of chapters and inserted these among the genuine Massoretic summaries at the ends of the books. From him these notes have been copied by Jablonski, Van der Hooght, and all the ordinary editions.

The Massoretico-critical editions of Baer (*Quinque Volumina*, Leipzig, 1886), and of Ginsburg (London, 1894), are revisions of the standard text of Jacob ben Ḥayyim, 1524-25, designed to conform it more closely to the teachings of the Massora. They differ from Jacob ben Ḥayyim and from one another only in trivial matters of accentuation and vocalization, and they represent substantially the standard codex of Ben Asher of the tenth century. The edition of Kittel (Leipzig, 1906) reproduces the text of Jacob ben Ḥayyim and gives in footnotes the more important variants of the MSS. and versions. No effort is made to emend the text, but only to give the materials on which an emendation may be based.

§ 5. THE MASSORA.

The Massora, or 'Tradition,' is a sort of text-critical commentary written in the margin of most of the codices. It contains observations and discussions of the Tiberian scribes during the period from the second to the tenth century of our era. It counts the number of sections, sentences and words in books. It notes their middle sentences and middle words. It enumerates passages in which unusual forms occur. It calls attention to abnormal letters, spelling, vocalization, or accentuation, and warns the scribe against changing these. Words that it regards as incorrect it marks with a small circle, and inserts in the margin the $Q^e r\hat{e}$, or supposedly correct reading, the vowels of which are placed under the $K^e th\hat{\imath}bh$, or form in the text. Similar in character are the $S^ebh\hat{\imath}r\hat{\imath}n$, or 'opinions,' that suggest an alternate reading to the one in the text. Variant readings of MSS. and of other rabbinical schools are also recorded. The Massora has been the means by which the extraordinary uniformity that now exists in the MSS. has been secured, and its authority must be final in deciding between variant readings of the Tiberian recension.

> The Massora is printed in connection with the Bible text, as in the MSS., in the great Rabbinic Bible of Jacob ben Ḥayyim (Venice, 1524–25), and in Buxtorf's Rabbinic Bible (Basel, 1618–19). There are also a large number of treatises which contain the Massora classified in various systematic ways either topical or alphabetic. The most important of these are the following:—from the tenth century, Aaron ben Moses ben Asher, *Diqduqe hat-Ṭe'amim* (ed. Baer and Strack, Leipzig, 1879); from an anonymous author of the same century, *Okhla we-Okhla* (ed. Frensdorff, Hannover, 1864); Moses the Punctuator, *Darke han-Niqqud wehan-Neginoth* (ed. Frensdorff, Hannover, 1847); Jekuthiel the Punctuator, '*En haq-Qore* (ed. Heidenheim in *Me'or 'Enayim*, Rödelheim, 1812–21, and in Ṣeder Yeme hap-Purim, Rödelheim, 1826); Elias Levita, *Sefer Massoreth ham-Massoreth*, Venice, 1536 (German transl. with notes by Semler, Halle, 1772; text, English transl. and notes by Ginsburg, London, 1867); Frensdorff, *Die Massora Magna*, Hannover, 1876; Ginsburg, *The Massorah compiled from manuscripts, lexically and alphabetically arranged* (London, 1880–85, 3 vols. fol.).

§ 6. CITATIONS IN JEWISH COMMENTARIES.

Besides these distinctively textual Massoretic treatises, there are numerous *midrashim* and later Jewish commentaries on the Book of Esther. All are based on the Tiberian text, and all contain more or less Massoretic material; they are of some value, therefore, in determining the true Tiberian readings. Their value is slight, however, and the additions of the *midrashim* have no text-critical importance. It seems better, therefore, to discuss these commentaries under the head of the history of interpretation where they play a much more important part (see § 34).

b. OTHER DESCENDANTS OF THE TEXT OF THE ṢOPHERIM.

§ 7. MSS. WITH BABYLONIAN VOCALIZATION.

Back of the pointed text of the seventh century lies the unpointed consonantal text that was established in the second century of the Christian era. The main witness to this is the Palestinian Massoretic recension whose various descendants we have just considered. Besides this there are several other recensions that must be taken into consideration in the effort to restore the original form of the consonantal text. Chief among these are MSS. with the Babylonian, or supralinear, system of punctuation. While the Palestinian scribes at Tiberias were elaborating and fixing in writing their tradition concerning the correct pronunciation of the Scriptures, the Babylonian scribes at Nehardea and Sura were engaged in the same occupation. Their tradition differed somewhat from that of the Palestinians, as numerous early statements prove. The Massora also records instances in which their readings differed from those of Tiberias (*cf.* Strack, *ZLT.* 1875, p. 622 *f.*). Their labours culminated in the tenth century in the standard codex of Ben Naphtali, which, according to the statement of Maimonides quoted above, was regarded as authoritative by the Babylonian Jews in the same way in which Ben Asher was regarded as authoritative by the Palestinian Jews. This codex has perished, and no immediate descendants of it are known; but in the Massora accompanying a number of Palestinian codices, lists are given of the differences between Ben Naphtali and Ben Asher. These differences are extremely trivial, and in only three cases do they affect the consonantal text of the OT.

In a MS. of the Pentateuch (Codex De Rossi 12) the statement is found that the accompanying Targum was copied from a MS. brought from Babylonia and "pointed above with the pointing of Asshur." In the *Maḥzor Vitry* (Hurwitz, p. 462) a Babylonian scribe says, "the Tiberian punctuation is not like ours, neither is it like that of the land of Israel." Çemaḥ ben Ḥayyim Gaon speaks of differences between the Babylonian punctuation in regard to the full or defective writing of the vowels, the open and closed sections, the verse-divisions, and the Massora. Saʻadia in his commentary on the Book *Yeçira* says that the Tiberians have 42 peculiarities in their treatment of the gutturals, the Babylonians only 17. A certain Isaac ben Eleazar, who lived probably in the twelfth or in the thirteenth century, states that by the Babylonians *Waw* before a letter with simple *Shewa* was pointed just as before other letters, and not with *Shureq*, as in the Palestinian system (see Dukes in the *Litteraturblatt zu " Orient,"* 1846, No. 45, p. 708).

This is all that was known about Babylonian MSS. until the middle of the last century, when codices with supralinear punctuation and other correspondences with the statements just quoted began to find their way into Europe from the Crimea and from Yemen in southern Arabia. Since that time a considerable number of these have been acquired by the Library of the British Museum and other great libraries of Europe, so that now it is possible to say something definite about the Babylonian Massoretic recension. The MSS. date from the twelfth to the seventeenth century. They exhibit three slightly variant systems of punctuation, all of which differ from the Tiberian system in the signs used for the vowels and accents and in being mainly supralinear. In spite of these differences, the Massoretic tradition represented by them is practically identical with that found in Palestinian MSS. They do not show the differences between the "Westerns" and "Easterns" and between Ben Asher and Ben Naphtali that the Palestinian Massora records, nor do they contain the peculiarities ascribed to Babylonian MSS. by ancient authorities. It is clear, therefore, that they date from a time after the decline of the Babylonian schools of scribes, when the Palestinian text triumphed and an effort was made to bring even Babylonian codices into conformity. These codices, accordingly, are of small text-critical value. Only occasionally they have retained by accident a genuine Babylonian reading.

One codex, however, is known which preserves more accurately the original Babylonian Massoretic tradition. This is the Berlin Codex, Or. Qu. 680. It is in an extremely fragmentary condition, but contains Est. 2^{14}–5^{13}. The original punctuation, which was written in a reddish brown ink, has been erased, and over it has been written the later supralinear vocalization which corresponds to the Palestinian system. Beneath the corrections the original readings may, however, still be recognized, and they have been collated and published by P. Kahle, *Der massoretische Text des A. T. nach der Ueberlieferung der babylonischen Juden* (1902). This codex partly confirms the lists of Babylonian variants given elsewhere, partly corrects them, and partly gives new variants not otherwise known. It is provided with a Massora that differs materially from the ordinary Palestinian Massora and corresponds with other fragments of Babylonian Massora. It is at present our best available source of information in regard to the Babylonian Massoretic recension. In the consonantal text of Esther it presents no variations. In the vocalization and accentuation it contains only unimportant differences that do not affect the sense of a single passage. This shows that not only the consonantal text but also its traditional pronunciation was established before the Babylonian Massoretic school diverged from the Palestinian. Even if Babylonian MSS. were older and more numerous, they would probably yield no important emendations of the current Palestinian text.

§ 8. THE PESHITTO, OR SYRIAC VERSION.

Passing now from the Heb. recensions and editions to their nearest relative among the versions, we come to the Syriac translation. This was made by various unknown persons, perhaps as early as the second century of our era, and was the Bible of the Syriac-speaking Christians. For the Book of Esther five editions of the text are accessible, that of the London Polyglot (1657), of Lee (1824), of the American missionaries at Urumia (1852), of the Codex Ambrosianus (1879–83), and of the Catholic missionaries at Mosul (1887). The first two contain identical texts and are referred to by me in the commentary as $\mathfrak{S}^L$. The Mosul Bible ($\mathfrak{S}^M$) is practically a reprint of the Urumia edition ($\mathfrak{S}^U$) with a few arbitrary alterations. As Rahlfs has shown (*ZATW*. 1889, pp. 161 *ff.*), for most of the books of the OT. the London Polyglot, Lee, and Codex Ambrosianus form a group representing the West-Syrian text, while Urumia and Mosul together represent the East-

Syrian, or Nestorian text. In the Book of Esther, however, the text of 𝔖^L scarcely differs at all from that of 𝔖^U. This is probably not due, as Grünthal thinks (*Die Syrische Uebersetzung zum Buche Esther*, 1900; cf. Barnes, *Apparatus Criticus to Chronicles*, 1897, Intr. § 1) to correction of the MSS. that underlie the Urumia edition by the London text, but to the fact that Esther was lacking from the Nestorian Canon and had to be supplied in later MSS. from West-Syrian prototypes. For this book, accordingly, we have only West-Syrian readings. In a number of cases 𝔖^A differs from 𝔖^LU, usually in the direction of closer conformity to the Massoretic text. Cornill (*Ezechiel*, p. 145 *f*.) thinks that the text of 𝔖^A has been systematically corrected from 𝔐, but this is denied by Rahlfs and Grünthal, who hold that in these cases 𝔖^A has preserved the better readings. Such variations are relatively few, and in the main the editions of 𝔖 present a homogeneous text. Variations of any importance between the editions are recorded in the critical notes of this commentary. Further details may be found in the work of Grünthal cited above.

The Syriac version of Esther is an extremely faithful translation of the original. Here and there a word is added for the sake of clearness, but ordinarily 𝔐 is followed with slavish fidelity. When possible, the translator even uses the same root that appears in Heb. Rarely, short additions are found that cannot have arisen from a mere interpretation of the text. Occasionally, as in 1⁶, these additions bear a slight resemblance to the Greek, but usually they are independent of it, and, whatever may be the case in other books, in Est. there is not a single clear instance of influence of 𝔖 by 𝔊. The parallels adduced by Grünthal, p. 19, are inconclusive. Accordingly, when 𝔖 agrees with 𝔊 against 𝔐 in a reading, this fact is of more significance than in other books of the Peshiṭto that have clearly been edited to conform to 𝔊. For this commentary I have made a new collation of 𝔖^L and 𝔖^U. The readings of 𝔖^A I have taken from Grünthal, as Ceriani's reproduction of the Codex Ambrosianus was temporarily absent from the Library of Hartford Seminary for use in the preparation of the forthcoming Hartford Concordance to the Syriac OT. A detailed exhibition of the departures of the Syriac version from the Massoretic text in the Book of Esther may be found in Grünthal, pp. 21–55. The significant variants will be found at appropriate points in the critical notes of the commentary. In general, it may be said that 𝔖 represents a consonantal text closely similar to that of the Massoretic recension, but not identical with it. There are a number of interesting variants that are found also in 𝔊, 𝔍, and the Targums. In some of these cases 𝔖 may have preserved a better text than 𝔐. The vocalization of proper names shows a different tradition from that of 𝔐. In other cases there is not much room for difference, since, in a simple historical narrative like that of Est., only one reading of the words is usually possible.

§ 9. THE FIRST TARGUM.

Closely akin in many respects to the Peshiṭto is the so-called *Targum Rishon*, or First Targum, a translation of the Book of Esther into the older Syriac dialect known as Biblical or Palestinian Aramaic. This Targum is found in the Bomberg Rabbinical Bible of Venice, 1517, in the Basel and London Polyglots, and in Lagarde, *Hagiographa Chaldaice*, pp. 201–223 (a reprint of the Bomberg text). Latin translations are found in the London Polyglot and in F. Tayler, *Targum prius et posterius in Esteram* (1655). These editions and the citations of Alḳabeẓ in the *Mānôth hal-Lēvî*, a collection of haggadic material (Venice, 1590), present a number of textual variants, which are gathered by S. Posner in the treatise entitled *Das Targum Rishon zu dem biblischen Buche Esther* (Breslau, 1896), pp. 71 *ff.* No critical edition has yet appeared, but the text on the whole is sound. In the translations in this commentary I have followed the London Polyglot.

In its relation to the Heb. original this translation is a curious compound of fidelity and freedom. On the one hand, it faithfully reproduces every word of the consonantal text. On the other hand, it interlards the version with all sorts of new material. Ordinarily, these additions consist of a few words added to make the sense clear, and constitute a sort of running grammatical commentary on the book. They show a fine feeling for the Hebrew idiom and are exceedingly suggestive to the modern interpreter. Other insertions are casuistical interpretations of words and phrases, analogous to the hallachic discussions of the Talmud, by which far more is deduced from the text than a literal interpretation would warrant; e.g., in 1¹, from a study of the phrase "and it came to pass," it is inferred that it always introduces a narrative of disaster; and in 1¹¹, from the fact that the King commands to bring Vashti with a crown on her head, it is inferred that she was to wear nothing but a crown. Besides these there are other long insertions that are pure *haggada*, or imaginary spinning out of incidents to supply gaps in the canonical history.

> Thus in 1¹ there is added an account of Vashti's descent from Nebuchadnezzar; 1², of Ahasuerus's throne; 1³ᶠ·, of the King's feast and the decorations of his garden; 1¹¹, of Vashti's wickedness; 1¹⁴, of the calling of the sons of Issachar to judge Vashti; 1¹⁹, of the execution of Vashti; 2¹, of the execution of the seven viziers; 2⁶ ᶠ·, of Mordecai's bringing up of Esther and the meaning of her name; 2⁹, of the names of Esther's handmaidens; 2¹⁰, of the reason why Mordecai commanded Esther to conceal her lineage; 2¹⁷, of the King's removal of the statue of Vashti from his bedroom; 2²⁰ of Esther's strict observance of the Law in the royal palace; 2²¹, of the reason why the two eunuchs conspired against Ahasuerus, and of Mordecai's discovery of the plot because he was able to speak seventy languages; 3¹ ᶠ·, of God's decree concerning Haman; 3², of the reason why Mordecai refused to bow to Haman; 3⁹, of the reason why Haman offered to pay 10,000 talents; 4¹, Elijah the priest's message to Mordecai; 4⁵, the identity of Hathakh and Daniel; 4¹², Haman's killing of Hathakh; 5¹, Esther's prayer; 5³, the King's promise not to rebuild the Temple; 5⁹, Mordecai's insult to Haman; 5¹⁴, the advice of Zeresh and the friends to Haman; 6¹, the visit of the angels to deprive the King of sleep and to make him suspicious of Haman; 7⁶, the genealogy of Mordecai; 8¹⁵, Mordecai's royal attire and triumph; 9¹⁴, the manner in which Haman and his sons were hanged; 9²⁷, the reading of the Roll of Est. at the feast of Purim.

These additions make the Book of Esther fully twice as long in 𝔗¹ as in 𝕳. They are inserted by abruptly breaking off the original narrative; and when they are ended, it begins again just where it was interrupted. It is thus easy to discriminate the amplifications and, for text-critical purposes, to fix one's attention upon the portions that constitute the real version.

In the Antwerp Polyglot (1569) and in the Paris Polyglot (1645) a shorter recension of this Targum is found that omits all the amplifications and gives merely a literal Aramaic translation of 𝔥. Apart from these omissions the text of this Targum is substantially the same as that of the London Polyglot. A tendency is noticeable, however, to substitute Aramaic words for the Heb. words that the London recension has retained, and to give more accurate translations of some of the words by the substitution of synonyms. The Paris Polyglot has taken this text from the Antwerp Polyglot. Whence the Antwerp Polyglot obtained it is not known. Arias Montanus, the editor, may have prepared this recension himself by elimination of those portions of the text that were not found in Heb., or he may have found this work already done for him by a predecessor. No MSS. or other editions of this short form are known, and it is certain that it was not the original text of the First Targum.

The major limit of age for this version is set by the fact that it makes extensive use of the haggadic material contained in the Tractate $M^e ghillā$ of the Babylonian Talmud. Nearly all the amplifications noted above are found also in $M^e ghillā$. This will appear in detail in the translations of the additions in the commentary, so that it is not necessary to dwell upon it here. In *Meg.* the amplifications are created by processes of rabbinical exegesis, in 𝔗¹ they are regarded as settled and are incorporated into the text; 𝔗¹, accordingly, must be later than *Meg.* The Talmud reached its final form toward the end of the sixth century, so that 𝔗¹ cannot be dated earlier than the seventh century. Apparently it is known to the *Pirqe Rabbi Eliezer* of the eighth century (see § 34). It shows no knowledge of Yosippon (Joseph b. Goryon's Heb. translation of Josephus), which dates from the tenth century; and, therefore, is presumably earlier. It is mentioned in the *Sepher ha-'Arukh*, a dictionary of the Talmud by Nathan b. Jehiel of Rome (11th cent.), and also frequently by Ibn Ezra and Alḳabeẓ. In view of all the facts Posner (p. 51) is probably right in dating it about 700 A.D. This, however, is only the date of the final literary fixing of the work. It bears internal evidence of being composed out of earlier targums, although in lack of quotations by ancient writers the precise limits of these sources cannot be determined. Back of them lay the oral targum of synagogal tradition. As early as the second century B.C. Hebrew was no longer understood by the common people in Palestine, and Aramaic versions became necessary. At first it was forbidden to write these, and the translators in the synagogues depended upon oral tradition. The popularity of Est. and the prescription that it should be read on the Feast of Purim must early have necessitated a version similar in character to the First Targum. The additions in 𝕲, 𝕷, and Jos., and the translations in 𝕵, show that the *haggada* that underlies this targum was already developed by the beginning of the Christian era. A targum on Est. is mentioned in the Mishna, *Meg.* ii. 1, and repeatedly in the Gemara of the same tractate. What the relation of this targum to 𝕿¹ is, is not known. These considerations lead one to believe that the oral Aramaic translation which underlies our targum, goes back to a high antiquity, and may preserve a memory of readings that differ from the official Massoretic text. In several places the consonantal text which 𝕿¹ preserves is different from that of 𝕸, and the vocalization also sometimes represents a different tradition. When these variants are confirmed by 𝕲, or by some of the other early versions, they possess some text-critical importance. Instances of this sort will be noted in the commentary. The additions of 𝕿¹ have, of course, not the least text-critical value. They are not found in 𝕲 or any of the other early versions, although passages similar to them do occasionally occur which show the beginning of the haggadic development. These additions belong to the latest stage of the growth of the targum tradition, and a discussion of them belongs in the history of interpretation rather than in the study of the text.

§ 10. THE SECOND TARGUM.

The Book of Esther alone among the books of the OT., except the Law, has a second independent Aramaic translation, the so-called *Targum Sheni*, or Second Targum. This is the favourite targum among the Jews and is found in all the Rabbinic Bibles, in Lagarde, *Hagiographa Chaldaice* (1874), pp. 223–270 (a reprint of the text of the Bomberg Bible of 1517); in Munk, *Targum Scheni zum Buche Est.*, *nebst Variæ Lectiones nach handschriftlichen Quellen erläutert u. mit einer literarhistorischen Einleitung versehen* (1876); in Cassel, *Aus Literatur u. Geschichte: Anhang, Zweites Targum zum Buche Est. im vocalisirten Urtext mit sachlichen u. sprachlichen Erläuterungen* (1885); and in David, *Das Targum Scheni zum Buche Est. nach Handschriften herausgegeben* (1898). The text of David is the best, and I have followed it in my translations of the targum. A German translation of 𝔗² is given in Cassel, *Das Buch Esther* (1891).

This targum contains a slavishly literal version of the Heb. interspersed in the same manner as 𝔗¹ with all sorts of legendary haggadic embellishments. When following the Heb. it is more faithful than 𝔗¹; when departing from it, it runs to fantastic excess. A number of its additions are verbally identical with those in 𝔗¹, others contain similar legends told in different language, and still others embody a totally divergent tradition. Some are similar in substance to the additions of 𝔊, but show no trace of having been derived from it. The majority are found only in this targum or in later midrashes based upon it. So numerous and so long are these additions that 𝔗² is more than twice as large as 𝔗¹, and four times as large as the Heb. Est. The principal additions are as follows:—

1¹, a list of the kings who have reigned or shall reign over the whole earth, the accession of Evil-Merodach and Daniel's dealings with him, the accession of Ahasuerus and his character, the location of Kush, and an account of the four kings who have reigned over as wide a territory as Ahasuerus; 1², a long addition, occupying eleven pages in David's edition, containing an acrostic on Solomon, a description of Solomon's throne, the visit of the Queen of Sheba, the destruction of Jerusalem and the Babylonian exile; 1⁴, the treasures which Ahasuerus showed his guests; 1⁵, a description of the King's feast; 1⁷, a description of the drinking at the feast; 1⁸, an account of Vashti's feast; 1¹⁰, the dispute of the King and his princes concerning beautiful women; 1¹¹, the command to strip Vashti and bring her naked; 1¹², Vashti's answer to the King; 1¹⁴, an account of the origin of the seven viziers; 1¹⁶, an identification of Memukhan with Daniel and some account of his activity; 1¹⁸, Memukhan's fear of Vashti's vengeance; 2¹, the King's execution of the seven viziers; 2⁵, the genealogy of Mordecai; and the reason why David spared the life of his ancestor

Shimei; 2⁶, further items in regard to Mordecai's travels; 2⁷, explanations of the meaning of the names Esther and Hadassah; 2⁸, Mordecai's effort to keep Esther from the messengers of the King; 2⁹, Esther's refusal to eat the King's food; 2¹⁷, the King's effort to ascertain Esther's origin; 2²¹, the plan of the eunuchs to kill the King; 3¹, the genealogy of Haman back to Esau; 3³, Mordecai's sermon to the King's servants against idolatry; 3⁷, Haman's efforts to find a suitable day for killing the Jews; 3⁸, Haman's argument against the Jews (occupies two pages in David's edition); 3⁹, an explanation of the 10,000 talents that Haman offered; 3¹¹, an apostrophe to Ahasuerus; 3¹⁵, the King's edict against the Jews; 4¹, the prayer of Mordecai; 4², the condition of the Jews after the royal edict was issued; 4¹¹, further messages that passed between Mordecai and Esther and the killing of Hathakh; 4¹⁷, Esther's command and the celebration of a great fast by the Jews; 5¹, Esther's dressing of herself and prayer before going to the King; 5⁸, the reasons why Esther invited Haman to her banquet; 5¹⁴, the advice of Zeresh and Haman's friends; 6¹, events in Heaven on the night after the issue of Haman's edict; 6¹⁰, Haman's argument with the King against honouring Mordecai; 6¹¹, Haman's carrying out of the King's command; 6¹³, Zeresh's exhibition of the futility of trying to strive against the Jews; 7⁹, the history of Ḥarbonah, Mordecai's interview with Haman before hanging him, and Haman's apostrophe to the trees; 8¹², the contents of the dispatch sent out by Mordecai; 9¹¹, the manner of the hanging of the sons of Haman; 9²⁴, the reason why Esther left the bodies of Haman and his sons on the gallows; 10³, the glory of Mordecai.

In regard to the age of this targum opinions differ. Cassel puts it in the time of Justinian. S. Gelbhaus, *Das Targum Scheni zum Buche Esther* (1893), on the strength of a citation in the BT. Tract. *Ṣopherim*, assigns it to the beginning of the fourth century; but this citation is now known to be a gloss. Gelbhaus' further argument for its antiquity from coincidences with the language of the Peshiṭto will apply equally well to 𝕋¹. The fact is, that two Aramaic translators, both endeavouring to give a faithful reproduction of the Heb., could not fail to use frequently the same expressions. Such coincidences prove nothing in regard to age or interdependence of the versions. A surer indication is found in the relation of this targum to the First Targum. Many passages are the same in both, and in all such cases it is more likely that the fuller work is the later. 𝕋², accordingly, probably borrows from 𝕋¹. (For evidence of this see Posner, pp. 18 *ff*.) Zunz, *Gottesdienst-*

liche Vorträge, p. 83, and David, in his introduction to the Second Targum, assign 𝕋² to the seventh century, but this is inconsistent with its dependence upon 𝕋¹. Posner finds evidences in it of the use of *Pirqe Rabbi Eliezer* (see § 34), and therefore dates it about 800 A.D. This is probably correct. It is first mentioned in RaShI's commentary on 1 K. 10¹⁹.

𝕋² bears clear evidence of being a compilation of several earlier targums. Frequently it contains two versions of the same passage. Its material is loosely strung together, and fully a fourth of it, particularly at the beginning, has nothing to do with the story of Esther. Munk, from a study of the quotations of Alḳabeẓ, comes to the conclusion that three earlier targums have been combined in this work. Back of these sources stood the same oral tradition that was used in 𝕋¹. Differences from the Massoretic text are not infrequent, and occasionally these may be reminiscences of a variant consonantal text. Where they agree with readings in the other Vrss., they may be text-critically important. Only where 𝕋² runs parallel to the Heb. has it any value for the text, the additions are all late *midrash* that never existed in any other language than Aramaic.

§ 11. THE LATIN VERSION OF JEROME.

A much more important witness than the targums for the official consonantal text is the Latin version of St. Jerome, made at Bethlehem between the years 390 and 405 A.D. The current Latin versions of this period were made from the Greek (see § 19) and were so incorrect that Jerome (Hieronymus) of Pannonia, the leading scholar of the day, was commissioned by Pope Damasius to prepare a better version for the use of the Western Church. At first he attempted a revision of the Old Latin, but soon becoming convinced that this was impossible, he set about making a complete new translation. In his prologue to the Book of Esther, which is printed in the Polyglots and in *Biblia Sacra Latina V. T. Hieronymo interprete*, ed. Heyse et Tischendorf (1873), Jerome speaks thus of this particular portion of his version:—

> It is well known that the Book of Esther has been corrupted by the various translators; but I, bringing it forth from the archives of the He-

brews, have translated it more literally word for word. The common version drags this book to and fro with rough ropes, adding on occasion whatever things can be said and heard; just as in school exercises it is customary to take a theme and to think out what words one can use who has suffered an injury, or one who has inflicted an injury. But you, Paula and Eustochium, since you have desired to enter the libraries of the Hebrews, and since you are judges of the disputes of interpreters, take the Book of Esther in Hebrew, and compare our translation of it word for word, that you may be able to testify that I have added nothing at all; but simply, as a faithful witness, have rendered the Hebrew history into the Latin tongue just as it stands in Hebrew. We do not covet the praises of men, nor are we afraid of their abuse, but as those who seek to please God we fear not the threats of men, because God will scatter their bones who seek to please men, as the Apostle says, "Those who are of this sort cannot be servants of Christ." Moreover, at various points we have placed red letters of the alphabet as far as Teth, in order by this means to suggest to the studious reader the order of the Septuagint; for we, alongside of the Hebrew form, have preferred to indicate the order that is also found in the Septuagint.

After this introduction, we should expect to find in Jerome's version of Esther as faithful a reproduction as possible of the Heb. text as it was known to him in the fourth century. He had a good knowledge of Hebrew, and was acquainted with the Jewish exegetical tradition of his day. He had access also to the Hexapla of Origen, and he was familiar with all the other early versions. Variations from the Massoretic text, accordingly, cannot be set down to ignorance, but indicate different readings in the MS. or group of MSS. that he used. The Vulgate, therefore, becomes an important aid in the correction of the Massoretic text.

After Jerome's solemn protest that he has added nothing to the Heb. original, it is surprising to find in how many places his translation contains words and sentences that are not found in 𝔐. The long additions of 𝔊, to be sure, are removed from the body of the book and placed in an appendix at the end; but other short additions are scattered quite evenly throughout the entire book. These additions are as follows:—

1[1], super; 1[3], igitur, grande; 1[5], quod regio cultu et manu consitum erat; 1[6], et pendebant ex omne parte tentoria, inserti erant, fulciebantur, quod mira varietate pictura decorabat; 1[7], qui invitati erant,

ESTHER

cibi inferebantur, ponebatur; 1⁸, præponens mensis singulos de; 1¹⁰, et post nimiam potationem incaluisset mero; 1¹¹, posito super caput ejus, cunctis; 1¹², mandaverat, contempsit; 1¹³, semper, et illorum faciebat, consilio, majorum; 1¹⁴, primi et; 1¹⁸, omnes; 1¹⁹, ultra; 1²², ac majores; 2³, et adducant eas, et tradant, et cetera ad usus necessaria; 2⁴, ut suggesserant; 2⁷, altero nomine vocabatur, nimis; 2⁸, juxta, pulchræ; 2⁹, et præcepit eunucho; 2¹⁰, de hac re omnino; 2¹¹, et scire volens; 2¹², vertebatur, ungerentur; 2¹³, ad ornatum pertinens, et ut eis placuerat compositæ; 2¹⁴, atque inde, deducebatur; 2¹⁵, evoluto autem tempore per ordinem; hæc ei ad ornatum dedit erat enim formosa valde et incredibili pulchritudine, et amabilis; 2¹⁸, pro conjunctione et nuptiis, universis; 2¹⁹, et congregarentur; 2²¹, janitores erant et in primo palatii limine, et occidere eum; 2²², qui ad se rem detulerat; 2²³, mandatumque est historiis; 3², solus; 3³, præter ceteros; 3⁵, quod cum audisset, experimento; 3⁶, nationem; 3⁷, in urnam, gens Judæorum deberet interfici et exivit mensis; 3⁸, et cæremoniis, et optime nosti; 3¹⁰, quo utebatur; 3¹¹, quod tu polliceris; 3¹⁵, et cunctis Judæis qui in; 4¹, spargens, ostendens, animi sui; 4³, crudele; 4⁴, quod audiens; 4⁵, ut iret; 4¹¹, pro signo clementiæ, igitur quomodo ad regem intrare potero; 4¹³, dicens, tantum; 4¹⁴, ut in tali tempore parareris; 4¹⁵, hæc, verba; 4¹⁶, non vocata; 5⁴, obsecro, ad me; 5⁷, sunt istæ; 5⁹, sedentem; 5¹⁰, ad se; 5¹¹, omnes; 6¹, sibi; 6², ad illum locum ubi; 6³, quod cum audisset; ei, ac; 6⁴, statim, et juberet; 6⁶, et reputans; 6⁸, imponi super; 6¹¹, equo præcedebat; 6¹³, quos habebat in consilio; 7⁴, esset tolerabile malum et gemens; 7⁶, quod, audiens illico, ferre non sustinens; 7⁷, de loco intravit; 7⁸, et intrasset, reperit; 8³, pessimas; 8⁴, ex more, quo signum clementiæ monstrabatur; 8⁵, obsecro; 8⁷, jussi, ausus est; 8⁸, hæc enim consuetudo erat; 8⁹, et librariis, qui, præsidebant; 8¹⁰, per omnes provincias, veteres litteras novis nuntiis prævenirent; 8¹¹, et in unum præciperent congregari, et in universis domibus; 8¹², et constituta est, ultionis; 8¹⁴, regis; 8¹⁵, de palatio, et; 8¹⁷, grandis; 9¹, vocari ante jam diximus, et se, vindicare; 9², et loca, et persecutores suos, magnitudinis; 9³, omnisque dignitas quæ singulis locis ac; 9⁴, et plurimum posse cognoverant, nominis; 9⁶, Agagitæ, quorum ista sunt nomina; 9¹⁰, quos cum; 9¹², putas, ultra; 9¹⁶, omnes; 9¹⁷, primus apud omnes interfectionis fuit, esse solemnem ut in eo omni tempore deinceps vacarent epulis; 9¹⁸, urbe, cædem exercuerant, idcirco, solemnem; 9²⁰, omnia, comprehensa; 9²¹, solemni, honore; 9²³, in solemnem ritum; 9²⁴, et adversarius, nostra lingua vertitur in; 9²⁵, Esther, obsecrans ut conatus ejus; 9²⁶, phur id est sors in urnam missa fuerint, id est libri hujus volumine continentur; 9²⁸, quæ his cæremoniis obligata est; 9²⁹, in posterum; 9³⁰, et sortium dies.

Some of these additions are nothing more than exegetical expansions to make the sense clear, such as we find in 🕭, but most of

THE VERSION OF JEROME

them cannot have originated in this way. In view of Jerome's solemn protest that he has added nothing to the Heb. original, we must assume that he had before him a text that contained many readings not found in the Massoretic recension. A large proportion of these occur also in 𝔖, 𝔊, and 𝔏, and this fact shows that they are not inventions of Jerome. Unfortunately we possess no really critical edition of Jerome's translation. The text of the Clementina is notoriously inaccurate, and in many cases of deviation from 𝔐 it is possible that we have to deal only with corruptions derived from the Old Latin or from the glosses of scribes. In the present state of knowledge of the Vulgate only those variants can be depended on which are confirmed by 𝔖 and 𝔊.

Jerome's omissions of readings found in our present Massoretic text are also interesting. Such omissions are found in $1^{1.\ 2.\ 5.\ 8.\ 10.\ 15.\ 18.\ 19}$ $2^{3.\ 6.\ 8.\ 9.\ 12.\ 13.\ 14.\ 15.\ 16.\ 18.\ 21}$ $3^{6.\ 8.\ 15}$ $4^{8.\ 14}$ $5^{2.\ 11}$ $6^{2.\ 5.\ 6.\ 7.\ 8.\ 9.\ 11.\ 13.\ 14}$ $7^{1.\ 2.\ 5.\ 9}$ $8^{3.\ 4.\ 5.\ 7.\ 9.\ 10.\ 11.\ 12.\ 13.\ 14.\ 15.\ 16}$ $9^{2.\ 4.\ 5.\ 6.\ 11.\ 12.\ 15.\ 16.\ 18.\ 19.\ 20.\ 24.\ 25.\ 27.\ 28.\ 30.\ 31}$ 10^{2}. In these cases 𝔍 sometimes agrees with 𝔊, more often with 𝔏 and L. The omissions, accordingly, cannot be regarded as accidental. In other passages 𝔍 gives a translation that does not correspond with the readings now found in the Massoretic text. Instances of this sort are as follows:—

1^2, civitas regni ejus exordium fuit; 1^4, ut ostenderet; 1^5, convivii invitavit, et nemoris; 1^6, ærii coloris, eburneis, depositi erant; 1^7, et aliis atque aliis vasis; 1^{10}, ejus; 1^{13}, ex more regio, ei aderant, leges; 1^{18}, exemplo parvipendens imperia maritorum, unde regis justa est indignatio; 1^{19}, accipiat; 1^{22}, regni sui ut quæque gens audire et legere poterat diversis linguis et litteris, viros, domibus, et hoc per cunctos populos divulgari; 2^3, qui est præpositus; 2^4, jussit fieri; 2^6, eo tempore; 2^7, fratris; 2^9, ornaret atque excoleret; 2^{12}, quæ ad cultum muliebrem pertinebant, uterentur; 2^{13}, transibant; 2^{15}, muliebrem cultum, virginum; 3^3, fores palatii; 4^4, perseveraret in sententia; 3^6, quod esset gentis Judæ; 3^7, quæ hebraice dicitur phur, quo die et quo mense; 3^8, novis utens; 3^{14}, summa autem epistolarum hæc fuit, ut omnes provinciæ scirent; 3^{15}, flentibus; 4^3, oppidis ac locis, pro strato utentibus; 4^8, reginæ; 4^{11}, et cunctæ quæ sub ditione ejus sunt, absque ulla cunctatione statim; 4^{12}, quod cum audisset Mardochæus; 4^{13}, rursum; 4^{15}, rursumque; 4^{16}, orate, tradensque me morti et periculo; 5^1, ille; 5^2, contra eam; 5^5, regina; 5^6, ei postquam vinum biberat abundanter; 5^9, palatii; 5^{14}, ei; 6^1, illo; 6^2, insidias; 6^3, illius; 6^8, de sella regis est, 6^9, primus; 6^{10-12}, palatii; 6^{14}, eum; 7^2, ei, postquam incaluerat; 7^4, nunc autem hostis noster est cujus crudelitas; 7^5, cujus potentiæ; 7^7, arboribus consitum; 7^8, nemoribus consito, ejus; 8^1, patruus suus; 8^2, suam; 8^4, ille, illaque, eum; 8^5, in occulis ejus, ei, novis epistolis veteres, eos; 8^6, et interfectionem; 8^7, affigi; 8^8, meo, mittebantur, illius; 8^9, erat autem, prout legere poterant et audire; 8^{10}, ipsæque epistolæ quæ regis nomine mittebantur; 8^{15}, omnisque; 8^{17}, epulæ, alterius gentis et sectæ eorum religioni et cæremoniis jungerentur, cunctos; 9^1, cunctis Judæis interfectio, eorum inhiabant sanguini; 9^3, nam; 9^4, quotidie et per cunctorum ora; 9^5, magna, quod sibi paraverant facere; 9^{12}, qui, exercere cædem; 9^{16}, interfectis hostibus ac persecutoribus suis; 9^{18}, hi, in cæde versati sunt; 9^{19}, in oppidis non muratis ac villis; 9^{20}, litteris comprehensa; 9^{21}, pro festis; 9^{25}, litteris regis irriti fierent; 9^{26}, id est sortium; 9^{27}, sustinuerunt, deinceps immutata sunt; 9^{28}, id est sortium non observentur; 9^{29}, etiam secunda epistolam ut omni studio dies ista solemnis sanciretur; 9^{31}, sortium, cum gaudio; 9^{32}, et omnia quæ libri hujus qui vocatur Esther historia continentur; 10^1, cunctas.

Some of these divergences can be explained as free paraphrases. In other cases the translation differs so completely from 𝔐 that we must assume that Jerome had an independent text, or else that he vocalized differently. Apart from the passages cited above, his text is identical with the Massoretic consonantal text, and the traditional pronunciation which he follows, *e.g.*, in proper names, is practically the same as that of 𝔐. Jerome does not carry us back of the codex adopted by the Jewish authorities in the second century, but for that he is one of the earliest and best witnesses.

§ 12. CITATIONS IN THE TALMUD.

Both the Babylonian and the Jerusalem Talmud in the Tractate *M^eghillā* contain a sort of running commentary on the Book of Esther, in which they frequently quote its language and discuss its meaning. These discussions presuppose in most cases our present consonantal text, but the vowel points are not yet known and the rabbis frequently suggest vocalizations that differ from those of 𝔐. The Talmud, accordingly, has some value as a witness to the pre-Tiberian text. Long additions to the story similar to those in 𝕿¹ and 𝕿² are also found in the Talmuds. These are translated in the commentary at appropriate points. They rest upon no textual authority; in fact, in most cases the process is exhibited by which they are elicited from the Heb. by ingenious methods of exegesis. They show that in the sixth century, when the Talmudic oral tradition first took literary form, a large part of the midrashic embellishments of Esther were already known.

These are all the descendants of the text of the Ṣopherim, since Aquila, Symmachus, and Theodotion, that are so helpful in other books, do not exist for Esther. By a comparison of the various forms of the text described thus far, namely, the Tiberian recension, the Babylonian recension, the Peshiṭto, First Targum, Second Targum, Vulgate and Talmud, it is possible to reconstruct with great certainty the consonantal text from which all are descended. The extraordinary similarity of the MSS. both of the Palestinian and of the Babylonian type—a similarity which extends even to the reproduction of errors and exceptional letters—and the close agreement of all the Vrss. made since the beginning of the Christian era, prove the thesis of Lagarde to be correct, that all these recensions are descendants from a single prototype, the so-called text of the Ṣopherim (*cf. Anmerkungen zur griechischen Uebersetzung der Proverbien*, 1863, pp. 1–2). At some time in the second century the exigencies of controversy with Christians, and the desire to have a fixed basis of discussion between the rabbis, led to the adoption by the Jewish authorities of an official standard codex of the OT. Since that time all copies have been made directly or indirectly from this codex and variant codices have been destroyed. The result is, that no ancient differences of reading have come down to us in this family, but only variants that have arisen since the standard codex was adopted.

c. OTHER DESCENDANTS OF THE ORIGINAL TEXT.
§ 13. THE GREEK VERSION.

Besides the text of the Ṣopherim, our only other witness to the original text is the Greek translation, the so-called Septuagint. This version was made before the adoption of the standard codex of the Ṣopherim. Its divergences from 𝔐 may represent an earlier form of the Heb. text. Esther is the only book of the Greek OT., except the Wisdom of Jesus son of Sirach, that has a subscription containing information about its authorship and date. According to addition F, verse [11] (=Vulg. and Eng. Apoc. Ad. Est. 11[1]), "in the fourth year of the reign of Ptolemy and Cleopatra, Dositheus, who said that he was a priest and Levite, and Ptolemy his son, brought the foregoing letter concerning Purim (Phrourai), which they said was genuine, and that Lysimachus, son of Ptolemy, one of the people in Jerusalem, had interpreted it." This can mean nothing else, than that the Book of Esther in Greek translation was brought from Jerusalem to Egypt in the fourth year of a king named Ptolemy, whose consort was Cleopatra. This is a very uncertain indication of age, inasmuch as four Ptolemies, namely Ptolemy V (Epiphanes), Ptolemy VI (Philometor), Ptolemy VII (Physcon), and Ptolemy VIII (Lathuros), were married to a Cleopatra. Most critics have supposed that Ptolemy VI is meant, because he was a friend of the Jews and permitted them to build a temple at Leontopolis. In that case the date of the version would be 178 B.C., but, as B. Jacob has shown ("Das Buch Esther bei den LXX," *ZATW*. x. (1890), pp. 241 *ff.*), the only Ptolemy who was married to a Cleopatra in the fourth year of his reign was Ptolemy VIII. The book must then be assigned to 114 B.C. This later date is more likely on account of the failure of the son of Sirach (*c.* 170 B.C.) to mention the Book of Esther (so Nöld., Wild., Rys.).

Kuenen (*Onderzoek*, i. p. 542), and many others following him, have doubted the genuineness of this subscription, because it represents the author as a resident of Jerusalem, while the book is written in the Egyptian dialect of Greek and seems to show knowledge of Egyptian conditions (so Jacob, *l. c.* pp. 280 *ff.*); but, as Nöld. points out (*EBi.* 1405), the name Lysimachus, son of Ptolemy, is Egyptian, and the author may well have been an Egyptian Jew, who, through residence in Jerusalem, became acquainted with Hebrew and was thus well qualified to make just such a version as we find in Est. A more serious objection to the genuineness of the subscription is the fact that it stands at the end of one of the long additions that seems to come from a different hand from that of the original translator. If added by a later glossator, this subscription may be only an invention designed to commend Purim to the Egyptian Jews by representing it as endorsed by one of the priests at Jerusalem. It is possible, however, that the subscription stood originally at the end of the book, and that the inserter of Addition F has merely removed it to the end of his addition. On the whole, there is no sufficient reason for doubting the genuineness of this testimony concerning the origin of the book. It dates the version just where for other reasons one would be inclined to put it. The Heb. Est. itself is hardly earlier than 150 B.C. and the Greek text is cited by Josephus *c.* 90 A.D. These, accordingly, are the major and the minor limits of age. The failure of Philo to quote Est. (Ryle, *Philo and the Holy Scriptures*, p. 32) does not necessarily show that the Greek translation was unknown to him. He may have regarded it as uncanonical.

§ 14. THE UNREVISED GREEK TEXT.

The Greek Book of Esther has come down to us in five main recensions, and only through a comparison of these can one hope to restore the primitive form of the text. Most important is the recension represented by the uncial codices B ℵ A N, and by the cursives 55, 108*a*, 249 (Holmes and Parsons). B, or *Codex Vaticanus*, Rome, Vatican Library, belongs to the middle of the fourth century. In 1890 it was published in photographic reproduction by the Vatican press. Its text is accurately printed by Swete, *The Old Testament in Greek*[2] (1896). On the whole it represents the current form of 𝔊 in the Christian Church before the revisions of Origen, Hesychius, and Lucian had been undertaken. In the book of Esther its text is neutral in relation to these three recensions. It cannot be supposed that it represents the κοινὴ ἔκδοσις of the third century, much less the original text of 𝔊, still it probably comes nearer to it than any other extant MS.

ℵ, or *Codex Sinaiticus*, also dates from the fourth century. The forty-three leaves containing Esther and portions of Ch., Esd., and Tob. were found by Tischendorf in 1844 among waste papers at the Convent of St. Catherine on Mt. Sinai, and are now in the Library at Leipzig. They were published in 1846 under the name *Codex Frederico-Augustanus*, by which name these fragments are cited by Field and by many German writers. Since the discovery of the rest of this MS. (now deposited at St. Petersburg), the earlier published portion has commonly been known as *Codex Sinaiticus*, and is indicated by the symbol ℵ or S. In Est. this codex agrees for the most part with B, although occasionally it shows the influence of Origen's Hexapla. Its deviations from B in the Book of Est. are given with extreme care by Lagarde, *Librorum V. T. canonicorum pars prior Græce* (1883), pp. 505 *ff.*, and by Swete, *The OT. in Greek*.

A, or *Codex Alexandrinus*, now in the British Museum, was written in the fifth century. This was used as the basis of Grabe's great edition (1707–20), and was published in facsimile (1881–3) by the Trustees of the British Museum. Its text is much more influenced by the Hexapla than that of B and ℵ, still it is far from being a mere transcription of Origen's recension. It has been revised from the Hexapla, yet it preserves many independent readings; and, on the whole, is to be regarded as a witness for the unrevised rather than the Origenic text. Its variants are given in the editions of Lagarde and Swete cited above.

N, or *Codex Basiliano-Vaticanus*, in the Vatican Library, dates from the eighth or the ninth century. Apart from obvious mistakes, its text in Est. presents few variations from that of B. The cursive 55 (=Rome, Vat. Reg. Gr. 1) is also exceedingly near to B. Its confusions of Λ and Δ and of Σ and E show that it was copied from an uncial MS. Codex 108 (=Rome, Vat. Gr. 330) exhibits two recensions of Est.; the first, known as 108*a*, contains a text similar to that of the uncials; the other, 108*b*, contains the Lucianic text. Codex 249 (=Rome, Vat. Pius I) belongs in the main to this family, but it shows many Hexaplaric readings, as is evident from its frequent agreement with the Hexaplaric MS. 93*b*. It is full of arbitrary alterations.

Closely akin to the text of the uncials, but forming a sub-group distinguished by common characteristics, are the codices 52 (=Florence, Laur. Acq. 44), 64 (=Paris, Nat. Reg. Gr. 2), 243 (=Venice, St. Mark's, cod. 16), 248 (=Rome, Vat. Gr. 346).

The Greek text of the Complutensian Polyglot (1514) is an exact reproduction of 248, agreeing with it even when it differs from all other codices (cf. $2^{23}\ 5^1$). The Aldine edition (1518–19) also belongs to this sub-group, probably through dependence upon 243, which was accessible to the editor, Andreas Asolanus, in Venice. In the few instances where these codices agree in differing from B, they are eclectic from all the other recensions.

The text of the recension of which B is the leading representative differs from 𝔐 chiefly in its numerous additions, which are without a parallel in other books of the LXX. There are 107 new verses not found in the Heb. Jerome in the Vulgate Lat. version translated the longer additions, but removed them from the body of the book and placed them at the end because they were not found in the Heb. This senseless arrangement is perpetuated in the English AV. and RV. In Swete's edition they are given in their proper place and are designated by the letters A, B, etc. A (=Lat. and Eng. 11^2–12^6) precedes 1^1 and narrates Mordecai's dream and the way in which he came to be promoted to honour at the court of Artaxerxes. B (=13^{1-7}) follows 3^{13} with a letter of Artaxerxes. C (=13^8–14^{19}) follows 4^{17} and contains the prayer of Mordecai. D (=15^{4-19}) follows C and precedes 5. It contains the prayer of Esther. E (=16^{1-24}) follows 7^{12} with a letter of Artaxerxes. F (=10^4–11^5) is an epilogue describing the establishment of the feast of Purim.

Besides these long additions, which form compact sections at various points in the book, there are numerous short additions inserted in the midst of verses. These are eliminated in Jerome's translation, and they do not appear in our English Apocrypha. In the commentary I have translated them in full. They occur in the following passages:—$1^{1.\ 6.\ 7.\ 8.\ 11.\ 14.\ 17}$ $2^{1.\ 3.\ 12.\ 18.\ 20.\ 21.\ 23}$ $3^{4.\ 7.\ 10.\ 12}$ $4^{1.\ 2.\ 4.\ 7.\ 8.\ 10.\ 12.\ 13.\ 15}$ $5^{4.\ 6.\ 8.\ 9}$ $6^{1.\ 2.\ 3.\ 8.\ 9.\ 11}$ $8^{5.\ 7.\ 13.\ 17}$ $9^{18.\ 19.\ 21.\ 22.\ 26}$ 10^2 (for details see the commentary). Some of these are short explanatory glosses analogous to those found in 𝔖 and 𝔘¹. Others are expansions of the story that have no foundation in the Heb. text.

No less striking than the additions are the omissions of this recension. There is scarcely a verse from which one or more words of 𝔐 are not deleted (details may be found in the critical notes of the commentary). Apart from these additions and subtractions the text of B follows 𝔐 closely. Ordinarily one can recognize the Heb. original word for word in the translation, just as in 𝔍, 𝔖, or 𝔘¹. Only occasionally the Greek fails to correspond with 𝔐. Sometimes this is due to reading a different Heb. word, at other times it is nothing but a textual corruption in 𝔊.

§ 15. THE RECENSION OF ORIGEN.

At the beginning of the third century Origen, desiring to perfect himself in exegesis, took up the study of Hebrew and soon made himself master of that language. In comparing the standard Jewish text of his day with the current Greek version, he noticed wide divergences and was convinced that the Greek text was very corrupt. In order to call attention to the errors and to aid scholars in correcting them, he prepared the huge work known as the Hexapla, in which in six parallel columns he exhibited the Hebrew, the Hebrew in transliteration, Aquila, Symmachus, the current Greek text, and Theodotion. Differences in order from 𝔥 in the current text he corrected by transposition, supposed errors he emended by the substitution of words that represented 𝔥 more closely. Omissions he supplied from 𝔥, or from one of the literal versions, and marked these with an asterisk to indicate that they were found in 𝔥, although missing in 𝔊. Insertions in 𝔊 he marked with an obelus ÷ to show that they were wanting in 𝔥.

This great work was completed about 240 A.D. and was long preserved at Cæsarea, where it was used by Jerome and many other scholars. Only fragments of copies of it have come down to us, and among these are no copies of Esther. The translations of Aquila, Symmachus, and Theodotion for this book, accordingly, are unknown to us. Copies of Origen's revised text in the fifth column of the Hexapla have, however, survived. Pamphilus and his friend Eusebius excerpted this from the Hexapla and gave it wide currency. Codex 93 (=British Museum, Reg. i. D. 2) contains two recensions of Esther; one, 93*a*, is that of Lucian; the other, 93*b*, has the asterisks, obeli, and other critical signs which mark it as belonging to Origen. Both texts are given by J. Ussher, *De Græca Septuaginta interpretum versione syntagma cum libri Estheræ editione Origenica et vetere Græca altera* (1655, 1695). In the Hexaplaric text the editor has taken great liberties in the insertion of the critical signs. The readings of this codex are also given in Holmes and Parsons. The form in 93*b* corresponds closely with 𝔐, inserting under an asterisk all the passages that are omitted by 𝔊, and obelizing the passages that are added by 𝔊. In Codex ℵ, a corrector of the seventh century, commonly designated as ℵ ᶜ·ᵃ, appends the following note at the end of the Book of Esther (Swete, ii. 780):—

> Compared with the exceedingly ancient copy corrected by the hand of the holy martyr Pamphilus. At the end of the same ancient book, which begins with First Kings and stops with Esther, there is found in an open space an autograph subscription of the martyr himself that reads as follows: Revised and corrected by the Hexapla, that was corrected by Origen himself. Antoninus the confessor compared it. Pamphilus corrected the copy in prison, through the abundant grace and bounty of God; and, if it be not presumptuous to say so, it is not easy to find a copy like this.

From this it appears that this corrector of ℵ made use of Pamphilus' copy of Origen's revised text in the fifth column of the Hexapla. His readings agree everywhere with those of 93*b* and thus confirm its Hexaplaric character. These readings are given in Lagarde's *Lib. Vet. Test. Canon.* and in Swete. The Hexaplaric material from 93*b* and ℵᶜ·ᵃ is collected by F. Field, *Origenis Hexaplorum quæ supersunt* (1875), i. pp. 793 *ff.* The fame of Origen, and the authority of the martyr Pamphilus and of the bishop Eusebius, gave Origen's revision of the Septuagint great currency among scholars, although it never supplanted the common text in the use of the Church. It resulted in a systematic re-editing of the ancient codices with the consequence that no MSS. have come down to us that have escaped Hexaplaric influence. The problem of the restoration of the original text of 𝔊 is thus greatly complicated.

§ 16. THE RECENSION OF HESYCHIUS.

Jerome in his preface to Chronicles and preface to the Gospel (*cf. Adv. Rufin.* ii.) says that Hesychius was the author of a recension of the Septuagint that enjoyed the same esteem in Egypt that Origen's recension enjoyed in Palestine. This Hesychius was probably a bishop who was martyred in the second half of the fourth century, and to his martyrdom was due the reputation which his text obtained. In lack of direct testimony ascribing manuscripts to this recension, we are compelled to fall back upon indirect evidence. It is reasonable to suppose that citations of the OT. made by the Alexandrian Fathers from the fifth century onward are based upon it, and that it was also used for the translations of the Bible into Ethiopic and the various dialects of Coptic. Applying these tests, a group of codices seems to be identified which represents in the main the Hesychian recension. For the Book of Esther these are the codices designated by Holmes and Parsons as 44 (=Zittau, A 1.1 = Lagarde's *z, cf. Gen. Gr.* 7 *ff.*), 68 (=Venice, St. Mark's, Gr. 5, *cf.* Scrivener-Miller, i. 219), 71 (=Paris, Nat. Reg. Gr. 1), 74 (=Florence, Laur. Acq. 700), 76 (=Paris, Nat. Reg. Gr. 4), 106 (=Ferrara, Bib. Comm. Gr. 187), 107 (=Ferrara, Bib. Comm. Gr. 188), 120 (=Venice, St. Mark's, Gr. 4), 236 (=Rome, Vat. Gr. 331). These codices agree with one another in numerous divergences from B, especially in omitting more matter that is found in 𝔐, and in making a number of new insertions (details are given in the critical notes of the commentary). They fall into a number of sub-groups; thus 44, 106, and 107 belong together; 74 and 76; and 120, 68, and 236 (see Jacob, *ZATW.* 1890, pp. 244 *ff.*). The Coptic versions of Esther, that would presumably show an underlying Hesychian text, have never been published, so far as I am aware; and the Ethiopic version, which might also throw light on the Hesychian recension, exists only in MSS. Dr. Littmann of Strassburg kindly informs me that there are two MSS. in the d'Abbadie Collection at Paris, one in Oxford, nine in the British Museum, and two at Frankfurt a. M. that contain the Ethiopic text of Esther. None of these have been accessible to me, so that I have been compelled to ignore their textual evidence.

§ 17. THE RECENSION OF LUCIAN.

According to the testimony of Jerome (*Pref. in Paral.; Ad Sunn. et Fret.* 2) the region from Constantinople to Antioch used a recension of the LXX, prepared by Lucian the martyr of Nicomedia (*c.* 311). In the Arabic Syro-Hexaplar, Field noticed that certain readings were designated as Lucianic, and that these also occurred in one group of cursive MSS. Readings of these MSS. were also found in Chrysostom and Theodoret of Antioch, who presumably used the Antiochan text. This created a strong probability that the codices in question belonged to the Lucianic recension. Similar conclusions were reached independently by Lagarde, and they have commended themselves to most subsequent scholars. The codices which Field and Lagarde recognize as Lucianic for the Book of Esther are Holmes and Parsons 19 (=Rome, Chigi, R vi. 38, which Lagarde designates as *h*), 93*a* (=the first recension in London, British Museum, Reg. i. D. 2, which Lagarde designates as *m*), and 108*b* (=the second recension in Rome, Vat. Gr. 330, which Lagarde designates as *d*). The text of 93*a* was published by Ussher in his *Syntagma* (1655) in connection with the Origenic text found in the same codex; also by O. F. Fritzsche, ΕΣΘΗΡ: *duplicem libri textum ad optimos codd.* (1848), and *Libri Apocryphi V. T. Græce* (1871), pp. 30 *ff.*, with use of the readings of 19 and 108*b* as given by Holmes and Parsons. Lagarde in his *Lib. V. T. Can. Græce* (1883) attempts a reconstruction of the Lucianic text of the historical books, and in the case of Est. gives also the text of the uncials in parallel columns. The Lucianic text here presented is constructed from a comparison of 19, 93*a*, and 108*b*, and in the critical apparatus all the variants are recorded. For the Lucianic readings this edition has completely superseded the clumsy and often inaccurate apparatus in Holmes and Parsons. Scholtz in his commentary on Est. reproduces the two texts of Lagarde, and gives also in parallel columns the narrative of Josephus and a German translation of 𝔐.

The text which these three late representatives of the Lucianic family contain differs so widely from the text of the uncials in the Book of Esther that Ussher, Fritzsche, and Langen ("Die beiden griechischen Texte des Buches Esther," *Tüb. Theol. Quartalschrift*, 1860, pp. 244 *ff.*) have been constrained to think that it is an independent translation from the Heb. A detailed comparison of the two texts, however, shows far too many correspondences to make this theory possible. This is a recension, not a version; nevertheless, it is the most widely variant recension that is found in the whole Greek OT.

> Although L has all the long additions to 𝔐 that are found in B, it has scarcely any of the shorter additions. In $1^{1.\ 6}\ 2^3\ 4^{2.\ 15}\ 5^{4.\ 6.\ 8.}\ 6^{1.\ 2.\ 11}$ L and B contain similar brief amplifications, but all the other amplifications mentioned in § 14 are lacking here. On the other hand, L has a long list of passages that are found neither in 𝔐 nor in B. These are as follows: $1^{5.\ 6.\ 9.\ 10.\ 12.\ 13.\ 16.\ 19.\ 20}\ 2^{1.\ 4.\ 7.\ 8.\ 9.\ 18}\ 3^{1.\ 2.\ 3.\ 7.\ 8.\ 9.\ 12.\ 15}$ $4^{1.\ 3.\ 4.\ 8.\ 10.\ 12.\ 14}\ 5^{4.\ 6.\ 9.\ 10.\ 12.\ 14}\ 6^{1.\ 3.\ 4.\ 8.\ 11}\ 7^{2.\ 4.\ 5.\ 8.\ 9}\ 8^{2.\ 3.\ 5.\ 7.\ 8.\ 12}$ $9^{4.\ 21}$. Some of these additions are of considerable length, as, for instance, the King's expression of regret that he has not rewarded Mordecai 6^3, Haman's conduct on being told to honour Mordecai 6^{11-12}, Esther's words to the King 7^5, the King's words to Esther 8^2, Esther's request of the King 8^7, the contents of Mordecai's letter 8^{12}. These are longer than the ordinary additions in B, apart from the six long passages, and resemble rather the amplifications in Josephus and the Targums. L also differs from B in its omissions. It leaves out not merely occasional words that seem superfluous in 𝔐, but also whole sentences and groups of sentences particularly in the latter half of the book, *e.g.*, $1^{12.\ 22}\ 2^{6.\ 8.\ 10-18.\ 19-23}\ 3^{14}\ 4^{5-7.\ 12}\ 5^{11}\ 6^3\ 7^{10}\ 8^{3.\ 4.\ 6.\ 13}\ 9^{1.\ 11.\ 15.\ 17-19.\ 24.\ 25.\ 27.\ 29-32}$. Here whole verses are omitted. There are also numerous cases where half verses are omitted.

In the passages where L runs parallel to both 𝔐 and B it frequently presents a different translation from that in B, or a translation which presupposes a different Heb. text. Here, as elsewhere in the OT., L has a curious and unexpected value as a witness to an independent Heb. original. Another peculiarity of L in Esther has often been noted in the other books, namely, a tendency to give side by side alternate versions of the same Heb. phrase (*cf.* Driver, *Text of the Book of Samuel*, pp. li. *ff.*).

§ 18. JOSEPHUS.

In the eleventh book of his *Antiquities of the Jews* (*c.* 90 A.D.), beginning with § 186 (ed. Niese), Josephus tells the story of Esther on the basis of the Greek version, transcribing at times its language verbatim. He thus becomes a witness of some importance to the original text of 𝔊. On the whole, his readings are nearer to those of the uncials than of any other recension. The dream of Mordecai and its interpretation he omits—apparently it did not stand in the MS. that he used—but the rest of the long additions in B he inserts. Most of the small additions of B are unknown to him, as to L. In his omissions he also agrees with L rather than B, but he leaves out more than L, and in this respect resembles the Old Latin. The most curious feature of his text is the numerous additions both short and long that it contains and that are not found in other recensions. Some of these are mere exegetical expansions. Others have no relation to the Greek text and are clearly derived from an early form of Jewish *midrash*. Thus in 205–206 he gives a long account of the law that the King made to prevent any members of his family approaching him without summons; in 207, of the way in which Barnabazos, a slave of one of the eunuchs, discovered the plot against the King and reported it to Mordecai; in 269, of how Sabouchadas, a royal eunuch, saw the gallows that Haman had prepared for Mordecai. Such embellishments can hardly have been invented by Josephus himself, but must have been derived from some traditional Jewish source. The short additions which occur in almost every verse, are too numerous to give here. They are translated in full in the commentary at the points where they occur in the text. Some of the additions Josephus has in common with L, and in other respects he often agrees with that recension against B. Other cases of the same sort in books v.–vii. of the *Antiquities* have been noted by Mez, *Die Bibel des Josephus* (1895). In general, Jos. gives such a free paraphrase of the story that it is difficult to draw certain conclusions from him except in regard to additions, omissions, and proper names.

§ 19. THE OLD LATIN VERSION.

The Old Latin version was made from the LXX in the middle of the second century A.D., and is, therefore, an important witness to the Greek before it underwent the revisions of Origen, Hesychius, and Lucian. The Old Latin Book of Esther, according to *Codex Corbeiensis*, is given by P. Sabatier, *Bibliorum sacrorum Latinæ versiones antiquæ, seu Vetus Italica*, i. (1751), pp. 796–825. For Addition A and chaps. 1–2 he gives also the variants of *Codex Oratorius* B vii.; and for the rest of the book, the variants of *Codex Pechianus*. S. Berger, "Notice sur quelques textes latins inédites de l'Ancien Testament," in *Notices et extraits des manuscrits de la Bibl. Nat. et autres bibl.* xxxiv. 2 (1895), pp. 145 *ff.*, publishes a specimen of an Old Latin text of Esther from MS. 356 at Lyons, that differs considerably from the other published texts, especially at the beginning and the end. J. M. Tommasi in his *Sac. Bibl. veteres tituli, etc.* (1688), found in tom. i. of his *Opera* (1747), gives the readings of *Codex Vallicellanus* (*cf.* Bianchini, *Vindiciæ*, pp. ccxciv. *ff.*). Unpublished MSS. of the Old Latin Esther exist in *Codex Complutensis* of the Madrid Natl. Libr., Munich 6225 and 6239, Monte Casino 35, and Milan, Ambros. E 26 inf. (see the article of Berger cited above, pp. 119 *ff.*).

𝕷 is a slavishly literal version of 𝕲, but its translator was not a very good Greek scholar; and, particularly in the more rhetorical passages, such as are found in the long additions, he fails to understand the meaning. Usually, it is easy to see what Greek words he had before him. The Old Latin contains all the long additions of the various Greek recensions, and has besides a number of interesting additions of its own. Thus after 3^{14} it appends a long prayer of the Jews (see com. *a. l.*); 4^4, Esther's distress on hearing that Mordecai is clothed in sackcloth; 4^{17}, Mordecai's proclamation of a fast; ^{16}, the deliverance of Noah, Abraham, Jonah, Hananiah, Azariah, Mishael, Daniel, Hezekiah, and Anna. These additions bear internal evidence of being translated from a Greek original; and in certain cases the mistakes show clearly that they are derived ultimately from a Heb. or Aram. source (*cf.* Jacob, *ZATW*.

1890, p. 257). The passage about the fast occurs in a very similar form in 𝕋²; and, according to a citation of Alḳabeẓ in his Commentary on Esther (Venice, 1585), it was found in a certain *Targum Rabbathi.* These additions must be fragments of ancient Jewish *midrashim* that were used to enrich the Greek codex from which this Latin version was made. They are thus an important witness to the antiquity of the *haggada* that has come down in the two Targums.

In its omissions 𝔏 rivals L, which is the shortest of the Greek recensions. The following entire verses are wanting:—A$^{12-17}$ 1^3· ^{4} 4$^{5.6}$ 5$^{5-8}$ 8^{13} 9$^{15-19.}$ $^{24-'7.}$ $^{30-32}$ 10^1. Besides these there are many short omissions of words and clauses. In most of these 𝔏 agrees with L. As a rule 𝔏 reproduces word for word a text similar to that of the uncials, but in other cases it follows the readings of L. The Greek MS. from which it was made must have belonged to a group similar to that which Lucian employed in his revision. The same phenomenon has been noticed in the Old Latin version of other books of the OT. Often the reading in 𝔏 has no counterpart in any of the Greek recensions; *e.g.,* 3^4 4$^{1.\ 7.\ 8.\ 9.\ 16.\ 17}$ 5^9 6^3 (see com.). In such cases it is difficult to say whether we have to deal with a variant in the Greek or with a corruption in the Latin. The text of *Corbeiensis* differs so widely from those of *Oratorius* and *Pechianus* that some have supposed that the latter are independent versions, and have appealed to Jerome's remark in his preface to Esther, "*Librum Esther variis translatoribus constat esse vitiatum.*" In this state of the text of 𝔏 it is impossible to draw certain conclusions from it in regard to the primitive form of 𝔊. Only when it agrees with one of the Greek recensions does its testimony become of any importance. In several cases 𝔏 has readings that are nearer to 𝔐 than those of any of the Greek recensions. These cannot be due to reediting of the Latin from the Hebrew, but must be survivals of better Greek readings than any found in our present codices.

§ 20. ORIGIN OF THE ADDITIONS IN GREEK.

The long additions to the Book of Esther described in § 14 are found, as we have seen, in all the recensions of the Greek and in the

Old Latin. This fact naturally raises the questions, whether they were not a part of the original Septuagint, and whether they did not stand in the Heb. codex from which this version was made. The presence of these additions in the LXX and Vulg. early led the Christian Church to regard them as canonical. They were sanctioned by the Council of Carthage in 397 A.D. and by several later councils, including that of Trent in 1546. In order to justify these decisions, Roman Catholic writers have been compelled to hold that the additions are translations from a Heb. or Aram. original that stood in a larger recension of Esther, or in the sources from which that book was derived. Many suppose the original to have been the Book of the Chronicles of the Kings of Media and Persia mentioned in Est. 10^2; so in recent times, J. Langen, "Die beiden griechischen Texte des Buches Esther," *Theol. Quartalschrift*, 1860, pp. 263 *ff.*; *Die deuterocanonischen Stücke im Buche Esther* (1862); Kaulen, *Einleitung in das A. T.*^{3} (1890), p. 271 *f.*; and Art. "Esther" in Wetzer and Welte's *Kirchen-Lexicon;* Scholz, *Kommentar* (1892), pp. xxi. *ff.*; Seisenberger, *Kommentar* (1901), p. 133; Willrich, *Judaica* (1900), p. 15. On this theory the Heb. Est. is an abbreviation of a fuller original which has been preserved by 𝔊.

The chief objections to this view are as follows:—(1) There is no evidence of the existence of Semitic originals for these passages. De Rossi (*Specimen variorum lectionum*, iv. 138–161) noted several MSS. of Esther in which the dream of Mordecai and the prayers of Mordecai and Esther in Aram. were appended to 𝔐 and regarded these as prototypes of the Greek additions (*cf.* § 3); but it is now known that these passages are a verbal translation of the first three chapters of Esther in Yosippon (10th cent. A.D.). Josephus knows the additions only in the Gr. text of the vulgar recension, and makes no use of Semitic sources. The Syr. version contains only the shorter text of the Heb. recension. Jerome knows only the present Heb. text, and the Talmud has none of the additions of 𝔊. The haggadic amplifications of the two Targums are all based upon 𝔐 and show no knowledge of the Gr. additions. Yosippon is the first Heb. writer that uses them, and he has evidently derived them directly from Josephus (*cf.* § 34).

ADDITIONS IN GREEK

Wherever analogues to the additions occur in the targumic or midrashic literature, the works are late and can be shown to have borrowed the material either directly or indirectly from 𝕲.

(2) The additions themselves bear no evidence of having been translated from Heb. or Aram. Certain familiar expressions of the OT. occur in them, such as a Jew would naturally use, but in general they are written in a florid style that cannot readily be translated into Heb. (*cf.* the attempt of S. I. Fränkel, *Hagiographa posteriora . . . e textu Græco in linguam Hebraicam convertit, etc.* (1830). The best modern authorities, such as Fritzsche, Nöldeke, Bertheau, Ryssel, Bissell, Schürer, André, Fuller, and the Jewish scholar Jellinek in *Beth ham-Midrash*, v. p. viii, are agreed that the additions of 𝕲 never existed in Heb. or Aram., but that they were written for the first time in Greek. This, of course, does not preclude the idea that they may have been derived from traditional Jewish oral sources.

(3) The interpolations contradict the Heb. text in so many particulars that it is impossible to regard them as having once formed an integral part of the Book of Est. For instance, in 2^{16-19} Esther becomes queen in the seventh year of Ahasuerus, and Mordecai does not appear at court until after this event, but in A^{2-12} (=11^3 12^1) Mordecai holds already a high position at court in the second year of Ahasuerus. In 2^{21-23} Mordecai has no access to the King, and is compelled to make use of the mediation of Esther to convey the news of his discovery of the plot, but in A^{13} (=12^2) Mordecai himself reveals the conspiracy. In $6^{3, 4}$ Mordecai receives no pay for his service, but in A^{16} (=12^5) he is at once richly rewarded. In 3^5 Haman is angry because Mordecai refuses to bow down to him, but in A^{17} (=12^6) it is because he denounced the two eunuchs. In 2^{15-18} Esther's marriage to the King is narrated with evident satisfaction, but in C^{26-27} (=$14^{15, 16}$) she describes her horror at union with one who is uncircumcised and her abhorrence of the royal crown. In 5^{4-8} Esther invites Haman twice to a banquet, but in C^{23} (=14^{17}) she declares that she has never eaten at Haman's table. In 3^1 Haman is called an Agagite and his father bears a Persian name, but in E^{10} (=16^{10}) Haman is a Macedonian. In 1^{19} 8^8 the royal edict is irrevocable, but in E^{17} (=16^{17}) the first

edict sent out by Haman is revoked. In 7^{10} Haman is hanged, but in E^{12} ($=16^{18}$) he is crucified. In 9^{20-32} the Jews alone are to keep Purim, but in E^{22} ($=16^{22}$) the Persians also are to keep the feast.

(4) The additions do not come from the hand of the original translator of Est., but are interpolations in 𝔊 itself. Their style is freer and more diffuse than that of the other parts of the book, and their author had a much better command of Greek than the original translator. Josephus does not know two of the additions, and the Lucianic recension bears evidence that one at least has been interpolated in it. After 8^{12} (8^{34} in Lagarde) L inserts: "And the letter which Mordecai sent out had the following contents: Haman sent you letters to the effect that you should hasten to destroy quickly for me the treacherous race of the Jews: but I, Mordecai, declare to you that he who did this has been hanged before the gates of Susa, and his property has been confiscated because he wished to slay you." This short addition was evidently the original draft of Mordecai's letter in L; and when some later editor desired to insert the long letter found in the text of the uncials he was unable to place it after 8^{12} on account of the presence of this short letter, and was obliged to insert it after 8^{7}. The different position of Addition E in L from that in B is witness, accordingly, that it was not an original part of L.

For these reasons the long additions of the Greek must be regarded as late interpolations that never stood in the Book of Esther or in any of its Heb. or Aram. sources. The main reason for them was the desire to supply the religious element that is so conspicuously absent from the Hebrew edition. Thus Addition A presents Mordecai to the reader at the outset as an inspired man who seeks to act in accordance with the will of God. The prayers of Mordecai and of Esther have the same purpose, and even the second letter of the King (E) is full of references to God and praises of the Jewish religion. This *Tendenz* extends so far that it causes a mistranslation of Heb. passages. Thus in 5^2 𝔐 says, "and she obtained favour in his sight"; but 𝔊 says, "and God changed the spirit of the King into mildness"; in 6^1 𝔐 says, "the sleep of the King fled"; but 𝔊 says, "the Lord drove away sleep from the King." The additions also serve the purpose of explaining difficulties in the conduct of Esther and Mordecai. Thus Mordecai's refusal to bow to Haman is due only to national pride in 3^{1-4}, but in C^{5-7} (=13^{12-14}) Mordecai says, "Thou knowest all things, and thou knowest, Lord, that it was neither in contempt nor pride, nor for any desire of glory, that I did not bow down to proud Haman. For I should have been content with good will for the salvation of Israel to kiss the soles of his feet. But I did this that I might not prefer the glory of man above the glory of God; neither will I bow down unto any but to thee, who art my Lord, neither will I do it in pride." Similarly in 2^2 Esther is willing to become a concubine of the King, receives the dainties that are sent her from the royal kitchen (2^9), goes cheerfully to the King's couch (2^{16}), is present at the King's feast (2^{18}), and carefully hides her race and her religion (2^{20}), but in C^{27-29} (=14^{16-18}) Esther prays: "Thou hast knowledge of all things; and thou knowest that I hate the glory of the wicked, and abhor the bed of the uncircumcised, and of every alien. Thou knowest my necessity; that I abhor the sign of my high estate, which is upon my head in the days wherein I shew myself. I abhor it as a menstruous rag, and I wear it not when I am in private by myself. Thy handmaid hath not eaten at Haman's table, neither have I honoured the King's feast, nor drunk the wine of the drink offerings. Neither had thy handmaid any joy since the day that I was brought thither to this present, but in thee, O Lord, thou God of Abraham." Apart from these religious and apologetic motives, the desire to fill up gaps in the Heb. story and to give specimens of fine Greek writing, such as are found in the two letters of Artaxerxes, are sufficient explanation of the invention of the longer Greek additions.

On the apocryphal additions to Est. reference may be made to the following literature: Fritzsche, *Kurzgefasstes exegetisches Handbuch zu den Apokryphen des A. T.* (1851–60); Keerl, *Die Apokryphen des A. T., ein Zeugniss wider dieselben* (1852), pp. 78 *ff.*, and *Die Apokryphenfrage auf's Neue beleuchtet* (1855), pp. 160 *ff.*; Stier, *Die Apokr., Vertheidigung ihres althergebrachten Anschlusses an die Bibel* (1853), p. 158; Dijserinck, *De Apocriefe Boeken des Ouden Verbonds* (1874) (not seen); Hengstenberg, *Für Beibehaltung der Apok.* (1853); Langen, *Die deuterocanonischen Stücke im Buche Esther* (1862); Fürst, *Geschichte der bibli-*

schen Literatur, ii. (1870), pp. 490 *ff.*; Bissell, *The Apoc. of the O. T.* (1880); Deane, "The Septuagint Additions to the Hebrew Text," *Expositor*, Sept., 1884; Fuller, *The Apoc.* in the *Speaker's Commentary*, pp. 361-402 (1888); Reuss, *Gesch. der heiligen Schriften A. T.*, 470; Zöckler, *Die Apok. des A. T.* (1891); Scholz, *Commentar über das Buch Est. mit seinen Zusätzen* (1892); Ball, *The Ecclesiastical or Deuterocanonical Books of the O. T.* (1892); König, *Einleitung in das A. T. mit Einschluss der Apok.* (1893), p. 481; Pförtner, *Die Autorität der deuterocanonischen Bücher des A. T.* (1893) (not seen); Schürer, *Gesch. des jüd. Volkes*[3] (1898), iii. pp. 330 *ff.*; and *PRE.*[3], i. p. 638; Ryssel, *Zusätze z. B. Est.*, in Kautzsch, *Die Apokryphen u. Pseudepigraphen des A. T.* (1900); André, *Les Apocryphes de l'Ancien Testament* (1903), pp. 195-208 (the clearest and completest recent introduction to the Apocrypha).

The short additions can make less claim than the long ones to be derived from a Heb. original. Few of them are found in more than one of the recensions, and this shows that they are not an integral part of 𝔊 itself. They are to be regarded as late glosses that have crept into the several recensions at a time subsequent to the insertion of the long additions.

As a result of our comparison of the Greek recensions we reach the conclusion that 𝔊 has little to offer for the emendation of the Hebrew text of Esther. None of its additions have critical value, except the short ones that are found in two or more of the recensions. When Jahn, *Das Buch Esther nach der Septuaginta hergestellt* (1901), attempts to reconstruct the Heb. text on the basis of 𝔊, this can only be pronounced a most uncritical procedure. Nöldeke, *EBi.* 1406, remarks: "The tendency, so common at the present day, to overestimate the importance of 𝔊 for purposes of textual criticism is nowhere more to be deprecated than in the Book of Esther. It may be doubted whether, even in a single passage of the book, the Greek MSS. enable us to emend the Hebrew text, which, as has been mentioned above, is singularly well preserved." This judgment seems to me to be too sweeping. As will appear in detail in the commentary, there are several passages where 𝔐 gives no good sense and where 𝔊 seems to have preserved the true reading. The middle course, followed by Haupt in his "Critical Notes on Esther" in *HM*. ii. pp. 113-204, avoiding the extremes both of Jahn and of Nöldeke in his treatment of 𝕲, seems to me to be the soundest method. It must be said, however, that, on the whole, the Massoretic text is unusually correct, and that 𝕲 has less to offer here than in the case of most of the other books of the OT.

In regard to the significance of the omissions in 𝕲 it is hard to form a positive opinion. These are found in all the recensions with a uniformity that is not true of the additions. This seems to prove that the original Greek Esther was shorter than the present Hebrew text, and thus raises the question, which form is the more primitive? In favour of 𝕲 being original is the fact that through the centuries the Book of Esther has constantly been receiving additions, and it is quite possible that this process went on before it was admitted to the Canon. In that case the Massoretic text will have to be regarded as a *midrash* upon an earlier nucleus that is common to both 𝔋 and 𝕲. In favour of the view that 𝔋 is original, is the fact that other books of the OT., *e.g.*, 1 S. Jb. Je., have been cut down in the Greek translation. I find myself unable to decide this question. Haupt, in the article just cited, omits many passages from 𝔋 on the strength of 𝕲, without formulating any theory of a shorter recension of 𝔋. I have recorded all these omissions in my notes, but in the majority of cases I have not felt sufficiently sure of them to adopt them as emendations. In general, 𝕸 unquestionably represents the purest form of the text that has come down to us, and it must be taken as the basis for all critical discussion of the book. The only attempts that have been made to construct a revised text of Est. on the basis of all the evidence are the works of Jahn and of Haupt cited above. The commentaries contain incidentally many textual emendations.

III. HIGHER CRITICISM.

§ 21. OUTLINE OF THE BOOK.

The book of Esther narrates the way in which Esther, a Jewish maiden, became queen of Ahasuerus, King of Persia, and saved her people from the destruction planned against them by Haman, the King's favourite; and how, in commemoration of this deliverance,

the feast of Purim was instituted. It falls into six main divisions:—
(1) The rejection of Vashti (1^{1-22}); (2) The choice of Esther to be queen (2^{1-23}); (3) The elevation of Haman and his plot to destroy the Jews (3^1-4^{17}); (4) The fall of Haman and the deliverance of the Jews (5^1-9^{19}); (5) The institution of the feast of Purim (9^{20-32}); and (6) An appendix telling something about the subsequent history of Ahasuerus and Mordecai (10^{1-3}).

The contents of the book in more detail are as follows:—Ahasuerus (Heb. *Ăḥashwērôsh*), King of Persia, in the third year of his reign, assembles all the dignitaries of the empire at Shushan (Susa) and feasts them for 180 days (1^{1-4}). During the seven days following he entertains the men of the fortress of Susa in a magnificent manner ($^{5-8}$). At the same time Vashti the Queen makes a banquet for the women (^{9}). On the seventh day Ahasuerus commands Vashti to show herself to the assembled guests; but this she refuses to do, and the King is very angry ($^{10-12}$). Thereupon he takes counsel with his seven ministers of state what to do to punish this disobedience ($^{13-15}$). Memukhan suggests that the example of Vashti will encourage women everywhere to rebel against their husbands; that, therefore, she ought to be deposed and a successor chosen; and that news of this decision should be disseminated in all parts of the empire and wives should be commanded to obey their husbands ($^{16-20}$). This advice pleases the King and he acts accordingly ($^{21-22}$).

When his wrath has subsided he misses Vashti, and his courtiers advise him to gather the most beautiful maidens from all the provinces in order to select from them another queen. This plan also meets with his approval (2^{1-4}). Among the girls who are brought to the palace is Esther, an orphan, who has been reared by her cousin Mordecai, a Jew of the tribe of Benjamin ($^{5-8}$). She is favoured by Hegai, the chief eunuch, and keeps it secret that she is a Jewess, although Mordecai comes every day to inquire how she is ($^{9-11}$). The maidens are obliged to submit to a twelve months' process of beautification and receive whatever ornaments they desire before they are brought to the King ($^{12-14}$). When Esther's turn comes, she asks for nothing, yet Ahasuerus regards her as the most beautiful of all the women and chooses her in the seventh year of his reign as queen in the place of Vashti, which event is celebrated with a feast and remission of taxes ($^{15-18}$). Mordecai, whose kinship with Esther still remains secret, soon after this discovers a plot against the life of the King. This he reports through the Queen, and the conspirators are hanged, but he is not rewarded, only the deed is recorded in the royal annals ($^{19-23}$).

Afterward Ahasuerus makes a certain Haman, the Agagite, chief over all his nobles and commands every one to do obeisance to him (3^{1-2a}). This Mordecai refuses to do, and the courtiers report it to Haman ($^{2b-5}$). In revenge Haman determines to destroy, not merely Mordecai, but the whole race of the Jews, and casts lots in the 12th year to determine a favourable day, either for laying the matter before the King, or for the execution of his plan. The lot falls, according to 𝔊 L, for the 14th (13th) of Adar, the 12th month ($^{6-7}$). Thereupon Haman goes to the King and asks that the Jews may be destroyed, offering to pay 10,000 talents of silver into the royal treasury if this be done. The King grants him free hand, and he issues a decree on the 13th day of the 1st month, that on the 13th day of the 12th month all the Jews throughout the empire shall be slain. Couriers are sent out with a dispatch to this effect, and it is published in Susa ($^{8-15}$). The Jews are filled with consternation, and Mordecai appears before the palace-gate clothed in sackcloth and ashes (4^{1-3}). Esther hears of this and sends other clothes in order that Mordecai may come into the palace, but he refuses to put them on. She then instructs Hathakh, one of the eunuchs, to find out what is the matter. Mordecai tells him, and charges Esther to go to the King and beg for a reversal of the decree ($^{4-9}$). Esther at first objects on the ground that the death-penalty is visited upon any one who appears before the King without a summons; but, being urged by Mordecai, she finally consents to run the risk three days later, asking that in the meanwhile all the Jews in Susa will fast with her ($^{10-17}$). On the third day she appears before the King and is graciously received. When he offers to grant any request, she asks only that he and Haman will come to a banquet that she has prepared (5^{1-5}). At the banquet the King offers again to grant any request, but Esther asks only that he and Haman will come to another banquet with her on the morrow (⁶⁻⁸). Haman goes out in high spirits, but when Mordecai refuses to bow to him, he hastens home and informs his family and friends that all his honours are worthless so long as this Jew is alive. They advise him to build a gallows 50 cubits high, and to ask the King the next day that Mordecai may be hanged upon it (⁹⁻¹⁴).

The following night the King cannot sleep, and has the annals of the kingdom read to him. He is thus reminded that nothing has been done to reward Mordecai (6¹⁻³). At this moment Haman arrives to beg that Mordecai may be hanged, and is asked, What shall be done to the man whom the King desires to honour? Supposing himself to be meant, he names a number of royal honours, and is amazed to be told to confer these upon Mordecai (⁴⁻¹⁰). This order he carries out and returns in despair to his home. There his family and his astrologers express their fear that this ill fortune is the beginning of his downfall (¹¹⁻¹³). While they are talking, eunuchs come to fetch Haman to the banquet with Esther (¹⁴). Here the King once more offers to give her anything that she may ask, and this time she tells him of Haman's plot and begs for her own life and the life of her people (7¹⁻⁶). The King goes out in wrath, and Haman falls upon Esther's couch to beg for his life. When the King returns, he is still more angered by Haman's posture, and commands to hang him on the gallows that he has built for Mordecai (7⁷⁻¹⁰). Mordecai is then installed in the place of Haman (8¹⁻²). Esther goes a second time unsummoned to the King, and being favourably received, begs for a reversal of Haman's edict of destruction. Full power is given Mordecai, and, although he cannot countermand Haman's orders, since the laws of the Medes and Persians are unchangeable, yet he directs that on the day appointed for their destruction the Jews shall everywhere defend themselves and slay their enemies (³⁻¹⁴). Mordecai then goes forth in royal apparel, and the Jews rejoice over their deliverance (¹⁵⁻¹⁷). When the thirteenth of Adar comes, the Jews assemble in accordance with Mordecai's directions and no one dares to oppose them. Helped by the governors of the provinces, they slay their enemies everywhere, and in Susa they kill 500 men, among whom are the ten sons of Haman (9¹⁻¹⁰). This the King reports to Esther and inquires if there is anything more that she would like to have done. She asks that another day be granted for slaughtering the Jew's enemies in Susa, and that the ten sons of Haman be hanged on the gallows ([11-15]). In the provinces 75,000 enemies of the Jews are slain on the thirteenth day and the fourteenth day is celebrated by the Jews as a festival; but in Susa the slaughter continues on the fourteenth day, and the fifteenth is kept as a holiday. This is the reason why the country Jews feast on the fourteenth, rather than the fifteenth of Adar ([16-19]).

After this Mordecai sends out letters commanding the Jews in all the provinces to celebrate both the 14th and 15th of Adar ([20-22]). This they undertake to do with repetition of the story of their deliverance ([23-25]). Thus the annual feast of Purim is instituted, and is made binding upon the Jews for all generations ([26-28]). Esther and Mordecai then write a second time to confirm the institution of Purim ([29-32]).

The story concludes with mention of a tax imposed by Ahasuerus, and of the greatness of Mordecai, for fuller information in regard to which the reader is referred to the Book of the Chronicles of the Kings of Media and Persia (10[1-3]).

§ 22. IDENTITY OF AHASUERUS.

For the interpretation of the book it is important to determine at the outset who is the king that is called Ahasuerus ('Ăhashwērôsh). On this point until recently opinions have differed widely. Every king of Media and of Persia, from Cyaxares to Artaxerxes Ochus, has been selected by some one for identification with this monarch.

(1) In Est. 2[6] it is stated that Mordecai was carried captive with Jeconiah (Jehoiachin) by Nebuchadnezzar, King of Babylon, and from this it has been inferred that the Ahasuerus of our book was one of the kings of Media contemporary with the period of the Babylonian captivity. Nickes, *De Estheræ libro*, i. (1856), pp. 43–49, identifies him with Ahasuerus, the father of Darius the Mede, mentioned in Dn. 9[1], whom he regards as the same as Cyaxares, son of Phraortes, the contemporary of Nebuchadnezzar and Jehoiachin. Similarly Ferrand, *Réflexions sur la religion Chrétienne*, i. p. 157; Marsham, *Canon Chroni-*

cus, p. 609; des Vignoles, *Chron. sac.*, ii. p. 274; Herbst-Welte, *Einl. in das A. T.*, ii. (1842), p. 253 *f.*; Kohlreif, *Chronologie liphrat katon* (1732), pp. 192 *ff.*, identify him either with Cyaxares I, or with a supposed Cyaxares II, his son. A similar view is held by Erbt (*Purim*, p. 47). The objections to this view are, that Darius the Mede in Dn. 9^1 is so uncertain a person historically that no safe conclusions can be based upon the name of his supposed father, and that Cyaxares reigned over no such vast territory as is assigned to Ahasuerus in 1^1. Moreover, the order of the words "Persia and Media" in $1^{14, 19}$ suggests that in the time of Ahasuerus Persia, and not Media, held the hegemony.

(2) G. Mercator, *Chronol.* iii., *Demonstr. Chron.*, p. 185; R. Walther, *Hommilarium sylva*, *Esther*, p. 2; P. Wokenius, *Commentatio in librum Esther* (1730); Aster, *Dissertatio Philologica de Esteræ cum Ahasuero conjugio* (1870), decide for Astyages; but this view has nothing in its favour, and is open to all the objections that apply to the identification with Cyaxares.

(3) Ezr. $4^{5-7, 24}$ names the kings of Persia in the following order: Cyrus, Ahasuerus, Artaxerxes, Darius, from which it has been inferred that Ahasuerus and Artaxerxes are Cambyses and Pseudo-Smerdis, who reigned between Cyrus and Darius. With this Ahasuerus, or Cambyses, the Ahasuerus of Est. is identified by Lyr., Vat., Genebrard, and Winck. (*AOF.* ii. 214). It is now generally recognized, however, that the order of the kings in Ezr. 4 is not chronological. The Chronicler supposed that the narrative of 4^{7-23} referred to the stopping of the building of the Temple, whereas really it referred to the stopping of the building of the wall. As a result, he has placed Xerxes I and Artaxerxes I between Cyrus and Darius. This passage, therefore, affords no safe basis for the identification of Ahasuerus with Cambyses.

(4) RaShI, IE., Tir., Lap., identify Ahasuerus with Darius Hystaspis. RaShI remarks, "He was the king of Persia who ruled after Cyrus, at the end of the seventy years of the Babylonian captivity." In support of this view is urged its correspondence with the statement about Mordecai's captivity in Est. 2^6, the extent of Darius' empire, and his invasion of India, as narrated by Megasthenes and Arrian. But the name Darius was well known to the Hebrews, and there is no reason why the author of Est. should not have used it if he had meant this king.

(5) The Lucianic recension of 𝕲 ordinarily transliterates the name of this king by Assueros, but in 9^{20}, codd. 19 and 108*b* read Xerxes (93*a*, Artaxerxes) and in 10^3 all the codd. agree in reading Xerxes. According to 𝕿² he was the son of Darius. Eusebius (*Chronicorum libri duo*, ed. Schoene (1875), i. 125; ii. 105) also identifies Ahasuerus with Xerxes. This view received a learned and elaborate defence from J. Scaliger, *Thesaurus temporum Eusebii* (1606), pp. 101 *ff.*; and

Opus de emendatione temporum (1629), pp. 587 *ff.* He has been followed by Drus., Mal., Jun., in their commentaries, and by Pfeiffer, *Dubia Vexata* (1704), pp. 257 *ff.*; Justi, "Versuch über den König Ahasverus im Buche Esther," in Eichhorn's *Repertorium*, xv. pp. 3-38; Carpzov, *Introd.* i. (1741), pp. 356 *ff.*; Baumgarten, *De fide libri Estheræ* (1839), pp. 122 *ff.*; F. M. Schultz, *SK.* (1853), pp. 624 *ff.*

(6) The common recension of 𝔊 translates 'Ăḥashwērôsh by Artaxerxes, and this has led to the identification of this king with each of the three monarchs who bore that name. Josephus, *Ant.* xi. 184 *ff.*, identifies him with Artaxerxes I (Longimanus); so also *Mid.*, Bel., Caj., Sanc., Sal., Bon., Men., Cler., and most Roman Catholic commentators down to modern times. See also Petavius, *Lib.* xv. *c.* 27; Lightfoot, *Complete Works* (1822), ii. pp. 317 *ff.* In support of this view is urged this king's good will toward the Jews, as evidenced by his kindness to Ezra and Nehemiah. The chief difficulty with this view, as with the following identifications, is the impossible age that it gives Mordecai, if he was carried captive under Jehoiachin, as narrated in Est. 6². This difficulty is avoided by the supposition that the statement about the captivity applies, not to Mordecai himself, but to one of his ancestors; but this is exegetically impossible (see com. *a. l.*). The Jewish Chronicle *Ṣeder 'Olam*, which is older than the Talmud, solves all chronological difficulties by the curious method of identifying all four kings of Persia mentioned in the OT., namely, Cyrus, Darius, Ahasuerus, and Artaxerxes, as titles of one and the same person (see chap. xxx. ed. Joh. Meyer, 1699).

(7) Jerome in his commentary on Ezek. 4; Bede, *De vi. mundi ætat.*, ad A. M. 3588; Rhabanus Maurus, and a few Catholic commentators think of Artaxerxes Mnemon.

(8) Serarius, Gordon, Huntley, Capellus (*Chronol. S.*, Tab. xi., ad A. M. 3743), prefer Artaxerxes III (Ochus). The only reason for this view is the fact that in the apocryphal addition E¹⁴ (=16¹⁴) Haman is said to have plotted to deliver the kingdom of the Persians to the Macedonians, which implies the later days of the Persian empire.

This controversy has been brought to a close by the decipherment of the Persian monuments, in which the name Xerxes appears in such a form as to leave no doubt that he is the king who is meant by Ahasuerus. In the Persian column of the trilingual inscriptions of this king from Persepolis, Elvend, and Van, he is called *Khshayarsha;* in the Babylonian equivalent, *Khishi'arshu* (see Bezold, *Achämenideninschriften* (1882), and Spiegel, *Altpers. Keilinschriften* (1881).

In Babylonian tablets such forms occur as *Akhshiyarshu*, *Akkashiarshi*, *Akkisharshu*, *Akhshiyawarshu*, *Akhshuwarshi*, and *Akhshiwarshu* (see Bezold, in *EBi*. i. 94). In an Aramaic inscription the consonants *Kh-sh-y-'-r-sh* appear. These forms are evidently the etymological equivalents of Heb. *'-kh-sh-w-r-sh*, which is the form that appears in Est. 1¹⁶ 2²¹ 3¹² 8¹⁰. In 10¹ the form is *'-kh-sh-r-sh*. The traditional pronunciation *'Ăkhashwērôsh* is inaccurate, and is probably due to Jewish effort to give the name a Heb. etymology. The original pronunciation may have been something like *'Akhashwarsh*. Instead of *w* the Persian and Bab. forms would lead us to expect *y*, and this is found in the Syriac spelling *'-kh-sh-y-r-sh*. From this Haupt, *HM.* ii. 119, infers that *w* is a corruption of *y* in the Heb. spelling; but, in the light of some of the Babylonian forms cited above, this cannot be regarded as certain (*cf.* Strassmaier, *Actes VII. Cong. Orient., Sect. Sém.* 18 *f.*, and Bevan, *Com. on Daniel*, p. 149).

With the identification of Ahasuerus with Xerxes all the statements of the Book of Est. agree. He was a Persian king who also ruled over Media (1³, ¹⁸), his empire extended from India to Ethiopia and contained 127 satrapies (1¹ 8⁹ 9³⁰), it also included the islands of the Mediterranean (10¹), his capital was at Susa in Elam (1², *etc.*). This is all true of Xerxes, but of no other Persian monarch. The character of Ahasuerus, as portrayed in the Book of Est., also agrees well with the account of Xerxes given by Herodotus and other Greek historians (see § 27). For these reasons there is general agreement among modern scholars, Jewish, Catholic, and Protestant, that by Ahasuerus the author of the Book of Est. means Xerxes.

§ 23. PURPOSE OF THE BOOK.

The purpose of the Book of Esther is to commend the observance of the feast of Purim by an account of the way in which this feast originated. The goal is reached in 9³⁰⁻³², where we read: "And [she] sent letters unto all the Jews, unto 127 provinces, the kingdom of Xerxes, containing friendly and faithful words, to establish these days of Purim at their appointed time, as Mordecai the Jew had established for them and Esther the Queen, and as they had established for themselves and for their descendants, the matters of the fastings and of their cry of distress. So the command of Esther established these matters of Purim and it was committed to writing." Toward this conclusion the whole narrative of the book tends. Xerxes' feast serves merely to give an opportunity for Vashti's degradation. Vashti is degraded in order that Esther may be brought to the throne. Haman's decree of destruction gives Esther an opportunity to interfere on behalf of her people. In 3^7 we are told that the lot which Haman cast was called *pur*. For this statement no reason appears, except that the author wishes to use this word later as an explanation of the name *Purim*. After Esther has interceded successfully for the Jews and the danger is averted, the author remarks $9^{17\ f.}$: "And they rested on its fourteenth day, and made it a day of banqueting and joy. Therefore the country Jews, that dwell in hamlets of the rural districts, keep the fourteenth day of the month of Adar as a joy, and a banquet, and a holiday, and a sending of dainties to one another." Immediately after in 9^{20} we read: "And Mordecai wrote the following words, and he sent letters unto all the Jews that were in all the provinces of King Xerxes, those near and those far, to establish for them, that they should continue to keep the fourteenth day of the month of Adar and its fifteenth day in every single year, like the days on which the Jews rested from their enemies and the month that was changed for them from sorrow unto joy and from mourning unto a holiday, to keep them as days of banqueting, and joy, and of sending dainties to one another. And the Jews made customary that which they had begun to do and that which Mordecai had written unto them." Again in $9^{26\ f.}$ we are told: "Therefore they called the days *Purim*, because of the name of the *pur*. Therefore, because of all the words of this message, and because of what they had seen in this respect, and because of what had come unto them, the Jews established and made it customary for themselves, and for their descendants, and for all who should join themselves to them, that it might not be repealed, to continue to keep these two days in accordance with the letter that prescribed them, and in accordance with the time set for them in every single year; and that these days might be remembered, and be kept in every single generation, and every single family, and every single province, and every single city; that these days of Purim might not be repealed by the Jewish community, and that the memory of them might not cease among their descendants." Then follows the concluding enactment of Esther (9^{30-32}), as quoted above. In the light of these facts it is clear that the book has one purpose from beginning to end, that is, the institution of the feast of Purim.

This is so obvious that it has been recognized by nearly all interpreters. As curiosities of exegesis it may be proper to mention a few divergent views. Advocates of an allegorical interpretation regard this book either as a prophecy, or as a symbol of sacred mysteries. Among the Jews this method has found little favour, for Purim is a cherished institution that has no basis in the Law, and they need to treat Est. as history in order to find a warrant for its observance. Still, Abraham Saba of the fifteenth century, in his unpublished commentary, and Moses Isserles of the sixteenth century, try in all earnest to carry through an allegorical interpretation. Hugo of St. Victor, in his *Appendix ad Opera Mystica de spirituali Christi convivio* in Migne, *Pat. Lat.* clxxvii. 1185–1191, understands the 180 days' feast of Ahasuerus as the period of preparation for the Gospel; and the seven days' feast that follows as the New Testament dispensation. Among Roman Catholics this kind of exegesis has lasted down to our own day. The most elaborate attempt of the sort is that of Didachus Celædeiis, *Comm. cum duplici tractatu de convivio Ahasueri mystico*, i.e., *de Eucharistia et de Esther figurata*, i.e., *beata Virgine* (London, 1646). Even commentators that follow in the main the historical method are prone to treat Esther as a type of the Virgin Mary. Scholz's *Commentar über das Buch Esther mit seinen Zusätzen* (1892) is a remarkable recent effort to allegorize the book. On p. xxxvi he says: "The Book of Esther is a prophetic repetition and further development of Ezekiel's prophecy concerning Gog. Ahasuerus is humanity that has entered into the Messianic kingdom, in which the Messianic God lives and works, with which also he is one, but which is prone to fall, and for the most part does actually fall more or less frequently." (See also §§ 35, 36.)

Against all such interpretations is the fact, that the book never suggests that it wishes to be taken in any other than a literal sense. It is a fundamental characteristic of genuine allegory that it is incapable of a complete literal interpretation, but this is not the case here. Est. is a plain, straightforward prose narrative, just like all the historical books of the OT., and it does not contain a single statement that cannot be understood literally. If the author had meant it to be a prophecy, he would have used the future tense, as all the prophets do, and would not have cast his message into a narrative form that was certain to be misunderstood by his readers. Moreover, if this were prophecy, analogy would lead us to expect the use of poetry rather than prose.

J. S. Bloch, *Hellenistische Bestandtheile im biblischen Schrifttum* (1877), advocates the extraordinary hypothesis that Est. was written during the Maccabæan period, and that its aim was "to justify the party that was friendly to the Greeks." This view emphasizes the absence of the name of God and of all distinctly Jewish religious colouring, also Esther's and Mordecai's friendly relations to Xerxes; but these features throw no real light upon the purpose of the book. It is hard to see how an author who was favourable to Greek heathenism could have represented Mordecai as refusing to bow down to Haman 3^2, or how he could have related with such evident satisfaction the slaughter of the heathen in chapter 9.

§ 24. INDEPENDENCE OF 9^{20}–10^3.

In regard to the unity of the larger part of the Book of Esther no doubt can be felt. The outline of contents given in § 21 shows that there is a systematic and harmonious development of thought at least as far as 9^{19}, and the discussion of purpose in § 23 shows that one aim dominates the entire book. Only in regard to the section 9^{20}–10^3 can doubt be felt whether it comes from the same hand as the rest of the narrative. J. D. Michaelis, *Deutsche Uebersetzung des A. T. mit Anmerkungen für Ungelehrte*, xiii. (1783), first noticed the peculiarities of this section, and concluded that they indicated that it was derived from an independent source. He has been followed by Bertheau in his commentary (1862) as far as $9^{20\text{-}32}$ is concerned, by Ryssel in the second edition of the same work (1887), by Kamphausen in Bunsen's *Bibelwerk* (1868), and by Wildeboer, *Kommentar* (1898). In support of this view the following facts may be noted:—

(1) In 10^2 the author refers to the Book of the Chronicles of the Kings of Media and Persia for additional information in regard to the matters that he has just been narrating. This suggests that he has derived his material from the work that he cites. In 9^{32} it is stated that "the commandment of Esther established these matters of Purim and it was committed to writing" (RV. "written in the book"). Here Pisc., Jun., Grot., Raw., see another reference to the Chronicle, but this is doubtful; the expression

probably alludes only to the letter of Esther mentioned in 9^{29} (see com. *a. l.*). This Chronicle of the Kings of Media and Persia was not the royal diary mentioned in 2^{23} 6^1, but was probably some Jewish compilation of the traditional history of the Medo-Persian kings, like the book of the Chronicles of the Kings of Judah and Israel that is so often cited by the Chronicler (see com. on 10^2). From it the author of Est. must have extracted some of the material that precedes 10^2, unless this reference be regarded as an invention designed to give additional authority to his book.

(2) 9^{24-25} contains an account of Haman's conspiracy that is a duplicate to chapters 3–7. Details vary in these two narratives in the manner that is usual in parallel accounts of the same events.

(3) In a number of particulars 9^{20}–10^3 contradicts the earlier part of the book to such a degree as to indicate that it comes from a different hand. According to 9^{19}, the Jews of the author's region kept partly the fourteenth and partly the fifteenth of Adar in memory of their escape, but in 9^{21-23} Mordecai commands, and the Jews agree, to keep both the fourteenth and the fifteenth of the month. The editor treats Mordecai's command as though it were only a modification of the observance of the Jews at the time of the first celebration of the feast, but 9^{19} indicates clearly that its author regarded this observance as an established practice. The two accounts show apparently the customs of the Jews in different regions. In $9^{24\,f.}$ Haman acts without the King's knowledge in planning the destruction of the Jews (*cf.* 9^{25}, "When it came before the King"); but in 3^{8-11} the King knows the plan from the beginning and aids Haman in carrying it out. In 9^{25} no reference is made to the part that Esther played in averting the disaster. The opening words of this verse cannot be translated, "when *she* came before the King," but mean only, "when *it* came before the King"; in chapter 7, on the contrary, the whole credit of the deliverance belongs to Esther. In 9^{25}, when the King learns of Haman's plot, he says, "Let his wicked plan, which he has devised against the Jews, return upon his own head." In $7^{8\,f.}$ a different account is given of the transaction and of the reason for the King's

sentence. In 9^{25} Haman and his sons are apparently hanged at the same time. In 7^{10} 9^{14} Haman is executed first, and his sons are not hanged beside him until after the massacre of the 13th of Adar. In 9^{22} the sending of gifts to the poor is prescribed as part of the observance of Purim, and in 9^{31} fasting and crying accompany the feast; but in $9^{17\text{-}19}$ these customs are not mentioned as part of the initial observance.

(4) The language of this section exhibits many points of similarity with that of the body of the book, as one would expect even in independent documents that belong to the same age and the same school of thought; on the other hand, a number of the most characteristic phrases of the body of the book are wanting here, and expressions are found here that do not occur in the body of the book. On the whole, the linguistic evidence is favourable to the literary independence of this section.

The following words and phrases are common to both parts of the book: אבר $Pi.$ $3^{9.\ 13}$ $9^{12.\ 24}$ and oft.; אֵבֶל 4^3 9^{22}; אָדָר 3^7 9^{17} $al.$; אֹיֵב 7^6 9^{22} $al.$; גְּדוּלָה 1^4 6^3 10^2; גּוֹרָל 3^7 9^{24}; הפך $Niph.$ $9^{1.\ 22}$; זֶרַע 6^{13} $9^{27.\ 28.\ 31}$ 10^3; חלל $Hiph.$ 6^{13} 9^{23}; חשב 8^3 $9^{24\ f.}$; יום טוב 8^{17} $9^{19.\ 22}$; כתב 1^{19} $9^{20.\ 29.\ 32}$ $+$ 13 t.; כָּתָב 1^{22} 9^{27} $+$ 6 t.; ל with inf. introducing a command 1^{22} 9^{21} and oft.; מֵאֲמַר 1^{15} 2^{20} 9^{32}; מְדִינָה 1^1 $9^{20.\ 28.\ 30}$ and oft.; מַחֲשֶׁבֶת $8^{3.\ 5}$ 9^{25}; מֶלֶךְ oft. in both; מִשְׁתֶּה oft. in both; מַלְכוּת in both; מָנוֹת 2^9 $9^{19.\ 22}$; מִשְׁלוֹחַ $9^{19.\ 22}$; סָפַר oft. in 1^3 9^{22} and oft.; נוח $9^{16.\ 17.\ 22}$; הפיל פור 3^7 9^{24}; נֶפֶשׁ 'self' 4^{13} 9^{31}; עבר 1^{19} $9^{27.\ 28}$; עִיר 3^{15} 9^{28} and oft.; עַם 1^5 10^3 and oft., עֵץ 2^{23} 9^{25} and oft.; עשׂה $9^{22.\ 23}$ $9^{17.\ 18}$; צוֹם 4^3 9^{31}; צָרַר 3^{10} 8^1 $9^{10.\ 24}$; קִבֵּל 4^4 $9^{23.\ 27}$; ראה 9^{26} and oft.; רֹאשׁ 9^{25} and oft.; רֹב 5^{11} 10^3; רע 9^{25} and oft.; שׂים 10^1 and oft.; שִׂמְחָה 9^{22} and oft.

The following common expressions of the body of the book are omitted in $9^{20}\text{–}10^3$:— אהב 1^{17} 4^{13} 9^{14}; בָּזָה 2^{17} $5^{10.\ 14}$ 6^{13}; אחר $3^{8.\ 13}$ 4^{11} 7^9 8^{12}; אמר ל 1^{17} 4^{13} 9^{14}; $9^{10.\ 15.\ 16}$; בזז 3^{13} 8^{11}; בִּירָה 1^2 and oft. to 9^{12}; בַּקָּשָׁה 7 times in $1^1\text{–}9^{19}$; דָּת 19 t. in body; הרג 10 t.; חֵמָה 6 t.; חֵן 6 t.; חפץ 7 t.; חצי המלכות 3 t.; חָצֵר 8 t.; יָד 3^{13} 8^{11}; טַף 7 t.; אם טוב 7 t.; טַבַּעַת 6 t.; חתם 3 t.; הרש 3 t.; ידע 7 t.; ירע 21 t.; לָשׁוֹן 5 t.; לקח 6 t.; לֵב 4 t.; יָקָר 9 t.; יָצָא 9 t.; יכל 3 t.; יַיִן 6 t.; יטב 5 t.; נפל 8 t.; נגע 14 t.; $Hiph.$ נגד 3 t.; קָקוּם 3 t.; מצא 8 t.; מלא 4 t.; מוֹלֶדֶת 3 t.; Qal 7 t.; נתן 26 t.; סוּס 6 t.; סוּר 3 t.; סָרִיס 12 t.; עֶבֶד 6 t.; עַיִן 12 t.; שָׂנֵא 3 t.; רכב 4 t.; רַב 7 t.; רָצִים 4 t.; קרא 11 t.; קבץ 6 t.; צוה 8 t.; פָּחָה 3 t.; שַׁעַר 10 t.; שמד 5 t.; שְׁאֵלָא 6 t.; שׂר 13 t.

The following expressions are found only in $9^{20}\text{–}10^3$:—אֶבְיוֹנִים 9^{22}; 10^3; דרש 9^{28}; דּוֹר 9^{30}; אֱמֶת 10^1; אִיִּים 10^1; אָח, of a fellow-Jew, 10^3; אִגֶּרֶת $9^{26.\ 29}$;

מָה רָאוּ Niph. 9²⁷; לוה 9²⁶; עַל כָּכָה 9²⁶; יָגוֹן 9²², 27· 31; זְמָן 9²⁸; זֵכֶר 9²⁴; הֲמַס 9²⁶; מַתָּנָה 9²²; מִשְׁפָּחָה 9²⁸; מְדִינָה 10³; (מְלָאכָה); מַעֲשֶׂה 10² (in 3⁹ 9³); מַס 10¹; סוֹף 9²⁸; פּוּרִים (plural) 9²⁶· ²³· ²⁹· ³¹· ³². קִיַּם *Pi.* 'made obligatory,' 9²⁷· ³¹· ³²; תֹּקֶף 9²⁹ 10². The use of the perfect with simple *Waw*, instead of the imperfect with *Waw* consec., is also peculiar to this part of the book (*cf.* 9²⁵).

In view of these facts it is difficult to think that 9²⁰⁻10³ comes from the same hand as the rest of the book. It is equally difficult to regard it as an interpolation. The purpose of the author is evidently to lead up to the establishment of Purim, as recorded in this section. If these verses be omitted, no adequate account of the origin of the feast is given, and the book is left without a head. The theory that best explains the facts, probably, is that the section 9²⁰⁻10¹ is quoted by the author of Est. from the Chronicle mentioned in 10², from which also he has derived the ideas that he has worked up in an independent fashion in the rest of the book. Erbt's analysis of Est. into a Mordecai story and an Esther story (*Purimsage*, pp. 19 *sq.*) is so obviously the product of his theory in regard to the origin of Purim that it demands no detailed consideration at this point (see pp. 78–81).

§ 25. AGE OF THE BOOK.

In regard to the age of Est. many opinions have been held. Josephus identifies Ahasuerus with Artaxerxes I, and assigns the book to the reign of that king. Augustine supposes that Ezra was the author; the Talmud (*Baba Bathra*, 15*a*), the men of the Great Synagogue. Clement of Alexandria conjectures on the basis of 9²⁰⁻³² that Mordecai was the author, and this view has been followed by many of the ancient Jewish and Christian scholars. R. Azariah de Rossi, in his Heb. Intr. to the OT., suggests that it was written by Jehoiakim b. Joshua. Conservative critics of the last generation assigned it to the reign of that particular king of Media or Persia with whom they happened to identify Ahasuerus. Modern critics are unanimous in believing that the book is a product of the Greek period. The only dispute is, whether it belongs to the earlier or the later part of that period. Most recent writers incline to the view that it dates from a time after the persecutions of Antiochus Epiphanes and the deliverance by Judas Maccabæus in 165 B.C.

For the solution of the problem the book contains the following data:—

(1) It makes no claim of age or authorship for itself. The statement of 9^{20}, "Mordecai wrote these things," does not refer to the foregoing narrative, but to the letter that follows. The "book" mentioned in 9^{32} is not Est., but the letter that Esther has just written.

(2) There is no external evidence for the existence of this book before the beginning of the Christian era. It is never cited by any pre-Christian writer. Ch., Ezr., Ne., Dn., Philo, and the apocryphal books contain no mention of it. The silence of the son of Sirach (c. 170 B.C.) is specially significant, since in Ecclus. 44-49 he gives a long catalogue of Hebrew worthies. The absence of Est. and Dn. from this list can be explained in no other way than that the books telling about them were not yet written. The earliest evidence of the existence of Est. is the LXX version, which is first cited by Josephus (*Cont. Ap.* i. 8). Purim is first mentioned in 2 Mac. 15^{36} as "the day of Mordecai" that follows the day of Nicanor. This reference does not show that Purim was observed in the time of Judas Maccabæus, but only that it was known to the author of 2 Mac. The earlier and better informed author of 1 Mac. 7^{49} mentions the 13th of Adar as the day of Nicanor, without reference to its proximity to the day of Mordecai. There is no evidence, therefore, that Purim was kept by the Palestinian Jews before the 1st cent. B.C.

(3) The historical standpoint of the book indicates its origin in the Greek period. In $1^{1.\ 13.\ 14}$ 4^{11} 8^8 the author speaks of the times of Xerxes as long passed. The halo of romance cast about the Persian empire also indicates that it had ceased to exist. In 3^8 the statement that the Jews are scattered abroad and dispersed among all peoples shows knowledge of the *Diaspora* of the Greek period. The conversion of multitudes to Judaism (8^{17} 9^{27}) did not occur in the Pers. period, but was a result of the proselyting zeal of Græco-Roman times (*cf.* Matt. 23^{15}). In the opinion of

many critics Ahasuerus' edict of destruction ($3^{12\,\text{f.}}$) shows **knowledge** of Antiochus' determination in 169 B.C. to root out the Jewish religion.

(4) The intellectual standpoint of the book also indicates its origin in the late Gr. period. There is no trace of the Messianic hope that characterized the early days of the restoration of the commonwealth. The bitter hatred of Gentiles, and the longing for their destruction that this book discloses, were first induced by Antiochus' resolve either to Hellenize or to exterminate the nation. Mordecai's refusal to bow before Haman (3^2) is not in accord with old Heb. usage, but shows a new spirit of independence awakened through contact with the Greeks. The prominence given to financial considerations (3^9) is also indicative of the commercialism that developed among the Jews during the Greek period. The national pride bereft of religious enthusiasm indicates that the book was not written at the time of the Maccabæan struggle, but in the period of worldliness and self-complacency that followed the attainment of national independence in 135 B.C.

(5) The language of the book leads to the same conclusion. Its Heb. is as late as any in the OT., and most resembles that of Ec., Dn., Ch. Many words are not found elsewhere except in the Mishna and other rabbinical writings. Aramaic influence is conspicuous in diction and construction. The style is awkward and laboured, and shows that the author used Heb. only as a literary language. The late words of the book are as follows:—

אֲבָרָן 8^6 9^5 ἁ.λ.=Syriac; אוֹרָה 8^{16} late, Mishnic; אִלּוּ 7^4 Ec. 6^6, as Aram. and Mishna; אמר לְ 'command to,' where early Heb. uses the *direct* address, 1^{17} 4^{13} 9^{14} 1 Ch. 13^4 15^{16} 21^{18} 22^2 2 Ch. $29^{21\text{b. 27. 30}}$ $31^{4.\ 11}$ 33^{16} Ne. 8^1 9^{15}; אנס 1^8, Aram. and Mishna; בחל *Qal* 2^9 Ec. 5^1 7^9 2 Ch. 35^{21}, *Pu.* 8^{14} Pr. 20^{21}, *Hiph.* 6^{14} 2 Ch. 26^{20} (in these late passages the word means 'hasten,' ordinarily 'terrify'); בּוּץ 'byssus' 1^6 8^{15} 1 Ch. 4^{21} 2 Ch. 2^{13} 3^{14} 5^{12} Ez. 27^{16}, a late word instead of the older שֵׁשׁ; בִּזָּה 'spoil' $9^{10.\ 15.\ 16}$ Dn. 11^{24} 2 Ch. $14^{13}+9$ t.; בְּנָיוֹן 1^{18} ἁ.λ.; הַבְזוֹת *Hiph.* inf. 1^{17} ἁ.λ.; בִּירָה 'fortress,' a late loan-word through the Aram. 1^2 and oft.; בִּיתָן only in Est. 1^5 $7^{7.\ 8}$, ph. Pers.; בעת *Niph.* 'be afraid,' only 7^6 Dn. 8^{17} 1 Ch. 21^{30}; בִּקֵּשׁ עַל 'ask for' 4^8 7^7, late usage, as Ne. 2^4 Ezr. 8^{23}; בַּקָּשָׁה $5^{3.\ 6.\ 7.\ 8}$ $7^{2.\ 3}$ 9^{12} Ezr. 7^6; גזר *Niph.* 2^1 2 Ch. 26^{21} La. 3^{54} Ps. 88^6 Ez. 37^{11} Is. 53^8, in the sense of 'was determined,' an Aramaism; גָּלִיל 'rod'

1^6 Ct. 5^{14}; גְּנָזִים 'treasury' 3^9 4^7, NH. and Aram.; דחף 'drive' 3^{15} 6^{12} 8^{14} 2 Ch. 26^{20}, NH. and Aram.; הֲנָחָה 'rest' 2^{18}, ἅ.λ.; הַצָּלָה 'deliverance' 4^{14}, ἅ.λ., an Aramaizing form; זוּעַ 5^9 Ec. 12^3, Aram.; זְמָן $9^{27.\ 31}$ Ne. 2^6 Ec. 3^1, Aram.; חוּל Hithpalp. 4^4, ἅ.λ.; חוּר 'white stuff' 1^6 8^{15}, Aram.; יהר Hithp. 8^{17}; יוֹם טוֹב 'holiday' 8^{17} $9^{19.\ 22}$, as in NH.; יוֹתֵר מִן 'more than' 6^6, cf. Ec. 2^{15} 7^{16} 12^9 and NH.; יְקָר $1^4 + 8$ t., a late word and Aram.; ישׁט Hiph. 'extend' 4^{11} 5^2 8^4, NH. and Aram.; כָּפָה עַל בְּכֵן 9^{26} ἅ.λ.; בְּכֵן 4^{16} Ec. 8^{10}, as in Aram.; כנס Qal 4^{16} Ec. $2^{8.\ 26}$ Ps. 33^7 1 Ch. 22^2 Ne. 12^{44}, as NH. and Aram.; כְּפָא מַלְכוּת 1^2 5^1, instead of כסא ממלכת in older books; כשׁר 'be legal' 8^5 Ec. 10^{10} 11^6, as NH.; כֶּתֶר 'turban' 1^{11} 2^{17} 6^8, only in Est. and NH.; לְ with inf., introducing the contents of a letter or command, 1^{22} and oft.; an Aramaism; מֵאֲמַר 1^{15} 2^{20} 9^{32}, an Aram. word; מְדִינָה $1^1 + 28$ t., an Aram. word found only in late Heb.; מָה רָאוּ 9^{26}, as in NH.; מַלְכוּת 24 t.; so regularly in Dn., Chr., Ezr., the ancient language does not use this word in similar constructions; נוח Hiph. inf. 3^8, constr. w. acc. as in Aram.; נֶזֶק 7^4, Aram. loan-word; נִשָּׂא חֵן $2^{15.\ 17}$ 5^2, instead of the ancient מצא חן, which occurs here only in the set phrase 5^8 7^3 8^5; עמד על 8^{11} 9^{16} Dn. 8^{25} 11^{14} 1 Ch. 21^1 2 Ch. 20^{23} 26^{18}, and in general the use of עמד instead of קום; פַּרְשָׁה 4^7 10^2, only in Est.; צוֹם 'fasting,' as in the late books; רְאוּיוֹת 'selected' 2^9, as in NH.; שׂבר 'think' 9^1, an Aram. loan-word; שַׂק וָאֵפֶר $4^{1.\ 3}$ Dn. 9^3; שׁוה 3^8 7^4, an Aramaism; שׁלט 9^1 Ec. 2^{19} 8^9 Ne. 5^{15}; שׁנה Pi. 'transfer' 2^9, an Aramaism; שַׁרְבִיט 4^{11} 5^2 8^4, Aram.; שֵׁשׁ 'alabaster' 1^6 Ct. 5^{15}; שְׁתִיָּה 1^8 ἅ.λ.; תַּכְרִיךְ 8^{15}, Aram.; תֹּקֶף 9^{29} 10^2 Dn. 11^{17}, Aram.

§ 26. AUTHORSHIP.

The intense national spirit of this book and its insertion in the Canon indicate that its author was a Jew. From 2^5 we may perhaps infer that he belonged to the tribe of Benjamin. In regard to his place of residence there is a difference of opinion. Willrich thinks that he lived in Egypt. Bloch thinks that he was a Palestinian Jew who sympathized with the Hellenizing movement in the days of Antiochus. Grätz and Meijboom hold that he was one of the Palestinian opponents of Antiochus. The absence of reference to Jerusalem and the mention of the Jews "scattered abroad and dispersed" (3^8) indicate rather that the author was himself one of the *Diaspora*. That Heb. could not be written outside of Palestine, except during the Babylonian captivity, as Grätz asserts, is more than doubtful. The Persian words and the knowledge of Persian customs that the book contains, suggest that its writer lived in Persia. Purim, as we shall see presently (§ 28), was a feast of foreign origin, and it is probable that its observance was learned outside of Palestine. It is a plausible conjecture that the author was a Persian Jew who had come to live in Judæa, and wished to commend the observance of Purim to the people of that land.

§ 27. HISTORICAL CHARACTER OF THE BOOK.

For the history of opinion, see § 39. In regard to the historical character of Est., the following facts may be noted:—

(1) The book wishes to be taken as history. It begins with the conventional formula "and it came to pass," which puts it into the sequence of the historical books. The argument for the observance of Purim also has no force unless the events narrated actually occurred. Similar claims, however, are made by Jon., Ru., and parts of Ch., that cannot be held to be historical.

(2) The book was regarded as historical by the Jewish authorities who admitted it to the Canon; but their opinion has no critical value, inasmuch as it is notoriously incorrect in regard to other books of the OT.

(3) A few of the statements of Est. are confirmed by external historical evidence. Ahasuerus is a historical personage (*cf.* § 22), and the picture of his character given in Est. as a sensual and capricious despot corresponds with the account of Xerxes given by Herodotus, vii. ix.; Aesch. *Pers.* 467 *ff.*, Juv. x. 174–187; yet monarchs of this type were common in the ancient Orient, and the narrative contains so little that is characteristic, that earlier scholars were able to identify Ahasuerus with every one of the kings of Media and Persia. The incidents of Esther can be fitted into the life of Xerxes without great difficulty. He reigned 20 years, and Est. goes no higher than his 12th, or possibly his 13th year ($3^{7.\ 12}$). The banquet in the 3d year (1^3) may plausibly be combined with the great council which Xerxes held before his invasion of Greece (Herod. vii. 8). The four years that intervened between the deposition of Vashti and the coronation of Esther

(1^3 2^{16}) may be identified with the four years during which Xerxes was absent on his expedition against Greece, only (2^{16}) Esther was taken to the palace by Xerxes in his 7th year (480 B.C.), when, according to Her., he was still in Greece, unless we assume that the years are reckoned in Babylonian fashion from the first full year.

Some of the statements of Est. in regard to Persia and Persian customs are confirmed by classical historians. Thus the arrangement of the banquet (1^{6-8}), the seven princes who formed a council of state (1^{14}), obeisance before the King and his favourites (3^2), belief in lucky and unlucky days (3^7), exclusion of mourning garb from the palace (4^2), hanging as the death-penalty (5^{14}), dressing a royal benefactor in the King's robes (6^8), the dispatching of couriers with royal messages (3^{13} 8^{10}). (For details see the commentary.) The palace of Xerxes as described in Est. is not unlike the palace of Artaxerxes Mnemon as excavated by Dieulafoy at Susa (see com. on 1^5). All that these facts prove, is that the author had some knowledge of Persia and Persian life which he used to give local colour. They do not prove that his story is historical any more than the local colour of the *Arabian Nights* proves them to be historical.

The following Persian words occur in the book:—אֲחַשְׁדַּרְפָּנִים 'satraps' (3^{12} 8^9 9^3) = Pers. *khshatrapâvan*, 'protectors of the realm'; אֲחַשְׁתְּרָנִים 'royal horses' ($8^{10, 14}$), from Pers. *khshatra*, 'realm'; בִּיתָן 'palace' (1^5 $7^{7, 8}$), according to Dieulafoy, *RÉJ*. 1888, cclxxvii. = Pers. *apadâna*, 'throne-room,' but this is very doubtful (see com. *a. l.*); גְּנָזִים 'treasury' (3^9 4^7), ph. = N. Pers. *kanja* (Vullers, *Lexicon*, ii. 1032; Lagarde, *Ges. Abhl.* 27); דָּת 'law' (1^8 + 18 t.) = Pers. *dâta;* כַּרְפַּס 'cotton' (1^6) = Skr. *karpâsa*, N. Pers. *karpâs* (Lagarde, *Armen. Stud.* § 1148); כֶּתֶר 'turban' (1^{11} 2^{17} 6^8), ph. Pers. loan-word (Lagarde, *Ges. Abhl.* 207); פַּרְתְּמִים 'nobles' (1^3 6^9) = Pers. *fratama*, 'first'; פִּתְגָם 'decree' (1^{20}) = Pers. *patigâma;* פַּתְשֶׁגֶן 'copy' (3^{14} 4^8 8^{13}) = פַּרְשֶׁגֶן (Ezr. $4^{11, 23}$ 5^6) = Pers. *paticayan* (Lagarde, *Ges. Abhl.* 79; *Armen. Stud.* § 1838). These words all belong to the language of government and of trade, and, therefore, do not indicate any peculiar knowledge of Persia on the part of the author of Est.

(4) Most of the statements of Est. are unconfirmed by external evidence. The chief personages of the book, Vashti, Haman,

Esther, Mordecai, are unknown to history. Ezr., Ne., the later Psalms, Sirach in his list of Hebrew worthies (Ecclus. 44–49), say nothing of the Jewish queen who saved her nation, or of the mighty Jewish chancellor who was "next unto King Ahasuerus, and great among the Jews, and accepted of the multitude of his brethren, seeking the good of his people and speaking peace to all his seed" (10³). Greek historians are equally silent about these two great personages.

The book of Est. gives many proper names; *e.g.*, the seven eunuchs (1¹⁰), the seven princes (1¹⁴), the chief eunuch (2³· ⁸), the ancestors of Mordecai (2⁵), and of Esther (2¹⁵ 9²⁹), the two conspirators (2²¹), the royal officials (2¹⁴ 4⁵ 7⁹), the relatives of Haman (3¹ 5¹⁰ 9⁷⁻⁹). This fact has often been claimed as proof of the historical character of the book, but similar lists are found in Ch., Judith, Tob., 𝕋¹, 𝕋², and other late and untrustworthy writings. Mere names prove nothing, except the inventive genius of an author, unless they are confirmed by external evidence. In the case of these names such evidence is not forthcoming. Not one of these persons is mentioned in the Greek account of Xerxes' reign, and their names cannot even be shown to have been in use in the time of Xerxes. In *Problèmes Bibliques,=RÉJ.* xxviii. (1894), J. Oppert makes an elaborate attempt to show that the proper names of Est. belong to the idiom of the Achæmenid dynasty, and could not have been invented by an author of the Gr. period; but in the opinion of the best authorities, he has not succeeded in proving his contention. He assumes extensive textual corruption, and even then finds hardly any Old Pers. names that are known to us. A number of the names are certainly Persian, but it is not clear that they are Old Pers. Some are probably of Bab., Aram., or even Heb. origin. In the lists of 1¹⁰· ¹⁴ 9⁷⁻⁹ some of the names are so much alike as to suggest that they are only traditional variants of a single form. All might have been gathered in the Gr. period by an author who knew something about Persia. The supposed Persian names are as follows:—

1⁹· ¹¹· ¹²· ¹⁵· ¹⁶· ¹⁷· ¹⁹ 2¹· ⁴· ¹⁷, וַשְׁתִּי: ܘܫܬܝ 𝔖: *Vasthi* 𝔏 𝔍: Αστιν 𝔊: Αστι C: αὕτη 55: Ουασθειν 9²ᵇ; Ουαστιν L. This is identified by Justi, *Handbuch der Zendsprache*, p. 271; Oppert, *Prob.*, p. 9, with

HISTORICAL CHARACTER

Pers. *Vahista*, 'best'; but as a proper name this form is unknown. Jensen (*WZKM*. 1892, p. 70) connects it with *Mashti* (= *Vashti*), an Elamite goddess, just as he connects *Haman* with *Humman*, an Elamite god, *Mordecai* with *Marduk*, and *Esther* with *Ishtar* (see § 28). This identification is regarded as possible by Wild., Sieg., Zimmern, Haupt. According to Cheyne (*EBi*. 5247), *Vashti* is a corruption of *Asshurith*, 'Asshur,' being often used as a synonym for Jerahmeel.

1¹⁰, מְחוּמָן: τω Αμαν 𝔊: *Maosma* (*Maosinan*) 𝔏: Μαουμαν 93*b*: Αζαν 249: *Mauman* 𝔍: ܡܚܘܡܢ ('eunuchs') 𝔖: om. L. The older comm. compare with Pers. *Meh-hum-van*, 'belonging to the great Hum' (Hum being one of the Izeds). Oppert identifies with Pers. *Vahumana*, 'the generous'; similarly Scheftelowitz (*Arisches im A. T.*, p. 47), Marquart (*Fundamente*, p. 71), comparing with the syllable *man* the Pers. names *Ariamnes*, *Arsamenes*, *Artamenes*, *Smerdomenes*, *Spitamenes*, as recorded by Gr. writers. The name admits of a natural Semitic etymology from the root אמן, and will then mean 'the trusty.' It is so understood by 𝔖.

1¹⁰, בִּזְתָא: *Bazatha* 𝔍: ܒܙܬܐ 𝔖: Μαζαν 𝔊 (Βαζαν א ᶜ·ᵃ: Βαζεα A: Ιαζαν 64: Αμαν 249: Βαζαθα C: Ζαβαθα 93*b*: Ζαβα(ν) 44, 71, 74, 76, 106, 120, 236: *Nabattha* (*Abathan*) 𝔏: om. L. This was formerly compared with N. Pers. *Bista*, 'castrated.' Oppert identifies with Pers. *Barita*, 'lucky'; Scheftelowitz, with *Vijita*, 'victory.' Marquart prefers the form in 𝔊, and supposes that the original text in 𝔐 was מזן or מזדן= Pers. *Mazdana* (*cf.* Βαζανης in the *Alexander-Romance*, 2¹⁹).

1¹⁰, חַרְבוֹנָא: (*H*)*arbona* 𝔍: ܚܪܒܘܢܐ 𝔖: Θαρρα 𝔊 (Αρβωνα 93*b*: Χαρβωνα C): (*N*)*arbona* 𝔏: om. L. In 7⁹ this appears as חרבונה: ܚܪܒܘܢܐ 𝔖: Βουγαθαν 𝔊: Βουγαζαν אᶜ·ᵃ: Βουταθαν N: Βουγαθα א* 71: Βουγαδαν 64: Γαβουθας 93*a*: Βουχαθαν 236: Αγαθας L: Αβουχαδας (Σαβουχαδας) Jos. xi. §§ 261, 266: *Buzatas* (*Baguas*) 𝔏: Αρβωνα 93*b*: Χαρβωνα C. Oppert identifies with Pers. *Uvarbāvā*, gen. *Uvarbauna*, 'splendour'; Schef., with O. Bactr. *Kahrpuna*, 'lizard'; Justi, with N. Pers. *Kherbân*, 'ass-driver'; Marq., on the basis of Jos. Σαβουχαδας, emends to חרבונא=Pers. *Huwar-baugana*.

1¹⁰, בִּגְתָא: *Bagatha* 𝔍: ܒܓܬܐ 𝔖: Βωραζη 𝔊 (Βαγαθα 93*b* C): *Thares* (*Tharas*) 𝔏: om. L. Apparently the same as (2²¹) בִּגְתָן: *Bagathan* 𝔍: ܒܓܬܢ 𝔖: om. 𝔊 (A¹² Γαβαθα): Ασταου L (A¹²): Γαββαθαν 93*b**: Βαταθαν 249: Βαγαθως Jos. xi. § 207 w. var.: Βαγαθαν א ᶜ·ᵃ ᵐᵍ ˢᵘᵖ: *Bartageus* (*Bastageus*) 𝔏: and 6² בִּגְתָנָא: *Bagathan* 𝔍: ܒܓܬܢܐ 𝔖: *Hastageo* (*Bastageo*) 𝔏: om. L𝔊 (exc. א ᶜ·ᵃ ᵐᵍ, 93*b* under *) (*cf.* 1¹⁴ *Meres* and *Marsena*). Justi identifies with *Bagadata* and *Bagadana*, 'gift of God'; Oppert, with *Bagita*, 'divine'; Schef., with Skr. *Vighāta*, 'defense'; Marq. emends to בגדתא=*Bagadata*.

1¹⁰, אֲבַגְתָא ܐܒܓܬܐ 𝔖: Αβταζα 𝔊 (Αβγαθα 93*a*): *Achedes*

(*Cedes*) 𝓛: om. L., Justi regards as the same as the last; Oppert, as Pers. *Abagita*, 'teacher'; Schef., as Skr. *Avaghāta*, 'blow.' Haupt (*HM*. ii. p. 125) regards as a gloss (or variant) to the preceding one; and thinks that the original name here was תֶּרֶשׁ, which is coupled with *Bigthan* in 2²¹ 6² 𝕲 A¹². 𝔖 reads *Teresh* here along with *Abhaghtha*, 𝕲 has Θαρρα as the equivalent of *Harbona*, and 𝓛 has it as the equivalent of *Bightha*.

1¹⁰, זֵתַר: *Zethar* 𝕵: *Zathi* (*Azatai*) 𝓛: ܙܐܬܝ 𝔖: Ζαθολθα 𝕲 (Ζηβαθαθα A: Ζαθολοα 249: Ζαραθ 93*b*: Ζηθαρ C: Ζαθολβα 71: Ζαθολα(ι) 44, 106): om. L. Oppert and Schef. identify with Pers. *Zatar*, Skr. *jētar*, 'victor.'

1¹⁰, כַּרְכַס: ܟܪܟܣ 𝔖: Θαραβα 𝕲 (Θαβαξ A: Βαρσαβα 249: Αχαρβας 93*b*: Χαραβας C: Αθαραβα 44, 71, 106)؛ *T*(*h*)*arecta* 𝓛: om. L. Justi, Oppert, Schef., identify with Pers. *Karkasa*, 'vulture.' Marq. compares the form in 𝕲 with *Tiribazos*.

1¹⁴, כַּרְשְׁנָא: *Charsena* 𝕵: ܟܪܫܢܐ 𝔖^LU ܟܪܫܢܐ 𝔖^A: Αρκεσαιος 𝕲 (Χαρσαν 93*b*: *Mardochæus* 𝓛: om. L. Justi identifies with Pers. *Keresna*, 'black'; Oppert, with Pers. *Karsana*, 'killer'; Schef., with O. Bactr. *Karasna*, 'the slender'; Marq. reads וכרשנא=*Warkačina*, 'wolfish.'

1¹⁴, שֵׁתָר: so N¹ S N² Br. C B¹ B² G: שְׁתָר Ba.: *Sethar* 𝕵: ܣܬܪ 𝔖: Σαρσαθαιος 𝕲 (Σαρεσθεος A: Σαραθαιος 249: Ασαθα 93*b*); *Soratha* (*Soratheas*) 𝓛: om. L. Formerly identified with *Sitâr*, 'star.' Oppert and Schef. identify with O. Bactr. *Shēthra*, Pers. *Kshathra*, 'lord.' Marq., on the basis of 𝕲, emends to שרשתי, in the second part of which he recognizes the Pers. word *shiyatish*, 'joy.'

1¹⁴, אַדְמָתָא: *Admatha* 𝕵: ܐܕܡܬܐ 𝔖: om. 𝕲 𝓛 L: Justi, Oppert, and Schef. identify with Pers. *Admata*, 'unconquered,'=Gr. Ἄδμητος. Raw. emends to ארתבנא=*Artabanus*.

1¹⁴, תרשיש: *Tharsis* 𝕵: ܬܪܫܝܫ 𝔖: *Pabataleus* 𝓛: om. 𝕲 L. According to Oppert,=Pers. *Darsis*, preserved in the Gr. form *Dadarsis*, a general under Darius. The Heb. form has been corrupted through influence of the geographical name *Tarshish*. Schef. identifies with O. Bactr. *Tarshush*, 'greedy.' On account of its absence from 𝕲, Marq. regards it as merely a variant form of שתר above.

1¹⁴, מֶרֶס: *Mares* 𝕵: ܡܪܣܡ 𝔖 (ܡܪܣܡ 𝔖^A): *Eas* 𝓛: om. 𝕲 L. According to Oppert, Schef., = Pers. *Marsa*, 'trial'; according to Marq., Haupt, it is a variant of the following name מרסנא (*cf*. above, 1¹¹⁰, *Bigtha* and *Bigthana*).

1¹⁴, מַרְסְנָא: *Marsana* 𝕵: ܡܪܣܢܐ 𝔖: Μαλησεαρ 𝕲: Ραμαθα 93*b*: *Malesar* (*Malesath*) 𝓛. According to Oppert,=Pers. *Marithna*, 'he who remembers'; according to Schef., derived from the same root as the last name; according to Raw., "Mardonius is *Marduniya* in Old Persian, and would have been best expressed in Hebrew by מרדוניא. It may, however, not improbably have been originally written by the author (without the *yod*) מרדונא. This form would easily become מרסנא, the ס replacing the two letters רו" (?). Marq. (*Fund*., p. 69) thinks that there were originally only three names in this list, as in 𝕲 and Dn. 6³, and that the list of seven has been manufactured in 𝔐 by insertion of variants and names borrowed from other parts of the book.

1¹⁴·²¹, מְמוּכָן: *Mamuchan* 𝔍: ܡܟܘܟܢ 𝔖: *Muchæas* 𝔏: om. 𝕲 L. In 1¹⁶, מוּמְכָן Q: מָמוּכָן: *Mamuchan* 𝔍: ܡܟܘܟܢ 𝔖: Μουχαιος 𝕲: Βουγαιος L: *Micheus* (*Mardochæus*) 𝔏. Oppert equates with Pers. *Vimukhna*, 'delivered'; Schef., with Skr. *Mumucāna*, 'cloud.'

2³, הֵגֶא: so S N² Br. C B¹ G Ba.: הֵגָא N¹ B² M Norzi: *Egei* 𝔍: ܗܓܐ 𝔖: om. 𝕲 (v. ⁸ Γαι): Γωγαιον L. In 2⁸·¹⁵, הֵגַי: *ei* 𝔍: Γαι 𝕲 (Γαην 249): Γωγαιον 93*b*: Βουγαιος L (Γωγαιος 93*a*): *Oggeo* 𝔏. Benfey (*Monatsnamen*, p. 192) compares Skr. *Âga*, 'eunuch'; Roediger (Ges. *Thes. Add.*, p. 83) compares 'Hγίas, an officer of Xerxes (Ctesias, *Pers.*, c. 24; Her. ix. 33); Schef. compares O. Bactr. *Hugāo*, 'possessing beautiful cows.'

2⁷, אֶסְתֵּר: commonly identified with Pers. *Stâra*, 'star'; but, according to Jensen, = *Ishtar*, the Babylonian goddess (see § 28).

2¹⁴, שֵׁשְׁבַן: some codd. S B¹: שַׁעַשְׁבַן C Ba. G: *Susagazi* 𝔍: ܫܥܫܓܙ 𝔖: Γαι 𝕲 (Σασαγας 93*b*): om. L. Schef. identifies with O. Bactr. *Sāsakshant*, 'one anxious to learn'; most commentators suggest no identification.

2²¹, בִּגְתָן, see above (1¹⁰) בִּגְתָא.

2²¹ ⁶², תֶּרֶשׁ: *Thares* 𝔍: ܬܪܫ 𝔖: om. 𝕲 (A¹² Θαρρα): Θεδευτου L (A¹²): Θαρας 93*b* *: Θαρραν 249: Θεοδεστος Jos. xi. § 207 w. var.: *Thedestes* 𝔏. Oppert compares with *Tiridates*; Justi, with N. Pers. *Tursh*, 'firm'; Schef., with Pers. *Tarsha*, 'desire,' see above (1¹⁰) אבגתא.

3¹ *sq*., הָמָן: Vrss. the same: Cod. 19 has Αμμαν. Oppert and most of the older comm. connect with N. Pers. *Hamayun*, supposing an O. Pers. form *Hamanā*, 'illustrious.' Raw. identifies with *Omanes*, a Pers. name in classical writers, which he regards as etymologically the same as *Eumenes*. Benfey (in Bert. *Com. a. l.*) compares Pers. *Homa*=Skr. *Soma*, the sacred drink. *Haman*,=*Soman*, will then mean 'offerer of the *Soma*' (so Schef.). Jensen, *WZKM*. 1892, pp. 58 *ff*., identifies with *Humban* or *Humman*, the chief god of the Elamites. In this view he is followed by many recent critics (see § 28).

3¹, הַמְּדָתָא: ܗܡܕܬܐ 𝔖: Αμαδαθου 𝕲 L: Αναμαθαδου A: Αμαθου 19: Αμαδαθουν 93*a*: Αμαθαδου 106: om. 𝔏. Benfey, Oppert, and Schef. identify with *Hāma-dāta*, 'given by *Hāma*' (the sacred drink). Oet. compares with *Mâh-dāta*, 'given by the moon.' Pott (*ZDMG*. 1859, p. 424) identifies with Μαδάτης. Jensen sees a compound of the same god *Humman* as in *Haman*.

3¹, הָאֲגָגִי: *qui erat de stirpe Agag* 𝔍: Βουγαιον 𝕲 L: Μακεδόνα L (A¹⁷):

ESTHER

Γωγαιον 93a: Ουγαιον C: om. 44, 106 𝕷. Oppert claims that it means 'belonging to the tribe *Agazi*' (= *Agagi?*), mentioned in the inscriptions of Sargon (*cf.* Winckler, *Sargon*, p. 110). Haupt regards it as a corruption of הגאגי, 'the Gogite' (*cf.* Ez. 38). Most comm. think that it means a descendant of the Agag mentioned in 1 S. 15 (see com. on 3¹).

4⁵· ⁶· ⁹· ¹⁰, הָתָךְ: הֲתָךְ var. Oc.: *Athach* 𝔍: ܐܬܢ 𝔖: Αχραθαιον 𝔊: Αχραθεον A: Εγχραδαιον 44: Αθακ 93b: Εγχραθαιον 106: Αθαχ C. Oppert identifies with *Hātaka*, 'good'; Schef., with O. Bactr. *Han-taka*, 'courier.'

5¹⁰· ¹⁴ 6¹³, זֶרֶשׁ: *Zares* 𝔍: ܐܪܙ̈ 𝔖: Ζωσαραν 𝔊 L: Σωσαραν A: Ζαρασαν (Γαζασαν, Γαζαγαν) Jos. xi. § 245: *Zosarra* (*Gozarra*) 𝕷: Ζωραν 93b. Oppert and Raw. connect with Pers. *Zara*, 'gold' (*cf.* Vullers, *Lexicon*, ii. 128b); Schef., with O. Bactr. *Zarsh*, 'desirous.' Jensen, *WZKM*. 1892, suggests that זרש may be a corruption of גרש (*cf.* the forms in some of the Vrss. above), and that גרש may be the same as the Elamite goddess *Kirisha*. Of late he has been inclined to identify her with *Siris*, the Babylonian goddess of wine (see § 28).

9⁷, פַּרְשַׁנְדָּתָא: so 𝔐 (with small ת): Φαρσαν και Νεσταιν B N 52, 248, Ald.: Φαρσαν(ν)εστα(ι)ν א A 55, 64, 243: Φαρσαν L: Φαρσαννεσιαν 108a: Φαρσανιστην 249: Φαρσενδαθα 93b: Φαρσανδαθα C: ܐܕܢܫܪܦ 𝔖ᴬ: ܐܕܢܫܪܦ 𝔖ᴸᴹᵁ: om. 𝕷. Benfey, *Keilinschr.*, and Oppert interpret as Per. *Frasna-dāta*, 'given to prayer'; Raw., as 'given to Persia, or the Persians'; Schef., as Pers. *Parshnodāta*, 'formed for defence.' According to Justi (*Eran. Namen*, p. 243), the name occurs in Ph. letters on a seal. *Cf.* also the Pers. name Παρσώνδης.

9⁷, דַּלְפוֹן: *Delphon* 𝔍: ܢܘܦܠܕ 𝔖ᴬ: ܢܘܦܠܕ 𝔖ᴸᴹᵁ: Δελφων 𝔊: αδελφων א*: και τον αδελφον αυτου L: Δελφον 93b, 108a: om. 𝕷. According to Raw. "*Dalphon*, which in Persian must have been *Darphon* or *Darpon*, is probably the Pers. representative of the Skr. *Darpin*, 'arrogant'" (similarly Oppert, Schef.).

9⁷, אַסְפָּתָא: *Esphatha* 𝔍: ܐܬܦܣܐ 𝔖: Φασγα 𝔊: Φιαγα א*: Φαγα A: Φαρνα L: Αφαρπαρ 93a: Φαστα 74, 76?: Αριφαθα 93b: Φαγγα 249: Ασφαθα C: om. 𝕷. Benfey, Raw., Schef., and Oppert connect with *aspa*, 'horse,' and regard as a shortened form of *Aspadāta*, 'gifted with a horse,' *i.e.*, 'horseman,' or 'given by the sacred horse' (*cf.* Ges. *Thes. Add.*, p. 71).

9⁸, פּוֹרָתָא: ܐܬܟܠܦ 𝔖ᴬ: ܐܬܟܠܦ 𝔖ᴸᴹᵁ: Φαραδαθα 𝔊: Φαρααθα א: Βαρδαθα A: Γαγαφαρδαθα L: Θαρδαθα 71, 74, 120, 236: Φουραθα 93b: Φαρδαθα 243, 249, Ald.: Φοραδαθα C: om. 𝕷. According to Benfey = *Pur-dāta*, 'given by lot, or fate'; according to Oppert, = Pers. *Puruvata*, 'aged'; according to Raw., = *Paru-ratha*, 'having many chariots'; according to Schef., = O. Bactr. *Pouruta*, 'mountain.'

9⁸, אֲדַלְיָא: ܐܡܠܟ 𝔖: Βαρσα B: Βαρελ א A: Βαρεα many codd.: τους ετερους 71: om. L 𝕷. According to Justi (*Eran. Namen*), ='Αδόλιος;

HISTORICAL CHARACTER

according to Schef., = *Ādārya*, 'honourable'; according to Oppert, = *Adalya* (for *Adardiya*), 'brave.'

9⁸, אֲרִידָתָא: ܐܪܝܕܬܐ ?: 𝔖ᴬ: ܐܪܝܕ ?: 𝔖ᴸᴹᵁ: Σαρβαχα 𝔊: Σαρβακα some codd.: Σαρμαχα 76: Σαρμακα 120: Σαραβαχα 236: Αριδαθα 93*b*, C: om. L, 71, 𝔏. According to Benfey, = *Hari-dāta*, 'given by Hari (Vishnu)'; according to Raw., = *Ari-dāta*, 'generous'; according to Oppert and Schef., = *Ariya-data*, 'sprung from the Aryan.'

9⁹, פַּרְמַשְׁתָּא: פרמשתא (both ש and ת small) G: *Phermesta* 𝔍: ܐܦܪܡܫܬܐ| 𝔖ᴬ: ܦܪܡܫܬܐ 𝔖ᴸᴹᵁ: Μαρμασιμα 𝔊: Μαρμασιμ א 55, 64, 243, 248, Ald.: Μαρμασιμνα A: Μαρμασιαν N: Σαρμασιν 74: Σαρμασιμ 76: Μαρμασαιμα L: Σααρμασιμ 120: Σααρμασειμ 236: Φαρμοσθα 93*b*: Φαρμασθα C: om. 𝔏. According to Benary, = Skr. *Parameshta*, 'the greatest'; similarly Raw., = Pers. *Fra-mathista*, '*præmagnus*' (so also Oppert and Schef.).

9⁹, אֲרִיסַי: ܐܪܝܣܝ ?: 𝔖: *Αρσαιον* 𝔊 (tr. with next): Αρσεον א: Αρισαι 93*b*, C: om. L 𝔏. Composed, according to Raw., from the intensive particle *ari* and *saya*, 'to conquer,' or 'to go.' According to Oppert, the true reading is אריז *Aryiz* = *Ariaçāya*, 'shade of an Aryan.' According to Schef., = Skr. *Ārya-śaya*, 'having Aryan property.'

9⁹, אֲרִידַי: ܐܪܝܕܝ? 𝔖: *Ρουφαιον* 𝔊: Ρουφανον A: Αρουφαιον N 55, 64, 74, 76, 108*a*, 120, 236, 243, 248, Ald.: Αριδαι 93*b*, C: om. L 𝔏. Raw. regards as composed of the intensive particle *ari* and the root *da*, 'give'; according to Ges. *Thes. Add.*, = *Hari-dayas*, 'pleasure of Hari'; according to Schef., = *Ārya-dāya*, 'gift of the Aryan.'

9⁹, וַיְזָתָא: large ו, small ו; so 𝔐: *Jezatha* 𝔍: ܐܙܝܕ 𝔖: Ζαβουθαιον 𝔊: Ζαβουδεθαν א: Ζαβουγαθα A: Ζαβουθαιθαν N 55, 64, 243, 248, Ald.: Ζαφονδαιδαν 52: Ζαβουθαθαν 108*a*: Ιζαθουθ L: Βαιζαθα C: Οναιζαθα 93*b*. Benfey identifies with Pers. *Wahyaz-dāta*, 'gift of the Mighty One'; similarly Oppert. Raw. identifies with *Vayu-zatha*, 'strong as the wind,' and Schef. with O. Bactr. *Vaya-zāta*, 'son of maturity.'

From the above survey it appears that the text of these names is very uncertain, that there is no agreement as to their Pers. identifications, and that none of the supposed Pers. names are otherwise known.

(5) Some of the statements of this book are contradicted by the Greek historians. For instance, during the period between the 7th and the 12th year (2^{16} 3^7) Xerxes' queen was not Esther but Amestris (Her. vii. 114; ix. 112). Since Scaliger's identification of Ahasuerus with Xerxes it has been customary to identify Esther with Amestris, but this is phonetically impossible. We know also from Her. vii. 61; Ctesias, 38*b*, that Amestris was not a Jewess, but the daughter of a Persian general, and that she married

Xerxes long before the action of this book begins. The suggestion of Sayce, that Esther was not the actual queen, but only a royal favourite, is contrary to the statement of 2^{17}.

According to 1^1 8^9, the Persian empire was divided into 127 satrapies, but Her. iii. 89 knows only 20, and the Achæmenian inscriptions name no more than 27 (but see com. *a. l.*). In 1^{9-12} it is assumed that Persian women were veiled, and that they could not show themselves at feasts, but this is contrary to the testimony of classical writers (*cf.* Her. ix. 110 *f.*). So far as we know, there was no reason why Vashti should refuse to show herself to the guests. The statement that the laws of the Medes and Persians could not be altered (1^{19} 8^8), which appears also in the late book of Daniel ($6^{9(8)}$), is unconfirmed by any ancient evidence. It is a Jewish legend that is introduced here for the sake of making the decree of Purim more binding. The idea that no person could approach the King without summons on pain of death (4^{11}), so that the only way in which Esther could communicate with her husband was by risking her life, is an effective feature in the story, but is contrary to all that we know of old Persian court life (for further details, see the commentary on these passages).

(6) There are a number of incidents in Est. which, although they cannot be shown to be unhistorical, are yet so contrary to Persian law and custom as to be improbable. Thus the suggestion of the King's servants (2^2) and the edict of the King ($2^{4,\ 8}$) that maidens of all nations should be gathered in order that from them he might select a successor to Vashti, and the choice of Esther without inquiry as to her race ($2^{10,\ 17}$), are contrary to the law of the Avesta and the testimony of Her. iii. 84, that the Queen might be selected only from seven of the noblest Persian families. Mordecai's free access to Esther (2^{11} 4^{2-17}) is contrary to the custom of Oriental harems. According to 4^2 he might have entered, but for the fact that he was dressed in sackcloth. The appointment of two foreigners, Haman the Agagite (*cf.* Nu. 24^7 1 S. 15^8), and Mordecai the Jew, as prime ministers (3^1 10^3) is not consistent with Persian usage. The issuing of decrees in the languages of all the provinces (1^{22} 3^{12}) was not the ordinary method of the Persian empire. For this purpose Aramaic was employed.

(7) The book contains a number of inconsistencies with itself. In 2^5 Mordecai is one of the captives carried away with Jehoiachin in 596 B.C., but in 3^7 8^2 he becomes prime minister in the 12th year of Xerxes, 474 B.C., *i.e.*, 122 years later, and apparently enjoys his office for a considerable time after this (10^{2-3}). In $3^{2,4}$ 4^1 Mordecai parades the fact that he is a Jew, but in 2^{10} he forbids Esther to make her kindred known. Esther successfully conceals the fact that she is a Jewess from the King, Haman, and everybody else ($2^{10, 20}$ $7^{3f.}$), and yet Mordecai, who is well known to be a Jew, is her uncle and comes to the palace every day to inquire after her (2^{11}), and all the Jews in Susa fast for her before she ventures to go to the King (4^{16}). Haman obtains an edict to destroy the Jews, because Mordecai the Jew will not do obeisance to him (3^6), but Haman's friends and family are ignorant of Mordecai's race (6^{13}). Xerxes delivers the Jews to destruction (3^{11}), yet heaps honours upon Mordecai ($6^{10f.}$). Haman is still the royal favourite, but he is given the menial task of conducting Mordecai through the streets ($6^{10f.}$). Xerxes authorizes the act of Haman (3^{11}), yet he is much surprised at the information Esther gives him of Haman's plot ($7^{6f.}$).

(8) The book contains a number of statements which cannot be proved to be untrue, but which are so intrinsically improbable that one has difficulty in believing that they are historical. Such are the gathering of nobles from all the provinces from India to Ethiopia for a feast of 180 days (1^{1-3}); Vashti's refusal to come at the King's command (1^{12}); the council of princes to determine what should be done to Vashti (1^{13-15}); the decision that her conduct endangered the authority of husbands throughout the empire, and the decree sent out to all the provinces that wives must obey their husbands (1^{16-22}); the gathering of droves of fair maidens out of all the provinces (2^{1-4}); the 12 months' rubbing-down with perfumes required of each maiden before she was brought to the King (2^{12}); the four years that Esther had to wait before her turn came (2^{16}); Haman a descendant of Agag, King of the Amalekites, the earliest enemies of Israel (Ex. 17^8 Nu. 24^7 1 S. 15^8); and Mordecai a descendant of Saul who overthrew Agag (3^1 2^5); the failure to reward Mordecai when he discovers the plot, but the writing of

his deed in the royal annals (2^{23}); the long toleration of Mordecai by Haman (3^6); the 10,000 talents offered the King by Haman for the destruction of the Jews, based apparently upon a calculation of a *mina* each for the 600,000 males of Nu. 26^{51} (3^9, *cf.* 𝔗¹ and 𝔗² *a. l.*); the edict for the universal destruction of the Jews and the promulgation of it a year in advance (3^{8-15}); the sorrow of the city of Susa over the edict (3^{15}); Esther's failure to ask for the life of her people when the King is favourable toward her (5^4), and again at the banquet (5^7); the gallows 83 feet high (5^{14}); the King's reading in the chronicles at night (6^1); Haman's coming at night to ask that Mordecai may be hanged (6^4); Haman's failure to plead ignorance of Esther's race (7^6); the way in which the King is brought to condemn him (7^8); the edict allowing the Jews to kill the Persians and take their property (8^{11}); and the non-resistance of the Persians ($9^{2\,f.}$); the second day of slaughter ($9^{13\,f.}$).

The account of the origin of Purim given by this book is also historically improbable. It represents this feast as instituted by Esther and Mordecai and as adopted by the Jews in commemoration of their deliverance from the destruction planned by Haman; but Purim is not a Heb. word, and it is not natural that a Jewish national commemoration should be called by a foreign name. In 3^7 9^{26} it is said that the feast is so called because "Haman cast *pur*, that is, the lot"; but it is unlikely that this trivial circumstance of the way in which Haman determined the day of destruction should give its name to the day of deliverance. The author also does not explain why the plural *Purim* is used. Moreover, there is no Pers. word *pur* with the meaning 'lot.' If Purim had originated in the time of Xerxes, as Est. represents, and had been enjoined upon all the Jews in all provinces of the empire (9^{20}), and had been accepted by the Jews for themselves and their posterity (9^{27}), there is no reason why it should not have been included in the Priestly Code as promulgated by Ezra. That code contains other late institutions, such as the Day of Atonement and Feast of Trumpets, that are unknown to the early codes. The oft-repeated argument, that the existence of the feast of Purim is a witness to the historical character of the Book of Est., since institutions do not come into existence without a reason, has no value. Purim, of course, must have had an origin, but it is not necessary that it should have been the origin recorded by Est. Religious tales are often a secondary invention designed to explain already existing religious institutions.

In view of these facts the conclusions seem inevitable that the Book of Est. is not historical, and that it is doubtful whether even a historical kernel underlies its narrative. It comes from the same age and belongs to the same class of literature as the Jewish romances Daniel, Tobit, Judith, 3 Ezra (1 Esdras) and the story of Ahikar. Its main ideas are derived from the same cycle of legends from which these works have drawn their materials, and in many particulars it bears a close resemblance to them.

In all these legends the scene is laid at the court of a powerful and splendour-loving king of ancient times (*cf.* Nebuchadnezzar and Belshazzar in Daniel; Darius, in 3 Ezr.; Holophernes, in Judith; Sarchedonus, son of Sennacherib, in Ahikar (*cf.* Tob. 1[21-22]). In all magnificent feasts are described, wise men who know the times and the seasons play an important part, numerous edicts are sent out by the King to all parts of his empire, and these decrees are irrevocable, even when the King himself wishes to change them. In all an enemy arises who seeks to destroy the Jews, and who has a special animosity against one leading Jew. In Esther it is Haman; so also in Tob. 14[10], according to one form of the text, in other recensions his name is Adam or Nadab; similarly in the story of Ahikar; in Daniel it is the officers and satraps of the King (*cf.* 6[3 ff.]); in Judith it is Holophernes, the general of Nebuchadnezzar. Esther, the deliverer of her people, has a counterpart in Judith; in fact, the resemblance between the two characters is so close that Jensen and Erbt hold that the Book of Judith was written for the same purpose as Est., namely, to be read at the celebration of the feast of Purim. Mordecai, the Jewish chancellor, who is next to the King, is the analogue of Daniel, who is set by Nebuchadnezzar over all the wise men of Babylon (Dn. 2[48]), who maintains this position under Belshazzar (5[1. 29]), under Darius (6[3 f.]) and Cyrus (6[29]); also of Zerubbabel, who in 3 Ezr. wins the first place among the pages in the reign of Darius; and of Ahikar, the cup-bearer, keeper of the seal, chancellor, and chief treasurer of Sarchedonus, King of Assyria, in the Story of Ahikar, and Tob. 1[21 f.] 2[10] 11[18] 14[10]. In all these stories the enemies of the Jews fail at the moment of their expected triumph, and perish by the same fate that they had planned for the Jews. So in Est. Haman is hanged on the gallows that he had prepared for Mordecai.

In Dn. the accusers of Daniel's three friends are cast into the fiery furnace that they had made ready, and the enemies of Daniel are flung into the lions' den to which they had condemned him. (For further details see Erbt, *Purimsage*, pp. 45–49.)

De Goeje, in the Dutch journal *De Gids*, iii. (1886), pp. 385–413, and in the article "Thousand and One Nights" in *EB.*[9], xxiii. (1886) traces parallels also between the Book of Esther and the tales of the *Arabian Nights*. In the article in *EB.* he speaks thus: "Persian tradition (in Firdausí) makes Princess Homái the daughter and wife of Bahman Ardashír, *i.e.*, Artaxerxes I. Longimanus. . . . Firdausí says that she was also called Shahrazád. This name and that of Dínázád both occur in what Mas'údí tells of her. According to him, Shahrazád was Homái's mother (ii. 129), a Jewess (ii. 123). Bahman had married a Jewess (i. 118), who was instrumental in delivering her nation from captivity. In ii. 122 this Jewish maiden who did her people this service is called Dínázád, but "the accounts," says our author, "vary." Plainly she is the Esther of Jewish story. Țabarí (i. 688) calls Esther the mother of Bahman, and, like Firdausí, gives to Homái the name of Shahrazád. The story of Esther and that of the original *Nights* have in fact one main feature in common. In the former the king is offended with his wife, and divorces her; in the *Arabian Nights* he finds her unfaithful, and kills her. But both stories agree that thereafter a new wife was brought to him every night, and on the morrow passed into the second house of the women (Esther), or was slain (*Nights*). At length Esther or Shahrazád wins his heart and becomes queen. The issue in the Jewish story is that Esther saves her people; in the *Nights* the gainers are "the daughters of the Moslems," but the old story had, of course, some other word than "Moslems." Esther's foster-father becomes vizier, and Shahrazád's father is also vizier. Shahrazád's plan is helped forward in the *Nights* by Dínázád, who is, according to Mas'údí, her slave girl, or, according to other MSS., her nurse, and, according to the *Fihrist*, the king's stewardess. The last account comes nearest to Esther ii. 15, where Esther gains the favour of the king's chamberlain, keeper of the women. It is also to be noted that Ahasuerus is read to at night when he cannot sleep (Esther vi. 1). . . . It appears that (at least in part) the book of Esther draws on a Persian source." This comparison finds the approval of Kuenen, *Onderzoek*, i. 551, and of A. Müller, in *Beitr. zur Kunde der indogermanischen Sprachen*, xiii. p. 223.

In the presence of these analogies there is no more reason why one should assume a historical basis for the story of Est. than for these other admittedly unhistorical works which it so closely resembles. If it is not historical, the question then rises, How did this story originate? It is connected in the closest way with the feast of Purim; and if the events here narrated did not create the feast, then the feast probably created the story, for comparative religion shows that institutions which do not have a historic origin, are often provided in course of time with a supposedly historical interpretation. That raises the question of the real origin of Purim; for if this can be discovered, it will probably throw light upon the genesis of the Esther-legend and of its counterparts in Jewish romances of the last two pre-Christian centuries.

§ 28. ORIGIN OF THE FEAST OF PURIM.

(1) *Theories that assign Purim a Jewish origin.*—A number of critics who have doubted the historical character of Est. have nevertheless believed that Purim must have a Jewish origin, and that it must be based upon some fact of deliverance in Jewish history, for otherwise they cannot explain its admission by the religious authorities into the sacred calendar.

Bleek, *Einleitung*[6], p. 238, suggests that the feast may originally have been a commemoration of the deliverance from the Babylonian Exile. H. Willrich, *Judaica* (1900), pp. 1–28, "Der historische Hintergrund des Buches Esther und die Bedeutung des Purimfestes," maintains that Est. was written in 48 B.C. and reflects the historical experiences of the Greek-speaking Jews in Egypt under the rule of the Ptolemies. Ahasuerus is the counterpart of Ptolemy Physcon (Euergetes II), Vashti is Cleopatra II, Esther is Cleopatra III, and Mordecai is Dositheus. Haman is the anti-Jewish party at the Egyptian court. The massacre of the enemies of the Jews is the massacre of the Cyreneans at the beginning of Physcon's reign (Diod. xxxiii. 13). The feast of Purim is the commemoration of the founding of Jewish military colonies by Ptolemy Philometor and the name 'lots' refers to the lots that were drawn at the distribution of lands. This fanciful theory rests upon the assumption that the Greek text of Est. is more original than the Hebrew (*cf*. § 20), and that the subscription at the end of the Greek recension is trustworthy (see § 13). It has found no favour thus far among critics.

According to T. K. Cheyne, *EBi*. iii. (1902), 3983, "Mordecai has no connection with Marduk, but is simply a corruption of a name such as Carmeli (one of the popular distortions of Jerahmeeli).... Hadassah and Esther seem to be equally remote from Ištar, being simply variants of the same name, which in its original form is Israelith (*cp.* Judith). Haman is Heman or Hemam. Hammedatha is an outgrowth of Hemdan (Gn. 36²⁶). In fact, the original Esther referred to *a captivity of the Jews in Edom* (*cp.* Obadiah).... The origin of 'Purīm' cannot be finally settled. In the view of the present writer, however, it is not improbable that Pur and Purīm are corruptions of a place-name, and that place-name very possibly was some collateral form of Ephrath, for there seems to have been an Ephrath in Jerahmeelite territory.... It is at Ephrath that the peril and the deliverance of the Jews are localized." This theory can be estimated only as a part of Cheyne's elaborate reediting of the OT. in the interest of Jerahmeel, on which see H. P. Smith, in *American Journ. Theol.*, Oct., 1907; N. Schmidt, in *Hibbert Journal*, Jan., 1908.

More plausible than any of the foregoing hypotheses is that of J. D. Michaelis, *Orient. Bibl.*, ii. (1772), p. 36, and in his German translation of Maccabees (1778), p. 168, that Purim was founded to commemorate the victory of Judas Maccabæus over Nicanor, the general of the Syrian king Antiochus Epiphanes, on the 13th of Adar 161 B.C. (*cf.* 1 Mac. 7³⁹⁻⁵⁰ 2 Mac. 15²⁰⁻³⁶; Jos. *Ant.* xii. 409; *Megillath Ta'anith*, c. 12). After this victory it was decreed that the 13th of Adar should be kept as a holiday (1 Mac. 7⁴⁹ 2 Mac. 15³⁶), but this is the day on which, according to the Book of Esther, Haman planned to destroy the Jews, and on which they were rescued by the intervention of Esther. According to Michaelis, Purim is derived from *pûrā*, 'wine-press,' with allusion to the victory, which is regarded as the wine-press of God's wrath against the enemies of his people.

This view has been followed by Reuss, *Geschichte*² (1890), p. 616, and by W. Erbt, *Die Purimsage in der Bibel* (1890), who also compares Esther's other name Hadassah with Adasa, the scene of Judas' victory over Nicanor (1 Mac. 7⁴⁰·⁴⁵; Jos. *Ant.* xii. 408). Following Halévy, Erbt derives the name Purim from the root *parar*, 'break in pieces.' On this view the Esther-legend stands in no genetic relation to the feast of Purim, but is a combination of a Persian saga with a late Babylonian myth, that has been taken by the author as a symbol of the victory over Nicanor.

This is also the theory of C. H. W. Johns in *EBi.* iv. 3980: "Whilst the Nicanor day is probably the starting-point of the specifically Jewish festival, which may be artificial and intentional, the older sources of the Megillah are probably Gentile, Babylonian, with some Persian influence, and a free adaptation of material."

A similar view is held by P. Haupt, *Purim* (1906). On p. 3 he says: "The Book of Esther was composed by a Persian Jew (under the reign of the nephew of Judas Maccabæus, John Hyrcanus, about 130 B.C.) as a festal legend for Nicanor's Day which was observed in commemoration of the great victory gained by Judas Maccabæus over the Syrian general Nicanor at Adasa on the 13th of Adar, 161 B.C. This commemoration of Nicanor's Day was combined with the observance of the ancient Persian New Year's festival which is celebrated at the time of the vernal equinox. The Persian spring festival, known as *Naurôz*, whose institution is ascribed to the mythical king Jemshîd, or Yim, is no doubt based on the Babylonian New Year's festival." On p. 21 he sums up his argument thus: "I believe therefore that Purim is derived from an Old Persian equivalent of Vedic *pûrti* 'portion.' *Pûrîm* 'portions, gifts' (Heb. *manôth* Est. 9[19, 22]) corresponds to the Latin *strenæ*, French *étrennes*. The explanation of *Yĕmê Pûrîm* as 'Days of the Lots' is a subsequent popular etymology suggested by the Heb. word for 'portion' in the sense of 'lot, destiny' as well as by oracular practices observed on New Year's Eve. The Book of Esther, just as the Book of Judith, is a festal legend for the Feast of Purim; it is not a historical book, or a historical novel, but entirely fictitious. The incidents related were suggested by the sufferings of the Jews during the Syrian persecution and their glorious victory over Nicanor on the 13th of Adar, 161 B.C. Nicanor is the prototype of Haman, and the honors bestowed on Mordecai correspond to the distinctions conferred on the Maccabee high-priest Jonathan, the younger brother and successor of Judas Maccabæus. The names of Haman and Vashti are Susian or Elamite, while Mordecai and Esther correspond to the Babylonian Marduk and Ištar. The antagonism between Haman and Vashti, on the one hand, and Mordecai and Esther on the other, may have been suggested by an ancient Babylonian festal legend celebrating a victory gained by the chief god of Babylon over the principal deity of the Elamites; and this may ultimately be a nature myth symbolizing the victory of the deities of Spring over the frost-giants of Winter who hate the sunshine and always plot to bring back Winter to the earth, just as the frost-giants of *Jötunheim* in old Norse mythology hated the beautiful god Balder, with whose presence Summer came back to the ice-bound earth. Mordecai, the god of the vernal sun, triumphed over the frost-giant Haman, who was a braggart like Hrungner, the strongest of the giants in *Jötunheim*, and the winter of Judah's discontent and oppression was made glorious summer by the sun of Judas Maccabæus."

The difficulties of this theory of an origin of Purim in Nicanor's Day are, first, that the feast of Purim does not fall on the 13th of Adar, the day of the victory over the Syrians, but, according to the Book of Est., on the 14th and the 15th of Adar (9^{17-21}); and on these days, according to all our historical evidence, they were always celebrated. 1 Mac. 7^{49} speaks of the institution of Nicanor's Day, on the 13th of Adar, but does not call it Purim or make any mention of the story of Esther and Mordecai. 2 Mac. 15^{36} says that, in memory of the victory over Nicanor, "They all ordained with a common decree in no wise to let this day pass undistinguished, but to mark with honour the thirteenth day of the twelfth month (it is called Adar in the Syrian tongue), the day before the day of Mordecai." Here the "day of Mordecai" on the 14th is carefully distinguished from the day of Nicanor on the 13th. In like manner Josephus, *Ant.* xi. 292 says, "The Jews that were in Susa gathered themselves together and feasted on the fourteenth day and the one that followed it; whence it is that even now all the Jews that are in the habitable earth keep these days as a feast by distributing presents to one another." The ancient Aramaic chronicle *Megillath Ta'anith*, which is old enough to be cited in the Mishna, gives a list of days on which it is forbidden to fast. In xii., lines 30–31, it says, "The 13th (of Adar) is the Day of Nicanor. The 14th and 15th are the Days of Purim. Fasting is forbidden" (see Derenbourg, *Histoire de la Palestine*, pp. 442 *ff.*). In these, our oldest authorities, there is no confusion between the Day of Nicanor and the Days of Purim, but the two are regarded as independent festivals. Reuss suggests that the feast of Nicanor commemorating a purely political event, was soon forgotten, and that then the 13th of Adar became a preparatory fast to the feast of Purim; but this does not explain why Purim is kept on the 14th and 15th of Adar, if it commemorates the victory over Nicanor on the 13th. Erbt, *Purimsage*, pp. 79 *ff.*, solves the difficulty by the assumption of an earlier shorter recension of Est. in which the keeping of the 13th day was prescribed. Subsequently the Jews dedicated the 14th to Mordecai; but in Jerusalem, where two Nicanor Days were kept, the Day of Mordecai could not be observed until the 15th. Afterward the Day of Nicanor, from which the whole development had started, was forgotten, and a late redactor tried to reconcile the differences of practice between Jerusalem and the rural districts by enjoining the keeping of two Days of Purim. All this is artificial in the last degree. It is simply a piling up of unlikely hypotheses in order to prove another unlikely hypothesis.

In the second place, Esther, the heroine of the book that bears her name, has nothing to do with the victory of Judas Maccabæus. If Haman is the counterpart of Nicanor and Mordecai of Judas, we should expect to find some woman conspicuously concerned in the overthrow of Nicanor, but this is not the case. Here once more Erbt comes to the rescue of his theory with another theory. He splits the Book of Est. into two narratives, a story of Mordecai and a story of Est., and maintains that the former was the original commemoration of the victory over Nicanor, and that the latter is an addition to the legend. According to Haupt (p. 7), "The prototype of Ahasuerus in the Book of Esther is Alexander Balas of Syria, while the prototype of Esther is Alexander's wife, the Egyptian princess Cleopatra, daughter of Ptolemy VI. Philometor and his sister Cleopatra, who both were very friendly disposed toward the Jews. . . . The figure of Esther also bears some traces of Ithaca or Irene (the favourite concubine of Ptolemy Philometor's coregent and successor, his brother Ptolemy Physcon) who besought Ptolemy Physcon to abandon his plan of exterminating the Alexandrian Jews." But the only point of similarity between Cleopatra and Irene and Esther is that both were favourable to the Jews. They had nothing to do with the overthrowal of Nicanor, and therefore it is hard to see why they should be dragged into a legend that is meant to commemorate Judas' victory.

A third objection to this theory is that it recognizes no organic connection between the feast of Purim and the festal legend composed for its celebration. The feast is of Jewish origin, but the legend associated with it is of Babylonian-Persian origin. How did this peculiar combination come about? If Purim were a Babylonian or a Persian feast, one could understand how the story that had been connected with it from time immemorial should still be attached to it when this feast was adopted by the Jews; but one cannot see how the Jews came to tell a Babylonian or a Persian story, that originally had an entirely different meaning, in connection with a Jewish historical anniversary. On p. 11 Haupt says, "The contemporaries of the author of the Book of Esther understood the allusions to Nicanor, Jonathan, Alexander Balas, Cleopatra, Irene, &c. . . . just as well as the readers of Heinrich von Kleist's *Hermannsschlacht* perceived the contemporary references in the patriotic drama of the Prussian poet. This can hardly be called a very good Hebrew or Semitic analogy. The Book of Job, that Haupt also alludes to, has no bearing on the case. Where have we another instance in the OT. of the observance of a holy day by the reading of a story that has no obvious connection with the meaning of the day in question? The deliverance from Egypt is celebrated by the reading of the story of the Exodus, not of an account of Marduk's victory over Tiâmat. The destruction of Jerusalem is commemorated by the reading of the Book of Lamentations, in which this event is described, not by an account of the fall of Humbaba before Gilgamesh. Why then should not Judas' victory over Nicanor be celebrated by a narrative of that event, instead of by an allegorical adaptation of a Persianized Babylonian myth?

A fourth objection to this theory is its failure to give a satisfactory Hebrew etymology for the name Purim. A feast that the Jews themselves had invented to celebrate an important event in their own history they would not have called by a Babylonian or Persian name for which no rational explanation can be given. This consideration applies with equal force to any theory that assigns Purim a Hebrew origin. A feast that bears a foreign name must have been derived from a foreign source—such is the opinion of the majority of critics of the present day. As Kuenen, *Onderzoek*, p. 545, also observes, this theory best explains the unhistorical character of the book. A feast that had a historical Jewish origin could best be justified by telling the true story of its institution, but a feast derived from the heathen could only be justified by a fiction. The *a priori* objection raised by König, *Einleitung*, p. 292, and Erbt, p. 76, that religious scruples would have prevented the post-exilic Jews from borrowing a heathen festival, is not weighty. In their early history the Hebrews adopted all the agricultural festivals of the Canaanites and transformed them into national memorials. Several Babylonian holy days have been similarly transformed in the Priestly Code. In later times difficulty would doubtless be felt in adopting religious festivals, but the same opposition would not be raised against secular anniversaries and holidays, such as the feast of Purim is. Many modern Jews keep Christmas and other national holidays as secular celebrations, and it is quite conceivable that in process of time they should make them a part of their calendar and give them a Jewish interpretation. The newspapers lately reported that a convention of Jewish rabbis had decided to keep the American national holiday of Thanksgiving Day, and to make it a celebration of the first landing of the Jews in America. This is a good illustration of the process that in all ages has been going on in Judaism of absorbing all sorts of alien elements and assimilating them to the national genius. There is no difficulty, therefore, in supposing that Purim was originally a heathen festival that the Jews learned to keep in one of the lands of their exile, and for which they subsequently invented the pseudo-historical justification that the Book of Esther contains. The history of religion is full of analogous instances in which heterogeneous institutions have been given a new interpretation by the sects which have adopted them.

(2) *Theory of a Greek origin of Purim.*—H. Grätz, "Der historische Hintergrund und die Abfassung des B. Est. und der Ursprung des Purimfestes," *MGWJ*. xxxv. (1886), pp. 425 *ff.*; 473 *ff.*; 521 *ff.*, maintains that Purim is the Greek feast of πιθοιγία, or 'the cask-opening,' the *Vinalia* of the Romans, a season characterized by wine-drinking and sending of presents just as Purim was. This he holds was introduced by Joseph, the tax-gatherer, in the reign of Ptolemy Philopator (222–205 B.C.) (*cf.* Jos. *Ant.* xii. 160 *ff.*). Following J. D. Michaelis, he explains Purim as an otherwise unknown plural of the Heb. word *pûrā*, 'wine-press,' and supposes that this name was given with reference to the opening of the wine-casks. But wine-presses are not wine-casks, and

they suggest rather the autumn than the spring-time, when the *Pithoigia* were celebrated. The intense reaction against everything Greek that obtained during the Maccabæan period makes it unlikely that a Greek festival, so recently introduced as this theory assumes, could have gained so strong a hold on the affections of the people that the religious authorities were unable to dislodge it. Moreover, this theory fails to give an explanation of the way in which the Esther-legend, which evidently is not of Greek origin, came to be connected with a Greek feast. This theory, accordingly, has found no favour among critics.

(3) *Theories of a Persian origin of Purim.*—If a foreign origin is to be sought for the feast of Purim, one naturally thinks first of Persia. The scene of the Book of Est. is laid in that land, and it contains a number of Persian words and allusions to Persian customs (*cf.* § 25, and § 27, 3). In 3^7 the word *pur*, from which Purim is supposed to come, is explained as though it were Persian. In 9^{17} *sq.* it is the Persian Jews who inaugurate the keeping of the feast. These facts suggest that Purim was originally a Persian feast that was learned by the Jews residing in Susa and its vicinity, and that from them it spread to the Jews in other parts of the world.

E. Meier, *Geschichte der poetischen National-Literatur der Hebräer* (1856), p. 506, speaks thus: "The name of this feast suggests at once its foreign origin. It is Persian, and our author interprets it as 'lot' (Pers. *bahr*), but incorrectly. Purim is clearly originally the great feast of the redemption of Nature, the spring festival (otherwise known as *neurúz* among the Persians), but here derived from Pers. *behâr*, 'spring.' In Persia the Jews became acquainted with this feast, took part in it, until at length it became quite their own, and then retained it even after the Persian dominion was past. Our author wishes to recommend this feast to his fellow-countrymen in Palestine, and seeks to give it, like the Passover, a historical basis, and thus to nationalize it" (*cf.* Meier, *Hebr. Wurzelwörterbuch*, p. 716).

F. Hitzig, *Geschichte des Volkes Israels* (1869), p. 280, says: "The Persian in our author's field of vision seems to be traversed by another language that is neither Aryan nor Semitic, in which *pur* meant 'lot' (3^7); but that the feast of Purim derived its name from this (9^{26}) does not sound probable. Adar (March) is the last month, and in the spring the Persians also began their year. Now, in modern Arabic New Year is called *phur;* the Persian *purdeghân* (intercalary days) belong here also, being derived from Skr. *pûrva,* 'the first, the preceding,' just as *sijâh,* 'black,' goes back to Zend *çjâva.* Since, moreover, on account of the description which 3[8] gives of the Jews, the book must be brought down to the times after the colonization by Seleucus Nicator, *etc.,* it was probably composed under Parthian rule after the year 238. The Parthians of Scythian stock may have had words like *pur,* 'lot,' *Agha,* from which perhaps comes *Agag,* and others."

Similarly J. Fürst, *Kanon des A. T.* (1868), pp. 104 *ff.,* and L. Zunz, *ZDMG.* xxvii. (1873), p. 686, hold that Purim is an adaptation of a Persian spring festival.

L. S. P. Meijboom (not Meyboom, as his name is spelled in all the handbooks) in his chapter on Esther in *Raadselachtige Verhalen uit het Oude en het Niewe Verbond* (1870), p. 114, also identifies Purim with the Persian New Year festival; and in addition to this seeks to give the characters in the Book of Est. a mythological interpretation: "The name Vashti may be the Persian *behischta,* 'belonging to Paradise,' Esther, the Sanskrit *stârâ,* which agrees with the Greek *astron,* our *star,* and may denote the star *par excellence, i.e.,* the sun. She is also called Hadassa, *i.e.,* 'the swift.' For Mordecai the dictionaries give the meaning of 'mannikin,' and this name of the faithful guardian of Esther is exceptionally appropriate to the moon. The conception of the moon as a man, sometimes as a woman, we find also among the Indo-Germans. It is better, however, to think of the Sanskrit *châyâ,* 'shadow,' and *mard,* 'make weak,' then 'melt'; and consequently to give the name Mordecai the meaning of 'shadow-melter,' which is not less appropriate to the moon. Haman's name finally is related to *hima, hiems, cheimôn,* which all mean winter, and all agree with the Sanskrit *heman.*" Meijboom then proceeds to show how the story of Esther depicts the victory of the gods of summer over the gods of winter.

A more important form of the Persian theory is that first proposed by J. von Hammer in the *Wiener Jahrbücher für Literatur* (1872), xxxviii. p. 49, namely, that Purim is the same as the Pers. *Farvardîgân,* a feast in memory of the dead, that was kept on the last ten days of the year and included the 5 intercalary days that were necessary to equalize the civil year of 360 days with the solar year. Lagarde, *Purim, ein Beitrag zur Geschichte der Religion* (1887), observed the fact that in the Lucianic recension of the Greek version *Purim* is represented by *Phourdaia* (in the common text *Phrourai*). This he regarded as the original form of the name, and as etymologically identical with Pers. *Farvardîgân.* In New Pers. this appears as *Pôrdigân,* which seems to be the same as *Phourdigan,* a feast of the Persians mentioned by the Byzantine historian Menander in the sixth century. The original Heb. form of the name he holds was *Purdaiya,* which has been preserved in the Lucianic text, and *Purim* is a late Jewish corruption of the name. The testimony of 3[7] that the feast was named after *pur*, 'the lot,' he rejects as a textual corruption. Similarly Renan, *Histoire du peuple d'Israel*, iv. (1892), connects the name with Pers. *Fourdi*=Aram. *Pourdai*=Heb. *Pourdim*=*Purim*.

F. Schwally, *Das Leben nach dem Tode* (1892), pp. 42-45, rejects Lagarde's etymology of the name Purim, but follows him in his identification of this feast with *Farvardîgân*, the Persian All Souls' Day. The avoidance of the name of God in Est. is best explained, he maintains, as due to the fact that this feast belonged to the cult of the dead. The fast and the feast of Purim must have had originally a religious meaning; but if they had been dedicated to the God of Israel, there would have been no reason for inventing a story to explain them. They cannot have been of heathen origin, for then they would not have been adopted by post-exilic Judaism. Midway between Yahwism and heathenism, however, stands the cult of the dead, that was practised in Israel from the earliest times and that never died out. In *Farvardîgân* the Jews found something congenial to their ancient beliefs and practices, and therefore adopted it more readily. The banquets that accompany Purim suggest the feasts of the dead, and the presents are a survival of offerings to the dead. In Jewish tradition the month Adar is specially connected with commemorations of the dead. In it fall the death-days of Moses, Elijah, and Miriam. In it the graves are whitewashed, and this is a custom that can be traced back to Persia. In a Purim-legend published by Sachau, Haman sits by the graveyard and exacts 3½ dirhams for every corpse. Purim is best explained as a "disguised feast of the dead." This view has found the approval of Wildeboer, *Lit. des A. T.*, pp. 445-450; *Commentar*, p. 176; Siegfried, *Com.*, p. 137; Haupt, *Purim*, p. 20, although these critics recognize also the presence of Babylonian elements in this festival.

So far as this theory depends upon an etymological identification of *Purim* with Pers. *Farvardîgân*, it rests upon a very insecure foundation. There is no reason why the notoriously incorrect text of Lucian should in this instance be preferred to the Heb. text. The Greek forms of the name can easily be explained as corruptions or attempted interpretations of the Heb. form, and there is no need of going to Persian for an explanation of *Phrourai*, *Phourdaia*, or any of the other variants of the name. Lagarde himself in his later writings abandoned this etymology and proposed to connect *Purim* with Mandaic *puhra*, 'meal.' With the failure of this identification there falls, however, the main reason for identifying *Purim* with *Farvardîgân*. Moreover, *Farvardîgân* came on the last ten days of the year, while Purim was celebrated on the 14th and 15th of Adar, the last month. It is difficult to see how or why the date of the feast was changed, if it was derived from *Farvardîgân*. In such matters religions are usually very conservative. It is also uncertain that *Farvardîgân* coincided regularly with the spring month of Adar. The Persian year had only 365 days, and consequently in the lapse of time New Year Day must have fallen in different seasons of the year (see Kuenen, *Onderzoek*, p. 546). The evidence that Purim was originally a feast of the dead, which is the only argument left for identifying it with *Farvardîgân*, is not very impressive (*cf.* Grüneisen, *Der Ahnenkultus und die Urreligion Israels* (1900), pp. 187 *ff.*).

(4) *Theory of a Babylonian origin of Purim.*—If Purim was derived by the Jews from a foreign source, it is natural to think that Babylonia may have been its original home. Even if it was learned in Persia, it may still be ultimately of Babylonian origin. The archæological discoveries of the last fifty years have demonstrated with ever-increasing fulness how much Hebrew civilization borrowed from Babylonia from the earliest down to the latest period. May it not be that Purim is one of the many elements derived from this source? Such is the opinion of a large number of recent critics.

F. Hommel, in an Appendix to N. Weisslovits, *Prinz und Derwisch* (1890); H. Zimmern, "Zur Frage nach dem Ursprunge des Purimfestes," *ZATW.* xi. (1891), pp. 157 *ff.* (*cf.* Muss-Arnolt, *Christian Intelligencer*, June 10, 1891); P. Jensen, "Elamitische Eigennamen," *WZKM.* vi. (1892), pp. 47 *ff.*, 209 *ff.*, and in Nowack, *Arch.* ii. 199, and Wildeboer, *Com.* p. 173; W. Nowack, *Archäologie* (1894), ii. pp. 194 *ff.*; Gunkel, *Schöpfung und Chaos* (1895), pp. 309 *ff.*; B. Meissner, "Zur Entstehungsgeschichte des Purimfestes," *ZDMG.* l. (1896), pp. 296 *ff.*; H. Winckler, *Altorientalische Forschungen*, ii. (1898), pp. 91 *ff.*, 182, 354 *ff.*; C. H. Toy, "Esther as a Babylonian Goddess," *New World*, 1898, pp. 130 *ff.*; H. Zimmern, *KAT*.[3] (1902), pp. 514 *ff.*; J. G. Frazer, *The Golden Bough*[2] (1903), pp. 138 *ff.* (*cf. EBi.* iii. (1902), 3980; H. Winckler, "Esther" in *Altorientalische Forschungen*, iii. (1902), pp. 1–66; all agree in tracing Purim and the Esther-legend to a Babylonian source.

Other critics, such as Erbt, Haupt, and Johns, who give Purim a Jewish origin, or Schwally, Wildeboer, and Smend, who give it a Persian origin, nevertheless recognize Babylonian influence in the story.

On this theory Purim is a Babylonian feast, and the story of Esther is the legend that belongs to this feast. The main characters are Babylonian and Elamite gods, and the narrative is transformed Babylonian mythology. *Mordecai* (Greek *Mardochaios*) is *Marduk* (*Merodach*), the chief god of Babylon. 𝕌[1] and 𝕌[2] on 10³ say that he was like the morning star. *Esther* is *Ishtar*, the chief Babylonian goddess. This is the regular form which her name assumes in Aramaic (*cf.* Haupt, "The name Istar," *AJSL.* xxviii. (1907), pp. 112 *ff.*). Her other name, *Hadassah*, is Bab. *ḥadaššatu*, 'myrtle,' then 'bride,' that is often used as a title of goddesses. She is the cousin of Mordecai, as Ishtar is of Marduk. In later Jewish literature there are many allusions to the connection of Esther and Ishtar. Thus the Babylonian Talmud, *Mᵉghilla* 13*a*, says, "According to Rabbi Nehemiah her name was originally Hadassah. Why then was she called Esther? Because the people of the world called her after the name of the planet Venus (אסתהר)." Similarly 𝕌[2] in Est. 2⁷ (ed. David, p. 19) says, "Her name was called after the name of a bright star, in Greek *Astêra* (אסתירא)" (*cf.* also *Yalquṭ* 44). *Haman* is *Humman* or *Humban*, the chief god of the Elamites. Strabo 512 says, "There were founded the sanctuaries both of Anaitis and of the associated gods Omanos and Anadatos, Persian divinities; and they celebrated a festival and yearly rites, namely, the Sakæa." In 733 he says, "These things were customary in the sanctuary of Anaitis and of Omanos." Anaitis is the chief Persian goddess, the counterpart of the Babylonian Ishtar, and Omanos and Anadatos bear a striking resemblance to Haman and Hammedatha, his father. *Midrash Esther Rabba* in its comments on 5¹⁰ says that "Haman had 365 counsellors, as many as the days of a solar year"; so also *Midrash Abba Goryon* on 5¹⁴. This seems to preserve a recollection that Haman was originally a solar deity. *Vashti* Jensen identifies with *Mashti* (*Vashti*), a deity of the Elamite inscriptions, who has the epithet *zana* that elsewhere is applied only to goddesses. Clay, *JAOS.* 1907, p. 137, notices certain Aramaic dockets on Babylonian tablets which seem to indicate that the much discussed ideographic divine name *NIN-IB* should be read *En-Mashti* (*Vashti*) 'Lord of Vashti,' and suggests that this may throw light on the origin of Vashti. The command of the King to Vashti in 𝔘² on 1¹¹, " Rise from thy royal throne, and strip thyself naked, and put a crown upon thy head, and take a golden cup in thy right hand, and a golden pitcher in thy left hand," suggests the representations of goddesses in West-Asiatic art. *Zeresh* of the Book of Est., Jensen conjectures, may be a textual corruption of *Geresh* (*cf. Gazasa* and *Gozarra* in some of the texts of Jos. and 𝔏 in Est. 5¹⁰), which he identifies with *Girisha* or *Kirisha*, an Elamite goddess, apparently the consort of Humman. In *ZDMG.* lv. (1901), p. 228, he suggests rather that *Zeresh* may be the same as *Siris*, the Babylonian goddess of wine.

These similarities of names are certainly striking and can hardly be accidental. If the leading characters of the Book of Est. be identified with the chief gods of Babylon and of Elam, then the conflict of Mordecai and Esther against Haman, Vashti, and Zeresh must be regarded as a euhemeristic version of an ancient Babylonian myth describing a conflict of Marduk and Ishtar against Humman, Vashti, and Kirisha (or Siris), and Purim must be identified with the Babylonian feast with which this myth was connected. There is general agreement concerning the main points of analogy just described, but in regard to the further interpretation of the myth and the identification of the Babylonian feast opinions differ.

> Jensen in Wildeboer's *Com.*, p. 174, finds the prototype of the story of Est. in the Gilgamesh Epic. Gilgamesh, the sun-god of Erech, the counterpart of Marduk, the sun-god of Babylon, is the hero of an expedition against Humbaba (a compound of Humman, Humban), King of Elam. Humbaba is the custodian of a lofty cedar that belongs to the goddess Irnina (=Ishtar), the prototype of Haman's gallows. Humbaba is killed by Gilgamesh with the aid of a goddess called Kallatu, 'Bride' (=Hadassah). (For the original of the Gilgamesh Epic, see Jensen in *KB.* vi. 1900, and *Das Gilgamesch-Epos in der Weltliteratur,* 1906.) With the unification of Babylonia under the rule of the city of

Babylon this legend became the national epic, and the exploits of Gilgamesh were transferred to his counterpart Marduk, the chief god of Babylon. As a Marduk-legend this epic eventually became known to the Jews, and was transformed by them into the story of Esther. By most critics these combinations are regarded as rather far-fetched, and it is a serious weakness in the theory that in the Book of Est. Esther plays the leading rôle as the ally of Mordecai and the overthrower of Haman, while in the Gilgamesh-Epic Ishtar is the enemy of Gilgamesh.

Gunkel, *Schöpfung*, p. 313, modifies this theory so that the Book of Est. becomes an account of the struggle between Babylonia and Persia rather than an individual episode of the Gilgamesh-legend. For him the conflict of Mordecai and Esther against Haman and Vashti is the conflict of the gods of Babylonia against the gods of Elam, which in its turn is a reflex of the century-long battle for supremacy between Babylonia and Elam, ending in the victory of Babylonia. The prominence given Esther-Ishtar is due to the fact that the city of Ishtar, not the city of Marduk, was the leader in the war of emancipation. The subsequent turning over of her authority to Mordecai and his exaltation correspond to the subsequent supremacy of Babylon, Marduk's city.

Zimmern finds the prototype of the Esther-legend in the Babylonian creation-myth. Humman and Vashti, the gods of the hostile Elamites, are the equivalent of Kingu and Tiâmat, the powers of darkness and disorder, who in the creation-story seek to reduce the world to chaos. Marduk and Ishtar are the gods of light and order, who vanquish Humman and Vashti and bring peace and blessing to the world. A trace of this origin of the legend still survives in the dream of Mordecai and its interpretation, Greek Add. A (=11) and F (=10), where the sun and a fountain and two dragons are interpreted to mean Mordecai, Esther, and Haman. The principal difficulty with this view is that in the Babylonian creation-story, as it has come down to us, Marduk alone is the hero, and Ishtar plays no such important part as is given Esther in our book. Meissner suggests that in late Babylonian times Ishtar began to supersede Marduk in popular esteem, and that in a late form of the creation-story Ishtar may have taken a more conspicuous part in the victory over the powers of darkness, but this is all conjecture.

Winckler is disposed to find analogies with the Tammuz-Ishtar myth. Haman is the deposed sun-god, who through the six winter months is condemned to dwell in the under-world. The 180 days of Ahasuerus' feast is the half-year period of Haman's reign. His name Agagite is connected with *agâgu*, 'be angry,' and corresponds to the myth of the drunken and tyrannical god whose rule is brought to an end with the vernal equinox. His death by hanging is a characteristic fate of solar-heroes. Vashti, the beautiful, who refuses to come at the command of the King, is the virgin Ishtar, who accompanies her lover to the under-world. She cannot come, because the period of her reign on earth is over. Mordecai and Esther are Marduk and Ishtar, the terrestrial counterparts of Haman and Vashti in the under-world. They release the earth from the tyranny of the powers of winter and darkness, and reign over the six summer months. The seven eunuchs and the seven viziers are the Annunaki and Igigi, the spirits of the upper and the lower world. The first seven are sent to bring up Ishtar out of Hades, the other seven advise that Vashti be deposed. Ahasuerus represents the *summus deus*, the abiding element in which the contradictions of nature find their reconciliation. This theory does not differ essentially from that of Zimmern, inasmuch as the gods of creation and of the springtime are closely connected in Babylonian thought.

The theories as to the particular Babylonian feast of which Purim is a descendant depend for the most part upon the form of mythical interpretation that is given to the Esther-legend. Lagarde, *GGA*. 1890, p. 403,=*Mittheilungen*, iv. p. 147, abandoned the identification of Purim with Pers. *Farvardîgân*, and connected it with the Mandaic word *puhra*, 'meal.' Hommel in the same year suggested that this might be the same as Bab. *puḫru*, 'assembly.' Zimmern then called attention to the fact that the Babylonian New Year feast was known as *puḫru*, and on the strength of this identified Purim with this feast. Under the name of *Zagmuk*, 'beginning of the year,' this feast in honour of Marduk was celebrated in the opening days of Nisan, the first month. It was the most solemn day in the whole year, for on it the gods were believed to meet in a *puḫru*, or 'assembly,' to determine the fates of men for the ensuing year. In symbol of this assembly the images of the gods were brought in festal processions from their various temples to meet with Marduk in the "Chamber of Fate." This assembly, which took place at the beginning of every year, the Babylonians also believed to have preceded creation. The creation-story narrates how, at the foundation of the world, a *puḫru* was held at which Marduk was given supreme authority, and the tablets of fate were placed in his hands. Thus, according to Zimmern, a creation-myth, such as he thinks underlies the Book of Est., was the original story that belonged to the *Zagmuk* feast. By this theory the explanation of Purim in Est. 3^7 9^{24} becomes intelligible. The "lots" of the Heb. narrative are a reminiscence of the lots or destinies of men that were determined on New Year Day. The banqueting on Purim is like the Babylonian celebration of *Zagmuk;* and this also had its divine counterpart, for at the assembly of the gods at creation they drank until they lost their senses and became stupefied (*cf.* Delitzsch, *Weltschöpfungsepos* (1896), pp. 79, 103, 139; Jensen, *KB*. vi. (1900), pp. 20, 135). In the name "Day of Mordecai" (2 Mac. 15[36]) Zimmern finds a strong evidence that Purim was originally a feast of Marduk.

A serious difficulty with this theory is its assumption that the strong guttural *ḫ* in *puḫru* could have been lost in Aram. and Heb. so that *Purim* could have arisen from it. It is generally thought that this change is phonetically impossible (*cf.* Jensen, *ZA*. x. (1896), p. 339 n.; Cornill, *Einleitung*, p. 255; Haupt, *Purim*, p. 20). Zimmern himself abandons this etymology in *KAT*.³ p. 518, but he still holds to the identification of Purim with the *Zagmuk* feast. Another difficulty with this theory is that *Zagmuk* was held in the first two weeks of Nisan, while Purim was celebrated on the 14th and the 15th of Adar, the preceding month. Zimmern thinks that it has been transferred to Adar from an original position in Nisan through the influence of Nicanor's Day, or through desire to avoid conflict with Passover, and in favour of this view he cites the facts that in Est. 3⁷ Haman casts lots in Nisan, and that in Greek A¹ (=11²) Mordecai's dream occurs on the first of Nisan. This is not a satisfactory explanation. Sacred days are not changed in this free fashion, but hold their original position, even though they may change their meaning. Another objection to this theory is that Ishtar plays no more important part in the ceremonies of the *Zagmuk* feast than she does in the creation-myth, while in the Book of Esther she is the central figure and Purim is instituted in her honour. Moreover, *Zagmuk* was so distinctly a religious celebration that it is hard to believe that the post-exilic Jews could ever have been brought to adopt it so completely.

Meissner's theory is a modification of Zimmern's. It assumes that *Zagmuk* is the prototype of Purim, but holds that it came to the Jews through the intermediate link of the Persian *Sakæa*, which is etymologically the same as *Zagmuk*. This feast is described by Berossus (in Athenæus, xiv. 639 *c*, *cf.* Dio Chrysostom, *Or*. iv. 6, 9, *f.* M.). Strabo, 512, as cited above, connects *Sakæa* with the gods Omanos and Anadatos, *i.e.*, Haman and Hammedatha. This feast was of a Bacchanalian character, and in it Ishtar, the goddess of love, played an important part. A slave or condemned criminal was made king for five days, ruled over the nobles, and had the right to use the royal concubines. At the end of that time he was hanged or crucified to typify the death of the god of winter. During this period all the usual social relations were reversed, as in the Roman Saturnalia and the Italian Carnival, which are survivals of this same feast. This feast the Jews came to know in Susa, and they were attracted to it because of the release that it brought them from their ordinary servile position. This accounts for their adoption of it, and for their subsequent development of it into a festival of national deliverance. Frazer, *Golden Bough*², iii. (1903), pp. 138–200, develops this theory still further. He holds that at the feast of *Sakæa*, at the close of the year, a mock-king and a mock-queen were chosen to impersonate the god and the goddess of winter, whose reign was now over, and that by sympathetic magic the union of these two persons was supposed to promote the fertility of the earth. When the brief period of the feast was ended, the mock-king was put to death and his bride was deposed, to represent the death of the god of winter. Haman and Vashti are the temporary king and queen who typify the god and goddess of fertility regarded as decaying and dying with the old year. A vestige of the right of the *Zoganes*, or king of the *Sakæa*, to use the royal concubines, is seen in the suspicion of Ahasuerus, Est. 7^8, that Haman intends to force Esther. Mordecai and Esther, on the other hand, are the representatives of the god and goddess of fertility, coming to life again with the beginning of the new year. A memory of the original conjugal relation between Mordecai and Esther is preserved in the Talmudic exegesis of 2^7 (*cf. Meg.* 13*a*; Schudt, *Jüdische Merkwürdigkeiten*, ii. p. 316).

Against this theory Zimmern, *KAT.*^{3} p. 516, argues that there is no sufficient evidence of the etymological connection of *Sakæa* with *Zagmuk*, and that the statement of Berossus cited above shows that the feast of *Sakæa* was celebrated on the 16th of Loos (July-August=the Bab.-Heb. month of Ab). Strabo, 512 and 733, also connects the *Sakæa* with Anaitis (=Ishtar) rather than with Marduk, which seems to show that this feast is to be identified with the Ishtar-feast in the month of Ab rather than with the Marduk-feast in Nisan. Jensen, who formerly adopted Zimmern's identification of Purim with *Zagmuk*, has latterly been moved by these considerations to identify it with the Ishtar-feast in Ab, which he regards as the prototype of the *Sakæa*. In support of this he urges the prominent position that Esther takes in the Book of Esther, which suggests that the feast of Purim was originally in honour of Ishtar. (*Cf.* Hoffmann in *ZA.* xi. 1897, p. 259.) Zimmern, *KAT.*^{3} p. 516, is so far influenced by Jensen's views as to hold that Purim has resulted from a mixture of the Marduk feast with elements derived from the Ishtar feast. The chief difficulty with this theory is that the *Sakæa* came in July-August, while Purim came in February-March. No satisfactory explanation can be given of this changing of the date of the feast, if it was derived from the Persian *Sakæa*.

Jensen in *Lit. Cent. Bl.*, 1896, No. 50, col. 1803, first suggested that there was an Assyrian word *pûru* with the meaning 'stone' or 'lot' (*cf.* Peiser, *KB.* iv., p. 106 *f.*). Following up this suggestion, Johns, *Expositor*, Aug., 1896, pp. 151–154, and *EBi.* 3997, maintains that in Assyrian this word also "denotes a 'term of office,' specially the year of eponymy. These offices were entered upon at the New Year feast in Assyria. Hence whilst that festival may have been called the *Puḫru* festival, it may also have been called the *Pūru* festival. Such a name for the New Year festival, however, remains undiscovered in cuneiform literature. If it were fully established, we should still have to account for the transference of the date. As on the New Year festival all officials entered on their offices, however, it is conceivable that those offices were previously fixed in Adar. Then the *Puḫru* and the *Pūru* festivals would be separate. Marduk's fixations of the fates may have been anticipated by a previous appeal to the 'lot.' True, in historical times, the eponyms appear to follow a regular order, and an appeal to the lot seems out of question. Still, in the later Assyrian times this order is widely departed from, and granting the royal favour to have 'loaded the dice,' we may imagine a formal appeal to the 'lot.' The Babylonian hemerologies have yet to be consulted as to the observances in Adar. Unfortunately, these await publication. But the 13th of Adar was so far a fast day that on it no fish or fowl might be eaten: in one tablet the 13th is marked 'not good,' whilst the 14th and 15th are 'good.'" On this view Purim, 'the lots,' was originally the Babylonian Election Day; and, as a secular occasion, was the more readily adopted by the Jews as a time of merrymaking. The great advantage of this theory is that it assumes a Babylonian prototype that corresponds with the days on which Purim has always been kept, so far as we have historical records. The difficulty with this theory is the doubt whether *pûru* really means 'lot' and 'eponymy.' Zimmern, *KAT*.[3] p. 518, gives the subject an elaborate discussion with full citation of the passages, and comes to the conclusion that *pûru* means 'a sacrificial bowl, or table' (*cf*. Haupt, *Purim*, p. 20). If so, then this attractive theory loses its foundation.

As a result of the survey of theories just given it appears that, while the feast of Purim is probably borrowed either directly from Babylonia, or indirectly by way of Persia, no certainty has yet been reached as to the precise Babylonian feast from which it is derived. The story which accompanies it has many points of similarity to Babylonian mythology, but no close counterpart to it has yet been discovered in Babylonian literature. For the history of the observance of Purim in post-biblical times, see the article of H. Malter on "Purim" in *JE*. and the literature that is there given.

IV. CANONICITY.

§ 29. OMISSION OF THE NAME OF GOD.

A curious phenomenon of the book is its omission of the name of God, even in passages like 4[14], where it seems almost impossible to avoid using it. In 167 verses the King of Persia is named 190 times, Persia 26 times, Ahasuerus 29 times, but Yahweh never. Some early Jewish exegetes attempted to remove this difficulty by the discovery of anagrams of the divine name in three passages of the book, and this theory has led to the enlargement of the initial letters of the words in question in a few codd. (see § 3). Jehring (1722), Bullinger (1889), and Cumming (1907) hail this as evidence that the author was a religious man, who wished to indicate that Yahweh is present in history, even though his working may be veiled. Such conceits need no refutation.

Steinthal, *Zu Bibel- und Religionsphilosophie* (1890), pp. 53 *ff.*, holds that the author's avoidance of the name of God is due to the fact that he is a skeptic. But belief in God is at least implied in the fasting and wailing of $4^{3, 16}$ and in the circumlocution of 4^{14}, "then will relief and deliverance arise to the Jews from another place." The author knows the story of Joseph, and probably other portions of the sacred literature of his people. His mention of proselytes (8^{17} 9^{27}) shows also that he was not indifferent to religion. He valued the feast of Purim, if no other feast, and its observance can hardly have been destitute of religious association.

The avoidance of the name of God cannot be due to residence in Persia (Scholtz, *Judith*, xvii.), since God is frequently named in the Persian inscriptions, and since Ez., Wisd., *etc.*, that were written in heathen lands, mention Him freely. This silence is not parallel to the substitution of Lord, Heaven, Highest, Name, *etc.*, for Yahweh in late Jewish literature, since these are not cases of omission but of substitution. It cannot be due to the fact that the author is writing about a godless age, or that Purim was originally a heathen, or a merely secular, institution.

The most probable explanation of the phenomenon is found in the occasion for which the book was written. Est. was meant to be read at the annual merrymaking of Purim, for which the Mishna lays down the rule that people are to drink until they are unable to distinguish between "Blessed be Mordecai!" and "Cursed be Haman!" (*cf.* $9^{19, 22}$). On such occasions the name of God might be profaned, if it occurred in the reading; and, therefore, it was deemed best to omit it altogether. The book is not irreligious, but it is non-religious. The author believes in God, but he has no such consciousness of his presence as appears in the Prophets and the Psalms. Alone of all the books in the OT. he ascribes deliverance to men instead of God. Fasting is the only religious rite that he mentions.

§ 30. MORAL TEACHING OF THE BOOK.

There is not one noble character in this book. Xerxes is a sensual despot. Esther, for the chance of winning wealth and power, takes her place in the herd of maidens who become concubines of the King. She wins her victories not by skill or by character, but by her beauty. She conceals her origin, is relentless toward a fallen enemy (7^{5-10}), secures not merely that the Jews escape from danger, but that they fall upon their enemies, slay their wives and children, and plunder their property (8^{11} 9^{2-10}). Not satisfied with this slaughter, she asks that Haman's ten sons may be hanged, and that the Jews may be allowed another day for killing their enemies in Susa (9^{13-15}). The only redeeming traits in her character are her loyalty to her people and her bravery in attempting to save them (4^{16}). Mordecai sacrifices his cousin to advance his interests (2^8), advises her to conceal her religion ($2^{10, 20}$), displays wanton insolence in his refusal to bow to Haman (3^{2-5}), and helps Esther in carrying out her schemes of vengeance (8^9 *sq.*). All this the author narrates with interest and approval. He gloats over the wealth and the triumph of his heroes and is oblivious to their moral shortcomings. Morally Est. falls far below the general level of the OT., and even of the Apocrypha. The verdict of Luther is not too severe: "I am so hostile to this book that I wish it did not exist, for it Judaizes too much, and has too much heathen naughtiness" (*Tischreden, W. A.* xxii. 2080).

§ 31. ESTIMATE OF THE CHURCH.

The Alexandrian Jews were so conscious of the religious and moral deficiencies of Est. that they tried to remedy them with the apocryphal additions noted above (§ 14). This free treatment shows that no sacred character was yet attached to the book. In Palestine there was long opposition before it was admitted to the Canon. It is never quoted by Christ, nor by any of the NT. writers. The early Christian Church made no use of it, and no Church Father attempted an exposition of it. Melito (*c.* 170 A.D.) omits it from his Canon, and Origen (*c.* 225 A.D.) does not include it among the historical books. The Syrian Christians regarded it as apocryphal, and the Nestorians never had it in their OT.

In significant contrast to this attitude of early Judaism and early Christianity stands the high esteem of this book in later Judaism. The Synod of Jamnia in the first century decreed it to be canonical. Later writers sought to explain away the opposition of their predecessors, and praised the book in most extravagant terms. Rabbi Simeon b. Lakish (*c.* 300 A.D.) ranked it next to the Law. Maimonides declared that although the Prophets and the Writings should pass away when Messiah came, yet this book and the Law should remain. Est. is inserted with the Law in the synagogue-rolls and is treated with the highest reverence. More targums and midrashes are based upon it than upon any other portion of the OT.

With this verdict of late Judaism modern Christians cannot agree. The book is so conspicuously lacking in religion that it should never have been included in the Canon of the OT., but should have been left with Judith and Tobit among the apocryphal writings.

V. INTERPRETATION.

§ 32. EARLIEST JEWISH EXEGESIS.

In the second century B.C., when the Book of Esther was written, two main types of exegesis were already fully developed among the Jews. These were known as *halakha*, 'walking,' *i.e.*, 'conduct,' and *haggada*, 'narrative.' The first was applied primarily to the Law, and consisted in a casuistical method of reasoning, by which new meanings, not naturally suggested by the language, were deduced from the words of Scripture, or by which justifications were found for existing ritual customs. The second was applied chiefly to the historical books, and consisted in an imaginative filling out of incidents not narrated in the original records. The Book of Esther lent itself to both these methods of interpretation. Although it was not a part of the Law, yet it instituted a feast that was regarded as equally binding with those of the Law, and that took its place among the feasts as a regular part of the sacred calendar. It was natural, therefore, that Est. should early become a basis for halakhic discussions analogous to those that were carried on over the Law. When, for instance, in 9^{19} it is enacted that the Jews in unwalled towns shall keep the fourteenth day of Adar, there is opportunity for protracted debate as to what towns are to be regarded as unwalled, and what is to be done in case that a town once had a wall but has lost it, or in case that it did not have a wall originally but has since received one. The *halakhoth* that arose in this way out of the discussions of the rabbinical schools were not written for fear of making additions to Scripture, but they were transmitted orally for several centuries. By the time of Christ an immense number of *halakhoth* to Esther, as well as to the Law, must have been in existence. Philo (in Eusebius, *Præparat. Evang.* viii. 7, 6) speaks of "ten thousand unwritten customs and rules," and Josephus, *Ant.* xiii. 10, 6, speaks of "many precepts which the Pharisees deliver to the people from the tradition of the elders" (*cf.* Mt. 15^2 Mk. 7$^{3,\ 5}$). In the case of Esther it was not possible to trace the origin of all the *halakhoth* back to Moses, as was done in the case of the *halakhoth* on the Law, yet the Babylonian Talmud comes very close to this in *M^{e}ghillā* 19b, when it says, "What is the meaning when it is written, Upon it stood all the words which the Lord spoke with you in the mount? From this it follows that the Holy One, blessed be He, revealed to Moses the careful investigation of the Law and the careful investigations of the scribes, and what new thing the scribes would one day introduce. What is that? The reading of the Roll of Esther."

In process of time the difficulty of remembering the vast number of detached *halakhoth* led to the attempt to arrange similar *halakhoth* in collections. Thus arose the form of tradition known as the *Mishna*. The rabbi to whom the chief credit is to be given for bringing the *Mishna* into its present form is Judah the Prince, who flourished *c*. 160–220 A.D. Of the 63 tractates, or collections, of the *Mishna* one entire tractate, *M^{e}ghillā*, is devoted to a collection of the *halakhoth* on the Book of Esther. It occupies the tenth place in the second *Ṣeder*, or 'arrangement,' that is known as *Mo'ed*. The contents of this tractate are mainly halakhic discussions concerning the proper observance of Purim, and the right dates, places, and manner of reading the Roll of Esther in connection with this feast.

The *Mishna* having received its final form from R. Judah, there at once began to grow up about it the further oral discussions of its meanings that constitute the *Gemara*. This bears the same relation to the *Mishna* that the *Mishna* bears to the original text. It is a casuistical commentary on the older commentary that discovers all sorts of new and unexpected meanings. The *Amorin*, or teachers of the *Gemara*, who flourished from about 220–500 A.D., were divided into two main schools, one at Tiberias in Palestine, the other at Sura in Babylonia. As a result of their division there grew up two independent but parallel forms of oral tradition of the combined *Mishna* and *Gemara*. One is known as the Jerusalem Talmud, the other as the Babylonian Talmud. The Babylonian tradition finally prevailed among the Jews, and as a result the Jerusalem Talmud has come down only in a fragmentary condition. The tractate *M^{e}ghillā*, however, has survived in both recensions.

Toward the close of the fifth century and the beginning of the sixth both Talmuds were at length reduced to writing. Their enormous size rendered it almost impossible to transmit them orally; and persecution, which cut off many of the leading rabbis, roused the fear that this learning might perish if steps were not taken to record it. With this literary fixing the Talmudic development reached its completion, and since that time there has been no further development of the *halakha*.

> The tractate *M^{e}ghillā* in the Jerusalem Talmud may be found in the editions, Venice, 1523–4; Cracow, 1609; Krotoschin, 1666; Shitomir, 1660–7. The Babylonian *M^{e}ghillā* may be found in all the numerous editions of the Babylonian Talmud (for a list of editions see Strack,

*Einleitung in den Thalmud*², pp. 73 *ff.*). German translations of the Babylonian *Mᵉghillā* are given by L. Goldschmidt, *Der Babylonische Talmud;* and by M. Rawicz, *Der Traktat Megilla nebst Tosaphoth vollständig ins Deutsche übertragen* (1883); English translation by M. L. Rodkinson, *New Edition of the Babylonian Talmud,* viii. (1899).

While this development of the halakhic exegesis was going on, another development of haggadic exegesis was also taking place. The Book of Esther was not merely a law establishing the feast of Purim, it was also a story describing the origin of that feast. The popularity of this story and the brevity of the original narrative early led to the growth of all sorts of legendary embellishments. At first these were transmitted like the *halakhoth* as detached oral traditions. Subsequently it was found more convenient to gather the legends that belonged to a single book, and to arrange them in the form of a commentary upon the original text. Thus arose what is known as *midrash*. It systematizes the *haggada* in the same way in which *mishna* systematizes the *halakha*. The numerous additions to the text of Esther in 𝔊 (see § 14), in Josephus (§ 18), in L (§ 17), and in 𝔏 (§ 19) show that the *midrash* to Esther had already attained a luxuriant development by the beginning of the Christian era. In fact, 𝔊, L, and Jos. may properly be described as Greek *midrashim* to the Book of Esther. The effort of this sort of exegesis is not interpretation in any true sense, but entertainment and edification. The original text is used merely as a foundation upon which all sorts of imaginary incidents are constructed.

Among the Jews of Palestine the haggadic tradition was not reduced to writing so early as among the Greek-speaking Jews of Alexandria. Haggadic legends similar to those found in 𝔊, L, and 𝔏 continued to be transmitted orally along with the *halakhoth* throughout the entire period of the Talmudic development. The ancient Jewish work on Chronology, Seder 'Olam, in which chapter xxviii. treats of Esther, makes use of this material (editions, Genebrard, 1577; Meyer, 1699; Ratner, 1897; Leitner, 1904). In the *Gemara* which follows the fifth *Mishna* in the first chapter of the tractate *Mᵉghillā* quite an extended *midrash* to the Book of Esther is inserted. This was put into writing along with the rest of the Talmud in the sixth century, and is the earliest Hebræo-Aramaic form of the *haggada* that is known to us.

> The haggadic portions of the Babylonian Talmud are translated into German by A. Wünsche, *Der babylonische Talmud in seinen haggadischen Bestandtheilen* (1886), and the corresponding portions of the Jerusalem Talmud by the same author in *Der Jerusalemische Talmud in seinen haggadischen Bestandtheilen* (1880). The two recensions differ widely from each other. The BT. has preserved the fuller collection of material. Both recensions contain only excerpts from a rich fund of oral tradition that continued to exist among the Jews and that was drawn upon by many later targums and midrashes.

§ 33. EARLIEST CHRISTIAN EXEGESIS.

During the period when both the halakhic and the haggadic exegesis of Esther were having such an elaborate development among the Jews, the book received almost no attention from Christians. Dislike of its revengeful spirit and doubts in regard to its canonicity led the Fathers of the Eastern and of the Western Church for the most part to ignore it. In discussions of the Canon the book is named by Epiphanius, Origen, Athanasius, Hilary, and Junilius (see § 31). Augustine alludes to the story of Esther in *Civ. Dei*, xviii. 36; also Clement of Alexandria, *Stromata*, i. p. 319; Eusebius, *Chronicorum libri duo*, ed. Schoene, i. 125; ii. 104; other Fathers contain passing references to Esther in sermons; but not a single Christian commentary was written on this book during the first seven centuries of our era.

§ 34. THE TARGUMS AND MIDRASHES.

In the period immediately after the completion of the Talmud there was great activity among the Jews in gathering the numerous halakhic and haggadic traditions connected with the Book of Esther and in reducing them to writing. The names of several old Esther midrashes and Esther targums are given by Alḳabeẓ (1585); but these have not survived, except as they have been incorporated into the First or the Second Targum or into some of the later midrashes. The First Targum, which dates from the seventh century, is also a *midrash* or 'commentary.' In § 9 the additions which this targum makes to the text have been described. As there stated, these additions have no text-critical value, but are merely examples of halakhic and haggadic interpretation of the Heb. original. The same oral tradition that is followed in the Tractate *Mᵉghillā* is also used here, and *Mᵉghillā* itself is frequently transcribed. This discloses, accordingly, the second stage in the literary fixing of the oral exegetical tradition connected with the Book of Esther. The third stage is seen in the Second Targum, which dates from the ninth century. Here the haggadic element so outweighs the version that it is more correct to speak of it as an Aramaic *midrash* than as a *targum*. The additions of 𝔗² have been described already in § 10. They are of the same general type as those found in *Meg.* and 𝔗¹, namely, a combined halakhic and haggadic commentary on the Heb. text.

To a somewhat later date than the two targums belong a series of midrashes on the Book of Esther that, for number and extent, are without a parallel in the case of any other book of the OT.

The first in order of time is the *Pirqe de-Rabbi Eliezer*, composed in the ninth century, and ascribed to Rabbi Eliezer b. Hyrcanus. It is a haggadic midrashic commentary on Gn., Ex., part of Nu., and selected later portions of the OT. Chapters xlix. *ff.* contain a *midrash* on the Book of Esther that has many points of similarity with the Talmud and Targums, but which contains also much new material. The editions of the *Pirqe* are as follows: Constantinople, 1518; Venice, 1548; Sabionetta, 1568; Amsterdam, 1712; Wilna, 1837; Lemberg, 1864.

The next *midrash* is that of Yosippon, or Joseph b. Goryon (Josephus Gorionides), which is now generally believed to be the work of a south Italian Jew in the tenth century. It is a history of the Jews from the fall of Babylon to the fall of Jerusalem, and is based in large measure either directly or indirectly upon Josephus, whose name "Yosippon" the author assumes. Book ii., chapters 1–5, contain the story of Esther. Here we meet for the first time in Heb. the dream of Mordecai, his high office in the palace and discovery of the plot of the eunuchs, Mordecai's prayer and Esther's prayer, just as in 𝔊. These additions seem to have been derived from the shorter form of the narrative given by Josephus, but the dream of Mordecai, which is not found in Jos., must have been taken from the Greek or Latin Apocrypha, unless it was interpolated in the copy of Josephus which Yosippon used. By the Jews of the Middle Ages Yosippon was highly valued, and in modern times there have been many editions of his work. The following may be mentioned: Mantua, 1476–9; Constantinople, 1510; Basel, 1541; Venice, 1544; Cracow, 1588–9; Frankfurt a. M., 1689; Gotha, 1707; Amsterdam, 1723; Prag, 1784; Warsaw, 1845; Jitomir, 1851; Lemberg, 1855. A Latin translation of Yosippon is given along with the Heb. text by J. F. Breithaupt, *Josephus Gorionides, sive Josephus Hebraicus* (1707), pp. 72 *ff*.

The *Midrash Esther Rabba*, found in all the current Midrash editions, was written apparently in the Eastern Roman Empire in the eleventh or twelfth century. It uses all the *midrashim* previously mentioned and also the *midrashim* on several of the other books of the OT. It is an extraordinary collection of halakhic and haggadic material of every description. Hair-splitting discussions of the meaning of words, long anecdotes concerning Esther, Mordecai, Ahasuerus, Haman, and the other characters of the book, sermons of famous rabbis on certain texts, fables, parables, and all other sorts of legends, relevant and irrelevant, are piled in here in wild confusion. The Heb. text serves merely as a thread on which stories of the most diverse origin are hung. Exegetically the *midrash* does not possess the least value, but as a repository of tradition, and as a monument of mediæval Jewish thought, it has considerable interest. A German translation is given by A. Wünsche, *Der Midrasch zum Buche Esther* (1881).

From the beginning of the twelfth century comes also the *Midrash Leqaḥ Ṭob* of Tobiah b. Eliezer. This is a partly grammatical, partly haggadic, commentary on the Pentateuch and the Five M*e*ghillôth. The portion covering the Book of Esther is given by S. Buber, *Sifre de-Agadta, Sammlung agadischer Commentare zum Buche Esther* (1886), pp. 85–112. The author stands under the influence of the literal school of interpretation that began to assert itself in this period, but he still values the ancient haggadic method. His excerpts from ancient midrashes, many of which are known to us only from his quotations, he arranges in logical order in connection with the verses to which they apply, abbreviates, and reedits so as to improve their Hebrew.

To the same century belongs *Midrash Abba Goryon*, printed by Jellinek, *Beth ham-Midrash* (1853–73), i. 1–18; Buber, *Sifre de-Agadta* (1886), 1–42; German translation by A. Wünsche, *Aus Israels Lehrhallen*, ii. 2 (1908), pp. 95 *ff*. Most of the material in this *midrash* seems to be derived from *Esther Rabba*, although it also contains much additional *haggada*. The author has subjected the *Rabba* to a rigid revision, rejecting irrelevant matter, and bringing the amplifications into closer conformity with the order of the Heb. text.

To the thirteenth century belongs the *midrash*-fragment known as *Midrash Megillath Esther*, published by A. Jellinek in *Beth ham-Midrash* (1853–73), i. pp. 18–24; German translation by A. Wünsche,

Aus Israels Lehrhallen, ii. 2 (1908), pp. 139 *ff*. This little *midrash*, which deals only with Est. 2⁵·¹⁴, is probably only a fragment of a larger work. It contains almost entirely new haggadic material. From the same period and bearing the same name is another *midrash* that is found in the Constantinople edition of 1519; also in Horowitz, *Sammlung kleiner Midraschim* (1881), pp. 56 *ff*. This contains an entirely different collection of *haggada* from the one just mentioned.

To the same or a little later period belong the *Midrash Ponim Aḥerim* to Est., given by Buber in *Sifre de-Agadta*, pp. 45–82; the *Midrash Shoḥer Ṭob*, on Ps. 22, which contains the Esther-legend (known to me only from the reference of André (*Les Apocryphes*, p. 198); the *midrash* from Yemen published by Buber in *Agadische Abhandlungen zum Buche Esther nach einer Handschrift aus Jemen* (1897), and the *midrash* published by M. Gaster in *Semitic Studies in Memory of A. Kohut*, pp. 167–178. This last *midrash* Gaster regards as the earliest of all the Esther *midrashim*, but in this opinion he is not followed by other critics. All these *midrashim* are little more than excerpts from earlier *midrashim* and *targumim*.

The *Yalquṭ Shim'oni*, a work of uncertain date, but later than those that have just been mentioned, is a huge compilation of all accessible halakhic and haggadic comments on the twenty-four books of the Hebrew Bible. In Esther the editor gives the best that is to be found in earlier *midrashim*, quoting in full, and stating the sources from which he has derived his material. On the *Dream of Mordecai*, which should be included in a list of the *midrashim* on Est., see § 3. On the story of Esther as given by the Persian Jewish poet Shahin, see Bacher, *Jahresbericht d. Rabbinerschule in Budapest*, xxx. 1906–7.

§ 35. OTHER MEDIÆVAL JEWISH COMMENTARIES.

The rise of Islam and the contact of Jewish scholars with Arabic learning gave a new turn to Biblical interpretation. Toward the close of the eighth century Anan b. David, a bitter opponent of the traditional rabbinic exegesis, founded the sect of the Karaites, which insisted upon a literal interpretation of Scripture without use of either *halakha* or *haggada*. This movement exerted a strong reflex influence upon orthodox Judaism, and in 928 Sa'adia, an advocate of the *peshaṭ*, or 'simple' interpretation, became head of the Babylonian rabbinical school at Sura. His Arabic version of the Pentateuch and other books of the Bible, unlike the *targumim* and *midrashim*, aims to give a clear, literal translation; and the accompanying commentary advocates everywhere the natural grammatical meaning. The Arabic version of Esther in Heb. characters from a prayer-book of Yemen, published at Vienna in 1896, comes either from his hand or from one of his disciples (see Poznansky, *MGWJ*. xlvi. 364). Aaron ibn Sargado († 942), a follower of Sa'adia, left a commentary on Est., parts of which are still extant in manuscript at St. Petersburg (see *JE*. i. 20).

In 1036 the schools of Jewish learning in Babylonia were closed and their rabbis were forced to seek refuge in other lands. Many of them migrated to Spain, where, under the protection of the Moors, they enjoyed peace and prosperity. Through the influence of Arabic scholarship a new scientific study of the Heb. language began, that was fruitful for later exegetical studies. Philological research reached its culmination in Abulwalid ibn Ganaḥ († *c.* 1050). He left no commentaries on the Bible, but his *Luma* and *Book of Roots* are so full of exegetical material as to constitute an almost complete exposition. Through this grammatical philological work the commentaries of the golden age of mediæval Jewish literature became possible. RaShI (=Rabbi Solomon ben Isaac († 1105), of Troyes in France, was the founder of the *peshaṭ* or literal school of interpretation in Europe. At a time when the Jews stood completely under the domination of the ancient *midrash* method of interpretation, he came under the influence of the Arabic-Spanish philological school and introduced a new type of grammatical exegesis. With him the literal sense is always the first consideration. He does not break entirely with the midrashic method, but uses it only when it is not in conflict with the literal meaning. To this policy of compromise RaShI doubtless owes much of the popularity that he has enjoyed among the Jews from that day to this. His commentary on Est. is found in all the Rabbinical Bibles (Latin translation by L. H. d'Aquine, 1622, and J. F. Breithaupt, 1714). It is full of sound lexical and grammatical remarks. Only the difficult points are discussed, and to the elucidation of these the author brings a wealth of biblical and of rabbinical learning that is without a parallel.

R. Menahem b. Ḥelbo, a contemporary of RaShI, belonged to the same literalistic school of interpretation. His com. on Est. is known only from the citations of his nephew Joseph Ḳara, in Hübsch, *Die fünf Megilloth* (1866). Joseph Ḳara († c. 1130) was a still more pronounced advocate of the *peshaṭ*. His com. on Est. is published by Hübsch (*l. c.*); by Berliner, in *MGWJ*. 1878; *cf. ib.* 1876, p. 158. Fragments of it are also found in Jellinek, *Commentarien zu Esther, etc.* (1855). It holds itself aloof from the *haggada* and gives an admirable grammatical philological interpretation. Abraham b. Meir ibn Ezra († 1167), the greatest of all the exponents of the *peshaṭ*, introduced a knowledge of Arabic-Jewish exegesis into Europe. His com. on Est. is found in all the large Rabbinic Bibles. A somewhat different recension is published by Zedner, *Abraham Aben Ezra's Commentary on the Book of Esther after another version* (1850). This lucid exposition ignores tradition, and gives the best fruits of the golden age of Jewish learning in Spain. It often criticises RaShI for his continued use of the haggadic method. RaShBaM (=Rabbi Samuel ben Meir) († c. 1174) was a grandson of RaShI and a thoroughgoing advocate of the literal method of exegesis. His com. on Est. is known only from the quotations of an anonymus given by Jellinek, *Commentarien zu Esther* (1855).

In the thirteenth century Jewish exegesis declined rapidly from the high standard set by RaShI and his successors through the entrance of the allegorical method of interpretation. Contemporaneously with the rise of mysticism in Christianity the Cabala developed in Judaism, and from Christian theologians the doctrine of a fourfold sense of Scripture was adopted. The four senses recognized by Jewish scholars were the *Peshaṭ*, or simple meaning; the *Midrash*, or traditional meaning; the *Ḥokhma*, or philosophic meaning; and the *Cabala*, or mystical, allegorical meaning. From this time onward all the commentaries combine these four methods, with a strong preference for the last, and the result is the death of genuine exegesis.

Eliezer b. Judah of Worms derived his mystical interpretations through cabalistic combinations of the Heb. words and calculations of the numerical values of their letters. His com. on Est. exists in manuscript, but has never been published, so far as I am aware. Joseph Naḥmias' com. on Est. (*c.* 1327) has been published by M. L. Bamberger, *Commentar des R. Josef Nachmias zum Buche Esther* (1891). The com. of Immanuel b. Solomon b. Jekuthiel († 1330) has been published in auto-lithograph by P. Perreau, *Commento sopra il libro di Ester del Rabbi Immanuel ben Salomo romano transcritto e publicato da Pietro Perreau secondo il codico ebreo-rabbinico derossiano No.* 615

(Parma, 1880). The com. of RaLBaG (=Rabbi Levi b. Gershom, otherwise known as Gersonides, Leon de Bagnols, or Magister Leo Hebræus), which was finished in 1329, has enjoyed considerable popularity. It was published at Riva di Trenta in 1560, and in the Rabbinic Bible of Frankfurter, Amsterdam, 1724–7. Isaiah b. Elijah di Trani in the fourteenth century wrote a com. on the Five M*e*ghillôth which exists only in manuscript (see Steinschneider, *Heb. Bibl.* ix. 137). Joseph Caspi († 1340) wrote a com. entitled *Gelile Keseph*, "Rings of Silver," which was published at Pressburg in 1903. These commentaries have some value on account of their preservation of fragments of otherwise lost *midrashim*, and on account of their quotations of the earlier literalistic school, but as independent contributions to the interpretation of Est. they have no value.

§ 36. MEDIÆVAL CHRISTIAN INTERPRETATION.

A few Christian comm. on Est. were produced during the Middle Ages. All are homiletical and devotional rather than exegetical, and all make free use of the allegorical method. The following may be mentioned:—

Rhabanus Maurus († 836), *Expositio in librum Esther*, in Migne, cix. 635–670; Wallafridus Strabus († 849), *Glossa Ordinaria, Liber Esther*, in Migne, *Pat. Lat.* xciii. 739–748; Rupertus Abbatis Tuitiensis (1135), *De Victoria Verbi Dei*, viii. cap. 1–26, in Migne, clxix. 1379–1395; Hugo of St. Victor, *Appendix ad Opera Mystica, De spirituali Christi convivio*, in Migne, clxxvii. 1185–1191; Nicholas de Lyra, *Postillæ perpetuæ, seu brevia commentaria in universa Biblia* (1293–1339); Paulus Burgensis, *Additiones ad postillam magistri Nicholai de Lyra* (1429); Petrus Comestor, *Historia Libri Esther*, in Migne, cxcviii. 1490–1506. The most important of these is the work of de Lyra, through which the exegesis of RaShI and Ibn Ezra became known to the Church. In this way the foundation was laid for the more scientific interpretation of the next period.

§ 37. THE REFORMATION PERIOD.

The revival of learning in the second half of the fifteenth century brought with it not only a knowledge of the Greek and Latin classics, but also of Hebrew. The Protestant Reformation, with its doctrine of the sole authority of Scripture, stimulated enormously the study of the Biblical books in the original tongues. Allegory and tradition were rejected, and an effort was made to obtain the literal, historical and grammatical sense. The result was the production of a large number of commentaries that have not yet lost their value.

> Luther and Calvin left no commentaries on Esther, but their contemporaries well supplied the deficiency. The following Protestant authors may be mentioned: A. Stenco (1529), S. Münster (1546), S. Castalio (1551), S. Pagninus (1556), Junius and Tremellius (1590), D. Pareus (1571), V. Strigel (1571-2), L. Osiander (1574), D. Wolder (1575), J. Brent (1576), C. Pellican (1582), L. Lavater (1586), J. Drusius (1586), R. Walther (1587), A. M. Jackson (1593), G. Diodati (1607), T. Cooper (1609), the *Dutch Annotations* (1618), J. Molder (1625), C. Sanctius (1628), H. Grotius (1644), J. Piscator (1646), L. de Dieu (1640), J. Trapp (1654), the *Westminster Assembly's Annotations* (1657), T. Wilson (1663), J. Richardson (1665), B. Kerner (1666), J. C. Zeller (1669), C. à Lapide (1669).

The most important of these are Münster, Drusius, and Grotius. The others are mainly practical and homiletic. All assume Est. to be strictly historical, and the main questions discussed are, whether Ahasuerus had a right to divorce Vashti, whether Esther had a right to marry a heathen, whether Mordecai was justified in advising Esther to conceal her nationality, whether Esther ought to have eaten of the King's food, whether the Jews did right to slay their enemies, and other similar moral and religious questions. A solid knowledge of Heb. is shown by most of these commentators, and their interpretations of difficult passages are full of acumen.

The Catholic comm. of the same period are also for the most part familiar with Heb., but they make the Vulgate the basis of their discussion, and in their interpretation follow the authority of the Fathers and the tradition of the Church. The apocryphal additions of 𝔊 are regarded as of equal authority with the Heb. text. The mediæval allegorical exegesis is not abandoned so thoroughly as among the Protestants, and by many Esther is treated as a type of the Blessed Virgin. In spite of these defects, some of these commentaries take a high rank for the historical and linguistic learning that they display. The Catholic comm. of the Reformation period are as follows:—

> Dionysius Carthusianus (1534), T. de V. Cajetanus († 1534) (Est. in *Opera Omnia*, ii. 1639, pp. 391 *ff.*), F. Vatablus (1545), J. Benter

(1547), J. Ferns (1567), F. Feuardentius (1585), P. Serarius (1610, see Migne, *Cursus Completus*, xiii.), T. Malvenda (1610), G. Estius (1614), J. Mariana (1619), E. Sà (1624), J. Couzio (1628), F. Haræus (1630), J. S. Menochius (1630), *Biblia cum Commentariis* (1632), J. Tirinus (1632), O. Bonart (1647), D. Celadæis (1648), Crommius (1648), Montanus (1648), A. Escobar et Mendoza (1667). The most important of these are Cajetanus, Feuardentius, Estius, Mariana, Serarius, and Menochius, who show sound exegetical judgment and make full use of Jewish and Protestant writers.

The close of the Reformation period is marked by three great compendia, which sum up the results of a century and a half of labour both on the Catholic and on the Protestant side. The first of these is the *Biblia Magna Commentariorium*, of J. de la Haye (1643) and the *Biblia Maxima* of the same author (1660), which contain an elaborate study of the texts and versions and the Esther comm. of the Catholic writers, Estius, Sà, Menochius, and Tirinus. The second is the *Critici Sacri*, a similar collection of the best comments of the Reformation period from the Protestant point of view (London, 1660). On the Book of Esther this contains the comments of Münster, Vatable, Castalio, Drusius, Amama, and the version of Pagninus. The third is the *Synopsis criticorum aliorumque S. Scripturæ interpretum*, of M. Poole (1669), which in the Book of Est. summarizes the views of Bonart, Cajetan, Drusius, de Dieu, Estius, Grotius, Junius, à Lapide, de Lyra, Malvenda, Mariana, Menochius, Münster, Osiander, Piscator, Sanctius, Sà, Serarius, Tirinus, Vatablus, and the versions of Montanus, Pagninus, Junius, and Tremellius, as well as the Tigurina and Genevan versions. Here the leading Catholic and Protestant commentators of the preceding century and a half are admirably collated.

The Jewish commentators of the Reformation period are unaffected by the work of Christian scholars, and exhibit the same degenerate type of exegesis that flourished during the Middle Ages. Most of them are destitute of originality, and simply excerpt from the earlier *midrashim* and from the great commentators of the eleventh and twelfth centuries. Some are interesting for their preservation of fragments of otherwise lost writings, but in

themselves they contribute nothing to the understanding of the
Book of Est. Their names are as follows:—

Solomon ibn Melech (Abenmelech), מכלל יוסף (Venice, 1518, and
oft.), grammatical scholia taken chiefly from Ḳimḥi; Joseph b. David
ibn Yaḥya, פירוש (1538); Meir b. Isaac Arama († 1556), Est. Com.
in MS. in *Cod. Rossi* 727; Zechariah b. Ṣeruḳ, פירוש על מ' אחשורוש
(Venice, 1565); Azariah de Rossi, מאור עינים (1573–5), a sort of general
introduction to the OT. The third part, אמרי בינה, treats of the origin
of Esther; Eliezer b. Elijah Ashkenazi, יוסף לקח (Cremona, 1576, and
oft.); Elisha b. Gabriel Galliko, פירוש מ' א' (Venice, 1583); Shemṭob
Melammed, מאמר מרדכי (Constantinople, 1585); Solomon Alḳabeẓ,
מגלת הלוי (Venice, 1585), important for its copious citations from lost
targums and midrashes; Samuel b. Judah Valerio, יד המלך (Venice,
1586); Solomon b. Ẓemaḥ Duran of Algiers († 1593), תפארת ישראל
(Venice, 1632), contains a discourse on the Amalekites and a com. on
Est.; Abraham b. Isaac Ẓahalon, ישע אלהים (Venice, 1595), compiled
entirely from earlier commentators with use of the fourfold method of
interpretation; Aaron Abayob, שמן המור (Salonica, 1596); Moses Almosnino, ידי משה, a diffuse haggadic commentary, completed in 1570,
first published, Venice, 1597; Moses Alsheikh of Safed, משאת משה
(Venice, 1601, and oft.); Joseph b. Solomon Ṭaiṭazaḳ, לחם סתרים (Venice,
1608); Judah Löw b. Bezalel, אור חדש (Prague, 1600, and subs.), contains also a discussion of Purim; Mordecai b. Jehiel Merkel, מירא דכיא
(Lublin, 1637); Abraham b. Moses Heilbronn, אהבת ציון (Lublin,
1639).

§ 38. THE POST-REFORMATION PERIOD.

In the second half of the seventeenth century and during the
entire eighteenth century few remarkable commentaries on Est.
were produced. This was a period of theological narrowness both
in the Protestant and the Catholic Church that was unfavourable
to exegetical progress. The comm. are mostly dogmatic, homiletic, and practical, and their authors are content to borrow their
materials mainly from the elaborate works of the previous period.
The following names may be mentioned:—

Among the Protestants, A. Calovius (1672), T. Pyle (1674), J. Mayer
(1683), G. Meissner (1687), S. Clarke (1690), F. Burmann (1695),
M. Henry (1706), E. Wells (1709), C. Adamus (1710, on Est. 2), T. Pyle
(1717), J. J. Rambach (1720), S. Patrick (1727), F. Wokenius (1730),

J. le Clerc (Clericus) (1733), S. Horsley (1733), J. Marchant (1745). Of these Clericus is probably entitled to the first rank as the ablest exegete of the period.

The Catholic commentators of this period are J. B. du Hamel (1706), A. Calmet (1707), J. Martianay (1708), C. Chais (1743), *Biblia Sacra Vulgata cum plur. interp.* (1745), C. Nestorideo (1746). Calmet is the chief of these, but all fall below the standard of the Catholic commentaries of the preceding period.

B. Spinoza in his *Tractatus theologico-politicus* (1670), x. 22, discusses the origin of Est. in a truly critical spirit, but here, as in so many other particulars, he is in advance of his age. His opinions made no impression upon his coreligionists, and little upon Christian thinkers. The only Jewish commentator of this period known to me is Meir b. Ḥayyim, משחת יי (1737).

§ 39. THE MODERN CRITICAL PERIOD.

In the middle of the eighteenth century there arose the remarkable movement of thought known as the *Aufklärung*. In all realms of knowledge men broke away from tradition, and subjected everything received from the past to a searching examination. The result was a revolution in Biblical exegesis. One of the first-fruits of this movement was a critical study of the text of the OT. As early as 1720 J. H. Michaelis in his *Biblia Hebraica* collected a number of variants in the Heb. text. He was followed by C. F. Houbigant, *Biblia Hebraica cum notis criticis* (1753), and *Notæ criticæ* (1777); B. Kennicott, *V. T. Heb. cum variis lectionibus* (1776–80); C. F. Schnurrer, *Variæ lectiones Estheris* (1783); and J. B. de Rossi, *Variæ lectiones V. T.* (1784–8). The importance of these works for the lower criticism of Est. has been noticed already in § 3.

At the same time a new interest was awakened in the problems of the higher criticism. The rationalists, who denied supernatural revelation, took a free attitude toward the Biblical books, and had no hesitation in questioning their historical character, if they found reason for so doing. The historical and moral difficulties of the Book of Est. early became objects of their attack. These assaults called forth replies in defence of the historical and religious value of the book from theologians of the traditional school. From this time onward scholars are divided into two hostile camps, the one attacking, and the other defending, the traditional Jewish conception of Est. The critical problems of composition, age, authorship, and historical credibility have been discussed for the most part in Biblical introductions, Biblical histories, and special introductions to the Book of Esther. These works have exerted so strong an influence upon modern interpretation, and are frequently so much more important than the commentaries, that it is proper to enumerate them at this point.

So far as I am aware, Semler, in 1773, was the first critic to make a formal attack upon the historical credibility of Esther; but in 1736 the adverse strictures upon this book in the writings of the English deists and early German rationalists were already sufficiently numerous to call forth the treatise of C. A. Heumann, *De in qua historiæ sacræ de Esthera Asiæ regina sua vindicatur auctoritas*. A similar position was held by Chandler, *Vindication of the History of the OT*. (1741); J. H. D. Moldenhauer, *Introductio* (1744), pp. 75 *ff.*; J. G. Carpzov, *Introductio*[3] (1741), pp. 350 *ff.*; T. C. Lilienthal, *Gute Sache der göttlichen Offenbarung*, xv. (1776), pp. 195–271. G. F. Oeder, *Freye Untersuchung über den Kanon des A. T.* (1771), pp. 12 *ff.*, and *Freye Untersuchung über einige Bücher des A. T.* (1771), p. 1 *f.*, denied that the book had any historical value. This called forth the replies of C. F. Sartorius, *De utilitate librorum V. T. historicorum apud Christianos* (1772); J. Aucher, *Disquisitio de canonica auctoritate libri Estheræ* (1772); E. A. Schulze, *De fide hist. lib. Est.*, in *Bibl. Hag.* v., vi. (1772); and C. A. Crusius, *De usu libri Estheræ ad praxin vitæ Christianæ* (1772), German edition, 1773. J. S. Semler, *Apparatus ad liberalem V. T. interpretationem* (1773), pp. 152 *ff.*, and *Abhandlung von freier Untersuchung des Kanons* (1771–5), ii. p. 251, renewed the attack with extraordinary ferocity. This called forth the replies of J. A. Vos, *Oratio pro libro Esther* (1775); J. J. Hess, *Geschichte der Israeliten* (1776–88); P. J. Bruns, *Entwurf einer Einleitung* (1784); F. S. Eckard, *Philos. u. krit. Untersuchung über das A. T. u. dessen Göttlichkeit* (1787); S. G. Unger, *De auctoritate librorum V. T. in familia Dei* (1785). In various forms the attack on the historical credibility of the book was renewed by J. D. Michaelis, *Bibl. Orient.*, ii. (1775), pp. 34 *ff.*; J. G. Eichhorn, *Einleitung* (1780); H. E. Güte, *Einleitung* (1787); H. Corrodi, *Versuch einer Beleuchtung d. jüdischen Bibelkanons* (1792), pp. 64 *ff.*; A. H. Niemeyer, *Characteristick der Bibel*, v. (1782), pp. 224 *ff.*, who remarks that Vashti is the only decent character in the book.

From the nineteenth century come the following works in which the problems of the higher criticism of Est. are discussed. Those marked with (C) are conservative treatises that defend the traditional conception of the book, the others regard it as wholly or in part a work of the imagination:—J. Jahn (Catholic), *Einleitung*, ii. (1803), pp. 295 *ff.* (C); G. L. Bauer, *Einleitung* (1806), pp. 364*ff.*; J. C. W. Augusti, *Einleitung* (1806); L. Bertholdt, *Einleitung*, v. (1815), pp. 2413 *ff.*; L. D. Cramer, *Hist. sent. de sac. lib. V. T. auctoritate* (1818) (C); C. G. Kelle, *Vindiciæ Estheris, libri sacri, ad castigatam histor. interpretationis normam exactæ* (1820), see *Theol. Anal.* (1822), pp. 431 *ff.* (C); F. Ackermann (Catholic), *Introductio* (1825), 4th ed. (1869), pp. 186 *ff.* (C); W. M. L. de Wette, *Einleitung* (1817, and oft.); M. Baumgarten, *De fide libri Estheræ* (1839); H. A. C. Hävernick, *Einleitung*, ii. 1 (1839), pp. 328 *ff.* (C); J. G. Herbst (Catholic), *Einleitung*, ii. (1842), pp. 249 *ff.* (C); F. C. Movers, *Loci quidam historiæ canonis V. T. illustrati* (1842), p. 27 *f.*; H. Ewald, *Geschichte* (1843), 3d ed. (1864), iv. pp. 296 *ff.*; Eng. Trans., v. 230; J. M. A. Scholz (Catholic), *Einleitung*, i. (1845), pp. 514 *ff.* (C); J. G. B. Winer, Art. "Esther" in *Bib. Realwörterbuch*[3] (1847); E. Meier, *Geschichte der poetischen National-Literatur der Hebräer* (1856), pp. 505 *ff.*; J. A. Nickes (Catholic), *De Estheræ libro* (1856), two large volumes (C); S. Davidson, *Introduction*, ii. (1862), pp. 151 *ff.*; iii. (1863), pp. 391 *ff.*; E. Riehm, *SK.* 1862, p. 407 *f.*; J. J. Stähelin, *Einleitung* (1862), pp. 170 *ff.*; H. H. Millman, *History of the Jews* (1863), ed. N. Y., 1881, pp. 472 *ff.* (C); A. P. Stanley, *History* (1863), iii. (1877), pp. 192 *ff.*; J. Oppert, *Commentaire historique et philologique du livre d'Esther d'après la lecture des inscriptions Perses,*= *Annales Phil. Chrét.* (1864) (C); Articles on Esther, *etc.*, in *Smith's Dictionary of the Bible* (1863 and 1893) (C); G. Weber and O. Holzmann, *Geschichte*, i. (1867), p. 418; T. Nöldeke, *A. T. Literatur* (1868), pp. 81 *ff.*; A. D. Aeschimann, *Étude sur le livre d'Esther* (1868); E. Reuss, Art. "Esther" in *Schenkel's Bibel-Lexicon* (1869); F. Hitzig, *Geschichte* (1869), pp. 279 *ff.*; E. Schrader, *Einleitung* (1869), pp. 396 *ff.*; Bleek-Kamphausen, *Einleitung* (1870), pp. 402 *ff.*; L. S. P. Meijboom, *Raadselachtige verhalen uit het O. en het N. Verbond* (1870), pp. 90 *ff.*; Articles on "Esther," *etc.*, in Hamburger, *Realencyklopädie* (1870–97); F. H. Reusch (Catholic), *Einleitung* (1870), pp. 132 *ff.* (C); H. Zschokke (Catholic), *Historia* (1872), pp. 308 *ff.* (C); Bertholdt and Zunz, *ZDMG.* 1873, p. 684; C. F. Keil, *Einleitung* (1873), pp. 487 *ff.*, 730 *ff.* (C); H. Grätz, *Geschichte der Juden*, ii. (1875), pp. 332, 339 *ff.*; A. Köhler, *Geschichte*, iii. (1893), p. 593 (C); L. Herzfeld, *Geschichte* (1870), pp. 108 *ff.*; A. Geiger (Jew), *Einleitung*, in *Nachgelassene Schriften*, iv. (1877), p. 170; J. S. Bloch (Jew), *Hellenistische Bestandtheile im biblischen Schriftthum, eine kritische Untersuchung über Abfassung, Character u. Tendenzen des B. Esther* (1877, 1882)=*Jüd. Lit. Bl.* 1877, Nos. 27–34; T. K. Cheyne, Articles on "Esther," *etc.*, in *EB.* (1878 *sq.*); P. Kleinert, *Abriss der Einleitung* (1878), pp. 56 *f.*,

68, 79; B. Hause (Jew), "Noch einmal d. B. Esther," *Jüd. Lit. Bl.* viii. (1879), No. 42 (C); E. Ledrain (Catholic), *Histoire*, ii. (1882), pp. 103, 170 (C); C. M. Horowitz, "Ueber die Peripetie im B. Est.," *MGWJ.* xxxi. (1882), pp. 49 *ff.*; R. P. Stebbins, *A Common-sense View of the Books of the O. T.* (1885), pp. 120 *ff.*; J. S. Bloch, "Der historische Hintergrund und die Abfassungszeit d. B. Est.," *MGWJ.* 1886, pp. 425 *ff.*, 473 *ff.*, 521 *ff.*; W. Vatke, *Einleitung* (1886), pp. 496 *ff.*; W. Schanz (Catholic), *Einleitung* (1887), pp. 480 *ff.* (C); F. W. Weber, *Einleitung* (1887), pp. 66 *ff.*; R. Cornely (Catholic), *Introductio* (1897), ii. 1, pp. 417 *ff.* (C); E. Riehm, *Einleitung*, ii. (1890), pp. 339 *ff.*; M. Vernes, *Précis d'histoire Juive* (1889), pp. 824 *ff.*; A. Scholz (Catholic), "Die Namen im B. Est.," *Tüb. Theol. Quartalschrift*, lxxii. (1890), pp. 209 *ff.*; P. H. Hunter, *After the Exile* (1890), pp. 237 *ff.*; F. Kaulen (Catholic), *Einleitung*[3] (1890), pp. 269 *ff.* (C); F. Robiou (Catholic), "Sur le charactère historique du livre d'Esther," *Science Cath.*, Dec., 1890; J. Mally (Catholic), *Hist. Sacra A. T.* (1890); E. Reuss, *Gesch. der heiligen Schriften A. T.* (1890), pp. 610 *ff.*; Steinthal, *Zu Bibel- u. Religionsphilosophie* (1890), pp. 53 *ff.*, "Haman, Bileam und der jüdische Nabi"; W. Gladden, *Who Wrote the Bible* (1892), pp. 161 *ff.*; A. F. Kirkpatrick, *Divine Library of the O. T.*[2] (1892), pp. 155 *ff.*; J. Robertson, "Esther," in *Book by Book* (1892); W. R. Smith, *The OT. in the Jewish Church*[2] (1892), p. 458; Germ. trans., p. 447; J. J. de Villiers, "Modern Criticism and the Megilla," *Jew. Chronicle*, Feb., 1893; T. K. Cheyne, *Founders of OT. Criticism* (1893), pp. 359 *ff.*; E. König, *Einleitung* (1893), pp. 289 *ff.*, 450 *ff.*, 481 *f.*; Articles "Esther," etc., in Riehm, *Handwörterbuch des biblischen Alterthums*[2] (1893-4); R. Smend, *A. T. Religionsgeschichte* (1893), pp. 331, 406 *ff.*; A. H. Sayce, *An Introduction to the Books of Ezra, Nehemiah, and Esther*[3] (1893) (C); A. Schlatter (Catholic), *Einleitung*[3] (1901), p. 138 *f.* (only the main points of the story are historical); J. Oppert, *Problèmes Bibliques* (1894) = *RÉJ.* xxviii. (1894); Ellicott, *Plain Introduction* (1894) (C); A. H. Sayce, *The Higher Criticism and the Verdict of the Monuments* (1895), pp. 469 *ff.*; H. Schultz, *A. T. Theologie* (1889), p. 417; H. L. Strack, *Einleitung*[5] (1898), pp. 146 *ff.*; Articles in Vigouroux, *Dictionaire de la Bible* (1895 sq., Catholic); K. Schlottmann, *Kompendium d. bibl. Theol.* (1895), pp. 66 *ff.* (Est. is inspired, but not to the same degree as other books); E. Kautzsch, *Abriss d. alttest. Schrifttums*, pp. 116 *ff.*, in Kautzsch's *Heilige Schrift* (1896); C. v. Orelli, Art. "Esther" in *PRE.*[3] (1896); K. A. Beck (Catholic), *Geschichte*[2] (1901), pp. 449 *ff.* (C); A. K. Fiske, *Jewish Scriptures* (1896), pp. 342 *ff.*; F. Hommel, *Ancient Heb. Tradition as illustrated by the Monuments* (1896), pp. 161 *ff.*; J. Marquart, *Fundamente* (1896), pp. 68–73; J. M. Whiton, "Esther," in Moulton and others, *The Bible as Literature* (1896), pp. 61 *ff.*; G. Wildeboer, *De letterkunde des Ouden Verbonds* (1893);

Germ. trans. (1895), pp. 444 *ff.*; F. de Moor, "Le livre d'Esther," *Science Cath.*, Oct., 1897; W. Gladden, *Seven Puzzling Bible Books* (1897), pp. 68 *ff.*; E. Schürer, *Geschichte d. jüdischen Volkes*[3] (1898–01), i. pp. 142, 156, 752; iii. pp. 330 *ff.*; E. Rupprecht, *Einleitung* (1898), pp. 439 *ff.*; C. H. H. Wright, *Introduction*[3] (1890), pp. 140 *ff.* (C); J. A. M'Clymont, "Esther" in *HDB.* (1899); D. Leimdörfer, *Zur Kritik d. B. Esther* (1899) (C); C. P. Tiele and W. P. Kosters, Art. "Ahasuerus" in *EBi.* (1899).

To the twentieth century belong the following introductory works: H. Willrich, *Judaica* (1900), chap. 1, "Esther und Judith"; I. Scheftelowitz, *Arisches im A. T.* (1901); T. Nöldeke, Art. "Esther" in *EBi.* (1901); S. R. Driver, *Introduction*[8] (1901), pp. 478 *ff.*; W. W. Baudissin, *Einleitung* (1901), pp. 305 *ff.*; H. P. Smith, *OT. History* (1903), pp. 485 *ff.*; G. W. Wade, *OT. History* (1904), pp. 473 *ff.*; W. S. Watson, "The Authenticity and Genuineness of the Book of Esther," *Princeton Theol. Rev.* i. (1903), pp. 64 *ff.*; J. D. Prince and E. G. Hirsch, "Esther" in *JE.* (1903); I. Scheftelowitz, "Zur Kritik des griechischen u. des massoretischen Buches Esther," *MGWJ.* xlvii. (1903), pp. 24 *ff.*, 110 *ff.*; J. Halévy, "Vashti," *JA.*, X. Sér., i. (1903), p. 377 *f.*; H. Chavannes, "Le livre d'Esther," *Rev. de Théol. et de Quest. Rel.* (1903); 2, pp. 177–192; 3, pp. 114–119; H. Willrich, *Juden und Griechen vor der maccabäischen Erhebung* (1905); H. Pope, "Why does the Protestant Church read the Book of Esther?" *Dublin Rev.* (1905), pp. 77 *ff.*; J. H. Raven, *Introduction* (1906), pp. 312 *ff.* (C); S. Jampel, *Das Buch Esther auf seine Geschichtlichkeit untersucht* (1907), reprinted from articles in *MGWJ.* 1905–6; L. B. Paton, "A Text-critical Apparatus to the Book of Esther," *Harper Memorial*, ii. (1908), pp. 1–52; P. Haupt, "Critical Notes on Esther," *Harper Memorial*, ii. (1908), pp. 113–204=*AJSL.* xxiv. (1908), pp. 97–186. For special treatises on the origin of Purim, see § 28.

The Protestant Commentaries on the Book of Esther that have been written since 1750, have all been compelled to notice the critical investigations mentioned in the previous paragraph, but in the main they have occupied a more conservative position than the introductory works. All the English commentaries until recently have been of the practical homiletical type, and have treated the critical problems that the book raises in a superficial manner. They have derived their material largely from the comm. of the Reformation and post-Reformation periods, and in scholarship they fall below the level of the leading English comm. of the seventeenth century. In Germany they have been more influenced by modern criticism, still many of them show no advance beyond the dogmatic standpoint of the seventeenth century. In the following list I have omitted titles where Est. forms part of a commentary on the whole OT.

J. G. Rinck (1755), com. on Est. 1; C. Simeon (1759); A. Clarke (1760); F. E. Boysen (1760); J. B. Koehler (1763), on Est. 1; A. Purver (1764); J. Wesley (1764); T. Haweis (1765); B. Boothroyd (1768); W. Dodd (1770); J. F. Ostervald (1772); J. A. Dathe (1773); C. B. Schmidt (1773); V. Zinck (1780); J. C. F. Schulze (1783); J. D. Michaelis (1785), one of the more important of the older commentaries; J. Yonge (1787); R. Gray (1792); J. C. W. Augusti (1797); D. Macrae (1799); J. Hewlett (1812), one of the more important early English comm.; C. Buckley (1802); J. Priestly (1803); G. Lawson, *Discourses on Est.* (1804); J. Hall (1808); S. Burder (1809); J. Gill (1809); J. Benson (1818); D'Oyley and Mant (1814); D. H. A. Schott (1816); A. G. F. Schirmer, *Observationes exeg. crit. in lib. Est.* (1817); J. Bellamy (1818); T. Scott (1822); J. Sutcliffe (1834); T. M'Crie, *Lectures on Esther* (1838); F. J. V. D. Maurer (1835), valuable gram. and text-critical remarks; J. Hughes, *Esther and her People, Ten Sermons* (1842); R. A. F. Barrett, *Synopsis of Criticisms*, iii. (1847), a learned and useful work; R. C. Morgan, *The Book of Esther typical of the Kingdom* (1855); E. P. L. Calmberg, *Liber Esther illustratus* (1857); J. Cordthwaite, *Lectures on Esther* (1858); A. D. Davidson, *Lectures on Esther* (1859); E. Bertheau (1862), a very important book; C. Wordsworth (1866); A. Kamphausen, Esther, in Bunsen's *Bibelwerk* (1868), brief and popular but scientific; C. F. Keil, in Keil and Delitzsch's Com. (1870), ultra-conservative, but one of the most scholarly and thorough of the modern commentaries; G. Rawlinson, in the *Speaker's Com.* (1873), brief and critically inadequate, but containing useful illustrations from Oriental sources; M. S. Terry, in *Wheedon's Com.* (1873); R. Jamieson (1876); F. W. Schultz, in Lange's Com. (1876), an elaborate and valuable work, Eng. trans. by J. Strong (1877); J. H. Blunt (1878); P. Cassel, *Das Buch Esther, ein Beitrag zur Geschichte des Morgenlandes* (1878), valuable exegetical remarks, and full of illustrative material derived from the targumic and midrashic literature, Eng. trans. by A. Bernstein; W. T. Mason, *Questions on Ezr., Neh., and Est.* (1880); A. Raleigh, *The Book of Esther, its Practical Lessons and Dramatic Scenes* (1880); G. Rawlinson, in Spence and Exall's *Pulpit Com.* (1880); J. W. Haley, *The Book of Esther, a new Translation with Critical Notes, etc.* (1885), very conservative, but useful; V. Ryssel, Second ed. of Bertheau's Com. in the *Kurzgefasstes exegetisches Handbuch zum A. T.* (1887), the most complete scientific commentary of modern times;

MODERN CRITICAL PERIOD

S. Oettli in Strack and Zöckler's *Kurzgefasster Kommentar* (1889), brief but valuable, represents a moderately conservative view; E. Reuss, *Das A. T. übersetzt, eingeleitet u. erläutert* (1892–4); W. F. Adeney, in the *Expositor's Bible* (1893), popular but scientific; V. Ryssel, in Kautzsch's *Heilige Schrift des A. T.* (1896); G. Wildeboer, in Marti's *Kurzer Handcommentar* (1898), much condensed, but thoroughly scientific and very important; C. Siegfried, in Nowack's *Handcommentar* (1901), also much condensed, but extremely useful; W. Harper, in the *Temple Bible* (1902); J. E. Cumming, *The Book of Esther, its Spiritual Teaching* (1906), a curious survival of mediævalism; A. W. Streane, in the Cambridge Bible (1907), a brief but scholarly little commentary.

The Catholic Church, during the modern period, has contented itself for the most part with reprints and compendia of the older commentators. The few new commentaries that have been written, have been relatively unimportant. They are as follows:—

J. N. Alber (1801–4), a very elaborate work; B. Neteler (1877); A. Arnaud (1881); L. de Sacy, *L'histoire d'Esther traduit* (1882); E. Ledrain, *La Bible, traduction nouvelle* (1891); L. C. Fillion (1891); A. Scholz, *Commentar über das Buch Esther mit seinen Zusätzen* (1892), a work of great learning, but disfigured by the constant use of allegorical exegesis; Cornely, Knabenbauer, Hummelauer, and others, *Commentaria in V. T.* (1907); M. Seisenberger, in *Kurzgefasster wissenschaftlicher Kommentar* (1901).

The new thought that roused Christendom in the middle of the eighteenth century also affected a small section of the Jews. Moses Mendelssohn, the philosopher, the father of modern liberal Judaism, projected a complete commentary on the Heb. Bible from a critical point of view. This is known as ספר נתיבות השלום, and was completed by a school of exegetes in sympathy with Mendelssohn and known as the "Biurists." The com. on Est. (1788) contains a German translation by A. Wolfsohn and a Heb. commentary by J. Löwe.

Similar in character, and aiming to convey to the Jews the best results of modern Biblical study, is L. Philippsohn, *Die Israelitische Bibel* (1858). I. Reggio's מפתח על מגלת אסתר, "Key to the Roll of Esther," is a modern critical introduction to the book of much merit. Other Jewish comm. of a modern type are S. Herxheimer, *Die vier und zwanzig Bücher der Bibel, u. s. w.* iv. (1848), pp. 449 *ff.* (many later separate editions of Est., last ed. 1902). S. Cahen, *La Bible, traduction nouvelle* (1848); J. Fürst, *Illustrirte Pracht-Bibel für Israeliten* (1874); U. M. P. Hillesum, *Het Boek Esther vertaald en verklaard* (1902), Heb. text with very brief but judicious notes.

Most of the Jewish commentaries of this period have remained on the traditional ground and have been content to make new collections of excerpts from the ancient *midrashim* and the great commentators of the Middle Ages. They are as follows:—

Moses Isserles מחיר יין (Offenbach, 1779), characterized by extreme use of the allegorical method; Aaron Bär Pereles שתי גלת הכתרת (Prague, 1784), and פתחי צדק (Prague, 1790); Jonathan Eybeschütz, ישועה גדולה (Warsaw, 1864); A. Hübsch, חמש מגלות (Prague, 1866); Elijah hag-Gaon, of Wilna, ספר מ' א' (Jerusalem, 1872); Jacob Ehrenpreis, מגלת א' (Lemberg, 1874); Joseph Zechariah, באור חדש מהריז (Wilna, 1875); Meir Malbin, מגלת א' (Warsaw, 1878), with RaShI, שׁ¹, *etc.*; Moses Isaac Ashkenazi (Tedeschi), הואיל משה (Livorno, 1880); H. D. Bawli, ספר דבר אסתר והוא מבוא (1880); D. Kohn, מפתח חדש אל מגלת אסתר למ' א' (Warsaw, 1881); Nathaniel Ḥayyim Pape, ספר מ' א' (Jerusalem, 1892).

A COMMENTARY ON THE BOOK OF ESTHER.

THE TITLE.

In Heb. manuscripts and printed editions the book bears the title *Esther*. In accordance with the analogy of other OT. books this title may mean either that Esther is the author or the heroine. The internal evidence shows the latter to be the correct interpretation.

אֶסְתֵּר in Gr. 'Εσθήρ (B A א L), or 'Αισθήρ (93*a*). Cod. 44 adds, *the twenty-second book*. A later hand in 108*b* adds, *that is Purim*. The Mishna (*Baba Bathra* 14*b*) calls the book מְגִלַּת אֶסְתֵּר, "Roll of Esther." This is a late designation due to the fact that Est., like the Law, was written on a scroll, rather than a codex, for use in the service of the Synagogue. In still later times the book was called simply *Mᵉghillā*, "the Roll," *par excellence*.

ADDITION A.

MORDECAI'S DREAM.

Between the title and 1¹, 𝕲𝕴L add the following section, A¹⁻¹⁷ (=Vulg. and Eng. Ad. Est. 11²–12⁶). The Gr. text and critical apparatus to it may be seen in *HM*. ii. pp. 6–7. In various distorted forms the passage appears in late Heb. and Aram. midrashes (see *Introduction*, § 34). For a discussion of the origin and character of the passage, see the *Introduction*, § 20. The addition is as follows:

¹ In the second year of the reign of Artaxerxes the Great, on the first day of the month of Nisan, Mordecai, son of Jair, son of Shimei, son of Kish, of the tribe of Benjamin, had a dream. ² He was a Jew dwell-

ing in the city of Susa, a great man, serving in the King's court. ³ He was of the captivity, which Nebuchadnezzar King of Babylon carried from Jerusalem with Jeconiah King of Judah; ⁴ and this was his dream: Behold, noise and tumult, thunderings and earthquake, uproar upon the earth: ⁵ and, behold, two great dragons came forth, both of them ready to fight, ⁶ and their cry was great. And at their cry all nations were prepared for battle, that they might fight against the righteous nation. ⁷ And lo, a day of darkness and gloom, tribulation and anguish, affliction and great uproar upon the earth. ⁸ And the whole righteous nation was troubled, fearing the evils that should befall them, and were ready to perish. ⁹ Then they cried unto God; and upon their cry, as it were from a little fountain, there came a great river, even much water. ¹⁰ The light and the sun rose up, and the lowly were exalted, and devoured the glorious. ¹¹ Now when Mordecai, who had seen this dream, and what God had determined to do, awoke, he bore it in mind, and until night by all means was desirous to understand it. ¹² And Mordecai slept in the court with Gabatha and Tharra, the two eunuchs of the King, the keepers of the court. ¹³ And he heard their communings, and searched out their purposes, and learned that they were about to lay hands upon King Artaxerxes; and he informed the King about them. ¹⁴ Then the King examined the two eunuchs, and after they had confessed, they were led to execution. ¹⁵ And the King wrote these things for a memorial; Mordecai also wrote concerning these things. ¹⁶ So the King commanded Mordecai to serve in the court, and for this he gave him gifts. ¹⁷ But Haman, son of Hammedatha, the Agagite, who was in great honour with the King, sought to injure Mordecai and his people because of the two eunuchs of the King.

THE REJECTION OF QUEEN VASHTI (1¹⁻²²).

XERXES MAKES A FEAST FOR HIS OFFICIALS (1¹⁻⁴).

1. *And afterward*]. This expression, by AV. and RV. rendered, *now it came to pass*, is used in continuation of a historical narrative, and implies a preceding verb in the perfect. Many of the books of the OT. are meant to be read in connection with those that precede them; but here, as in Jon. 1¹, no such connection is possible. The phrase cannot be due, as perhaps Jon. 1¹, to the fact that Est. is an extract from a larger history (Scho.); nor that in late Heb. *and afterward* had lost its original meaning (Keil, Wild., and the older comm. in general); nor that knowledge of the earlier history of Xerxes is presupposed in the reader (Bert., Oet.); but it is an imitation of the beginnings of the older histories, designed to suggest that Est. belongs to this class of literature.—[𝔊 L + After these events]. This addition is made with reference to the section A[1-17] that has just been inserted by 𝔊 L.—*In the days of*], the usual expression for the period of a king's reign, *cf.* Gn. 14¹ 1 S. 17¹² 2 S. 21¹ 1 K. 10²¹ 21²⁹ and often.—*Xerxes*] Heb. 'Aḥashwērôsh (*Ahasuerus*). On the identity of this monarch with Xerxes I, see *Introduction*, § 22. Xerxes was the son of Darius by Atossa, the daughter of Cyrus. He was not the oldest son; but, as the first born after his father became king, and as the grandson of the great Cyrus, he succeeded in making good his claim to the throne upon the death of Darius in 486 B.C. He had the reputation of being the tallest and the handsomest man among the Persians (Her. vii. 187). In spite of many noble characteristics, he showed on the whole a weak and passionate disposition that unfitted him for his high office, and made his rule inglorious. The most important event of his reign was the unsuccessful war with Greece in 480–470 B.C., rendered forever memorable by the narrative of Herodotus in books vii.–ix. of his history.* The architectural undertakings of Xerxes were numerous, and in Persepolis the ruins of several of his buildings are still to be seen.† In these buildings a number of trilingual inscriptions of this King have been discovered.‡ He was assassinated in 465 B.C. by the officers of his palace. After the name of Xerxes, 𝕋² gives a long addition in regard to the ten kings who have ruled, or shall rule, the earth; the accession of Evil-Merodach, his relations to Daniel and Jehoiachin, and the accession of Darius. As this has nothing to do with the story of Esther, it is not inserted here.—*He is the Xerxes*]. This and what follows to the end of v. ¹ is a parenthesis breaking the connection between ¹ᵃ and ¹ᵇ. The writer knows other historical personages by the name of 'Aḥashwērôsh, and, therefore, finds it necessary to define which one he means. It is not likely that he knew Xerxes II, who reigned

---

* See Meyer, *Geschichte des Altertums*, iii. pp. 337–417; Justi, in Geiger-Kuhn, *Grundriss der Iranischen Philologie*, ii. pp. 457–460.

† See Niebuhr, *Reisebeschreibung*, vol. ii.; Flandin et Coste, *Perse ancienne; Voyage en Perse* (1851–52); Stolze, *Persepolis* (1882); Perrot et Chipiez, *Hist. de l'Art*, v. (1890), p. 403 ff.

‡ See Spiegel, *Altpers. Keilinschr.*, pp. 59–67.

for only a few months in 424 B.C.; but he must have known 'Ăhashwērôsh, the father of Darius the Mede (Dn. 9¹), and 'Ăhashwērôsh, King of Persia, who stopped the building of the Temple, whom Ezr. 4⁶ places between Cyrus and Darius. From one or both of these he distinguishes this 'Ăhashwērôsh by the fact that "he reigned from India to Ethiopia." The father of Darius the Mede is not said to have been a king, and the 'Ăhashwērôsh of Ezr. 4⁶ is perhaps regarded as living before the great expansion of the Persian empire. Here, accordingly, Xerxes the Great must be meant. At this point the Targums insert the following passages:

[𝕿¹ + In whose days the work upon the house of our great God ceased and was interrupted until the second year of Darius, on account of the advice of the wicked Vashti, the daughter of Evil-Merodach, the son of Nebuchadnezzar. And because she did not permit the building of the house of the sanctuary, it was decreed concerning her that she should be put to death naked; and he also, because he gave heed to her advice, had his days cut short and his kingdom divided; so that, whereas before all peoples, races, languages, and eparchies were subject to his authority, they now served him no longer because of this. But after it was revealed before the Lord that Vashti was to be slain, and that he was to accept Esther, who was of the daughters of Sarah, who lived 127 years, a respite was granted to her.]

[𝕿² + The son of Cyrus, King of Persia, son of Darius, King of Media. He was the Xerxes who commanded to bring wine from 127 provinces for 127 kings who were reclining before him, that every man might drink of the wine of his own province and not be hurt. He was the Xerxes whose counsel was foolish, and whose decree was not established. He was the Xerxes, the corrupt king. He was the Xerxes who commanded to bring Vashti, the queen, naked before him, but she would not come. He was the Xerxes, the wicked king, the fool, who said: Let my kingdom perish, but let not my decree fail. He was the Xerxes in whose days the children of Israel were sold for no money, as it is written, "Behold ye shall be sold for naught." He was the Xerxes who commanded to bring cedars from Lebanon and gold from Ophir, but they were not brought. He was the Xerxes in whose days the faces of the house of Israel were black, like the outside of a pot. He was the Xerxes in whose days that was accomplished upon the house of Israel which is written in the Book of the Law of Moses, "In the morning thou shalt say: Would that it were evening," . . . and because of what he said, and because of what he did, his days were shortened. . . . He was the Xerxes who killed his wife for the sake of his friend. He was the Xerxes who killed his friend for the sake of his wife. He was the Xerxes.]

1ᵇ. *Who used to reign from India*].   *Hôddû*, 'India,' is Old Pers. *Hiñd'u*, Skr. *Sindhu*, 'river,' *i.e.*, the Indus, and refers only to the northwest portion of the peninsula, that drained by the river Indus. This is also the meaning of India in classical geography. The modern application of the name to the whole peninsula has arisen by a process of extension similar to that by which Palestine (Philistia) has come to be the name of the whole of Canaan.* According to Arrian (*Ind.* i. 1), Cyrus extended his conquests to the border of India (Duncker, *Geschichte des Alterthums*,⁴ iv. p. 370). The conquest of India by Darius, the father of Xerxes, is recorded in Her. iii. 94–106; iv. 44. Indian troops fought in the armies of Darius and of Xerxes (vii. 65, 70).—*Even unto Kush*]. Neither the Babylonian nor the Arabian Kush is meant, but the African, *i.e.*, Ethiopia, the modern Nubia. Ethiopia was subdued by Cambyses (Her. iii. 97), and was part of the empire of Darius and of Xerxes (Her. vii. 9, 65, 69*f.*). In iii. 97 and vii. 70, Her. combines India and Ethiopia in a manner similar to this passage. They are also given as the confines of the Babylonian empire in 𝕲 Dn. 3¹ and 1 Esd. 3². In Xerxes' own inscriptions he speaks of himself as "the great King, the King of Kings, the King of the lands occupied by many races, the King of this great world" (Spiegel, *Altpers. Keilinschr.*, p. 59).—[𝕮¹ + Which is east of great India, and unto the west of Kush:] [𝕮² + From India which is in the west unto Kush which is in the east.] These insertions are due to the idea that Kush lay in the neighbourhood of India.—*Seven and twenty and a hundred provinces*]. This clause is not the object of *used to rule*, since this verb is regularly construed with the preposition *over*. It must be taken as an appositive, explaining the meaning of the foregoing clause *from India even unto Kush*. The 127 provinces are mentioned again in 8⁹ and in 𝕲 in B¹ E¹ 1 Esd. 3². In Dn. 6² ⁽¹⁾ Darius the Mede appoints satraps over 120 provinces. By the addition of 7 provinces the author perhaps intends to convey the idea that the empire of Xerxes was even greater than that of Darius. Her. iii. 89 says that Darius divided the empire into

---

*See von Bohlen, *Das alte Indien*, pp. 9, 17; Wahl, *Vorder- und Mittelasien*, i. p. 359 *ff.*; Lassen, *Indische Alterthumskunde*, i. p. 2; Spiegel, *Altpers. Keilinschriften*, p. 246.

20 satrapies. Jos. *Ant.* x. 249 gives Darius the Mede 360 provinces, but in the story of Esther he has the same number as 𐤄. In his own inscriptions, Darius enumerates in the earliest period 21 provinces, later 23, and finally 29 (Spieg., pp. 3–59), confirming thus the statement of Herodotus. To explain the discrepancy between Est. and Her., comm. generally assume that the provinces of Est. are smaller racial groups into which the satrapies of Her. were divided. This view derives some support from 3[12], "unto the satraps of the King and the governors of the provinces" (*cf.* 8[9] 9[3]), which suggests that the provinces were smaller than the satrapies. In Ezr. 2[1] Ne. 7[6] 11[3] "the province" means no more than Judæa, but this was only a part of the great satrapy of Trans-Euphrates, which included Syria, Phœnicia, and Cyprus. Other comm. regard the 127 provinces as an exaggeration similar to those found elsewhere in this book (see § 27). Scho. regards the number as symbolic; 12, the number of the tribes; × 10, the number of completeness; + 7, the number of perfection, means that all nations were subject to Xerxes. This view finds some support in the fact that *Meg.* 11*a* interprets the 127 provinces as meaning that Xerxes reigned over the whole earth.*

2. *In those days*], a resumption of the thought of [1a], which has been interrupted by the parenthesis in [1b].—*When King Xerxes took his seat*]. The language suggests the beginning of his reign, but 1[3] says that it was in the third year. *Meg.* 11*b* solves the difficulty by taking the phrase in the sense of "when he was established," and this view has been extensively followed by later Jewish comm. So also Lyra, Mar., Vat., Cler., Ramb., Hew., Clark. Those who regard 'Aḥashwērôsh as identical with Artaxerxes Longimanus, see in this an allusion to the political disturbances that followed the assassination of Xerxes II, and take it to mean "when King Artaxerxes enjoyed peace." This, however, is an impossible translation. The phrase, accordingly, must be regarded as referring, not to the absolute beginning of the King's reign, but to the beginning of his reign in Susa. The Medo-Persian empire

---

*On the organization of the Persian empire, see Brisson, *De reg. Pers. principatu*, i. 169 (for references in classical writers); Meyer, *Gesch. d. Altertums*, chap. i.; Justi, in Geiger-Kuhn, *Iran. Phil.*, pp. 432–438; Buchholz, *Questiones de Persarum Satrapis satrapiisque* (1895).

had three capitals, Susa, Ecbatana, and Babylon, besides the royal residence at Persepolis. These events occurred at the time when Xerxes took up his residence in Susa (so Drus., Cas., Sanc., Rys.). Will. (pp. 16, 21) understands the phrase of the official coronation. The Pers. monuments represent kings seated upon a lofty chair, and Gr. writers record that they travelled, and even went into battle, seated upon a throne (see Baum., p. 85 *ff*.). This was not a distinctively Pers. custom. Among the Hebrews, and throughout the Orient, sitting was the official posture for kings and judges.—*Upon his royal throne*]. Instead of (*malkhûthô*), *his royal* (lit. *of his kingdom*), some codd. read *m^elakhtô*, 'his work.' On this slight foundation 𝔗¹, 𝔗², and *Mid.* construct the story that Xerxes could not sit upon the throne of Solomon, and therefore had to sit upon "the throne of his own workmanship." The insertion in 𝔗¹ is as follows:—

[𝔗¹ + King Xerxes wished to sit upon the royal throne of Solomon, which had been carried away from Jerusalem by Shishak, King of Egypt; and had been brought away from Egypt by Sennacherib; and had been captured out of the hands of Sennacherib by Hezekiah, and had been brought to Jerusalem; but had again been carried away from Jerusalem by Pharaoh the Lame, King of Egypt; and from Egypt had been carried away by Nebuchadnezzar, and had been brought to Babylon. When Cyrus devastated the province of Babylon, he transported it to Elam; and afterward, when Xerxes reigned, he tried to sit upon it, but was not able. Accordingly, he sent and brought artisans from Alexandria in order that they might make one like it, but they were not able. So they made another inferior to it; and after two years had been spent in its production, at length he sat upon his royal throne which the artisans had made for him.]

𝔗² has a similar but much more elaborate addition describing the wisdom of Solomon, the construction of his throne, the visit of the Queen of Sheba, and Nebuchadnezzar's capture of Jerusalem. The legends here gathered are largely of Babylonian origin (*cf.* Wünsche, "Salomo's Thron u. Hippodrom, Abbilder des babylonischen Himmelsbildes," *Ex Oriente Lux*, ii. (1906).— *Which was in Susa*], added to distinguish this throne from the others which were in Ecbatana, Persepolis, or Babylon. *Susa* (Heb. and As. *Shushan*, 𝔊 Σούσοι, Old Pers. *Shushin* or *Shushim*) is the modern mound of Shush, 15 mi. S.W. of Dizful in Persia. Its history is known from references in Bab. and As. inscriptions, from classical historians, and from the inscriptions and other remains discovered in the excavations recently undertaken on its site by the French government under the direction of Dieulafoy and De Morgan.—*The fortress*], so also Dn. 8^2 Ne. 1^1 Est. 1^5 2$^{3.\ 5.\ 8}$ 3^{15} 8^{14} 9$^{6.\ 11.\ 12}$. This distinguishes the acropolis, in which the palace lay, from the less strongly fortified surrounding "city of Susa" (3^{15b} 6^{11}), which lay on the other side of the river Choaspes, the As. *Uknû*. The excavations show that the main city had a circumference of 6 or 7 mi. At a height of 72 ft. above the general level lay the *fortress*, or *citadel*, a rectangular platform inclosed with a massive wall 2½ mi. in length. This was the palace-quarter, in whose midst, at an elevation of 120 ft., stood the royal castle, or "house of the king" (1^5 2^8 4^{13} 7^8). The strength of this inner city is repeatedly affirmed by Gr. writers (*cf.* Strabo, xv. 3^2; Polybius, v. 48).

3. *In the third year of his reign*]. According to the Ptolemaic Canon (see Wachsmuth, *Alte Geschichte*, p. 305) Xerxes' first full regnal year began Dec. 23, 486 B.C. It thus coincides practically with 485 B.C. His third year must then have been 483 B.C. At the time of his accession Egypt was in revolt (Her. vii. 4); not under the leadership of Habisha, as has commonly been supposed (Birch, *TSBA.* i. p. 24; Petrie, *History of Egypt*, iii. p. 369; Erman, *Zeitsch. f. Aegypt.*, xxxi. p. 91); for, as Spiegelberg has lately shown (*Papyrus Libbey*, 1907), Habisha belonged to a time about 324 B.C. (see *Or. Lit. Zeitung*, 1907, cols. 422, 439). Egypt was reduced to submission in Xerxes' second year (484 B.C.), and was placed under the rule of his brother Achæmenes (Her. vii. 7). In the following year the action of the Book of Est. begins. According to 𝕌^1, 𝕌^2 and *Mid.*, Xerxes was obliged to wait until the third year because his throne was not yet ready. Mid. notes that this was the third year after the interruption of the building of the Temple (Ezr. 4^6).—*He* [𝕌^1 + Xerxes] *made a* [Gr. codd. + great] *banquet*]. The word means primarily a drinking-bout. It occurs 20 times in Est. and only 24 times in all the rest of the OT.—*To all his officials*], not 'princes' (*i.e.*, members of the royal family), as AV. and RV. translate, but 'officers' appointed by the King; so L correctly τοῖς ἄρχουσι (*cf.* Buhl, *Die socialen Verhältnisse der Israeliten*, p. 83 *ff.*).—*And courtiers*]. The word means primarily 'slaves.' The 'slaves of the King' in OT. usage are not 'subjects' in general, as 𝔊 translates here; nor are they those who do the menial work of the palace, but they are the members of the royal household, the *courtiers*, as we should say (*cf.* 3²¹· 4¹¹ 5¹¹ 1 K. 5¹⁵ 20²³ 22³ 2 K. 19⁵ Je. 36²⁴).—[*With the officers of*] *the army of Persia and Media*]. ³ᵇ is a circumstantial clause describing the nature of the feast, and specifying the classes of dignitaries included under the *officials and courtiers* of ³ᵃ. *The army* is unrelated grammatically to the preceding clause. At least *and* is needed before it. Even with this insertion it does not make good sense, for it is inconceivable that Xerxes should invite the whole army of Persia and Media along with the dignitaries of the realm. Bert., Kamp., Schu., Rys., Or., seek to explain the difficulty by taking *army* to mean the picked body-guard of 2,000 cavalry, 2,000 lancers, and 10,000 infantry described in Her. vii. 40 *f.*); but, as Keil points out, the phrase *force of Media and Persia* cannot naturally be limited in this way. If this were the meaning, we should expect "force of the King." Keil holds that the army was present in its élite representatives, but in that case we should expect "the mighty men of valour." It is necessary, therefore, with Jun. and Trem., Pisc., Rys., Buhl, Haupt, to supply *and the officers of* before *army* (*cf.* 2 S. 24⁴ 1 K. 15²⁰ 2 K. 25²³ Je. 40⁷· ¹³, *al.*). The Medes and Persians were the principal subdivisions of the Iranian branch of the Indo-European race, and were closely akin in language, customs and religion to the Aryans of northern India. In the eighth century B.C., according to the As. records, they first began to push into the regions east of Assyria and Babylonia. By the sixth century their conquest of ancient Elam and the territory northward to the Caspian was complete, and a Medo-Persian empire was founded by Phraortes the Mede (647–625 B.C.). Under his successor Cyaxares (624–585 B.C.), Media was strong enough to destroy Nineveh and to divide the Assyrian empire with Nabopolassar of Babylon. Under Astyages (584–550 B.C.) Media declined, and Cyrus the Persian (549–530 B.C.) was able to seize the throne. Henceforth we have a Perso-Median instead of a Medo-Persian empire. Cyrus conquered Babylon (539 B.C.), and soon made himself master of the whole of western Asia. His son Cambyses (529–523 B.C.) added Egypt to the empire. Darius I (522–466 B.C.) did not enlarge his domain, but brought it into a splendid state of organization. His son and successor was Xerxes, the 'Ăḥashwērôsh of Est. In this passage the Persians are named before the Medes, corresponding to the fact that at this time Persia held the hegemony in the double kingdom (so also 1[14. 18. 19] and in the Achæmenian inscriptions *Parsa uta Mada*). In Dn. 5[28] 6[9(8). 13(12). 16 (15)] 8[20] the order is reversed, because Daniel lived at the time of the Median hegemony. In Est. 10[2] the order Media and Persia is due, either to the use of a different source (see *Introduction*, § 24) or to the fact that chronicles are mentioned which naturally treated of the two kingdoms in chronological order. From these two orders in Est., *Meg.* 12a infers that there was a bargain between the two peoples, so that, when the kings were Medes, the satraps were Persians, and *vice versa*.—*The nobles and the officials of the provinces before him*] [Jos.[186] + as became a king]. The provinces are the conquered portions of the empire in contrast to the home-lands of Persia and Media that have just been mentioned. The comm. make many guesses as to the reason for this banquet. According to *Meg.* 11b, Xerxes perceived that Belshazzar had miscalculated the 70 years of Je. 29[10], and had brought ruin upon himself by using the Temple vessels at his feast. Xerxes calculated more correctly, and found that the 70 years were up in his second year; therefore, in his third year he ventured to make a feast and to use the Temple vessels. 𝕋[1] holds that it was to celebrate the quelling of a rebellion, or was an anniversary; so also L, ἄγων τὰ σωτήρια αὐτοῦ. 𝕲 and IE. think that it was because of his marriage to Vashti; Cler., that it was to conciliate the empire at the beginning of his reign; Sanc., to initiate his residence at Susa; Mal., Scho., to celebrate his victory over the Egyptians; Lap., to observe his birthday (*cf.* Her. i. 133); Ser., to display his wealth (*cf.* 1[4]). Jun., Mal., Keil, Häv., Baum., *al.* identify this banquet with the council which Xerxes convened when he was planning to invade Greece (Her. vii. 8), and quote the remark of Her. i. 133

that the Persians discuss the most important affairs of state over their cups (*cf.* Strabo, xv. 3^{20}; Curt. vii. 4; Xen. *Cyrop.* viii. 8^{12}). There is, however, no hint in Est. of deliberating over an impending war. These speculations in regard to the reason for the feast are of interest only if one is convinced of the strictly historical character of the book.

[𝕋¹, 𝕋² + Why did he make a feast? Some say that his governors had revolted against him, and that he went and conquered them; and after he had conquered them he returned and made a feast. Another says, This was a feast-day for him, so he sent letters into all the provinces to come and celebrate it in his presence with joy. He sent and invited all governors of the provinces that they should come and rejoice with him. There assembled in his presence 127 princes from 127 provinces, all adorned with crowns on their heads, and they reclined on woollen couch-covers, and feasted, and rejoiced before the King. And while the princes and the governors of the provinces were before him, certain also of the rulers of Israel came thither, who wept and mourned because they saw the vessels of the house of the sanctuary. And they ate and drank and enjoyed themselves.]

4. *While he showed* [*them*] *his glorious royal wealth*], lit. *the wealth of the glory of his kingdom.* The wealth of the Persian court is celebrated by the classical writers. Her. iii. 95 *f.* speaks of 14,560 Eubœic talents (£3,549,000, or $17,248,140) as the annual tribute collected by Darius, and states that he was accustomed to melt the gold and pour it into earthen jars, then to break off the clay and store away the ingots. Her. vii. 27 speaks of a golden plane-tree and a golden vine that Darius received as a present from Pythius of Celænæ. In the spoil of Xerxes' camp the Spartans found tents covered with gold and silver, golden couches, bowls and cups, and even gold and silver kettles (Her. ix. 80 *f.*). Æschylus (*Persæ*, 161) speaks of the gold-covered chambers of the palace (*cf.* Curt. iii. 13; v. 6; Athenæus, xi. 14; other references in Baum., p. 16). The Targums and Midrash make the following additions:—

[𝕋² + It is not written that he showed his wealth, but, "While he showed his glorious royal wealth," that is, the wealth that had come from the sanctuary, for flesh and blood cannot possess wealth, but all wealth belongs to the Holy One, blessed be He! as it is written, "Mine is the silver and mine the gold, saith the Lord of hosts." Every day he showed them six treasure-chambers, as it is written, "wealth, glory, kingdom, costliness, ornament, greatness," that is, six things. But when the Israelites saw there the vessels of the house of the sanctuary, they were not willing to remain before him; and they told the King, the Jews are not willing to remain because they see the vessels of the house of the sanctuary. Then the King commanded his servants to bring them other vessels.]

[*Mid.* + He showed them his great household. . . . He showed them his various revenues from the land of Israel. . . . He showed off with what belonged to him and with what did not belong to him, like the crow that struts on its own and on somebody else's ground. How did the wretch get so much wealth? R. Tanḥuma said, the cursed Nebuchadnezzar had brought all the wealth of the world together for himself, and his eye feared for his wealth. When he saw that he was near death, he said: Shall I leave all this wealth to this fool Evil-Merodach? He loaded it upon great copper ships and sunk them in the Euphrates. They were then disclosed by God to Cyrus when he gave command to rebuild the Temple, as it is written: "So saith the Lord to his anointed, to Cyrus, 'I will give thee the treasures of darkness, and hidden riches of secret places'" (Is. 45³)].

[𝔗¹ + This was left in the hand of Xerxes by Cyrus the Mede, who had found this treasure. When he captured Babylon, he dug into the bank of the Euphrates, and found there 680 chests full of pure gold, diamonds, beryls, and emeralds. With these treasures then he displayed his wealth.]

And the costliness of his kingly apparel], lit. *the costliness of the ornament of his greatness*. The language of this and of the preceding clause is as redundant as the statements are exaggerated. —*Many days* [𝔗¹ + and the feast for his officials lasted] 180 *days*]. *Many days* is an acc. of time that joins on to *made a banquet* [3a]; 180 *days* is an appositive, defining more precisely what is meant by *many days*. The extraordinary length of this banquet, 180 days, or half a year, has aroused the wonder and the incredulity of comm. in all ages. *Mid.* absurdly suggests that *many* may be 3, and *days* may be 2, so that really there were only 5 days; and that they are called 180 because they seemed that long to the oppressed Jews. Scho. takes 180 as symbolic of the duration of the Messiah's kingdom. Bon., Sal., Cler., West., Eich., Baum., Scott, Raw., Stre., *al.*, think that the governors could not have left their provinces for 180 days, and, therefore, were entertained by Xerxes in relays;

but there is not the least foundation for this view in the text. Lyra, Keil and Winck. (*AOF*. iii. 1, p. 31 n.) take v. ⁴ as a parenthesis describing the events which preceded the feast, rather than those which occurred during its progress, and regard the 7-day feast of v. ⁵ as the same as the one whose description is begun in v. ³ᵇ. This is not a natural interpretation, since *while he showed them* (v. ⁴) does not properly mean 'at the end of a 180 days' display.' Besides, if the nobles were present for 180 days looking at the treasures, no reason appears why the feast might not have lasted during that period. Moreover, *all the people that were found in Susa* (v. ⁵) is not the same as *his officials and his courtiers* (v. ³), which shows that the banquet of v. ⁵ is different from that of v. ³. In support of their identity, Keil urges that the officials and the courtiers of v. ᵇ are present at the feast of v. ⁵ (*cf.* v. ¹¹); but this is easily explained by the supposition that, although the multitude was invited, the nobles also remained to the second banquet. In fact, the *peoples and the officials* are named together in v. ¹¹. Keil's view also demands the arbitrary assumption of an anacoluthon at the beginning of v. ⁵ to resume the thought of v. ³. We must hold, therefore, with the majority of comm., that the author means to say that there was a feast of 180 days, followed by another feast of 7 days. As to the probability of such a celebration, opinions differ. Ser. cites a 90-day debauch of Dionysius of Syracuse, and Fryar, *Travels*, p. 348, reports that he found feasts of six months' duration among the modern Persians; nevertheless 180 days remains an incredibly long time for the King and all the officials of the empire to spend in drinking.

1. ויהי] καὶ ἐξήτησε 108*a*: om. 44 𝔍: many of the historical books of the OT. begin with ו: thus Ex., 1 K., Ezr., with a simple ו conjunctive; Lv., Nu., 2 K., 2 Ch., with ו consecutive and the impf.; Jos., Ju., 1 S., 2 S., Ne., with ויהי. In all these cases, the book is meant to be read in connection with the one that precedes it (so also possibly Ru. 1¹ and Ez. 1¹); here, however, such a connection is impossible. *Meg.* 10*b*, 𝔗¹, *Mid.* 1*a*, *Yalquṭ Est.* § 1044, claim that everywhere in Scripture ויהי introduces a narrative of disaster. This conceit has its origin in the similar sound of Gr. οὐαί, Latin *væ*, 'woe.'—בימי] καὶ ἐκράτησεν 108*a*: om. 44.—אחשורוש] *Assueri* 𝔍: *Artaxerxis* 𝕷: اسمانه 𝔖: Ἀσσυήρου L: Ἀρταξέρξου 𝔊 (so 𝔍 𝔖 L 𝔊 elsewhere): om. 44, 108*a*.—הוא]

om. K 151, R 899, 𝔍: סו‸ כס 𝔖: οὗτος δὲ 44: τοῦ βασιλέως L.—אחשורוש ‸2] om. K 151, R 899, 𝔍: τοῦ μεγάλου L: +ὁ βασιλεύων 93b under *: Haupt deletes as a gloss.—הַמֹּלֵךְ] om. 106: here pointed as a ptc., as in Je. 22¹¹, but it might equally well be pointed as a noun, הַמֶּלֶךְ 'the king.' The ptc., if correct, expresses the continuance of Xerxes' rule. From this unusual vocalization *Meg.* 10b, *Mid.*, *Yalq.* § 1045, RaShI, infer that Xerxes was an upstart who had usurped the throne. This opinion is justified neither by the Heb. expression nor by the facts of history.—הֹדּוּ] τῆς Ἰνδικῆς 𝔊: *India* 𝔏: +χώρας 108a: is derived by assimilation of ו from הִנְדוּ, which corresponds to Ar. and N. Pers. *Hind*, Syr. *Hendu*, Aram. *Hindya*, O. Pers. *Hiñd'u*, Skr. *Sindhu*. The Massoretic vocalization is peculiar. From the analogy of the cognates we should expect rather *Hiddû*, or *Heddû*, with the accent on the ultima. Bert. and Scho. conjecture that it has been pointed in this way to make it resemble הֹהוּ, and thus to suggest that the heathen world is doomed to destruction. The word occurs only here and in 8⁹. See Ges. *Thes. s. v.*; Rödiger, *Thes. Add. s. v.*; Scheftelowitz, *Arisches im A. T.*, p. 43. —וְעַד כּוּשׁ] so L 𝔏 ℵ a. c mg, 93b under *: om. 𝔊.—כּוּשׁ]. Three Kush's are known in the OT.: (1) a Babylonian people from which sprang Nimrod, the founder of Babylon, Erech, Accad, Calneh in the land of Shinar, Nineveh, Rehoboth-Ir, Calah and Resen, all cities or regions of Babylonia and Assyria (Gn. 10⁸⁻¹² J). This doubtless is the same as the *Kašše*, a people often mentioned in the Babylonian or Assyrian inscriptions, whose original seat was in the mountains east of Babylonia; from which they emerged about 1700 B.C., conquered Babylonia, and established the third dynasty of Babylon, which reigned from about 1700 to 1100 B.C. Perhaps the same people is meant in Gn. 2¹³. This *Kush* was well known to the Jews in Babylonia; and in *Meg.* 11a R. Samuel identifies the *Kush* of Est. 1¹ with it, and comments on the fact that it lay near to India. He explains the difficulty by saying that the passage means, that, just as Xerxes ruled over India and Kush, so he also ruled over 127 provinces, and compares 1 K. 5⁴ (Eng. 4²⁴). This view is also followed by 𝔘¹, 𝔘², and *Mid.*, but it is not the natural meaning of the language. India and *Kush* are evidently meant to be the opposite extremes of the empire. Moreover, *and* must be inserted before *over* 127 *provinces* on this interpretation. Rab is therefore correct, in opposition to Samuel, in saying that *Hôddû* lay at one end of the world and *Kush* at the other end. (2) There is a *Kush* in South Arabia (Gn. 10⁶ f. P; Nu. 12¹ E; *cf.* Ex. 2¹⁶. ²¹ J; Hb. 3⁷ 2 Ch. 21¹⁶; ph. also Gn. 2¹³ Am. 9⁷ Is. 20³ 2 Ch. 14⁹ ff. This appears as Kûšu in four inscriptions of Esarhaddon (Winckler, *Altorientalische Forschungen*, ii. 8, 18; Knudtson, *Gebete an den Sonnengott*, No. 108; *KAT.*³, p. 89). On the Arabian *Kush* see Winckler, *Alttestamentliche Untersuchungen*, p. 165 *f.*; "Muṣri, Meluḫḫa, Maʿin," *MVG.* 1898, 1, p. 47; 4, pp.

XERXES' FEAST

1–10; *KAT.*³ p. 144; Cheyne, Art. "Cush" in *EBi.*). With this South Arabian *Kush*, the *Kush* of Est. 1¹ is identified by Mar. and Cler., chiefly because they regard 'Ăḥashwêrôsh as the same as Artaxerxes Longimanus, and in his day Persian rule extended no further than Arabia. (3) *Kush* denotes Ethiopia, the modern Nubia (Is. 18¹ 37⁹= 2 K. 19⁹ Zp. 3¹⁰ Ez. 29¹⁰). In Egypt. it appears as *Kš*, in As. as *Kûšu*. This is probably the *Kush* meant by our author (so Ser., San., Mal., and all recent commentators). (Cas. thinks that *Kush* is a general name for nomadic peoples, and understands it of the Scythians on the northwest border of the Persian empire.)—יֶשְׁבֵּי] pr. *super* 𝔍: om. 𝔖.— וְעֵשְׂרִים] pr. ܠ 𝔖.—מְדִינָה] χῶραι 𝔊 L: פַּלְכִין 𝔗¹: an Aram. loan-word that occurs ten times in Aram. sections of the OT. (*cf.* Syr. *medînta*, Ar. *medîneh*, 'city'). It does not appear in Heb., except in the later books of the OT. (*cf.* 1 K. 20¹⁴·¹⁵·¹⁷·¹⁹ Ezr. 2¹ Ne. 1³ Ec. 2⁸ 5⁷ Lam. 1¹ Ez. 19⁸ Dn. 8² 11²⁴ and 29 times in Est.).

2. בימים ההם] om. 𝔍 𝔏 L: Haupt rejects as a gloss.—כישבת] here only in OT. בשבת seems more natural, but כשבת is supported by 𝔊 ὅτε ἐθρονίσθη and L *ἐν τῷ καθῆσθαι*. The phrase expresses the beginning rather than the continuance of the action (*cf.* Müller, *Syntax*, § 111). On the use of כ, *cf.* 1 S. 5¹⁰. See Winckler, *MVG.* xi. p. 21, and Jacob, *ZATW.* x. p. 281.—המלך אחשורוש] om. א * 𝔍 N 55, 108*a*: Haupt deletes אחשורוש.—המלך] om. L.—על־מלכותו] om. 𝔊 (93*b* has under *): this phrase is used only in later books of the OT. (*e.g.*, 1 Ch. 22¹⁰ 28⁵ 2 Ch. 7¹⁸. In earlier books we find על כסא ממלכה (1 K. 9⁵).—אשר] om. 𝔍 𝔊 𝔏 L.—בשושן הבירה] om. L 𝔏: *Susan civitas regni ejus exordium fuit*, 𝔍.—שושן] Susa was the capital of ancient Elam as early as the third millennium B.C., and was the sanctuary of the great goddess Shushinak. At first it was subject to Babylonia, and was ruled by a *patesi* or vice-king; but in 2280 B.C. it declared its independence, and from this time forward became a formidable antagonist of Babylon. About 2800 B.C., according to the annals of Ashurbanipal (*Rassam Cylinder*, vi. 107; *KB.* ii. p. 208 *f.*), Kutirnaḫunte, King of Elam, carried thither the image of the goddess Nana of Erech. It was doubtless also the residence of Kutir Laḫgamar, the Chedorlaʿomer of Gn. 14. About 1350 B.C. it was conquered by Kurigalzu II, King of Babylon, and some of the spoil taken in 2280 B.C. was recovered (*cf.* Hilprecht, *Old Bab. Inscr.* I, part i. p. 31). In the twelfth century the tables were again turned, Shutruk-Naḫunte, King of Elam, and his son Kutir-Naḫunte conquered Babylonia and carried its spoil to Susa. Among the objects plundered was the stele containing the famous code of Ḫammurabi, discovered in Susa by the French expedition in 1897–9 along with other important Bab. monuments. After the rise of Assyria, Susa became the ally of Babylon against Nineveh. This led to prolonged and bloody wars, which ended with the capture of Susa by Ashurbanipal about 625 B.C. The image of Nana, which had been carried off 1635 years before, was brought back, and an enormous booty was captured (*Rassam Cylinder*, vi.). Susa, however, soon revived from the disaster, and with the decline of Assyria became again the capital of Elam. About 596 B.C. it fell a prey to the Medo-Persian migration (*cf.* Je. 49[31-39]), and the old Elamitic population gave way to a new Indo-European race. During the Median supremacy, Susa was less important than Ecbatana (Heb. Achmetha, Ezr. 6[2], the modern Hamadan) in Media; but when the hegemony passed to Persia under Cyrus and his successors, Susa again became the chief capital of the empire (*cf.* Dn. 8[2] Ne. 1[1]). Xenophon (*Cyrop.* viii. 6[22]) says that it was the winter residence of the kings, while Ecbatana and Babylon were the summer residences (*cf.* Ezr. 6[1 f.]). The classical writers contain many allusions to its wealth and to the splendour of the buildings erected by the kings of Persia (*cf.* Baum., p. 18 *ff.*). The city continued to exist under Sassanian rule and was not abandoned until some time in the Middle Ages. The vast size of the mounds that now mark its site is a witness to its antiquity and former glory (see Loftus, *Chaldea and Susiana* (1857), p. 343 *ff.*; Neubauer, *Géographie du Talmud* (1868), p. 381; Delitzsch, *Wo lag das Paradies*, p. 326; Mme. Jane Dieulafoy, *A Suse, Journal des Fouilles* (1887); *La Perse et la Susiane* (1887), chap. xxxix; M. Dieulafoy, *L'Acropole de la Suse* (1890), translated in part in Jampel, *Das Buch Esther;* Winckler in Helmolt, *Weltgeschichte,* iii. (1901), pp. 91-109; Billerbeck, *Susa, eine Studie zur alten Geschichte Westasiens* (1893); De Morgan, *Délégation en Perse* (gives an account of the French excavations; vol. ii., by Scheil, contains the *Textes Élamitiques et Sémitiques*); Curzon, *Persia,* ii. p. 309.—בירנהא [בירה] 𝔗¹: *bîrta* 𝔖: is a loan-word from the Aram. that appears only in late Heb. (apart from Est. in Ne. 1[1] 2[8] 7[2] 1 Ch. 29[1. 19] Dn. 8[2]). In As. it appears in the f. form *bîrtu* as early as the inscriptions of Shalmaneser II (Delitzsch, *As. HWB.* p. 185). In Pers. it appears as *bāru,* and in Skr. as *bura, bari* (*cf.* BDB. *s. v.*). In Ne. 2[8] the name is applied to a stronghold near the Temple, probably the same as the later Akra of the Syrians in 1 Mac. and Jos. After the destruction of this fortress by Simon in 142 B.C., another citadel was built north of the Temple, which was also known as בירה (𝔊 βάρις). This was subsequently rebuilt by Herod under the name of Antonia. 𝔊 and 𝔍 here, and L in 1[5], have πόλις and *civitas,* which leads Jahn to conjecture that the original reading in 𝔐 was העיר, but 𝔏 in 1[5] 2[3. 5] has *Thebari,* which represents τῇ βάρει in the Gr. from which it was translated.

3. om. 𝔏.—[בשנת שלוש] om. L.—[למלכו] καὶ ὁ βασιλεὺς L.—[משתה] +*grande* 𝔍 𝔖 44, 74, 76, 120, 236.—[לכל־] so 93*b*: om. 𝔊 L.—[שריו] τοῖς φίλοις 𝔊: τοῖς δούλοις 236: τοῖς ἄρχουσι L: τοῖς φίλοις αὐτοῦ 44, 71, 74, 76, 120.—[ועבריו] καὶ τοῖς λοιποῖς ἔθνεσιν 𝔊: om. L.—[חיל־ומדי] om. 𝔖[u]

THE SECOND FEAST 135

(𝔖ᴬᴸᴹ have).—חיל] καὶ τοῖς ἐνδόξοις 𝔊: τῆς αὐλῆς (היכל) L: before חיל we must supply וְשָׁרָי. 𝔊 καὶ τοῖς λοιποῖς represents an original ושאר, which is a corruption of ושרי.—פרס] פָּרָס some codd. incorrectly.— הפרתמים] καὶ τοῖς ἄρχουσιν 𝔊: καὶ οἱ ἄρχοντες L. הפרתמים is commonly regarded as the Pers. word *fratama*, which is the equivalent of Skr. *prathama* and Gr. πρῶτος 'first.' It occurs elsewhere in the OT. only in 6⁹ and Dn. 1³ (*cf.* the glossary in Spiegel, *Die altpers. Keilinschr.*, p. 232; Lagarde, *Armenische Studien*, § 2289; Ges. *Abhandlungen*, p. 282 *f.*). Haupt, *Am. Journ. Phil.*, xvii. p. 490, proposes to connect it with As. *paršûmûti*, 'elders' (Delitzsch, *As. HWB.* p. 546). Mid. and other comm. incorrectly regard הפרתמים as the royal body-guard. RaShI and Kimḥi know that it is Pers. and interpret it correctly.— ושרי] τῶν σατραπῶν 𝔊: om. L.—המדינות] ܡܟܠܟ̈ܐ 𝔖: om. 𝔊.—[לפניו καὶ μετὰ ταῦτα 𝔊 (93*b* under ÷): + ܡܢ̱ܒܠܐ ܣܘܣܢ 𝔖.

4. om. 𝔏.—בהראתו] μετὰ τὸ δεῖξαι αὐτοῖς 𝔊: εἰς τὸ ἐπιδειχθῆναι L: ἔδειξεν αὐτοῖς 44, 71, 76, 106, 120, 236: the inf. with בְּ denotes continuation of the action, *i.e.*, the display went on all the time that the feast lasted. Instead of בְּהַרְאֹתוֹ, 'in his showing,' we should naturally expect בְּהַרְאֹתָם, 'in showing them' (*cf.* Jos. 5⁶). This is supported by αὐτοῖς in 𝔊, and is adopted by Buhl. Haupt regards this as gratuitous.— כבוד]—ܐܫܬܡܥ 𝔖: om. 𝔊 (93*b* has under *).—מלכותו] τοῦ βασιλέως L.—יָקָר] so Mas. (Baer): יְקָר var. G C (see Norzi, *ad loc.*): aft. גדולתו 𝔍. יקר is commonly used in Est. in the secondary sense of 'honour' (*cf.* 1²⁰ 6³· ⁶ 8¹⁶), but here the parallelism with עשר in the preceding clause demands that it should be given its primary meaning of 'preciousness.'—תפארת], primarily 'beauty,' 'ornament,' is used of women's finery Is. 3¹⁸, of garments Is. 52¹, of jewels Ez. 16¹⁷· ³⁹ 23²⁶, and of the apparel of the high priest Ex. 28²· ⁴⁰. Here it seems to refer to the regalia of the Persian monarch. On the basis of Ex. 28², *Meg.* 12*a* and *Mid.* infer that Xerxes put on the robes of the high priest that had been carried off by Nebuchadnezzar.—ואת יקר-גדולתו] om. 44, 106.— גְּדוּלָתוֹ] so many edd.: גְּדוּלָתוֹ B¹ C Ba. G: om. L 52, 64, 243, 248, C, Ald.—ימים רבים] om. 𝔊 L: Haupt regards as a gloss, or alternate reading, to the following.—שמונים] pr. ἐν B, pr. ἐπὶ א L N, 44, 71, 74, 76, 106, 120, 248, Ald., 55, 108*a*.—ומאת] om. 70.

XERXES ALSO MAKES ANOTHER BANQUET FOR THE MEN OF THE FORTRESS OF SUSA, AND VASHTI FOR THE WOMEN (1⁵⁻⁹).

5. *And when these days were completed*]. R. Samuel holds (*Mid. ad. loc.*) that the feast of 7 days whose description begins here, is included in the 180 days of the previous feast, *i.e.*, after 173 days the common people were admitted to dine with the nobles;

so also Jun., Drus., Pisc., Mal. In defence of this view it is said that there is no description of the feast of 180 days unless v.⁵ be included in it, that the nobles were present (v.¹¹), and that all that were found in Susa were invited (v.⁵), *i.e.*, the nobles as well as the common people. On the other hand, Rab (*Mid. ad loc.*) and most comm. hold that the seven days followed the 180 days.—[𝕋² + The King said, Now I will make a banquet for the inhabitants of my city and] *the King made a banquet during seven days*]. Net. thinks that this was the wedding feast of Vashti, and compares it with the wedding feast of Esther (2¹⁸). Cas. compares the seven-day feasts in the Shahnameh of Firdusi.—*For all the people*], *i.e.*, for all the men. The women were invited to another banquet given by Vashti (v.⁹).—[𝕋¹ + of the house of Israel]. The addition is due to an ancient inference from the words *all the people*, that Jews must have been present at the banquet (*cf. Meg. 12a*).—*That were found* [𝕋¹ + sinners] *in Susa the fortress* [𝕋¹ + who were counted among the uncircumcised inhabitants of the land]. *Were found* is not the same as *lived*, but denotes those who at the time happened to be in the place, whether residents or visitors (*cf.* 1 Ch. 29¹⁷ 2 Ch. 34³² Ez. 8²⁵); that is, this second feast included not only those who had come up out of the provinces to the first feast, but also the rest of the men that were present in the palace-quarter known as "Susa the fortress" (see v.²).—*From the great to the small*], *i.e.*, not from the oldest unto the youngest, but from the highest unto the lowest; both the nobles, who had been present at the previous banquet, and all the members of the royal household, who had not hitherto been included, were now invited. Ctesias (a poor authority) states that 15,000 guests were entertained by Artaxerxes Mnemon at a cost of 400 talents (*Frag.* xxxvii., ed. Lion).—*In the enclosed garden of the King's palace*]. Persian palaces stood usually in the midst of a παράδεισος, or 'park,' which was surrounded with a fortified wall (*cf.* Xen. *Cyrop.* i. 3, 11; *EBi.*, Art. "Garden"). The phrase *court of the garden* indicates a court belonging to the garden, rather than a court that is used as a garden, because in v.⁶ it is paved with mosaic. Dieulafoy thinks of the mosaic-paved court in front of the palace at Susa.

Under the name of the Memnonium the palace at Susa is frequently mentioned by classical writers (*cf.* Her. v. 53 *f.*; vii. 151; Strabo, xv. 3²; Polyb. v. 48). The early explorers observed extensive ruins of this edifice on the top of the mound of Susa, and copied there the trilingual inscription of Artaxerxes Mnemon, which reads: "Darius, my ancestor, built this palace (*apadâna*) in ancient times. In the reign of Artaxerxes, my grandfather, it was destroyed by fire. Through the favour of Ahura-Mazda, Anahita, and Mithra, I have restored this palace. May Ahura-Mazda, Anahita, and Mithra protect me" (*Journ. of the Roy. Asiat. Soc.*, xv. p. 159; Spiegel, *Altpers. Keilinschr.*, p. 68 *f.*; Bezold, *Achämenideninschr.*, p. 44 *f.*; Oppert, *Mèdes*, 229–230; *Records of the Past*, vii. p. 79). In 1884-6 Dieulafoy excavated the ruins of this palace of Artaxerxes. The acropolis as a whole occupied a roughly rectangular space about 300 acres in area. This was divided into four quarters. In the S. W. corner was a fortified gate that was the main entrance (the "gate of the King" in Est.), and a large open space (the "outer court" of Est.). In the S. E. corner stood the royal residence (the "house of the King" in Est.). The N. E. corner was occupied by the harem (the "house of the women" in Est.); and the N. W. corner, by the *apadâna*, or throne-room, surrounded with an open space that may have been used as a garden. Dieulafoy thinks that the *bîthān*, or 'palace,' of this verse and 7[7f.] is a Heb. adaptation of the Pers. word *apadâna* and refers to this throne-room. This is extremely doubtful (see critical note). The *apadâna* occupied a square space 250 feet on each side. Its roof of cedar-wood was supported by slender, fluted limestone columns with carved capitals, arranged in six rows of six columns each. The front was open. The rear and side walls were of brick, encrusted with mosaic of white and reddish gray cement, or with enamelled tiles. Each side was pierced with four doors. Flanking the main entrance were pylons, ornamented on one side with a line of lions on enamelled tiles, similar to those found at Khorsabad and at Babylon; and on the other side with a line of soldiers of the royal body-guard.*

---

* See the works cited on p. 134, and Dieulafoy, "Le livre d'Esther et le Palais d'Assuèrus," *Rev. des Études Juives*, xvi. (1888), *Actes et Conférences*, pp. cclxv. *ff.*; translated by F. Osgood, *Bibl. Sacra*, lxvi. (1889), pp. 626–653; Mme. Jane Dieulafoy, *Harper's Monthly*, June, 1887; Jastrow, "The Palace of Artaxerxes Mnemon and the Book of Esther," *Sunday-school Times*, Nov. 17, 1888.

[𝔊 + planted by the royal care and hand.] [𝔗¹ + Which was planted with trees bearing fruits and spices, overlaid for half their height with pure gold and set with inlays of precious stones, that yielded them shade. But the righteous Mordecai and his companions were not there.] [𝔗² + He made arbours, and cut down spice-trees to make seats, and strewed precious stones and pearls before them, and set out shady trees.] [L + While he celebrated his deliverance.] [Jos. 87 + And the banquet was made for them in this manner.]

6. The description of the feast in v.⁶ is unconnected grammatically with the foregoing. It begins abruptly with *white stuff*, without a predicate. The comm. generally regard the sentence as a series of exclamations, *white stuff! cotton! purple!* but this is very un-Hebraic. The subsequent descriptive clauses in vv.⁷·⁸ are introduced in the ordinary way with *and*, followed by a predicate. The Vrss. all insert at the beginning of the v. such words as "and awnings were stretched"; AV. and RV. supply "and there were hangings of"; Rys. and Sieg., "and there were." A comparison of the Vrss. suggests that the original beginning of the v. may have been, "and the curtains were" (see critical note).— *White cotton cloth*]. The first word is written in 𝔐 with a large initial letter, which is probably intended to call attention to a suspected omission before it (*cf.* De Wette-Schrader, *Einl.*⁸ p. 210; Ginsburg, *Intr.* pp. 334 *ff.*). Similar extraordinary letters occur in 9⁹·²⁹.—[𝔗¹ + With sapphire and green] *and violet*], *i.e.*, blue purple, a colour extracted from a mollusk of the Mediterranean, probably the *Helix Ianthina* (*cf. HDB.* i. 457; *EBi.* i. 875). Violet and white were the royal colours (*cf.* 8¹⁵; Curt. vi. 6⁴).— [L + And scarlet intertwined with flowers, and the tent was] *caught up with cords of linen and red purple*]. The idea is, that the curtains which served as awnings were suspended by means of these cords upon the framework set up to support them. So the Vrss., Keil, Wild., Schu., Sieg. On the other hand, Bert., Rys., Haupt, translate 'bound,' 'bordered,' instead of 'caught up.'—*Upon rods of* [𝔊 Jos. + gold and] *silver*]. These rods formed a trellis to which the white and violet awnings were tied by the cords. The author has in mind the structure of the Tabernacle in Ex. 26–27, but there is no hint that he means this to be an allegory of the Messianic feast that God will make for his people (Scho.).—*And* [𝔗¹ + round

THE SECOND FEAST 139

beams of silver placed upon] *pillars of marble* [𝕲 + and stone] [L + gilded] [𝕿¹ + red, green, flame-colour, yellow, and white] [𝕵 + were gleaming]. The first addition of 𝕿¹ is an alternate translation of the preceding clause. The word *pillars* is the same that is used in Ex. 26³²·³⁷ 27¹⁰·¹¹·¹⁷ 36⁵⁶·²³ *al.* for the supports of the Tabernacle; in 1 K. 7²·³·⁶, for the columns in Solomon's palace; and 1 K. 7¹⁵, for the two bronze columns that stood before the Temple. The word for *marble* is the same that is used in the description of Solomon's Temple (1 Ch. 29²). From this *Mid.* infers that these pillars were part of the spoil of the Temple carried off by Nebuchadnezzar. The columns in the ruins of the *apadâna* at Susa are of a dark-blue limestone that might easily be described as *marble*. In *Mid.* it is said that Xerxes' columns were of a bluish-black colour, and R. Mathna makes the curious remark that he had slept on the top of one of them, and that it was broad enough for him to lie at full length. This seems to indicate that the ruins of Susa were known to the Babylonian rabbis. Benjamin of Tudela, a Spanish Jew, visited Susa in the twelfth century and speaks of the ruins of Xerxes' palace (ed. Asher, 1840, i. p. 117).

[𝕿¹ + He made them lie upon] *beds of* [𝕿¹ + fine woollen stuffs, which were spread upon bedsteads whose heads were of] *gold and* [𝕿¹ + their feet of] *silver* [Jos.¹⁸⁷ + so that many tens of thousands could recline]. The clause is without conjunction or predicate in the same manner as 6ᵃ, and the Vrss. all find it necessary to supply something. Probably we should read, *and the beds were gold and silver*, after the analogy of the descriptive clauses that follow in vv.⁷·⁸. Haupt supplies the prep. *on*. The word *bed* is ambiguous in Heb., as in Eng. It may mean either the mattress, or the frame which supports it. Ordinarily it means only the rug, or mat, which the peasant spreads upon the ground; but in Am. 6⁴ 'beds of ivory' must mean 'bedsteads.' In this case Keil, Rys., Sieg., think of cushions covered with cloth of gold and cloth of silver. It seems more natural, however, with *Meg.* 12*a*, 𝕿¹, and *Mid.*, to think of frames of gold and silver on which the cushions were laid. Her. ix. 82 speaks of couches and tables of gold and silver that the Greeks captured from the Persians (*cf.* Plutarch,

Vit. Alex. 37). Reclining at table was not the custom of the ancient Hebrews, but in the time of Amos it began to come in from the East (Am. 6⁴). In later days it was the universal practice of the Jews. Classical references show that Est. is correct in ascribing this custom to the Persians.—[𝔍 𝔖 𝔗¹ + placed] *upon a mosaic pavement of porphyry and marble, and mother-of-pearl, and dark marble* [𝕲 + and transparent coverings gayly decorated with roses strewn in a circle]. On *marble*, *cf.* ⁶ᵃ. The other names of materials occur only here and are of very doubtful meaning. We are to think of four kinds of stone of different colours that were set in ornamental patterns. Such pavements were greatly admired in the ancient Orient, and have been found in the excavations in Babylonia, Assyria, and Persia. The versions presuppose a different text (see note).

7. [𝔗¹ + And he commanded] *and drink was brought* [𝔍 + for those who were present] *in vessels of gold* [𝕲 𝔗² + and silver] [Jos.¹⁸³ + adorned with precious stones for pleasure and for display] [𝔗¹ + from the House of the Sanctuary, which wicked Nebuchadnezzar had carried away from Jerusalem;] [𝔗² + and he who drank out of a cup did not drink again out of the same cup, but they took that one away from him and brought him another;] [𝕲 + and a ruby beaker was displayed at a cost of 30,000 talents]. Golden drinking-vessels are mentioned among the spoil taken from the Persians by the Greeks (Her. ix. 80, 82). Xen. *Cyrop.* viii. 8, 18, says that the Persians prided themselves on the number of their drinking-vessels (*cf.* Athen. xi. 465; Strabo, xv. 3, 19). According to *Mid.*, the vessels were of crystal as costly as gold. It is curious that in this description no mention is made of food as well as of drink. The additions of the versions are all imaginary embellishments that have no text-critical value. —*And the vessels* [𝔍 + for food] *were different from one another.*

[𝔗¹ + And the other vessels of King Xerxes himself which were there, were changed in their appearance to the likeness of lead, and in the presence of the vessels of the Sanctuary they were transformed;] [*Meg.* 12a + and a voice was heard from Heaven, saying, The former kings perished on account of their use of the Temple-vessels, and you follow their example.]

THE SECOND FEAST

The idea of the Heb. is, that no two drinking-cups were alike, an extraordinary evidence of the wealth of the King. 𝕿¹, 𝕿², and *Mid.* take the expression *vessels differed from vessels* in the sense that the Temple-vessels differed from the other vessels, and so develop the extraordinary idea that Xerxes' cups were turned to lead. *Meg.* takes the verb in the sense of 'repeating' instead of 'differing,' and so gains the notion that Xerxes was 'repeating' the sin of Nebuchadnezzar (Dn. 5². ³⁰).— [𝕿¹ + And they drank] *royal wine* [𝕿¹ + of surpassing aroma, and most pleasant taste,] [𝕲 𝕿¹ + and sweet,] [𝕿¹ + not scanty, but] *abundant, with royal liberality* [𝕿² + and the wine was older than each one that drank of it, for the cup-bearer asked each man, How old art thou? and if he said I am 40 years old, he gave him wine that was 40 years old, and so with every one]. By *wine of kingdom* the versions and comm. generally understand such wine as the King himself drank. The older comm. think of the Chalybonian wine that the Persian kings are said to have drunk, and compare Ez. 27¹⁸; Plutarch, *Alexander.—According to the hand of the King*]. 𝕲 𝕷 L understand this to mean such wine *as came to the King's hand;* Mont., *according to the ability of the King;* Tig., *according to the royal command;* Pag., Vat., Pisc., Jun., and Trem., and most modern comm., *according to the generosity of the King,* i.e., *with royal liberality* (*cf.* 2¹⁸ 1 K. 10¹³ Ne. 2⁸). 𝕵 translates correctly, *ut magnificentia regia dignum erat*.

8. *And the drinking was according to the law. There was no one to compel* [Jos. + by bringing wine to them continually, as is the custom of the Persians.]

> [𝕿² + At the feasts of the Persians they used to bring to each one a great cup that held four of five *heminæ* (that is what is called a *pithqa*), and they made every man drink it down at one draught, and they did not let him go until he had finished it in one draught. So the cup-bearer who served the Persians became an exceedingly rich man; because, when he brought the cup to a man and he was not able to drink it, he winked to the cup-bearer to take the cup away from him, and paid him a sum of money because he was not able to drink it. But now Xerxes was not willing that they should drink out of such cups.]

The two clauses seem to be contradictory. One says that the

drinking was regulated by law; the other, that there was no constraint. *Meg.* 12a solves the difficulty by supposing that *according to the law* means *according to the Law of Moses*, in which the altar receives more food than drink. 𝕋¹ thinks that it means *according to the habit of each man; Mid., according to the custom of each nation;* Cler., *according to judgment*, i.e., *moderately.* Most comm. interpret it as meaning *according to the special rule made for this feast.* Ordinarily the guests drank together at a word of command from a toast-master, but now they were allowed to drink as they pleased. This interpretation can hardly be regarded as satisfactory. In the place of these two clauses 𝔊 has, *and the drinking took place according to no prescribed law*, which suggests that *law* should be pointed as a construct without the article; and that we should translate, *and the drinking was according to the law of no compeller*, i.e., *was unrestrained.*—For so the King [𝔊 + willed and] *had enjoined upon every officer of his house* [Jos. + to permit them to enjoy themselves and] *to do according to* [𝔊 + his wish and according to] *the wish of every man* [𝕋¹ + that was an Israelite, and according to the wish of the men of every kindred and tongue.] [*Meg.* 12a + And every man received the wine of his own province.] [Jos.[189] + And sending messengers through the provinces he commanded that they should have a release from their labours, and should feast on account of his kingdom many days.] The idea of the passage as a whole is, that there was neither any compulsion to drink, nor any restraint from drinking: every man was free to do as he pleased, and the servants were required to execute his orders. This verse concludes the description of Xerxes' feast for all the people of Susa the fortress. Its splendour was so great that one wonders what more could have been done for the nobles at the previous banquet. Persian feasts were proverbial in antiquity for their magnificence (*cf.* Her. i. 126; Athen. xii. 512; Horace, *Odes*, i. 38).

9. *Also Vashti the* [𝕋¹ + wicked] *Queen*, [*Meg.* 10b + the granddaughter of the wicked Nebuchadnezzar who had burnt the house of God,] *had made a* [L 𝕷 𝔖 + great] *feast* [L 𝔖 + for all] *the women in* [𝕋¹ + the place of the bedroom of] *the royal house that belonged to King Xerxes* [*Meg.* 12a + for she wished to sin as well

THE SECOND FEAST

as Xerxes, as the proverb says, The man reads and his wife holds the light.]

[𝕿² + She gave them dark wine to drink, and seated them within the palace, while she showed them the wealth of the King. And they asked her, How does the King sleep, and she told them everything that the women wished to know. She showed them the King's bedroom, and how he ate, and how he drank, and how he slept.] [𝕿¹ + But the righteous Mordecai prayed before the Lord from the first day of the feast unto the seventh day, which was the Sabbath.]

For the different theories in regard to the identity of Vashti, see p. 88. A separate feast for the women was not demanded by Persian custom (see v.¹²). We must suppose, either that the author has wrongly ascribed a Jewish custom to the Persians, or that he thinks that the number of the guests necessitated dividing them into two companies. *The house of the kingdom*, where the women were feasted, is evidently different from the *bîthān*, or *palace*, where the men were assembled. Whether it is also to be distinguished from the *house of the King* and from the *house of the women*, as Dieulafoy thinks, is not clear (*cf.* 2¹⁶ 5¹).

5. וּבִמְלֹאות [ובמלואת Q: om. 19 𝕷. The spelling in 𝔐 is simply a mistake that is corrected by Q (*cf.* Baer, p. 71).—מלאות shows a transition from ל״א to ל״ה forms, that is common in late Heb. (*cf.* Stade, *Heb. Gram.* § 201 *b* A; Siegfried, *Neuheb. Gram.* § 98 *c*, 105). במלאות does not mean 'in the fulfilling,' and so does not refer to a time within the 180 days; but means 'in the being full,' *i.e.*, in the time when the 180 days were over (*cf.* Lv. 12⁶). It is thus practically synonymous with כמלאות 'at the fulfilment' (2 K. 4⁶ Je. 25¹² Ez. 5²). 𝔊 translates correctly ὅτε δὲ ἀνεπληρώθησαν αἱ ἡμέραι. The 7-day feast follows the 180 days, at the same time the nobles are supposed to remain for this feast also.—הימים] om. 19 𝕷.—האלה] ἃς L: τοῦ γάμου 𝔊 (πότου A א c. a mg, 93*b* under ÷: + αὐτοῦ 93*b*): om. 𝕷: *convivii* 𝔍.—המלך] om. 𝕷 𝔍 44, 106.—לכל] om. 𝕷.—העם] om. L 𝕷.—הַנִּמְצָאִים] the word is regularly so pointed as if from a ל״ה root, except in Ezr. 8²⁵, where it is in pause. On the form *cf.* Maur. on Jos. 10¹⁷. The pl. is used because the preceding word is collective (*cf.* Kautzsch, § 145 *c*, *β*).—בשושן] εἰς 𝔊 (ἐν 44, 93*b*, 106): הבירה] *Thebari* 𝕷: om. 𝔍.—למגדול-קטן] om. 𝔊: to end of v., om. 𝕷.—שבעת] ἐξ 𝔊. מִשְׁתֶּה is pointed as an absolute; שבעת ימים, accordingly, must be taken as an acc. of time, 𝔊 correctly ἐπὶ ἡμέρας. Haupt points as a cstr. 𝔊 ἐξ has probably arisen out of regard for the Sabbath, since the Jews were included among *all the people* that were invited.—בחצר גנת] Winck. (*AOF.* iii. 2) deletes as a gloss to the next two words.—גנת] om. 𝔊 L: *cf.* 7[7f.] Ct. 6[11]. Cstr. to גִּנָּה, *cf.* Stade, § 193 *c*.—ביתן] om. 𝔏: οἴκου 𝔊: + συμφοίτου 93*b* under *: *et nemoris* 𝔍: om. 𝔏: ܒܣܶܕܪܳܐ 𝔖: גְּוָאָה 'interior,' 𝔗¹: found only in Est. It is commonly supposed to be a derivative from בית, 'house,' by appending the ending ן, (*cf.* Stade, *Heb. Gram.* § 294 *b*). Zimmern, *KAT.*³ p. 649, regards it as a loan-word from As. *bîtânu*, 'palace' (*cf.* Delitzsch, *HWB.* p. 172; Haupt, *ad loc.*). ביתן is not very similar in sound to Pers. *apadâna*, and to regard it as derived from the latter is unnatural, inasmuch as *apadâna* is already represented by Heb. אַפֶּדֶן (Dn. 11[45]). Cheyne (*EBi.* 4500) proposes to read בְּטָנֵי instead of בְּיתָן, and to translate 'in the royal pistachio-nut orchard.'—[המלך *quod regio cultu et manu consitum erat* 𝔍: + ἄγων τὰ σωτήρια αὐτοῦ. ἦν δὲ ἐξεστρωμένα L: + κεκοσμημένη 𝔊: + καὶ ἦν ἡ αὐλὴ κεκοσμημένη 44, 71, 74, 76, 120, 236: καὶ ἦν κεκοσμημένη 106: + *erant autem strata stragula regis derpina* 𝔏: + *et pendebant ex omne parte tentoria* 𝔍: + ܡܶܢ ܣܶܕܪܳܐ 𝔖.

6. חוּר] ח large, so Mas.: *aerii coloris* 𝔍: ܘܚܶܠܒܳܢ 𝔖: βυσσίνοις 𝔊. The word occurs only here and in 8[15]. 𝔊 translates 'fine white linen'; 𝔖, 'wool'; 𝔍, 'sky-blue.' Rab connects it with *ḥôr*, 'hole,' and regards it as perforated work; but Samuel says that it means 'something white' (*Meg.* 12*a*), similarly 𝔗¹. The root means 'to be white,' and occurs in Is. 29[22]. This word is probably cstr. before the next, so that we must translate 'white cloth of cotton,' not 'white cloth, cotton.' Haupt regards it as an explanatory gloss to כרפס that has taken the place of an original תחת.—כרפס] ܣܶܕܺܝܢܶܐ 𝔖: om. 44, 106: καρπασίνοις 𝔊: *i.e.*, 'cotton,' is the Skr. word *karpâsa*. It is found in Pers., Ar., and Aram., and appears in Gr. as κάρπασος and in Lat. as *carbasus* (*cf.* Lagarde, *Armen. Studien*, § 1148; BDB. p. 502). The Vrss. have for the most part the same word. 𝔖 has the equivalent, and 𝔗¹, 'fine linen.' *Meg.* 12*a* renders 'covers of coloured stuffs.' The word should be pointed כַּרְפָּס.—ותכלת] om. 𝔊: καὶ ὑακίνθινα + καὶ κόκκινα ἐμπεπλεγμένα ἐν ἄνθεσιν καὶ σκηνῇ L: *et hyacinctina* + *et super organa* 𝔏: *ac hyacinthini* 𝔍: ܘܬܶܟܶܠܬܳܐ 𝔖. Haupt transposes this word with בוץ (*cf.* 8[15]).—אחוז] sg., but refers to both of the preceding nouns (*cf.* Müller, *Syntax*, § 138). 𝔊 and 𝔖 read the pl.—אחוז־בוץ] om. 44, 71, 106.—בוץ] בְּחַבְלֵי־בוּץ] מְטַכְסִין 'in rows' 𝔗¹.—בוץ] *id*. 𝔖: βυσσίνοις 𝔊 L: *carbaseis* 𝔏. According to some it is derived from the root בוץ, Ar. *bâḍa*, 'to be white'; according to others, from Egypt. *hbos*, 'clothe.' It denotes properly 'fine linen,' such as was made in Egypt, but is often confused with כַּרְפַּס 'cotton cloth' (*cf.* BDB. *s. v.*). Haupt regards the word as a gloss to כרפס, that originally stood immediately after כרפס. —וארגמן] *id*. 𝔖 𝔗¹: καὶ πορφύροις 𝔊 L: *et purpureis subrotis* 𝔏.

THE SECOND FEAST

This was a red purple obtained from the mollusk *Murex Trunculus*, found on the Phœnician coast, and from the *Murex Brandaris*, found in the western Mediterranean. The etymology of the word is uncertain, but it is presumably of Phœn. origin, inasmuch as the manufacture of this colour was long a Phœn. monopoly. The word is found in As., Ar., Aram., Pers., and ph. in Skr. *râgaman*, 'red,' bearing witness to the extent of the Phœn. export trade (see Plin. *Nat. Hist.* ix. 124, 133–135; *HDB*. i. p. 457; *EBi*. i. 875; Moore, *Judges*, p. 234; BDB. *s. v.*; Haupt, *Transact. Hamburg Congress Orientalists*, p. 220; *KAT*.³ p. 649, n. 2).—[גלילי] ἐκ κιόνων, 'pillars,' Jos.: אונקלון, *i.e.*, ὄγκινον, 'hook,' 𝔗¹: *qui circulis inserti erant* 𝔍. This word is derived from גלל 'roll,' and has ordinarily the meaning of 'circuit' or 'district.' Here it might mean 'rings,' as 𝔍 and most modern versions; but Ct. 5¹⁴, where the hands (fingers) are compared to גלילי זהב, suggests rather that it means 'cylinders,' or 'rods.' Gr. κύβοις arises from confusion with גלילי 'stocks,' 'blocks.'—[כסף] *eburneis* 𝔍: om. 𝔏.—[ועמודי] ἐπὶ στύλοις 𝔊: καὶ στύλοις L: ܘܥܡܘܕܐ ܣܡܟܐ 𝔖: *columna* 𝔏: om. 71.—[שש] ordinarily means 'fine linen.' Here and Ct. 5¹⁵ it appears as a material from which pillars were made, in ⁶ᵇ as material in a pavement. In 1 Ch. 29² the alternate form שַׁיִשׁ is used of a stone employed in the Temple. The versions generally translate 'marble': παρίνοις 𝔊 L: *eparina* (*electa*) 𝔏: *marmoreis* 𝔍: מרמרין 𝔗¹. 𝔖 has ܐܫܟܪܥܐ 'acacia,' which is the word by which שטים is regularly translated. This suggests that it read here עמודי שטים. This reading is adopted by Canney (*EBi*. 2936), but 𝔐 is supported by the weight of evidence. The word appears also as the name of a kind of stone in Aram., Syr., and ph. in As. *šaššu* (see BDB. 1010). According to the last-cited work it means 'alabaster.'—[מטות] pr. καὶ L 𝔍 𝔖.—[וכסף] om. L: + ܘܣܐܡܐ 𝔖.—[רצפת] רִצְפַת Ben Asher: רְצָפַת Ben Naphtali (Buhl): λιθόστρωτον 𝔊 L: *pavimentum stratum* 𝔍: *lapides* 𝔏: סטיו כביש 'a trodden stoa,' 𝔗¹. The root, which appears in As. *raṣapu*, Ar. *raṣafa*, means 'to join together.' רצפה is a pavement composed of small pieces of stone. It is used of the pavement in Solomon's temple, 2 Ch. 7³, and in Ezekiel's temple, Ez. 40¹⁷ᶠ·—[בהט] om. 𝔏 𝔖: σμαραγδίτου λίθου 𝔊, *i.e.*, a stone like the emerald in colour, perhaps 'malachite,' 'serpentine,' or 'verd-antique': σμαράγδου L: *smaragdino* 𝔍: קרוסטלינין 'crystals,' 𝔗¹. In Ar. *baht* means 'alabaster' (Dozy, *Suppl*. i. p. 121). In Egypt. *behet* means ph. 'porphyry' (Brugsch, *Dict*. v. 438; Wendel, *Altäg. Bau- u. Edelsteine*, p. 77 *f.;* BDB. p. 96). The word occurs only here, and its meaning is quite doubtful.—[ושש] om. L 71, 106: tr. w. next 𝔊: see above.—[ודר] καὶ πιννίνου, 'and of pearl,' 𝔊: ודרא דרכרכי ימא רבא, 'and pearl of the cities of the great sea,' 𝔗¹. These renderings presuppose the same text as 𝔐. In Ar. *durr* means 'pearls.' In a pavement we must think rather of mother-of-pearl. Haupt thinks of shell-marble which may have been obtained from the neighbourhood of Astrakhan. 𝕷 has *varia*, and 𝕴 *quod mira varietate*, which seem to presuppose וְרֻבֵּי, 'and multitudes,' instead of 𝔐 ודרו. 𝔖 omits.—וסחרת] apparently the same as As. *siḫru*, a precious stone of an unknown sort (Delitzsch, *HWB.* 495). The name is perhaps connected with שחר 'to be dark.' Instead of this 𝕴 reads *pictura decorebat*, and 𝕷 *pictura*, which seems to indicate that they read סָכִיּוֹת, which they took as the Aram. equivalent of שְׂכִיּוֹת 'imagery,' 'pictures.' In Is. 2¹⁶ 𝕴 renders this word *quod visu pulchrum est*. 𝔊 has καὶ στρῶμναι διαφανεῖς ποικίλως διηνθισμέναι, 'and transparent coverings gayly decorated.' 𝔖 has ܘܟܣܝ̈ܐ ܕܟܬܢܐ ܘܕܫܐܪܝ 'and coverings of linen and of silk.' Both of these versions presuppose כָּסוּת 'covering' instead of סחרת in 𝔐 and סכית in 𝕴𝕷. The rest of the phrase in both cases is free amplification designed to explain what is meant by 'covering.' 𝕿¹, 𝕿², read ואטונין מצירין מקפין להון חזור חזור 'and coloured ropes enclosed them on this side and on that.' This presupposes 𝔐 וסחרת. The word is regarded as derived from סחר 'go about, surround,' and is here freely interpreted as an enclosure of ropes that surrounded the feasters. Instead of ודר וסחרת L reads καὶ κύκλῳ ῥόδα, 'and roses in a circle,' which represents an original ורדי סחרת. This then has come into 𝔊, κύκλῳ ῥόδα πεπασμένα, as a conflate reading alongside of the other translation of the phrase. There is no reason to regard the text of either 𝕴𝕷 or 𝔊𝔖 as superior to 𝔐. What we expect here is not a mention of pictures nor of couches, which have been described in a previous clause, but of the materials of the pavement. Regarding 𝔊 as original, Jahn emends ודר וסחרת to read thus: ומכסות ברומים דקים ציצים סביבותיה ורדים סחרים. For ושחרת Canney (*EBi.* 2936) reads: ושש ודר ומפרשי שש ברקמה לסחרת 'and mother-of-pearl and screens of fine linen in the form of shields.'

7. [והשקות] *Hiph.* inf. cstr., literally 'and the giving to drink.' The inf. is used because only the action is prominent, and it is cstr. because closely connected with the following words: *bibebant autem qui invitati erant* 𝕴: to שונים om. 𝕷.—שונים–וכלים] om. 𝔊: ἔξαλλα L: *et aliis atque aliis vasis cibi inferebantur* 𝕴.—ויין] om. ו 𝔊.—מלכות] om. 𝔊𝕷: *præcipuum* 𝕴: the form without the article is peculiar. Jahn emends to מתוק] after 𝔊 ἡδύς.—רָב] so Mas. on 2 Ch. 28⁸ (*cf.* Dn. 11²): *cf.* Stade, § 193 *b*, n. 2: om. L:+ καὶ ἡδύς 𝔊:+ *et suave valde* 𝕷.—כיר] ὃν αὐτὸς ἔπινεν 𝔊𝕷: ὃν πίνει L.

8. [והשתיה] *et ad jucunditatem bibere* 𝕷: *ponebantur* 𝕴: this f. form of the noun occurs here only, the m. in Ec. 10¹⁷:+ οὗτος 𝔊.—כדת] the word דָּת is Old Pers. *dâta*, 'law' (*cf.* Spiegel, *Altpers. Keilinschr.*, p. 225). It is found in the OT. only in writings of the Persian period or later. It occurs 19 times in Est. and also in Ezr. 8³⁶, in all cases with reference to a royal decree. In the Aram. parts of Ezr. and Dn. it is

XERXES SUMMONS VASHTI 147

used both of the law of the King and the law of God. (See Lagarde, *Abhandlungen*, 36 *f.*; *Armen. Stud.* § 579; Marti, *Aram. Gram.*, p. 59.)—
[כדת אין אנס] οὐ κατὰ προκείμενον νόμον ἐγένετο 𝔊. This shows that 𝔊 pointed כדת without the article and regarded it as cstr. before אין אנס, or else that it read כדת אין אנסת. This gives a better sense than 𝔐. 𝔏 has *secundum legem nemini vim fieri*, which also implies that דת is cstr.—[אנס] not 'hinder' (Schu., Haupt), but 'constrain,' *i.e.*, either to drink or not to drink.—[סר על:] here only in the meaning 'enjoin upon,' like חיס על $9^{21.\ 27.\ 31}$ (*cf.* 1 Ch. 9^{22}): ἠθέλησεν ... καὶ ἐπέταξεν 𝔊.—[המלך] om. 𝔏.—[על] *præponens mensis singulos* 𝔍.—[כל רב ביתו] τοῖς οἰκονόμοις 𝔊: *actoribus domui* 𝔏: *de principibus suis* 𝔍: om. L.—כרצון + αὐτοῦ καὶ 𝔊.

9. [גם] om. 𝔖.—[ושתי] Ἀστὶν 𝔊: Ἀστὶ C: αὕτη 55: Οὐασθεὶν 93*b*: Οὐαστὶν L: *Vasthi* 𝔏 𝔍 (so subsequently in all these recensions).—[עשתה] pf., instead of impf. w. ו consec., because antecedent in time (*cf.* $2^{5.\ 10}\ 4^1$). —[בית] pr. ἐν 𝔊 L 𝔏 𝔖: ב has accidentally fallen out of the text (*cf.* 1^{22} $5^1\ 9^4$).—[המלכות] βασιλείοις 𝔊: τοῦ βασιλέως L.—[אשר למלך] om. L 𝔏: ἵπου ὁ βασιλεὺς 𝔊: Haupt deletes.—[אחשורוש] om. L: Haupt deletes.

XERXES COMMANDS VASHTI TO SHOW HERSELF TO THE GUESTS, BUT SHE REFUSES TO COME (1^{10-12}).

10. [L + And it came to pass] *on the seventh day,* [𝔗¹ + which was the Sabbath, his cry and the cry of the Sanhedrin came before the Lord, and] *when the King's mood grew merry from wine,* [𝔍 + and when, after too deep drinking, the wine-bibber became heated,] [𝔗¹ + the Lord sent unto him a disturbing angel to trouble their feast.]

[𝔗² + When also the 127 kings wearing crowns who were with him grew merry, and the conversation turned to improper subjects, a violent dispute arose among them.] [*Meg.* 12*b* + Some said, The Median women are the most beautiful; others said, The Persian women are the fairest. Then said Xerxes to them, The wife that I enjoy is neither a Mede nor a Persian, but is a Chaldean. If you wish, you may see her. Yes, they said, but she must appear naked, for with what measure one metes, it shall be measured to him again. The shameless Vashti had taken Israelitish maidens and stripped them naked, and had made them work on the Sabbath (similarly 𝔗¹, 𝔗², *Mid.*).]

The seventh day is, of course, the last day of the seven-day feast (**v.**⁵) and not the Sabbath. With the phrase *mood grew merry,* *cf.* Ju. 16^{25} 1 S. 25^{36} 1 K. 8^{66} Pr. 15^{15} Est. 5^9.—[L + The King] *commanded M*ᵉ*hûmān, Bizz*ᵉ*thā, Ḥarbhônā, Bighthā, and Ăbhagh-thā, Zēthar, and Karkaṣ, the seven eunuchs*]. On the attempts to explain these names from the Pers., see p. 67. The names differ widely in the Vrss., and the correct text is very uncertain. Eunuchs were employed as custodians of the women of the Persian court, as in Babylonia, Assyria, Egypt, and other countries of the ancient and the modern Orient (*cf.* Her. viii. 105; Petron. *Satyr.* 157; Terence, *Eunuch.*, Act. 1, Sc. 11; Brisson, ii. p. 234). The old controversy whether this word may not also mean 'officers,' does not come up here, inasmuch as these individuals who have access to the women's quarters must be eunuchs. The number *seven*, which appears also in v.¹⁴ and 2⁹, was sacred among the Persians, as among the Hebrews. Ahura-Mazda and the six Amesha-Spentas constituted a heavenly council of seven; or, according to another conception, there were seven Amesha-Spentas (*cf.* Geiger-Kuhn, *Iran. Philologie*, p. 634). The royal court was patterned on a similar model.— *Who served* [𝕋¹ + *during these seven days*] *before King Xerxes*], lit. *who served the face of King Xerxes* (*cf.* Gn. 19¹³· ²⁷ 1 S. 2¹⁸).

11. To bring Vashti the Queen before the King with the royal turban [𝕲𝕷𝕵 + placed upon her head] [𝕋¹ + in recompense for the good deed of Nebuchadnezzar, her paternal grandfather, who had clothed Daniel in purple] *to show* [some codd. 𝕲𝕷𝕵 + all] *the peoples and the officials her beauty, for she was very fair.* [𝕋² + And the King said to them, Go, say to Queen Vashti, Rise from thy royal throne, and strip thyself naked, and put a crown upon thy head, and take a golden cup in thy right hand, and a golden pitcher in thy left hand, and come before me and before the 127 crowned kings, that they may see that thou art the fairest of women.] [*Mid.* + And she wished at least to wear a girdle like a harlot, but her husband would not permit that.] From the fact that only a turban is mentioned, *Meg.*, 𝕋¹, 𝕋², and Jewish comm. generally infer that this was all that Vashti was permitted to wear. In reality the author means, in full regal attire, including the crown. Having displayed all his other treasures to his guests, Xerxes is now anxious to show his most precious possession, his beautiful wife. The remark that he did this when he was heated with wine, indicates the opinion of the author that he would not have acted so if he had been in his right mind. *To show her beauty* is a reason for the sending, not a reason why the Queen should come. On the question who were present at this feast, see 1⁵. According to some of the Rabbi's, Vashti was one of the four beautiful women of the world, the other three being Sarah, Rahab, and Abigail (*Meg.* 15a).

12. *But Queen Vashti refused* [𝔍 + and scorned] *to come at the command of the King which* [𝔍 𝔖 𝔗¹ + he sent unto her] *by the eunuchs,* [Jos.¹⁹¹ + for she was mindful of the laws of the Persians, which do not permit strangers to look upon wives,] [*Meg.* 12b + because she had become leprous, or because Gabriel had come and caused a tail to grow on her.]

> [𝔗² + And Queen Vashti answered and said unto them, Go, say unto your foolish master, whom you resemble in folly: Thou groom of my father, I am Vashti, the Queen, the daughter of the kings of Babylon from of old. My father drank wine enough for a thousand men, yet wine never enticed him to speak such senseless words as thou speakest. So they went and gave the King the answer which Queen Vashti sent unto him; and when the King heard these words, he was very angry, and his wrath was kindled within him. And he sent again unto her by the seven royal eunuchs who sat before him in the kingdom, saying: Go now and say to Queen Vashti, If thou dost not hearken unto my words and come before me and before these kings, I will slay thee and take away thy beauty from thee. But when the officers of the King told this to her, she paid no attention to them, but answered and said unto them, Go, say to this foolish king, whose counsels are vain and whose decrees are worthless: Am not I Vashti, the Queen, the daughter of Evil-Merodach, the granddaughter of Nebuchadnezzar, King of Babylon? From my birth until now no man has seen my body, except thou, the King, alone. If now I come before thee and before the 127 crowned kings, they will kill thee and marry me. And one of the noble Persian ladies answered and said unto Queen Vashti: Even if the King slay thee and take away thy beauty from thee, thou canst not disgrace thy name and thy father's name by showing thy body to any person except the King alone.] [Jos.¹⁹¹ + And though he sent the eunuchs often to her, she none the less remained away and refused to come.]

No good reason appears for Vashti's refusal to show herself to the guests. It was not Persian custom to seclude the women as in the modern Orient. According to Est. 5⁴ ᶠ· and Ne. 2⁶, the Queen could be present at banquets (*cf.* Her. v. 18), where the Persians say, "It is the custom with us Persians, when we give a great feast, to bring our concubines and lawful wives to sit by our sides." In Her. ix. 110, Queen Amestris is present at the birthday-feast of Xerxes; so also Stateira at the table of Artaxerxes (Plutarch, *Artax.* v.). It is a mistake, accordingly, when later writers assert that wives were not present at Persian feasts (*e.g.*, Plutarch, *Sympos.* i. 1; Macrobius, *Sat.* i. 1.). The assumption of Jos., Drus., and many others, that Vashti refused to come because it was contrary to Persian custom, is therefore untenable. There is no hint of this in Est. *Meg.*, 𝔗¹, 𝔗², and *Mid.* assume that she declined to show herself because she was commanded to appear naked, but of this also there is no suggestion in the text. Even this explanation did not satisfy the Rabbis, for they could not see why such a shameless creature as Vashti was painted by tradition should be unwilling to come even in this condition. Hence the notion that she had a disfigurement which she was unwilling to reveal. Par. suggests that she refused because she thought her feast as good as that of Xerxes, and was unwilling to depreciate hers by gracing his. Keil and Bert. conjecture that the refusal was due to the fact that the men were drunk, and that Vashti feared to be insulted by them (*cf.* Her. v. 18 *f.*); but, according to Lucian, the women were guarded by eunuchs when they attended banquets (*cf.* Brisson, i. 103); and surely a Persian queen must have been accustomed to the spectacle of drunkenness. The author of Est. apparently regards the refusal as merely a whim, for which he offers no explanation. The added words, *which he sent unto her by the eunuchs*, show that the summons was delivered in the proper, formal way, and, therefore, enhance the disrespect of Vashti.— [𝔗² + And when the officers of the King told the King that Queen Vashti refused to come at the command of the King sent by the eunuchs (similarly L),] *then the King was exceedingly angry, and his wrath was kindled within him;* [Jos.[192] + and he broke up the banquet.] The anger of the King was due to the public affront put upon him by the Queen's refusal to obey a formal command given in the presence of all the dignitaries of the empire.

THE COUNCIL CONCERNING VASHTI 151

10. ביום] pr. ἐγένετο δὲ L: pr. *itaque* 𝔍: pr. ○ 𝔖.—כטוב] cstr. inf. with כ, as כשבת (1¹) *q. v.*, not the *Qal* pf., or the adj., as some comm.— לב] om. 𝔊 L 𝔏.—ביין] om. 𝔊 𝔏: *et post nimiam potationem incaluisset mero* 𝔍.—שבעת הסריסים] om. L.—המשרתים] om. 52, 64, 243, 248, C, Ald.—את פני] om. 𝔊 L: τοῖς πρώτοις 71.—המלך] *ejus* 𝔍: αὐτοῦ L 44, 106.—אחשורוש] om. 𝔍 L N 44, 55, 74, 76, 106, 108a, 120, 236: Haupt deletes.

11. את ושתי] om. 𝔊 𝔏.—לפני - מלכות] πρὸς αὐτόν, βασιλεύειν αὐτὴν καὶ περιθεῖναι αὐτῇ τὸ διάδημα 𝔊 𝔏: εἰς τὸ συνεστηκὸς συμπόσιον ἐν τῷ διαδήματι τῆς βασιλείας αὐτῆς L: *coram rege posito super caput ejus diademate* 𝔍.—כתר] διάδημα 𝔊 L 𝔏 𝔍: תגא 𝔖 𝔗²: כלילא 𝔗¹: from כתר 'surround,' is a turban twisted up to a high point, Gr. κίδαρις (see Marti, *Aram. Gram. Glos.*, *s. v.* כרבלא). Lagarde, *Armen. Stud.* 1003; Ges. *Abhl.* 207, regards it as a Pers. loan-word. It is found only in Est., here, and 2¹⁷ of the Queen's turban, 6⁸ of the ornament on the head of the King's horse.—להראות] + πᾶσιν א A N 44, 55, 64, 71, 74, 76, 106, 108a, 120, 243, 248, 249, 𝔏 𝔍: κατὰ πρόσωπον L.—העמים] τῆς στρατιᾶς αὐτοῦ L.—והשרים - היא] om. L.

12. המלכה] om. 𝔍 L.—וישתי] om. 𝔍 𝔏 44, 106: Haupt deletes.—לבוא] ποιῆσαι L.—בדבר - אשר] om. 𝔊 𝔏.—אשר] om. L: + *mandaverat* 𝔍: + ܡܚ ܠܚܡ 𝔖.—ביד הסריסים] μετὰ τῶν εὐνούχων 𝔊: *cum eis* 𝔏: om. 44, 106: + ὡς δὲ ἤκουσεν ὁ βασιλεὺς ὅτι ἠκύρωσεν Οὐαστὶν τὴν βουλὴν αὐτοῦ L.—המלך] om. L.—מאד] om. 𝔊.

XERXES TAKES COUNSEL WITH HIS MINISTERS WHAT OUGHT TO BE DONE TO VASHTI (1¹³⁻¹⁵).

13. *And* [Jos. + *standing up*] *the King said to* [L + *all*] *the wise men* [𝔖 + *the discerning*] [𝔗¹ + *the sons of Issachar* (*cf.* 1 Ch. 12³²)] *who knew the times* [*Meg.* 12b, 𝔗¹ + *and the seasons in the Book of the Law and in the calculation of the world*]. This did not take place at the feast, apparently, but on another occasion, as the officers and the people are not mentioned in this connection. There is no reason, therefore, to regard the following deliberation and decree as the acts of drunken men. Only one class of counsellors is mentioned here, for *knowers of the times* is in apposition with *wise men*. By *knowers of the times*, *Meg.*, 𝔗¹, 𝔗², *Mid.*, and most comm. understand *astrologers* (*cf.* Is. 44²⁵ 47¹⁰⁻¹⁵ Je. 50³⁵ Dn. 2²⁷ 5¹⁵); but the next clause equates them with *knowers of law and justice;* they must, therefore, be those who are familiar with historical precedents that have the value of law (so Vit.,

Pag., Drus., Pisc., Osi., Ramb., Patr.; *cf.* 2 Ch. 12³²). In a case of this sort no reason appears why astrologers should be called in. —*For so was the King's procedure* [𝕋¹ + wont to be discussed] *before all* [𝕋¹ + the wise men and] *those who knew law and custom*]. The addition of 𝕋¹ gives the true sense. The translation of AV. and RV. *for so was the King's manner toward all* is incorrect. On *dāth*, 'law,' see v.⁸.

[*Meg.* 12*b* + Then they considered what they ought to say, saying, If we say, Let her be put to death; to-morrow, when the King is sober, he may become reconciled to her and put us to death: if we say, She is innocent, that will be an insult to the King. So they said to him, Since the Sanctuary has been destroyed and we have been exiled out of our land, we are no longer allowed to pronounce sentences of life or death. Go to Ammon and Moab, which have remained in their places like wine upon its lees. [𝕋¹ + And the sons of Issachar prayed before the Lord and spoke thus: O Lord of the world, confound their feast, and be mindful of the righteous who offered before thee in the House of thy Sanctuary lambs of a year old, two young pigeons, and turtle-doves upon an altar of earth, by the hand of the high priest, clad with the breast-plate, in which was the chrysolite, while the crowds of priests sprinkled and mingled the blood and arranged the shew-bread before thee. So the King turned and sought again advice from his princes.]

This addition of 𝕋¹ is a series of plays upon the names of the seven counsellors based upon *Meg.* 12*b*. Vv. ¹³ᵇ⁻¹⁴ form a parenthetical explanation inserted between ¹³ᵃ and ¹⁵.

14. *And those who were* [𝕵 + first and] *near to him* [𝕋² + in counsel, some from afar and some from near by] *were* [𝕋¹ + named] Karshᵉnā [𝕋² + from Africa], Shēthar [𝕋² + from India], Adhmāthā [𝕋² + from Edom], Tarshîsh [𝕋² + from Egypt], Mereṣ [𝕋² + from Mereṣ], Marṣᵉnā, Mᵉmûkhān [𝕋² + from Jerusalem]. This clause is not to be connected with the foregoing, so as to read, *those who knew law and custom and were near unto him* (𝕋¹), for in that case the adj. would be pl., since it would follow the noun with which it agrees; nor is it to be translated *the King said to the wise men and to those near to him* (𝔖), for in that case the preposition *to* would be repeated. This clause must be taken as an independent sentence, *And the near to him were.* The predicate is singular because it precedes its subjects

(Müller, *Syntax*, § 133; see note). These *near ones* belong to the class of the *wise*, because they answer the question just put to them. This is a further evidence that the *wise* are not astrologers. The author's idea is, that out of the class of the wise men seven enjoyed a special proximity to the King. *Near* does not refer to relationship or to rank, but, as the following words show, to physical propinquity. On the names of these viziers, see p. 68. In BT., 𝔗¹, *Mid.*, these names receive a host of allegorical explanations.—*The seven viziers of Persia and Media*]. The statement that there were *seven* is confirmed by Ezr. 7¹⁴; Her. iii. 31, 84, 118; Xen. *Anab.* i. 6⁴; Jos. *Ant.* xi. 31. According to these passages seven chief judges held offices for life and decided all questions that affected the conduct of the King. On *Persia and Media*, see v. ³.—*Who continually beheld the face of the King*], i.e., who were intimately associated with him (*cf.* 2 S. 14²⁴·³² Mt. 18¹⁰). According to Her., these seven chief nobles had access to the King at all times, except when he was in the company of one of his wives. —*Who sat next to the royal throne*], lit., *who sat first in the kingdom.* Their thrones were probably set in the same relation to that of Xerxes as those of the Amesha-Spentas to that of Ahura-Mazda, namely, three on each side and one in front of the King. 𝔗¹ paraphrases correctly, 'in the first row of the thrones of the kingdom.'

15. [Jos.¹⁹² + And he accused his wife, and told how he had been insulted by her, and how, although she had been summoned many times by him to the banquet, she had not once obeyed. Then he commanded that some one should state] *according to law, what was to be done with Queen Vashti*], a resumption of the thought of ¹³ᵃ that has been interrupted by the parenthesis ¹³ᵇ⁻¹⁴. The words *according to law* are placed first for emphasis. Haupt, against the testimony of 𝔊 𝔏 𝔖, joins *according to law* to the end of the preceding v. The art. is omitted because no particular law is meant. On *law*, see 1⁸. *Because she did not execute the order of King Xerxes* [𝔗¹ 𝔖 + which he sent] *by the eunuchs*], a recapitulation of the offence already described in vv.¹⁰⁻¹². Nothing could be more improbable than that a despot like Xerxes should seek the advice of his wise men before dealing with a refractory wife. Judging from Herodotus' narratives, he would have made quick work with her.

13. [המלך] om. 𝕲.—[לחכמים] τοῖς φίλοις αὐτοῦ 𝕲 𝕷: + ܐܢܠܝ 𝕾.—[ידעי העתים] om. 𝕲 𝕷 𝕵.—[ידעי]‑² [העתים] om. L.—[כי כן] κατὰ ταῦτα 𝕲: qui ex 𝕵.—[דבר] more 𝕵: ἐλάλησεν 𝕲.—[המלך]² 'Αστίν 𝕲: + ܐܢܠܝ 𝕾.—[לפני] semper ei aderant 𝕵: et dixit rex 𝕷: ποιήσατε οὖν 𝕲.—[כל] et illorum faciebat cuncta consilio 𝕵: περὶ 𝕲: omnibus L.—[ידעי] τούτου 𝕲: principibus 𝕷.—[דת ודין] νόμον καὶ κρίσιν 𝕲 L: leges ac jura majorum 𝕵: ܢܡܘܣܐ ܘܕܝܢܐ 𝕾. דת is an edict promulgated by the King, דין is customary law. On the etymology of the two words see Haupt, a. l. According to Sieg., ודין is an explanatory gloss upon the preceding Pers. word דת.

14. [ויהקרב] pr. ܣܠܩ 𝕾: καὶ προσῆλθεν (θον) 𝕲 L: Sieg. emends to וְהִקְרֵב (cf. 1 K. 5⁷); Haupt, to וְהִקְרַב.—[שבעת] om. 𝕾 𝕲 𝕷 L.—[ראי] tr. with הישבים 𝕾: οἱ ἐγγὺς 𝕲: καὶ οἱ ὁρῶντες L: qui proximi 𝕷.—[הישבים] pr. καὶ L.—[ראשנה] ܩܕܡܝܐ 𝕾: om. L 𝕷. The f. of the adj. is used as an adv., usually with a prep., but also without prep., Gn. 38²⁸ 1 K. 18²⁵ Je. 16¹⁸ Lv. 5⁸ Nu. 2⁹ Jos. 21¹⁰, in the sense of 'first in time,' here and Gn. 33² in the sense of 'first in place.'—[במלכות] post eum 𝕵: τῷ βασιλεῖ 𝕲: + καὶ ἀπήγγειλαν αὐτῷ 𝕲: om. 𝕷.

15. [כדת] om. 𝕵 L.—[מה-המלך] tr. to v. ¹³ after ודין L.—[וישתי] om. L 𝕷: Haupt deletes.—[לא עשתה] μὴ τεθεληκέναι αὐτὴν ποιῆσαι L.—[אחשורוש] om. 𝕲 L 𝕷: Haupt deletes: + ܡܠܟܐ 𝕾: + dicta erunt L.—[ביד הסריסים] om. L.

THE ADVICE OF THE MINISTERS (1¹⁶⁻²⁰)

16. *Then spoke Mᵉmûkhān before the King and the viziers* [44, 106 + *and the King's officers*].

[*Meg.* 12b, 𝕿¹ + He was Haman the descendant of the wicked Agag.] [𝕿² + He was Daniel. And why was he called Mᵉmûkhān? Because, when the tribe of the house of Judah was carried captive to Babylon, there were carried captive with them Hananiah, Mishael, and Azariah; and Daniel also was among the exiles, and signs and wonders were wrought by his hands. Also by means of Daniel it was decreed from on high that Queen Vashti should be slain; therefore his name was called Mᵉmûkhān ('appointed'). This was the decree of the King in the council, that the younger nobles should give their advice first; and if the advice was good, they followed it; and if it was not good, they followed the advice of the seniors. Now, since Mᵉmûkhān was the youngest of all, he gave his advice first before the King. Mᵉmûkhān had married a rich Persian wife, and she was not willing to speak with him except in her language, so Memûkhān said within himself, Now the opportunity has come to compel the women to honour their husbands.]

From the fact that Memûkhān is named last in v.¹⁴, *Meg.* 12b and *Mid.* infer that he was the lowest in rank and thrust himself forward on this occasion. 𝕌², in the passage just cited, thinks that he was the youngest. Others suppose that he appeared as the spokesman of the council after deliberation with the rest.— [L + Saying,] *Not against the King only has Queen Vashti sinned, but against all the officials and all the peoples in all the King's provinces*]. The charge is twofold, that Vashti has wronged the King, and that she has set a dangerous example. The second charge is amplified in vv. ¹⁷⁻¹⁸. The wily Memûkhān insinuates that in punishing Vashti the King will not be gratifying a private grudge, but will be consulting public welfare. On *officials*, see 1³. *Peoples* is in contrast to *officials;* the lower as well as the upper classes are wronged (*cf.* v. ¹¹). The pl. is used on account of the number of races in Xerxes' empire. *Provinces of the King* is the usual formula in Est. (2³ 3⁸ *provinces of the kingdom*). By these are meant the 127 provinces of 1¹.

17. *For the conduct of the Queen will become known to all the women*]. The nobles of the provinces from India to Ethiopia will go home after the feast, and will tell how Vashti refused to obey her husband, so that the scandal will soon become known to all women of the empire. *Conduct*, lit. *word, matter* (*cf.* 1¹³ 9²⁰).— *With the result of making them* [𝕊 + scorn and] *despise their husbands*,] [Jos.¹⁹³ + and lead them a wretched life,] [𝕌² + saying to them, Art thou more honourable than King Xerxes?] Lit. the phrase means, *unto causing to despise their husbands in their eyes.* *Baʻal,* 'owner,' 'lord,' is here used for 'husband' as in Gn. 20³ Dt. 24⁴ Ho. 2¹⁶ and often.—*While they say* [𝕌¹+each to the other, Verily] *King Xerxes commanded to bring Queen Vashti before him, but she did not come.*] The idea, which the Targums seek to make more clear, is that wives throughout the empire will say, The Queen did not obey, therefore we need not obey.

18. *And this very day*]. Prompt action is necessary, since the trouble is likely to begin at once among the women in Susa.—*The* *ladies of Persia and Media, who have heard of the conduct of* [𝕿¹ + Vashti] *the Queen* [Jos.¹⁹⁴ + *toward thee who rulest over all*]. Verse ¹⁷ spoke of women in general throughout the empire, this v. speaks of women of the aristocracy. They were in Susa with their husbands, and were present at Vashti's feast (v.⁹), so that they would be corrupted at once by her example. On *Persia and Media*, see 1³.—*Will say* [𝕿¹ + *that they may do thus to their husbands, and will take counsel to do thus*] *to all the King's officials.*] *Say* has no object. Most comm. follow 𝕿¹ and 𝕿² in supplying one from the preceding v., and translate, *will say the like*, AV. and RV.; or *will tell it* (*i.e.*, the conduct of the Queen), Keil, Oet., Kau., Sieg., Schu. and others go back to *while they say* (¹⁷ᵇ), and regard the clause which there follows as the object of *say* in this v. 𝔖, Bert., Rys., find the object in the next clause, and translate, *will speak—and that in abundance—scorn and indignation.* All these constructions are unnatural, and one must suspect corruption of the text. Instead of *say* 𝕲 has *will dare similarly to dishonour;* 𝕷, *will neglect and treat with contumely;* 𝕵, *will make light of.* With the omission of a single letter the v. reads, *will rebel against all the King's officials* (see note).—*Then there will be enough contempt and wrath* [𝕿¹ + *and who will be able to bear it*]. If the text be sound, *enough* is ironical; Mᵉmûkhān means, far too much. *Contempt, i.e.*, on the part of wives toward their husbands; *wrath, i.e.*, on the part of husbands toward their wives. Instead of *enough*, Haupt, by a slight textual emendation reads *whenever*, and translates, *whenever there is contempt then there is wrath.* This greatly improves the sense. This absurd advice, that the example of Vashti is politically dangerous, can hardly be taken as sober history.

[Jos. ¹⁹⁴ + And he exhorted him to punish her who had so insulted him, with a great punishment.] [𝕿² + But, when Mᵉmûkhān had given this opinion, he feared for his life, and said: Perhaps the King will not carry out this advice; and when Vashti comes to hear of this advice which I have given against her, she will judge me harshly, if I do not secure that King Xerxes says that Vashti shall not come before him, and cause him to swear an oath which the Persians are afraid to break. Therefore Mᵉmûkhān said,]

19. *If it seems good to the King* [L 𝕷 + and agreeable to his mind,] [*Mid.* + my lord the King needs but to speak the word and I will bring her head in a dish.] This is the regular formula for making a proposition to the King (*cf.* 3⁹ 5⁴⁻⁸ 7³⁻⁹ 8⁵ 9¹³ Ne. 2⁵). After the exposition of the nature of Vashti's offence in vv.¹⁶⁻¹⁸, Mᵉmûkhân is now ready to say what ought to be done with her.—*Let a royal edict go forth from him, and let it be written* [𝕿² + and the oath] *among the laws of Persia and Media that it may not be repealed*]. *Cf.* 1³⁻⁸. As 𝕿² rightly perceives, the motive in making Vashti's deposal irrevocable is to escape the consequences that will ensue if she returns to power. The idea that the laws of the Medo-Persian empire could not be changed, appears again in 8⁸ and Dn. 6⁹⁻¹³, but is not attested by any early evidence. It is extremely improbable that such a custom existed.—*That Vashti* [𝕾 + the Queen] (the omission of Queen after Vashti's name in 𝕳 is intentional) *may not come* [𝕵 𝕾 𝕲 + again] *before King Xerxes* [𝕿¹ + and if she comes before the King, let the King decree that her head be cut off.] This is the law that the King is advised to enact. Thus, as 𝕿² emphasizes, Mᵉmûkhân secures that Vashti may have no chance to reinstate herself in the King's favour and then to avenge herself on her enemies.—*And her place as Queen let the King give to another who is better than she.*] This is not part of the law, but a suggestion that makes its enactment easier. The King will readily find another woman to take Vashti's place. *Place as Queen*, lit. *kingdom*, or *royalty*, is in an emphatic position. *Another*, lit. *fellow*, or *companion*, is not necessarily one of the palace-women, for *fellow*, whether male or female, is used in the widest way of any person who belongs in the same category with another (*cf.* 1 S. 15²⁸, "Yahweh hath given the kingdom to thy fellow," *i.e.*, to another person; also Ex. 11² 1 S. 28¹⁷). *Better* may mean either *more beautiful*, or *more virtuous*. From the context it must mean here *more obedient*.

20. *And when the King's decree which he makes shall be heard in all his kingdom*]. Having suggested how Vashti may be punished for her offence against the King and the nation, Mᵉmûkhân now proceeds to show how the effect of her bad example may be counteracted by making her punishment as widely known as her disobedience. *In all his kingdom* is more naturally connected with *heard* than with *makes*.—*Though it be great*], *i.e.*, the kingdom, not the decree, as 𝔊¹ takes it, for *decree* is m. and *great* is f. (*cf.* Albrecht, *ZATW*. xvi. (1896), p. 115). This flattering parenthetical remark serves no other purpose than to expand the idea already expressed in *all*.—*Then all the women from great to small will give* [L 𝔊¹ + reverence and] *honour to their husbands*.] Xerxes' empire is so great that it includes practically *all the women*. *From great to small* means here, as in v.⁵, *from high to low*, both the ladies and the common women (*cf.* 1¹⁷ᶠ·); so Vrss., Schu., Sieg., Haupt. Other comm. translate less correctly *from old to young*. With this v. Mᵉmûkhān's speech ends. The comm. indulge in much speculation as to the reason for the severity of his advice. 𝔊², in the passage previously quoted, says that he had had trouble with his own wife, and wished to discipline her by this indirect method. *Mid.* thinks that he had a personal grudge against Vashti; either she had struck him in the face with a shoe-lace, because it says, "Not against the King alone hath Vashti sinned"; or she had not invited his wife to her feast, because it says, "The conduct of the Queen will become known to all the women"; or he thought that he could get his own daughter made Queen, because it says, "Let the King give her place as Queen to another." Others think that the viziers as a body were jealous of Vashti's influence; so Cas., who gives numerous instances of the way in which Turkish viziers have intrigued against favourites. Most comm. suppose that Mᵉmûkhān advised what he knew Xerxes wished to hear, and compare the servility of Cambyses' counsellors, Her. iii. 31. There is much discussion among the older comm. as to whether Xerxes was justified in putting Vashti away on this occasion. The arguments on both sides may be found in Par. *ad loc.*

16. המלך] αὐτὸν L: + ܀ܣܡܠ 𝔖.—והשרים] + καὶ τοὺς ἡγουμένους τοῦ βασιλέως 44, 106: καὶ πάντας τοὺς ἄρχοντας 64: καὶ πρὸς τοὺς ἄρχοντας 248, C, Ald.: λέγων L.—לבדו] om. 64.—עותה] ܚܛܐ 𝔖: ἠτίμασεν A. This is a denom. from עָו 'sin,' found only in Aram. and late Heb. Construed with עַל ἀ.λ.—ושתי] om. 44, 106.—כל] om. L 𝔏.—ועל כל העמים] καὶ τοὺς ἡγουμένους 𝔊: Περσῶν καὶ Μήδων L: om. 44, 106: *et gentes* 𝔏.

THE ADVICE OF THE MINISTERS 159

אשר-מדינות—] om. L 𝕲 𝕷.—המלך [³ om. L 𝕷.—אחשורוש] om. L 𝕲: Haupt deletes.

דבר המלכה [17. כי .—𝕷 ‎ܒܠܗ ‎𝕾: καὶ γάρ 𝕲: καὶ L.—יצא] + ‎ܒܠܗ ‎𝕾.
ἡ ἀδικία αὐτῆς L: eo contumelia regis 𝕷.—על כל הנשים] + ‎ܠܗܘܢ ‎ܟܠܗܘܢ
𝕾: αὐτοῖς 𝕲: εἰς πάντας τοὺς λαούς L: etiam ab omnibus mulieribus 𝕷: instead of על Haupt reads אל, but the two are often confused in late Heb.—להבזות-לפניו] om. 𝕲 L.—להבזות] ‎ܢܫܬܛܘܢ ‎𝕾: quod contemnat 𝕷: Hiph. inf. cstr., ἀ.λ.—באמרם] the m. suf. is used because men and women alike will say this. Even if the suffix referred to the women alone, the m. form would be possible.—המלך] regina 𝕷.—אחשורוש-לפניו] om. 𝕷.—אחשורוש] Haupt deletes.—להביא] inf. cstr. w. ל after אמר, as in 6¹, frequent in late Heb., but also 1 S. 24¹¹.—ולא באה] καὶ ὡς ἀντεῖπεν τῷ βασιλεῖ ὡς οὖν ἀντεῖπεν τῷ βασιλεῖ Ἀρταξέρξῃ 𝕲: ὅτι ἠκύρωσε τὸ πρόσταγμα τοῦ βασιλέως L: neglexit enim et contempsit 𝕷: the reading of 𝕲 is a combination of two parallel texts.

18. om. L.—והיום הזה] exemplo hoc 𝕵: ‎ܒܗܢܐ ‎𝕾: quomodo non 𝕷.— תאמרנה] parvipendentes omnes 𝕵: ‎ܢܐܡܪ̈ܢ ‎𝕾: τολμήσουσιν (καὶ αὐταί) ὁμοίως ἀτιμάσαι 𝕲: negligent et contumeliam facient 𝕷. Instead of האמרנה we should probably read תמרנה, Qal or Hiph. from מרה 'rebel,' or, less probably, from מרר 'be bitter.' In that case it may be necessary to read בכל instead of לכל, but the change is perhaps unnecessary in this late Heb.—שרות] αἱ τυραννίδες αἱ λοιπαὶ τῶν ἀρχόντων 𝕲: ‎ܘܪܘܪ̈ܒܢܐ ‎𝕾.—פרס—] some codd. incorrectly פרס.—ומרדי] om. 𝕷.—אשר-המלכה] om. 𝕵: ἀκούσασαι τὰ τῷ βασιλεῖ λεχθέντα ὑπ' αὐτῆς 𝕲: aut quomodo non infamia tradetur adversus regem 𝕷: Haupt deletes.—לכל] imperia 𝕵: ‎ܡܠܟܗܝ ‎𝕾:om. 𝕲 𝕷.—שרי המלך] maritorum 𝕵: τοὺς ἄνδρας αὐτῶν 𝕲: viris suis L.—וכדי-וקצף] om. 𝕲: unde regis justa est indignatio 𝕵: etiam his qui extra regnum sunt 𝕷: ‎ܣܓܝܐܬܐ ‎ܡܣܟܬܐ ‎𝕾: ומי ייכול לוברא כמיסח חוך דין ורגוז 𝕿¹. No help can be gained from the Vrss., all of which fail to understand this phrase. Haupt's conjecture of כדי instead of וכדי is probably correct. In Jb. 39²⁵ בדי is used in the sense of 'whenever,' for which ordinarily we find מדי (1 S. 1⁷ 18³⁰ 1 K. 14²⁸ 2 Ch. 12¹¹ 2 K. 4⁸ Is. 28¹⁹ Je. 31²⁰). In that case ו before קצף must be regarded as introducing the predicate (Kau. § 143 d).—בזיון] ἀ.λ. from בזה 'despise.'—על] late Heb. for אל (cf. 1¹⁷ 3⁹ 5⁴. ⁸ 7³).

19. [הלמך] tibi 𝕵: τῷ κυρίῳ ἡμῶν L: tibi maxime rex 𝕷.—יצא-מלפניו] προσταξάτω βασιλικὸν 𝕲: jube 𝕷: om. L.—מלכות] used frequently in Est. in the sense of 'royalty' as a substitute for מלך, e.g., 1⁷· ⁹ 2¹⁶ 5¹ 6⁸ 8¹⁵.—ויכתב-יעבור] γραφήτω εἰς πάσας τὰς χώρας καὶ πρὸς πάντα τὰ ἔθνη καὶ γνωσθήτω L.—בדתי] κατὰ τοὺς νόμους 𝕲.—פרס ומדי] so N 55, 93b, 249 א ᶜ· ᵃ: Μήδων καὶ Περσῶν 𝕲.—ולא יעבור] et de malitia Vasthi reginæ quomodo abusa sit te 𝕷.—יעבור] in the sense of 'pass away,' 'cease to exist,' as in 9²⁷ ᶠ· (BDB. 718 § 6). In the parallel passage, Dn. 6⁹, the Aram. equivalent is עדא.—אשר לא תבוא] pr. ‎ܘܬܥܘܠ ‎𝕾: μηδὲ εἰσελ-

θάτω ἔτι 𝔊: ἠθετηκυῖα L: *quoniam non introiit* 𝔏.—וישתי] + מחכמא
𝔖: ἡ βασίλισσα 𝔊: om. 𝔏.—לפני-אחשורוש] so A, 93*b* under *, 𝔏: πρὸς αὐτόν 𝔊: τὸν λόγον τοῦ βασιλέως L: Haupt deletes אחשורוש.—ממנה] *et meliori* 𝔏.

20. [ונשמע-מלכותו] καὶ φαινέσθω ὑπακούουσα τῆς φωνῆς τοῦ βασιλέως καὶ ποιήσει ἀγαθὸν πάσαις ταῖς βασιλείαις L.—פִּתְגָם] פִּתְגָּם Ba. G: פְּתָגָם al.: ὁ λόγος A: *verbo* 𝔏: *hoc* 𝔍. This is a loan-word from the O. Pers. *patigâma* (*cf.* BDB. 834; Marti, *Aram. Gram.* p. 79); here cstr. in spite of the long vowel in the ultima.—יעשה-המלך] om. 𝔍.—אשר] 𝔖. ○.—[נכל om. 𝔊.—מלכותו] om. suffix 𝔖.—כי רבה היא] *quoniam verum est* 𝔏: om. 𝔊 𝔏: כי is concessive, 'although,' as Je. 4³⁰ 14¹² 49¹⁶. ¹⁹ ᶠ. 50¹¹ Ho. 13¹⁵ Zc. 8⁶ Ps. 37²⁴ 49¹⁹ ᶠ. 137³ Na. 1¹⁰ 2³ (*cf.* BDB. p. 473, 2 *c*).—[וכל + יקר.—𝔊 οὕτως + καὶ δόξαν L.—למגדול] tr. w. next 𝔊 L 𝔏.

XERXES ACTS ACCORDING TO THIS ADVICE (1²¹⁻²²).

21. *And the advice seemed good to the King and the viziers, and the King acted in accordance with the advice of M^emûkhān*], *i.e.*, he accepted both propositions, to degrade Vashti, and to send notice of this decree throughout the kingdom. In regard to the execution of the first proposition no details are given. Vashti does not appear again in the story, and the book does not inform us what became of her. 𝔗¹, 𝔗², and Jewish comm. hold that she was put to death. The execution of the second proposition follows in the next v.

22. *And he sent dispatches* [𝔗¹ + written and sealed with his seal] *unto all the King's provinces*]. *Cf.* 3¹²⁻¹⁵ 8⁹⁻¹⁴. According to Her. v. 14, viii. 98; Xen. *Cyrop.* viii. 6, 17, the Persian empire had a highly organized system of posts.—*Unto every single province in its script, and unto every single race in its language*]. A vast number of languages were spoken in the Persian empire in the time of Xerxes. In Persia itself there were the Iranian dialects spoken by the ruling race, and the Elamitic, Babylonian, and Aramæan dialects of the older subject-races. The inscriptions of Xerxes and other Achæmenian rulers at Persepolis and elsewhere are mostly trilingual, containing in parallel columns Old Persian, Babylonian, and Susian. In India, Sanskrit and cognate tongues were spoken, together with numerous Dravidian and other aboriginal languages. In Babylonia and Assyria, Assyrian was spoken, together with Aramaic and possible survivals in certain quarters of Sumerian and Kassite. In Armenia there was old Vanic, along with later Indo-European dialects; in Asia Minor, Greek, together with Lydian, Carian, Cappadocian, and a host of other aboriginal tongues. In Mesopotamia and Syria, Aramaic prevailed, and also in Palestine, although Phœnician and other local idioms still held their own. East and south of Canaan Arabic was spoken; and in Egypt, Egyptian. It is inconceivable that Xerxes should have had at his court scribes who were able to write all these and the other languages that were spoken in various parts of the empire. We have no evidence that this was Persian custom, and the trilingual inscriptions of Persepolis lend no support to the idea. Even in Assyrian days Aramaic had become the language of trade and of diplomacy, and in the Persian period was ordinarily employed for official dispatches, *cf.*, for instance, the Aramaic letter of the Jewish Chief of Elephantine in Egypt to the Persian governor Bagoas lately published by Sachau in *Drei aramäische Papyrusurkunden aus Elephantine* (1907).

[𝕌¹ + And he proclaimed and spoke thus: You, O peoples, nations, and tongues, who dwell in all my dominion, be advised] *that every man should show himself ruler in his own house*], lit., *unto each man's becoming ruler*. This clause gives the contents of the dispatches.—*And should* [𝕌¹ + compel his wife to] *speak according to the tongue* [𝕌¹ + of her husband and according to the speech of] *his people*]. This clause has given great perplexity to the Vrss. and comm. 𝕌¹, 𝕌², *Mid.*, RaShI, IE., and Jewish comm. generally understand it to mean, that, if a man has married a wife of another race, he is to compel her to speak his language, instead of speaking hers (*cf.* Ne. 13²³ ᶠ·); so Pisc., Dieu., Gen., Baum., Keil, Schu., Haupt, *al.* Pag., J. & T., Cler., and many of the older comm. and versions, supply an object for *speak* from the preceding clause and translate, *and should proclaim it* (*the dispatch*) *in the language of his people;* so AV. and RV.; similarly Oet., except that he points the ptc. as a passive. This is an impossible rendering of the Hebrew, and the idea which it yields is irrelevant. What we expect, is not directions for the promulgation of the decree, but for a man's regulation of his household. If the text be sound, it must be rendered as the Jewish comm. have done. It cannot be denied that this yields a passable sense, still it is not what we should expect in this connection. Haupt regards it as a late gloss, meaning that he is to talk plainly to her. Most modern comm. regard the text as corrupt. Maur. makes no attempt to emend it. Bött. also offers no suggestion. Hitzig, in a private communication to Bert., makes a slight alteration in the text and reads, *and should speak what suited him*. This emendation meets the approval of Bert., Raw., Rys., Buhl. Wild. and Sieg. mention it with reserve. Scho. finds a historical interpretation impossible, and concludes that the passage is symbolic of the gift of tongues at Pentecost (see note). The absurdity of this solemn edict commanding wives to obey their husbands struck even the doctors of the Talmud. Raba said: "If this first letter had not been written, the enemies would have left nothing of Israel. But the people said, What sort of decree is this that is sent unto us, that every man should show himself ruler in his own house? Even the weaver is master in his own house (so when the decree came to destroy Israel they took it also as a joke)" (*Meg.* 12*b*).

21. [הדבר] + בן הם 𝔖.—[בעיני] ἐν καρδίᾳ L.—[ויהשר] ס + suff. סום 𝔖: om. L.—[המלך] ἑτοίμως L.—[נדבר] καθὰ ἐλάλησεν 𝔊 𝔏: τὸν λόγον L.—[ממוכן] Mamuchan 𝔍: ܡܟܘܟܢ 𝔖: Μουχαιος 𝔊: *Mardochæus* 𝔏: τοῦτον L.

22. om L—[וישלח] + ὁ βασιλεὺς Α א c a mg 93*b* und * 𝔏.—[ספרים] om. 𝔊. ספר is an ancient loan-word from As. *šipru*, 'sending,' 'missive,' then 'letter.' It occurs frequently in the sense of 'letter' in the *Tell-el-Amarna Letters*. The root *šapâru* from which it comes is ph. itself a Shaphel from פר (see Haupt, *a. l.*). In Est. it is commonly used in the sense of 'letter' (*cf.* 3¹³ 8⁵· ¹⁰ 9²⁰· ²⁵· ³⁰). In 2²³ 6¹ 9³² 10² it means a book in scroll form—[מדינות המלך] *provincias regni sui* 𝔍: τὴν βασιλείαν 𝔊: *regno suo* 𝔏.—[ומדינה] so A: om. 𝔊 𝔖: *gens* 𝔍.—[ככתבה] κατὰ τὴν λέξιν αὐτῶν 𝔊: *secundum interpretationes eorum* 𝔏: *audire et legere poterat* 𝔍: + κατὰ τὸ γράμμα αὐτῆς 93*b* under *.—[ואל־כלשונו] so 93*b* under *: om. 𝔊 𝔏: *diversis linguis et litteris* 𝔍.—[להיות־בביתו] *esse viros principes ac majores in domibus suis* 𝔍: ὥστε εἶναι φόβον αὐτοῖς ἐν ταῖς οἰκίαις αὐτῶν 𝔊: *ut esset unusquisque in domum suam* 𝔏.—[להיות] inf. w. ל introducing the contents of the dispatches as in 3¹³ 8¹³. An Aram. construction found in late Heb.—[שרר] denominative from שר 'officer,' 'ruler,' ptc., ἀ.λ.—[ומדבר־עמו] so 93*b* under *: om. 𝔊: *et fuit timor magnus in omni muliere* 𝔏: *et hoc per cunctos populos divulgari* 𝔍.

𐤔, 𝕿¹, and 𝕿² presuppose the same text as 𝕳. Hitzig's emendation, וּמְדַבֵּר כָּל־שָׁוֶה עַמּוֹ, which he translates, 'and should speak everything that he pleased,' is unlikely, because שָׁוֶה means 'fitting,' 'proper,' rather than 'acceptable,' 'pleasing,' and because it is construed with לְ and not with עִם (cf. 3⁸ 5¹³). Haupt reads בלשׁן instead of כלשׁון, and deletes the whole clause as a gloss.

THE CHOICE OF ESTHER TO BE QUEEN (2¹⁻²³).

XERXES RESOLVES TO SEEK A SUCCESSOR FOR VASHTI (2¹⁻⁴).

1. *After these events* [𝕿¹ + when he had grown sober, and had slept off his wine-debauch, and] *when the anger of King Xerxes had subsided*]. 𝕿¹ suggests that Vashti's condemnation occurred while the King was still drunk, but 𝕳 indicates rather that this decree was made at a later meeting of the Privy Council (*cf.* 1¹³). The drunkenness was over when the decree was made, but the anger lasted longer.—*He* [𝕲 + no longer] *remembered* [𝔖 + Queen] *Vashti and* [𝕲 + was mindful of] [𝔖 + all] *that she had done and* [𝔖 + all] *that had been decreed against her*.

[*Mid.* + Then he broke out in anger against her and caused her to be put to death] [𝕿¹ + Then his officers answered and spoke thus: Art not thou he who didst condemn her to death on account of what she did? And the King said to them: I did not decree that she should be slain, but only that she should come into my presence; but when she did not enter, I commanded to deprive her of royal dignity. They answered him: It is not so, but thou didst pronounce sentence of death upon her at the advice of the seven viziers. At this his anger waxed hot.] [𝕿² + He sent and called all the officers and said to them: Not against Queen Vashti am I angry, but against you am I angry because of the sentence. I spoke a word in wine; why have you urged me to slay Queen Vashti and to remove her name from the kingdom? I also will slay you, and will remove your names from the kingdom.] [𝕿¹ + And he commanded that the seven viziers should be hanged upon the gallows.] [Jos.¹⁹⁵ + But being lovingly disposed toward her, and not bearing the separation, he nevertheless could not now be reconciled to her; so he was grieving over the things that he wished to accomplish as impossible.]

Comm. differ as to the sense in which *remembered* is to be understood. 𝕿¹, 𝕿², and *Mid.* take it in the sense of *recalled unfavourably*, and so gain a basis for the idea that he inflicted further punishment upon her. The same conception underlies the interpolations of 𝕲. This view gains some support from the following words, *what she had done and what had been decreed against her*, but it is in conflict with the context. *When his anger had subsided* suggests that he was ready to be reconciled, and the advice of the servants contemplates the same possibility. Accordingly, RaShI, IE., Ashk., Men., Bon., take *remembered Vashti* in the sense of *called her beauty to mind,* and understand the rest of the v. as referring to the good that she had done on other occasions and the honour that the King had once put upon her; but the words *what had been decreed* can scarcely refer to anything else than the irrevocable condemnation that had just been published. For this reason, Jos., Drus., Cler., and most modern comm. take the clause to mean that Xerxes had the rejection of Vashti constantly in mind and was uncomfortable on account of it. Vit. and Pisc. take *remembered* in the sense of *made mention of*, and thus find a reason for the remark of the servants in the next v.

2. *Then said the King's pages who waited upon him*]. The courtiers make haste to drive Vashti out of the King's mind, lest she may return to power and their lives be endangered. From the non-mention of the viziers here and subsequently, 𝕿¹ and 𝕿² infer that they had been put to death.

[𝕿² + After she was killed, in order that he might not remember Vashti, and what she had done, and what had been decreed against her: Vashti did not deserve a sentence of death, but this was the will of Heaven in order to destroy the seed of Nebuchadnezzar, King of Babylon.] [Jos. 195 + Let the King cast out the memory of his wife and his useless love for her, and let him send through the whole inhabited world.]

And let there be sought for [𝕿¹ + *the use of*] *the King beautiful young virgins*], lit., *girls, virgins, good of looks.* Only virgins might be taken by the King (1 K. 1²), as by the High Priest (Lev. 21¹³ ᶠ·). Vv. ³⁻⁴ explain in detail how this plan for gathering virgins is to be carried out.

3. *And let the King appoint commissioners in all the provinces of his kingdom*]. *Meg.* 12b contrasts the account of the seeking for a young virgin for David (1 K. 1²⁻⁴). In that case no commissioners were necessary, for men brought their daughters gladly. In this case the King had to appoint officers to search, because men hid their daughters from him.—*And let them gather all the beautiful young virgins*], lit., *every virgin*. *Gather unto* is a pregnant construction for *gather and bring unto*.—[𝔍 𝔏 + And bring them] *unto Susa the fortress*]. *Cf.* 1². —*Unto the house of the women* [𝔗¹ + where there are hot baths and swimming-baths]. *Cf.* 2¹¹· ¹³. According to Dieulafoy, *the house of the women*, or harem, lay in the N. W. corner of the palace-enclosure (*cf.* 1⁵).— [𝔊 𝔏 L + And deliver them] *into the charge of Hēghē, the King's* [𝔗¹ + chief] *eunuch, the keeper of the women*]. Here, as in 1¹⁰, only eunuchs have access to the women's apartments. On the name *Hēghē*, see p. 69.—*And let him give their cosmetics* [𝔊 𝔍 + and the other things that they need], *i.e.*, for the twelvemonth's process of beautification that they have to undergo before they can be presented to the King (*cf.* 2¹²).

4. *And the girl who pleases the King, let her reign instead of Vashti*, [Jos.¹⁹⁶ + for his longing for his former wife will be quenched, if he introduces another; and his affection for her gradually diminishing, will turn to the one that is with him.] The courtiers realize that the only way to get the King to forget Vashti is to make him fall in love with another woman. The gathering of the maidens will divert him, and out of the number they hope that one will win his heart.—*And the advice seemed good to the King and he* [L + readily] *acted thus* [𝔍 + as they had suggested]. This method of selecting a queen is in the highest degree improbable. According to the Avesta, the King might marry only a Persian. According to Her. iii. 84, his wife must come from one of seven noble families; but by this plan of the pages a woman of low birth from one of the subject-races might come to the throne. Such a scheme may have been followed to obtain concubines, but surely never to select the Queen of Persia. One wonders why another of the wives, that Xerxes already had, was not elevated to Vashti's place.

1. אחשורוש–אחר] om. L.—אחר] καὶ μετὰ 𝔊.—כשך] ἐκόπασεν 𝔊: *cf.* כשבת 1². שכך (*cf.* 7¹⁰) is used of the subsiding of waters, Gn. 8¹. *Mid.* infers from כ that it was not a real subsidence, but only 'like' one.—[אחשורוש] so א c. a mg, 93*b* under *: om. 𝔊 𝔏: Haupt deletes.—[זכר] καὶ οὐκέτι ἐμνήσθη 𝔊 (καὶ οὐκέτι under ÷ 93*b*): ἐμνήσθη γὰρ A: καὶ οὕτως ἔστη τοῦ μνημονεύειν L: to end of v. om. 𝔏.—[וישחי] *cf.* 1:9.—[ואת] om. ו 𝔊: ܟܠܗܝܢ 𝔖.—[עשתה] ἐλάλησεν 𝔊: ἐποίησεν A L.—[ואת־עליה]2 καὶ ὡς κατέκρινεν αὐτήν 𝔊: Ἀσσυήρῳ τῷ βασιλεῖ L: ὅσα αὐτῇ κατεκρίθη A.—[ואת]2 ܟܠܗܝܢ 𝔖.—[נגזר] ἀ.λ., an Aramaism.

2. [ויאמרו] + ܟܠܗ 𝔖.—[המלך] πρὸς τὸν βασιλέα A: *ejus* 𝔏.—[משרתיו] pr. ס 𝔖: om. 𝔊 L 𝔏 (93*b* has under *).—[יבקשו] ζητηθήτω 𝔊: *quaerantur* 𝔏: ζητήσωμεν L: the subj. is impersonal, 'let them seek'= 'let there be sought,' as 𝔊 𝔏.—[למלך נערות] om. L 𝔏.—[נערות בתולת] *cf.* Dt. 22:23 Ju. 21:12.—[בתולת] so C: בתולות Ba. G: ἄφθορα 𝔊.

3. [מלכותו] om. 𝔍 𝔖.—[פקידים] om. 𝔍.—[המלך] om. 𝔏 L.—[ויפקד־טובת] om. 𝔍 𝔖: om. ו A.—[ויקבצו] ἐπιδειξάτωσαν A.—[את כל] om. 𝔊 𝔍. Kau. § 117*d*, Sieg., delete את because the obj. is undefined. Haupt, on the other hand, defends its correctness and compares Ec. 3:11. 15 7:7.—[מראה־הנשים] om. L: *et adducant eas ad civitatem Susan et tradant eas in domum feminarum* 𝔍: *et perducantur in Susis Thebari in conspectu mulierum* 𝔏.—[אל־הבירה] om. 𝔖.—[אל יד] ܟܠܗ 𝔖: καὶ παραδοθήτωσαν 𝔊: *et tradentur* 𝔏: καὶ δοθήτωσαν προστατεῖσθαι ὑπὸ χεῖρα L.—[אל] Or. MSS., על to end of v. Haupt deletes as a gloss derived from v. 8.—[הגא] so S N² Br. C B¹ G Ba.: הגֶא N¹ B² M Norzi: *Egei* 𝔍: ܗܢ 𝔖: om. 𝔊 (v.8 Γαί): Γωγαίου L.—[המלך] *qui est propositus et* 𝔍: om. 𝔖 L.—[הנשים] + *regiarum* 𝔍.—[ונתון] ܟܠܗܝܢ 𝔖: om. L: + αὐταῖς 44, 71, 74, 76, 106, 120, 236: inf. abs. instead of the finite vb., as 6:9 and often in Est. (*cf.* Kau. § 113, 2).—[תמרקיהן] so Norzi, Mich. N² B² G: תמרוקיהן N¹ S Br. C B¹ Ba.: om. L: from מרק 'scour,' 'polish,' lit. 'their rubbings': σμῆγμα 𝔊: *et nitores* 𝔏: *mundum* 𝔍: ܟܠܗ ܠ 𝔖: סמתר משחהון 𝔗¹.

4. [וייטב־המלך] om. 𝔏.—[ויעש] + ἑτοίμως L.

MORDECAI AND ESTHER ARE INTRODUCED TO THE READER (2⁵⁻⁷).

5. *A man of Judah had been living in Susa the fortress.* [𝔗² + He was called a Judæan because he was sinless; and concerning him David prophesied and said, This day a hero dies in Israel and one who was a just man.] The abrupt transition is designed to make the new actor in the story more conspicuous. *A man of Judah*, lit. *a man, a Judæan*, is placed before the predicate to render it emphatic. Mordecai is here called a man of Judah, although in the next clause he is said to belong to the tribe of Benjamin, because, after the fall of the northern kingdom, Judah gave its name to the nation; and, during the Exile and subsequently,

BIOGRAPHY OF MORDECAI 167

men of all the tribes were known as Jews, *i.e.*, Judæans. This obvious explanation is ignored by *Meg.* 12*b*, 13*a*, which offers a number of far-fetched interpretations. On *Susa the fortress, cf.* 1². How this Jew happened to be in the *fortress* (not the city) *of Susa*, the book does not explain. 𝕲 (in A²) and 𝕿¹ say that he was one of the officers of the King. This conjecture, which is based upon the fact that in 2¹⁹ 3² he sits in the King's gate and appears among the courtiers, has been followed by many comm. According to Jos., he lived, not in Susa, but in Babylon (see v. ¹¹).—*And his name was Mordecai*]. On this name and the historical identifications proposed for it, see p. 88.—*Son of Jair, son of Shimei*,

[𝕿² + He was the Shimei who cursed David, King of Israel, and said to King David, Go out, thou wicked man, and man worthy of death. Then answered Abishai son of Zeruiah and said to David, Let me go up and take off Shimei's head. But David discerned prophetically that Mordecai would spring from him; and because King David perceived this, he commanded his son Solomon, and said to his son Solomon, that he should slay Shimei, when he had ceased from begetting sons, that he might triumph and go to Heaven; and because from him should spring a righteous son by whose hands should be wrought signs and wonders in their four captivities. . . . Shimei was put to death justly, because it is written in the law of Moses, "A just judge thou shalt not despise, and shalt not curse a ruler of thy people"; but he cursed David, King of Israel. But David spared him and did not put him to death, because he saw that two saints would spring from him, through whom deliverance would come to the house of Israel. (𝕿¹ has a similar, though briefer interpolation.)]

The son of Kish]. *Jair, Shimei,* and *Kish* are regarded by Cler., Ramb., Raw., as the immediate ancestors of Mordecai; and in the case of *Jair* this view may be correct. By all the older comm., as by Jos., *Meg.*, 𝕿¹, 𝕿², and *Mid.*, *Shimei* and *Kish* are regarded as remote ancestors; one, the Shimei of 2 S. 16⁵ ᶠᶠ· 1 K. 2⁸· ³⁶⁻⁴⁰; the other, Kish the father of Saul (1 S. 9¹ 14⁵¹ 1 Ch. 8³³). This view is probably correct. Haman, the enemy of Mordecai, is of the family of Agag, whom Saul overthrew (1 S. 15); and, therefore, in this genealogy it is probably the author's intention to represent the victorious Mordecai as of the family of Saul. For this reason he wastes no time on the intermediate links, but leaps back at once to the well-known Shimei and Kish of 1 S. Scho. follows *Meg.* in allegorizing all these names as epithets of Mordecai.

[𝕿² + son of Shemida, son of Baanah, son of Elah, son of Micha, son of Mephibosheth, son of Jonathan, son of Saul, son of Kish, son of Abiel, son of Zeror, son of Bechorath, son of Aphiah, son of Shecarith, son of Uzziah, son of Shishak, son of Michael, son of Eliel, son of Ammihud, son of Shephatiah, son of Pethuel, son of Pithon, son of Meloch, son of Jerubbaal, son of Jehoram, son of Hananiah, son of Zabdi, son of Eliphael, son of Shimri, son of Zebadiah, son of Merimoth, son of Hushim, son of Shechorah, son of Gezah, son of Bela, son of Benjamin, son of Jacob, the first-born, whose name was called Israel (similarly 𝕿¹ after 7⁶).]

A Benjamite [𝕿¹ + a righteous and penitent man, who prayed to God for his people,] [Jos.[198] + one of the chief men among the Jews,] [𝕲 (A²) + a great man, who served in the court of the King]. By the addition of *Benjamite* the author identifies Mordecai's ancestors with the ancient Shimei and Kish, who belonged to the tribe of Benjamin, and carries back the genealogy to one of the sons of Jacob.

6. *Who had been carried away from Jerusalem with the exiles who were deported with Jeconiah, King of Judah, whom Nebuchadnezzar, King of Babylon, took captive*]. Jeconiah (*cf.* Je. 24¹ 27²⁰ 28⁴ 29² 1 Ch. 3¹⁶ ᶠ·) is an alternate form of Jehoiachin, the name of the last but one of the kings of Judah (2 K. 24⁶⁻¹⁷). He came to the throne and was deported by Nebuchadnezzar (in older documents more correctly Nebuchadrezzar) in 596 B.C. According to Burg. in Estius, West., Patr., Cler., Ramb., Raw., the relative pronoun *who* refers, not to Mordecai, but to his great-grandfather Kish. Against this view are the facts, that, as just remarked, Kish is probably not an immediate ancestor, but is the father of King Saul; and that Heb. usage demands the reference of *who* to Mordecai. The appositives *ben Jair, ben Shimei, ben Kish,* like Johnson or Jackson, serve merely as surnames to Mordecai. If, however, Mordecai himself was carried away with Jehoiachin in 596, he must have been at least 113 years old in the third year of Xerxes (483 B.C.), supposing him to have been an infant in arms at the time of his deportation. When he became grand vizier in

BIOGRAPHY OF MORDECAI

the twelfth year of Xerxes (3^7 8^2), he was at least 122 years old. An appointment at such an age seems very unlikely, although most Jewish and some Christian comm. have not hesitated to accept it. This difficulty has led many of the older critics to identify Ahasuerus with Cyaxares, Darius, or one of the early kings of Persia. Such identifications are, however, impossible (see p. 51). 𝔊, 𝔏, Esti., Grot., Men., Mar., May., Kamp., Bert., Keil, Schu., Oet., think that *carried captive* means only that his ancestors were exiled by Nebuchadnezzar, and compare Gn. 46^{27}, where the sons of Joseph are spoken of as coming to Egypt with Jacob, although they were born in Egypt; Ezr. $2^{2\,ff.}$ Ne. $7^{7\,ff.}$, where the later inhabitants of Jerusalem are said to have returned with Joshua and Zerubbabel; Heb. $7^{9\,f.}$, where Levi pays tithes in the loins of Abraham. These cases, however, are not parallel, and the fact remains that *who was carried captive* is not a natural way of saying *whose ancestors were carried captive*. Most recent comm. frankly admit that the author has here made a blunder in his chronology. So Wild., Sieg., Stre. (see p. 73).

> [𝔗² + But Mordecai went back again with the people who freely offered themselves to rebuild the House of the Second Sanctuary. Then Nebuchadnezzar, King of Babylon, carried him captive a second time, and then in the land of the children of the captivity his soul did not cease from signs and wonders.] [𝔗¹ + But when Cyrus and Darius carried Babylon captive, Mordecai went forth from Babylon, with Daniel and the whole company of Israel who were there in Babylon, and they went forth and came with King Cyrus to dwell in Susa the fortress.]

These additions assume, as also IE. and Light., that Mordecai is identical with the Mordecai of Ezr. 2^2 Ne. 7^7, who returned to Jerusalem with Zerubbabel. In these passages his name is followed by Bilshan, from which it is inferred that he spoke many tongues. According to *Meg.* 10b, 15a, *Hul.* 139b, he was identical with Malachi, and prophesied in the second year of Darius. According to *Shek.* v. 1, *Men.* 64b–65a, he was a member of the Great Sanhedrin and was able to speak seventy languages. He decided all difficult matters of the Law, and, therefore, was known as Pethahiah. According to 𝔊 (A^2), he was a high official of the

King. According to *Meg.* 12*a*, he and Haman were the two chief cup-bearers. Other legendary embellishments of his history will be noted in connection with later passages of the book (*cf.* Seligsohn, Art. "Mordecai," in *JE.*).

7. *And he had adopted Hadassah, she is Esther*]. In *Meg.* 13*a*, 𝕿¹, 𝕿², and later Jewish comm., opinions differ as to whether *Hadassah* or *Esther* was the original name. Those who hold that *Esther* was original, regard *Hadassah*, 'myrtle,' as a title, and suppose that it was given to her, either because she was of medium height like a myrtle; or because the righteous are compared to myrtles (Zc. 1¹⁰); or because Is. 55¹³ says, "instead of the brier shall come up the myrtle," *i.e.*, instead of Vashti shall come up Esther; or because the myrtle does not dry up in summer or winter, so Esther enjoyed both this life and the life to come. Those who hold that *Hadassah* was original regard *Esther* as a title given because she concealed (*sāthar*) her nationality. Only R. Nehemiah (*Meg.* 13*a*) seems to have suggested that the name *Esther* was given by the Persians, "because the tribes of the earth called her by the name of *Istahar*," *i.e.*, Pers. *sitâr*, 'star,' particularly the planet Venus, the Babylonian *Ishtar* (*cf.* Levy, *Neuheb. W.-B.*, *s. v.*); similarly 𝕿². This view has been followed by the older Christian comm., namely, that *Hadassah* was the girl's original Heb. name and *Esther* her Persian name, or the name that she received when she became Queen. For the modern view, according to which *Esther* is the same as the Bab. goddess *Ishtar*, and *Hadassah* a Bab. title of this goddess, see p. 88.

The daughter of [𝕲 + Amminadab] *his paternal uncle* [𝕷 + and Mordecai had cherished her like an adopted daughter]. That is, Esther was an own cousin of Mordecai, not his niece, as is persistently stated incorrectly by the comm. Those who suppose that Mordecai was carried captive with Jehoiachin, and that he was now upward of 120 years old, have some difficulty in explaining how his own cousin Esther, who must have been at least 50 or 60, should have been so beautiful as to have won the heart of Xerxes. Jewish comm. explain it by the hypothesis that Esther, like Sarah, remained perennially young; Christian comm. by the assertion that in the seclusion and care of an Oriental harem, beauty lasts

BIOGRAPHY OF MORDECAI

to an extreme age (?). Others suggest that Mordecai's uncle may have been 20 years younger than his father, and that he may have taken a young wife when he was 60 years old. 𝔏 and 𝕵 avoid the difficulty by making Esther's father the *brother*, not the *uncle*, of Mordecai. That the word *uncle* can have the wider sense of *kinsman*, has not been proved. According to 2[15] his name was Abîḥayil, for which 𝕲 here and elsewhere substitutes Amminadab.—*For she had neither father nor mother* [𝕿[1] + when her father died, she was left in her mother's womb; and as soon as her mother had borne her, she died also]. This addition, which is found also in *Mid.*, is based by *Meg.* 13*a* upon the repetition in 7[b] of the statement that her father and mother had died.

And the girl had a fine figure and was [𝕵 𝔏 L + very] *good looking,* [Jos.[199] + so that she drew the eyes of all beholders upon her]. [*Meg.* 12*b* + She was neither tall nor short, but of moderate height like a myrtle. Her complexion was sallow, but she had charms.] According to some of the Rabbis, the four beautiful women of the world were Sarah, Rahab, Abigail, and Esther, but others gave the fourth place to Vashti (*Meg.* 14*b*).—*And, after her father and her mother had died, Mordecai took her unto him* [𝕿[1] + into his house and spoke of her] *as a daughter*]. The older comm. were troubled to see how Mordecai could take a girl of his own generation into his house as a daughter. According to Semitic custom, a cousin on the father's side is the most suitable of all persons to take as wife (*cf.* Ar. *bint 'amm,* 'daughter of paternal uncle,' as a synonym for 'wife'). *Meg.* 13*a* solves the difficulty by reading *l*ᵉ*bhēth,* 'for a wife,' instead of *l*ᵉ*bhath,* 'for a daughter' (in Rab. Heb. *bēth,* 'house,' has the secondary meaning of 'wife'), and justifies this interpretation by 2 S. 12[3], where 'like a daughter' is parallel to 'slept in his bosom.' This view has been followed by 𝕲, and has found wide acceptance in the Targums, Midrashes, and comm. It must be admitted that nowhere else is a wife of Mordecai mentioned; but it cannot have been the intention of the author to represent Esther as his wife, since in 2[3] he says that only virgins were collected for the King. Raw. thinks that Mordecai may have been a eunuch.

[𝕋² + On account of Esther Mordecai went into captivity, for he said, It is better that I should go and bring up Esther than that I should live in the land of Israel. ... She was the same Esther in her youth and in her old age, and did not cease to do good deeds.] [𝕋¹ + She was chaste in the house of Mordecai for seventy-five years, and did not look upon the face of any man, except that of Mordecai, who had brought her up.]

5. אִישׁ] pr. καί 𝕲 L 𝕾.—יְהוּדִי] om. 𝕷.—הָיָה] cf. Jb. 1¹, not equivalent to a simple 'was' (cf. BDB. 226, III.).—הַבִּירָה] Thebari 𝕷 = τῇ βάρει.—מָרְדֳּכַי] so B² everywhere exc. 4¹², see Norzi: מָרְדֳּכַי Baer everywhere: מָרְדְּכַי Ginsburg everywhere: Μαρδοχαῖος 𝕲 L.—בֶּן־קִישׁ] cf. A¹.—אִישׁ] de stirpe 𝕴: ܡܢ ܫܒܛܐ 𝕾: ἐκ φυλῆς 𝕲: τῆς φυλῆς L.—יְמִינִי] Jemini 𝕴: Βενιαμείν(μιν) 𝕲 L 𝕾: an abbreviation of בן ימיני, cf. 1 S. 9¹·⁴ 2 S. 20¹.

6. om. L.—אֲשֶׁר הָגְלָה] ex captivitate 𝕷.—עִם הגלה] de captivitate 𝕷: eo tempore 𝕴: om. 𝕲 (93b has under *).—אֲשֶׁר־יְהוּדָה] om. 𝕲 𝕷 (93b has under *): Haupt deletes.—הָגְלְתָה עִם] om. 𝕴.—אֲשֶׁר] om. 𝕴.—נְבוּכַדְנֶצַּר] Ναβουχοδονοσόρ 𝕲 𝕷. The Bab. original Nabû-kudurrî-uçur is most closely represented by נבוכדראצור (Je. 49²⁸). The form נבוכדראצר is common in Je. and Ez.; in later writings נבוכדנ(א)צר, with change of ר to נ, is the regular form. 𝕲 suggests that the original vocalization was נְבוּכַדְנֶאצַר (cf. Haupt, a. l.).

7. אֹמֵן־הֲדַסָּה] τούτῳ παῖς θρεπτή 𝕲: ἐκτρέφων πιστῶς L: illi 𝕷.—הִיא אֶסְתֵּר] so 93b under *: καὶ ὄνομα αὐτῇ Ἐσθήρ 𝕲: τὴν Ἐσθήρ L: tr. to end of v. (Hester) 𝕷: quæ altero nomine vocabatur Esther 𝕴.—בַּת־דֹּדוֹ] θυγάτηρ Ἀμειναδάβ (Ἀμιναδάβ א A) ἀδελφοῦ πατρὸς αὐτοῦ 𝕲: filia fratris ejus et nutrierat eam Mardochæus sicuti adoptatam filiam 𝕷: filiæ fratris sui 𝕴.—וּאָם] om. 𝕲 L: 𝕷 has.—הַנַּעֲרָה] + σφόδρα א ᶜ·ᵃ ᵐᵍ L: + nimis 𝕷 𝕴.—וְטוֹבַת מַרְאָה] so L א ᶜ·ᵃ ᵐᵍ, 93b under *: om. 𝕲 𝕷.—וּבְמוֹת־לְבַת] om. L.—מָרְדֳּכַי] so א ᶜ·ᵃ ᵐᵍ, 93b under *: om. 𝕲.—לְבַת] εἰς γυναῖκα 𝕲 (εἰς θυγατέρα 93b).

ESTHER IS TAKEN TO THE PALACE (2⁸⁻¹¹).

8. *And afterward, when the King's word and law became known, and when many* [𝕴 + *pretty*] *girls were gathered (and brought) to the fortress of Susa,* [𝕴 + *and were delivered*] *into the charge of Hēgai,* [𝕾 + *the eunuch,*] a resumption of the thought of v. ⁴, which has been interrupted by the account of Mordecai and Esther vv. ⁵⁻⁷. The language is almost a verbal repetition of v. ³. According to Josephus ²⁰⁰ (cf. 2¹²), the number of the girls was 400. The interval of four years (2¹⁶), during which one girl was pre-

ESTHER TAKEN TO THE PALACE

sented every day to the King, suggests that there were as many as 1460 girls.

[𝔗² + Mordecai heard that virgins were being sought, and he removed Esther and hid her from the officers of King Xerxes, who had gone out to seek virgins, in order that they might not lead her away. And he hid her away in the closet of a bedroom that the messengers of the King might not see her. But the daughters of the heathen, when the commissioners were sent, danced and showed their beauty at the windows; so that, when the King's messengers returned, they brought many virgins from the provinces. Now the King's messengers knew Esther; and when they saw that she was not among these virgins, they said one to another, We weary ourselves unnecessarily in the provinces, when there is in our own province a maiden fairer of face and finer of form than all the virgins that we have brought. So, when Esther was sought and was not found, they made it known to King Xerxes, and he wrote in dispatches, that every virgin who hid herself from the royal messengers should be sentenced to death. When Mordecai heard this, he was afraid, and brought out Esther, the daughter of his father's brother, to the market-place.]

And Esther [𝔖 + also] *was taken* [𝔗¹ + by force and brought] *unto the house of the King*, [Jos. + and was delivered] *into the charge of Hēgai*, [Jos. L + one of the eunuchs,] *the keeper of the women*]. 𝔥 contains no hint that Mordecai was unwilling to sacrifice his cousin to his political ambition, or that Esther was unwilling to be made a concubine of the King on the chance of becoming Queen. The form *was taken*, instead of *went*, does not naturally suggest compulsion. It is the regular expression for marrying a wife (*cf.* also 2¹⁵, where Mordecai 'takes' Esther as a daughter). 𝔗¹ and 𝔗² excuse their conduct by the foregoing interpolations. 𝔊, in the prayer of Esther (C¹²⁻³⁰), makes Esther protest that only under compulsion has she had anything to do with Xerxes. The older Christian comm. defend Esther, either on the ground that Xerxes, not being a Canaanite, was not so wicked that marriage with him was a sin; or that the end justified the means; or that Mordecai was inspired to do on this occasion what under ordinary circumstances would not have been permissible. By the *house of the King* Dieulafoy understands the private quarters of the monarch on the east side of the palace at Susa, in distinction from the *house of the women* in the N. E.

corner. Here *house of the King* seems to be the same as *house of the women* in 2³, but in 2¹³ and elsewhere they are carefully distinguished. If the text be sound, *King's house* is used in two senses; in one case, of the private apartments; in the other, of the whole palace-complex (*cf.* 2⁹ 4¹³).

9. *And the girl pleased him* [L + more than all the women,] *and* [L 𝕷 + Esther] *gained his favour* [L + and pity]. Hēgai, who was a connoisseur in such matters, discerned in her the most likely candidate for Vashti's place.—*And he* [𝕵 + commanded a eunuch, and he] *hastened to give her her cosmetics* [Jos.²⁰⁰ + which she used for anointing her body,] [𝕿¹ + and her necklaces and royal clothing,] *and her dainties*]. Thinking that she was likely to become Queen, he did his best to ingratiate himself by promptness. Since at least a year must be spent in preparation before she could go to the King (2¹²), it was well to begin at once. On *cosmetics*, see 2³. *Dainties* are lit. *portions*, i.e., *choice parts of dishes* (*cf.* 9¹⁹·²² 1 S. 14 f. Ne. 8¹⁰·¹²; Wellhausen, *Skizzen*, iii. p. 114). The girls who were to be presented to the King were not merely beautified with cosmetics, but were also given a special diet (*cf.* Dn. 1⁵). There is no trace in 𝕳 of any objection on Esther's part, such as Daniel and his friends manifested, to eat these heathen viands; but the interpolations in 𝕿² and 𝕲 (C ²⁸) make her refuse to touch them. According to R. Samuel, she was offered flitches of bacon; according to R. Johanan, she finally obtained vegetables like Daniel. Rab held that she was given Jewish food from the first (*Meg.* 13*a*). Jos. translates *portions* by 'abundance of ointments'; others, more generally, 'the things that she needed'; so Mal., Men., Ser., Lyr., Bon., AV.—*And to give her the seven picked maids out of the King's house.*

[𝕿¹ + They served her on the seven days of the week. Ḥôltā on the first day of the week, Rôqʻîthā on the second day of the week, Gĕnûnîthā on the third day of the week, Nĕhôrîthā on the fourth day of the week, Rôḥāshîthā on the fifth day of the week, Ḥûrpîthā on the sixth day of the week, and Rĕgoʻîthā on the Sabbath. All were righteous and were worthy to bring her food and drink in their hands.] [𝕿² + And the dainties which were given to her, Esther gave these heathen maids to eat, for Esther would not taste anything from the King's house.]

The article with *seven maids* shows that this was the prescribed number allotted to every one of the candidates for royal favour. The addition of *picked* shows that Esther's seven were better than those assigned to the other beauties. That these maids came from the *house of the King*, rather than the *house of the women*, is surprising (*cf.* 2⁸). Perhaps the meaning is merely, that they were supplied and maintained by the King.—*And he transferred her and her maids to the good (rooms)* [𝕋¹ + and to the delicacies] *of the house of the women*], *i.e.*, he did not allow her to remain in the ordinary quarters of prospective concubines, but assigned her apartments such as were reserved for royal favourites.

10. *Esther had not disclosed her race nor her descent*]. This is a parenthetical remark relating to an earlier period, and therefore not expressed by the impf. with *Waw* consec. Wherever they have lived, the Jews have made themselves unpopular by their pride and exclusive habits (*cf.* the additions to 3⁸ and C⁴ᶠ·). Esther, accordingly, knew that she would not be treated so well if she revealed the fact that she was a Jewess. This concealment involved eating heathen food and conforming to heathen customs (in spite of 𝔊 and 𝕋²), yet the author sees nothing dishonourable in it. L and Jos. save her reputation by omitting this v. How Esther was able to conceal her race from the officers who collected the girls and from the eunuchs and jealous rivals in the harem, especially when her cousin Mordecai the Jew (3⁴ 5¹³) came every day to inquire after her (2¹¹), the author does not try to explain. —*For Mordecai had bidden her not to tell* [𝕵 + anything about this matter].

[𝕋¹ + For he thought in his heart, Vashti, who sought honour for herself and was not willing to come and show her beauty to the King and the nobles, he condemned and put to death; . . . and he feared lest the King, when he was angry, might both slay her and exterminate the people from which she was sprung.]

There is nothing of the martyr-spirit in Mordecai, as in Daniel and his friends, who display their Judaism at all cost. So long as there is any advantage in hiding it, he does not let Esther tell her race; only when secrecy is no longer useful, does he bid her disclose it (4⁸). The addition of 𝕋¹ shows consciousness that this is not the noblest sort of conduct. The older comm. are much concerned to show that Mordecai was justified in giving this advice, and that Esther showed a beautiful spirit of filial obedience in following it. According to Cas., Mordecai displayed singular unselfishness in not letting his relationship to Esther be known.

11. [Jos.²⁰⁴ + Removing also from Babylon to Susa in Persia, her uncle lived there,] *and every day Mordecai used* [𝕿¹ + to pray and] *to walk in front of the court of the house of the women,* [𝕵 + in which the chosen virgins were kept,] *to inquire after Esther's health and* [𝕵 + to ascertain] *what had been done with her,* [Jos.²⁰⁴ + for he loved her like an own daughter]. This is another parenthetical remark, which serves the purpose of showing how subsequently Mordecai is able to advise Esther in an emergency (4²⁻¹⁶). Although he does not allow her to disclose her origin, yet he keeps in touch with her; both because he is interested in her fate, and because he wishes to retain her loyalty so that she may carry out his directions. How he could thus gain daily access to her after she had been taken to the royal harem, is a question that puzzles the comm. Bert. and Wild. suggest that women were not secluded so carefully in ancient Persia as in the modern Orient, and that Mordecai might have been permitted to hold a brief daily interview with his cousin under the supervision of a eunuch. Only later, when he was in mourning, was he unable to enter the palace-precincts. 𝕲, 𝕿¹, Jewish comm., Bon., San., *al.*, suppose that Mordecai was of princely rank, because he was one of those carried away with Jehoiachin (2 K. 24¹²); so that, as officer or courtier, he had free access to the palace (*cf.* 2⁵). From the fact that no wife of Mordecai is mentioned, Raw. infers that he was a eunuch and, therefore, could enter the women's quarters. Haupt also regards this as possible. Keil, Haupt, *al.*, think that he did not see Esther after she was taken to the palace, but that he used the servants as intermediaries, as in 4²⁻¹⁶. See further on 2²¹. How Esther could keep it secret that she was a Jewess, when she was daily inquired after by Mordecai, who was well known to be a Jew, no commentator has yet explained. Haupt's reflections *a. l.* do not help the case. *In front of the court of the house of the women* probably means at the entrance of the passage which led

ESTHER TAKEN TO THE PALACE

into the inner court of the harem. *What had been done with her*, *i.e.*, how she was progressing in the process of beautification. 𝔊² translates, "What miracles were wrought by her hand." *Mid.* understands it of magic arts practised against her.

8. ויהי-הגי] om. L.—ודהתו] om. 𝔊 𝔏 (93*b* has under *): *et juxta mandatum illius* 𝔍.—נערות] ܣܒܰܐܟܳܐܢ 𝔖.—הבירה] om. 𝔍.—אל יד] pr. *et traderentur* 𝔍: ܟܰܡܠ 𝔖.—הגי] Egeo 𝔍: + ܡܚܣܓܒܢ 𝔖: Γαὶ 𝔊 (Γωγαίου 93*b*: Γαιη 249 Ἄγαι C): *Oggeo* 𝔏.—אל יד הגי] Haupt deletes in 8ᵃ, *cf.* 8ᵇ.—אסתר] 𝔖 ܐܣ + ܘܬלקה.—το κοράσιον L: Haupt deletes.—אל-המלך] so L, 93*b* under *: om. 𝔊 𝔏: *inter ceteras puellas* 𝔍.—אל יד הגי] *ei* 𝔍: πρὸς Γαὶ 𝔊 (Γάην 249): ἐπὶ τὸν Γωγαῖον 93*b*: καὶ εἶδε Βουγαῖος ὁ εὐνοῦχος L (Γωγαῖος 93*a*): *ab Oggeo* 𝔏.—הגי] om. 𝔖.—שמר הנשים] *ut servaretur in numero feminarum* 𝔍: ὁ φυλάσσων τὸ κοράσιον L.

9. ותיטב-בעיניו] om. 𝔏: a favourite expression in Est., *cf.* 1²¹ 2⁴ 5¹⁴.—הנערה] om. 𝔍 L.—ותשא חסד] ἀ.γ., *cf.* נשא חן 2¹⁵· ¹⁷ 5², the usual expression is מצא חסד or מצא חן.—ויבהל] *Pi.* in the sense of 'hasten' is found only in late Heb., *cf.* 2 Ch. 35²¹ Ec. 5¹ 7⁹. Haupt objects to the translation 'hasten' on the grounds that Esther's treatment with cosmetics lasted a year in any case, and could not be 'hastened,' and that she did not need to have her food 'hastened,' and translates 'and he took a special interest'; but the beginning of the treatment could be 'hastened,' even if the process itself could not be abbreviated, and it was not her 'food' but her 'dainties' that he 'hastened.' The meaning 'hastened' is attested by 𝔊 ἔσπευσεν, 𝔍 *accelerare*, 𝔖 ܡܗܓܒ, and by all the passages in the OT. where this form occurs, *cf.* 8¹⁴ מבהלים ודחופים, 'hastened and impelled'; 6¹⁴ ויבהלו להביא, 'they hastened to bring.'—תמרוקיה] *mundum muliebrem* 𝔍: ܣܡܓܒܐ 𝔖: τὸ σμῆγμα 𝔊: προστατῆσαι αὐτῆς L: *ad omnes nitores ejus* 𝔏.—את מנותה] so B² Ba.: ואת מנוהיה G: om. L 𝔏.—ואת] ܣܒܐܠ 𝔖.—לתת לה] καὶ ἐπέδωκεν ὑπὲρ L: om. 𝔏. The inf. with ל preceded by its objects is a pure Aram. construction. Another object being introduced after this, the phrase is repeated (*cf.* Dn. 2¹⁰· ⁴⁶ 6²⁴); so the versions, Keil, Bert., Oet., Schu., Wild. Kau. § 115*c* and Sieg., *Com. a. l.*, hold that the phrase does not depend upon ויבהל, but upon the preceding noun, and should be translated 'which ought to be given to her.'—ואת²] om. L.—הנערות] + ܣܡ 𝔖.—הראיות] הראויות] τὰς ἄβρας L.—] on the insertion of *Daghesh*, *cf.* Kau. § 75 *v.* Ba. G om. *Daghesh* (*cf.* Ba., p. 72). This use of the pass. part. of ראה is not found elsewhere in the OT., but is common in BT.—לתת²om. 𝔍 𝔊 L 𝔏.—לה] om. 𝔍 𝔏.—מבית-הנשים] om. L.—המלך] *ejusdem* 𝔏.—לתת לה מבית המלך] Haupt deletes as a misplaced correction of the preceding לתת לה.—וישנה] *et tam ipsam ornaret* 𝔍: ܣܒܣܡ 𝔖: καὶ ἐχρήσατο αὐτῇ 𝔊. In 1⁷ 3⁸ the *Qal* of this vb. is used in the sense of 'be different'; here the *Pi.* in the sense of 'change.' The construction

12

with acc. of the person and ל of the place is Aram., *cf.* Levy, *Aram. W.-B.* iv. 586; Payne-Smith, *Thes.* 4234. There is no reason to suspect that the text is corrupt in spite of the variations of the versions.—[וישנה–נערותיה] om. 𝔏.—[לטוב–הנשים] *atque excoleret* 𝔍: καλῶς ἐν τῷ γυναικῶνι 𝔊 (+ εἰς ἀγαθόν 93b under *): *ætatis ipsius in conventu mulierum* 𝔏.

10. om. L.—[לא] pr. ο 𝔖: pr. καί 𝔊𝔏.—[אסתר] *quæ* 𝔍.—[עמה] ܐܡܪܐ.—[תגיר] 𝔖.—ܘܡܠܕܬܗ [מולדתה] 𝔖. + *de hac re omnino* 𝔏.

11. om. L.—[ובכל] om. ו 𝔊 (A 93b have).—[מרדכי] *qui* 𝔍.—[לפני] ב R 2.—[בית] om. 𝔖.—[הנשים] *in qua electæ virgines servabantur* 𝔍.—[לדעת] not merely of an attempt to know, but of the attainment of knowledge (*cf.* Dt. 8² 13⁴).—[את–שלום] ܐܡܪܐ 𝔖: τί συμβήσεται 𝔊𝔏: usually construed with שאל rather than with ידע (*cf.* 1 S. 10⁴).—[אסתר] *ei* 𝔏.—[ומה–בה] om. 𝔊𝔏.—[בה] לה some codd. (R).

THE PREPARATION OF THE GIRLS TO GO TO THE KING (2¹²⁻¹⁴).

12. *And whenever each girl's turn came to go to King Xerxes*]. So, according to Her. iii. 69, the wives of the false Smerdis came to him in turn. How the turn was determined, is not stated. The next clause narrates merely that no girl could go to the King until she had been twelve months in the palace. Presumably, as the girls arrived at the palace, their names were recorded; and, at the expiration of twelve months, they were called in the order of their arrival. Those who came from Susa would naturally begin their preparation sooner than those who came from India or Kush, and so would be ready earlier to go to the King.—*After she had been treated in the manner prescribed for the women* [𝔘¹ + *while they tarried in their delicacies*] *twelve months* [𝔘¹ + *of the year*]. Lit., *at the end of its being to her, according to the law of the women.* What the *law of the women* was, is explained in the next clause. It was a twelvemonth's process of beautification with cosmetics. Cler. wrongly explains the phrase after the analogy of Gn. 18¹¹ 31³⁵. On *law,* see 1⁸.—*For this was the regular length of their period of massage; six months* [𝔊 𝔍 + *they were anointed*] *with oil of myrrh,* [𝔘¹ + *which removes the hair and makes the skin soft,*] *and six months with perfumes and feminine cosmetics;*] [Jos.²⁰⁰ + *and the number of the girls was 400.*] This parenthetical remark gives the contents of the *law of the women* mentioned in the preceding clause. From this it appears, that every maiden was re-

THE PREPARATION OF THE GIRLS 179

quired to take this twelvemonth's treatment before she could be admitted to the King. Hēgai could not shorten the period in Esther's case; the best that he could do was to begin it as soon as possible. In regard to the credibility of this long period of preparation opinions differ.

13. *And whenever* [Jos.²⁰¹ + Hēgai thought that the virgins had done all that was necessary in the aforesaid time, and were now ready to go to the King's couch,] [𝕌¹ + after they had completed twelve months of the year and] *each girl was going unto the King*, a resumption of the thought of the first part of ¹²ᵃ, which has been interrupted by the long parenthesis in the rest of the v. The connection is, *whenever each girl's turn came to go to the King, . . . and in this* (i.e., *in turn*) *each girl was going to the King*. The second clause is not the apodosis, but is a continuation of the temporal clause. The apodosis follows in ¹³ᵇ.—*Every thing that she demanded* [𝔍 + that belonged to her adornment,] [𝕌¹ + whether a noble or an officer,] *used to be given her* [𝕌¹ + at once] *to go with her from the house of the women unto the house of the King*. Each girl was given a chance to make the best impression, and to this end was allowed to select any garment or jewel that she thought would enhance her beauty. Whether she was permitted to retain these after her visit to the King, we are not told. Haupt thinks that she had to return them. Probably the idea is, that she kept them as a *mohar*, or wedding-gift. V. ¹⁵ suggests that most of the girls used the opportunity to load themselves with jewels. Here the *house of the women*, or harem, is distinguished from the *house of the King*, or private apartments, in which Xerxes received the women in turn (see 1⁵).

14. *In the evening she used to go in* [𝕌¹ + to wait upon the King], a circumstantial clause, defining more precisely the manner of presentation, and also preparing the way for the future action of the book. The girls were not merely shown to the King when their turns came, as we should expect; but in each case the marriage union was consummated, as appears from ¹⁴ᵇ, where they return to the *house of the concubines*.—*And in the morning she used to return unto the second house of the women, into the charge of Sha'ashgaz, the King's eunuch, the keeper of the* [𝔍 + royal] *con-*

cubines]. Having received the honour of admission to the King's couch, no girl could return to the company of candidates in charge of Hēgai; but went now to another section of the harem, under the custody of a different eunuch; where, as a concubine of the King, she was kept presumably under stricter surveillance. On *Sha'ashgaz*, see p. 69.—[𝔗² + Her name was recorded and] *she did not go in again to the King unless the King longed for her and she was summoned by name* [𝔗¹ + distinctly and in writing.] Most of the girls, apparently, never got a second summons; but remained in practical widowhood in the house of the concubines. Only occasionally one made sufficient impression on the King for him to remember her and to wish to see her a second time. How many girls preceded Esther, we are not told; but evidently no one had such charms that the King thought of her as a possible successor to Vashti. This story bears marked resemblance to that of Shehriyar at the beginning of the *Arabian Nights*. He also had a new wife every evening, and did not suffer one to come to him a second time (see p. 76).

12. om. L.—[ובהגיע] οὗτος δὲ ἦν 𝔊: καὶ ὅταν A: *et quando esset* 𝔏: *cf.* 4¹⁴ 6¹⁴ 9¹·²⁶. ב is used instead of כ because the turns kept coming. The inf. takes its time from ינתן v. ¹³, *i.e.*, it denotes recurring action in the past.—[ונערה] om. 𝔖 𝔊 𝔏.—[נערה] om. 𝔏: ܐܟ̈ܬܒܕܐ 𝔖. ܘܫܡܥ.—[אחשורוש] om. 𝔍 𝔊 𝔏 (93*b* has under *): Haupt deletes.—[מקץ] is regularly followed immediately by the time-limit (*cf.* Gn. 4³ Ju. 11³⁹ 2 S. 14²⁶). Here an equivalent of the time-limit comes first and the time-limit follows in apposition.—[לה-הנשים] *omnibus quæ ad cultum muliebrem pertinebant* 𝔍: *tempus puellæ* 𝔏: om. 𝔊 (93*b* has under *): καιρὸς κοράσια A.—[שנים עשר] *undecimo* 𝔏: ἐπὶ ἕξ Jos.—[חדש] + *vertebatur* 𝔍: ܐܡܠܐ 𝔖.—[ימלאו ימי] of the completion of a prescribed period, as Gn. 25²⁴ 29²¹ 50³ *et al.* The impf. is used to express recurring action in the past, 'the days used to be fulfilled,' *i.e.*, in each individual case.—[מרוקיהן] *á.λ.*, *cf.* תמרוק (2³·⁹·¹²) and the n. on 2³.—[ימלאו-מרוקיהן] om. 𝔍.—[חדשים] ܡܥܒܕܐ 𝔖: + ἀλιφόμεναι 𝔊: + *ut ungerentur* 𝔍.—[בשמן המר]. The meaning 'oil of myrrh' is certain from the versions and the cognate languages. *Meg.* 13*a* translates it סטכת 'stacte' (cinnamon oil) or אנפקינון 'omphacinum' (green olive oil). 𝔗¹ combines both renderings. Myrrh had a healing and purifying effect upon the skin.—[וששה-הנשים] om. 𝔏.—[חדשים] + *aliis* 𝔍: ܡܥܒܕܐ 𝔖.—[הנשים] *uterentur* 𝔍.

13. om. L.—[ובזה] om. 𝔍. 'And in this,' *i.e.*, 'in turn,' refers back to the first words of v. ¹². In this case ובזה is a continuation of the tem-

poral clause of v. ¹² and the apodosis follows in 13*b* (so Bert., Rys., Wild.). Others make this the apodosis of the sentence. In that case ובזה must be taken temporally, 'and in this time,' 'then' (so 𝔊, 𝔗¹, J. & T., Pisc., Sieg., Haupt). Others understand ובזה to mean 'and in this condition,' *i.e.*, 'prepared,' as described in the previous verse (so 𝔖, Mün., Tig., Vat., AV.); but the expression for this is בכן (4¹⁶). RV. seems to suggest that 'and in this' means 'under the following conditions,' and refers to the permission to take with her whatever she pleased.—[הנערה] הנער codd., הנערה Q: om. 𝔍𝔊𝔏 (93*b* has under *).—[בָּאָה] ptc. f., not pf., on account of the accent (*cf.* Ewald, § 331; König, i. 643 *f.*). It takes its time from the following impf. used to express recurring action in the past.—[את-המלך] om. 𝔏.—[את כל-] καί 𝔊. This can hardly be taken as the obj. of תאמר. It is rather the subj. of the pass. ינתן construed with את (Kau. § 121 *a*).—[האמר] 'commanded' as in 1¹⁰. This verb and the following one are impf. to express recurring action in the past (Kau. § 107 *e*). They govern the time of the protasis in ¹²⁻¹³.—[ינתן] on the pointing, see Ba., p. 72.—[לבוא עמה] *et ut eis placuerat compositæ transibant* 𝔍. We should expect rather להביא, but the reading is sustained by 𝔊 συνεισέρχεσθαι. This has suggested to 𝔗¹ the idea that persons, not things, accompany the girl to the King. So Ramb. *al.*, but v. ¹⁵ shows that this is impossible.

14. [בערב-באה] *et cum introiret mulier ad domum regis* 𝔏: tr. to v. ¹⁶ L.—[באה] ptc., taking its time from the preceding impf. as a frequentative in the past.—[ובבקר] *cf.* Ba., p. 72.—[ובבקר היא שבה] *ad diem unum et recurrebat* 𝔏: tr. to v. ¹⁶ L.—[שבה] + *atque inde deducebatur* 𝔍.—[אל-בית המלך] om. L.—[הנשים] om. 𝔍.—[שני] שנית S*ᵉ*bhîr: om. 𝔖. This word is grammatically unrelated to the rest of the sentence, as in Ne. 3³⁰. We must either read שֵׁנִית 'a second time,' or (הַשֵּׁנִי(ת 'the second,' agreeing with בית הנשים (so Ba., Rys., Wild., Sieg.). Buhl suggests מִשְׁנֶה. Haupt deletes as a gloss, as in 2¹⁹ 7² 9²⁹, and supposes that the girls returned to the same building from which they set out, only to the care of a different eunuch.—[אל-הפילגשים] pr. *quæ* 𝔍. Var. Or.: pr. על om. 𝔏.—[אל יד] οὗ 𝔊.—[המלך] om. 𝔍 44, 106.—[הפילגשים] a foreign word of unknown origin. For the theories as to its etymology, see BDB. 811.—[לא חבוא] pr. καί 𝔊𝔖: *non habebat spado potestatem inducendi* 𝔏.—[עור-המלך] om. 𝔏.—[כי אם] ὡς δὲ L.—[חפץ-המלך] κατεμάνθανεν ὁ βασιλεύς L: om. 𝔊𝔏 (93*b* has under *).—[ונקראה בשם] om. ו 𝔊𝔏: πάσας τὰς παρθένους L.

ESTHER IS BROUGHT TO THE KING AND IS CHOSEN QUEEN (2¹⁵⁻¹⁸).

15. *And when* [𝔍 + the time had gone round in order,] *the turn came of Esther, the daughter of 'Ăbîhayil, Mordecai's uncle, whom Mordecai had adopted as a daughter, to go in to the King*]. *Cf.* v. '.

These genealogical details are mentioned in order to distinguish Esther from the nameless herd of girls that had gone before her. For 'Ăbîḥayil (*cf.* 9²⁹) 𝕲 has everywhere in Est. 'Αμειναδάβ, which is used elsewhere for both 'Ăbînādāb and 'Ammînādāb in 𝕳. How this could have arisen out of 'Ăbîḥayil, it is difficult to see. On the other hand, it is possible that 'Ammînādāb was original, but was objectionable to Jewish ears on account of its connection with the name of the heathen god 'Amm, and therefore has been changed in 𝕳 (*cf.* Paton, Art. " 'Amm" in *Hastings' Dict. Rel.*).— [𝕷 + And it came to pass, when she went in to the King,] *she did not request* [𝕿¹ + the use of] *any thing, except that which Hēgai, the King's eunuch, the keeper of the women, advised* [𝕵 + and gave her as ornament, for she was exceedingly shapely and incredibly beautiful], *i.e.*, she did not take the chance that was offered her, according to v. ¹³, to enrich herself at the King's expense. Vat., Keil, and most comm. see in this an evidence of Esther's extraordinary modesty; Grot., of her confidence in her beauty; Mal., of protest against this heathen alliance. Others see in it a sign of her good judgment in leaving everything to Hēgai, who was experienced in such matters and knew the King's taste. The passage does not say that she went unadorned, but only adorned in the manner that Hēgai regarded as most becoming.—*And Esther won the admiration* [𝕵 𝕿¹ + and love] *of all beholders.* [*Meg.* 13a + Every one thought that she belonged to his nation.] This was not on account of her modesty, but on account of her beauty, as dressed by the master-hand of Hēgai. This is an anticipation of the favour that she finds with the King (2¹⁷). From this passage *Meg.* 7a infers the inspiration of the Book of Est. How else but by inspiration could it be known that *all* admired her?

16. *And Esther was taken unto King Xerxes* [𝕿¹ + as wife, and he brought her] *unto* [𝕿¹ + the house of the bed-chamber of] *the royal house*]. In *taken* there is no suggestion of force, any more than in 2⁸, *q. v. Royal house* is here evidently the same as *house of the King*, 2¹³ (*cf.* 1⁹). Perhaps the change in expression is due merely to the desire to avoid the repetition of *King*.—In the *tenth month, that is, the month Ṭēbhēth*]. The name is derived from

Bab. *Ṭêbêtu*, and occurs here only in the OT. It equals Dec.-Jan. The Bab. names of the months, together with the numbering from Nisan, were adopted by the Jews after the Exile (*cf.* KAT.³ p. 330 *f.*).—*In the seventh year of his reign*]. According to 1³, the deposition of Vashti occurred in the third year. The appointment of a commission to gather girls followed speedily, "when the anger of King Xerxes had abated" (2¹). Four years, accordingly, elapsed from the time that the King set out to seek a successor to Vashti until Esther was brought to him. Why was her presentation delayed so long? Her home was in Susa (2⁵), so that she must have been one of the first to be taken to the palace; and Hēgai did everything to hasten her preparation (2⁹). Bon. thinks that the delay was due to the number of girls that preceded her. At the rate of one a day for four years, there must have been 1460 maidens on the waiting-list ahead of her. This is a goodly number, and it is a tribute to Esther's beauty that out of so many she was the first to captivate the King. Bert. thinks that, if time be allowed for the abating of Xerxes' wrath, for the appointing of a commission, for the collecting of girls, and a year for Esther's preparation (2¹²), four years is not too long. Making all allowances, however, it seems incredible that Xerxes should have been willing to remain four years without a queen. 𝔖 solves the difficulty by changing the *seventh* year to the *fourth*. San. thinks that v. ¹⁵ refers to a first visit of Esther to the King at an earlier date, and v. ¹⁶ to a second visit after he had tried the rest of the girls; but v. ¹⁷ shows clearly that only one visit is meant. Baum., Häv., Keil, Raw., and other defenders of the strict historicity of the book, hold that the delay was due to Xerxes' absence in Greece during the sixth and the seventh year of his reign (480–479 B.C.). It is possible that, after the battle of Platæa, Xerxes returned to Susa by Dec.-Jan., in time to take Esther as Queen before the end of the year; but the Book of Est. contains no suggestion of a two years' interruption of the presentation of girls, while the King was absent on a great military expedition; on the contrary, 2¹²⁻¹⁶ assumes that the girls were brought regularly one after the other until Esther's turn came. If the King had been away two years, and the preparation of the girls had lasted one year, there would not have been time for the extensive testing that the book assumes before the selection of Esther (*cf.* 2⁸ 'many,' 2¹⁷ 'all') (see p. 73).

17. *And the King loved Esther* [L 𝕊 + exceedingly] *more than all the wives* [𝕋¹ + that he had taken], *and she gained his grace and favour more than all the virgins.* [*Meg.* 13*a* + If he wished to enjoy a virgin, he enjoyed her; if he wished to enjoy a matron, he enjoyed her]. The sense is not, as Bert. suggests, that he loved her better than both the older and the younger women, but, as 𝕋¹ and *Meg.* indicate, better than the wives that he had already, and better than the girls that he had just gathered.—*And he placed the royal turban upon her head*, [𝕋¹ + and he cast out from the bedroom of the house where he slept the statue of Vashti, and placed there a statue of Esther. And he seated her upon the second throne,] *and he made her Queen instead of Vashti.* [Jos.²⁰³ + So Esther was married without disclosing her race.] After the King had seen Esther he had no desire to investigate further. The presentation of girls came to a sudden end; and Esther, apparently, was made Queen at once. On *royal turban*, see 1¹¹. There can be no doubt as to the author's intention to represent Esther as wife and queen, in contrast to the other women who were only concubines (see p. 71).

18. [Jos.²⁰² + And he made a wedding-feast for her, and sent *angaroi*, as they are called, to every race, commanding them to celebrate the nuptials;] *and the King made a great banquet* [𝕵 + because of his union and marriage] *for all his officials and courtiers* [𝕲 + for seven days] [𝕲 L 𝕋¹ + and celebrated] *Esther's banquet* [L + publicly]. [𝕋² + And he gave gifts to the provinces; and he said to her, Tell me now whether thou art sprung from the Jewish people? And she said to him, I do not know my race nor my descent, because, when I was a child, my father and my mother died and left me an orphan (*cf. Meg.* 13*a*).] On *banquet, officials, courtiers*, see 1³. Apparently this banquet followed immediately after the choice of Esther as Queen in the seventh year of Xerxes.—*And* [𝕋² + when Xerxes heard this word] *he made a release* [𝕋¹ + from paying tribute] *for* [L 𝕷 𝕵 + all] *the provinces*]. *Release*, lit. *a causing to rest*, although understood by 𝕋¹ and many comm. of a release from tribute, probably means a release from prison (*cf.* 1 Mac. 10³³ Mt. 27¹⁵; see Haupt *a. l.*). Others think of a release from work, a holiday (so 𝔖, 𝔍, Bert., Sieg.), or a release from military service, as Her. iii. 67 (Drus.).—*And he gave a largess* [𝔘¹ + and a present] *with royal liberality* [𝔘² + for he thought in his heart, and said within him, I will do good to all peoples and kingdoms because among them is the people of Esther. . . . And the princes of the King said to him, If thou dost wish Esther to tell her race and her descent, arouse her jealousy with other women, and she will tell thee her race and her descent (so the King made a second gathering of girls)]. *Largess* is lit. *a lifting up*, *i.e.*, either something taken from one, or something given to one. Here the latter meaning is demanded. In Am. 5¹¹ Jer. 40⁵ the word is used more specifically of *gifts of food* (*cf.* Xen. *Cyrop.* viii. 27; *Anab.* i. 9, 25). *With royal liberality*, see 1⁷.

15. ובהגיע תר] ἐφάνη ἐπιφανεστάτη L: + introeundi 𝔏: *cf.* v. ¹².—בת—end of v. om. L.—הר־לבת Haupt deletes as a gloss derived from v. ⁷ and 9²⁹.—אביחיל] so 𝔐: *Abihail* 𝔍: ܐܚܣܒ 𝔖ᴬ: ܐܚܣܒ 𝔖ᴸᴹ: ܐܚܣܒ 𝔖ᵁ: *Abihel (Chihel)* 𝔏: Αμειναδάβ 𝔊 (Αβιχάιλ C).—דד] *fratris* 𝔍𝔏.—אשר־לבת] om. 𝔊𝔏 (93b has under *).—לבוא] ἐν τῷ εἰσελθεῖν A: pr. ὅν ἔμελλεν 44: *introibat* 𝔏.—המלך] + *et factum est cum introiret ad regem* 𝔏.—דבר] *muliebrem cultum* 𝔍.—כי־את] om. 𝔊𝔏.—אשר] ὧν 𝔊: ὧν αὐτῇ ℵ A N 55, 64, 71, 74, 76, 106, 108a, 243, 248, 249, C Ald.: ἐκ πάντων ὧν αὐτῇ 44: *ex quibus* 𝔏.—הגי] om. 𝔊𝔏 (93b has under *).—סרים המלך] Haupt deletes.—המלך] om. 𝔍𝔖𝔊𝔏 (93b has under *).—שמר הנשים] om. 𝔏 106: + *hæc ei ad ornatum dedit erat enim formosa valde et incredibili pulchritudine* 𝔍.—ותהי אסתר] om. 𝔍.—אסתר] Haupt deletes.—נשאה] with quiescent א, *cf.* Ba. 73, Stade, § 112c. On the phrase *cf.* v. ⁹. The periphrastic form with the ptc. expresses the constancy of the favour that she enjoyed.—ראיה] see Ols. § 176c.

16. ותלקח־המלך] tr. aft. 2⁹ L.—אסתר] om. 93b 𝔍.—אחשורוש] om. L 𝔏 44, 106: Haupt deletes.—אל בית to end of v.] om. L.—מלכותו] om.—אל] om. 𝔊𝔏 (93b has under *).—העשירי] τῷ δωδεκάτῳ 𝔊𝔏 (δεκάτῳ 93b C).—טבת] מֶבֶת Ba.: ܐܣܦܢ ܚܠܛ 𝔖: 'Αδάρ 𝔊𝔏: 'Αδέρ 248 (so always): Τηβήθ ℵ ᶜ·ᵃ C: Βήθ 93b.—שבע] ܐܢܙ 𝔖.—היא חדש] om. 𝔏.

17. ויאהב־אסתר] ἤρεσεν αὐτῷ σφόδρα L (tr. aft. 2⁹).—אסתר] + ܒܓ 𝔖: αὐτῆς 44, 76, 106.—מכל הנשים] om. 𝔊 L 𝔏 (93b has under *).—וחסד] om. 𝔖 𝔊 𝔏 (93b has under *).—לפניו] om. 𝔊 (93b has under *).—מכל הבתולות] *super omnes mulieres* 𝔍: om. L.—וישם] ܘܣܒܡܗ 𝔖.—מלכות] τὸ γυναικεῖον

𝔊: om. 𝔏.—וימליכה-ושתי [בראשה] αὐτῇ 𝔊𝔏.—וימליכה-ושתי] om. 𝔊 L: 𝔏 has, and 93*b* under *.

18. גדול] om. 𝔊 𝔏 (93*b* has under *).—המלך] om. 𝕵.—ויעש-ועבדיו] om. L.—ועבדיו] ܣܟ̈ܡܐ 𝔖: καὶ ταῖς δυνάμεσιν + ἐπὶ ἡμέρας ἑπτά, καὶ ὕψωσεν 𝔊: + καὶ ἤγαγεν ὁ βασιλεὺς L.—משתה] *pro conjunctione et nuptiis* 𝕵: τοὺς γάμους 𝔊𝔏: τὸν γάμον L.—את משתה אסתר] Haupt deletes.—וְהֲנָחָה] καὶ ἄφεσιν 𝔊: καὶ ἀφέσεις L: ܘܢܝܚܐ 𝔖: *et requiem* 𝕵: *Hiph.* inf. from נוח. The form is Aram. rather than Heb. (*cf.* Stade, §§ 244, 621 *c*). Haupt regards it as an inf. abs. used instead of a finite vb., as 2³ and often in Est., and deletes the following עשה.—למדינות] τοῖς ὑπὸ τὴν βασιλείαν αὐτοῦ 𝔊: pr. πάσαις L 44, 71, 74, 76, 106, 𝔏 𝕵.—ויתן-המלך] om. 𝔊 L 𝔏.—מַשְׂאֵת] Haupt reads מַשְׂאָת, 'portions,' 'rations' (see also on 10¹). Winck. (26–29) proposes to transpose 2¹⁷ᶠ· to a position before 10¹, on the grounds that the elevation of Esther to be Queen is the proper climax of the book, and that מַשְׂאֵת is the same as מַס in 10¹, and the same gathering of tribute is meant. He then reads the s. מדינה instead of the pl., and finds in it an allusion to Seleucia as the capital of the empire. All this is utterly fanciful.

MORDECAI DISCOVERS A PLOT AGAINST THE KING (2¹⁹⁻²³).

19. *And when virgins were being gathered a second time*]. What is meant by *second* is a *crux interpretum*. (1) 𝔗², Tir., Bon., Lap., Mal., Osi., Caj., Hez., Maur., Keil, Schu., Raw., Oet., Wild., Stre., think of a gathering that followed the selection of Esther as Queen; and suppose, either that these were girls from a distance who arrived after the game was over; or that the King, although he made Esther Queen, was not content with her charms, but demanded continually a fresh supply of concubines; or that the courtiers, being jealous of Esther's influence, tried to lead him to select another favourite; or, as 𝔗² maintains, that Xerxes made this second gathering so as to rouse Esther's jealousy and to get her to tell her race. The objections to this view are, that 2¹⁶ᶠ· suggests that Xerxes was so well satisfied with Esther that he tried no new candidates; and that there is no reason why a gathering after Esther's marriage should be called the *second*, since many gatherings must have preceded it.

(2) Drus. and Bert. think that *second* refers to a gathering of concubines into the second house of the women, either after visiting the King, or after attending Esther's wedding; but why in this

case should they be called *virgins*, instead of concubines, as in 2¹⁴? It is not a sufficient answer to say that *virgins* means only young women, or that they are so called because they were lately virgins. *Gather* must also have the same sense here as in 2³·⁸.

(3) In view of these facts, Grot., Vat., Mar., Cler., Ramb., hold that this is a parenthetical remark referring to a time previous to Esther's marriage. Vat., Mar., think that there was a similar gathering of girls before Vashti was chosen, and that *second* refers to the gathering from which Esther was taken. Cler., Ramb., suppose that the first gathering occurred in the provinces, and the second at Susa. Others suppose that *second* means the second detachment of girls that arrived in Susa in accordance with the order of 2²⁻⁴. The difficulties with this view are that on this interpretation we should expect an art. with *virgins*, since they have been mentioned before; that v. ²⁰, which follows immediately, does not refer to the past but to the present; and that v. ²² shows that these events occurred after Esther became Queen.

(4) Dat., Bar., Jahn, despair of an interpretation, and follow 𝕲 in deleting the passage; but the omission by 𝕲 does not prove that the words did not stand in the original text, but only that 𝕲 could make nothing out of them. Haupt deletes the whole of v. ¹⁹ as a misplaced gloss to v. ²¹.

(5) Sieg. explains the clause as due to the clumsiness of the author, who wanted to say something about Mordecai's discovering the plot, and knew no better way in which to introduce it. If we must choose between these theories, the first probably offers the least difficulty; but there is strong ground for suspicion that the text is corrupt (see crit. note).

Why this statement about a gathering of virgins is introduced at this point, is also a puzzle. Schu. thinks that the confusion attending the arrival of the girls gave the conspirators a chance to discuss their plans (v. ²¹), and gave Mordecai a chance to observe them without being noticed, since they supposed that he was merely an ordinary member of the throng; but a crowded gate is surely not the place that conspirators would choose for discussing plans to murder the King. It is better with Keil, Raw., and most comm. to regard the clause as introduced solely for the purpose of

giving the time of the events. It is parallel to *in those days*, v. ²¹.—
While Mordecai [𝕿¹ + was praying, and having gone forth] *was
sitting in the King's gate*]. The verse-division in 𝕸, 𝕾, 𝕵, and
most modern versions and comm. treat this clause as the apodosis
and translate, *when virgins were gathered—Mordecai was sitting;*
but the same expression occurs in v. ²¹, and there it is temporal.
It is better, accordingly, with Cas., Rys., Stre., to regard this as
a second subordinate clause. What Mordecai's sitting in the
King's gate has to do with the gathering of virgins, is not clear.
The older versions and comm. suppose that he was a royal official
who had charge of the reception of the girls (see 6¹⁰, where the
King knows that he sits in the gate), but this is not a fair inference
from the text. Schu., Wild., think that, when a company of girls
arrived, people crowded into the King's gate to see them, and that
Mordecai took this opportunity to penetrate farther into the palace
than he could ordinarily go; but this hypothesis is unnecessary,
since in 2¹¹ he walks daily before the court of the women, and in
3² 5¹³ he sits in the King's gate when no virgins are being brought.
If we regard this clause as subordinate, like the first, there is no
need of seeing any causal nexus between the two. *The King's
gate* is presumably a large fortified entrance to the palace-enclosure,
such as Dieulafoy discovered at Susa. Such gates have always
been used in the Orient as courts of justice and as lounging-places
for the rich (see *HDB*. Art. "Gate"). From 2²¹ 3² ᶠ· 5⁹· ¹³ 6¹⁰· ¹²
(*cf.* 4²· ⁶) it appears that this was Mordecai's favourite haunt.
This shows him to have been a man of leisure, but not necessarily
a royal official. His reason for sitting here may have been solely
his desire to pick up news concerning Esther (see 2⁵· ¹¹). Haupt
thinks that he may have been a money-changer who placed his
table here.

20. *Esther had never disclosed her descent nor her race, as Mordecai had enjoined upon her* [𝕲 𝕷 + to fear God] [𝕷 + every day].
The sentence begun with the two temporal clauses in v. ¹⁹ is broken
off to insert this parenthetical remark, which shows why Mordecai
still sat an idler in the King's gate, although his cousin had become
Queen; and also explains why he could spy upon the conspirators
(v. ²¹) without being detected. *Descent* is here put before *race* be-

cause the main point is Esther's relationship to Mordecai (*cf.* 2¹⁰). *Meg.* 13*a*, 𝕿², regard this as the apodosis of the sentence, and take it to mean that, although Xerxes tried to arouse Esther's jealousy by gathering other girls, yet still she did not reveal her origin, through loyalty to Mordecai, who sat in the King's gate. This is a very forced interpretation.—*But Esther had always obeyed the injunction of Mordecai.*

[𝕿¹ + She had kept sabbaths and fast days, she had taken heed to the days of her separation, she had avoided the food of the heathen, and had not drunk their wine, and she had observed all the commandments which Israelitish women ought to keep, according to Mordecai's instructions,] [𝕿² + for she showed herself humble when she became Queen.]

Just as when she grew up in his house [𝕲 + and Esther had not changed her manner of life]. This continuation of the parenthesis restates in positive form the thought of the preceding clause. The *injunction of Mordecai* was, of course, to conceal her race, not, as 𝕿¹ thinks, to keep the Jewish Law, which would have resulted in the immediate disclosure of her origin. The author wishes us to admire Esther's filial obedience even after she has become Queen. This is important in the further development of the plot.

21. [Jos. ²⁰⁵ + Now the King had enacted a law that, when he sat upon his throne, none of his household should approach him, without being called; and men with axes surrounded his throne ready to cut down any that approached the throne without a summons. The King, however, sat with a golden sceptre in his hand; and when he wished to save any one who came uncalled, he held it out to him; and he that touched it was safe (*cf.* 4¹¹): but enough of this matter.]

In those days while Mordecai was sitting [𝕿¹ + in the sanhedrin which Esther had established for herself] *in the King's gate*]. This is a resumption of the sentence begun in v. ¹⁹, but interrupted by the parenthesis in v. ²⁰. *In those days* corresponds to *and when virgins were being gathered.* The second clause is the same in both vv.—*Bigthan and Teresh, the two royal eunuchs,* [𝕵 + doorkeepers at the entrance of the palace,] *who guarded the threshold,* [𝕿¹ + noticed this and met together and] *were angry* [𝕲 + because Mordecai was promoted].

[𝕿¹ + And they said one to another: Does not the Queen with the consent of the King seek to remove us and to put Mordecai in our place? It is not fair to remove two officers in order to substitute one. Then they took counsel in their language.] [*Meg.* 13*b* + Bigthan and Teresh were Tarsees and spoke the Tarsee language, and they said one to the other: Since this (Esther) has come to court we can get no sleep at night; therefore let us put poison into the King's drink, that he may die. They did not know that Mordecai belonged to the Great Sanhedrin, every member of which understood 70 languages (similarly 𝕿²).] [Jos. ²⁰⁷ + And Barnabazus, a Jew, a servant of one of the eunuchs, becoming aware of the plot, revealed it to the uncle of the King's wife;] [𝕲 (A¹³) + and he heard their discussions and investigated their schemes and learned them (similarly L in A¹³).]

And they sought [𝕿¹ + to give a deadly poison to Queen Esther and] *to lay hands on King Xerxes* [L 𝕵𝕿¹ + to slay him] [𝕿¹ + with the sword in his bed-chamber]. The object of all these additions is to explain why Bigthan and Teresh were angry with the King. 𝕲 and 𝕿¹ think that it was because of the promotion of Mordecai, so Tir., Drus., *al*. *Meg*. holds that jealousy of Esther was the cause. Others have supposed that the two eunuchs were friends of Vashti and resented her degradation. Lap., Men., Cler., suppose that this was part of a plot of Haman to seize the throne (*cf*. 6⁸ᶠ·). Oet. brings the anger into connection with the gathering of virgins (v. ¹⁹), and thinks that then the wishes of the eunuchs were thwarted. The author gives no indication of his opinion. On *Bigthan* and *Teresh*, see p. 69. *The two royal eunuchs*, not *two of the King's chamberlains*, as AV. and RV. The *threshold* which these eunuchs guarded was presumably the entrance to the King's private apartments. They were the most trusted watchmen; and, therefore, their treason was doubly dangerous. *Lay hands on*, lit. *send forth a hand upon*, is the equivalent of *kill* (*cf*. Gn. 37²² 1 S. 24⁷· ¹¹). Such conspiracies were common in the ancient Orient, and were the only way to get rid of a despot. Several of the kings of Judah and of Israel perished in this way (*cf*. 1 K. 15²⁷ 16⁹ 2 K. 9¹⁴ 15¹⁰· ²⁵ 21²³); also of Damascus (2 K. 8¹⁵), and Assyria (2 K. 19³⁷). Xerxes himself perished through such a conspiracy (Diod. Sic. xi. 69, 1; Ctesias, *Pers*. 29), and a like fate befell Artaxerxes Ochus.

22. *And the affair became known to Mordecai* [𝔗² + through a holy spirit] [𝔗¹ + because he was able to speak 70 languages]. How Mordecai knew this plot, 𝔥 does not say. The additions supply a variety of reasons. The comm. have conjectured that he overheard the conversation of the eunuchs because he sat in the King's gate, but this would not be a likely place for the concocting of a plot. Mordecai's sitting in the gate has no other connection with this v. than as an indication of time.—*And* [L + having considered well,] *he disclosed it to Queen Esther, and Esther told it to the King* [𝔗¹ + and it was written] *in the name of Mordecai* [𝔍 + who had reported the matter to her]. Mordecai still managed to keep in communication with Esther, even after she had become Queen; but how this was done, or how it could be carried on without revealing Esther's race, the author does not explain. Mordecai was well known to be a Jew (2⁵ 3⁴·⁶ 5¹³ 6¹⁰); and, if he used the Queen to communicate his intelligence to the King, it must have been conjectured that they were related. It is also hard to understand how Xerxes could have forgotten so promptly (6³), if the news of this great service had been communicated by the Queen. Haupt solves the difficulty by changing the text of the v. to read, "And he disclosed it to Haman, son of Hammedatha, the Gogite, keeper of the threshold" (see note).

23. [Jos.²⁰⁸ + And the King was alarmed] *and the affair was investigated and was found* [𝔗¹ + true,] *and* [𝔊 L + having confessed,] *both of them were hanged upon a gallows*]. *Cf.* 5¹⁴ 6⁴ 7⁹·¹⁰ 8⁷ 9¹³·¹⁴·²⁵. The word translated *gallows* is lit. *tree* or *pole;* hence it has been inferred that impaling is meant (so L in 6¹¹, Haupt). Jos., 𝔖, 𝔍, *al.* think of crucifixion (*cf.* E¹⁸), but both of these methods of execution seem to be precluded by the fact that *the tree* of 5¹⁴ is 50 cubits high. This can only have been a gallows. [Jos.²⁰⁸ + But at that time he gave no reward to Mordecai who had been the means of his escape, only] [L + Xerxes,] [𝔊 + the King, commanded] [Jos. + the scribes to record his name] *and it was written* [𝔊 + for a memorial] *in the book of the chronicles* [𝔗¹ + which was read continually] *before the King* [𝔊 + with praise concerning the good will of Mordecai.] [𝔊 L (A¹⁶) + And the King commanded that Mordecai should serve in the King's court and should guard every door publicly. And he gave him gifts on account of this] [Jos. + as though he were a most intimate friend of the King.] Why Mordecai should not have been rewarded at once, but his services merely recorded in the annals, is hard to understand. Literary rather than historical considerations have here shaped the narrative. 𝕲 solves the difficulty by inserting rewards. The *book of the chronicles*, lit. *book of the acts of the days*, was a sort of royal diary recording memorable events (6¹ 10²). Such annals were kept by the ancient kings of Babylonia and Assyria, by the Hebrew kings (1 K. 14¹⁹ 15⁷ and oft.), and by the kings of Persia (Ezr. 4¹⁵; Her. vii. 100; viii. 85, 90; Diod. Sic. ii. 32). *Before the King* indicates that the annals were kept in his apartments, so that anything important might at once be jotted down (*cf.* 6¹). Haupt arbitrarily translates 'at the disposal of the King,' but *cf.* the passages just cited from Her.

19. om. L.—ובהקבץ-שנית] om. 𝕲 𝕷 (93*b* has under *):+ *et congregarentur* 𝕵:+ اعلم 𝕾: perhaps instead of שֵׁנִית 'a second time,' we should read שֹׁנוֹת 'different, various' (*cf.* 1⁷ 3⁸).—ומרדכי] om. ו 𝕾.—וישב] here only in book written defectively, 𝕸: ἐθεράπευεν 𝕲: *sedebat* 𝕷.—המלך] om. 𝕲 (93*b* has under *).

20. om. L. Haupt deletes the whole v. as made up of two tertiary glosses to ותאמר אסתר למלך בשם מרדכי v. ²².—מגרת] *Hiph.* ptc. f. expressing the continuation of E.'s refusal to tell her origin (*cf.* Kau. §§ 107 *d*, 116 *c*)—ואת עמה] om. 𝕲 (exc. 93*b* *).—מאמר] *omnia* 𝕷: a late word, as in 1¹⁵ 9³².—מרדכי] *ille* 𝕵: αὐτοῦ 𝕲: om. 𝕷.—אסתר] om. 𝕲 𝕷.—עשה] ποιεῖν 𝕲: *servaret* 𝕷.—באמנה] om. 𝕲 𝕷 (exc. 93*b* *).

21. om. L.—בימים-המלך] om. 𝕲: ἕως τῆς νυκτὸς καὶ ἡσύχασεν Μαρδοχαῖος ἐν τῇ αὐλῇ 𝕲 (A¹¹ᶠ.): ἕως τῆς ἡμέρας ἧς ὕπνωσε Μαρδοχαῖος ἐν τῇ αὐλῇ τοῦ βασιλέως L (A¹¹).—בימים] pr. ο 𝕾.—ומרדכי] om. ו 𝕾.—קצף] pr. καὶ 𝕲 𝕾: om. 𝕷: μετὰ 𝕲 (A¹²) L (A¹²). The vb. is singular because it precedes the two subjects.—משמרי הסף] Haupt deletes from this connection and inserts in the emended text of v. ²², on the ground that בגתן ותרש is the correct text in 1¹⁰ instead of בגתא ואבגתא, and that in 1¹⁰ these are body-servants of the King, not door-keepers (see p. 67). The present text is supported by all the Vrss. except L.—הסף] τὴν αὐλήν 𝕲 (A¹²): *atrium* 𝕷 (A¹²).—ויבקשו] וַיְבַקֵּשׁ Ba.—לשלח יד] ἀποκτεῖναι 𝕲 𝕷.—אחשורש] so Oc.: אחשורוש Or.: om. 44, 106 𝕷: Haupt deletes.

22. om. L.—ויודע-למרדכי] καὶ ὑπέδειξεν τῷ βασιλεῖ περὶ αὐτῶν 𝕲

MORDECAI DISCOVERS A PLOT

(A¹³): εὖ δὲ φρονήσας ὁ Μαρδοχαῖος ἀπήγγειλε περὶ αὐτῶν L (A¹³).— [ויגד
+ αὐτὸν 248 C: + *Mardochæus* 𝕃.— [ויגד-מרדכי om. 𝕲 in A¹³, L in A¹³.
לחמן בן המדתא הגאגי [לאסתר-מרדכי instead of this Haupt substitutes
משמרי הסף, and after v. ²³ he inserts והמלך לא ידע כי מרדכי הגיד הדבר.
His reasons are, that the King's neglect of Mordecai is inexplicable, if
the news of his service was reported by Queen Esther herself, as the
present text relates, and that the subsequent action of the book becomes
clearer, if we suppose that Mordecai told Haman of the plot, and that
the latter took the credit of the discovery to himself. This will explain
why Haman was exalted (3¹), why Mordecai refused to bow down to
him (3²), and why Haman was afraid to put Mordecai to death at once
(Haupt, *Purim*, p. 37). The theory is ingenious, but is wholly unsupported by the Vrss., all of which offer substantially the same text as
𝕳. It is unsafe to assume that the inconsistencies which Professor
Haupt would have avoided, if he had written the Book of Est., were necessarily avoided by the author. Moreover, this theory does not remove all
difficulties. If, as Haupt assumes, Mordecai's service was written in the
royal chronicle (2²³ 6¹ ᶠ·), then it would have been impossible for Haman
to claim the honour of discovering the plot for himself.—[המלכה om. 𝕲 𝕃
(exc. 93*b* *).—[ותאמר om. תאמר 𝕵.—[אסתר αὐτῇ 𝕲: ἡ βασίλισσα A: *illa* 𝕵
—[למלך + :'Αρταξέρξῃ א ᶜ·ᵃ ᵐᵍ A, 93*b* ÷.—[בשם מרדכי τὰ τῆς ἐπιβουλῆς 𝕲:
et nomen Mardochæi 𝕃.

23. om. L.—[ויבקש-וימצא om. 44, 106.—[ויבקש + ὁ βασιλεύς 𝕲.—
[הדבר τοὺς δύο εὐνούχους 𝕲.—[וימצא καὶ εὗρε τοὺς λόγους Μαρδοχαίου
L (A¹⁴): *et invenit sic* 𝕃: om. 𝕲: + καὶ ὁμολογήσαντες 𝕲 (A¹⁴), 𝕃 (A¹⁴):
+ καὶ ὁμολογήσαντες οἱ εὐνοῦχοι L (A¹⁴).—[ויתלו ἀπήχθησαν 𝕲 (A¹⁴),
L (A¹⁴).—עץ על] om. 𝕲 𝕃.—[ויכתב *mandatum est historiis et traditum*
𝕵: ܡܠܟܐ ܗܘ 𝕊: καὶ προσέταξεν ὁ βασιλεὺς καταχωρίσαι εἰς μνημόσυνον
𝕲: καὶ ἔγραψεν ὁ βασιλεὺς εἰς μνημόσυνον 𝕲 (A¹⁴): καὶ ἔγραψεν 'Ασσυ-
ῆρος ὁ βασιλεὺς L (A¹⁴): *et scriptum est memoriale* 𝕃.—[בספר-המלך ἐν τῇ
βασιλικῇ βιβλιοθήκῃ 𝕲: τοὺς λόγους τούτους 𝕲 (A¹⁵): περὶ τῶν λόγων
τούτων L (A¹⁵): *legis* 𝕃: + ὑπὲρ τῆς εὐνοίας Μαρδοχαίου ἐν ἐγκωμίῳ 𝕲:
+ καὶ ἐπέταξεν (ἐνετείλατο L) ὁ βασιλεὺς (+ περὶ τοῦ L) Μαρδοχαίῳ
(Μαρδοχαίου L) θεραπεύειν (+ αὐτὸν L) ἐν τῇ αὐλῇ (+ τοῦ βασιλέως
καὶ πᾶσαν θύραν ἐπιφανῶς τηρεῖν L) καὶ ἔδωκεν αὐτῷ δόματα (om. L)
περὶ τούτων 𝕲 (A¹⁶) L (A¹⁶). According to Winck. (*AOF*. iii. 5), vv. ²¹⁻²³
are in their right place in 𝕲, and their insertion here is a gloss. Similarly Erbt, *Purim*, p. 22.

HAMAN'S ELEVATION AND HIS PLOT (3¹–4¹⁷).

HAMAN IS EXALTED AND ALL MEN ARE REQUIRED TO BOW DOWN TO HIM (3¹⁻²ᵃ).

1. [L 𝕷 + And it came to pass] *after these events*]. This is a vague indication of a later date (*cf.* 2¹). This may have happened at any time between the seventh and the twelfth year of Xerxes (2¹⁶ 3⁷).

[𝕿¹ + The measure of judgment came before the Lord of the whole world and spoke thus: Did not the wicked Haman come down from Susa to Jerusalem in order to hinder the building of the house of thy Sanctuary? but behold now how] *King Xerxes magnified Hāmān, son of Hamm^edhāthā, the Agagite,* [𝕿² + son of Ṣadda, son of Kuza, son of Eliphaloṭ, son of Dios, son of Dioses, son of Peros, son of Ma'adan, son of Bal'aqan, son of Antimeros, son of Hadros, son of Segar, son of Negar, son of Parmashta, son of Wayzatha, son of Amalek, son of the concubine of Eliphaz, the first-born of Esau (*cf.* 𝕿¹ on 5¹).]

On *Haman* and the other proper names, see p. 69. According to *Meg.* 12*b*, 𝕿¹, Haman was the same as M^emûkhān (1¹⁴). For other legends concerning him, see Seligsohn, Art. "Haman" in *JE*. The only Agag mentioned in the OT. is the King of Amalek (Nu. 24⁷ 1 S. 15⁹ *sq.*). Jos. ²¹¹, *Meg.* 13*a*, 𝕿¹, 𝕿², all Jewish, and many Christian comm. think that Haman is meant to be a descendant of this Agag. This view is probably correct, because Mordecai, his rival, is a descendant of Saul ben Kish, who overthrew Agag (1 S. 15⁷ᶠ·). Amalek was the most ancient foe of Israel (Ex. 17⁸⁻¹⁶), and is specially cursed in the Law (Dt. 25¹⁷). It is, therefore, probably the author's intention to represent Haman as descended from this race that was characterized by an ancient and unquenchable hatred of Israel (*cf.* 3¹⁰, "the enemy of the Jews"). When 93*a* makes him a Gogite (*cf.* Ez. 38–39), and L makes him a Macedonian, these are only other ways of expressing the same idea (see p. 69*f*). In 1 Ch. 4⁴²ᶠ· it is recorded that the last remnant of the Amalekites was destroyed in the days of Hezekiah, but this creates no difficulty for our author in assigning Haman to this race. That an Amalekite should be raised to the highest rank in the Persian empire, is very improbable. The cases of favour to Greek exiles adduced by Baum. (p. 26 f.) are not parallel.—*And exalted him* [𝕌¹ + prince over everything,] *and placed his throne above all the officials that were with him*], *i.e.*, made him grand vizier.—[L + so that all stooped and bowed down to the earth to him.]

[𝕌¹ + And the Lord of the world replied: It is not yet revealed in the world. Let me alone until he magnifies himself: then shall it be revealed to all peoples; and afterward recompense shall be taken from him for all the sufferings which he and his fathers have inflicted upon the people of the house of Israel.]

2ᵃ. *And all the King's courtiers that were in the gate* [𝕌¹ + of the house] *of the King used to bow down* [𝕌¹ + to an idol which he had placed upon him,] [*Mid.* + embroidered upon his garment and worn over his heart, so that all who did homage to him, worshipped it]; *and they used to prostrate themselves before Haman* [Jos.²⁰⁹ + when he went in to the King], *for so the King had commanded concerning him*]. On *King's courtiers,* lit. *slaves of the King,* see 1³. Prostration before high officials was a universal custom in the ancient Orient. In the case of the Persians it is attested by Her. i. 134 (for other references, see Bris. i. 10). From this passage it cannot be inferred that Mordecai was a royal official (*cf.* 2⁵· ¹⁹).

1. אחר] pr. καὶ ἐγένετο L 𝕃.—האגגי-גדל] καὶ ἦν ᾿Αμὰν ᾿Αμαδάθου Βουγαῖος ἔνδοξος ἐνώπιον τοῦ βασιλέως 𝕲 (A¹⁷): ᾿Αμὰν ᾿Αμαδάθου Μακεδόνα κατὰ πρόσωπον τοῦ βασιλέως L (A¹⁷).—גִּדַּל] *Pi.* with *pathach* (Stade, § 386 b).—אחשורוש] Haupt deletes.—אֶת־הָמָן] so Ben Asher: אֶת־הָמָן Ben Naphtali (Ginsburg).—וישׁתחוו] om. 𝕁𝕾.

2ᵃ. עבדי המלך] om. 𝕲 L 𝕃 (exc. 93b *).—אשׁר בשׁער] om. L.—המלך] ² om. 𝕲 L 𝕃 (exc. א c. a, 93b *).—ומשׁתחוים] om. 𝕲 L 𝕃 (exc. 93b *).— להמן] αὐτῷ 𝕲 L (᾿Αμάν A 𝕃).—כי—end of v.] om. 106.—לו] *eis* 𝕁: ποιῆσαι 𝕲: *fieri* 𝕃: αὐτοῖς ποιῆσαι 93b: om. L.

MORDECAI REFUSES TO BOW DOWN TO HAMAN (3²ᵇ⁻⁵).

2ᵇ. *But Mordecai* [𝕁 + alone,] [Jos.²¹⁰ + because of his wisdom and the law of his nation,] *would never bow down* [𝕌¹ + to the idol] *and would never prostrate himself* [𝕌¹ + before Haman, because he had been a field-slave who had sold himself to him for a loaf of bread]. Mordecai's refusal to bow down to Haman is quite inexplicable. In 3^4 he tells the courtiers that it is because he is a Jew, but the Hebrews prostrated themselves, not only before kings (1 S. $24^{9(8)}$), but before all superiors (Gn. 23^7 27^{29} 33^3). There was nothing repugnant to their feelings in doing obeisance to such a great man as a grand vizier.

(1) The oldest explanation of Mordecai's refusal is that of 𝔊 in C^7 (= 13^{14}), namely, that Haman claimed divine homage, which Mordecai, as a pious Jew, could not render. This view has been followed by Jos., 𝔗², RaShI, San., Lap., Ser., Bon., Men., Tir., Jun., Mal., Drus., Kamp., Bert., Keil, Net., Schu., Hal., Raw., Scho., Wild., *al.* In its support it is claimed that the Persian kings assumed divine honours, according to Æsch. *Pers.* 644 *ff.*; Plutarch, *Themist.* xxvii.; Curtius, viii. $5^{6\text{ ff.}}$; and that Haman, as the King's vizier, shared this assumption of divinity. But no such claim on the part of the kings is found in the Pers. monuments; and, if they had made it for themselves, it is hard to see why it should have extended to their viziers. Even granting this assumption, Jews must have been able to bow before Persian rulers without regarding this as an act of worship. Ezra and Nehemiah could not have come into the close relations which they maintained with the Persian court without observing the rules of Persian etiquette. Esther and Mordecai also must have observed them when they came before the King. Mordecai could not become vizier without rendering to Xerxes precisely the homage that he here refuses to Haman, and he must himself have received it after his elevation (8^{15}).

(2) 𝔗¹ (*cf.* 6^1), the Midrashes, IE., and Jewish comm. in general suppose that Haman had an idol ostentatiously embroidered upon his robe, so that Mordecai could not bow to him without worshipping the idol (*cf. Pirq.* lxix); but this is a gratuitous assumption.

(3) *Meg.* 15*b*, 16*a*, and 𝔗¹ say that Haman had been a slave of Mordecai and had been a barber for 22 years in the town of Kefer Qarçum, and that this was the reason why Mordecai would not bow down to him.

(4) Kuen. and many modern comm. see in this act the influence upon the author of Greek ideas of freedom. Thus the Spartan ambassadors Sperthies and Bulis refused to prostrate themselves before Xerxes (Her. vii. 136).

(5) Caj., Burg. in Bon., Jun., Osi., Grot., Oet., hold that Mordecai refused to bow because Haman was an Amalekite (*cf.* 3¹). This idea is suggested also by 𝕋² on 3³, where the courtiers ask Mordecai why he refuses to bow to Haman, when his ancestor Jacob bowed to Haman's ancestor Esau (Gn. 33³). Such a motive is quite in accord with the spirit of the book; but here, as elsewhere, it is not necessary to seek for historical reasons. The literary reason is clear enough. Mordecai must do something to provoke Haman in order that he may seek to destroy the Jews; and this refusal to bow down, unreasonable as it is, serves the purpose.

3. [L + And the King's courtiers saw that Mordecai did not bow down to Haman,] *and the King's courtiers who were in the gate* [𝕋¹ + of the palace] *of the King said to Mordecai,* [𝕃 + saying,] [𝔊 + O Mordecai,] [𝕋² + What dignity hast thou above us who have to bend and bow before Haman that thou dost not bow down before him?] *Why dost thou* [𝔍 + unlike the rest] *disobey the command of the King* [L𝕃 + by not bowing down to Haman?] [𝕃 + and he would not answer them.]

[𝕋² + Then Mordecai answered and said to them, O fools, destitute of intelligence, hear a word from me; and tell me, you villains, where is there a son of man who can exalt and magnify himself? for he is born of a woman, and his days are few, and at his birth there is weeping, and woe, and distress, and groaning, and all his days are full of trouble, and at the end he returns to the dust; and I, should I bow down to such a one? I will not bow down, except to the living and true God; who is a flame of consuming fire; who has hung the earth upon his arm, and spread out the firmament through his might; who by his will darkens the sun, and at his pleasure makes the darkness light; who in his wisdom has set a bound to the sea with sand, while he gives its waters the taste of salt and its billows the smell of wine; who has enclosed it with a barrier and shut it within boundaries in the treasuries of the deep that it may not cover the earth, and that when it rages, the deep may not pass over its bounds; who by his word created the firmament, and expanded it in the air like a cloud, spread it like a mist above the clouds, like a tent over the earth, which by its strength sustains both the upper and the lower world. Before him run the sun and moon and the Pleiades, the stars and the planets; they miss not their time, they rest not, but all of them run like messengers to the right and to the left to do the will of him that created them. Him it is meet that I should praise, and that before him I should bow down. They answered and said to Mordecai, we have heard that thy forefather bowed down before Haman's forefather. Mordecai answered and said to them, Who was it that bowed down before the forefather of Haman? They replied, Did not thy forefather Jacob bow down before his brother Esau, who was the forefather of Haman? (Gn. 33³). He answered, I am of the seed of Benjamin; but when Jacob bowed down to Esau, Benjamin was not yet born; and from that day onward he never bowed down to a man. Therefore God has made with him an eternal covenant, from his mother's womb until now, that he should inhabit the land of Israel, and that the Holy House should be in his land, and that his habitation should remain within his borders, and that all the house of Israel should gather there, and that peoples should bend and bow down in his land. Therefore I will not bend or bow down before this wicked Haman, the enemy.]

In 𝔊 it does not appear whether the courtiers spoke to Mordecai to warn him of the risk that he ran in disobeying the King, or because they were jealous of his assumed superiority to them; nor does Mordecai make any reply to them. Both deficiencies are well supplied by the long addition of 𝔗².

4. *Afterward, when they had spoken to him day after day without his listening to them, they told Haman, so as to see whether Mordecai's conduct would be tolerated* [𝔗¹ + in opposition to the orders of Haman]. The courtiers bear Mordecai no grudge, and give him fair warning of his danger; but, when day after day he refuses to heed their advice, they become irritated and resolve to bring him to his senses by calling Haman's attention to him. *Be tolerated*, lit. *stand* (*cf.* Pr. 12⁷), *i.e.*, whether it would be judicially approved as legal conduct. Others following 𝔍 translate, "whether Mordecai would persist in his conduct."—*For he had told them that he was a Jew* [𝔗¹ + and that he did not bow down to Haman, because he had been his slave, who had sold himself to him for a loaf of bread; and that he would not bow down to the idol that he wore upon him, for the Jews do not serve nor bow down to such].

MORDECAI DEFIES HAMAN 199

From this it appears that Mordecai's reply to the courtiers was, that, being a Jew, he could not bow down to Haman. Why his Judaism was inconsistent with this act of homage, we are not told (*cf.* v. ²).

5. *And when Haman* [𝔍 + had heard this and] *saw that Mordecai never bowed* [𝔘¹ + to the idol] *nor prostrated himself before him,* [*Mid. A. G.*¹²ᵃ + he came toward him from another direction, and acted just as if Mordecai had saluted him, and said, My lord, peace be upon thee; but Mordecai said, There is no peace, saith the Lord, to the wicked.] [Jos.²¹⁰ + And he inquired whence he came; and, when he learned that he was a Jew,] *then Haman was full of wrath* [L + against Mordecai, and anger was kindled within him,] [Jos. + and he said to himself, that the free Persians did not hesitate to bow down to him, but that this slave did not see fit to do so.] Apparently Haman had not noticed Mordecai's conduct until the courtiers called his attention to it. This explains why so many days passed without Mordecai's getting into trouble.

2ᵇ. ומרדכי] om. ו L.—[יכרע] + αὐτῷ 𝔊 L 𝔏: + ἐπὶ τὴν γῆν πάντας, πάντων οὖν προσκυνούντων 93*a*: the impf. is used to express recurring action in the past. [ולא ישתחוה] om. 𝔊 L 𝔏 (exc. 93*b* *): + καὶ εἶδον οἱ παῖδες τοῦ βασιλέως ὅτι ὁ Μαρδοχαῖος οὐ προσκυνεῖ τὸν 'Αμάν L.

3. [עבדי המלך] om. 𝔊 𝔏 (exc. 93*b* *).—[אשר] om. 𝔖 L.—[בשער המלך] om. L.—[למרדכי] *cui* 𝔍: Μαρδοχαῖε 248: + Μαρδοχαῖε 𝔊 (exc. 44, 106: 93*b* ÷).—[עובר את מצות] *cf.* 9²⁷ 2 Ch. 24²⁰. In Dt. 26¹³ עבר ממצוה.—[את מצות] om. L.

4. [ויהי] om. 𝔊: om. יהי 𝔖.—[ויהי – אליהם] om. L.—[באמרם] כְּאָמְרָם Q. The Ḳ°thîbh is preferable to the Qᵉrê. The latter would mean 'as soon as they spoke.' ἐλάλουν 𝔊.—[אליו] om. 𝔖 𝔏.—[יום ויום] *cf.* 2¹¹.—[ויגידו – מרדכי] om. 44, 106.—[ויגידו] καὶ οὐκ ὑπέδειξαν 108*a*.—[לראות – מרדכי] Μαρδοχαῖον τοῖς τοῦ βασιλέως λόγοις ἀντιτασσόμενον 𝔊: *quoniam Mardochæus non obedit regi ut adoret te* 𝔏: περὶ αὐτοῦ L: *scire cupientes utrum perseveraret in sententia* 𝔍.—[כי] καὶ 𝔊 L.—[כי – יהודי] tr. after v. ³ L: καὶ εἶπε Μαρδοχαῖος Ιουδαῖος εἰμί 71: *eo quod sit Judæus* 𝔏: Haupt deletes the clause as an erroneous explanatory gloss to דברי מרדכי.—[הגיד] pluperf. as in 2¹⁰ 3⁶.—[להם] + ὁ Μαρδοχαῖος 𝔊 (exc. 106: 93*b* ÷).

5. [כי – לו] om. L.—[מרדכי] om. א 44, 71, 74, 76, 106, 236.—[ומשתחוה] om. 𝔊 𝔏 (exc. 93*b* *).—[וימלא – המה] + [על מרדכי] K 76, 117, 166. 188, 218, 249 𝔘¹ 𝔘² 𝔖: ἐθυμώθη σφόδρα 𝔊 𝔏: ἐθυμώθη τῷ Μαρδοχαίῳ καὶ ὀργὴ ἐξεκαύθη ἐν αὐτῷ L: *iratus est valde* 𝔍: Haupt deletes המן.

HAMAN CASTS LOTS TO DESTROY THE JEWS (3⁶⁻⁷).

6. *And it seemed to him beneath his dignity to lay hands on Mordecai alone* [𝕿¹ + to kill him,] *for they had told him* [𝕿¹ + that Mordecai was a descendant of Jacob, who had taken away from Esau, the ancestor of Haman, the right of the first-born and the blessing, and that the Jews were] *the race of Mordecai. So Haman sought to destroy all* [𝕵 + the nation of] *the Jews that were in all Xerxes' kingdom, the race of Mordecai* [L + in one day] [Jos.²¹¹ + for he was naturally hostile to the Jews, because the race of the Amalekites to which he belonged had been destroyed by them.] [L + And Haman, being jealous, and being stirred in his inmost soul, grew red, thrusting Mordecai out of his sight.] 𝕿¹ and Jos. think that Haman wished to destroy the Jews because he was an Amalekite, but 𝕳 suggests rather, that it was because Mordecai had based his refusal of homage on the ground that he was a Jew. If being a Jew prevented his bowing down, then other Jews might be expected to act similarly. That Haman should conceive this preposterous plan of destroying all the Jews for the offence of one, is perhaps possible. Raw. compares the massacre of the Scythians (Her. i. 106) and of the Magi (Her. iii. 79). No reason, however, appears why Haman should postpone his vengeance on Mordecai. He would naturally dispatch him at once, even if he intended to kill the other Jews later. The delay is due solely to literary reasons.

7. *In the first month, that is Nisan, in the twelfth year of King Xerxes*]. The month is numbered and named in the Babylonian style that was adopted by the Jews after the Exile (*cf.* 2¹⁶); the old Hebrew name of this month was *Abib*. It corresponds to our March-April. *The twelfth year, i.e.,* of the King's reign, was 474 B.C., five years after Esther had been made Queen (2¹⁶).— *They cast pur, that is, the lot, before Haman*]. The verb is singular, and Pisc., Bert., Oet., think that Haman is the subject. This is natural after v. ⁶, but does not correspond well with the next words, *before Haman*. Keil, Schu., Rys., Sieg., and most of the older versions and comm. take the subj. as impersonal, *one cast,* *they cast* (*cf.* Müll., *Syntax*, § 123, 2). Perhaps a slave was designated for this purpose, or perhaps the casting of lots was the function of a particular sort of diviner. Haman, like the King, must have had astrologers and soothsayers attached to his court. For the various theories in regard to the origin and meaning of *pur*, see *Introduction*, § 28. From the earliest times the lot has been employed in all lands as a means of ascertaining the will of the gods. Its use among the Persians is attested by Her. iii. 128; Xen. *Cyrop.* i. 6⁴⁴; iv. 5⁵⁵ (*cf.* Baum. 101 *f.*).

What Haman wished to learn from the lot, we are not told. It is commonly assumed that he sought to discover an auspicious day for ordering the destruction of the Jews, and this view is favoured by the fact that the massacre is planned (3¹³) in the same month for which the lot fell (3⁷); but the first thing that Haman would wish to ascertain would be, not the day of destruction, but a lucky day for going to the King to make his request; and, so soon as a day had been pronounced lucky, we are told that he went to the King (v. ⁸). This looks as if the lot were cast in the first instance to find a suitable time for presenting his petition; and as if, after this day had proved itself unfavourable for the Jews, it was selected in the following year as the date for their massacre.
—*From day to day and from month to month* [L 𝔍 + to know the day of their death,] [𝕲 𝕷 + so as to destroy in one day the race of Mordecai.]

> [*Mid.* (abbreviated) + The first day was unfavourable because in it God made heaven and earth. The second day was unfavourable because in it the waters were separated, as Israel is separated from the nations. The third day was unfavourable because in it seeds were created that the Israelites bring as offerings. The fourth day was unfavourable because in it the heavenly bodies were created to give Israel light. The fifth day was unfavourable because in it beasts were created for Israel to sacrifice. The sixth day was unfavourable because in it the first man was created. The seventh day was unfavourable because it was the Sabbath. Then he tried the months. Niṣan was unfavourable because of the merit of Passover; Iyar, because the manna was given in it; Sivan, because of the merit of the Law; Tammuz, because of the merit of the land; Ab, because they had already suffered enough in that month; Elul, because in it the walls of Jerusalem were finished; Tishri, because of the merit of the Feast of Trumpets, Day of Atone-

ment, and Tabernacles; Marchesvan, because Sarah died in it; Chislev, because of the Feast of Dedication; Ṭebeth, because of the merit of Ezra; Shebaṭ, because of the merit of the men of the Great Synagogue. But in Adar no merit was found.]

If the view suggested above be correct, that Haman was trying to find a lucky day for going to the King, we must suppose that he cast lots on each successive day to see whether this were favourable for his plans. Those who hold that he was trying to determine the date for the massacre, suppose that the lots for the different days were all cast at one time; but this is hardly a natural interpretation of the words *he cast the lot from day to day and from month to month*. In that case we should expect, *for day and day and for month and month*.—[𝕲 L + *and the lot fell for the fourteenth* (L, *thirteenth*) *of the month*] *the twelfth one, that is, the month of Adar*]. The text of 𝔐 makes no sense at this point, and it is necessary with Bert., G, Rys., Wild., Sieg., Buhl, Haupt, to supply the words inserted by 𝕲 L. The reading *thirteenth* in L is probably correct in view of 3[13] (see crit. note). Thirteen is an unlucky number in the Book of Est. as it was also among the ancient Babylonians. Adar is mentioned only in Est. It corresponds to February-March.

6ª. om. 𝕲 (exc. 93*b* *) L.— [ויבז בעיניו] ܠܐ ܚܣܡ̈ܘ ܘܠܐ ܣܝܢ 𝕾: *et pro nihilo duxit* 𝕵: *et quærebat* 𝕷.— [ויר] + 𝕳 𝕾.— [במרדכי] *ei* 𝕷.— [לבדו] *ut perderet eum* 𝕷.— [כי-מרדכי] Haupt deletes as a gloss.— [המן] om. 𝕵𝕲L: Haupt deletes.— [להשמיר] om. 𝕾.— [את כל-אחשורוש] om. L.— [נכל] om. כל 𝕵𝕲𝕷.— [עם מרדכי] *et Mardochæum et genus ejus* 𝕷: τὸν Μαρδοχαῖον καὶ πάντα τὸν λαὸν αὐτοῦ L: om. 𝕵𝕲: Haupt deletes as a gloss to the preceding [עם מרדכי]—היהודים] *Daghesh forte dirimens* (Ewald[8] § 28).

7. Haupt deletes the entire v. as a misplaced later addition to v. [13], but the larger part of it is sustained by the Vrss.— [בחדש-אחשורוש] om. L.— [בחדש-ניסן] om. 𝕲 (exc. א c. a mg.— [הראשון] + *neomeniæ* 𝕷.— [חדש] om. 𝕾 𝕷.— [למלך] τῆς βασιλείας 𝕲: *regnante* 𝕷.— [הפיל-המן] καὶ ἐποίησεν ψήφισμα καὶ ἔβαλεν κλήρους 𝕲: *decretum fecit et misit sortem* 𝕷: καὶ ἐπορεύθη Ἀμὰν πρὸς τοὺς θεοὺς αὐτοῦ L aft. v. [10]: *missa est sors in urnam, quæ Hebraice dicitur phur* 𝕵.— [פור] ܦܽܘܓ 𝕾: φοῦρ 93*b* *.— [הוא] ܣܬܶܡ 𝕾.— [לפני המן] so 93*b* *: om. 𝕲 𝕷.— [מיום-לחדש] om. L.— [לחדש] לחדש var. Oc.: + *gens Judæorum deberet interfici et exivit mensis* 𝕵: + ὥστε ἀπολέσαι ἐν μιᾷ ἡμέρᾳ τὸ γένος Μαρδοχαίου καὶ ἔπεσεν ὁ κλῆρος εἰς τὴν τεσσαρεσκαιδεκάτην τοῦ μηνὸς 𝕲 (93*b* om.): + τοῦ ἐπιγνῶναι ἡμέραν θανάτου αὐτῶν καὶ βάλλει κλήρους εἰς τὴν τρισκαιδεκάτην τοῦ μηνὸς L aft. v. [10]:

+ *perdere gens Mardochæi quæ cecidit sors in quarta decima die mense* 𝕷: + ܚܡܝܐ 𝕾.—שנים עשר] om. 𝕲 L (𝕷 has).—הוא] om. L.—הרש] om. 𝕲 𝕷 L 𝕾.—ארר] + Νισάν L (Νεισάν 93a) aft. v. ¹⁰.

HAMAN OBTAINS AN EDICT TO DESTROY THE JEWS (3⁸⁻¹¹).

8. [*Meg.* 13*b* + When the lot fell on the month of Adar, Haman rejoiced greatly, for he said, It is the month in which Moses died, but he forgot that it was also the month in which Moses was born. Now there was no one who could slander so well as Haman.] *And Haman spoke to King Xerxes* [𝕷 L + with base heart, evil things concerning Israel, saying,] [*Meg.* 13*b* + Let them be destroyed; but he answered, I am afraid of their God, lest he treat me as he has those who have gone before me. Haman replied, They no longer keep the commandments. But, said the King, there are rabbis among them. Haman answered,] *There is a single* [Jos.²¹² + wicked] *people* [*Meg.* + and if thou sayest, I shall make a bare spot in my kingdom, (I reply,) They are] *scattered and* [*Meg.* + if thou sayest, We have advantage from them, (I reply,) They live] *separated (although) among the races,* [𝕿¹ + and nations and tongues] [*Meg.* + like mules that are unproductive. And if thou sayest, they live in one country, (I reply,) They are] *in all the provinces of thy kingdom.*] *Scattered* refers to the *Diaspora*, which began with the Exile and reached its height in the Greek period. The statement that Jews are found *in all the provinces* shows that the author lived later than the Persian period. *Separated* refers to the barrier of the Law, which the Jews erected in the post-exilic period to save themselves from being absorbed by the heathen world. The language of Dt. 4⁵⁻⁸ is in the author's mind. What is there the boast of the Jew, Haman here uses as a reproach.—[L + They are a warlike and treacherous people,] [Jos.²¹² + unadaptable, unsociable, not having the same sort of worship as others.] [𝕿² + They are proud and haughty of spirit. In January they gather snow and in July they sit in (hot) baths, and their customs are different from those of every people,] *and their laws differ from (those of) every race.*

[*Meg.* + They will not eat with us, nor drink with us, nor will they intermarry with us.] [𝕿¹ + Our bread and our food they do not eat, our wine they do not drink, our birthdays they do not celebrate, and our laws they do not keep,] *and the laws of the King they do not obey*, [*Meg.* + because they observe now Sabbath, now Passover, and other feasts different from ours.] [L 𝕷 + They are known among all nations to be wicked and to disregard thine injunctions.] [𝕌² + When they see us, they spit on the ground, and regard us as an unclean thing; and when we go to speak to them, or to summon them, or to make them render some service to the King, they climb over walls, or break through hedges, or ascend to rooms, or get through gaps; and when we run to seize them, they turn and stand with flashing eyes, and gnashing teeth and stamping feet, and they frighten people, so that we are not able to seize them. They do not give their daughters to us as wives, and they do not take our daughters unto them; and whoever of them is drafted to do the King's service makes an exception of that day with excuses; and the day on which they wish to buy from us they say is a lawful day, but on the day when we wish to buy from them they shut the bazaars against us, and say to us, It is a forbidden day. In the first hour they say, We are repeating the *Shema;* in the second, We are praying our prayers; in the third, We are eating food; in the fourth, We are blessing the God of heaven because he has given us food and water; in the fifth, they go out; in the sixth, they return; and in the seventh, their wives go out to meet them and say, Bring split beans, because you are weary with working for this wicked king. They go up to their synagogue and read in their scriptures and interpret their prophets, and curse our king and revile our rulers, and say, This is the day in which the great God rested. Their unclean women on the seventh day go out at midnight and defile the waters. On the eighth day they circumcise their sons and do not spare them, but say that they are distinguishing them from the heathen. (The rest of the passage which relates to the Jewish feasts is too long to insert.)]

No better commentary on the meaning of the v. could be found than these additions of the Vrss. They show why anti-Semitism was as prevalent in antiquity as in modern times (*cf.* Ezr. 4^{12-16}). —*And it is not proper for the King to tolerate them*, [*Meg.* + because they eat and drink in a manner to disgrace the King; for if a fly fall into a goblet of wine, they take it out and drink it; but if the King touches the goblet of wine, they pour it out.] Haman's real argument, which is obscured by the additions of the Vrss., is, that Mordecai's Judaism has made him disobey the King's command; therefore all Jews may be expected to be lawbreakers. This is a good deal like Mᵉmûkhān's argument in 1^{16-18}.

9. *If it seems good to the King,* [L 𝔏 + and the decision is good in his heart,] [Jos.²¹³ + and if thou wilt do a favour to thy subjects]. This is the regular formula for presenting a proposition to the King (*cf.* 1¹⁹).—*Let it be written* [𝔗¹ + in a writing] *to destroy them,* [Jos. + and that no remnant of them be left, nor any of them be preserved in slavery or in captivity. But, that thou mayest not lose the revenue that accrues from them, I will make it up out of my own fortune,] *and I will weigh out* 10,000 *talents of silver* [Jos.²¹⁴ + whenever thou commandest] *into the hands of the proper officials to bring into the King's treasuries.*

> [Jos. + And I will pay this money gladly that the kingdom may be delivered from these evils.] [*Mid.* 13*b* + It was known to him who said one word and the world was created, that Haman would one day offer money for Israel. Therefore he had commanded before, that they should pay shekels of silver to the Lord, as we have learned in a *mishna*, that on the first of Adar it was announced that the shekels should be given (*cf.* JT. *Meg.* 1⁵).] [𝔗¹ 𝔗² + And what does the sum equal? It equals the 600,000 minas that their fathers paid when they went up out of the bondage of the Egyptians.]

The unit of measure for silver in the Persian empire was the light Babylonian royal shekel weighing 172.8 gr. troy and worth almost exactly 2 shillings. The mina was composed of 60 shekels and the talent of 60 minas. The talent thus contained 3,600 shekels and was worth about £360 (see *HDB.* iii. 421; *EBi.* iv. 4443 *ff.*; Weissbach, *ZDMG.* 1907, p. 402). The 10,000 talents that Haman promised were thus worth about £3,600,000 or $18,000,000. The purchasing value of this sum was, of course, much greater in antiquity than at the present time. How the author came to hit upon this amount is shown by the additions of *Meg.*, 𝔗¹, and 𝔗². In Nu. 2³² the total number of the children of Israel is set at 600,000. By paying a mina apiece for their destruction, instead of the half shekel that they paid for their redemption (Ex. 30¹¹⁻¹³), the sum is obtained (*cf.* Nöldeke in *EBi.* ii. 1401).

According to Her. iii. 95, the total revenue of the Persian empire was 14,560 Euboeic talents or nearly 17,000 Babylonian talents. Haman thus offered almost ⅔ of the annual income of the empire. How he proposed to raise this vast sum we are not told. Tir., Bert., Keil, Oet., Wild., Sieg., suppose that he intended to secure it from the plunder of the slaughtered Jews (*cf.* 3¹³), and that this indicates the author's estimate of the wealth that was in their hands; but 3¹³ suggests that the plunder was offered to those who did the work of killing, and in 8¹¹ 9¹⁵ the Jews are permitted to keep the spoil of their enemies. We must suppose, therefore, with Jos. and most comm., that the author means to represent Haman as promising this sum out of his own private fortune. In regard to the probability of such an offer opinions differ. Raw. compares Pythius' offer of 4,000,000 gold darics to Darius (Her. vii. 28) and Tritæchmes' income of an *artabe* of silver daily (Her. i. 192). Monarchs must have been juster in the ancient Orient than they are in the modern Orient, if a subject could safely make such a display of wealth. Haman hopes that his generous offer will tempt the King to look with favour upon his plan. Those who regard the book as historical point out that Xerxes' finances must have been greatly impoverished by his unsuccessful war with Greece, and that he would naturally be glad to recoup himself in this manner.

10. *And the King drew off his signet-ring* [𝔍 + which he used] *from his hand and gave it to Haman, son of Hamm^edāthā the Agagite, the enemy of the Jews*, [𝕲 + into his hand to seal what had been written concerning the Jews.] In ancient times the seal took the place of the written signature, hence to give a man one's seal was equivalent to allowing him to sign one's name (*cf.* 8². ⁸. ⁹ Gn. 41⁴² 1 Mac. 6¹⁵). The Jews were now at Haman's mercy. Originally seals were worn on cords hung around the neck. Subsequently they were set in rings (*cf. HDB.* Art. "Seal"; *EBi.* Art. "Ring"). On the proper names, see p. 69. *The enemy of the Jews* defines more precisely what is suggested in the title *Agagite* (*cf.* 3¹).

11. *And the King said to Haman, The silver* [𝔍 + which thou hast promised] *is given to thee*]. It is beneath the King's dignity to take a bribe for doing something that will promote public welfare. Those who think that Haman proposes to raise the money by confiscating the property of the Jews, hold that the King bestows this sum upon him as a reward for his service in denouncing the traitors.—*And the people* [𝔗¹ + is delivered into thy hand] *to do with it as seems good to thee.*] There is not the least delay or hesitation on the part of the King in handing over the entire Jewish race to destruction. Not merely the Jews in Susa and in the provinces of the Persian empire, but also those in Palestine are included in the edict. Despot as Xerxes was, it may well be questioned whether such an insane project ever met with his approval.

8. וַ] om. 𝔖.—[הָמָן om. 𝔊 (exc. 44, 71, 74, 76, 106, 120, 236: 93*b* *) 𝔏.—[אֲחַשְׁוֵרוֹשׁ] *ficto corde propter genus Judæorum et dixit* 𝔏: καρδίᾳ φαύλῃ κακὰ περὶ Ἰσραὴλ λέγων L: + λέγων 𝔊 (om. 93*b*): Haupt deletes.—[יֶשְׁנוֹ] with ו inserted before the suf. as in Dt. 29¹⁴ 1 S. 14³⁹ 23²³ (*cf.* König, *L.* ii. 1, 102; Ols. § 97*b*; Stade, § 370*b*; Brockelmann in *ZA.* xv. pp. 347 *ff.*). The form should probably be pointed יֶשְׁנוּ (*cf.* Haupt *a. l.*).—אחד] om. 𝔖𝔊𝔏 L. —[וּמְפֹרָד om. 𝔊 (exc. 93*b* *) L: *incredibile* 𝔏.—מפזר ומפרד] both *Pual* ptc. ܐ.ܠ.—[בֵּין הָעַמִּים] om. 𝔍 𝔏 L.—[מדינות] om. 𝔊𝔏 L.—[מַלְכוּתֶךָ] ܡܠܟܐ ܐܣܡܝܢ 𝔖: ταῖς βασιλείαις L: + λαὸς πολέμου καὶ ἀπειθής L.—[וְדָתֵיהֶם + *et cæremoniis* 𝔍.—[מִכָּל עָם] om. 𝔍 𝔏 L.—[הַמֶּלֶךְ σοῦ βασιλεῦ L: *tuis* 𝔏.— [עֹשִׂים] + *et optime nosti* 𝔍: + *qui cognoscuntur in omni pestilentia et præcepta tua spernunt* 𝔏: + γνωριζόμενοι ἐν πᾶσι τοῖς ἔθνεσι πονηροὶ ὄντες καὶ τὰ προστάγματά σου ἀθετοῦσι L.—[וְלַמֶּלֶךְ-לְהַנִּיחָם πρὸς καθαίρεσιν τῆς δόξης σου L; *in diem munitionis gloriæ tuæ* 𝔏.—[לְהַנִּיחָם] on the Aramaizing *Hiph.* inf. with *Daghesh*, see BDB. 628 B. The word has rather an Aram. than a Heb. meaning.

9. [טוב] + καὶ ἀγαθὴ ἡ κρίσις ἐν καρδίᾳ αὐτοῦ L: + *et optimum est sensui tuo* 𝔏.—[יִכָּתֵב לְאַבְּדָם δοθήτω μοι τὸ ἔθνος εἰς ἀπώλειαν L: *detur mihi genus hoc in perditionem* 𝔏.—[לאבדם] om. ס 𝔍 𝔖. The *Pi.* of this vb. is used of massacres on a large scale (*cf.* 3¹³ 2 K. 11¹), Winck. 26 deletes as a gloss.—[כסף]om. 𝔍 𝔏.—[עַל-לְהָבִיא] om. 𝔊 (exc. 93*b* *, א ᶜ·ᵃ ᵐᵍ) L 𝔏.—[על]so Oc.: אל var. Or.—[עֹשֵׂי הַמְּלָאכָה] of royal officials in general 9³ (*cf.* 1 Ch. 29⁶). Here the following words show that treasury officials are meant.—[לְהָבִיא om. 𝔍.—[גנזי] pl. as in 4⁷.—[הַמֶּלֶךְ²] *tuæ* 𝔍: *tuo* 𝔏: om. L.

10. aft. 3¹¹ L.—[טַבַּעְתּוֹ] + αὐτοῦ A.—[מֵעַל יָדוֹ] om. 𝔊𝔏.—[וַיִּתְּנָהּ] + εἰς χεῖρα(ς) 𝔊𝔏 (exc. א *).—[בֶּן-הַיְּהוּדִים] om. 𝔊𝔏 L: Haupt deletes as a gloss.

11. [הַמֶּלֶךְ] om. 𝔏.—[לְהָמָן] *eum* 𝔍: αὐτῷ L: om. 𝔖 𝔏.—Instead of הכסף נתון לך והעם Haupt proposes to read העם נתון לך and to regard הכסף as a gloss, on the ground that no Oriental monarch would thus make a present of 10,000 talents to his vizier. The conjecture is unsupported by the Vrss., and it is unnecessary to make any emendations in Est. on the ground that a statement is historically improbable.

AN EDICT TO DESTROY THE JEWS IS SENT OUT (3$^{12-15}$).

12. *And*, [Jos. + when Haman had gained what he desired,] *the King's scribes were called* [𝔖 + on that day] *in the first month, on its thirteenth day.*] The *scribes* had charge of the engrossing of royal edicts (*cf.* 8⁹). If every language and script of the Persian empire was used, as the following clause asserts, there must have been a large body of clerks. Those who suppose that Haman cast lots (3⁷) to determine the date for the destruction of the Jews, think that the scribes were called in the same month. If, however, the lots were cast to determine a time for asking this favour of the King, then the scribes were called in Nisan of Xerxes' thirteenth year (see on 3⁷).

[𝔗¹ + And the (heavenly) King sent unto his Temple by his righteous servants unto Haggai, Zechariah, and Malachi, who sat in the chamber of hewn stones and prophesied there concerning the great wall of Jerusalem. And after 72 of its towers had been built, the wicked Xerxes sent and brought 127 scribes out of 127 provinces, every man with a scroll and a tablet in his hand; and they sat in the gate of Susa; and they wrote, and they sent out hard edicts against the Jews and against their laws.]

And a dispatch was prepared in accordance with all that Haman commanded [𝕷 + the scribes] *unto* [𝔍 + all] *the King's satraps and unto the governors,* [𝔗¹ + who had been appointed rulers] *over every single province* [𝔊𝕷 + from India to Ethiopia, 127 provinces,] *and unto the officials of every single race*]. Here there are three grades of officials: *the satraps*, ruling over the 20 great divisions of the empire; *the governors*, ruling over the smaller subdivisions; and *the officials*, serving under the governors (*cf.* 1¹·³).
—*To every single province in its script, and every single race in its language*], see 1²².—*In the name of King Xerxes it was written, and it was sealed with the King's seal,* [L + for no one can annul that which is sealed.] This is the use to which Haman puts the seal that is given him v. ¹⁰ (*cf.* 8⁸).

13. *And dispatches were sent out by means of couriers*], *cf.* 1²² 3¹⁵ 8¹⁰·¹⁴. These are the ἄγγαροι of Her., Xen., and Jos., who were stationed at intervals of four or five parasangs, and who forwarded dispatches with extraordinary rapidity. In 8¹⁰ they ride on thoroughbred royal race horses; but that is not stated here, as there was no need at this time for special haste.—*Unto all the King's provinces, to destroy, to slay, and to annihilate all the Jews, from boy to old man, children and women*]. The heaping up of synonyms is in imitation of the legal style, and is common in Est. (*cf.* 8¹¹). On the probability of this wholesale slaughter, see v. ¹¹.—*In one day, on the thirteenth of the twelfth month, that is, the month of Adar*]. If, as suggested above, Haman cast lots to determine the day for presenting his petition to the King (3⁷) and decided on the 13th of Adar, in Xerxes' 12th year, then the day for the massacre was set one year later, on the 13th of Adar in the 13th year.

The reason for this extraordinary delay of nearly a year is hard to find. If the Jews had been warned a year in advance of their impending destruction, they would have found means to escape. The massacre of St. Bartholomew would not have been a great success if the Huguenots had been informed a year beforehand. Schu. thinks that this long time was needed for the preparation and sending out of the dispatches to remote provinces, but this does not accord with what we know of the excellence of the Persian postal system. Bert. thinks that it was to enhance the suffering of the Jews by keeping them in suspense as long as possible. Cler., Keil, Raw., suppose that it was to give the Jews an opportunity to leave the country, but Haman is hardly to be credited with any such benevolent intention. The reason probably is merely literary. The author wishes to put the massacre on the unlucky 13th of Adar in the 13th year, and also to gain time for the development of Haman's pride and for the issuing of the counter edict by Mordecai.—*And to plunder their goods* [$\mathfrak{S}$ + In one day, in the month of Adar, on the thirteenth it was written.] This is offered as an inducement to all people to attack the Jews. There is no suggestion that the plunder is to be gathered into the royal treasuries or to be given to Haman (*cf.* 3⁹). According to *Meg.* 12*a* the reason why God sent this disaster upon the Jews was because they had attended Xerxes' feast.

ADDITION B.

XERXES' LETTER.

At this point 𝕲 𝕷 L insert what purports to be a copy of Haman's letter (B[1-7]). Jos. gives a free reproduction of the substance of 𝕲. 𝕿[2] gives under 4[1] a letter similar in substance but differently expressed. It is probably derived indirectly from 𝕲. In regard to the authenticity of the addition, see *Introduction*, § 20. For a critical apparatus to the text, see **Paton** in *HM*. ii. pp. 18-20. The addition reads as follows:—

> [1]Now this is the copy of the letter: The great King Artaxerxes writes these things to the governors of 127 provinces from India to Ethiopia, and to the officials that are subject to them. [2]After I became lord over many nations, and had dominion over the whole world, without being lifted up with presumption of my authority, but carrying myself always with equity and mildness, I purposed to settle my subjects continually in a quiet life; and, by making my kingdom peaceable, and open for passage to the utmost coasts, to renew peace, which is desired by all men. [3]Now when I asked my counsellors how this might be brought to pass, Haman, that excelled in wisdom among us, and was approved for his constant good will and steadfast fidelity, and had the honour of the second place in the kingdom, [4]declared unto us, that in all nations throughout the world there was scattered a certain malignant people, that had laws contrary to all nations, and continually set aside the commandments of kings, so that the union honourably intended by us, cannot be established. [5]Seeing then we understand that this nation is alone continually in opposition to all men, following by their laws an alien life, and evil-affected to our state, working all the mischief they can, that our kingdom may not be firmly established: [6]therefore have we commanded, that they that are indicated in writing unto you by Haman, who is ordained over the affairs, and is a second father unto us, shall all, with their wives and children, be utterly destroyed by the sword of their enemies, without any mercy or pity, on the fourteenth day of the twelfth month Adar of this present year: [7]so that they who of old and now also are malicious, may in one day with violence go down to Hades, and so ever hereafter cause our affairs to be well settled, and without trouble.

14. *The contents of the edict (were), Let it be given out as law in every single province, published to all the races, to be ready for this day* [Jos. + for the destruction of the Jews]. *The contents* is lit.

the copy, not *a copy*, as AV. and RV. render, because the following genitive is definite. The purpose of the dispatches has been indicated so fully already in v. ¹³ that only a brief summary of their contents is given here. If the long addition of 𝔊 had stood in the original text, this v. would have been unnecessary; or, at least, the addition must have followed it instead of preceding it, as it is clumsily inserted in 𝔊. *This day* means the 13th of Adar, as indicated in v. ¹³.

15. *The couriers went out expedited by the King's order*]. Haman hastens the matter as much as possible so as to get the law promulgated before the King changes his mind. If there was such haste, the postponement of the execution of the Jews cannot have been due to the need of a long time for circulating the edict. —*And the law was given out in Susa the fortress*], *i.e.*, simultaneously with the dispatching of the couriers. On *Susa the fortress*, see 1². [𝔏 + And all the gentiles made a feast,] *and the King and Haman sat down to drink* [𝔗¹ + wine]. This is a very effective piece of contrast. Orders have been sent out that will throw the empire into confusion, but the King and his prime minister enjoy themselves after finishing this troublesome business. Perhaps, as in 7¹, we should translate *banquet* instead of *drink*, regarding the verb as a denominative from the word 'banquet,' lit. 'drinking.' *And the city of Susa was perplexed* [L + at these events] [𝔗¹ + on account of the joy of the heathen and the mourning cry of the people of the house of Israel]. *The city of Susa* is the metropolis in contrast to Susa the fortress (see 1²). That the people of Susa would feel any great grief over the destruction of the Jews is improbable. The author here ascribes his own emotions to them.

[𝔏 + And the Jews invoked the God of their fathers and said: Lord God, thou alone art God in heaven above, and there is no other God besides thee. If we had kept thy Law and thy precepts, we should perhaps have dwelt in peace all our life long; but now, because we have not kept thy precepts, all this trouble is come upon us. Thou art just, and calm, and exalted, and great, O Lord, and all thy ways are justice. And now, O God, do not give thy children up to captivity, nor our wives to violation, nor to ruin; for thou hast become favourable to us from Egypt even until now. Pity thy chosen people and give not our heritage up to shame, that our enemies should rule over us. And in Susa, the city nearest to the King, a copy was displayed and the writings became known.]

12. ויקראו - בו] om. L.— הראשון] + αὐτὸς ὁ μὲν Νισὰν (καὶ) א c. a mg inf, 93b ÷.—יום בו] om. 𝕲 (exc. א c. a mg, 93b ÷): τοῦ μηνὸς 44, 71, 74, 76, 106, 120, 236: ܚܣܝܢܐ ܗܘ 𝕾: *die* 𝕷.—ויכתב] om. ו 𝕾: λέγων γράφε L: καὶ ἔγραψαν 𝕲: *et scripta sunt* 𝕷.— אשר - ככל 2] om. L.— ככל] om. 𝕲𝕷 (exc. 93b *).—אל] + *omnes* 𝕵.— אחשדרפני] τοῖς στρατηγοῖς 𝕲: *et ducibus* 𝕷: *satrapes* 𝕵: ܐܣܛܪܛܝܠܘܣ 𝕾: אסטרטילוסי 𝕿[1]: יקירוי 𝕿[2]. (*Cf.* 8[9] 9[3].) The word is Pers. khshatra-pāvan, Gr. σατράπης, 'protectors of the realm' (*cf.* Spiegelberg, *Altpers. Keilinschr.*, p. 215. Lagarde, *Ges. Abhl.*, p. 68, 14; *Sem.*, i. 42 *f.* reads אֲהַשְׁדַּרְפָּן.— המלך] om. 2 𝕲 (exc. 93b *).— הפחות] a loanword through the Aram. of As. *paḫāti*, an abbreviation of *bêl-paḫāti*, 'lord of the province' (see BDB. 806).—על] + כל 𝕾 𝕲 𝕷.— מדינה] τὰς χώρας L: πόλεις 93a.— ומדינה] om. 𝕲 (exc. א c. a) L (exc. 93a).—ואל - נכתב] om. L.—ואל ערי] om. 𝕵.— עם ועם] ܠܥܡܡܐ 𝕾: τῶν ἐθνῶν κατὰ τὴν αὐτῶν λέξιν 𝕲: *uniuscujusque loci gentium secundum interpretationem eorum* 𝕷.— מדינה - כלשנו] om. 𝕲𝕷.— אהשורש] so Oc.: var. Or. אחשורוש: Haupt deletes.— נכתב] 𝕵 𝕲: pr. καὶ 93b 𝕷.— ונחתם - המלך] om. 𝕲 (exc. 93b *). — ונחתם [ונחתם] Ba. G: καὶ σφραγίζου L: *Niph.* pf. or ptc. If pf., it is an instance of the late use of pf. with ו connect. instead of impf. with ו consec.— המלך] 4 *ipsius* 𝕵.

13. Winck. 26 deletes the whole v. as a late addition.— ונשלוח] *Niph.* inf. abs. in continuation of the narrative after impf. with ו consec. (see Kau. § 113, *z*).— ונשלוח - הרצים] καὶ ἀπεστάλη διὰ βιβλιαφόρων 𝕲 (βιβλιογράφων 243, 248, C, Ald.): καὶ ἔσπευσε καὶ ἔδωκεν εἰς χεῖρας τρεχόντων ἱππέων L (tr. aft. 3[13b]): *et dimissæ sunt litteræ per librarios* 𝕷.— אל - המלך] om. L 44, 106: εἰς τὴν Ἀρταξέρξου βασιλείαν 𝕲𝕷.— להרג ולאבד] om. 𝕲𝕷 L (exc. 93b *).— להרג] pr. ו 𝕾 𝕵.— ולאבר] om. 𝕵.— אח כל] τὸ γένος 𝕲𝕷.— מנער - ונשים] om. 𝕲𝕷 (exc. 93b *): ἀπὸ ἀρσενικοῦ ἕως θηλυκοῦ καὶ διαρπάζειν τὰ νήπια L.— ביום - לבוז] om. L.— בשלושה עשר] om. 𝕲𝕷 (exc. 93b *).— שנים עשר] *undecimo* 𝕷: om. 𝕾.— הוא] om. 𝕾.— חדש] om. 𝕾 𝕲𝕷 (exc. 93b *). — ושללם] ܘܣܝܒܗܘܢ 𝕾: καὶ τὰ ὑπάρχοντα αὐτῶν 𝕲𝕷.— לבוז] *diarpásai* 𝕲𝕷: + ܘܢܚܡܘܢ ܐܢܘܢ ܐܝܟ ܚܝܘܬܐ ܒܪܬܐ 𝕾.

14. om. L 71.— פתשגן הכתב] *summa epistolarum hæc fuit* 𝕵: τὰ δὲ ἀντίγραφα τῶν ἐπιστολῶν 𝕲: om. 𝕷.— פתשגן] *cf.* 4[8] 8[13]. In Ezr. 4[11. 23] 5[6] 7[11] it appears as פרשגן. It is a loan-word through the Aram. from O. Pers. *paticayan* (see Andreae, in Marti, *Aram. Gram.*, p. 79*; Gildemeister, *WZKM.* iv. 210; Lagarde, *Ges. Abhl.* 79; *Armen. Stud.* § 1838; Meyer, *Ent.* 22; BDB. 1109).— להנתן [להנתן] Ba. G: *ut scirent* 𝕵: ἐξετίθετο 𝕲: *et imperatum est* 𝕷. The inf. with ל is regarded by Sieg. as introducing the contents of the edict, as in 1[22]. Haupt regards the clause להנתן דת בכל מדינה ומדינה as equivalent to a relative clause modifying הכתב.— דת] see 1[8. 15] 2[12] 3[8]: om. 𝕵 𝕾 𝕲 𝕷 (exc. 93b *).— בכל] om. כל 𝕲: *omnibus* 𝕷.—

THE TERROR OF THE JEWS

גלוי – העמים] om. 𝖏.— העמים] om. 𝕲 (exc. 93*b* *).— ומדינה] om. 𝕷.— מדינה – העמים
גלוי] **صفه** 𝕊: καὶ προσετάγη 𝕲: not in agreement with דת which is f. (*cf.*
3⁸·¹⁵ 4¹¹), but with the impersonal subj. of יהי understood before להנתן.
Keil, Haupt, take it in agreement with פתשגן, and regard the clause beginning with להנתן as a parenthesis explaining the contents of the edict;
but on this interpretation the publication of the law takes place before
the sending out of couriers (v. ¹⁵). Keil avoids this difficulty by translat-
ing גלוי 'unsealed' (*cf.* Je. 32¹¹·¹⁴), but this is less natural than the construction proposed above which is that of Bert., Rys., Sieg.— להיות – הוה]
Winck. (26) deletes as a late addition.— עתידים] so N¹ S Br. C B¹: עתדים
Ba. G.— הוה] *statutum* 𝕷.

15. הרצים – המלך] om. L.— הרצים – יצאו] om. 𝕲 𝕷 (exc. 93*b* *).— דחופים
בדבר] ἐσπεύδετο δὲ τὸ πρᾶγμα 𝕲 𝕷 (γράμμα 52, 64).— דחופים] lit. 'driven,'
'impelled.' The vb. occurs only here and 6¹² 8¹⁴ 2 Ch. 26²⁰.— המלך] om.
𝕲 𝕷 (exc. 93*b* *).— בְּשׁוּשָׁן] בְּשׁוּשָׁן some
codd. and edd.: + *et convivium fecerunt omnes gentes* 𝕷.— הבירה] om. 𝖏
𝕲 𝕷 L (exc. 93*b* *).— והמלך – לשתות] om. L: *Aman autem cum introisset
regiam cum amicis luxuriabatur* 𝕷.— לשתות] + **صه.** 𝕊.— והעיר – נבוכה]
tr. aft. 4¹ L: om. 𝕷 (*cf.* 4³): *et cunctis Judæis qui in urbe erant flentibus* 𝖏.
— שׁוּשָׁן] so B²: שׁוֹשָׁן Ba. G: om. 𝖏 𝕲 (exc. 93*b* *).

MORDECAI AND ALL THE JEWS ARE FILLED WITH TERROR (4¹⁻³).

1. *When Mordecai had learned* [𝕿¹ + through Elijah the high
priest] *all that had been done*] [𝕿¹ + in the highest heavens], *i.e.*,
not merely the royal edict published in Susa and the consequences
of his arrogant refusal to bow down to Haman, but also the circumstances of the issuing of the edict. In 4⁷ Mordecai is able
to tell Esther how Haman obtained the decree. The same secret
sources of information that helped him in the case of the two
eunuchs (2²²) apparently still stood at his disposal.

> [𝕿¹ + And that the people of the house of Israel had been condemned
> to be destroyed from the world; and that, just as it was written and sealed
> to destroy them from off the face of the earth, so it was written and sealed
> in the highest heavens, because they had enjoyed the feast of the wicked
> Xerxes (however the seal was sealed with clay); then the Lord of the
> world sent Elijah the high priest to declare to Mordecai himself that he
> should continue praying before the Lord of the world for his people: and
> when he knew this,] [L + coming to his house,]

Mordecai rent his garments, and clothed himself with a hair garment [𝕿¹ + upon his flesh] *and* [𝕲 𝕷 𝕵 𝕿¹ + strewed] *ashes* [𝕷 𝕿¹ + upon his head]. These were familiar signs of mourning among the Hebrews (Gn. 37²⁹· ³⁴ 1 S. 4¹² 2 S. 1² 13¹⁹ 15³² 1 K. 20³¹ ᶠ· 2 K. 6³⁰). *The garments* were *rent* when bad news first arrived. *Haircloth* and *ashes* were put on later. The ellipsis of a verb before *ashes* is supplied by the Vrss., but the insertion is unnecessary. These rites belonged originally to the cult of the dead, being designed to protect one from the attacks of malevolent spirits; subsequently they became general signs of grief, and were believed to be efficacious in turning away the divine wrath (1 K. 21²⁷ 2 K. 19¹ᶠ· Dn. 9³ Jon. 3⁶). Nothing is said by the author of any religious significance in Mordecai's conduct, but it can hardly be doubted that this was in his mind (see p. 95).—*And Mordecai went out into the midst of the city and raised a loud and bitter cry* [𝕷 + from the court of the men even unto the gate of the women,] [𝕿¹ + and wept in the bitterness of his spirit with the voice of one afflicted.] *Cf.* Gn. 37³⁴ 2 S. 13¹⁹ Ez. 27³⁰; Her. viii. 99; ix. 24.— [𝕲 𝕷 + saying, An innocent people is condemned to death.] [*Meg.* 14*b* + Haman is greater than Xerxes, an earthly king is more esteemed than a heavenly.] [𝕿² + Alas! how terrible is this edict that the King and Haman have decreed against us. Not a half is cut off and a half spared, not even a third or a fourth; but concerning the whole body of us he has decreed to destroy and to uproot (followed by a long account of an assembly of the Jews and Mordecai's address to them).]

2. *And* [Jos. + having spoken thus,] *he came as far as the space in front of the gate* [𝕿¹ + of the palace] *of the King* [𝕲 L + and stood], *for no one could enter the gate* [𝕿¹ + of the palace] *of the King in hair clothing* [𝕲 + and ashes]. Haircloth was a sign of mourning for the dead and, consequently, was ceremonially unclean (among the Persians?), so that Mordecai could not enter the palace; but he was anxious to come as near as possible in order to establish communication with Esther. On the question whether he would have had access if he had not been dressed in mourning, see 2¹¹. On *King's gate*, see 2¹⁹.

3. *And in every single province* [𝕿¹ + and in every single city] *wherever the King's command and his law arrived,* [Jos. + all did the same as Mordecai;] *there was great* [L + and bitter] *mourning* [𝕷 + and grief] *among* [L 𝕷 + all] *the Jews, and fasting, and weeping, and lamentation* [Jos. + on account of the calamities decreed against them]. These are probably to be understood as religious acts performed in unison by the Jewish communities when the fatal news reached them. After the fall of Jerusalem days of mourning and fasting became a regular part of the Jewish calendar (*cf.* Zc. 7³⁻⁵ 8¹⁹ Lev. 23²⁷ ᶠᶠ·). In 9²²· ³¹ laments and fasts are contrasted with "good days" or holidays.—*Haircloth and ashes were spread out by most of them* [𝔊¹ + that were righteous], that they might lie and sit upon them as the expression of deepest grief (see note). Here also there is no mention of God, yet it cannot be doubted that the acts have a religious significance (see p. 95).

1. ומרדכי] *et hic* 𝕷.—כל] om. 𝔊 𝕷.—אשר נעשה] *scripta quæ erant in epistola* 𝕷: + 3¹⁵ 4³ in part *q.v.* L.—ויקרע] περιείλετο L.—מרדכי] om. 𝔍 𝔊 𝕷: Haupt deletes.—שק] appears also as a sign of mourning in Babylonia (*cf.* III. R. 36, 3*d*; Winckler, *Altor. Forsch.* ii. p. 44; Jensen, *KB.* vi. p. 400), from which Zimmern (*KAT.*³ pp. 603, 650) concludes that it is a Bab. loan-word in Heb. It seems to have been a loin-cloth of goat or camel hair, the original dress of the desert, that survived in later religious rites.—ואפר] καὶ σφοδαθεὶς L: om. 71.—ויצא - ומרה] om. L.—ויצא] om. יצא 𝔍.—בתוך] διὰ τῆς πλατείας 𝔊: *per totam plateam* 𝕷.—ויזעק] + ἐν Σύσοις τῇ πόλει 93*b* ÷.—זעקה] *et vociferans* 𝕷: om. 71.—גדולה] om. 𝕷 71.—ומרה] om. 𝔊 𝕷: *ostendens amaritudinem animi sui et hoc ejulatu* 𝔍.

2. ויבוא] *et sedit* 𝕷.—עד] *in* 𝕷.—לפני] om. 𝔖: *atrio* 𝕷.—שער] τὴν αὐλὴν L: *aulæ* 𝕷: τῆς πόλεως 93*b*: τῆς αὐλῆς A.—המלך] τὴν ἔξω L: *muliebris* 𝕷: om. 93*b*.—אין] + נלבוש 𝔖.—אין לבוא] *cf.* Kau. § 114 *k*.—שער] τὴν αὐλὴν 𝔊 𝕷: πύλην א ᶜ·ᵃ ᵐᵍ, 93*b*: om. L.—המלך] om. 𝔊 𝕷: τῆς πόλεως 93*b*: τὰ βασίλεια L.—שק] + καὶ σποδόν 𝔊 (93*b* ÷).

3. tr. to 4¹ L: tr. to 3¹⁵ end 𝕷.—מדינה] πόλει L: om. 𝕷.—ומדינה] *oppidis* 𝔍: om. 𝔊 𝕷 𝔖 (exc. א ᶜ·ᵃ ᵐᵍ, 93*b* *).—ומדינה - מגיע] om. L.—מקום] *ac locis* 𝔍.—מקום] cstr. before the relative clause (Kau. § 130*c*).—דבר] τὰ γράμματα 𝔊: *exemplum epistolæ* 𝕷 (τὸ πρόσταγμα א ᶜ·ᵃ ᵐᵍ).—המלך] om. 𝔊 𝕷 (exc. א ᶜ·ᵃ ᵐᵍ, 93*b* *).—ודתו] *crudele* 𝔍: om. 𝔖 𝔊 𝕷.—מגיע] intrans. 'arrived,' *cf.* 6¹⁴ Gn. 28¹².—אבל] pr. καὶ 𝔊 L: tr. aft. ומספד 𝔊.—גדול] + ἐγένετο 44: + ἐγίνετο 74, 76, 106, 236.—וצום - לרבים] om. L 𝕷.—וצום] om. 𝔊 (exc. 93*b* *).—ובכי] κραυγὴ 𝔊 (κλαυθμός 93*b* *).—ומספד] + ἦν καὶ A: + καὶ 44, 74, 76, 106, 120, 236, C.—יצע] *pro strato utentibus* 𝔍.—לרבים] ἑαυτοῖς 𝔊. If the text be sound, לָרַבִּים must be translated 'by most of them.' For ל expressing the agent after a passive vb., see Kau. § 121 *f*. The presence of the article precludes the translation 'many' of AV. and RV. Haupt reads יָצַע (ptc. = מֻצָּע, cf. Kau. § 53 s) and translates 'most of them had a sack-cloth and overspread ashes.' In this case יָצַע agrees only with אפר, and ל with רבים denotes possession.

ESTHER INQUIRES WHAT IS THE MATTER, AND IS CHARGED BY MORDECAI TO GO TO THE KING, AND TO PLEAD FOR HER PEOPLE (4^{4-9}).

4. *And Esther's maids and her eunuchs came in and told her* [Jos. + that Mordecai stood thus in mourning garb before the court]. The *maids* have been mentioned before (2^9); the *eunuchs* were assigned after her marriage (*cf.* 4^5). These people all know that Esther is a relative of Mordecai (*cf.* 2^{22}) and understand that she will be glad to hear news of him; yet, strange to say, none of them suspects that she is a Jewess (*cf.* 2^{20}). How this is possible, the author does not explain. What they tell Esther, apparently, is merely the fact that Mordecai is in mourning (*cf.* vv. 7 *ff.*).— *And the Queen was exceedingly shocked* [𝔊 + when she heard what had happened], not, as Haupt thinks, at the fact that Mordecai was so slightly clad, for this was customary, but at the grief of which it was a sign. Jewish authorities differ as to the way in which Esther's distress showed itself (see *Meg.* 15a). According to *Mid.* she gave birth to a still-born child.—*And she sent* [𝔗¹ + royal] *garments to clothe Mordecai, and to take his haircloth off from him*], so that he might come into the palace and tell her more fully what had happened. The author assumes that Esther could hold an interview with Mordecai, provided that he were properly dressed (see 2^{11}).— [L 𝔏 + And she said, Bring him in] [𝔏 + that I may know what my brother wishes, why I hear the voice of my brother, a loud voice of trouble and mourning and weeping and distress and need; and the eunuch went out and told him,] *but he would not receive them* [Jos. + nor put off his haircloth, because the sad occasion that made him put it on had not yet ceased.] This addition of Jos. gives correctly the reason for the refusal. Since nothing had yet been done to relieve the Jews, Mordecai could not take off the dress of a suppliant.

5. *So Esther called* [*Meg.* 15a, 𝔗¹ + Daniel, who was surnamed]

Hathakh [*Meg.* 15a, 𝕿¹ + because by the utterances of his mouth the affairs of the kingdom were decided,] *one of the King's eunuchs whom he had put at her disposal*]. Since Mordecai will not lay aside his haircloth and come to her, Esther is compelled to send a messenger to him. On the name *Hathakh*, see p. 70.—*And charged him concerning Mordecai,* [𝕵 + that he should go] *to learn* [𝕵 + from him] *what this meant* [𝕿¹ + that he was weeping with such a lamentable cry,] *and why it was* [𝕿¹ + that he did not receive the royal garments that she had sent unto him.] [*Meg.* 15a + Have the Jews perchance transgressed the five books of Moses?] The additions of 𝕿¹ indicate admirably the scope of Esther's inquiries. Two things puzzle her, why Mordecai is in mourning, and why he will not put off his mourning. Both problems Mordecai solves in vv.⁷⁻⁸.

6. *And Hathakh went out* [𝕿¹ + to speak] *to Mordecai, into the city-square that was in front of the gate* [𝕿¹ + of the palace] *of the King*]. The *square*, lit. the *broad place*, denotes the open space, outside of the gates of all Oriental cities, that is used as a marketplace. On the *gate of the King*, see 2¹⁹.

7. *And Mordecai told him all that had happened to him* [𝕿¹ + because he had not bowed down to Haman and had not worshipped his idol], *i.e.*, he explained the circumstances that had led him to put on mourning. What these were, the next clauses describe more fully.— [Jos. + And the dispatch which had been sent by the King into all the country,] *and the exact amount of silver which Haman had offered to weigh* [𝕿¹ + into the hands of the collectors of the revenue] *for the King's treasury,* [𝕲 𝕷 + namely, 10,000 talents] *for the Jews, in order that he might destroy them*]. Cf. 3⁹. *Happened* is used as in 6¹³; *exact amount*, as in 10². Mordecai shrewdly calculates that this buying of the Jews will rouse Esther's wrath more than anything else. The King's refusal to take the offer he does not mention, so that money seems to be the only cause for the Jews' destruction. How Mordecai came to know of this private transaction between the King and Haman, we are not informed.

8. *And the copy of the draft of the law to destroy them, which had been published in Susa, he gave him to show to Esther and to explain* *to her* [𝔗¹ + what the wicked Haman had devised against the people of Judah]. In order that there may be no doubt in Esther's mind as to the gravity of the situation, Mordecai gives her documentary evidence. On *copy*, see 3¹⁴; on *law*, 1⁸. Contrary to the accents, Bert. attaches *to explain* to the following clause, but this does not improve the sense. Perhaps we may infer from it that Esther was unable to read Persian, so that Hathakh needed not merely to show her the edict, but also to interpret the contents.—*And to enjoin upon her to go to the King to implore mercy of him*, [Jos. + and, for the deliverance of her people, not to think it beneath her to assume a humble mien,] *and to entreat him* [𝔗¹ + for pity] *on behalf of* [L + himself and] *her race* [some codd. 𝔊 + and her native land,] [𝔊 L + remembering her lowly days, when she was brought up by his hand, because Haman, the next in rank to the King, had sentenced them to death; and to call upon the Lord, and to speak to the King on their behalf, and to rescue them from death.] Hitherto Mordecai has counselled Esther to conceal her origin (*cf.* 2¹⁰), now that nothing is to be gained by secrecy, he advises her to reveal the fact that she is a Jewess in hope that through love for her the King will be moved to spare her people.

9. *And Hathakh came and told Esther* [𝔊 + all] *the words of Mordecai.* [𝔏 + And it came to pass, when Esther had read her brother's letter, that she rent her garment, and cried out with a bitter and loud voice, and wept copiously, and her body was made to tremble and her flesh became exceedingly weak.] This passage in 𝔏 takes the place of v. ⁹ in 𐤄, but logically it follows it.

4. תבואינה – וסריסיה] καὶ ἐκάλεσεν εὐνοῦχον ἕνα καὶ ἀπέστειλε πρὸς Ἐσθήρ L: *et audivit Hester regina vocem Mardochæi fratris sui Hebraica voce lingua* 𝔏.— ותבואנה [ותבואינה Q Oc.: ܣܠܩܬ 𝔖.—[נערות om. 𝔖.— [וסריסיה om. ו 𝔖.— [ויגידו – מאד om. L 𝔏.— [ותתחלחל *Hithpalp.* from חול (see Stade, § 518 c) = 'writhe.'— [המלכה מאד *quod audiens* 𝔍: ἀκούσασα τὸ γεγονός 𝔊.— [ותשלח – מעליו καὶ εἶπεν ἡ βασίλισσα περιέλεσθε τὸν σάκκον L: *et misit spadonem, qui præsto erat in conspectu ipsius, dicens; vade, exi celerius hinc, et auferes vestimenta quæ est indutus, et indue illum vestimenta alia* 𝔏.—[בגדים om. 𝔊 (exc. 93b *).—[את מרדכי *eum* 𝔍.— [ולא קבל *et noluit Mardochæus deponere saccum et omnem humilitationem suam* 𝔏. קְבֵל is an Aram. form. *Cf.* 9²³. ²⁷.

ESTHER IS CHARGED BY MORDECAI

5. om. L 𝕷.—[הַמֶּלֶךְ] aft. אשר 𝕵: αὐτῆς 𝕲: om. 249.—[אשר-לפניה] om. 71.
—[העמיד] 𝔖. [על] is not equivalent to אל v.[10] (AV. RV.), but means 'concerning' (cf. Gn. 12[20] Nu. 8[22] 1 Ch. 22[12f.]), Haupt emends to אל.—
[לדעת] + ab eo 𝕵: + αὐτῇ 𝕲 (93b ÷): + αὐτόν א c. a A, N, 71, 74, 76, 120, 236, 249.—[מה זה] τὸ ἀκριβές 𝕲: ÷ τὸ ἀκριβές * τί τοῦτο 93b: om. 71.—
[ועל-זה] om. 𝕵 𝕲 (exc. 93b *).—[זה ?] om. 𝔖.

6. om. 𝕲 𝕷 L (exc. 93b *): א c. a mg has εἰς τὴν πλατεῖαν τῆς πόλεως ἡ ἐστὶν κατὰ πρόσωπον τῆς πύλης τῆς πόλεως: A has ἐπὶ τὴν πλατεῖαν πρὸς τῇ (τῇ A * τὰ sup. ras. Aᵃ) βασιλέᾳ.—[הַמֶּלֶךְ] palatii 𝕵.

7. om. L.—[ויגד-קרהו] om. 𝕷.—[כל] om. 𝕲 (exc. א c. a mg, 93b *).—ואת —end of v.] simul de decem millibus talentorum quae dedit Aman pretium perditionis Judaeorum 𝕷 (tr. aft. 4[8]).—[הכסף] om. 𝕲 (exc. א c. a mg, 93b *).—[לשקול] om. 𝕲 (exc. א c. a, 93b *).—[על] + 𝔖. [גנזי] אֶל 𝔖: עַד: γάζαν 𝕲: pl. as in 3[9].—[הַמֶּלֶךְ] om. 𝔖.—[ביהודיים] Q Oc.: בַּיְּהוּדִים var. Oc. ב of the price as Lv. 17[14].

8. [ואת-אסתר] om. L, 71: tr. w. rest of v. 𝕷.—[כתב־] so Ben Asher: כְּתָב Ben Naphtali (Ginsburg): om. 𝔖 𝕲 (exc. א c. a, 93b *): with Qamets in the cstr., cf. Kau. § 93 w. w.—[הדת] om. 𝔖 𝕲 𝕷 (exc. א c. a, 93b *).—
[להשמידם] om. 𝕵 𝔖:—[אשר-להשמירם] om. 𝕷.—[נתן] om. 44, 74, 76, 106, 236.—[נתן] misit 𝕷.—[לו] inf. w. ל giving the contents of the law, cf. 3[14] 4[11] 6[4].—[נתן] misit 𝕷.—
confestim 𝕷.—[להראות-אסתר] om. 𝕷.—[אסתר] reginae 𝕵.—[ולהגיד] καὶ εἶπεν 𝕲 𝕷: ἀλλ' εἶπεν L: om. 𝕵 𝔖.—[לה] αὐτῷ 𝕲: οὕτως L: spadoni 𝕷: om. 𝕵 𝔖.—
[ולצוות] ἐντείλασθαι 𝕲: ἐρεῖτε L: vade dic 𝕷.—[ולצוות עליה] cf. 2[10] Gn. 2[16] 28[6] 1 K. 2[43] al.—[לבוא]-end of v.] surge, quid sedes et taces? quoniam venundata es, tu et domus tua et patris tui, et gens et omnis progenies: surge si poterimus pro gente nostra laborare et pati, ut Deus propitius fiat genti nostrae 𝕷.—[לבוא-לא] μὴ ἀποστρέψῃς τοῦ εἰσελθεῖν πρὸς τὸν βασιλέα L.—
[לבוא] εἰσελθοῦσαν A.—[להתחנן לו] cf. 8[3] Hos. 12[5] Jb. 9[15] 19[16].—[ולבקש מלפניו] om. 𝕵 71.—[בקש על] cf. 7[7] Ne. 2[4] Ezr. 8[23], in the sense of 'beg (favour) for,' a late usage.—[עמה] τοῦ λαοῦ 𝕲 L: + καὶ τῆς πατρίδος א c. a mg, A, 44, 71, 74, 76, 106, 120, 236, 249, 93b *.

9. Factum est autem cum legisset Hester litteras fratris sui, scidit vestimentum suum et exclamavit voce amara et gravi, et ploravit ploratione magna, et corpus ejus formidolosum factum est, et caro ipsius concidit valde 𝕷.—[ויבוא התך] om. L.—[התך] cf. 4[5]: Ἀχραθαῖος א * A: Ἀγχραδαῖος 44.—[להתך 4[10]-ויגד] om. 93b.—[לאסתר] so א * A, 64, 243, 249, C, Ald.: αὐτῇ 𝕲 L.—[את-מרדכי] τὴν ὀδύνην τοῦ Ἰσραήλ L.—[את] + πάντας 𝕲 (exc. 44, 71, 74, 76, 106.—[מרדכי] τούτους 𝕲.

ESTHER FEARS TO GO TO THE KING, BUT IS URGED BY MORDECAI TO DO SO (4¹⁰⁻¹⁴).

10. *And Esther instructed Hathakh and ordered him* [𝕲 𝕿¹ + to go and to say] *unto Mordecai*]. The pregnant construction of 𝕳 is rightly interpreted by 𝕿¹.

> [𝕿¹ + That he should not stir up strife with Haman by taking upon himself the enmity that existed between Jacob and Esau. Esther also put words into Hathakh's mouth, saying to him: Speak thus to Mordecai, Has not the wicked Haman decreed through the command of Xerxes that no one may go in unto the King into the inner court without permission?]

11. *All the King's courtiers and the people of the King's provinces know, that for every man or woman who goes in unto the King into the inner court without being called*] [𝕿¹ + by the mouth of Haman] *one penalty is prescribed, namely, to put (him or her) to death, except that person to whom the King* [𝕁 + in token of clemency] *may extend the golden sceptre in order that he may live,* [Jos. + for whenever the King does this to one who has come in uncalled, he not only does not die, but obtaining pardon, is saved.] The law that no man might approach the King without summons, was designed to give dignity to his person and to protect him from assassination. According to Her. i. 99, it was first enacted by Dioces the Mede. According to Her. iii. 72, 77, 84, 118, 140; Corn. Nep., *Conon* 3; it was also enforced by the Persian monarchs (see Baum., pp. 82 *ff.*). Her., however, is careful to state that people might send in a message to the King and request an audience. If this had not been permitted, the King would have been shut off from communication with the outer world. The Book of Est. knows no such qualification. According to it, even the Queen had no way of obtaining an interview with her husband, except by waiting for a summons. This is most improbable. Either the author does not know Persian custom, or he intentionally suppresses his knowledge in order to make Esther's going to the King more heroic. Jos. tries to solve the difficulty by the assumption that this law applied only to members of Xerxes' household (see the addition in 2²¹). This is very unlikely. 𝕿¹, followed by Lyr. Ser., adds the hypothesis that Haman had enacted this law recently to keep Esther from getting word to the King; but Haman evidently has no suspicion that Esther is a Jewess (5¹² ᶠ.), and the words *all the people of the provinces know* show that the law had long been in force. Keil and Schu. suppose that Esther might have requested an audience of the King, but feared to do so because she was not in special favour, not having been summoned for thirty days. If, however, she were out of favour, why was it wiser to go to the King at the risk of her life than to request an audience? These theories all fail to render the narrative probable. The *inner court* is in contrast to the *outer court* of the King's house (6⁴). From it (5¹) one could see the King sitting upon his throne (see on 1⁵).

> [𝕿² + And for thirty days I have been praying that the King may not desire me and may not cause me to sin; because, when I grew up in thy house, thou usedst to say to me, that every woman of the house of Israel who is taken and brought to the house of a heathen of her own accord, has neither part nor lot with the children of the tribes of Israel.]

And now for thirty days I have not been summoned to go in to the King, [L 𝕷 𝕵 + and how can I go without being summoned?] These words clearly assert that Esther knows no way to obtain an audience with the King, except by waiting for a summons; and this she has no reason to expect, since she has not been called for a month. The case of Phædyma (Her. iii. 69) is not parallel, since the question there is not the obtaining of an interview with the false Smerdis, but the obtaining of a chance to see whether his ears have been cut off. The reason for the cooling of Xerxes' affection is not given. The comm. suppose that another woman now enjoyed his favour.

12. [𝕿¹ + Now when the wicked Haman saw Hathakh, whose name was Daniel, going to and fro to Esther, his anger waxed great against him, and he slew him; but instantly there came thither the angels Michael and Gabriel (similarly 𝕿²),] *and they told Mordecai* [𝕲 + all] *Esther's words,* [𝕷 + and Mordecai was angry.] In v. ¹⁰ Hathakh was sent to Mordecai; here the subject changes suddenly to the pl. and Hathakh is not again mentioned. From this 𝕋¹, 𝕋², and Jewish comm. infer that Hathakh was killed by Haman. We should probably follow the Vrss. in reading the sg.

13. *Then Mordecai told* [𝕋¹ + Michael and Gabriel] *to reply to Esther* [𝕋¹ + speaking thus to her]:

[𝕋² + perhaps thou fanciest and sayest to thyself, I am called to sovereignty merely to be Queen; and perhaps thou thinkest and sayest to thyself, I do not need to ask pity for the house of Israel; but, if the foot of one Jew stumbles, do not suppose that thou alone of all the Jews shalt escape out of the King's house, because Saul thy ancestor brought this evil upon Israel. If he had carried out that which the prophet Samuel commanded him, this wicked Haman of the seed of the house of Amalek would not have come against us, and this son of Hamm^edāthā would not have come against us, and would not have bought us from the King for 10,000 talents of silver, and the Holy One, blessed be he, would not have delivered us into the power of two wicked men (followed by a long account of God's deliverances in the past).]

Do not imagine that thou wilt [𝕋¹ + get away and] *escape* [𝔊 𝔏 𝔍 + alone] (*in*) *the King's house apart from all the Jews*]. Mordecai does not reproach Esther with indifference to the fate of her people, but shows her that she is in the same peril as they. Going to the King may be dangerous, but staying away is just as dangerous. Although she is the King's wife, Haman will not allow her to escape, when he knows that she is a Jewess, particularly as she is a relative of the hated Mordecai. No allowance is made for the possibility that the King may make an exception in Esther's favour. *Imagine* is lit. *form in thy soul.*

14. *For if thou dost persist in remaining silent at this time,* [L 𝕋¹ + and dost not make intercession for the Jews,] *relief and deliverance will appear for the Jews from some other quarter* [𝕋¹ + on account of the merits of thy forefathers; and the Lord of the world will deliver them out of the hands of their enemies]. Here, as elsewhere, the author goes out of his way to avoid mentioning God. On the reason for this, see *Introduction,* § 29. L, Jos., 𝕋¹, 𝕋², supply the religious deficiency by the insertion of the name of God. Although the author does not mention God, there is little doubt that he thinks of the ancient promises that Israel shall **never perish.** Sieg. supposes that he thinks rather of the help of

ESTHER FEARS TO GO TO THE KING

some other nation, as, for instance, of Rome in the Maccabæan period (1 Mac. 8¹⁷ 12¹). Even that, however, he might have regarded as providential.—*But thou and thy family will perish* [Jos. + at the hands of those that are lightly esteemed] [𝕶¹ + on account of this fault]. Jos. and Lap. suppose that the Jews themselves will avenge Esther's disregard of them. Most comm. think of a special divine judgment inflicted upon her for neglect of her opportunity. Even though the other Jews may be rescued, she and her family will not be suffered to go unpunished. Bert. and Sieg. suppose the meaning to be, that many Jews will avoid the consequences of Haman's edict, but that he will not allow Mordecai and Esther to escape him. *Family*, lit. *house of thy father*, is *family* in a wider sense, or clan.—*And who* [𝕶¹ + is the wise man who] *knows if* [𝕶¹ + in the coming year] *at a time like this thou* [𝕾 + art called and] *hast come unto* [𝕶¹ + the possession of] *royalty,* [𝕵 + that thou mayest be ready] [𝕷 + that thou mayest deliver thy people]. The meaning of this sentence is uncertain, and there is reason to suspect textual corruption (see critical note).

10. להתך – ותאמר] om. L.—ותאמר] *et misit* 𝕷: 'command,' as 1¹⁷ 4¹³. ¹⁵ 6¹ 9¹⁴.—אסתר] om. 𝕵 𝕷.—להתך] *spadonem suum* 𝕷: πρὸς αὐτόν 44, 106: *ei* 𝕵.—ותצוהו] πορεύθητι 𝕲: om. 𝕷.—אל על] S⁽ᵉ⁾bhîr *cf.* 4⁵: κατὰ L: the construction with acc. of the person and אל is correct, *cf.* 8ʲ Ex. 6¹³.—מרדכי] τάδε L: ταῦτα 93*a*: *eum* 𝕷: + καὶ εἶπον (+ αὐτῷ 44, 71, 74, 76, 106, 236) ὅτι 𝕲: + λέγουσα L: + *dicens* 𝕷: + كملحبى 𝕾.

11. כל – מדינות] om. L 𝕷.—המלך – ועם] om. 𝕲 𝕾 (exc. א c. a mg, 93*b* *).—ועם] *et cunctæ* 𝕵.—המלך] *quæ sub ditione sunt* 𝕵: Artaxerxes rex 𝕷: σύ L.—יודעים] so N¹ N² Br.: ידעים Ba. G: γινώσκεις L: *dixit* 𝕷.—כל] παρὰ πάντας L.—איש ואשה] *homo omnis gentis* 𝕷: om. L.—אל²] הפנימית] om. L.—החצר] here f. (*cf.* 5¹ 6⁴), see Albrecht, *ZATW*. xvi. 49.—הפנימית] so A 𝕷: τὴν ἐσωτέραν 𝕲.—להמית – אחת] *absque ulla cunctatione statim interficiatur* 𝕵: οὐκ ἔστιν αὐτῷ σωτηρία 𝕲 𝕷: θανάτου ἔνοχος ἔσται L (aft. הוזהב).—אחת דתו] lit. 'one is his law.' An anacoluthon. After 'every man or woman' we should expect 'has one law,' or 'is under one law.' The indirect object implied in the suffix of דתו is placed absolutely at the beginning of the sentence, 'as for every man . . . one is his law.' אחת is placed first for emphasis.—לבד מאשר] instead of מלבד אשר (Nu. 6²¹) or מאשר Ec. 3²².—ויושיט] *cf.* 5² 8⁴, an Aramaism.—לו] om. 𝕲 𝕷 L (exc. א c. a, 93*b*).—המלך] om. L.—שרביט] *cf.* 5² 8⁴, the Aram. equivalent with inserted ר of Heb. שֵׁבֶט

(see Stade, § 243, 6; Strack-Sieg. § 18 c; Kau. § 85 w; Krauss, *Gr. u. lat. Lehnwörter im Talmud*, p. 142. All the authorities read שָׂרָבִיט (ב *Raphe*), but the As. equivalent is *šabbiṭu*, which shows that רב has come from resolution of ב (*cf.* Haupt, *a. l.*).—[וחיה om. L.—[לבוא om. L.— 𝔖.—[שלושים] אלחגן .—[זה] L. αὐτόν [5] המלך 'now' (*cf.* BDB. p. 261, § 4 *h*).—[ויום] + *igitur quomodo ad regem intrare potero* 𝔍: + *et quomodo introibo ad regem et exiit* 𝔏 + καὶ πῶς εἰσελεύσομαι νῦν ἄκλητος οὖσα L: + καὶ ἀπελθῶν 71.

12. om. L.—[ויגידו] סמא 𝔖: καὶ ἀπήγγειλεν 𝔊: Buhl and Haupt read וַיַּגֵּד: + 'Αχραθαῖος 𝔊 ('Αρχαθαῖον A: *cf.* 4⁵): + *spado* 𝔏.—[למרדכי] *illi* 𝔏: + πάντας 𝔊 (93 *b* ÷).—[את-אסתר] om. 𝔍: ταῦτα 71: *verba ipsius* 𝔏.

13. [ויאמר] καὶ ἀπέστειλε L.—[מרדכי] om. 𝔍𝔏: + πρὸς 'Αχραθαῖον ('Αχθραθαῖον א) πορεύθητι καὶ 𝔊 (93 *b* ÷) (om. πρὸς 'Αχραθαῖον A, 71: αὐτῷ 44, 106): + πρὸς αὐτήν L: + *spadoni intra* 𝔏.—[להשיב] *rursum* 𝔍: εἶπον 𝔊𝔏: καὶ εἶπεν L.—[אל] αὐτῇ 𝔊𝔏 L.—[אסתר]+ *dicens* 𝔍: om. L 𝔏 44, 71, 74, 76, 106, 236.—אל—end of v.] om. L.—[להמלט] *salva fiar* 𝔏: + *tantum* 𝔍: + ܐܢܬܝ 𝔖: + μόνη 𝔊𝔏.—[בית המלך] pr. ܒܩܡ 𝔖: ἐν τῇ βασιλείᾳ 𝔊𝔏: + ܐܢܬܝ 𝔖.—[בית המלך] generally regarded as acc. of place. Is it possible that we have here an instance of the late Heb. use of בית in the sense of 'wife' (see on 2⁷)? In that case the clause would mean 'that thou shalt escape as wife of the King.' This rendering is suggested by the addition in 𝔏, *quoniam uxor regis sum*. Haupt reads בבית as in 1⁹.—[מכל] מן in the sense of separation, 'away from,' 'as an exception to,' as Ru. 1⁶ (see BDB. p. 578 *b*).

14. [כי] ὡς ὅτι 𝔊: ὅτι A, 44, 71, 74, 76, 106, 120, 236: om. 𝔖 L.—[החרש] om. 𝔊𝔏 L (exc. א c. a mg, 93 *b* *).—[תחרישי] παρακούσῃς 𝔊: ὑπερίδῃς L: *non præmiseris* 𝔏.—[בעת הזה] τοῦ ἔθνους σου + τοῦ μὴ βοηθῆσαι αὐτοῖς ἀλλ' L.—[רוח] ܘܣܝܥܐ 𝔖: om. 𝔍: βοήθεια 𝔊𝔏: βοηθός L: lit. 'interval,' 'respite,' only here and Gn. 32¹⁷. According to Haupt, *JBL*. xxvi. p. 33, the word should be pointed רֶוַח.—[והצלה] καὶ σκέπη 𝔊: *et defensor* 𝔏: καὶ σωτηρία L.—[יעמוד] pr. οὐκ 106.—[יעמוד] in the sense of 'stand forth,' 'appear,' 'as Ezr. 2⁶³ Ne. 7⁶⁵, a late usage.—[ליהודים] G: αὐτοῖς L (ἐν αὐτοῖς 93 *a*).—[ממקום אחר] *per occasionem aliam* 𝔍: ἄλλοθεν 𝔊𝔏: ὁ θεὸς L.—[ומי יודע אם-לעת כזאת] *Who knows*, followed immediately by an impf., is equivalent to *perhaps*. Most comm. assume that *who knows if* has the same meaning. לְעֵת is commonly rendered *for a time*, and the whole sentence is translated, *perhaps for a time such as this thou hast attained to royalty*, *i.e.*, thou hast providentially been raised to the position of Queen in order to help thy people in this emergency (*cf*. Gn. 45⁷ 50²⁰). No other instance occurs, however, where *who knows if* is equivalent to *perhaps*. If this were the meaning, instead of אם we should expect אם לא or הֲלֹא, *whether not*. Moreover לְעֵת ordinarily means *at a time*. Accordingly Bert., Keil, Reuss, insist that אם must be given full conditional force, and that an implied apodosis must be supplied from the context. Bert.

ESTHER RESOLVES TO GO TO THE KING

and Reuss translate *who knows (what may happen), if at a time like this thou goest to royalty?* (i.e., *to the King*). Keil translates, *who knows, if at a time like this thou hast attained royalty, (what thou shouldst do?)*. Schu. translates, *who knows whether for a time like this thou hast come to royalty?* in the sense, who knows whether thou hast sufficient courage to act like a queen in this emergency. 𝔗¹ takes לְעֵת temporally, and understands *like this* to refer to the corresponding season of another year, so that the whole sentence means, *who knows whether a year from now thou wilt be Queen?* These interpretations are all unnatural, and one is compelled to suspect textual corruption, although the Vrss. support the reading of 𝔐. Perhaps for יוֹדֵעַ *knowing*, we should read יָרֵעַ *will harm* (Zp. 1¹²), and translate, *and who will harm, if at such a time as this thou hast drawn near to the royal presence?* i.e., how can any one hurt thee, when he learns what impelled thee to this step? The clause will thus be an encouragement to Esther to run the risk. For הגיע in the sense of 'draw near,' see 4³ 6¹⁴ 8¹⁷ 9¹·²⁶. For מלכות 'kingdom,' as a synonym for 'king,' see 1⁹·¹⁹ 2¹⁶ 5¹ 6⁸ 8¹⁵. It is analogous to the English use of 'majesty.'—[כזאת + .ە ܐܶܠܨܰܒ݂ 𝔖.—[ולמלכות + *ut in tali tempore parareris* 𝔍: + *ut gentem tuam liberes. Et introiit spado, et renuntiavit verba Mardochæi Hester reginæ* 𝔏: + καὶ ἀπελθὼν ἀνήγγειλεν αὐτῇ 71.

ESTHER RESOLVES TO GO TO THE KING (4¹⁵⁻¹⁷).

15. [𝔏 + And the eunuch went in and reported to Queen Esther all the words of Mordecai.] *Then Esther told* [𝔗¹ + Michael and Gabriel] *to reply to Mordecai* [𝔊 L + *saying*] [𝔍 + as follows,] [𝔏 + Master, brother, if it seems best to thee, I will go in, though I may die].

16. *Go, gather all the Jews that are found in Susa* [𝔖 + the fortress,] *and fast for me, and eat nothing for three days,* [𝔏 + and tell the elders to keep a fast; let them separate the sucking babes at night from their mothers, and let not cattle or sheep graze during these days,] [𝔗¹ + and pray before the Lord of the world night and day]. Mordecai's argument is convincing, and Esther resolves to go to the King at once; but since she appears on behalf of the Jews, she desires their spiritual support. On *found*, see 1⁵. The number of the Jews in Susa must have been considerable, since, according to 9¹⁵, they were able to slay 300 men. Fasting can only be a religious act designed to propitiate God. Normally, it is followed by prayer (2 S. 12¹⁶⁻²³ 1 K. 21²⁷⁻²⁹ Dn. 9³ Jo. 1¹⁴

Jon. 3⁵⁻⁹). Here, however, in accordance with the author's custom, no mention is made either of God or of prayer (*cf.* 4³·¹⁴ and see *Introduction*, § 29). By *three days* only parts of three days are meant. Esther begins to fast on the day that Mordecai gives her information about Haman's plot, continues to fast the following day, and on the third day goes to the King (5¹). This consideration detracts somewhat from the observation of the old comm. that she trusted in God rather than in her beauty, which would be impaired by three whole days of fasting.—*I also and my maidens will fast likewise*]. Although the maids given by Hēgai (2⁹) must have been heathen, yet Esther values the help of their fasting; and they are loyal enough to her to be willing to undertake it. Bon. supposes that under the religious instruction of Esther they had become proselytes to Judaism.—*And in this condition I will go to the King* [𝕵 + uncalled], *although this is not in accordance with the law; and if I perish* [𝕿¹ + from my women's quarters and am taken away violently from thee (*cf. Meg.* 15*a*),] *I perish* [𝕿¹ + from the life of this world for the sake of the salvation of the people of the house of Israel;] [𝕿² + but I shall have a part in the world to come]. *If I perish, I perish* is a despairing expression of resignation to the inevitable, as Gn. 43¹⁴, "If I am bereaved, I am bereaved." No religious enthusiasm lights up Esther's resolve. She goes, as one would submit to an operation, because there is a chance of escaping death in that way.

17. *And Mordecai* [𝕿¹ + was sad and indignant and he] *crossed over and acted in accordance with all that Esther had enjoined upon him.*] Ordinarily 'cross over' means 'transgress.' Assuming that the fast began on the 13th of Nisan (3¹²), and that Mordecai fasted three days, he must have continued to fast until the 15th of Nisan, which was the feast of Passover; thus he transgressed the law of Ex. 12 (so Rab in *Meg.* 15*a*, 𝕿¹, 𝕿², *Mid.*, and Mich.). There is nothing, however, to show that Esther's fast began on the same day on which the scribes began to write (3¹²), and it is quite unnecessary to put this meaning upon 'crossed over.' Most recent comm. assume that this means no more than 'proceeded' (*cf.* Gn. 18⁵ Nu. 22²⁶ *al.*), and this is certainly a possible interpretation. In *Meg.* 15*a* R. Samuel asserts that a sheet of water lay between the palace and the city, which Mordecai was obliged to cross. It is a fact that the Acropolis of Susa was separated from the city by the river Choaspes, the As. Uknû and the modern Ab-Kharkha, and to this fact the author of Est. may allude in the expression *crossed over*.

[𝕿¹ + And he transgressed against the joy of the feast of Passover, and he appointed a fast and sat in ashes.] [𝕷 + And the bridegrooms went forth from their couches, and the brides from their dainties; the elders also and the old women went out to pray. He prescribed that the cattle and the sheep should not graze for three days and three nights. All put on ashes and invoked God most high that he would take pity upon their humility. Mordecai, moreover, rent his garments, and spread haircloth beneath him, and fell upon his face to the earth with the elders of the people from morning until evening (similarly 𝕿²).] [𝕿² + At that time they investigated and found in the assembly 12,000 young priests, and they gave them trumpets in their right hands and books of the Law in their left hands; and, weeping and lamenting, thus they cried toward heaven: O God of Israel, this is the Law which thou hast given us. If thy beloved people perishes from the world, who will stand and read from this and will make mention of thy name? The sun and the moon will be darkened, and their light will no longer shine, because they were created solely for the sake of thy people. And they fell upon their faces and said: Answer us, our Father, answer us! Answer us, our King, answer us! And they blew upon their trumpets, and the people responded after them, until the hosts of heaven wept and the forefathers forsook their graves.]

ADDITION C.

THE PRAYERS OF MORDECAI AND ESTHER.

At this point 𝕲𝕷L insert the following prayers of Mordecai and Esther (Addition C¹⁻³⁰ = Vulg., Eng. 13⁸–14¹⁹). Jos. has the passage in a different and greatly abbreviated form. Yos. ii. 3 and *Mid.* also give distorted versions of it. 𝕿² inserts a different prayer of Esther after 5¹. In regard to the authenticity of the passage, see *Introduction*, § 20. For the Greek text and variants see Paton, *HM.* ii. pp. 24-27. The addition reads as follows:

¹Then he made his prayer unto the Lord, calling to remembrance all the works of the Lord, ²and said, O Lord, Lord, thou King Almighty, the whole world is in thy power, and if it be thy will to save Israel, there

is no man that can gainsay thee: ³for thou hast made heaven and earth, and all the wondrous things that are beneath the heaven; ⁴and thou art Lord of all, and there is no man that can resist thee, who art the Lord. ⁵Thou knowest all things, and thou knowest, Lord, that it was neither in contempt nor pride, nor for any desire of glory, that I did not bow down to the proud Haman. ⁶For I should have been glad for the salvation of Israel to kiss the soles of his feet. ⁷But I did this, that I might not place the glory of man above the glory of God: neither will I bow down to any but to thee, who art my Lord, neither will I do it in pride. ⁸And now, O Lord, thou God and King, the God of Abraham, spare thy people: for they watch us to bring us to naught, and they desire to destroy the heritage that has been thine from the beginning. ⁹Despise not thy portion, which thou didst redeem out of the land of Egypt for thine own self. ¹⁰Hear my prayer, and be merciful unto thine inheritance: and turn our mourning into feasting, that we may live, O Lord, and sing praises to thy name: and destroy not the mouth of those that praise thee, O Lord. ¹¹And all Israel cried out mightily, because their death was before their eyes.

¹²Queen Esther, also, being seized with the agony of death, fled unto the Lord: ¹³and laid away her glorious apparel, and put on the garments of anguish and mourning, and instead of fine ointments she covered her head with ashes and dung, and she humbled her body greatly, and all parts (of her body) that she (ordinarily) rejoiced to adorn, she covered with her dishevelled hair. ¹⁴And she prayed unto the Lord, the God of Israel, saying, O my Lord, thou only art our King: help me that am desolate and have no other helper but thee: ¹⁵for my danger is at hand. ¹⁶From my youth up I have heard in the tribe of my family, that thou, O Lord, tookest Israel from among all the nations, and our fathers from all their progenitors, for a perpetual inheritance, and didst perform for them whatsoever thou didst promise. ¹⁷And now we have sinned before thee, and thou hast given us into the hands of our enemies, ¹⁸because we glorified their gods: O Lord, thou art righteous. ¹⁹Nevertheless it satisfies them not that we are in bitter captivity: but they have joined hands with their idols, ²⁰that they will abolish that which thou with thy mouth hast ordained, and destroy thine inheritance, and stop the mouth of them that praise thee, and quench the glory of thy house, and thine altar, ²¹and open the mouths of the heathen to celebrate the virtues of idols, and that a fleshly king shall be magnified forever. ²²O Lord, give not thy sceptre unto those that do not exist, and let them not laugh at our fall: but turn their device upon themselves, and make him an example that has begun this against us. ²³Remember, O Lord, make thyself known in the time of our affliction, and give me boldness, O King of the gods, and holder of all dominion. ²⁴Give me eloquent speech in my mouth before the lion: and turn his heart to hate him that fights against us, that there may

THE PRAYER OF ESTHER

be an end of him, and of those that are like-minded with him: [25]but deliver us with thine hand, and help me who am desolate and have no one but thee, O Lord. [26]Thou hast knowledge of all things; and thou knowest that I hate the glory of him who does not keep the Law and abhor the bed of the uncircumcised, and of every alien. [27]Thou knowest my necessity: that I abhor the sign of my high estate, which is upon mine head in the days when I shew myself. I abhor it as a menstruous rag, and I do not wear it when I am quietly by myself. [28]And thine handmaid has not eaten at Haman's table, neither have I honoured the King's feast, nor drunk the wine of the drink-offerings. [29]Neither has thy handmaid had any joy from the day that I was brought hither to the present, but in thee, O Lord, thou God of Abraham. [30]O God, that art mighty above all, hear the voice of the despairing and deliver us out of the hands of the wicked, and deliver me out of my fear.

15. ותאמר] καὶ (ἐξ)απέστειλεν 𝕲 L.— אסתר] ἡ βασίλισσα L.— להשיב] rursum 𝕵: τὸν ἥκοντα πρὸς αὐτὴν 𝕲 (om. πρὸς αὐτὴν A): denuo cum misisset qui ad eam venerat 𝕷: om. L.— אל מרדכי] a Mardochæo 𝕷: om. L: + λέγουσα 𝕲 L.

16. לך] om. L 𝕷.— היהודים - כנוס] παραγγείλατε θεραπείαν L: prædica igitur sanitatem 𝕷.— כל] om. 𝕲 (exc. א ᶜ·ᵃ, 93b * μοι πάντας).— הנמצאים] וּ𝐋ܐ S: om. 𝕲 𝕷 L.— בשושן] om. L 𝕷.— ויום - וצומו] καὶ δεήθητε τοῦ θεοῦ ἐκτενῶς L.— וצומו] et orate 𝕵.— ואל] om. ו 57 codd. R, N¹ 𝕿¹ 𝕵.— גם] וגם 72 codd. R, 𝕿¹ 𝕵 S 𝕲 L: om. 𝕷.— אצום] ποιήσομεν L.— כן] om. 𝕷 𝕲 (exc. א ᶜ·ᵃ, 93b *).— ובכן] om. 1 S: καὶ τότε 𝕲 𝕷: καὶ L: according to Bert., Wild., with so-called *Beth essentiæ*, which is used either with the primary or secondary predicate to express an essential state of the subj.; 'as such,' *i.e.*, 'as one who has fasted three days' (*cf*. Lv. 17¹⁴ Ez. 13¹⁹ Ec. 8¹⁰; Kau. § 119 ii; BDB. p. 88, I. 7). According to others, ב has the ordinary meaning, and the phrase means simply 'in such a state.'— אשר] the antecedent is the previous clause *I will go to the King*. Others regard אשר לא as equivalent to Syr. ܕܠܐ 'without.'— אשר - כדת] παρὰ τὸν νόμον 𝕲: ἄκλητος L: + *non vocata* 𝕵: om. 𝕷.— אברתי -² וכאשר] ἐὰν καὶ ἀπολέσθαι με ᾗ (δέῃ) 𝕲: εἰ δέοι καὶ ἀποθανεῖν με L: *habens in manu animam meam* + *exiit spado et dixit verba ejus* 𝕷: *tradensque me morti et periculo* 𝕵.

17. ויעבר] om. יעבר L.

THE DELIVERANCE OF THE JEWS (5^1–9^{19})

ADDITION D.

ESTHER GOES TO THE KING AND IS GRACIOUSLY RECEIVED (5^{1-2} = D$^{1-16}$).

These verses are expanded in 𝕲 𝕷 L into Addition D = Chap. 15 in 𝕵 and AV. For the Gr. text and variants, see Paton, *HM*. ii. pp. 27–29. *Mid.* has a similar passage.

1 (= D$^{1-6}$ = 15$^{1-6}$). *Afterward, on the third day* [𝕿^1 + of the Passover,] [𝕲 𝕷 L + when she had ceased praying, she put off her garments of worship,] [𝕿^2 + after she had fasted three days in succession, and she arose from the dust and ashes where she had bowed herself without ceasing,] [𝕷 + and washed her body with water, and anointed herself with ointment;] *then Esther clothed herself* [Vrss. + in garments of] *royalty,* [𝕿^2 + adorned with pure gold of Ophir, made of fine Frankish silk, ornamented with precious stones and pearls brought from the province of Africa. And she put on her head a crown of pure gold, and shod her feet with sandals of fine gold,] [𝕷 + and adorned herself with ornaments,] [𝕿^1 + and the Holy Spirit rested upon her (*cf. Meg.* 15*a*).] Although Esther has besought the favour of God through fasting, she does not fail to make use of her own charms. On *the third day, cf.* 4^{16}.

> [𝕲 𝕷 L + ²And being majestically adorned, after she had called upon the all-seeing God and saviour, she took her two maids with her: ³and upon the one she leaned, as though she were delicate; ⁴and the other followed bearing her train. ⁵And she gleamed in the perfection of her beauty, and her countenance was cheerful, as though she knew that she was lovable, but her heart was in anguish for fear. ⁶Then she passed through all the doors.]

And she stopped [𝕿^1 + and prayed] *in the inner court of the King's house* [𝕿^1 + which was built] *over against the King's house* [𝕿^1 + that was in Jerusalem.] On *inner court, cf.* 4^{11}. *Over against* refers to Esther, not to *court* or *house*. 𝕿^1 refers it to *house*, and understands it to mean that the palace in Susa was the counterpart of the palace (or temple) in Jerusalem. On *King's house*, see 2⁸·⁹·¹³ 4¹³.

[*Meg.* 15*b* + And as she passed by the house of idols the divine presence left her. Then she said, My God, my God, why hast thou forsaken me? Dost thou judge a sin committed accidentally as one done intentionally, and one committed under compulsion as one done willingly? Or is it perhaps because I have called him a dog?]

And the King was sitting upon his royal throne in the royal house, [𝕋¹ + *and he saw everything*] *over against the door of the house.*] From the inner court Esther can look through the open door and see the King seated on his throne at the farther end of the throne-room. He can look out and see her standing in the court. Here she pauses to see what the King will do. She has already violated the law in coming as far as the inner court (4¹¹). On *royal throne*, see 1². The *royal house* is regarded by Dieulafoy as the throne-room in distinction from the *King's house*, or royal residence, but in 1⁹ 2¹³·¹⁶ the two are identified. Probably the expression is chosen merely for variety.

[𝕲 𝕷 L + ⁶And he was clothed with all his robes of majesty, all covered with gold and precious stones; and he was very terrible. ⁷Then he lifted up his countenance that was flushed with glory in fierce anger.] [𝕋¹ + Then Esther answered and spoke thus: Lord of the world, do not deliver me into the hands of this uncircumcised one, nor accomplish the desire of the wicked Haman upon me, as he accomplished it upon Vashti, whom he persuaded the King to put to death, because he wished him to marry his daughter. But it was the will of Heaven that she should be afflicted with a loathsome disease so that her mouth stank exceedingly, and they led her forth as quickly as possible. So she was excluded in order that I might be married to him. Now, then, render me acceptable in his sight, that he may not slay me, but may grant my desire and my petition which I am about to ask of him. Thou also in the multitude of thy mercies be favourable to my people, and do not deliver the children of Jacob into the hands of Haman, son of Hammᵉdāthā, son of 'Ādā, son of Biznai, son of Aphliṭus, son of Deioṣoṣ, son of Peroṣ, son of Hamdān, son of Talyon, son of Atniṣomus, son of Ḥarum, son of Ḥarṣum, son of Shĕgar, son of Nĕgar, son of Parmashtā, son of Wayzāthā, son of 'Āgag, son of Ṣûmqar, son of 'Āmālēḳ, son of 'Ĕlîphaz, son of the wicked Esau (*cf.* 𝕋² on 3¹).]

2 ($= D^{7\text{-}16} = 15^{7\text{-}16}$). *Presently, as soon as the King saw Queen Esther standing* [𝕿¹ + sorrowfully] *in the court* [𝕿¹ + with both her eyes streaming with tears, and looking up toward heaven,] [𝕷 + he was enraged and determined to destroy her, and he shouted uncertainly, and said, Who has dared to enter the court uncalled?]

[𝕿² + And Haman, the bodyguard of the King, wished to slay Esther.] [𝕲 𝕷 L + ⁷And the Queen fell down, and turned pale, and fainted, and she bowed herself upon the head of the maid that went before.] [*Meg.* 15*b* + And three angels came to her aid in that hour. One lifted up her head, the second endued her with grace, the third lengthened the King's sceptre. How much? According to R. Jeremiah it was 2 cubits long, and he extended it to 12 cubits; others say 16, others 24, a Baraitha says 60. R. b. Uphran said in the name of R. Eliezer, who had heard it from his teacher, and he from his, that it became 200 cubits long; and] [𝕲 𝕷 L + ⁸God changed the spirit of the King to mildness, and in an agony he leaped from his throne, and took her in his arms, till she came to herself again, and he comforted her with soothing words, ⁹and said unto her, Esther, what is the matter? I am thy brother, be of good cheer: ¹⁰thou shalt not die, for our commandment is for the common crowd only: come near.]

And she won his favour, and the King extended to Esther the golden sceptre that was in his hand, [Jos. + and laid his staff upon her neck, thus legally delivering her from alarm.] *And Esther approached and* [𝕿¹ + grasped his hand and] *touched the head of the sceptre.*

[𝕲 𝕷 L + ¹²And he kissed her, and said, Speak unto me. ¹³Then she said unto him, I saw thee, my lord, as an angel of God, and my heart was troubled for fear of thy glory. ¹⁴For wonderful art thou, my lord, and thy countenance is full of grace. ¹⁵And as she was speaking, she fell down for faintness. ¹⁶Then the King was troubled, and all his servants comforted her.]

The simple statement of 𝕳 that Esther succeeded in her venture is not enough for the Vrss. which find here a rare opportunity for embellishment. Instead of the colourless expression *she won his favour*, 𝕲 𝕷 L say that God changed the spirit of the King.

ESTHER'S REQUEST 233

1 (= D¹). וַיְהִי] om. יהי 𝔍 𝔖.—וַתִּלְבַּשׁ] καὶ περιεβάλετο 𝔊 L 𝔏.—אסתר]
+ vestimentis 𝔍: om. 𝔊: + ܠܒܫܬ 𝔖: τὰ ἱμάτια L: vestimento 𝔏.—
מלכות] τὴν δόξην αὐτῆς 𝔊: τῆς δόξης L: gloriæ suæ 𝔏: so also 6⁸ 8¹⁵.
Possibly, with Bert., Rys., Wild., we should follow the Vrss. in inserting
לְבוּשׁ. Others think that מלכות may be an adverbial acc. = 'royally,' or
that it may mean 'regalia.'—**1** (= D⁶). וַתַּעֲמֹד] κατέστη 𝔊: ἔστη L: in
the sense of 'came to a stand' (cf. Jos. 10¹³ Ju. 9³⁵).—הַמֶּלֶךְ ²-וַתַּעֲמֹד] om.
𝔏.—בחצר] om. 𝔊 L.—נכח] ἐνώπιον 𝔊 L: κατενώπιον 93b א ᵒ· *.
—בית] om. 𝔊 L.—וְהַמֶּלֶךְ] et ille 𝔍: καὶ αὐτὸς 𝔊: et invenit Artarxerxem
regem 𝔏: οὗ αὐτὸς 93b.—מַלְכוּתוֹ] om. מלכות 𝔍 19: gloriæ suæ 𝔏.—[בבית-הבית
om. 𝔊 L 𝔏.—הַמַּלְכוּת-בבית] om. 𝔖.

2 (= D⁷). וַיְהִי] om. יהי 𝔍 𝔖: om. 𝔊 𝔏 L.—כִרְאוֹת] so Ben Asher (Ginsburg): כְּרְאוֹת Ben Naphtali, B²: ἔβλεψεν 𝔊 𝔏: ἐνέβλεψεν L (aft. D⁷ᶜ):
om. א * A.—הַמֶּלֶךְ] om. 𝔍 𝔊 L 𝔏.—אֶת אֶסְתֵּר] om. 𝔊: αὐτῇ L: eam 𝔏.—
[נשאה-בעיניו cf. 2¹⁷.—נשאה חן] om. 𝔍.—בחצר] om. 𝔊 L 𝔏.—הַמַּלְכָּה-בחצר
καὶ μετέβαλεν ὁ θεὸς τὸ πνεῦμα τοῦ βασιλέως εἰς πραΰτητα 𝔊: καὶ μετέβαλεν
ὁ θεὸς τὸ πνεῦμα τοῦ βασιλέως καὶ μετέθηκε τὸν θυμὸν αὐτοῦ εἰς πραότητα
L: Deus autem iram convertit in miserationem et furorem ipsius in tranquillitatem 𝔏.—**2** (= D¹²). וַיּוֹשֶׁט] καὶ ἄρας 𝔊 L 𝔏: see 4¹¹.—הַמֶּלֶךְ] om.
𝔍 𝔊 L 𝔏.—לְאֶסְתֵּר] contra eam 𝔍: om. 𝔊 L 𝔏.—שַׁרְבִיט se ׳ ׳ ׳ ׳ ׳ ׳ ׳ ׳.—הב ׳ ׳.—om.
L.—אֲשֶׁר בְּיָדוֹ] om. 𝔊 L: et extendit in manu ipsius 𝔏.—וַתִּקְרַב אֶסְתֵּר] quæ
accedens 𝔍: om. 𝔊 L 𝔏.—וַתִּגַּע] osculata est 𝔍: ܢܫܩܬ 𝔖: ἐπέθηκεν 𝔊 L:
om. 𝔏.—בְּרֹאשׁ הַשַּׁרְבִיט] ἐπὶ τὸν τράχηλον αὐτῆς 𝔊 L: om. 𝔏: + ܘܢܫܩܗ 𝔖.

THE KING OFFERS TO GRANT ANY REQUEST, BUT ESTHER ASKS ONLY THAT HE AND HAMAN WILL COME THAT DAY TO A BANQUET (5³⁻⁵).

3. *And the King said to her, Whatever thou dost wish, Queen
Esther*]. Lit. *whatever is to thee*. In Jos. 15¹⁸ this is used of a
desire and is so understood here by the Vrss.—*And whatever thy
petition is*]. A clearer statement of the thought of the preceding
clause. The King recognizes that only a pressing need can have
led Esther to run the risk of coming unsummoned. [𝔘¹ + Even
if thou dost ask] *as much as half of the kingdom, it shall be given
thee*.] *Cf*. 5⁶ 7² 9¹². This is a polite formula, like the Oriental
"take it for nothing," that is not meant to be understood too literally, *cf*. Her. ix. 109, where Xerxes offers to give Artaynte whatever she asks, and is much distressed when she takes him at his
word; also Salome's request of Herod (Mk. 6²³). The construction is elliptical to express the King's haste in reassuring Esther.

[𝕋¹ + Except the rebuilding of the House of the Sanctuary, which stands in the border of half of my kingdom, I cannot grant, for so I have promised with an oath to Geshem the Arabian, Sanballat the Horonite, and Tobiah the Ammonite, the slave, that I would not permit it to be rebuilt; for I am afraid of the Jews, lest they rebel against me. This request then I cannot grant thee, but whatever else thou shalt ask of me, I will decree that it shall be done for thee immediately, and that thy desire shall be granted.]

4. *And Esther said,* [𝔊 L + To-day (to-morrow) is a notable day for me.] *If it seems good to the King, let the King and Haman* [L 𝕷 + *his friend*] *come to-day to the banquet which I have prepared for him.*] That Esther should thus postpone her request, when the King was in good humour, is psychologically most improbable. Instead of asking for the life of the Jews, she asks only that he will come to a banquet. At the banquet she still refuses to present her petition (5⁷). Not until a second banquet does she speak out (7³ ᶠ·). The older comm. suppose that she wished to make the King merry with wine before she offered her request, or that she desired greater privacy, or that Haman was not present, and that she needed him for the *dénoûment*. These explanations are all unsatisfactory. The true reason for Esther's delay is purely literary; the author needs time for the humiliation of Haman and the exaltation of Mordecai before the final blow falls. Why Haman should be invited with the King is hard to see. Such an invitation would only rouse suspicion, and his presence might counteract all of Esther's influence. Lyr. thinks that it was to rouse the jealousy of the other princes of Persia who were not invited. *Meg.* 15*b* gives twelve explanations offered by the rabbis. No one of them commanded general assent. Even the prophet Elijah could not tell Rabba b. Abuhu the reason. Here again the motive is purely literary. The author wishes to heap honours upon Haman in order to heighten the contrast with his impending fall.

[𝕋² (v. ⁸) + There were three reasons why Esther invited Haman to supper. The first was that Esther knew that Haman had seen how Hathakh had been a messenger between Esther and Mordecai; so Esther said, I will invite Haman to supper. The second reason was, that she might uproot hatred from his heart; and then, said she, I will provoke jealousy between Xerxes and Haman, since the King will say, How comes it that of all my princes Esther has invited no one but Haman to supper? The third reason was that Esther said, The eyes of all the house of Israel are turned upon me, that I may ask King Xerxes to kill Haman. I will surely invite him to supper, that the hearts of the children of Israel may be changed, and that they may turn to their Heavenly Father and may implore his pity.]

The initial letters of the words *let the King and Haman come to-day* spell the divine name יהוה. In a few codd. they are written large to call attention to this fact. Jehring, Bullinger, Cumming, *al.* assume that this is intentional, and is designed by the author to offset his usual avoidance of the name of God! (see *Introduction*, § 29). On *prepare a banquet*, see 1[3. 5. 9] 2[18].

5. *And the King said* [𝔍 + *at once*], *Fetch Haman quickly that Esther's wish may be gratified.*] Lit. *for the doing of the word of Esther* (*cf.* Dn. 8[24]). *And the King and Haman came to the banquet which Esther had prepared*, [L + *a costly repast*].

3. לה] om. 𝔊 L 𝔏 (exc. א [c. a mg] A 44, 71, 93*b*, 106).— [המלך] om. 𝔏.— [מה לך] τί ἔστιν L 71: τί θέλεις 𝔊: *quæ est postulatio tua* 𝔏: מה is indefinite = 'whatever' (*cf.* Kau. § 137 *c*; BDB. 553, 1 *e*).— [אסתר] *succedanea et consors regni mei* 𝔏.— [המלכה] om. 𝔊 L 𝔏 (exc. א [c. a], 93*b* under *).— [ומה בקשתך] ἀνάγγειλόν μοι L.— [בקשה] *cf.* 5[6. 7. 8] 7[3] 9[12]. Only in Est. and Ezr. 7[6].— [וינתן] καὶ ἔσται 𝔊: καὶ ποιήσω L: *et faciam* 𝔏.

4. [אסתר] *illa* 𝔍: *regina* 𝔏: + ἡμέρα μου ἐπίσημος σήμερόν ἐστιν 𝔊: ἡμέρα ἐπίσημός μοι αὔριον L (𝔏 om.).— [אם-טוב] *postulatio mea rex* 𝔏: + *obsecro* 𝔍.— [יבוא] in agreement with the nearest subj. bec. preceding, *cf.* v. [5].— [היום והמן המלך בוא] a few codd.— [המלך] om. 𝔍: καὶ αὐτὸς 𝔊: ὁ βασιλεὺς א [c. a mg] A 52, 108*a*, 243, C, Ald., 64, 93*b*: σὺ L 𝔏.— [והמן] + ὁ φίλος σου L: + *amicus tuus* 𝔏.— [היום] om. K 101, 158, 180, R 562, 593, 667, 850, 𝔖: αὔριον L: *cras* 𝔏.— [לו] *ad me* 𝔍: om. 𝔊 L: *apud me* 𝔏: לכון 𝔗[1].

5-8. Winck. (36) deletes as an erroneous repetition of 7[1].

5. [מהרו] ܣܡ̈ܟܐ 𝔖: om. 𝔏: *Pi.* 'hasten,' in the sense of 'bring in haste,' as Gn. 18[6] 1 K. 22[9] 2 Ch. 18[8] Est. 6[10].— [את המן] om. 𝔏.— [את דבר המלך והמן] om. 𝔏.— [אסתר] *reginæ* 𝔏.— [ויבא]—end of v.[8] om. 𝔏.— أَسِرْ وَأَعْجِلْ 𝔖.— ἀμφότεροι 𝔊 L.— [אשר - אסתר] om. 𝔖.— [עשתה] εἶπεν 𝔊.— [אסתר] *eis regina* 𝔍: + δεῖπνον πολυτελές L (93*b* under ÷): om. 249.

AT THE BANQUET THE KING AGAIN OFFERS TO GRANT ANY REQUEST, BUT ESTHER ASKS ONLY THAT HE AND HAMAN WILL COME TO ANOTHER BANQUET ON THE FOLLOWING DAY (5⁶⁻⁸).

6. *And the King said to Esther during the wine-drinking, Whatever thy request is,* [𝕲 𝕿¹ + Queen Esther,] *it shall be granted thee; and whatever thy petition is,* [𝕿¹ + Even if thou dost ask] *as much as half of the kingdom, it shall be done.*] After the meal wine-drinking began (*cf.* Her. i. 133; Est. 7². ⁷ Dn. 1⁵. ⁸). This put the King in good humour, and he repeated his offer. The language is almost identical with that of v. ³, *q.v.*

> [𝕿¹ + Except the building of the House of the Sanctuary, which stands in the border of half my kingdom, I cannot grant thee, because I have promised with an oath to Geshem the Arabian, Sanballat the Horonite, and Tobiah the Ammonite, the slave, that I would not permit it to be rebuilt, lest the Jews may revolt against me.] [Jos. + But she put off the stating of her petition to the next day.]

7. *And Esther said* [𝕿¹ + I do not ask for half of the kingdom as] *my request and* [𝕿¹ + I do not ask for the building of the House of the Sanctuary as] *my petition;* [𝕵 + they are these.] Esther starts to tell the King what is in her heart, *My request and my petition*—then suddenly recollecting herself, or changing her mind, she resolves to put the matter off to another day.

8. [𝕿² + And Esther answered, O King,] *if I have obtained the King's favour, and if it seems good to the King to grant my request and to accede to my petition*]. The usual formula for presenting a matter to the monarch (*cf.* 1¹⁹ 3⁹ 5⁴ 7³ 8⁵).—*Let* [𝕲 codd. + my lord] *the King and Haman come* [𝕲 L + to-morrow also] *to the banquet which I will prepare for them, and to-morrow I will do as the King wishes*]. This delay in presenting her petition is even more unlikely than her previous unwillingness to tell the King what she wanted (v. ⁴). Whatever reasons may then have caused her to wait, existed now no longer, and a second banquet could be no more favourable occasion than the first. The reason for the delay is that the author needs time for the disgrace of **Haman**.

6. om. 𝕴.—[לאסתר] *ei* 𝕵: om. 44, 106.—[במשתה] *postquam biberat abundanter* 𝕵: om. L.—[היין] om. 𝕲 L (exc. א ᶜ·ᵃ ᵐᵍ, 93*b* under *).—[מה] + ἐστιν βασίλισσα Ἐσθήρ 𝕲: + ἔστι σοι βασίλισσα Ἐσθήρ 52, 64, 74, 106, 120, 243, 248, C, Ald.: + ἡ βασίλισσα L: + σοι Ἐσθήρ 44.—[שאלתך]om. 𝕲 (exc. א ᶜ·ᵃ ᵐᵍ, 93*b* under *): τὸ θέλημά σου L.—[וינתן - המלכות] om. 𝕲 (exc. א ᶜ·ᵃ ᵐᵍ, 93*b* under *).—[ינ־תן לך] om. L: om. י 𝕾.—[ומה בקשתך] αἴτησαι L (καὶ τί τὸ ἀξίωμά σου 93*a*).—[וְתֵעָשׂ] καὶ ἔσται (σοι) ὅσα ἀξιοῖς 𝕲 L: ܚܒ ܚܣܡܠ 𝕾. *Niph.* impf. of the jussive form in pause (*cf.* Kau. § 109*f*.). So also 7² 9¹².

7. om. 𝕴.—[אסתר] om. 𝕲 (exc. A 44, 93*b*, 106).—[ויאמר] om. 𝕵 𝕲 L.—[בקשתי] καὶ τὸ ἀξίωμα 𝕲 (+ μου א A N L 71, 74, 76, 93, 243, 248, C, Ald.): om. 44, 106.

8. om. 𝕴.—[בעיני] ܚܣܡܠܒܝ 𝕾: ἐνώπιον 𝕲: ἐναντίον A L.—[המלך] σου βασιλεῦ L.—[להת־] ܚܣܡܠ 𝕾.—[אם - בקשתי] om. 𝕲 (exc. א ᶜ·ᵃ ᵐᵍ ⁱⁿᶠ, 93*b* *).—[על] ܚܣܡܠ 𝕾.—[יבוא] + ὁ κύριός μου 44, 71, 74, 76, 106, 120, 236.—[ולעשות] ܚܠ ܥܒܕܐ ܚܒ ܘܠܥܐ 𝕾.—[והמן] + ἔτι τὴν αὔριον 𝕲: + ἐπὶ τὴν αὔριον A 52, 64, 248, C, Ald.: + καὶ τῇ αὔριον L.—[ומחר] ו 𝕾.—[אעשה] om. 𝕾.—[כדבר] τὰ αὐτά 𝕲: κατὰ τὰ αὐτά L: κατὰ ταῦτα 44, 71, 74, 76, 106, 120, 236.—[⁴המלך] om. 𝕲 L.

HAMAN PLANS TO HANG MORDECAI (5⁹⁻¹⁴).

9. [L + And the King said, It shall be done as thou willest.] *And Haman went out that day* [𝕲 𝕿¹ + from the King] *glad and good-natured*, [Jos. + because he alone was asked to sup with the King at Esther's banquet, and because no one else received such honour at the hands of kings.] The reason for Haman's joy is well stated by Jos. (*cf.* v. ¹²). On *good-natured*, *cf.* 1¹⁰ 1 S. 25³⁶.—[𝕴 + And there were 300 men with him and they all worshipped him, but Mordecai would not worship him.] *And as soon as Haman saw Mordecai* [𝕲 + the Jew] [𝕾 𝕴 + sitting] [𝕿¹ + and the children busying themselves with the precepts of the Law in the sanhedrin, which Esther had made for them] *in the King's gate*]. Mordecai has returned to his old place (*cf.* 2¹⁹· ²¹ 3² ᶠ· 5¹³ 6¹⁰· ¹²). This means that he has heard of Esther's successful entry to the King, and has put off his sackcloth in confidence that all is going well.—*While he* [𝕿¹ + Mordecai] *neither rose up* [𝕿¹ + before his idol] *nor trembled before him*, [𝕿¹ + but, with the palm of his right hand extended, showed him the deed of sale by which he had sold himself to him for a loaf of bread, wherein was written on leather the defect that he had in his knee; immediately his wrath waxed great,] *and Haman was full of fury against Mordecai.*] In spite of all the trouble that it has brought upon the Jews, Mordecai still persists in his insolent behaviour toward Haman (*cf.* 3²). No wonder that Haman is angry, since even his edict of destruction has failed to humble this man.

10. *And Haman restrained himself and went to his house* [𝔏 + sad]. This delay in taking vengeance upon Mordecai is just as unnatural as is Esther's delay in taking vengeance upon Haman. The author wishes to keep the reader in suspense as long as possible, and to give Haman time to devise an exceptional penalty for Mordecai.—*And he sent and brought his friends* [𝔏 + and his sons] *and Zeresh his* [𝔗¹ + wicked] *wife,* [𝔗¹ + the daughter of Tatnai, the prince of the region beyond the river.] [*Mid.* + He had 365 counsellors, one for each day of the solar year, but no one could give such good advice as Zeresh his wife.] The guests are probably *brought* to a banquet (*cf.* 6¹⁴). The *friends* are the same as the *wise* of 6¹³. Like the King, Haman has his council of advisers (*cf.* 1¹³). Neither Esther nor Haman dares to make a move in the game of state without consulting experts. On *Zeresh*, see pp. 70, 89.

11. *And Haman recounted to them the greatness of his wealth, and* [𝔗¹ + how he was reckoned among the King's princes, and how there ran before him] *the multitude of his sons* [𝔗¹ + 208 in number, besides 10 others who were polemarchs over the provinces, and Shammāshê who was the King's scribe (*cf. Meg.* 15*b*);] *and all the ways in which the King had honoured him,* [Jos. + and the Queen as well;] *and how he had exalted him above* [Vrss. + all] *the officials and the King's courtiers.*] *Cf.* 3¹ ᶠ· where the elevation of Haman is first described. On his *wealth, cf.* 3⁹, where he is able to offer 10,000 talents for the destruction of the Jews. According to Her. i. 136, those Persians were held in highest honour who had the largest number of sons. According to 9¹⁰, Haman had ten, but see the addition of 𝔗¹. On *officials* and *courtiers,* see 1³.

12. And Haman [L 𝔏 + boasted and] *said: Queen Esther brought no one with the King to the banquet which she had pre-*

pared except me, [𝕷 + and the Queen mentioned nobody but me, and I am his favourite among all his friends, and my seat he has placed above all others and it is honoured by all;] *and to-morrow also I am invited by her* [𝕿¹ + *to feast*] *along with the King*.] It is most surprising that, in spite of all Esther's dealings with Mordecai (2¹¹· ²² 4⁴⁻¹⁶), Haman has no suspicion that she is a Jewess, but regards her invitations as tokens of signal favour. Esther must have dissembled with consummate skill at the first banquet. The first half of the v. refers, not to the coming banquet (Sieg.), but to the one just finished. *Brought* refers to the custom of sending slaves to escort a guest to a feast (5¹⁰ 6¹⁴ Lu. 14¹⁷).

13. *But all this fails to satisfy me all the time that I see Mordecai the Jew sitting* [𝕿¹ + *in the sanhedrin with the young men*] *in the King's gate* [L 𝕷 𝕾 + *and he does not bow down to me*.] One wish ungratified poisons the whole cup of life for Haman. With all that he has, he cannot be happy until Mordecai is punished (*cf.* 3² 5⁹). *Fails to satisfy me*, i.e., lit. *is not adequate for me*. Mordecai's race is here well known to Haman (*cf.* 2⁵ 6¹⁰ 8⁷). This makes it all the more surprising that he does not know that Esther is a Jewess. On *King's gate*, *cf.* 2¹⁹· ²¹ 3³ 5⁹ 6¹⁰· ¹².

14. *And Zeresh his wife and all his friends said to him:*

[L + He belongs to the Jewish race. The King has permitted thee to destroy the Jews, and the gods have granted thee a day of destruction in order to punish them.] [𝕿¹ + If it please thee, let us speak one word in thy presence. What are we to do to this Mordecai the Jew? If he be one of the righteous who are created in the world, and we try to kill him with the sword, the sword will perhaps turn and fall upon us. If we seek to stone him, once with a stone David slew Goliath the Philistine. If we cast him into a chain of bronze, Manasseh once broke it and escaped from it. If we throw him into the great sea, the children of Israel once divided it and passed through its midst. If we cast him into a furnace of flaming fire, Hananiah, Mishael and Azariah once extinguished it and went forth from it. If we fling him into a lion's den, the lions once did Daniel no harm. If we cast him alive to dogs, the mouth of dogs was once shut in the land of Egypt on account of the children of Israel. If we send him into captivity, they were once carried into captivity and multiplied there. By what penalty then can we kill him, or what sort of death can be inflicted upon him? If we cast him into prison, Joseph was once brought from prison to royal dignity. If a knife be thrust at his throat, the knife was once turned away from Isaac. If we put out his eyes and let him go, he will kill some of us as Samson killed the Philistines. We do not know what punishment we can inflict upon this man unless this: (similarly 𝔗², *Mid.*, *Mid. A. G.*).]

Let them prepare a gallows fifty cubits in height [L + and let it be set up.] They are so sure that the King will give Haman whatever he wishes that they advise that all be made ready for the execution of Mordecai. The word *tree* does not signify *stake* or *cross* but *gallows*, as is evident from its height (*cf.* 2²³). Its enormous size, over 83 feet, is one of the characteristic exaggerations of the book (*cf.* 1¹· ⁴⁻⁸ 2¹² 3⁹· ¹²).—*And in the morning speak to the King* [L + about him,] [𝔗¹ + and let his blood be poured out at the door of his house,] *and let them hang Mordecai upon it*, [𝔗¹ + that all the Jews and all his companions and friends may see him, while heaven and earth together behold the gallows which Haman has prepared for Mordecai.] So Amestris asks Xerxes to kill the wife of Masistes (Her. ix. 110). See also Plutarch, *Artax.* 14 *f.*, 17, 23. Is it possible that the grand vizier could not put an obscure Jew to death without first obtaining permission from the King?—*Then go merrily with the King to the banquet.*] Having destroyed his enemy, there will be no barrier to Haman's perfect enjoyment of Esther's feast.—*And the advice seemed good to Haman and he prepared the gallows* [Jos. + and gave orders to his servants to place it in the court for the execution of Mordecai.] *Cf.* 1²¹ 2⁴. *Mid.* here appends a long discussion of God with the trees as to which one should furnish wood for the gallows.

[𝔗¹ + Haman waited impatiently for the morning to go before the King and ask for the gallows. At this time Haman son of Hammᵉdāthā did not put off his garments, nor did he lie down until he had gone and brought carpenters and smiths; the carpenters to make the gallows, and the smiths to forge an iron knife. And the sons of Haman exulted and rejoiced, and Zeresh his wife played on the lyre with the wicked Haman. He said also, I will pay wages to the carpenters and I will prepare a feast for the smiths on account of this gallows. That same hour, when Haman arose to try the gallows with his own length, there went forth a daughter-voice from the highest heaven and said to him, It is good, wicked Haman; and fits thee, son of Hammᵉdāthā.] [Jos. + And God laughed to scorn the hope of the wicked Haman; and knowing what was about to happen, he was delighted that it would be so.] [𝕿¹ + And from the day in which Esther invited Haman to the banquet the children of Israel were distressed, saying thus among themselves: We expect daily that Esther will ask the King to put Haman to death, but instead of this she invites him to a banquet. At this same time the whole family of Jacob poured out their soul, and had faith in their Heavenly Father, speaking thus: Answer us! Answer all the afflicted! As the eyes of servants wait upon their masters, and as the eyes of a handmaid wait upon her mistress, so our eyes wait upon thee until thou wilt appear and deliver us. For, behold, an enemy and a foe pursues us and says, Who are these Jews? Then He hearkened unto the voice of their prayer and answered their petitions, for every time that He rescued them from their enemies He rescued them at night, from Pharaoh, and from Sennacherib, and from all that rose up against them.]

[𝕿¹ 𝕿² + "In that night" went forth deliverance to the Jews. "In that night" Sarah was taken to the house of Abimelech. "In that night" all the first born of the Egyptians were slain. "In that night" their oracles were revealed to the Prophets and visions to the dreamers of dreams. That same night the whole world was shaken, cities and all their inhabitants; and there was great mourning in all cities, lamentation and crying in all provinces, young men girding themselves with sackcloth, old men and women beating upon their breasts, and all weeping bitterly and crying with a loud voice: Alas! because we see destruction upon destruction and breach upon breach. From our first breach we have not yet recovered, nor is healing restored from our wound, nor have we received consolation from our sorrow, nor have the afflictions of our heart departed from us. The city of our fathers lies upon the ground, and the enemy has closed our Sanctuary, and our foes have trampled our Temple-courts. Neither Pharaoh nor the Egyptians took counsel against us after this manner, nor did the kings of the heathen devise plans against us in this way, that they should be ready against that day to cut us off from the face of the earth (He who reveals secrets has revealed this secret to Mordecai that a decree of death has been issued against us, the house of Israel), nor did they sell us as man servants or as maid servants.

In that night the sleep of the Holy One, the Supremely Blessed, forsook him; but if the following Scripture were not written, it would be impossible to say this, for it is written, "Awake! why sleepest thou, Lord?" Do not say that, for sleep is never present with Him; but when the house of Israel sins, He acts as if He were asleep; but when they do His will, "He who keepeth Israel neither slumbers nor sleeps." In that night the sleep of Mordecai the just also forsook him; for he was awake and did not lie down; or if he lay down, he did not sleep, because the house of Israel were gathered and sat before him, saying: Thou thyself hast been the cause of all this evil that has come upon us. If thou hadst risen up before the wicked Haman and hadst done obeisance and hadst paid homage to him, all this distress would not have come upon us. Mordecai answered and said to them: The outer garment which Haman wears has two idols depicted upon it, the one on the front, the other on the back. If then I should rise up and do obeisance to him, I should be found to have worshipped idols; but you yourselves know that he who worships idols shall perish from this world and shall be excluded from the world to come. Then they all kept silence before him. In that night sleep forsook the wicked Haman, for when he was awake, he did not lie down; and when he lay down, he could not sleep, from the time when he prepared the gallows on which to hang Mordecai, without knowing that he was preparing it for himself. In that night sleep forsook the righteous Esther, because she had prepared food to invite Haman to a feast with King Xerxes. In that night sleep forsook the foolish Xerxes, for when he was awake he did not lie down; and when he lay down, he could not sleep, because a spirit possessed him which possesses kings and disturbed him the whole night. At length he spoke and addressed his nobles thus: Whatever I eat does not agree with me, whatever I drink I cannot retain. The heavens have thundered against me and the heaven of heavens lifts up its voice. Is it because I have not remitted the tribute which I promised to remit to the provinces? Or have Esther and Haman planned to kill me, because Esther invites no one to the feast with me except Haman? In that night the memory of Abraham, Isaac, and Jacob came before their Heavenly Father, so that an angel was sent from the height, Michael himself, the commander of the army of Israel, who, sitting at the head of the King, drove sleep away from him the whole night long.]

9. ביום ההוא] κατὰ τὰ αὐτά L 93b ÷ : om. 𝔊 𝔏 (exc. א c. a mg, 93b under *).—יצא המן] καὶ ἀπηγγέλη τῷ Ἀμάν L, 93b ÷.—שמח] ὑπερχαρὴς 𝔊: καὶ ἐθαύμασεν L, 93b ÷ : om. 𝔏: + ἀπὸ τοῦ βασιλέως 𝔊 (exc. 93b): + a cœna 𝔏: + καὶ ὁ βασιλεὺς ἀναλύσας L, 93b ÷.—ב ט] εὐφραινόμενος 𝔊: ἡσύχασεν L: om. 𝔏.—לב] om. 𝔊 𝔏 L (exc. א c. a, 93b under *).—וכראות—end of v.] et trecenti viri cum eo, et omnes adoraverunt eum: Mardochæus autem non adoravit eum 𝔏: om. L.—כראות] inf. with ב introducing the precise moment of time. See on 1² כיבת.—בשער] ἐν τῇ αὐλῇ 𝔊.—ממנו—המלך] om. 𝔊 (exc. א c. a mg sup, 93b under *).—המלך] palatii 𝔍.—קם—זע] Pf. because a parenthetical circumstantial clause (Kau. § 106 d. e.). According to Haupt the two forms are participles in the acc. as עָמְדָה (5²).—נו] de loco sessionis suæ 𝔍.—המן על מרדכי] om. 𝔊 (exc. א c. a mg, 93b under *: A has Ἀμάν): Haupt deletes המן.—חמה על] here only in OT.

10. ויתאפק] om. 𝔊 L 𝔏 (exc. א c. a mg, 93b under *).—המן] om. 𝔊 (exc. א c. a mg, 93b under *): Haupt deletes.—וישלח] om. 𝔊 𝔏 L (exc.

HAMAN PLANS TO HANG MORDECAI 243

א c. a mg, 93*b* under *).— [ויבא] + *ad se* 𝕵.— [אהביו] τοὺς φίλους 𝕲 (+ αὐτοῦ L 𝕷).

11. om. L.— [המן]om. 𝕵 𝕲 (exc. א c. a) 𝕷.— [את כבוד]om. 𝕲 (exc. 93*b*).— [כבוד עשרו] in 1⁴ in reverse order.— [ורב בניו] om. 𝕲 𝕷 (exc. א c. a mg, 93*b* under *).— [ורב בניו] Hitzig in Bert. finds this expression peculiar and proposes to read ורב פניו, 'and his abundant dignity.' This is very unlikely.— [ואת] introducing clauses that are objects to ויספר (Kau. § 157 *c*.). — [ואת]—end of v.] om. 𝕷.— [את כל]om. 𝕾.— [כל] δόξαν 𝕲: πάντα 93*b*: Haupt regards כל as impossible in this connection and transposes to a position before השרים.— [גדלו] αὐτῷ περιέθηκεν 𝕲: om. 𝕵.— [את אשר]² om. 𝕵 𝕾.— [על השרים] om. 𝕲.— [על] + כל K 117, 252, R 379, 𝕋¹ 𝕋² 𝕵.— [ועברי] [המלך]— 𝕾.— [ועברי המלך] καὶ ἡγεῖσθαι τῆς βασιλείας 𝕲.— ܣܒ̈ܐ ܟܠ ܐܚ̈ܐ *suos* 𝕵.

12. [ויאמר המן] καὶ ἐκαυχᾶτο λέγων L: *et gloriabatur dicens* 𝕷.— [המן] om. 𝕵: Haupt deletes.— [אף] *post hæc* 𝕵: ὡς L: om. 𝕲 𝕷.— [אסתר] om. 𝕲 L 𝕷 (א c. a A 93*b* have).— [המלכה] *rex* 𝕷: om. 𝕾.— [עם - עשתה]om. 𝕷.— [עם] εἰ μὴ L.— [אל - עשתה] ἐν ἐπισήμῳ ἡμέρᾳ αὐτῆς L: om. 𝕾.— [אשר עשתה] om. 𝕵 𝕲 (exc. א c. a): αὐτῆς 74, 76.— [כי אם אותי] καὶ ἐμὲ μόνον L.— [וגם - המלך] *regina autem nullius mentionem fecit, nisi mei: et ego sum necessarius tuus inter omnes amicos ejus, sedile autem meum supra omnes, et ab omnibus adoratur* 𝕷.— [גם] om. 𝕲 L.— [לה עם המלך] om. 𝕲 L (exc. א c. a mg, 93*b* under *). — [לה] ל in the meaning of 'by,' after a passive (*cf.* 4³ Ru. 3¹⁰).

13. [וכל] om. 𝕲 L (𝕷 has).— [זה - לי] τοῦτο δὲ λυπεῖ με μόνον L.— בכל אשר עת] ὅταν 𝕲 L 𝕷: ἐν παντὶ χρόνῳ ὅταν א c. a mg, 93*b* under*: ܟܡܐ ܕ— 𝕾: *quamdiu* 𝕵: Bert., following 𝕲 L 𝕷, regards עת as indefinite on account of the absence of the art. and translates 'every time that,' but this is not necessary, since עת is cstr. before the following relative clause (*cf.* מקום אשר 4³ 8¹⁷), and, therefore, may be definite even without the art. The phrase means, accordingly, 'all the time that,' 'so long as' (so 𝕾 𝕵 AV. RV. Sieg., Rys.).— [יושב] om. 𝕲 L 𝕷 (exc. א c. a, 93*b* under *).— [בשער] ἐν τῇ αὐλῇ 𝕲 L: om. 𝕷.— [המלך] om. 𝕲 (exc. א c. a, 93*b* under *) 𝕷: + ܘܠܐ ܣܓܕ ܠܝ ܘܐܦ 𝕾: + καὶ μὴ προσκυνεῖ με L: + *non adorantem me* 𝕷.

14. [זרש] *cf.* 5¹⁰.— [וכל]om. כל 𝕲 L 𝕷 (exc. א c. a, 93*b* under*): *ceteri* 𝕵. — [אהביו] οἱ φίλοι 𝕲 (+ αὐτοῦ א c. a, 93*b* under *): om. L.— [יעשו] κοπήτω σοι 𝕲 L 𝕷 (om. σοι A 44, 71, 74, 76, 106, 236).— [גבה] om. 𝕲 L 𝕷 (exc. א c. a mg).— [אמה] *pedum* 𝕷.— [בבקר - למלך] tr. aft. עליו L.— [אמר למלך]om. 𝕷.— [ויתלו] *ut appendatur* 𝕵: καὶ κρεμασθήτω 𝕲 𝕷: καὶ κρέμασον L.— [את מרדכי] αὐτὸν L.— [עליו] ἐπὶ τὸν ξύλον 𝕲 L: *in eo* 𝕷.— [ובא - המן] om. 𝕷.— [עם] πρὸς L.— [המשתה אל] om. L.— [שמח] καὶ εὐφραίνου 𝕲 (om. καὶ L).— [הדבר]om. L. — [לפני] בעיני some codd., 𝕾.— [המן] *ei* 𝕵: + ܚܫܒ 𝕾.— [וייטב העץ] καὶ ἐποίησεν οὕτως L: the idea, of course, is not that Haman constructed the gallows with his own hands. 'Made' may equal 'had made,' or ויעש may be regarded as impersonal, as הפיל (3⁷).

THE KING IS REMINDED THAT NOTHING HAS BEEN DONE TO REWARD MORDECAI (6¹⁻³).

1. *That night the King's sleep fled.*] Here, as everywhere, the author goes out of his way to avoid mentioning God. 𝕲 𝕷 L 𝕿¹ 𝕿² correct the defect and say that God took away his sleep.— [Jos. + Now he was not willing to pass the sleepless time idly, but chose to devote it to something that was profitable for the kingdom,] *so he ordered* [𝕲 𝕿² + his secretary] *to bring the book of memorable events, namely, the chronicles* [Jos. 𝕿² + of the kings that had reigned before him and of his own deeds.] This is not a natural way of passing a sleepless night—with his numerous wives the King might have found something livelier, but the author chooses it because this was the book in which Mordecai's service in discovering the plot against the King was recorded (see 2²³). According to this passage the book was kept in the King's room. —*And they kept on reading before the King* [𝕿¹ + the decrees of the kings that had reigned before him.] The periphrastic form of the verb expresses the duration of the action. Since the King could not sleep, the reading lasted all night.

> [𝕿¹ 𝕿² + And Michael sat over against him, and the King looked and saw as it were the form of a man, who addressed the King thus: Haman desires to slay thee and to make himself king in thy stead. Behold, he will present himself in the morning and will wish to ask thee to give him the man who saved thee from death in order that he may kill him; but say thou to Haman, What shall be done for the man whom the King wishes to honour? and thou wilt see that he will ask for nothing else from thee but royal garments, the crown of the kingdom, and the horse on which the King rides. And the man who was reading was one of the scribes.] [Jos. + And when he had brought the book and was reading it, it was found that one, on account of his virtue on a certain occasion, had received a country, and its name was stated; and another was recorded to have received a present on account of his fidelity.]

2. [𝕷 + And the God of the Jews and Lord of all creation guided the hand of the reader to the book which the King had written to remind him of Mordecai,] *and it was found written* [𝕲 𝕿¹ + in the book] *how Mordecai had informed* [𝕲 L + the King] *concerning Bigthan and Teresh, the two eunuchs of the King who* *guarded the threshold, who had sought to lay hands on King Xerxes* [𝕿¹ + to kill him in his bedroom.] [*Meg.* 16a + And the secretary blotted it out, but the angel Gabriel wrote it again a second time (similarly *Mid. A. G.*).] See 2²¹. At the very moment when Haman is planning to hang Mordecai the King's attention is unexpectedly directed to Mordecai's service and he determines to heap honours upon him. This is the way that things happen in story-books, but not in real life.

3. [Jos. + And when the record stated no more than this and passed on to another matter,] *then the King said,* [𝕲 codd. + to his servants,] *What honour or dignity has been conferred upon Mordecai because of this? and the King's pages who served him said,* [𝕿¹ + As yet] *nothing has been conferred upon him.* [*Meg.* 16a + This they said, not because they loved Mordecai, but because they hated Haman.] Improbable as it is that Mordecai's service should be merely recorded, instead of being at once rewarded (2²³); it is much more improbable that Xerxes should utterly forget the man who saved his life, particularly when he was a friend of his beloved Esther (2²²). It was a point of honour with the Persian kings to reward promptly and magnificently those who conferred benefits upon them (*cf.* Her. iii. 138, 140; v. 11; viii. 85; ix. 107; Thuc. i. 138; Xen. *Hell.* iii. 1, 6). According to Her. viii. 85, the Persians had a special class of men known as *Orosangai,* or 'benefactors of the King.' See on 2²³. On *pages,* see 2².

[Jos. + And he commanded to stop reading.] [L + and the King gave close attention, saying: That faithful man Mordecai, the protector of my life! He it is that has kept me alive until now, so that I sit to-day upon my throne, yet I have done nothing for him! I have not done right. And the King said to his pages, What shall we do for Mordecai the saviour of the situation? And, reflecting, the young men were envious of him, because Haman had put fear in their hearts; and the King perceived. Then day broke.] [Jos. + And he inquired of those appointed for the purpose, what hour of the night it was; and when he was informed that it was dawn, he commanded that, if they found any of his friends who had come already before the court, they should tell him.] [𝕲 + And, at the moment when the King learned about the kindness of Mordecai, behold, Haman arrived in the court,] [𝕷 + for Haman watched in the royal palace and 300 men with him.]

246   ESTHER

1. נדדה שנת המלך] ὁ δὲ Κύριος ἀπέστησεν τὸν ὕπνον ἀπὸ τοῦ βασιλέως 𝕲: ὁ δὲ δυνατὸς ἀπέστησε τὸν ὕπνον τοῦ βασιλέως καὶ ἦν ἀγρυπνῶν L: *Judæorum autem Deus et universæ creaturæ Dominus percussit regem vigilantia* 𝕷ᴾ (𝕷ᶜ om. 6¹).— ויאמר] καὶ εἶπεν τῷ διδασκάλῳ αὐτοῦ 𝕲: καὶ ἐκλήθησαν οἱ ἀναγνῶσται L: *et dixit rex* 𝕷.— להביא] + *sibi* 𝕵: εἰσφέρειν 𝕲: εἰσφέρων A: *legite mihi* 𝕷 : om. L.— ויאמר להביא] inf. w. ל after אמר, as 4¹³ 1 Ch. 22² 2 Ch. 1¹⁸ Ne. 9¹⁵ ᵇ.— את ספר] γράμματα 𝕲: καὶ τὸ βιβλίον L: *librum* 𝕷.— הזכרנות - המלך] *et oculi mei somnum capiant et extendit lector manum suam in bibliotheca* 𝕷ᴾ.— דברי] om. 𝕲 L (exc. א ᶜ⁻ ᵃ, 93b under *).— היםים] om. L. Haupt, in defense of his singular emendation of 2²², arbitrarily rejects דברי הימים as a gloss derived from 2²³ and 10².— ויהיו נקראים] ἀναγινώσκειν 𝕲: ἀνεγινώσκετο L.— לפני המלך] αὐτῷ 𝕲 L: αὐτὰ ἐνώπιον τοῦ βασιλέως א ᶜ⁻ ᵃ, 93b under *.

2. וימצא כתוב] *ventum est ad illum locum ubi scriptum est* 𝕵: εὗρεν δὲ τὰ γράμματα τὰ γραφέντα 𝕲: καὶ ἦν ὑπόθεσις L: *Judæorum autem Deus gubernavit manum lectoris ad librum quem scripserat rex memoriam facere Mardochæo* 𝕷.— הגיד] ἐποίησε εὐεργέτημα L: *liberavit eum* 𝕷.— מרדכי] *de periculis* 𝕷.— על] *insidias* 𝕵: om. L.— שני] om. 𝕵 L.— המלך] αὐτοῦ A: om. 𝕵 L 𝕷 44, 106.— משמרי הסף] ἐν τῷ φυλάσσειν αὐτοὺς 𝕲: om. 𝕵 L 𝕷: Haupt deletes, as in 2²¹, *q.v.*— הסף] נכבד 𝕊.— אשר] *end of v.*] om. L.— אשר בקשו] καὶ ζητῆσαι 𝕲.— במלך] om. 𝕷 𝕲 (exc. 44, 71, 74, 76, 106, 120, 236).— אחשורוש] + *quod cum audisset* 𝕵: *eum* + *et legit lector benefactum Mardochæi et commemoratus* 𝕷: Haupt deletes.

3. om. L.— המלך] + τοῖς διακόνοις αὐτοῦ 44, 71, 74, 76, 93b, 120, 236.— מה] *dic nondum* 𝕷.— נעשׂה] ἐποιήσαμεν 𝕲, as if נָעֲשָׂה. Here followed by ל and עִם, in 2¹¹ by ב, all in substantially the same meaning.— יקר וגדולה] om. 𝕷: both words are genitives depending on מה. So 𝕵, *quid, pro hac fide, honoris ac præmii* (Haupt).— יקר] 'honour,' as 1⁴· ²⁰ 6⁶.— למרדכי] *huic homini* 𝕷.— על זה] om. 𝕲 (exc. א ᶜ⁻ ᵃ, 93b under *): *secundum quod fecit nobis* 𝕷.— ויאמרו] + *ei* 𝕵: + ܠܗ 𝕊.— ויאמרו— *end of v.*] om. 𝕷.— משרתיו] om. 𝕲 (exc. 93b): pr. *ac* 𝕵 𝕊.— נעשׂה] ἐποίησας 𝕲.

THE KING COMMANDS HAMAN TO CONFER ROYAL HONOURS UPON MORDECAI (6⁴⁻¹⁰).

4. *And* [𝕵 + straightway] *the King said, Who is* [𝕌¹ + the man who stands] *in the court? just after Haman had entered the outer court of the King's house* [Jos. + earlier than the customary hour] *to speak to the King about hanging Mordecai on the gallows which he had erected for him,* [𝕷 + but the Lord did not permit him to speak.] Haman apparently cannot wait until morning to ask permission to hang Mordecai on his high gallows, but comes in the middle of the night to the palace, although there is no reason to expect a summons from the King at that hour (*cf.* v. ⁵). His coming coincides with the moment when the King learns of Mordecai's service and wishes to find a courtier to execute his commands. This sounds more like fiction than history. The improbability is somewhat relieved by the Vrss. which represent Haman as coming the next morning; still, even on this hypothesis, the coincidence is too lucky to be natural. Haman waits in the *outer court* because he dares not enter the inner court without a summons (see 4¹¹). He hopes that, if he is on hand, the King may soon call for him. *To speak to the King*, as in 5¹⁴. On the erection of the gallows, *cf.* 5¹⁴.

5. *And the King's pages said unto him, Behold, Haman is waiting in the court; and the King said, Let him enter.*] The fact that Haman alone is found in the court suggests that it is an unusual hour, when none of the other courtiers are present (*cf.* v. ⁴). *Enter*, *i.e.*, into the King's bedchamber.

6. *And Haman entered; and the King said to him,* [Jos. + Because I know that thou alone art a faithful friend to me, I beseech thee to advise me,] *what is to be done with the man* [L 𝕷 + who honours the King,] *whom the King longs to honour* [Jos. + in a manner worthy of his generosity?] It is a fine stroke of literary art by which Haman himself is made to decide what honours shall be paid to the man whom he has decided to hang. The King does not give him time to present his petition, but immediately asks him the question, *What is to be done?* lit. *What to do?* as in 1¹⁵. In 2¹⁴ the same verb, *longed*, is used of the King's craving for one of his wives.—*And Haman said to himself,* [Jos. + Whatever advice I give will be on my own behalf, for] *on whom besides me does the King long to bestow honour?*] Haman's total lack of suspicion makes the blow that falls in v. ¹⁰ all the more crushing. *To himself*, lit. *in his heart*. This is one of the passages from which *Meg.* 7a infers the inspiration of the Book of Est. How could the author know what Haman said *in his heart*, if he were not inspired?

7. *And Haman said to the King,* [Jos. + If thou wishest to cover with glory] *the man* [𝕷 + who honours the King] *whom the*

King longs to honour]. The sentence thus begun is not completed in the next vv., but Haman constructs a new sentence in which *the man* is object. For similar anacolutha, see 4¹¹ 5⁷. The insertion of Jos. removes the anacoluthon.

8. [𝔗¹ + Let the King make a decree, and] *let them bring a royal garment which the King has worn* [𝔗¹ + on the day of his accession to the throne,] [𝔏 + and a golden crown]. Haman proceeds to enumerate the things that were counted tokens of highest honour among the Persians. The *garment* is not merely such a one as the King is accustomed to wear (AV., RV.), but, as the perf. indicates, and as 𝔗² understands, one that he has actually worn. Plutarch (*Artax.* 24) relates that a certain Tiribazos asked the King to take off his mantle and give it to him. The King acceded, but forbade him to wear the mantle. From this it appears that to wear the King's own robe was accounted one of the greatest favours (*cf.* 1 S. 18⁴).—*And* [𝔏 𝔍 + place him upon] *a* [L 𝔏 + royal] *horse on which the King has ridden* [𝔗¹ + on the day of his accession to the throne]. There is no ancient record of this method of rewarding service to the King of Persia, but it is analogous to the wearing of the royal garment. *Cf.* 1 K. 1³³, where Solomon is seated on David's horse; and Gn. 41⁴³, where Joseph rides in the second chariot.—*And on whose head a royal turban has been placed*]. This clause has given great trouble to the older comm. because they have supposed it impossible that a *royal turban* should be placed on the horse's head, and because in 8¹⁵ such a turban is placed on Mordecai's head. 𝔊 L Jos. omit. 𝔏 substitutes *clad as I have said above*. 𝔍 renders *he ought ... to receive a royal crown upon his head;* Mün., Tig., Cler., Ramb., *and let a royal crown be placed upon his head;* Jun. & Trem., Pisc., *and when a royal crown is placed upon his head, then let them give the garment, etc.;* Pag., RV. mg., *and the crown royal which is set upon his head*. All these renderings are grammatically impossible. *On whose head* can only refer to the horse. In the following narrative the crown does not appear as part of Mordecai's attire, which shows that it belongs to the horse's outfit. So 𝔗¹, 𝔗², IE., and Jewish interpreters generally, Dieu., Caj., Vat., and most modern comm. There is no real difficulty in this idea. The

As. reliefs depict the King's horses with tall, pointed ornaments like a royal turban on their heads (see Layard, *Nineveh*, vol. ii. pl. 9). It is likely that a similar custom prevailed in Persia. On *royal turban*, see 1[11].

9. *And let them give the garment* [𝕌¹ + of purple] *and the horse into the charge of one of the King's noble officials*], to see that the ceremony is carried out properly, and to add dignity to it by his presence.—*And let them clothe the man whom the King longs to honour*, [Jos. + and put a gold chain about his neck,] *and make him ride on the horse* [L 𝔖 + and lead him about] *in the city-square.*] The subject may still be impersonal, as in the preceding clauses, or it may be the *noble officials* of the last clause. The account of Joseph's elevation (Gn. 41[38-44]) is in the author's mind. From this source Jos. derives his addition (Gn. 41[42]). See Rosenthal, "Der Vergleich Ester-Joseph-Daniel," *ZATW*. xv. (1895), pp. 278 *ff.*; xvii. (1897), pp. 125 *ff.* The purpose of the riding is to display the man's honour to all the inhabitants of Susa. On *city-square*, see 4[6].—*And* [Jos. + let one of the King's most intimate friends precede him and] *proclaim before him, This is what is done for the man* [L 𝔏 + who honours the King] *whom the King longs to honour.*] A crier explains the meaning of the procession as it advances (*cf.* Gn. 41[43]). From this advice of Haman 𝕌¹, 𝕌², and the Midrashim infer that he was plotting to seize the throne (*cf.* 𝕌¹ 𝕌² on 6[1]).

10. [Jos. + Thus Haman advised, supposing that the reward would come to him.] [𝕌² + And the King regarded Haman closely, and thought in his heart and said to himself, Haman wishes to kill me and to make himself King in my stead: I see it in his face.] *Then the King*, [Jos. + being pleased with the advice,] *said to Haman*, [𝕌² + Haman! Haman!] *make haste*, [𝕌² + Go to the King's treasury and fetch thence one of the fine purple coverings and] *take the garment* [𝕌² + of fine Frankish silk adorned with precious stones and pearls, from all four of whose sides hang golden bells and pomegranates; and take thence the great crown of Macedonian gold which was brought me from the cities of the provinces on the first day that I was established in the kingdom; and take thence the fine sword and armour that were brought me from the province of Kush, and the two fasces covered in royal fashion with pearls which were brought me from the province of Africa. Then go to the royal stable] *and* [𝕿² + lead out] *the horse* [𝕿² + that stands in the chief stall, whose name is Shifregaz, upon which I rode on the first day that I was established in the kingdom;] [Jos. + and take the neck-chain] *as thou hast said, and do thus unto Mordecai* [*Meg.* 16a, 𝕿¹, 𝕿² + Haman answered, Which Mordecai? The King replied] *the Jew.* [*Meg.*, 𝕿¹, 𝕿² + But, said Haman, There are many of that name among the Jews. I mean, said the King, the one] *who sits in the King's gate* [𝕿¹ + in the sanhedrin which Queen Esther has established.] [*Meg.* + Give him, said Haman, a town or (the toll of) a river. Give him that also, said the King.] [𝕿¹ + Haman answered, I ask thee to slay me rather than to impose this duty upon me. Make haste, said the King,] *omit nothing of all that thou hast said,* [Jos. + for thou art my intimate friend; be, therefore, the executor of those things which thou hast so well advised. This shall be our reward to him for having saved my life.] Thus with a word the King blights Haman's hope. The sudden climax is very artistic and is not improved by the additions of the Vrss. The King is aware that Mordecai is a Jew. Perhaps we may suppose that this was recorded in the royal annals that were read before him (6^1). He is also aware that Mordecai habitually *sits in the gate of the King* ($2^{19, 21}$ 3^2 $5^{9, 13}$), although this fact would not naturally be mentioned in the annals. This lends some support to the theory of the Vrss. that Mordecai was a royal official (*cf.* $2^{11, 19}$), or we may suppose that the King had noticed him as he passed to and fro through the gate. How the King knows so much about Mordecai without suspecting that his friend Esther (2^{22}) is a Jewess, is hard to understand. It is also difficult to explain how he can honour Mordecai the Jew in this signal fashion, when he has just condemned all the Jews to destruction (3^{11-13}); or, at least, how he can avoid making some provision to exempt Mordecai from the edict of death. All these honours would be of little use to him, if he were to be executed a few months later. Perhaps the author supposes that Xerxes had a short memory; and had forgotten his edict against the Jews, as he had forgotten Mordecai's service (2^{23} 6^3).

HAMAN ADVISES XERXES   251

4. בחצר] ἐστιν ἔξω L.— והמן – end of v.] aft. 6[5] 𝕷.— [והמן בא parenthetical subordinate clause giving the time of the previous vb.— [בא עֻיֵהּ L. Instead of בא לחצר Haupt reads בא אל חצר.— החיצונה – לחצר] om. 𝕲: Ἀμὰν δὲ ὤρθρικει L: *ad regem et cogitabat* 𝕷.— [החיצונה] *interius* 𝕵.— +[למלך *et juberet* 𝕵.— [להלוח] inf. with ל giving the contents of the conversation with the King (*cf.* 3[14]; Kau. § 114 *g*).— [על – לו] om. L.— [לו] om. 𝕲 (exc. א [c. a mg], 93*b* under *).

5. ויאמרו – בחצר] om. L.— [אליו] om. 𝕵𝕲 (exc. א [c. a mg], 93*b* under *).— [הנה] om. 𝕵𝕷.— [עׂשר בחצר] om. 𝕷.

6. לו המלך] om. [ויבוא המן 𝕷𝕲 (exc. א [c. a mg], 93*b*).— [המן] om. 𝕵L.— [מה] 𝕵.— [ומלך] om. 𝕷.— [למלך להמן R 593: ὁ βασιλεὺς τῷ Ἀμάν 𝕲𝕷.— 𝕾.— [לעשוח] ποιήσω 𝕲: ποιήσομεν L: *fiet* 𝕷.— [באיש] + τῷ τὸν βασιλέα τιμῶντι L: + *qui regem honorificat* 𝕷. The ב in באיש is ב of the instrument after עשה (BDB. p. 89, III. 2 *b*). In 1[15] 'what to do with' means 'how to punish,' here it means 'how to reward.'— [אשר – ביקרו] om. 𝕷.— [2 המלך] 𝕲.— [חפץ] 'long,' 'desire,' as 1 K. 13[33] 21[6] Est. 2[14].— [ובלבו] + *et reputans* 𝕵: λέγων L: *cum cogitatione sua* 𝕷.— [למי] *neminem* 𝕷.— יחפץ – יקר] *habet rex necessarium* 𝕷.— [יוחר] 'excess' is a late Heb. word found only in Ec. and Est. יוחר מן 'excess from' (Ec. 12[12] and here) does not mean 'more than' (Wild., Sieg., BDB.) but 'other than,' 'besides' (so Haupt); 𝕲, εἰ μὴ ἐμέ; 𝕵, *nullum alium nisi*.

7. המן] om. 𝕵𝕷𝕲 (exc. א [c. a], 44, 71, 74, 76, 106, 120, 236, 93*b*): Haupt deletes.— אל המלך] *domine rex* 𝕷: om. 𝕵 L 44, 106.— [איש] 𝕊: حَبَـ: *honorificanti regem* 𝕷.— [אשר] om. 𝕷: for the construction, *cf.* Kau. § 143 *c*, note.

8. יביאו] ἐνεγκάτωσαν οἱ παῖδες τοῦ βασιλέως 𝕲 (ἐνεγκάτω A): ληφθήτω L: *accipiatur* 𝕷.— [מלכות] βυσσίνην 𝕲.— [אשר – 1 המלך] om. 𝕵 L 𝕷.— [בו] om. 𝕲 (exc. א [c. a mg], 93*b* under *). Here only construed w. ב instead of the acc. [וסום] *et imponi super equum* 𝕵: *et equo regali vehatur* 𝕷: καὶ ἵππος βασιλικὸς L.— [2 אשר – 2 המלך] om. 𝕷: *qui de sella regis est* 𝕵.— [עליו] om. L 𝕲 (exc. א [c. a mg], 93*b* under *).— [ואשר – בראשו] om. L 𝕲 (exc. א [c. a mg], 93*b* under *): *indutus quæ supra dixi* 𝕷: *et accipere regium diadema super caput suum* 𝕵: Haupt deletes as a tertiary gloss based upon a secondary gloss in 8[15].— [נתן] Maur. regards as *Qal*, impf. 1 pl. for נִתֵּן (*cf.* Ju. 16[5]); but there is no *Maqqeph* here, and therefore no reason for shortening the vowel. The 1 p. would also be inappropriate in the mouth of Haman. The form is *Niph.* pret. 3 sg.

9. ונחון] καὶ λαβέτω ταῦτα L: om. נחון 𝕷: inf. abs. instead of finite vb. in lively discourse (*cf.* 2[3]). Here preceded by jussive and followed by perf. with ו cons. (Kau. § 113 *z*).— [הלבוש – יד] om. 𝕷 L 𝕲 (exc. א [c. a mg], 93*b* under *).— [הלבוש] om. 𝕵.— [על יד] 'into the charge', *cf.* 2[3. 8. 14] 3[9].— [הפרחמים – הסום] see on 1[3].— [הפרחמים] *primus* 𝕵: ἐνί 𝕲: εἷς L: *unus* 𝕷.— [איש] om. 𝕷.— [והלבשו] Oort, Haupt, read the sg.— [ביקרו] om. 𝕵.— [והלבישו] om. L 44, 106.— [והרכיבוהו על הסוס] *et incedens* 𝕵.— [ברחוב] [אשר – ביקרו] om. L 44, 106.—

ܠܒܘܫܐ ܣܘܣܝܐ ܕܡܠܟܐ 𝔖: διὰ τῆς πλατείας 𝔊: *in tota* 𝔏: καὶ περιελθέτω L.— [העיר om. 𝔖.—[וקראו κηρυσσέτω 𝔊 (κηρυσσέτωσαν א c. a) κηρύσσων L: *prædicet* 𝔏: Oort, Haupt, read the sg.—[לפניו λέγων 𝔊: *et dicat* 𝔍.—[איש παντὶ ἀνθρώπῳ 𝔊: *omni* + *honorificanti regem* 𝔏: τῷ τὸν βασιλέα τιμῶντι L: in 6⁶ באיש.—ביקרו - אשר] om. 𝔏.

10. [לחמן *ei* 𝔍: om. 44, 71, 106.—[מהר - הסוס] om. 𝔊 (exc. א c. a mg inf, 93*b* under *).—[מהר קח] 'take swiftly,' *cf.* 5⁵.—[קח - הסוס] om. 𝔏.—[את הסוס pr. סוסא 𝔖.—[כאשר καλῶς 𝔊: *bene* 𝔏.—[ועשה] om. ו 𝔊𝔏.—[כן *sicut dixisti* 𝔏.—[היהודי] om. 𝔏.—[הויׁשב בשער τῷ θεραπεύοντι ἐν τῇ αὐλῇ 𝔊𝔏: ὃν δοξάζει 106.—[בשער] ἐν τῇ βουλῇ 249: ὃν εἶπεν A.—[המלך] *palatii* 𝔍: om. L 𝔊 (exc. A 106).—[אל תפל] 'do not let fall,' *i.e.*, 'do not omit' (*cf.* Jos. 21⁴⁵ Ju. 2¹⁹).—[דבר] + σου 𝔊 L 𝔏.—[מכל] om. L 𝔊 (exc. א c. a, 93*b* under *).— [אשר דברת om. L.

HAMAN EXECUTES THE KING'S COMMAND AND GOES HOME IN DESPAIR (6¹¹⁻¹³).

11. [L + Now, when Haman perceived that he was not the one who was to be honoured, but Mordecai, his heart was completely crushed and his courage was changed into faintness.] [𝔏 + And Haman mourned at these words.] [𝔗² + And when the wicked Haman saw that his arguments availed nothing with the King, and that his words were not heeded, he went to the King's treasury with bowed head, without looking up, mourning, and with his head covered, with stopped ears, and closed eyes, and pouting mouth, and an agonized heart, and wounded feelings, and loosened girdle, and knees knocking against each other]

And Haman took the [𝔗¹ + purple] *garment* [𝔗² + of royalty that was brought King Xerxes on the first day that he was established in the kingdom; and he took thence all the rest of the royal apparel, as he had been commanded; and he went out in haste to the royal stable] *and* [𝔗² + took thence] *the horse* [𝔗² + that stood in the chief stall, from which golden stirrups hung down; and he laid hold of the horse's bridle, and all the royal apparel he carried upon his shoulders; and they put on the harness and adjusted the saddle.]

[Jos. + And he took the golden neck-chain] [L, Jos., *Meg.* + And he found Mordecai] [L + on the very day on which he had determined to impale him] [Jos. + clothed in sackcloth before the court,] [*Meg.* 16*a* + with the Rabbis seated before him, while he taught them *halachoth* as to how the handful of meal of the meal-offering of firstlings ought to be offered at Passover. When Mordecai saw that he came toward him leading a splendid horse, he was frightened and said to the Rabbis, This wretch comes, no doubt, to kill me. Avoid him, that you may not be harmed also. Thereupon Mordecai wrapped himself in his prayer-mantle and stood up to pray. And Haman entered, and sat down before him, and waited until Mordecai had finished praying. Then he said to him, What were you doing just now? Mordecai answered, We were learning that, so long as the Temple stood, every one who had vowed a meal-offering brought a handful of meal and obtained atonement thereby. Then said Haman, your handful of meal has outweighed my 10,000 talents of silver. Wretch, said Mordecai, When a slave acquires wealth, to whom do he and his wealth belong?] [L, Jos. + Then he said to Mordecai, Take off thy sackcloth,] [Jos., *Meg.* + and put on the royal apparel.] [𝔏 + Arise, servant of God, and be honoured.] [L + and Mordecai was dismayed as one about to die, and was pained to lay aside his sackcloth.] [Jos. + And not knowing the truth, but upposing that he was mocked, he said, O basest of all men, dost thou thus laugh at our misfortunes? But when he was convinced that the King bestowed this honour upon him as a reward for the deliverance which he had wrought for him by convicting the eunuchs who had plotted against him,] *Meg.* + Mordecai said, I cannot put on the royal garments until I have gone to the bath and have had my hair cut, for in this condition it is not proper for me to put on royal garments. Esther meanwhile had sent and had forbidden all baths and all barbers (to serve Mordecai). So Haman himself went into he bath-house and bathed him. Then he brought a pair of scissors from his home and cut his hair, groaning and sighing all the time. Why sighest thou? said Mordecai. Alas! said Haman, to think that the man who was honoured by the people more than all the nobles has now become a bath-attendant and barber! Wretch, answered Mordecai, Wast thou not a barber in the village of Karçum for 22 years?]

And he clothed Mordecai, [L + and it seemed to Mordecai that he saw a miracle, and his heart was toward the Lord, and he was speechless from astonishment.] [*Meg.* + Then Haman said to him, Mount the horse and ride! But Mordecai replied, I cannot, I am too weak from long fasting. So Haman crouched down, and Mordecai mounted on his back, giving him a kick as he went. Then said Haman, Is it not written, "Rejoice not when thine enemy falleth?" That, said Mordecai, holds good only of an Israelite. Of you it is written, "Thou shalt tread upon their high places."] [L + And Haman hastened] *and he made Mordecai*

ride [Vrss. + upon the horse, and led him about] *in the city-square.*
[L, Jos. + And Haman went before him] *and he proclaimed before him, This is what is done to the man* [L + who honours the King] *whom the King* [Jos. + loves and] *longs to honour.*

> [𝔗² + And there were sent him from the King's house 27,000 choice youths, with golden cups in their right hands and golden pitchers in their left hands, and they marched before the righteous Mordecai crying, This is what is done for the man whom the K ng, the creator of heaven and earth, longs to honour. And when the Israelites saw, they walked on the right and on the left crying, This is what is done for the man whom the King, the creator of heaven and earth, longs to honour. And when Esther looked and saw Mordecai, her cousin, clothed in the royal garment, with the royal crown upon his head, riding upon the King's horse, she gave thanks and praised the God of heaven for their deliverance, because Mordecai had put on sackcloth and had placed ashes upon his head in the sight of the oppressors. And when she saw Mordecai, her cousin, she answered and said unto him, In thee is fulfilled the word of Scripture by the holy prophets: "He raiseth up the poor out of the dust, and lifteth up the needy from the dunghill; that he may set him with princes, even with the princes of his people." Mordecai also gave thanks, saying: "Thou hast turned for me my mourning into dancing; thou hast loosed my sackcloth, and girded me with a royal garment. I will praise thee, O Lord God, my redeemer, because thou hast not rejoiced the heart of my enemies (similarly 𝔗¹ on 8¹⁵).] [*Meg.* 16a + And as he passed by Haman's house, Haman's daughter looked down from the roof, and supposed that her father was riding and that Mordecai was accompanying him on foot; so she fetched a slop-jar and poured it upon her father's head. But when she perceived that it was her father, she flung herself from the roof and killed herself.] [𝔏 + And Haman walked in his disgrace, but Mordecai was highly honoured; and God broke the heart of Haman.]

12. *And* [Jos. + when he had traversed the city,] *Mordecai returned unto the King's gate* [𝔗¹ + unto the sanhedrin that was there, and he put off the purple raiment, and put on sackcloth, and sat in ashes, confessing and praying until the evening.] After this extraordinary and unexpected honour Mordecai is brought back to his old haunt (2¹⁹) from which he set out (6¹⁰).—*And Haman hurried to his house, mourning* [𝔗¹ + for his daughter,] *and with his head covered* [𝔗¹ + like one mourning for his daughter and his disgrace (*cf. Meg.* 16a).] Haman feels the need of getting home at once to hide his shame and to pour out his sorrows to sympathetic ears. The *covered head* was a sign of mourning among the Hebrews (7⁸ 2 S. 15³⁰ Je. 14⁴); so also among the Persians, according to Curt. iv. 10, x. 5.

13. *And Haman recounted* [Jos. + with weeping] *to Zeresh his wife and to all his friends all that had happened to him.*] The *friends* (*cf.* 5¹⁰· ¹⁴) are in the next clause called *his wise men*, from which, says *Meg.* 16*a*, we may infer that even a heathen may be wise.—*And his wise men* [𝔍 + that he had in council] *and Zeresh his wife said to him,* [*Meg.* 16*a* + If Mordecai be descended from other tribes, thou canst overcome him; but] *if Mordecai be of the seed of the Judæans* [*Meg.* + Benjamin, Ephraim, or Manasseh] *before whom thou hast begun to fall* [𝔗¹ + as the kings fell before Abraham in the Plain of the Field, as Abimelech fell before Isaac, as the angel was vanquished by Jacob, and as by the hands of Moses and Aaron, Pharaoh and all his hosts sank in the Red Sea, and as all kings and princes who did them harm were delivered by God into their hand, so also] *thou wilt accomplish nothing* [𝔗¹ + harmful] *against him, but wilt fall completely before him,* [𝔊 + for the living God is with him.]

[𝔗¹ + For of Judah it is written, "Thy hand is upon the neck of thine enemies"; and of Ephraim, Benjamin, and Manasseh it is written, "Before Ephraim, Benjamin, and Manasseh stir up thy might."] [𝔗² + Thou hast heard long ago that there were three Judæans in the province of Babylon, Hananiah, Mishael, and Azariah, and because they did not obey the commands of Nebuchadnezzar, he cast them into a fiery furnace, yet they went forth from the midst of the flame unharmed; and a tongue of flame came out from the furnace and devoured those who had eaten their bread. If now Mordecai is one of the descendants of those men, his deeds will be like theirs.]

The *wise men* are counsellors, like those of the King (1¹³), not necessarily astrologers in either case, or identical with those who cast lots 3⁷ (Grot.). Here as in 2⁵ *Judæan*, Jew, has become a national name. It is hard to see how there could be any doubt at this late date whether or not Mordecai were a Jew (*cf.* 2⁵ 3⁴· ⁶). In 5¹³ Haman himself says that this is the case. Perhaps the author's idea is, that Mordecai's being a Jew made no impression upon the counsellors until Haman began to fall before him, and then they bethought themselves of the significance of this fact. It is also hard to see why Haman's Persian advisers should find anything alarming in his sustaining a temporary reverse before a Jew. The Jews were a despised, subject race, whose destruction had been decreed by the King, and there were no indications yet that he would change his mind. Lap. supposes that they had a touch of genuine inspiration like the Sibyl and Caiaphas (Jn. 11[49-52]); Mal., that they obtained the information from an evil spirit; Lap., Bert., that shrewd human calculation showed them that Mordecai's star was in the ascendant; Mar., Men., Jun., that they had learned from the Jews of God's wonderful deeds in the past; Grot., Wild., Sieg., Stre., that they knew the oracles condemning Amalek to fall before Israel (Ex. 17[16] Nu. 24[20] Dt. 25[17-19] 1 S. 15 2 S. 1[8 ff.]; see on 3[1]). This is probably the author's idea. He knows the curses of Amalek in the Jewish Scriptures, and assumes that they are equally well known to Haman, the descendant of Agag, and his friends. At first they have disregarded these predictions, but now they see that they have retained all their ancient vitality. That they should really have known Jewish literature so well is, of course, impossible. This advice of the wise men is of one piece with the additions of the Targums, which make them quote the OT. freely.

11. [הסוס] pr. 𝔖. ܣܘܣܐ.— [וילבש את מרדכי] καὶ ἐνεδύσατο τὰ ἱμάτια δόξης L.— [ויךכיבהו] ܘܐܣܩܗ 𝔖: + על סוס K 118, 202; R 486: + ἐπὶ τὸν ἵππον 𝔊𝔏: + ἐφίππον L.— [ברחוב העיר] καὶ ἐξήγαγεν Ἀμὰν τὸν ἵππον ἔξω + καὶ προσήγαγεν αὐτὸν ἔξω L: pr. καὶ διῆλθεν 𝔊𝔏.— [לפניו] λέγων 𝔊𝔏: om. 𝔍 L.— [לאיש] παντὶ ἀνθρώπῳ 𝔊𝔏: τῷ ἀνδρὶ τῷ τὸν βασιλέα τιμῶντι L, 93*b* ÷.

12. [וישב-המלך] aft. אבל L.— [אל שער המלך] εἰς τὸν οἶκον αὐτοῦ L: εἰς τὴν αὐλήν 𝔊 (+ τοῦ βασιλέως ℵ c. a mg, 93*b* under *, 𝔏).— [המלך] *palatii* 𝔍.— [נדחף] *Niph.* 'urge oneself,' *i.e.*, 'hasten'; *cf.* דחופים of the royal couriers 3[15] 8[14].— [וחפוי ראש] κατὰ κεφαλῆς 𝔊 (κατακεκαλυμμένος (τὴν) κεφαλήν ℵ c. a, 93*b* *): *et percusso corde* 𝔏: om. L.

13. [ויספר] *misit et narravit* 𝔏.— [המן] om. 𝔍𝔏: Haupt deletes.— [לזרש] *cf.* 5[10]: om. L.— [ולכל אהביו] om. 𝔖 L: om. כל 𝔍𝔊𝔏.— [כל[2]] om. 𝔊 (exc. 93*b*).— [קרהו] of misfortunes (*cf.* 4[7] Gn. 44[29]).— [לו] so N[2] C B[2] G: לי S Br. Ba. (p. 75), om. L: + Ἀμάν ℵ. When *Daghesh* is inserted, it is the so-called *Daghesh forte conjunctivum* (Kau. § 20 *c*).— [חכמיו] ܚܟܝܡܐ̈.

𝔖: οἱ φίλοι 𝔊 𝔏 (+ αὐτοῦ ℵ ᶜ·ᵃ, 93b under *).— [וזרש] om. וזרש 𝔍 L 𝔏 𝔊 (exc. ℵ ᶜ·ᵃ ᵐᵍ, 93b under *).—[אשתו] ἡ γυνή 𝔊 (+ αὐτοῦ ℵ ᶜ·ᵃ ᵐᵍ, 93b under *).—מרדכי - אם]om. L.—אשר - end of v.] ἀφ' ὅτε λαλεῖς περὶ αὐτοῦ κακά, προσπορεύεταί σοι τὰ κακά· ἡσύχαζε L.—[אשר] om. 𝔊 𝔏.—[לו כי] ܣܡܠܟ 𝔖: αὐτὸν ἀμύνασθαι 𝔊 𝔏.—[נפול הפול] om. 𝔏.—[נפול] נפל N¹ a few codd.: ܒܩܕܡ 𝔖.—[לפניו] om. 𝔊 L 𝔏 + ὅτι θεὸς ζῶν μετ' αὐτοῦ 𝔊 (93b ÷): + ὅτι ὁ θεὸς ἐν αὐτοῖς L: + *quia jam propheta est* 𝔏.

ESTHER DENOUNCES HAMAN TO THE KING (6¹⁴–7⁶).

14. *While they were still talking with him, the King's eunuchs appeared, and brought Haman with speed to the banquet that Esther had prepared.*] Lit. *hastened to bring Haman.* There is no suggestion here that Haman in his grief had forgotten his appointment with Esther, or, as *Meg.* 16a suggests, that he was afraid to go, so that eunuchs had to be sent to fetch him. It was the custom to send servants to escort guests (*cf.* 1¹⁰ 5¹⁰·¹² Lu. 14¹⁷), and the expression *hastened* means no more than *brought expeditiously.* With what different emotions Haman went from those that he had anticipated (5¹⁴)!

[Jos.²⁶¹ + And one of the eunuchs named Sabouchadas saw the gallows that was erected at Haman's house, which Haman had prepared for Mordecai, and he inquired of one of the domestics for whom they were preparing this. And when he learned that it was for the Queen's uncle, since Haman was about to beg the King that he might be punished, he for the present held his peace.]

1. *So the King and Haman came to banquet with Queen Esther.*] *To banquet* is lit. *to drink.* Here, as perhaps in 3¹⁵, the verb is used as a denominative from the noun *banquet,* lit. *drinking* (*cf.* Jb. 1⁴ 1 K. 20¹²).

2. *And on the second day also the King said to Esther during the wine-drinking*]. The *wine-drinking* was the later part of the meal after food had been served (see on 5⁶).—*Whatever thy request is, Queen Esther, it shall be granted thee; and whatever thy petition is, even as much as half of the kingdom, it shall be done.*] See 5³·⁶, where almost the same language is used. Esther has already put the King off twice when he has offered to grant her request (5⁴·⁸), but his good nature is unbounded.

[𝕿¹ + Except the rebuilding of the House of the Sanctuary which stands in half the border of my kingdom, I cannot grant thee, because so I have promised with an oath to Geshem, and Tobiah, and Sanballat; but wait until Darius thy son shall grow up and shall inherit the kingdom; then it shall be done.] [L + And Esther was in an agony of fear at the thought of telling him, because her enemy was before her.] [𝕿¹ + And Esther raised her eyes toward Heaven.] [L + And God gave her courage, when she called upon him.]

3. *And Queen Esther answered,* [Jos. ²⁶² + lamenting the danger of her people, and said:] [𝕷 + Neither silver nor gold do I seek.] *If I have obtained thy favour, O* [𝕿¹ + exalted] *King, and if it seems good to the King* [𝕿¹ + of the world]. See on 5⁸.—*Let* [𝕿¹ + the saving of] *my life* [𝕿¹ + from the hand of those that hate me] *be given me as my request, and* [𝕿¹ + the deliverance of] *my people* [𝕿¹ + from the hands of their enemies] *as my petition.*] Now at last the author allows Esther to speak the words for which she risked her life (4⁸). The only reason for the delay has been to give an opportunity for Mordecai's triumph over Haman (see on 5⁴·⁸). The ellipses in Esther's rapid utterance are accurately supplied by 𝕿¹.

4. *For I and my people* [𝕿¹ + of the house of Israel] *have been sold* [𝕿¹ + for naught] *unto destruction, slaughter, and annihilation;* [Jos. ²⁶² + and on this account I make my petition.] Lit. *to destroy, to slay, and to annihilate.* The same language is used in the King's edict (3¹³). The expression *sell into the hand* for *deliver up to enemies* is a favourite one with the editor of Judges (2¹⁴ 4⁹, etc.). Here the author is thinking of Haman's offer and the King's refusal (3⁹·¹¹).—*And if only we had been sold as slaves and as maids,* [𝕵 + groaning] *I should have kept silent,* [L + so as not to trouble my lord,] [Jos. ²⁶³ 𝕵 + for the evil would have been bearable,] *for the enemy is not sufficient for the injury of the King.*] This last clause is one of the most difficult in the book. No satisfactory rendering has yet been proposed. For suggestions in regard to its interpretation and emendation, see the following critical note.

5. *And King Xerxes said* [𝕿² + to an interpreter,] *and he said to Queen Esther*]. The verse has two beginnings, due doubtless to a combination of alternate readings. The Vrss. omit the second clause wholly or in part. 𝔗² and *Meg.* 16a help out the abnormal construction by inserting an interpreter. The fact that the King addresses himself to Esther gives Haman no opportunity to justify himself.—*Who is it, and where is he,* [𝔗¹ + the shameless, guilty, and rebellious man,] *whose heart has impelled him to do thus?*] [L + to degrade the emblem of my sovereignty so as to cause thee fear?] *Impelled* is lit. *filled, cf.* Acts 5³, "Why hath Satan filled thy heart to lie to the Holy Ghost?"

[L + And when the Queen saw that it seemed dreadful to the King, and that he hated the wrong-doer, she said, Be not angry, my lord! It is enough if I have gained thy pity. Enjoy the feast! To-morrow I will act in accordance with thy command. And the King adjured her to tell him who had dared to do thus, and with an oath he promised to do for her whatever she wished.]

6. *And Esther said, An enemy and foe, this wicked Haman,*

[𝔗¹ + who wishes to slay thee this evening in thy bedchamber, and who even to-day has asked to be clothed with a royal garment, and to ride upon thy horse, and to place the golden crown upon his head, and to rebel against thee, and to take away thy kingdom from thee. But the heavenly voice brought to pass in that hour that honour was rendered to the righteous Mordecai, my paternal uncle, the son of Jair, son of Shimei, son of Shemida‘, son of Ba‘ana, son of Elah, son of Micha, son of Mephibosheth, son of Jonathan, son of King Saul, son of Kish, son of Abiel, son of Zeror, son of Bekhorath, son of Aphiya, son of Sheḥarim, son of Uzziah, son of Sason, son of Michael, son of Eliel, son of ‘Ammihud, son of Shephatiah, son of Penuel, son of Pithaḥ, son of Melokh, son of Jerubba‘al, son of Jeruḥam, son of Hananiah, son of Zibdi, son of Elpa‘al, son of Shimri, son of Zebadiah, son of Remuth, son of Ḥashom, son of Shehorah, son of ‘Uzza, son of Guza, son of Gera, son of Benjamin, son of Jacob, son of Isaac, son of Abraham, whom the wicked Haman sought to hang (*cf.* 𝔗² on 1⁵);] [𝔗² + therefore is his name called Ha-man (this is the one), for this is the one who has wished to lay hands upon the Jewish people, who are called children of the Lord of all, and who has wished to slay them.] [*Meg.* 16a + All the time she pointed at Xerxes, but an angel came and turned her hand toward Haman.]

The two parts of Esther's answer correspond to the two parts of the King's question. The fatal word is now spoken which will decide whether Haman or Esther has the greater influence with the King. *The enemy* is a standing title of Haman (*cf.* 7⁴ and the synonymous word 3¹⁰ 8¹ 9¹⁰·²⁴). As a descendant of Agag (3¹), he was characterized by an inveterate hostility to the Jews.— *Haman meanwhile was in terror* [𝔍 + straightway] *before the King and the Queen*]. He might well be terrified, since he suddenly discovered that he had affronted both the King and the Queen; the King, by condemning his wife to death; the Queen, by attempting to destroy her and her people.

14. 'ועדם וגו'] a nominal clause at the beginning of a sentence (Kau. § 116 u); followed by pf.— [עמו ܥܡܗ 𝔖: om. 𝔍 𝔏 𝕷 𝔊 (exc. א c. a mg, 249, 93b under *).— [וסריסי] ܠܗ̈ܢ 𝔖: τις L.— [המלך] *reginæ* 𝔏: om. L 𝔊 (exc. א c. a mg, 93b under *, 71, 74, 76, 106, 120, 236, 249).— [הגיע] παρῆν L: 'arrived,' as 4³·¹⁴ 8¹⁷ 9¹·²⁶.— [ויבהלו] *Hiph.* 'hastened,' as *Qal* 2⁹ 8¹⁴.— [להביא] om. 𝔖 L 𝕷 𝔊 (exc. א c. a mg, 93b under *).— [המן] *eum* 𝔍 L.— [אשר אסתר] *καὶ οὕτως ἱλαρώθη* L.— [אסתר] *regina* 𝔍: + ἡ βασίλισσα 71, 74, 76, 120, 236.

1. [ויבא - לשתות] *καὶ πορευθεὶς ἀνέπεσε ἐν ὥρᾳ* L.— [לשתות] ܠܚܡܫܐ 𝔖: *ad cœnam* 𝕷.— [עם] ܘܚܡܪܐ 𝔖.— [אסתר] om. 𝔍 L 𝕷 𝔊 (exc. א c. a mg, 93b under *).— [המלכה] *eo* 𝕷: αὐτῶν L.

2. [ויאמר] pr. *factum est* 𝕷: [לאסתר] *ei* 𝔍: + *reginam* 𝕷: om. A.— [גם - במשתה] ὡς δὲ προήγεν ἡ πρόποσις L.— [גם ביום השני] Haupt deletes.— [גם] om. 𝕷 𝔊 (exc. א c. a, 93b under *).— [ביום] om. 44 𝕷.— [השני] ܣܒ 𝔖.— [במשתה] *postquam incaluerat* 𝔍: ? for ב 𝔖: *in bona propinatione* 𝕷.— [היין] om. L 𝕷 𝔊 (exc. א c. a, 93b under *): + τί ἐστιν καὶ 𝔊 (τί ἐστί σοι καὶ 71, 74, 76, 106, 120: τί ἔσται σοι καὶ 44: 93b om.).— [שאלתך] ὁ κίνδυνος L.— [אסתר - לך] om. 𝔖 L 𝕷.— [המלכה] om. 𝔍 44, 106.— [וינתן לך] om. 𝔊 (exc. א c. a mg, 93b under *).— [ומה] om. 𝔍.— [בקשתך] *relatio* 𝕷.— [המלכות] + *mei* 𝔍 𝔖 𝔊 L 𝕷.— [ותעש] + ܠܟܝ 𝔖: + σοι 𝔊: + *tibi* 𝕷: om. L.

3. [ותען] om. L 44, 106.— [אסתר] *illa* 𝔍: om. 𝔊 (exc. א c. a mg sup, 93b under *).— [ותאמר] om. [המלכה] om. 𝔍 L 𝕷 𝔊 (exc. א c. a mg sup, 93b under *).— om. 𝔍: + τῷ βασιλεῖ 71, 74, 76, 120.— [מצאתי הן בעיניך] δοκεῖ L: εὗρον χάριν ἐνώπιον 𝔊.— [המלך] pr. τοῦ κυρίου μου 44, 74, 76, 120, 236.— [ואם - טוב] *καὶ ἀγαθὴ ἡ κρίσις ἐν καρδίᾳ αὐτοῦ* L: *et si videtur animæ tuæ* 𝕷: om. 𝔊 (exc. א c. a mg, 93b under *).— [לי] om. 𝔖 L 𝕷 𝔊 (exc. א c. a, 93b under *).— [נפשי - end of v.] *desiderium meum, neque aurum, neque argentum ego peto* 𝕷.— [נפשי] om. ܝ 𝔊 (exc. א c. a mg, 93b under *): ὁ λαός μου L.— [בשאלתי] ܒ *essentiæ* (*cf.* 4⁷), according to Wild., Sieg., *i.e.*, 'life' is identical with 'request.' According to Bert., Keil, Rys., it is ܒ of the price; according to Haupt, ܒ of the instrument.— [ועמי] *καὶ ὁ λόγος μου* 𝔊 (a few codd. λαός): *καὶ τὸ ἔθνος* L.— [בבקשתי] τῆς ψυχῆς μου L.

4. [להשמיד] ܠܚܒܠܐ 𝔖: εἰς ἀπωλείαν 𝔊 𝕷: om. L.— [להרוג] ܀ 𝔖: *καὶ διαρπαγὴν* 𝔊 𝕷: om L A 44, 71, 106.— [ולאבד] *καὶ δουλείαν* 𝔊 𝕷: εἰς

δούλωσιν L.— ואלו] *utinam* 𝕁: this word, compounded of אִין (אִם) לִי, is used only here and Ec. 6⁶. It is common in Aram. and late Heb. introducing a supposition that is regarded as desirable (Kau. § 159 b). Followed here by the perf. because the condition is contrary to fact (Kau. § 106 p).— [ואלו] + ܘܒܢܝܢ 𝕊: ἡμεῖς καὶ τὰ τέκνα ἡμῶν 𝕲: καὶ τὰ νήπια αὐτῶν L: *et filii nostri* 𝕃.— [לעברים] om. 𝕃. 𝕊: εἰς διαρπαγήν L: *in captivitatem* 𝕃.— [ולשפחות] om. ל 𝕊: om. 𝕃 L.— [נמכרנו] om. L 𝕁 𝕲 (exc. א c. a mg, 93b under *).— [הרשתי] καὶ παρήκουσα 𝕲: καὶ παρθένους 52: καὶ παρήκας 64, Ald.: καὶ παροικοῦσα 106: καὶ παρηκούσας 108a, 243, 248, 249, C: καὶ οὐκ ἤθελον ἀπαγγεῖλαι L: om. 𝕃.— [כי – המלך] *nunc autem hostis noster est cujus crudelitas redundat in regem* 𝕁: οὐ γὰρ ἄξιος ὁ διάβολος τῆς αὐλῆς τοῦ βασιλέως 𝕲: *et non est dignum regiæ regis* 𝕃: ἐγένετο γὰρ μεταπεσεῖν τὸν ἄνθρωπον τὸν κακοποιήσαντα ἡμᾶς L: ܘܠܐ ܫܟܚ ܗܠܝܢ ܠܡܐܡܪ ܠܡܠܟܐ 𝕊: παρεκάλει τὲ τούτων ἀπαλλαγῆναι Jos.: ארום לית מעיקא טימין 𝕋². ארום לית בעיל דבבא שתיק שוי בטננא דמלכא: 𝕋u: ורוחא באנזיקא דמלכא. These all presuppose the text of 𝔐. The additions in L 𝕁 Jos. look like conflate readings containing a translation of 𝔐 in which צר is rendered 'calamity': ἵνα μὴ λυπήσω τὸν κύριόν μου L: *esset tolerabile malum* 𝕁: μέτριον γὰρ τοῦτο τὸ κακόν Jos. In this passage most comm. assume that, הַצָּר means *the enemy*, as in 7⁶ and everywhere else in Est. Their translations then vary according to the meaning that they put upon שֹׁוֶה 'equal' and נֵזֶק 'injury.' *Meg.* 16a renders, *for the enemy is not satisfied with the loss of the King; i.e.,* he was jealous of Vashti and killed her, now he is jealous of me and wishes to kill me. Similarly Mar., not content with plundering the King's treasury, he must needs kill the King's subjects; Osi., *for the enemy would not then cause loss to the King, i.e.,* if we were made slaves, I should still be kept alive; Jun. & Trem., *since the enemy proposes nothing for (averting) the loss of the king;* Sol. b. Melekh, Drus., Grot., Pisc., Vat., Cler., Ramb., Ges., Will., AV., RV., most modern Vrss., *although the enemy cannot compensate for the loss of the King, i.e.,* cannot make up the tribute that will cease when the Jews are killed; Bert., Keil, Haupt, *for the enemy is not worth troubling the King about;* Schu., *for (the punishing of) the enemy is less important than (the averting of) the injury to the King.* All of these translations are unsatisfactory, since they give no reason for Esther's keeping silence, as the context requires. Most of them demand the supplying before them of the words *but I cannot keep silence,* which are not in the text. All assume artificial meanings either for כִּי, for שֹׁוֶה, or for נֵזֶק. IE., Dieu., Pisc., Drus., Buhl., *al.* suggest reading צַר 'adversity,' 'calamity,' instead of צַר 'enemy,' and translate *for the calamity is not so great as the injury of the King,* or, *for the calamity would not be sufficiently great to trouble the King about it;* but this is just as unsatisfactory as the other renderings. צַר never has the meaning of 'calamity' in Est., and it is very doubtful whether נֵזֶק *injury,* can be weakened into meaning *an-*

noyance to the King through mentioning the business, as several modern comm. assume (but see Haupt, *a. l.*). The text is probably corrupt. Oet., Wild., read כִּי אֵין הַצָּלָה שׁוֶה בְּנֶזֶק הַמֶּלֶךְ, 'for the deliverance is not worth the injury of the King,' but this does not relieve the difficulty. There is an ancient corruption of the text at this point for which no satisfactory emendation has yet been proposed.— בְּנֵזֶק] so B²: בְּנֶזֶק Ba. G.

5. ויאמר]— καὶ ἐθυμώθη L.—[אחשורוש om. L 𝕃 𝕲 (exc. א c. a mg, 93*b* under *): Haupt deletes.—[ויאמר ²] om. 𝕃 𝕲 (exc. א c. a mg, 93*b* under *): Haupt deletes.—[לאסתר המלכה] om. 𝕁 L 𝕲 (exc. א c. a mg, 93*b* under *).— אי זה הוא] *et cujus potentiæ* 𝕁: om. L 𝕃 𝕲 (exc. א c. a mg, 93*b* under *). — מְלָאוֹ] *Qal* perf. of the transitive form of the vb. מָלָא (Kau. § 74 *g*) with suf. Jahn, Haupt, read מְלָא.

6. ותאמר]— καὶ θαρσήσασα εἶπεν L.—[איש צר] ὁ ψευδὴς οὑτοσί L.—[הַצַּר here pointed with *Pathach;* Ju. 7⁴ הַצֵּר (see Baer, *a. l.*). Pred. put first for emphasis.—[ואויב] + *noster* 𝕁: *regis* 𝕃: ὁ φίλος σου L: om. 𝕲 (exc. א c. a mg, 93*b* *).—[והמן] *quod ille audiens* 𝕁: *Aman autem audiens verba* 𝕃.—והמן – end of v.] om. L.—[והמן] *ille* 𝕁.—[נִבְעָת] so N¹ S N² Br. C B¹ B² G: נִבְעָת̈ Ba.—[נבעת] *Niph.* only in late books, *e.g.*, 1 Ch. 21³⁰ Dn. 8¹⁷. This clause and those that follow as far as ויאמר (8*b*) are circumstantial clauses with participles.—[מלפני – והמלכה] *vultum regis ac reginæ ferre non sustinens* 𝕁: *et cecidit vultus suus* 𝕃.

THE KING SENTENCES HAMAN TO DEATH (7⁷⁻¹⁰).

7. [𝕿¹ + And the King lifted his eyes and looked, and saw ten angels like unto the sons of Haman cutting down the trees in the inner garden.] *Now the King was rising in his wrath from the wine-drinking,* [𝕃 + flinging away his napkin,] [Vrss. + to go] *into the palace-garden* [𝕿¹ + to see what this thing was (similarly *Meg.* 16*a*).] *Rising into* is a pregnant construction for rising to go into. On *wine-drinking*, see 5⁶ 7². On *palace* and *garden*, see 1⁵. As to the reason for the King's going into the garden opinions differ. 𝕿² supposes that it was to work off his anger by cutting down trees; Men., that it was to avoid sight of the hated Haman; Lyra, Haupt, to take time to think about his decision; Drus., because he was still friendly to Haman and hesitated to condemn him; Bon., Bert., Oet., Sieg., because he was uncomfortably heated with wine and anger, and wished to cool off in the outer air; Schu., Stre., because of the natural restlessness of anger. The true reason is probably to give the author a chance to insert the episode in v. ⁸.—*But Haman was staying to beg Queen Esther* [𝔊¹ + for mercy] *upon his life,* [Jos. ²⁶⁵ + and to entreat her to pardon his offences,] *for he saw that evil was determined against him by the King*.] On *staying, cf.* 5¹. The ellipsis after *beg* is rightly supplied by 𝔊¹ (*cf.* 4⁸). *Determined*, lit. *completed*, is used of something that is fully settled in a person's mind (*cf.* 1 S. 20⁷· ⁹ 25¹⁷ Ez. 5¹³). It is clear to Haman, at least, that the King's going into the garden is not to devise means of saving him, but to think out some terrible punishment to inflict upon him.

8. *And as the King was returning* [𝔊¹ + in his wrath] *from the palace-garden to the banquet-hall,* [*Meg.* 16*a*, 𝔊¹ + behold the angel Gabriel gave the wicked Haman a push in sight of the King, and] *Haman* [L + was dismayed and] *was lying prostrate* [L + at the feet of Queen Esther] *upon the couch on which Esther* [L 𝔖 + was reclining.] The King's wrath is not abated by his visit to the garden, but impels him to return in a few minutes to the banquet-hall that he has just left. Meanwhile Haman, in an agony of fear, has fallen at the feet of Esther as she reclines upon her couch, to beg her to save him. Falling down and laying hold of the feet was a common attitude of suppliants (*cf.* 8³ 1 S. 25²⁴ 2 K. 4²⁷, also frequently in the Assyrian inscriptions). It was impossible under the circumstances for the King to misunderstand the gesture; but he had come back with the determination to kill Haman, and was ready to put the worst construction on anything that he might do. This interpretation seems more natural than that the author means to represent the King as hitherto in doubt, but now decided by Haman's supposed assault upon the Queen. On *couch*, see 1⁶. —*And,* [𝔏 Jos. + seeing him upon Esther's couch,] *the King* [𝔏 𝔊¹ + was enraged and] *said,* [*Meg.* 16*a* + Woe within and woe without!] [Jos. + O wickedest of all men!] [L 𝔏 + Is not his crime against the kingdom enough?] *Is he also (going) to violate the Queen while I am present in the house?* [𝔊¹ + Now, all peoples, nations, and tongues, judge what ought to be done with him?] *Also* is used with reference to Haman's first crime against Esther. Not satisfied with attacking her life, he must *also* attack her honour. Esther has now a chance to intercede for Haman, but she does not take it. All his entreaties are in vain, and she looks on in silence while he is condemned to death. The older commentators labour hard to show that Haman deserved no mercy, and that Esther would have done wrong to intercede for him; but it must be admitted that her character would have been more attractive if she had shown pity toward a fallen foe. The author might have represented her as interceding for Haman, even if the King did not grant her request; but such an idea is far from his mind. Here, as everywhere, he gloats over the destruction of the heathen.— *Before the word left the King's mouth they had covered Haman's face.*] The watchful eunuchs need nothing more than the King's last remark to see that Haman is condemned to death, and they *cover his face* preparatory to leading him out to execution. Curtius (vi. 8²²) mentions this as a Greek custom; and Livy (i. 26²⁵) as a Roman custom. It is not attested among the Persians, but is not improbable. *Cf.* 6¹², where Haman covers his head as a sign of grief (see critical note).

9. *Then said Ḥarbônā, one of the eunuchs* [𝔍 + who stood] *before the King*]. This is the same person doubtless as Ḥarbônā of 1¹⁰, although the spelling is slightly different (see p. 67). Those who have hitherto flattered Haman are now ready to give him a shove when they see that he is falling.—*There is the gallows too that Haman erected for* [Vrss. + hanging] *Mordecai who spoke a good word on behalf of the King* [𝔘¹ + by whose means also he was saved from being killed. That gallows is] *standing in the house of Haman.* [𝔊 codd., Jos.²⁶⁶ + This he knew, because he had seen the gallows in the house of Haman when he was sent to summon him to the royal banquet, and inquiring about it from one of the servants, he learned for what it was intended (*cf.* 6¹⁴).] *Too* adds another reason to those already given by the King why Haman should be executed, and incidentally suggests a method of carrying out the sentence. On Mordecai's service, see 2²² 6²; on the erection of the gallows, 5¹⁴.—[L 𝔘¹ + Now, if it seems good to the King, let the gallows be brought from his house, and let him be lifted up and fastened upon it] *fifty cubits high.* [*Meg.* 16a + The wicked Ḥarbônā had been involved in Haman's plans; but when he saw that their scheme could not be carried out, he took to flight (similarly 𝔘²).] [Jos.²⁶⁷ + When the King heard this, he determined that Haman should be put to death in no other way than that which he had devised for Mordecai.] *And the King said* [𝕋² + to Mordecai] [𝕋¹ + go] *hang him upon it,* [𝕃 + and his wife and his ten sons.] The King is easily influenced by the suggestions of his courtiers (*cf.* 1²¹ 2⁴ 3¹¹ 5⁵ 6¹⁰ 7⁵). The author intends to represent him as a weak character moved by the whim of the moment. The poetic justice of hanging Haman on the gallows that he had reared for Mordecai naturally catches his fancy.

[𝕋² + So the word of Holy Scripture was fulfilled for Mordecai, "When the Lord is pleased with a man's ways, even his enemies shall depend upon him." And the King answered and said to Mordecai, O Mordecai, the Jew, who hast saved the King from being killed, rise, go and take Haman, the wicked enemy, the oppressor of the Jews, and hang him on the gallows which he prepared for himself. Inflict a terrible penalty upon him, and do to him whatever seems good to thee. Then Mordecai went out from before the King and took Haman from the gate of the King's house. And Mordecai spoke to Haman, saying, Come with me, Haman, thou foe and wicked enemy and oppressor of the Jews, that we may hang thee upon the gallows which thou hast erected for thyself. Then the wicked Haman answered the righteous Mordecai, Before they bring me to the gallows, I beg thee, righteous Mordecai, that thou wilt not hang me as they hang common criminals. I have despised great men, and governors of provinces have waited upon me. I have made kings to tremble at the word of my mouth, and with the utterance of my lips I have frightened provinces. I am Haman; my name was called Viceroy of the King, Father of the King. I beg thee, righteous Mordecai, not to do to me as I thought to do to thee. Spare my honour, and do not kill me or hew me in pieces like Agag my father. Thou art good, Mordecai; deal with me according to thy goodness, and do not take my life; do not kill me like a branch so that my life shall be destroyed. Do not remember against me the hatred of Agag, nor the jealousy of Amalek. Do not regard me as an enemy in thy heart and do not cherish a grudge against me, as Esau my father cherished. Great wonders have been wrought for thee as they were wrought for thy fathers when they crossed the sea. My eyes are too dim to see thee, and my mouth I am not able to open before thee, because I have taken the advice of my friends and of Zeresh my wife against thee. I beg thee to spare my life, my lord Mordecai, the righteous, and do not blot out my name suddenly like that of Amalek my ancestor, and do not hang my gray head upon the gallows. But if thou art determined to kill me, cut off my head with the King's sword, with which they kill all the nobles of the provinces. Then Haman began to cry and to weep, but Mordecai did not give heed to him. And when Haman saw that no attention was paid to his words, he set up a wail and a weeping in the midst of the garden of the palace (followed by an address of Haman to the trees who refuse in turn to furnish a gallows for him until the cedar is reached).]

10. *So they hanged Haman upon the gallows which he had erected for Mordecai*, [249 + who spoke on behalf of the King,] [𝕷 + and his wife and his ten sons.] *And the wrath of the King subsided*], *cf.* 2¹.

[Jos. ²⁰⁸ + Which event compels me to wonder at the divine providence, and to learn his wisdom and justice, not merely in punishing the wickedness of Haman, but in bringing it about that he should suffer the same penalty that he had devised for another; so teaching, that whatever evil one plans for another, he is unconsciously preparing for himself first of all. Haman, accordingly, who had not used discreetly the honour that he had received from the King, was destroyed in this manner.]

7. [בחמתו] ἔκθυμος δὲ γενόμενος L: om. 𝕷 𝕲 (exc. א ᶜ·ᵃ ᵐᵍ, 93*b* under *) —[ממשתה היין] *de loco suo* 𝕷: *de loco convivii* 𝕵: καὶ πλησθεὶς ὀργῆς L: + *et intravit* 𝕵: + ܐܠܚܡܬܐ 𝕾: + καὶ ἦν περιπατῶν L: + *et exiit* 𝕷.— [גנת הביתן] *hortum arboribus consitum* 𝕵: τὸν κῆπον 𝕲 (+ τὸν σύμφυτον א ᶜ·ᵃ ᵐᵍ, 93*b* under *): *hortum* 𝕷: om. L.—[והמן]—end of v.] om. L.— [עמד] om. 𝕷 𝕲 (exc. א ᶜ·ᵃ, 93*b* under *, 249): παρεκάλει 52, 64, 243, 248, C, Ald.—[לבקש] παρῃτεῖτο 𝕲: καὶ ᾐτεῖτο 52, 64, 243, 248, C, Ald.: παρεκάλει 55, 71, 74, 76, 106, 120, 236.—[על נפשו] om. 𝕷 𝕲 (exc. א ᶜ·ᵃ, 93*b* under *, 249).—[מאסתר] om. 𝕷 𝕲 (exc. א ᶜ·ᵃ ᵐᵍ, 93*b* under *).—[כי כלתה] om. 𝕲 𝕷. —[אליו] with Haupt read עליו.—[אליו הרעה] ἑαυτὸν ἐν κακοῖς ὄντα 𝕲 𝕷.— [מאת המלך] om. 𝕷 𝕲 (exc. א ᶜ·ᵃ, 93*b* under *).

8. [והמלך – יין] tr. aft. עליה L.—[והמן] *qui cum* 𝕵.—[מגנת] om. L.— [הביתן] *nemoribus consito* + *et intrasset* 𝕵: om. L 𝕷 𝕲 (exc. א ᶜ·ᵃ ᵐᵍ, 93*b* under *).—[אל – היין] *ad locum suum* 𝕷: om. 𝕲 (exc. א ᶜ·ᵃ ᵐᵍ, 93*b* under *).—[והמן] *reperit Aman* 𝕵.—[נפל] + ἐπὶ τοὺς πόδας Ἐσθὴρ τῆς βασιλίσσης L. — [נפל] in the sense of 'lying prostrate' as Jos. 7¹⁰ 1 S. 5³⁻⁴ Am. 9¹¹ (see BDB. p. 657, § 6; Kau. § 116 *d*).—[עליה] [אשר] ἀξιῶν τὴν βασίλισσαν 𝕲: *reginæ et deprecabatur eam tenens* 𝕷: ἔτι ἀνακειμένης L.—[אסתר] + ܠܐܣܬܪ 𝕾.—[לכבוש] with ellipsis of היה, as 𝕌¹, 'he has not come except to violate' (Kau. § 114 *i*). According to Haupt, it is impf. with prefixed emphatic ל (*cf. AJSL.* xxii. p. 201). כבש means ordinarily 'subdue' (Ne. 5⁵). Here the context demands the special sense of 'violate.'—[עמי] μου L 𝕷 𝕲 (μετ' ἐμοῦ א ᶜ·ᵃ ᵐᵍ).—[בבית] ἐνώπιόν μου L: om. 𝕷.—[הדבר – חפו] ἀπαχθήτω Ἀμὰν καὶ μὴ ζήτω· καὶ οὕτως ἀπήγετο L: om. 𝕷: Ἀμὰν δὲ ἀκούσας διετράπη τῷ προσώπῳ 𝕲 (pr. ὁ λόγος ἐξῆλθεν ἐκ τοῦ στόματος τοῦ βασιλέως א ᶜ·ᵃ ᵐᵍ,

93*b* under *). חפו] Condamin (*Rev. Bibl.* vii. pp. 258–261) and Perles (*Analekten*, p. 32) propose on the basis of 𝔊 to read חָפְרוּ 'his face grew red' (*cf.* Ps. 34⁶ Jb. 6²⁰, 𝔊 διετράπη τῷ προσώπῳ). Haupt adopts this emendation. It is not necessary with Sieg. to regard חפו (pf. with ו) as an Aramaizing construction instead of impf. with ו consec. The clause is circumstantial and expresses the idea that the covering had taken place before the word was fairly out of the King's mouth.

9. [הסריסים + *qui stabant* 𝕴: + ܘ̈ܐܡܢ] ܘܩ̈ܡܝܢ 𝔖: τῶν παίδων αὐτοῦ L: — [לפני המלך πρὸς τὸν βασιλέα 𝔊: τοῦ βασιλέως A: *regis* 𝔏: om. L.— [גם καὶ 𝔊: *Domine rex* 𝔏: om. 𝕴 L.— [אשר–המלך tr. aft. אמה L.— [אשר om. 𝔖 𝔊.— [המן om. 𝕴: + ܨܠܝܒܐ 𝔖: + ἵνα κρεμάσῃ L: + *ut illum suspenderet* 𝔏.— [למרדכי τὸν Μαρδοχαῖον L: + ܚܟ̈ܝܡܐ 𝔖.— [אשר–המן om. 𝔏.— [אשר ܓ̇ܒܪ 𝔖.— [דבר טוב על *cf.* 1 S. 25³⁰ Je. 32⁴². The phrase means 'to speak well of one.' This Haupt finds inappropriate as a description of Mordecai's service, and emends to read גָּמַל דָּבָר טוֹב עַל 'rendered a good deed on behalf of.' The change is unsupported by the Vrss.— [טוב om. 𝕴 𝔊 (exc. א ᶜ·ᵃ ᵐᵍ, 93*b* under *).— [עמד pr. καὶ 𝔊 𝔖: om. L 44, 106.— [בבית המן ἐν τῇ αὐλῇ αὐτοῦ L: om. 44, 106.— [גבה גבוה Br.: ξύλον 𝔊 (pr. ὑψηλόν א ᶜ·ᵃ, 93*b*) om. A L: *erectum* 𝔏.— [אמה *pedum* 𝔏: + κέλευσον οὖν, κύριε, ἐπ' αὐτῷ αὐτὸν κρεμασθῆναι L.

10. om. L.— [ויתלו–המן καὶ ἐκρεμάσθη Ἀμὰν 𝔊: *et suspensi sunt sicut præceperat rex* 𝔏.— [למרדכי + τῷ λαλήσαντι περὶ τοῦ βασιλέως 249.— [שָׁכָכָה pausal form for שָׁכְכָה (Stade § 401 *b*).

MORDECAI IS INSTALLED IN THE PLACE OF HAMAN (8¹⁻²).

1. *On that day King Xerxes gave Queen Esther the property of Haman, the enemy of the Jews* [𝔗¹ + *and the men of his house, and all his treasures, and all his riches.*] The property of criminals was confiscated by the state, according to Her. iii. 129; Jos. *Ant.* xi. 17. Haman's property the King bestows upon Esther in compensation for the injury done her. *Property*, lit. *house*, is used in the sense of all a man's belongings, as Gn. 39⁴ 44¹·⁴ 1 K. 13⁸ Jb. 8¹⁵; so rightly the addition of 𝔗¹. On *enemy*, see 3¹⁰.—*And Mordecai came before tne King*], *i.e.*, he was raised to the rank of the high officials who saw the King's face (1¹⁰·¹⁴ 7⁹).—*For Esther had disclosed what his relationship to her was.*] Now for the first time the King discovers that Mordecai is a connection of Esther; but *cf.* 2⁷·¹¹·²² 4⁴⁻¹⁶. How the King could have remained in ignorance of this fact until this late date is as extraordinary as Haman's ignorance up to the moment when the blow falls. To his relationship to Esther Mordecai owes his present promotion. His service to the King has already been rewarded.

2. *And the King drew off his signet* [𝔘¹ + ring] *which he had taken away from Haman* [L + and with which his life was sealed, and the King said to Esther: Did he plan also to hang Mordecai who saved me from the hand of the eunuchs? He did not know that Esther was his relative on the father's side.] *And he gave it to Mordecai.*] On the *signet-ring*, see 3¹⁰. The removal of the ring must have preceded the leading of Haman out to execution; but since it was not mentioned in 7⁹, it is inserted here as an afterthought. The bestowal of this ring made Mordecai grand vizier and clothed him with all the powers that Haman had hitherto possessed (3¹⁰⁻¹⁵).—*And Esther appointed Mordecai* [𝔘¹ + master and steward] *over Haman's property.*] According to 3⁹, ¹¹ 5¹¹ 9¹⁰ the estate must have been very great, so that the administration of it and disposal of its revenues gave Mordecai wealth suitable to his new dignity. How much he possessed before, we are not told, only that he had leisure to sit most of the time in the King's gate. [L + And he said to him, What dost thou wish? and I will do it for thee.]

1. [ביום - היהודיים] om. L.—[אחשורוש] om. 44, 71, 106: Haupt deletes.—[המלכה] om. 𝔊 (exc. 93b under *).—[המלך ²- צרר] om. 𝔏.—[היהודיים - היהודיים] Q: om. 𝔊 (exc. א ᶜ·ᵃ ᵐᵍ, 93b under *).—[ומרדכי - המלך] καὶ ἐκάλεσεν ὁ βασιλεὺς τὸν Μαρδοχαῖον (tr. aft. 8² למרדכי) L: καὶ Μαρδοχαῖος προσεκλήθη ὑπὸ τοῦ βασιλέως 𝔊.—[כי - לה] om. L.—[הגידה אסתר] *cognoverat rex* 𝔏: + τῷ βασιλεῖ 44, 71, 74, 76, 106, 236.—[מה הוא לה] ὅτι ἐνοικείωται αὐτῇ 𝔊 (+ Μαρδοχαῖος 44, 71, 74, 76, 106, 120, 236): *quod Mardochæus erat de genere reginæ* 𝔏: *quod esset patruus suus* 𝔍.

2. [טבעתו] + [מעל ידו] K 18, 95; R 42, 405: + ἀπὸ τῆς χειρὸς αὐτοῦ L.—[אשר - מהמן] om. L.—[העביר] + *rex* 𝔏.—[העביר] 'to transfer from one person to another' (*cf.* Nu. 27⁷), here from Haman to the King.—[ויתנה למרדכי] om. L.—[ותשם - מרדכי] καὶ ἐχαρίσατο αὐτῷ L.—[המן] *suam* 𝔍.

ESTHER OBTAINS PERMISSION TO COUNTERACT HAMAN'S EDICT AGAINST THE JEWS (8³⁻⁸).

3. *And Esther spoke again before the King*]. The overthrow of Haman and the elevation of Mordecai do not satisfy Esther so long as Haman's edict of destruction remains unrevoked. Although Mordecai held the signet-ring, he did not venture to use it to save the Jews until express permission had been obtained. From v. 4 it appears that Esther once more risked her life in going to the King unsummoned (*cf.* 5¹). It is hard to see why this was necessary, now that Mordecai was grand vizier and could bring all matters before the King. It is also hard to see why Esther should run this risk when the day for slaughtering the Jews was set nearly a year later (see on 4¹¹). The author wishes to magnify Esther's patriotism by representing her as willing to risk her life twice for her nation.—*And she fell at his feet, and wept, and besought him*]. Esther's supplication is much more passionate in this case than in 7³⁻⁴ because her petition concerns not herself but her people (*cf.* 7⁸).—*To counteract the evil of Haman the Agagite and his* [𝔍 + *wicked*] *plan which he had devised against the Jews.*] Counteract is lit. *cause to pass over.* On *Agagite*, see 3¹; on the *plan*, see 3¹²⁻¹⁴.

4. *And the King extended to Esther the golden sceptre* [𝔍 + *in his hand as a sign of clemency,*] *and Esther arose and stood before the King.*] See on 5².

5. *And she said, If it seems good to the King, and if I have won his favour, and the thing is proper in the King's opinion, and I am pleasing unto him*]. The first two formulas of introduction have been used frequently before (*cf.* 1¹⁹ 5⁴· ⁸ 7³), the last two are new.—[𝔘¹ + *Let him make a decree and*] *let it be written to revoke the dispatches, the device of Haman son of Hammᵉdāthā, the Agagite, which he wrote to cause the destruction of the Jews that are in all the King's provinces.*] Revoke is lit. *cause to return* (*cf.* 8⁸). On *dispatches, cf.* 1²² 3¹³ 8¹⁰ 9²⁰· ²⁵· ³⁰. On the contents of these dispatches, *cf.* 3¹²⁻¹⁴. The added words, *the device of Haman*, bring out the thought that the former edict had not been issued for the good of the state, but to gratify Haman's private vengeance.

6. *For how can I gaze upon the calamity that has befallen my people, and how can I gaze upon the destruction of my kindred?*], *i.e.*, I cannot be a silent spectator while this tragedy is being enacted. Here Esther reiterates the petition that she began to present in 7³· ⁴, from which the King's attention was diverted by his wrath against Haman (*cf.* 7⁸). *Kindred* is used as in 2¹⁰· ²⁰.

On the similarity of this v. to Gn. 44³⁴, see Rosenthal, *ZATW*. xv. p. 281 (see on 6⁹).

7. [Jos. ²⁷¹ + And the King promised her that he would not do anything that would be displeasing to her, or that would be contrary to her desire.] *And King Xerxes said to Queen Esther and to Mordecai the Jew.*

> [𝔘² + Behold, thou didst wrong at the beginning, when I asked thee saying, From what race art thou sprung? that I might make thy family kings and rulers; and when I asked, From what stock art thou? that I might make thy family generals and polemarchs; that thou didst say, I know not, for my father and mother died leaving me a little girl.]

Esther alone comes before the King and she alone is addressed by him, so that the words *and Mordecai the Jew* look like an interpolation. They are omitted by 𝔊 L 𝕷 𝔖 Jos., but *cf.* v. ⁸.— *Behold, the house of Haman I have given to Esther, and him they have hanged upon the gallows* [𝕷 + with all his house] *because he laid hands upon the Jews*], *cf.* 7¹⁰–8¹. The King reminds Esther of the two favours already granted, not to suggest that he has done as much as can reasonably be expected, but to show that he is kindly disposed toward the Jews, and is ready to do all that the law will allow to avert the consequences of Haman's edicts.

> [𝔊 + What dost thou still desire?] [L + And Esther said to the King, Grant me to punish mine enemies with death. And Queen Esther begged the King for the sons of Haman that they also might die with their father. And the King said, Let it be so. And she smote a multitude of her enemies. In Susa also the King granted the Queen to put men to death; and he said, Behold, I give thee the right to hang them. And so it was done.]

8. *Now* [𝔘¹ + make haste,] *write ye yourselves on behalf of the Jews, as seems good to you, in the King's name, and seal it with the King's signet,*] [Jos. ²⁷¹ + to send into all the kingdom,] *for the document that is written in the King's name and that is sealed with the King's signet cannot be revoked* [Jos. ²⁷¹ + by those who have read it.] The addition of Jos. suggests that the clause beginning with *for* gives only a reason for the sealing that has just been mentioned (so Schu.); but the word *revoked* suggests rather that

ESTHER OBTAINS A NEW EDICT

it is a reason for the whole activity of Esther and Mordecai commanded by the King. Esther had asked (v. ⁵) that the edict of Haman might be revoked; the King now says, It is impossible to revoke a law that has been made (*cf.* 1¹⁹), but you may devise measures to counteract its operation. This v. is a counterpart to the permission given to Haman in 3¹¹.

3. om. L 106.— אסתר] om. 𝕃 𝕲 (exc. א ᶜ·ᵃ, 93*b* under *, 71, 74, 76, 120, 236).— ויתרבר] finite vb. instead of inf. after ויתוסף.— המלך] *eum* 𝕁.— ויתבך] 𝕊: καὶ ἤξίου 𝕲.— ויתבך-מחשבתו] om. 𝕃.— ויתחנן] om. 𝕲 (exc. א ᶜ·ᵃ ᵐᵍ, 93*b* under *).— האגגי] om. 𝕲 (exc. 93*b* under *).— ואת-היהודים] Haupt deletes as a tertiary gloss derived from 9²⁶.— מחשבתו] om. 𝕲 (exc. 93*b* under *).— אשר חשב על] *de quo impetraverat Aman adversus genus* 𝕃: + συμπᾶσι 93*b* ÷.

4. om. L.— המלך¹] *ille ex more* 𝕁.— לאסתר] om. 𝕁 44.— שַׁרְבֵט [שַׁרְבִיט Ba.: שרביט Var. Or. (Ginsburg) N¹ S.— הזהב] + ἣ ἦν ἐν χειρὶ αὐτοῦ 93*b* under ÷.— ותקם] 𝕊 ܣܥܒ̈ܐ ܠܡܐ.— אסתר] *illa* 𝕁: om. 106.— המלך²] *eum* 𝕁.

5. ותאמר] καὶ εἶπε(ν) 𝕲 L 𝕃: + אסתר K 117 𝕲: + Μαρδοχαῖος L: + *regi* 𝕃.— יכתב] om. L.— המלך¹] σοι 𝕲: κυρίῳ μου τῷ βασιλεῖ 44, 74, 76, 106, 120, 236: *domino meo* 𝕃.— ואם-לפניו] tr. aft. המלך² 𝕊.— ואם] om. אם 𝕲 (exc. 44, 93*b*, 106, 108*a*).— לפניו] om. 𝕲: ἐνώπιόν σου א ᶜ·ᵃ ᵐᵍ, A, 44, 108*a*, 249, 93*b* under *: ἐν ὀφθαλμοῖς σου N: *in conspectu tuo* 𝕃: *in oculis ejus* 𝕁.— וכשר-בעיניו] om. 𝕲 𝕃 (exc. א ᶜ·ᵃ ᵐᵍ, 249, 93*b* under *).— כשר] an Aram. word found only in late Heb. (*cf.* Ec. 11⁶), and ordinarily used of the ceremonially clean (*cf.* Siegfried, *Neuheb. Gram.* § 44).— המלך²] *ei* 𝕁.— וטובה אני בעיניו] om. 𝕁 𝕊.— יכתב] *obsecro ut novis epistolis* 𝕁: ܢܬܟܬܒܘܢ 𝕊: πεμφθήτω 𝕲: *mittantur a te litteræ* 𝕃.— להשיב] ἀποστραφῆναι 𝕲: ἀποστρέψαι א A: ὅπως ἀνέλῃs L.— להשיב] cstr. inf. with ל giving the contents of the writing as 3⁹ and often.— הספרים] *τὴν ἐπιστολὴν* L.— מחשבת] *veteres* 𝕁: pr. ○ 𝕊: τὰ ἀπεσταλμένα 𝕲: om. L 𝕃.— מחשבת-האגגי] om. 𝕁 L 𝕃 𝕲 (exc. א ᵃ·ᶜ ᵐᵍ, 93*b* under *): ܟܢ 𝕊.— האגגי] Haupt deletes as a gloss derived from v. ².— אשר — end of v.] om. L.— לאבד] *perire* 𝕁.— את] + כל many codd. (KR) 𝕊 𝕌¹ 𝕌² 𝕃.— היהודים] *eos* 𝕁.— בכל מדינות המלך] ἐν τῇ βασιλείᾳ σου 𝕲: *in regia tua in nomine tuo* 𝕃.

6. om. L 106: ⁶ᵃ Haupt deletes as a gloss or variant to ⁶ᵇ.— וראיתי] finite vb. after אוכל instead of the usual inf. cstr. or inf. cstr. with ל (*cf.* Kau. § 112 *p*).— ראה ב] ברעה means to look intently upon something that inspires joy or horror. *Cf.* Gn. 21¹⁶ "gaze upon the death of the child." — ימצא] here only in the book in the sense of 'befall.' For this the author generally uses קרה (*cf.* 4⁷ 6¹³).— אשר ימצא] om. 𝕲 𝕃 (exc. 93*b* *): *et interfectionem* 𝕁.— ימצא] המצא K 245 R 196, *Sebhîr* in some codd.—

272   ESTHER

ואיככה – מולדתי] om. 𝔍.— ²וראיתי] σωθῆναι 𝔊: liberari 𝔏.— בְּאָבְדַן] sola 𝔏: in 9⁵ אָבְדָן. The correct form is אָבְדָן. On the formation, see Ols. § 215 b; Stade, § 274 b.— מולדתי] de patria mea 𝔏.

7. ויאמר – היהודי] אחשורש] so Oc. (Ginsburg): אחשורוש] Or. N¹ S Br. B¹: om. 𝔊𝔏: Haupt deletes.— לאסתר] illi 𝔏: om. 44, 106.— המלכה – היהודי] om. 𝔊𝔏 (exc. 93b under *): τῇ βασιλίσσῃ A 𝔖.— הנה –]לאסתר καὶ ἐνεχείρισεν αὐτῷ ὁ βασιλεὺς τὰ κατὰ τὴν βασιλείαν L.— [הנה om. 𝔍𝔏.— בית] πάντα τὰ ὑπάρχοντα 𝔊: omnes facultates 𝔏.— לאסתר] καὶ ἐχαρισάμην σοι 𝔊: tibi 𝔏 𝔖.— ואתו – ביהודיים] om. L.— חלו] jussi affigi 𝔍: ἐκρέμασα 𝔊: suspendi 𝔏.— על – ביהודים] Haupt deletes to correspond with his restoration of 2²²ᶠ.— על אשר] + ausus est 𝔍.— שלח – ביהודיים] cogitavit super me mala inferre regno meo 𝔏.— שלח יד ב'] as 2²¹ 3⁶ 6² 9².— ביהודיים] ביהודים Q.

8–13. tr. aft. v. ¹⁴ L.— ואתם] καὶ ὁ βασιλεὺς ἐνεχείρισε τῷ Μαρδοχαίῳ L: om. אתם 𝔏. אתם is emphatic both in its insertion and in its position.— כתבו] γράφειν L: scribe 𝔏: om. 𝔖.— על] not 'unto' but 'concerning' (cf. v.⁹ 9²⁰).— על היהודים] 𝔊𝔏.— כטוב בעיניכם] ὡς δοκεῖ ὑμῖν 𝔊: ὅσα βούλεται L: quemadmodum tibi placet et Mordochæo 𝔏.— בשם – end of v.] om. L.— ¹המלך] μου 𝔊 (exc. 93b).— ונחתמו] om. 𝔖.— ²המלך] meo + hæc enim consuetudo erat 𝔍: μου 𝔊 𝔏.— כי] 𝔖.— כתב אשר נכתב] ὅσα γράφεται 𝔊: quæcunque scribuntur 𝔏.— כתב] see on 1²².— נכתב] mittebantur 𝔍.— בשם המלך] ἐπιτάξαντος τοῦ βασιλέως 𝔊𝔏.— ונחתום] inf. abs. instead of finite vb. as 3¹³ and often in Est. On the formation, cf. Kau. § 63 c. Haupt regards this as impossible in a coördinated relative clause and reads נֶחְתָּם as in 3¹².— ⁴המלך] illius 𝔍: μου 𝔊 𝔏.— אין] pr. ל 𝔖.— להשיב] αὐτοῖς ἀντειπεῖν 𝔊 𝔏.

MORDECAI SENDS OUT DISPATCHES TO COUNTERACT THE EDICT OF HAMAN (8⁹⁻¹⁴ᵃ).

9. *And the King's scribes* [𝔍 + and secretaries] *were called at that time*]. On the scribes, see 3¹². Mordecai does not delay in availing himself of the King's permission.—*In the third month, that is, the month Sivan, on its twenty-third day*], i.e., two months and ten days after the issuing of Haman's edict of destruction (3¹²). The intervening time is supposed to be filled with the events of 4¹–8². On the Babylonian names of the months, see 2¹⁶. —*And a dispatch was prepared in accordance with all that Mordecai commanded, unto the Jews, and unto the satraps, and the governors, and the officials* [𝔘¹ + who had been appointed rulers] *of the provinces that (extended) from India all the way to Kush*, 127 *provinces, to every single province in its script, and to every single race in its language*]. See on 3^{12} and 1^1, which are in almost verbal agreement with this passage. Just as the dispatches were formerly prepared at Haman's dictation, so now at the dictation of Mordecai. —*And unto the Jews in their script and their language*]. Incredibly large as the number of scribes was that Haman required, Mordecai required still more, for he had to send also to the Jews in all the provinces (see on 1^{22} and 3^{12}). From this passage Blau draws the unwarranted inference that, as late as the time of the writing of this book, the Jews had not yet adopted the Aramaic alphabet, but still made use of the old "Phœnician" character. Baer calls attention to the fact that this is the longest v. in the Hagiographa, containing 43 words and 192 letters.

10. *And he wrote in the name of King Xerxes and sealed it with the King's signet* [𝔊¹ + ring.] See on 3^{12b}.—*And he sent dispatches by the mounted couriers*]. These are the well-known Persian royal messengers, who have been mentioned already in 3^{13}, q.v. (cf. 3^{15} 8^{14}). *Mounted couriers* are lit. *runners on the horses.*—*Riding on the coursers, the royal steeds, bred from the stud*, [𝔊¹ + whose spleens were removed, and the hoofs of the soles of their feet were cloven.] The word translated *coursers* is used in Mi. 1^{13} of a chariot-horse, and in 1 K. 5^8 (Eng. 4^{28}) of the royal horses. It must, therefore, denote a superior sort of horse. The next word *'aḥashtᵉrānîm* is probably a loan-word from the Pers., derived from *khshatřa*, 'kingdom' (cf. Spiegel, *Altpers. Keilinschr.*, p. 215), and means something like 'royal steeds.' The old Vrss. can make nothing out of it and leave it untranslated. The doctors of the Talmud also confess their ignorance of its meaning, and say, "If we read the Book of Esther, although we do not understand this; why should not other Israelites read it, even if they understand no Hebrew?" (*Meg.* 18a.) The word translated *stud* is also uncertain (see note). These fast horses are not mentioned in the sending out of Haman's decree, $3^{13. \; 15}$. Apparently they are granted as a special favour to Mordecai, in order that the news of their deliverance may reach the Jews more speedily.

11. *To the effect that the King granted* [𝔊¹ + help] *to the Jews,* *who were in every single city to assemble and to stand for their life*]. According to the edict of 3¹³, they were to submit quietly to being killed. That edict cannot be revoked, but now they are allowed to defend themselves. The knowledge that the King favours them will strengthen them and will weaken the attack of their enemies, so that there is hope that they may come out safely. Thus far the edict is what one would expect, if the previous law could not be repealed. On *stand for their lives, cf.* 9¹⁶ Dn. 12¹.—*To destroy, to slay, and to annihilate every armed force of race or city that might be hostile to them*]. *Cf.* 3¹³. The clause contains a series of objects to *granted*. From 8¹³ 9¹⁻¹⁶ it appears that the Jews are here permitted not merely to defend themselves against attack, but also to carry on an aggressive campaign against their enemies. A contrary opinion is maintained by Haupt only by an arbitrary changing of the text. The former situation is now reversed (9¹); whereas before the Jews had to submit to being killed by their foes, the foes have now to submit to being killed by the Jews. Improbable as it is that Xerxes should devote the whole Jewish race to destruction, it is vastly more improbable that he should give up his Persian subjects to be massacred by the Jews.—*Children and women*] might grammatically be the subject of the preceding infinitives, but this gives no good sense. Sieg. suggests that it is another object to *granted*, and translates *granted children and women and their goods as plunder;* but in that case we should expect *their children and their women*. This construction is contrary to the analogy of 3¹³, where the Jewish women and children are to be killed. Accordingly, in spite of the absence of a conj., we must regard *children and women*, like *armed force*, as objects to *kill, slay, and annihilate*. The older comm. are more troubled than the author over the question, whether it was right for the Jews to kill the women and children. Bon. infers from the statement that the Jews did not take the spoil (9¹⁰· ¹⁶), that *a fortiori* they did not kill the women and children; but it is questionable whether this inference is valid.—*And to plunder their goods*]. See on 3¹³.

12. *On one day in all King Xerxes' provinces,*

[L + And the letter which Mordecai sent out had the following contents: Haman sent you letters to the effect that you should hasten to destroy quickly for me the treacherous race of the Jews; but I, Mordecai, declare to you that he who did this has been hanged before the gates of Susa, and his property has been confiscated, because he wished to slay you]

On the thirteenth of the twelfth month, that is, the month Adar,] see on 3^{13b}.

ADDITION E.

MORDECAI'S LETTER.

At this point 𝕲 𝕷 insert Mordecai's letter, E^{1-24} (𝕵 and Eng. Apoc., Ad. Est. 16^{1-24}). L inserts after 8^7. Jos. gives it in a much modified form. 𝕿² also inserts a letter similar in substance. In some indirect way it must be derived from 𝕲. For a critical apparatus to the Greek text, see Paton in *HM*. ii. pp. 39-42.

¹The following is a copy of the letter: The great King Artaxerxes unto the governors of countries in 127 provinces from India unto Ethiopia, and unto those that are concerned with our affairs, greeting. ²Many who are honoured too much with the great bounty of their benefactors, desire yet more, ³and endeavour not only to hurt our subjects, but also, not being able to bear abundance, undertake to plot against those that do them good: ⁴and not only take thankfulness away from among men, but also, being lifted up with boastful words, as though they had never received good, they think to escape the evil-hating justice of God, who always sees all things. ⁵Oftentimes also the fair speech of those that are put in trust to manage their friends' affairs, has caused many that are in authority to be partakers of innocent blood, and has involved them in remediless calamities: ⁶beguiling with the false deceit of their lewd disposition the innocent good will of princes. ⁷Now you may see this, not so much from the ancient histories that have come down to us, as you may, if you search, what has been wickedly done through the pestilent behaviour in your presence of those that are unworthily placed in authority. ⁸And we must take care for the time to come, to render our kingdom quiet and peaceable for all men, ⁹both by paying no attention to slanders, and by always judging things that come before our eyes with the greatest possible gentleness. ¹⁰For Haman the son of Hammᵉdāthā, a Macedonian, an alien in truth from the Persian blood, and far distant from our goodness, being received as a guest by us, ¹¹had so far obtained the favour that we shew toward every nation, that

he was called our father, and was continually honoured by all men, as the next person unto the royal throne. [12]But he, not bearing his high estate, went about to deprive us of our kingdom and our life, [13]having by manifold and cunning deceits sought the destruction both of Mordecai, who saved our life, and continually procured our good, and also of Esther the blameless partaker of our kingdom, together with their whole nation. [14]For by these means he thought, catching us unguarded, to transfer the kingdom of the Persians to the Macedonians. [15]But we find that the Jews, whom this thrice guilty wretch has delivered to utter destruction, are no evil-doers, but live as citizens by most just laws: [16]and that they are children of the most high and most mighty living God, who has established the kingdom both for us and for our progenitors in the most excellent manner. [17]Wherefore ye shall do well not to put in execution the letters sent unto you by Haman the son of Hammedāthā. [18]For he, that was the worker of these things, is hanged at the gates of Susa with all his family: God, who ruleth all things, speedily rendering vengeance to him according to his deserts. [19]Therefore ye shall publish openly the copy of this letter in all places, to let the Jews live after their own laws, [20]and to aid them, that on the aforesaid day, being the thirteenth day of the twelfth month Adar, they may defend themselves against those who set upon them in the time of their affliction. [21]For Almighty God hath made this day to be a joy unto them, instead of the destruction of the chosen people. [22]And ye shall, therefore, on the feast days called "Lots"* keep it a high day with all feasting: [23]that both now and hereafter it may be safety for you and for the well-affected Persians: but for those who conspire against us a memorial of destruction. [24]Therefore every city or country whatsoever, which shall not do according to these things, shall be utterly destroyed without mercy with fire and sword; it shall be made not only unpassable for men, but also most hateful to wild beasts and fowls forever.

13. *The contents of the edict (were), Let it be given out as law in every single province, published to all the races, that* [𝕲 + all] *the Jews be ready for this day*]. See the almost identical passage, 3[14]. —*To avenge themselves on their enemies*.] This shows that the Jews are granted not merely the right of self-defense, but also to do to their enemies as the enemies intended to do to them (*cf.* 8[11]).

14[a]. *The couriers went forth* [Jos. + bearing the letters,] *riding upon the coursers, the royal steeds*]. See on v. [10].—*Hastened and expedited by the King's order*.] See on 3[15].

* Reading with Grotius, Fritzsche and Ryssel κλήρων, as a translation of **Purim**, **instead of** the meaningless ὑμῶν.

MORDECAI SENDS OUT DISPATCHES

9. [ויקראו – ככל אשר] om. L.— [המלך – ההיא] om. 𝔊 (exc. א ^{c. a mg}, 93*b* under *): *regis* 𝔏.— [בעת ההיא] *erat autem tempus* 𝔍.— [השלישי] τῷ πρώτῳ 𝔊 𝔏 (τρίτῳ א ^{c. a mg}, 93*b*).— [חרש] om. 𝔖 𝔊 𝔏.— [סיון] *Siban* 𝔍: ܣܝܘܢ 𝔖: Νισά(ν) 𝔊 (Σιουάν א ^{c. a mg}, 93*b*): om. 𝔏.— [בשלושה] ἐν τετάρτῃ 249.— [ועשרים] om. 𝔏.— [בו –] τοῦ αὐτοῦ ἔτους 𝔊: τοῦ δευτέρου ἔτους א *: τοῦ αὐτοῦ μηνός Α, Ν, 76: *ipsius mensis* 𝔏: + ܚܡܫܬ 𝔖.— [ויכתב –] 𝔖.— [צוה – ܚܕܐ 𝔖: ἐπέστειλε δὲ L.— [מרדכי] om. 𝔏 𝔊 (exc. א ^{c. a mg}): Μαρδοχαῖος διὰ γραμμάτων L: Ἐσθήρ 44, 71, 74, 76, 106, 120, 236: om. 𝔏.— [אל –] end of v.] om. L.— [אל] ܠܐ 𝔖.— [ואל] om. ו 𝔖: Haupt follows 𝔖 in this and the preceding reading.— [האחשדרפנים] *principes* 𝔍: ܠܪ̈ܒܝ ܚܝܠܐ 𝔖: τοῖς οἰκονόμοις 𝔊: *actoribus* 𝔏.— [ושרי] + *qui praesidebant* 𝔍: τῶν σατραπῶν 𝔏 𝔊.— [המדינות] om. 𝔊 𝔏.— [אשר] om. 𝔖 𝔏 𝔊 (exc. א ^{c. a mg}, 93*b*).— [כוש] + [אל several codd., K and R.— [מדינה] *satrapis* 𝔏.— [מדינה ומדינה 2] *gentium imperantibus* 𝔏.— [ככתבה] κατὰ τὴν ἑαυτῶν λέξιν 𝔊: *secundum* 𝔏.— [ועם ועם כלשנו] ܘܠܟܠ ܐܡܐ ܐܝܟ ܠܫܢܗ 𝔖: *gentem et gentem secundum uniuscujusque eorum linguam* 𝔏: om. 𝔊 (exc. 93*b* under *).— [ואל – וכלשונם] *et Judæis prout legere poterant et audire* 𝔍: om. 𝔏 𝔊 (exc. 93*b* under *): Haupt deletes on the ground that the Jews needed no special dispatches, since those sent to the satraps were to be published, and since the Jews understood the languages of the provinces where they resided.

10. [ויכתב – אחשורש] om. L.— [ויכתב] ܘܟܬܒ ܀ 𝔖: ἐγράφη δὲ 𝔊 𝔏: καὶ ἐγράφη A, 71, 74, 76, 236. This vb. and the following may be impersonal (*cf.* 3⁷), but it is not necessary with 𝔖 to read them as *Niphal*.— [בשם] διὰ 𝔊 𝔏.— [אחשורש] so Oc.: אחשירוש Or. N¹ S Br. B¹: Haupt deletes.— [ויחתם] ܘܛܒܥ 𝔖: καὶ ἐσφραγίσθη 𝔊 𝔏: κ.. ἐσφραγίσατο L.— [המלך 2] τοῦ βασιλέως L: αὐτοῦ 𝔊 𝔏.— [וישלח] end of v.] om. L.— [וישלח] καὶ ἐξαπέστειλαν 𝔊 (ἐξαπέστειλεν א^{c. a} A).— [ספרים] om. 𝔏.— [ביד] διὰ 𝔊 𝔏.— [הרצים] βιβλιαφόρων 𝔊: *librarios currentes* 𝔏.— [בסוסים] ܒܛܒ̈ܐ 𝔖.— [רכש] ܀ 𝔖: om. 𝔊: Haupt deletes as a gloss to the next two words.— [רכבי – הרמכים] *qui per omnes provincias discurrentes veteres litteras novis nuntiis prævenirent* 𝔍: om. 𝔏 𝔊: τοῖς ἐπιβάταις τῶν ἁρμάτων οἱ μεγιστᾶνες υἱοὶ τῶν Ραμαχείμ 93*b* under *.— [רכש] ܀ܒܐ 𝔖: רכסא 𝔗¹: ריכשא 𝔗²: om. 𝔊 𝔏 𝔍: ἁρμάτων 93*b*. The general meaning 'horse' is established by Aram., Syr., and the apposition to סוסים here, and 1 K. 5⁸ (*cf.* Mi. 1¹³) shows that it must be a special kind of horse. The word רְכוּשׁ 'property' is from the same root.— [אחשתרנים] om. 𝔊 L 𝔏 𝔍: οἱ μεγιστᾶνες 93*b* *: ערטלוני 𝔗¹: ערטילא 𝔗² (Haupt regards these last two forms as corruptions of ארטבלא = טבלרא, ܛܒܠܪܐ, *tabellarius*, 'courier'). RaShI translates 'camels'; IE. 'mules.' Gesenius, *Thes.* 76, connects with New Pers. *astar* or *astâr*, 'mule'; but this corresponds with Old Pers. *açpatara*, Skr. *açvatara*, which does not resemble the above form. Equally impossible is the etymology of Pott (*Forschungen*, p. lxvii) from *esahyo*, 'king,' and *shutur*, 'camel.' The derivation from *khshatra*, 'kingdom,' was first suggested by Haug in Ewald's *Jahrbücher*, v. 154 (see Rödiger, *Suppl. to Ges. Thes.*, p. 68), and is now generally accepted. Haupt deletes this word as an antiquarian gloss, and also the following two words as a tertiary explanation of this gloss.—[הרמכים] 𝔖: רמכין 𝔘¹: רמכאי 𝔘²: Ῥαμαχείμ 93b: om. 𝔊 L 𝔈 𝔍. In Syr. and New Pers. the word means 'herd,' in New Heb. 'mule.' In Ar. 'mare.' Whether it means here 'studs,' 'mares,' or 'stallions' is uncertain. With Haupt we should point הָרְמָכִים instead of הָרַמָּכִים. The latter means properly 'herdsmen.'

11. [אשר]= 'that,' introducing the contents of the dispatches, as 1¹⁹ 2¹⁰ 3⁴ 4¹¹ 6², a late usage.—[אשר המלך]¹ om. L: ܡܟܬܒܐ ܘܒܐ 𝔖: ὡς ἐπέταξεν 𝔊 𝔏.—[ליהודים] αὐτοῖς 𝔊 𝔏: τὸ ἔθνος αὐτοῦ L.— [אשר]² om. 𝔊 L 𝔏. —[בכל עיר ועיר] ἐν πάσῃ (τῇ) πόλει 𝔊: κατὰ χώρας ἕκαστον αὐτῶν L: om. 𝔏: [להקהל] 𝔖.— et in unum præciperent congregari 𝔍: χρῆσθαι τοῖς νόμοις αὐτῶν 𝔊 𝔏: ἑορτάζειν τῷ θεῷ L.—[ולעמד]—end of v.] om. 𝔏.—[ולעמד על נפשם] βοηθῆσαι τε αὐτοῖς 𝔊: καὶ μένειν L.—[להשמיד— end of v.] om. L.—[להשמיד—ולאבד] καὶ χρῆσθαι ὡς βούλονται 𝔊 (+ ἀφανίζειν καὶ φονεύειν ὡς βούλονται καὶ ἀπολαύειν 93b under *).—[ולהרג] om. ו many codd. KR, B².—[ולאבד] om. 𝔍.—[את כל-ומדינה] τοῖς ἀντιδίκοις αὐτῶν 𝔊 (+ πᾶσαν δύναμιν λαοῦ καὶ χώρας τοὺς θλιβόντας αὐτούς א c. a mg, 93b under *): omnes 𝔍: ܚܝܠܐ 𝔖.—[חיל] cf. 1³. Haupt deletes.—[הצרים אתם] καὶ τοῖς ἀντικειμένοις αὐτῶν 𝔊: Qal ptc. from צור 'be hostile,' not from the noun צר 'enemy,' which cannot govern the acc. (BDB. 849, III.). Haupt changes unnecessarily to הצררים אתם (cf. Nu. 10⁹).—[טף-לבוז] pr. ס 𝔖: om. 𝔊 (exc. א c. a mg, 93b under *): Haupt deletes as a gloss derived from 3¹³.—[ונשים] + et universis domibus 𝔍.— [לבוז] + et constituta est 𝔍.

12. [מדינות] τῇ 𝔍.—[ביום ב 𝔍.—[ביום-אחשורוש om. L: [ביום אחד] om. 𝔏: τῇ βασιλείᾳ 𝔊.—[המלך] om. 𝔍 𝔊 𝔏.—[אחשורוש] om. 𝔍: Haupt deletes.— [בשלושה] quarta 𝔏.—[שנים עשר] om. L.—[חדש] om. 𝔍 𝔊 L 𝔏.

13. om. L 𝔏.—[פתשגן] ܦܬܓܡܐ 𝔖.—[הכתב] om. 𝔊 (exc. א c. a, 93b under *).—[להנתן] ἐκτιθέσθωσαν 𝔊: ἐκτιθέσθω א: ἐκτεθείσθω A.—[דת] om. 𝔖 𝔊 (exc. 93b under *).—[מדינה] τῇ βασιλείᾳ 𝔊.—[ומדינה] om. 𝔖 𝔊 (exc. 93b under *).—[גלוי] om. 𝔍: ܣܦܝܩ 𝔖: ὀφθαλμοφανῶς 𝔊.—[לכל העמים] om. 𝔍 𝔊.—[ולהיות] + πάντας Q.—[עתודים] Q.—[היהודים] Q.—[ולהיות] om. 𝔍 𝔊.—[ליום הזה] om. 𝔍.—[להנקם] πολεμῆσαι 𝔊.

14a. [הרצים המלך] om. L.—[הרצים] pr. ס 𝔖: οἱ μὲν οὖν ἱππεῖς 𝔊.— [רכבי-האחשתרנים] om. 𝔍 𝔊 𝔏 (exc. א c. a mg, 93b under *): pr. ܘܐܣܬܚܦܘ 𝔖. —[האחשתרנים] om. 𝔖: Haupt deletes.—[יצאו] om. 𝔏.—[מבהלים] ܚܠܣܐ 𝔖: festinanter 𝔏: Pu. ptc. pl. (cf. 2⁹ 6¹⁴).—[ורחופים] perferentes 𝔍: ܡܣܬܪܗܒܝܢ 𝔖: ἐπιτελεῖν 𝔊: καὶ διωκόμενοι ἐπιτελεῖν א c. a mg, 93b under *. Cf. 3¹⁵ 6¹²: Jahn, Haupt, delete.—[בדבר המלך] Haupt deletes as a gloss derived from 3¹³.—[בדבר] nuncia 𝔍: τὰ λεγόμενα 𝔊: præcepta 𝔏.—[המלך] om. 𝔍 𝔖. —[והדת]—end of v.] om. 44, 106, 107, 236: Haupt deletes as a scribal expansion derived from 3¹⁵.

THE JEWS REJOICE OVER THEIR ESCAPE (8¹⁴ᵇ⁻¹⁷).

14ᵇ–15. *Meanwhile the law had been given out in Susa the fortress, and Mordecai had gone out* [𝕵 + *from the palace and*] *from the King's presence in a royal garment of violet and white*]. On *royal garment*, see 6⁸; on *violet* and *white*, see 1⁶.—*And a big golden crown*]. The word *crown* is different from the one used for the royal turban in 1¹¹ 2¹⁷ 6⁸, but the idea is the same. Not only the King, but also his favourites were allowed to wear the royal head-dress, and in Mordecai's case this was specially large. —*And a mantle of fine linen and purple*]. See on 1⁶. When Mordecai received these decorations, we are not told, presumably at the time when he became grand vizier (8¹ ᶠ·). He is now privileged to wear continually what before he received for a short time only (6¹¹).

> [𝕿¹ + Rejoicing and glad of heart because of his great honour and abundant dignity, clothed in royal garments of wool, linen, and purple, with a chain of fine gold of Ophir in which were set pearls and precious stones, clad in a mantle made from the young of the bird of paradise(?) of the western sea, under which was a purple tunic with embroidery of all sorts of birds and fowls of the heavens, and this tunic was valued at 420 talents of gold. And he was girt about the loins with a girdle on which were fastened throughout its length beryl stones. His feet were shod with Parthian socks imported by the Macedonians, woven of gold and set with emeralds. A Median sword hung by his side, suspended on a chain of rings of gold, on which was engraved the city of Jerusalem, and on whose hilt the fortune of the city was depicted. A Median helmet painted with various colours was put on his head, and above it was placed a great crown of Macedonian gold, and above the crown was placed a golden phylactery, in order that all peoples, nations, and tongues might know that Mordecai was a Jew, that the Scripture might be fulfilled where it is written, "And all peoples of the earth shall see that the name of the Lord is named upon thee." And when Mordecai went out from the gate of the King, the streets were strewn with myrtle, the court was shaded with purple extended on linen cords, and boys with garlanded heads, and priests holding trumpets in their hands, proclaimed, saying, "Whoever is not reconciled to Mordecai and reconciled to the Jews, shall be cut in pieces and his house shall be turned into a dung-hill." And the ten sons of Haman came with lifted hands, and spoke before the righteous Mordecai, saying, "He who gives wages to the Jews brings also the wages of the wicked upon their heads. This Haman our father

was a fool because he trusted in his riches and in his honour. The humble Mordecai has defeated him through his fasting and his prayers." And the righteous Esther looked out at the window, for the Queen was not permitted to go among the people in the street. And Mordecai, turning his eyes, saw her and said, "Blessed be the Lord who did not give me a prey to their teeth." Esther answered, saying, "My help is from the Lord who made heaven and earth." Many people rejoiced at the fall of the wicked Haman and gave thanks and praise on account of the deliverance which was wrought for the Jews, and they celebrated the deliverance and the glory which the righteous Mordecai had at this time (similarly 𝔗², *cf.* 𝔗² on 6¹¹).]

And [Jos. + when they saw him so honoured by the King, the Jews who were in] *the city of Susa had shouted and rejoiced*], in contrast to 3¹⁵, where the capital is perplexed at the edict of destruction. Here, as in 3¹⁵, the author ascribes to the whole population the emotions of the Jews. The *city* of Susa is here distinguished from the *fortress* of Susa as in 3¹⁵ 4¹· ⁶ 6⁹ (see on 1⁵).

16. *Unto the Jews there came light, and joy, and rejoicing, and honour.*] *Light* is a figure for prosperity, as in Jb. 22²⁸ 30²⁶ Ps. 97¹¹. 𝔗¹, following *Meg.* 16*b*, translates *light*, "freedom to busy themselves with the Law"; *joy*, "and to keep the Sabbaths"; *rejoicing*, "the set feasts"; and *honour*, "to circumcise the foreskins of their sons, and to place phylacteries upon their hands and upon their heads." On *honour*, see 1⁴. The Jews in Susa are still meant. Now that they had become the King's favourites, all men hastened to flatter them.

17. *And in every single province and in every single city, wherever the King's command and his law arrived*]. See on 4³.—*There was joy and rejoicing* [𝔗¹ + of heart] *among the Jews, and banqueting and holiday*], in contrast to the fasting, weeping, lamentation, haircloth, and ashes of 4³, when Haman's edict was promulgated.—*And many of the heathen* [𝔊 𝔏 L + were circumcised and] *became Jews*, [Jos. + to secure safety for themselves by this means,] *for the fear of the Jews had fallen upon them.*] So completely were the tables turned, that it was now dangerous not to be a Jew. *Heathen* is literally *peoples of the earth;* not *people of the land,* AV.; or *peoples of the land,* as RV. (see note). On *fear had fallen upon them, cf.* 9²ᶠ· Gn. 35⁵ Ex. 15¹⁶ Dt. 11²⁵ Ps. 105³⁸ *al.*

THE JEWS REJOICE 281

The allusion to proselyting in this v. is one of the many indications of the late date of the book. There is no evidence that this took place before the Greek period.

14b. [והדת] + *regis* 𝕵: ܠܢ ܣܕܦܣ 𝕾: *exemplum epistolæ* 𝕷.—[נתנה ודאתם 𝕾: pf. with ו in a circumstantial clause. 𝕾 takes it as a relative clause, 'in the word of the King and the law which had been given out in Susa.'—[הבירה] om. 𝕵 𝕲 (exc. א ^{c. a}, 93b under *): *civitate regis* 𝕷: περιέχον τάδε L (here L inserts 8⁸⁻¹³).—[ומרדכי יצא] not impf. with ו consec. in sequence with the foregoing, but another circumstantial clause, unless regarded as an instance of the late use of the pf. with ו connect. instead of impf. with ו consec., as 9²³ (*cf.* Driver, *Tenses*, § 313). Here, however, the subject precedes the vb., as normally in a circumstantial clause.

15. [מלפני המלך] om. 𝕷 𝕲 L (exc. א ^{c. a mg}, 93b under *).—[תכלת וחור om. 𝕷 L 𝕲 (exc. א ^{c. a mg}, 93b under *).—[וחור] ܣܪܩܝ 𝕾: *et aereis* 𝕵: ἀερίνην א ^{c. a}, 93b.—[ועטרת–גדולה] om. L (exc. 93a): Haupt deletes. עטרת here only in Est., elsewhere כתר (1¹¹ 2¹⁷ 6⁸).—[גדולה] om. 𝕵 𝕾 𝕲 𝕷. —[ותכריך] *et amictus* 𝕵: καὶ διάδημα 𝕲 L: מכריך 𝕿¹: ἀ.λ. from Aram. כרך 'enclose.' It denotes a sort of spacious outer mantle.—[בוץ] *serico pallio* 𝕵: *et byssinum* 𝕷.—[וארגמן] om. 𝕷: om. ו 𝕲 L.—[והעיר שושן] ἰδόντες δὲ οἱ ἐν Σούσοις 𝕲 L 𝕷.—[צהלה] usually 'neigh,' here of a shrill cry of joy, as Is. 12⁶ 54¹; pf. in continuation of the series of circumstantial clauses.— [ושמחה] om. L 𝕷 𝕲 (exc. א ^{c. a mg}): + ὅτι A: pausal form of pf. 3 f. s. of stative vb. Haupt deletes as an explanatory gloss to the preceding word.

16. [אורה] om. 44, 106, 107: *cf.* Ps. 139¹². Aram. and late Heb. for אור, and used with the same literal and figurative meanings. The translation of 𝕿¹ is a play upon the similar word אוריתא 'law.'—[ושמחה] πότος L. —[וששן] κώθων L: τῷ κυρίῳ θεῷ 19: κυρίῳ τῷ θεῷ 108b: om. 𝕷 𝕲 (exc. א ^{c. a}, 93b under *).—[ויקר] om. L 𝕷 𝕲 (exc. א ^{c. a}, 93b under *).

17. [ומדינה] om. L.—[ובכל¹ om. 𝕲 (exc. 108a): om. ו 𝕾.—[ובכל² om. 𝕲 𝕷.—[עיר] om. 𝕷.—[ועיר] om. 𝕾 𝕷 𝕲 (exc. 93b under *).—[ובכל²] om. 𝕲 𝕷.—[מקום–end of v.] om. 71.—[מקום–טוב] om. 44, 106, 107.—[מקום–המלך] om. A N 52, 74, 76, 243.—[מקום] om. 𝕲 𝕷.—[דבר om. 248, C, Ald.—[המלך ודתו] om. 𝕷 𝕲 (exc. א ^{c. a mg}, 93b under *).— [ודתו] om. 𝕵.—[מגיע] + οὗ ἂν ἐξετέθη τὸ ἔκθεμα 𝕲 (exc. א): + τὸ ἔκθεμα 248, C, Ald.—[וששון] 𝕾 ܘܢܒܐ.—[ליהודים–טוב] om. 𝕷.—[ליהודים] *epulæ* 𝕵: + ○ 𝕾.—[ויום טוב] καὶ εὐφροσύνη 𝕲: καὶ ἀγαλλίασις 74, 76, 120, 236: om. 249.—[יום טוב] Here as in 1 S. 25⁸ of a day of feasting. In 9¹⁹, ²² Zc. 8¹⁹, as in late Jewish usage, of the feast days of the religious calendar.—[עמי הארץ] *alterius gentis* 𝕵: τῶν ἐθνῶν 𝕲: τῶν Ἰουδαίων L. The singular עם הארץ means 'people of the land,' and is used either of the aboriginal Canaanites, as Gn. 23⁷, ¹² f. (P) Nu. 14⁹ (JE) Ezr. 4⁴, or of the Israelites, as Ex. 5⁵ (J) Lev. 4²⁷ 20², ⁴. The plural עמי הארץ means always 'the

peoples of the earth,' and is used of the heathen in contrast to Israel. So Dt. 28¹⁰ Jos. 4²⁴ 1 K. 8⁵³·⁶⁰ 1 Ch. 5²⁵ 2 Ch. 6³³ 32¹⁹ Ezr. 10² Ne. 10³¹ ᶠ· Ez. 31¹² Zp. 3²⁰. Similarly עַמֵּי הָאֲרָצוֹת 'peoples of the lands,' 2 Ch. 13⁹ Ezr. 3³ 9¹ ᶠ· ¹¹ Ne. 9³⁰ 10²⁹. From this plural a singular is formed in New Heb. with the meaning of 'one ignorant of the Law,' who is no better than a heathen (*cf.* Jn. 7⁴⁹).— מתיהדים] *eorum religioni et cæremoniis jungerentur* 𝕴: ܡܬܬܠܡܕܘ 𝕾: om. to end of v. L. This word is a *Hithp.* denom. from יהודי (Stade § 164), ἁ.λ., and rare in New Heb. 𝕿¹ 𝕿² have מתגיירין, which is the usual later word for 'become a proselyte.'— כי נפל] διὰ 𝕲 (καὶ διὰ א *): *propter* 𝕷.— פחד] + *grandis* 𝕴: *timorem qui factus erat adversus inimicos* 𝕷.— עליהם] *cunctos* 𝕴: om. 𝕷 𝕲 (exc. 93*b* under *).

ON THE APPOINTED DAY THE JEWS DESTROY THEIR ENEMIES (9¹⁻¹⁰).

1. *And in the twelfth month, that is,* [Jos.²⁸⁶ + among the Jews] *the month of Adar,* [Jos. + but among the Macedonians Dustros,] *on its thirteenth day*]. The nine months that intervened since the second edict was sent out (8⁹) are passed over in silence.—*When the King's command and his law went into operation*], lit. *arrived to be done* (*cf.* 4³ 8¹⁷). According to the irrevocable law of 3¹³, the heathen are to kill the Jews; and, according to the equally irrevocable law of 8¹¹, the Jews are to kill the heathen. Lively times are to be anticipated.—*On the day, when the enemies of the Jews expected to domineer over them, it was changed* [𝕿¹ + by Heaven on account of the virtue of the forefathers] *so that the Jews domineered over their enemies.*] According to AV., Rys., the second clause is a continuation of the preceding temporal clause, and the apodosis does not come until the next v., but this is not so natural. *It* is impersonal (Keil, Sieg., Haupt). The characteristic avoidance of the name of God is seen here as in 4³· ¹⁴· ¹⁶ 6¹.

2. *The Jews had assembled in their cities in all King Xerxes' provinces to lay hands upon those who wished them ill.*] This is in accordance with the edict of 8¹¹. *To lay hands*, lit. *to stretch forth a hand*, is a synonym of *kill*, as in 2²¹ 3⁶. The persons killed are not merely those who attack them, but also those who are known to be hostile, "their haters" (v. ¹). See on 8¹¹.—*And no man had stood out against them*], lit. *had stood before them.* Stood might

THE JEWS KILL THEIR ENEMIES 283

mean *took a stand*, as in 4^{14} 5^1 7^7; but from $9^{3. 16}$ it appears that the Jews encountered opposition, so that we must translate *had kept a stand*, as in 8^{11} 9^{16} Jos. 10^8 21^{44} 23^9. The enemies of the Jews attacked them in accordance with the edict of 3^{13}, but they had no enthusiasm and were easily defeated.—*For the fear of them had fallen upon all the races.*] See on 8^{17}.

3. *And all the officials of the provinces and the satraps and the governors,* [𝔍 + and every dignitary in every place,] *and those who did the King's business had been helping the Jews, for the fear of Mordecai had fallen upon them.*] See on $3^{9. 12}$. The royal officials have no difficulty in seeing which edict they would better enforce. They everywhere take the side of the Jews and help them kill the heathen. Granted that such an edict could be sent out, this is doubtless the natural result.

4. *For Mordecai was* [𝕌¹ + overseer and] *great* [𝕌¹ + and steward] *in the King's house,* [𝔍 + and had much power,] *and the report of him kept going through all the provinces, for the man Mordecai* [𝕌¹ + was master of the house and father to the King and] *grew greater and greater.*] This is an explanation of the last clause of the preceding v. All the provinces learned that Mordecai was so powerful that his vengeance would surely overtake any one who showed himself hostile to the Jews. On *King's house*, see 2^8. *Grew greater and greater* is lit. *was growing and was great*.

5. *So among all their enemies the Jews made a smiting with the sword, and a slaughter* [𝕌¹ + with maul-clubs] *and a destruction* [𝕌¹ + of lives.] *Made*, lit. *smote*, is followed by the cognate acc. *smiting* and the synonyms *slaughter* and *destruction*. Cf. the terms of the decree in 8^{11}.—*And they did with their enemies as they pleased.*] *Did with* is used in the sense of *did to* as 1^{15} 6^6. This is more than self-defence. All that were known to be hostile to the Jews were hunted out and killed.

6. [Jos.^{288} + So the King's decree was carried out in all the country that was subject to him] *and in Susa the fortress the Jews slew and annihilated* 500 *men* [𝕌¹ + all the chieftains of the house of Amalek.] On *Susa the fortress*, see 1^2. This slaughter took place in the palace-quarter under the King's very eyes. It indicates the presence of a considerable body of Jews in Susa (*cf.* 4¹⁶).

7–10. *Meanwhile they slew Parshandātha, and Dalphôn, and 'Aspātha, and Pôrātha, and 'Ădalyā, and 'Ărîdhātha, and Parmashtā, and 'Ărîsay, and 'Ărîday, and Wayzātha, the ten sons of Haman, son of Hammᵉdātha,* [Vrss. + the Agagite,] *the enemy of the Jews,* [𝔍 + whose names are these.] On the origin and meaning of these names, see p. 70. The Massora prescribes that they are to be written in a perpendicular column on the right side of the page, with *and* on the left side. This arrangement is followed in most of the printed editions. The reason for it is found in haggadic legends as to the way in which the sons of Haman were hanged. See on 9¹⁴, and Buxtorf, *Synag. Jud.*, Basel, 1680, pp. 557–559. In the first name, the Massora prescribes that *th* shall be written smaller than the other letters; in *Parmashtā*, that *sh* shall be small; and in *Wayzātha*, *w* large and *z* small. These peculiar letters may indicate early attempts to correct the text (*cf.* Baer-Strack, *Diqduqe haṭṭeʿamim*, 61, p. 48 *f.*). They are known already to BT., for *Meg.* 16*b* directs that the ו of Wayzātha shall be written large, to show that the ten sons were all hanged on one gallows (*cf.* v. ¹⁴). *Meg.* also directs that the names of the ten shall be uttered in one breath, because their souls left their bodies at one time.—*But on the plunder they did not lay their hands*], although permitted to do so by the King (8¹¹). According to RaShI they left this for the King, so that he would not permit the princes of Trans-Euphrates to disturb their brethren. Similarly IE., Esti. According to Men., Tir., Lap., it was to avoid suspicion of having attacked their enemies for mercenary reasons; according to Grot. *al.*, to prevent the heathen from saying that they had enriched them, as Abraham in Gn. 14²² ᶠ.

1. om. L 𝔏.— הוא] *quem vocari ante jam diximus* 𝔍.— חרש] om. 𝔍 𝔖 𝔊.— ‍יום בו] om. 𝔖: τοῦ μηνός 𝔊.— להעשות – אשר] *quando cunctis Judæis interfectio parabatur* 𝔍.— אשר] om. 𝔊.— אשר הגיע] here of time, in 4³ 8¹⁷ of place. On אשר = 'when' after words expressing time, see BDB. 82*b*.— הגיע] + ‍[דבר] 𝔖.— [דבר τὰ γράμματα τὰ γραφέντα ὑπὸ 𝔊: τὰ γράμματα 44, 106, 107.— ודתו להעשות] om. 𝔊 (exc. א ᶜ·ᵃ ᵐᵍ, 93*b* under *).— [ביום – בהם Haupt deletes as a scribal expansion.— [ביום – שברו] om. 𝔖.— [ביום אשר *et* 𝔍.— [אשר – אשר] om. 𝔊 (exc. 93*b* under *).— [שברו] *inhiabant* 𝔍: a late word

[היהודים] borrowed from Aram.—איכי היהודים] 𝔖.— ܒܥܠܕܒܒܝܗܘܢ eorum 𝔍.—לשלוט] sanguini 𝔍: om. 𝔖.—לשלוט] found only in post-exilic literature and NH.—נהפך] om. 𝔍𝔖.—ונהפוך] versa vice 𝔍: om. ו 𝔖.— ונהפוך] Niph. inf. abs. as a substitute for the finite vb., as so often in this book, e.g., 6^9 8^8 (cf. Stade, §§ 251, 626 c); here apparently as a substitute for the impf. with ו consec.—הוא] 𝔖.— ܟܡܐܕ.—אשר בשנאיהם] Haupt deletes as a scribal expansion.—אשר] = 'so that,' as Gn. 11^7 13^{16} Ex. 20^{26} Dt. $4^{10.\ 40}$ 6^3 al.—ישלטו בשנאיהם] ἀπώλοντο οἱ ἀντικείμενοι τοῖς Ἰουδαίοις 𝔊: Judæi superiores esse cœperunt et se de adversariis vindicare 𝔍.—ישלטו] 𝔖. ܘܢܡܐܟܘܢ.

2. om. 𝔏.—נקהלו - רעתם] om. L 𝔊 (exc. 93b under *): pr. ו 𝔍𝔖.— נקהלו] pf., as עמד in the next v., instead of impf. with ו consec., because these events are not subsequent to v. ¹, but are a *résumé* in detail of what is there stated in general.—היהודים] om. 𝔍. 𝔖 et loca 𝔍.—אחשורוש] om. 𝔍: Haupt deletes.—במבקשי] 𝔖. ܟܠܗܘܢ — et persecutores suos 𝔍.—לפניהם בפניהם 110 codd. KR, N¹ Br. B²: om. 𝔊 (exc. 93b under *, א c. a mg): αὐτοῖς L.—כי נפל פחדם] φοβούμενος αὐτούς 𝔊: ἐφοβοῦντο γὰρ αὐτούς L.—פחדם] formido magnitudinis eorum 𝔍.—על כל העמים] om. 𝔊 L: Haupt deletes the whole clause from כי to העמים as an illogical scribal expansion.

3. וכל] nam et 𝔍: γάρ 𝔊: et 𝔏: δὲ L.—המדינות] τῶν σατραπῶν 𝔊 𝔏: om. L.—והפחות] om. 𝔊 𝔏.—ועשי המלאכה] καὶ οἱ γραμματεῖς 𝔊 𝔏: om. 44, 71, 106.—אשר למלך] om. 𝔍: βασιλικοί 𝔊 L: regis 𝔏: om. 44, 71, 106.— כי - עליהם] 𝔖: ἐτίμων 𝔊 𝔏.—היהודים] Deum 𝔏.—מנשאים] 𝔖: ܡܝܩܪܝܢ. Haupt deletes as a scribal expansion.—מרדכי] ܘܠܡܪܕܟܝ 𝔖.

4. כי - המלך] om. L 𝔊 𝔏 (exc. א c. a mg, 93b under *).—כי] + cogno- verant 𝔍.—מרדכי] quem 𝔍.—הבית] ܒܝܬܐ 𝔖.—וׁשמעו הולך] fama quoque nominis ejus crescebat 𝔍: προσέπεσεν γὰρ τὸ πρόσταγμα τοῦ βασιλέως ὀνο- μασθῆναι 𝔊: præceptum enim erat timorem regis nominari 𝔏: καὶ προσέ- πεσεν ἐν Σούσοις ὀνομασθῆναι Ἀμὰν καὶ τοὺς ἀντικειμένους L.—שמעו] ܫܡܥ 𝔖: from שמע (cf. Jos. 6^{27} 9^9 Je. 6^{24}), a rarer form with the same meaning as שָׁמַע.—בכל המדינות] quotidie 𝔍.—ܡܕܝܢܬܐ 𝔖: ἐν πάσῃ (τῇ) βασιλείᾳ 𝔊 L: in omni civitate ejus 𝔏: + αὐτοῦ 44, 74, 76, 106, 120, 236.—כי וגדול] ²¹ et per cunctorum ora volitabat 𝔍: om. L 𝔏 𝔊 (exc. 93b under *): Haupt deletes as a scribal expansion.—הולך וגדול] in 2 Ch. 17^{12} הוֹלֵךְ וְגָדֵל, which suggests that גָדוֹל may be an adj. It is probably better, however, to regard it as an inf. abs., since this construc- tion is such a favourite with the author.

5-19. om. 𝔏.—5. om. L 𝔊 (exc. 93b under *).—ויכו ב'] 'smote among,' as Jos. 10^{10} 2 S. 23^{10} 24^{17}.—בכל] om. 𝔍.—חרב] magna 𝔍.—ויהרג ואבדן] Haupt deletes as a gloss derived from the next v.—ויהרג] et occiderunt eos 𝔍.—ואבדן] om. 𝔍: see on 8^6.—כרצונם] quod sibi paraverant facere 𝔍.

6. om. 𝔏.—ובשושן] om. ו 𝔖: καὶ ἐν αὐτῇ 𝔊.: καὶ ἐν Σούσοις א * א c. a mg inf A L.—הבירה] om. א * L 44, 106 𝔍: Haupt deletes as a gloss.

286   ESTHER

היהודים—] om. 𝔍.—ואבד] om. 𝔍 𝔖 L 𝔊 (exc. ℵ ᶜ·ᵃ, 93*b* under *): inf. abs., as so often in this book.— חמש מאות] ἑπτακοσίους L.

   7. om. 𝔏 106: tr. aft. 9¹⁰ᵃ 𝔍.

   8. om. 𝔏 106.

   10. om. 𝔏.—עשרת] pr. *extra* 𝔍: pr. καί L, 44, 106, C.—בן המדתא] om. 𝔍 𝔖: + *Agagitæ* 𝔍: + ‎ ‎ 𝔖: + (τοῦ) Βουγαίου 𝔊 L: + καὶ Βουγαίου 44, 106: + Βουδέου ℵ *.—צרר] τοὺς ἐχθροὺς 249.— הרגו] pr. *quos cum* 𝔍: om. L 𝔊 (exc. ℵ ᶜ·ᵃ A, 93*b* under *).—ובבזה ידם] καὶ διήρπασαν 𝔊: καὶ διήρπασαν πάντα τὰ αὐτῶν L: καὶ οὐ διήρπασαν C: καὶ ἐν τοῖς σκύλοις οὐκ ἀπέκτειναν τὰς χεῖρας αὐτῶν 93*b* under *: om. 106.

THE KING GRANTS ESTHER ANOTHER DAY OF SLAUGHTER IN SUSA (9¹¹⁻¹⁵).

11. *On that day the number of those slain in Susa the fortress came to the knowledge of the King.*] According to IE. the enemies of the Jews reported it in order to turn the King against the Jews. If so, they failed in their effort.

12. *And the King said to Queen Esther, In Susa the fortress the Jews have killed and annihilated* 500 *men,* [𝔗¹ + chieftains of the seed of Amalek,] *and also the ten sons of Haman. In the rest of the King's provinces what have they done?* [*Meg.* 16*b* + Then came an angel and smote him on the mouth.] The idea is, if as many as 500 men have been killed in the palace-quarter, how vast must have been the slaughter throughout the empire. The addition of *Meg.* assumes that the question is put in anger, and only because of supernatural intervention does the King change his mind and ask Esther what more she wishes. Of this there is no trace in the original. Xerxes tries to please Esther by showing her how precisely her desire has been carried out, and then proceeds to inquire what more she wants.—[44 + And the King said to Esther,] *Now whatever thy request is shall be granted thee, and whatever is still thy petition shall be done.*] See on 5³·⁶ 7². The King is so well disposed that he is ready to grant Esther permission to massacre a few more thousands of his Persian subjects, if she sees fit (*cf.* 8¹¹).

13. *And Esther said, If it seems good to the King*]. See on 1¹⁹.— *Let it be granted to-morrow also to the Jews that are in Susa to act in accordance with the law of to-day* [𝔗¹ + by keeping a holiday

THE SECOND MASSACRE

and rejoicing as ought to be done on a famous day.] The explanation of 𝔗¹ is inadmissible, since nothing has yet been said of any celebration of the thirteenth of Adar as a holiday (*cf.* v. ¹⁷). *In accordance with the law of to-day* can only mean with a slaughter, such as has been permitted to-day (*cf.* 8¹¹ 9⁶⁻¹⁰); so Jos., "To treat their remaining enemies in the same manner." For this horrible request no justification can be found. A second massacre was in no sense an act of self-defence, since the power of the enemies of the Jews had already been broken by the events of the thirteenth of Adar. This shows a malignant spirit of revenge more akin to the teaching of the Talmud (*e.g.*, in Tract. '*Abhoda Zara*) than to the teaching of the OT. On law, see 1⁸.—*And let them hang the sons of Haman upon the gallows*], although they have already been killed, according to vv. ⁷⁻¹⁰. The vengeance of Esther pursues them even after they are dead. We must suppose that their bodies are suspended with their father's (7¹⁰ 8⁷), in order to complete the degradation of the house of Haman and to serve as an additional warning to the enemies of the Jews (*cf.* 1 S. 31¹⁰; Her. iii. 125; vi. 30; vii. 238).

14. *And the King commanded that this should be done*, [Jos.²⁹⁰ + because he was unable to deny Esther anything,] *and a law was given out* [246 + on the fourteenth of Adar, and they slew 300 men] *in Susa.*] See on 3¹⁵. The complaisant King at once issues a new edict granting the two points that Esther requested, namely, another slaughter of his Persian subjects, and the hanging of the sons of his former friend. No improbability is too great for this author. The next two clauses show how this law was executed.—*So they hanged the ten sons of Haman* [codd. + upon the gallows.]

[𝔗¹ 𝔗² + And this is the order in which they were hanged with Haman their father on the gallows which Haman had prepared for Mordecai:— Its height was 50 cubits. It was set three cubits deep in the ground, and Parshandāthā was 4½ cubits above the ground, and Parshandāthā was hanged in a space of 3 cubits, and between him and Dalphôn was ½ cubit. Dalphôn was hanged in a space of 3 cubits, at a distance of ½ cubit from 'Aspāthā. 'Aspāthā was hanged in a space of 3 cubits, at a distance of ½ cubit from Pôrāthā. Pôrāthā was hanged in a space of 3 cubits, at a distance of ½ cubit from 'Ădalyā. 'Ădalyā was hanged in a space of three

288   ESTHER

cubits, at a distance of ½ cubit from 'Ărîdhāthā. 'Ărîdhāthā was hanged in a space of 3 cubits, at a distance of ½ cubit from Parmashtā. Parmashtā was hanged in a space of 3 cubits, at a distance of ½ cubit from 'Ărîsay. 'Ărîsay was hanged in a space of 3 cubits, at a distance of ½ cubit from 'Ărîday. 'Ărîday was hanged in a space of 3 cubits, at a distance of ½ cubit from Wayzāthā. Wayzāthā was hanged in a space of 3 cubits, at a distance of ½ cubit from Haman. Haman was hanged in a space of 3 cubits, and above his head 3 cubits were left, so that the birds might not eat of it.] [𝔗¹ + And Zeresh fled with 70 sons who were left to Haman, and they earned their living by becoming doorkeepers, and also Shimmeshe, the scribe, was slain with the sword, and 108 sons, who were rulers in the King's streets, died with the 500 men slain in Susa.] [𝔗² + And when Mordecai came and saw Haman and his sons hanging on the gallows, Mordecai addressed Haman thus: Thou thoughtest to do evil to the people of the house of Israel, but He who knoweth the hidden things and the thoughts, hath brought thy plan upon thy head. Thou wast desiring to kill us and to remove us from under the wings of our Heavenly Father. Now they are treating thee so, and are hanging thee with thy sons under thy wing.]

15. *And the Jews that were in Susa assembled also on the fourteenth day of the month of Adar.*] In this way the author seeks to explain the fact that in his day the city Jews kept the feast of Purim on the fifteenth of Adar, instead of the fourteenth, the day observed by the country Jews (*cf.* 9¹⁸ ᶠ·). History here arises from custom, not custom from history.—*And they slew in Susa three hundred men* [𝔗¹ + *of the house of Amalek*,] *but on the plunder they did not lay their hands.*] See on v. ¹⁰ᵇ.

11. om. L𝔗.— [ביום ההוא] om. 106.— [הבירה] om. 𝔍𝔊 (exc. א ᶜ· ª, 93b under *).— [לפני המלך] om. 52, 93b.
12. om. 𝔗.— [המלך] *qui* 𝔍.— [לאסתר] om. 𝔍.— [המלכה] om. L𝔊 (exc. א ᶜ· ª ᵐᵍ, 93b under *).— [בשושן הבירה] om. L: Haupt deletes הבירה.— [הרגו היהודים] ἀπώλεσαν οἱ Ἰουδαῖοι 𝔊: πῶς σοι οἱ ἐνταῦθα (ἐνταῦτα ἡ 19, 108b) L.— [ואבד] om. L𝔊 (exc. א ᶜ· ª ᵐᵍ, 93b under *): Haupt deletes.— [חמש - המן] om. L.— [ואת - המן] om. 𝔊 (exc. א ᶜ· ª ᵐᵍ, 93b under *).— בשאר [מדינות] ἐν δὲ τῇ περιχώρῳ (χώρᾳ A) 𝔊: καὶ οἱ ἐν τῇ περιχώρῳ L.— [המלך] om. 𝔍𝔖L𝔊 (exc. 93b under *).— [מה עשו] *quantam putas eos exercere cædem* 𝔍: πῶς οἴει ἐχρήσαντο (κέχρηνται א ᶜ· ª A) 𝔊: κέχρηνται L: + καὶ εἶπεν ὁ βασιλεὺς πρὸς Ἐσθήρ 44.— [ומה ¹] om. ו 54 codd. K R, 𝔍𝔖.— ומה - end of v.] om. L (*cf.* 8² end).— [שאלתך] ἀξιοῖς + ἔτι 𝔊: *postulas* + *ultra* 𝔍.— [וינתן] 𝔖: καὶ ἔσται 𝔊: om. 𝔍.— [לך] om. 𝔍.— ומה² - end of v.] om. 𝔊 (exc. 93b under *).— [עוד] om. 𝔍𝔖.— [ותעש] *ut fieri jubeam* 𝔍: ܘܢܬܠ 𝔖.

13. om. 𝕷.— שׁוּב-[אִם] om. 𝕾 L: τῷ βασιλεῖ 𝕲: αὐτῷ 44: ἐὰν τῷ βασιλεῖ φανῇ 93b under *.— גם om. 𝕾 𝕲 L.— [אשר בשושן] om. 𝕾 𝕲 (exc. 93b under *): οὓς ἐὰν θέλωσιν L.— [לעשות] χρῆσθαι 𝕲: ἀνελεῖν L.— [כדת היום] ܐܦ ܒܡܚܪܐ 𝕾: ὡσαύτως 𝕲: καὶ διαρπάζειν L.— [את-העץ] om. L (cf. 8⁷ end).— [על העץ] om. 𝕲 (exc. א ᶜ·ᵃ, 93b under *).

14. om. 𝕷 106.— [ויאמר] καὶ ἐπέτρεψεν 𝕲: καὶ συνεχώρησεν L: ἐπέστρεψεν א *.— [המלך]—end of v.] om. L.— [המלך] om. 𝕲 (exc. 93b under *).— [להעשות] Niph. inf. here only in book. The Qal inf. is the regular construction.— [תנתן] καὶ ἐξέθηκε(ν) 𝕲.— [דת] τοῖς Ἰουδαίοις 𝕲: + τῇ τεσσαρεσκαιδεκάτῃ τοῦ Ἀδὰρ καὶ ἀπέκτειναν ἄνδρας τρισκοσίους 236.— [בשושן] τῆς πόλεως 𝕲: om. א *.— [ואת עשרת] τὰ σώματα 𝕲: om. א *.— [תלו] κρεμάσαι 𝕲: + על העץ K 147, 180; R 443, 𝕾, 249.

15. om. L 𝕷.— [היהודיים] היהודים Q.— [אשר] om. 𝕵 𝕲.— [¹בשושן] om. 71.— [גם ביום] om. 𝕲 (exc. 93b under *).— [ביום-איש] tr. aft. דת, v. ¹⁴, 236.— [לחדש] ܣܒܼܗ ܡܢ ܒܠܚܘܕ 𝕾: om. 𝕲 (exc. א ᶜ·ᵃ, 93b under *).— [אדר] om. 𝕾 *.— [²בשושן] om. 𝕲 (exc. א ᶜ·ᵃ ᵐᵍ, 93b under *): + οἱ Ἰουδαῖοι א ᶜ·ᵃ ᵐᵍ, 93b under ÷.— [ובבזה-ידם] καὶ οὐδὲν (οὐθὲν A) διήρπασαν 𝕲: καὶ οὐθὲν διήρπασεν 93b under ÷: + καὶ οὐκ ἐξέτειναν τὰς χεῖρας αὐτῶν εἰς διαρπαγήν 93b under *.

THE ORIGIN OF THE TWO DATES ON WHICH THE FEAST OF PURIM IS KEPT (9¹⁶⁻¹⁹).

16–17ᵃ. *Now the rest of the Jews that were in the King's provinces had assembled, and had stood for their life, and had rested from their enemies, and had slain among their foes* 75,000 *men* [𝕌¹ + of the house of Amalek], *without laying hands on the plunder, on the thirteenth day of the month of Adar* [Jos. 𝕌¹ + the slaughter took place] [𝕌¹ + among the descendants of Amalek;] [𝕌² + And the men whom the Jews killed in Susa were the enemies of Israel, who said to the house of Israel, Within a few days from now we will kill you and dash your children upon the ground.] This v. does not continue the narrative of v. ¹⁵, but is a supplementary statement in regard to the events of the thirteenth of Adar already related in vv. ²⁻⁵. Hence the tenses are properly rendered by the pluperfect. On the phraseology, *cf.* 8¹¹ ᶠ· 9⁵· ¹⁰· ¹⁵. The phrase *stood for their life* is mechanically repeated from 8¹¹, although, according to 8¹⁷ 9², they encountered little opposition. The new item, that 75,000 men were killed, contains an incredibly large number. 𝕲 changes it to 15,000 and L to 10,107. The clause,

19

and on the plunder they did not lay their hands, is not the conclusion of the sentence, as the Massoretic division of the verses suggests, but is a parenthetical remark separating the verbs of v. ¹⁶ from the adverbial clause at the beginning of v. ¹⁷, *on the thirteenth day of the month of Adar*. To this faulty verse-division are due the additions of Jos. 𝕋¹ AV. and RV.

17ᵇ. *And they rested on its fourteenth day.*] Not until the day after the fight could they have rest (*cf.* vv. ¹⁸·²¹·²²). Hence it is a mistake when Sieg., following the Massoretic division, translates, "On the thirteenth day of the month of Adar, then they found rest, and on the fourteenth."—*And they made it* [𝔍 + a solemn occasion that for all time to come they should keep as a day of feasts and] *a day of banqueting and joy.*] *Cf.* 8¹⁷.

18. *But the Jews that were* [𝔍 + making the slaughter] *in Susa* [𝕲 𝔍 + the fortress] *had assembled* [𝕋¹ + to cut off the children of Amalek] *on its thirteenth day and on its fourteenth day*], as already narrated in vv. ⁶·¹⁰·¹⁵. In contrast to the Jews of the provinces, who had only one day for slaughtering their enemies, those of Susa had two days, and therefore could not enjoy themselves until one day later than their brethren.—*And they rested on its fifteenth day, and made it a* [𝔍 + solemn] *day of banqueting and joy.*] *Cf.* 8¹⁷ 9¹⁷.

19. *Therefore the country Jews, that dwell in hamlets of the rural districts, keep the fourteenth day of the month of Adar as a joy, and a banquet, and a holiday, and a sending of dainties to one another.*] Here we find the reason for the foregoing stories of the different days of slaughter. In the author's time there was a diversity of practice, the country Jews keeping Purim on the fourteenth of Adar and the city Jews on the fifteenth. This he seeks to explain by the theory that the Jews of the provinces had only one day of vengeance, while those of Susa had two. On *banquet*, see 1³; on *holiday*, 8¹⁷; on *dainties*, 2⁹. This v. has all the value of a *tôrā*; it is not surprising, therefore, that in the Talmud it has become the basis of an elaborate halachic development. In addition to the celebration here recorded, *Meg.* 2a prescribes that the roll of Est. must be read in hamlets on the fourteenth of Adar, or on the preceding market-day that falls on the eleventh, twelfth, or thirteenth; but that it must not be read earlier than the eleventh or later than the fourteenth. This raises the question, What may legally be regarded as a hamlet? According to *Meg. 3b*, a town that was originally unwalled, but subsequently has been surrounded with a wall, is still to be regarded as a hamlet. A place with less than ten men whose whole time is devoted to prayer is also to be regarded as a hamlet (*cf.* 5*a*).—[𝕲 codd. + But those who dwell in the cities keep also the fifteenth of Adar as a joyous and good day by sending dainties to their neighbours.] This is exactly what we should expect, but do not find in the Heb. It is implied in v. ²¹, and once must have stood at this point in the text. Whether the reading of 𝕲 is a survival, or is a happy conjectural emendation, it is impossible to say. It did not stand in the text used by the doctors of the Talmud; but they felt the need of it, and supplied it by a process of casuistical reasoning (*Meg.* 2*a, Mishna;* 2*b, Gemara*). By *cities* the *Mishna* teaches we are to understand places that have been surrounded with a wall since the days of Joshua (*cf.* Dt. 3⁵). Other authorities hold that it means places that have been fortified since the days of Xerxes (2*b*). The rule of the *Mishna* gives rise to extended discussions over the question, which cities of Palestine were walled in the days of Joshua (*cf. Meg.* 5*b*).

16. om. 𝕷.—[אשר במדינות] 𝕵.—[ושאר] om. L.—[ושאר - מאיביהם] om. 𝕷.—[אשר במדינות] בכל [במדינות] 248.—om. 44, 106: οἱ ἐν τῇ βασιλείᾳ 𝕲: πᾶν ἐν τῇ βασιλείᾳ 248.—מדינות 15 codd. K R, 𝕵.—[המלך] om. 𝕲: Ἀρταξέρξου 71, 74, 76, 236.—[נקהלו] om. 𝕵.—[ועמד] καὶ ἑαυτοῖς ἐβοήθουν 𝕲: inf. abs. instead of finite vb., as throughout this v. and the next. A very common construction in this book (*cf.* Kau. § 113 *f.*).—[על נפשם] om. 𝕲 (exc. א ᶜ·ᵃ, 93*b* under *).—[ונוח] inf. abs. as vv. ¹⁷·¹⁸. The statement that they had rest from their enemies, although supported by all the Vrss., does not come in naturally before the statement that they slew their enemies, and v. ¹⁷ states that they did not rest until the fourteenth day. Accordingly, after the analogy of 8¹³, Bert., Reuss, G, Rys., Wild., Buhl, propose to read either וְהִנָּקֵם or וְנָקוֹם, 'and were avenged.' The reading ונוח has probably come in from the next v. Haupt deletes the whole phrase ונוח מאיביהם as a misplaced gloss.—[והרוג] ܣܚܠܟ 𝕾: ἀπώλεσαν γὰρ 𝕲: καὶ ἀπώλεσαν L.—[בשניהם] ܡܠ for ב 𝕾: αὐτῶν 𝕲: δυνάτων א *: om. L.—[חמשה ושבעים אלף] μυρίους πεντακισχιλίους 𝕲: μυριάδας ἑπτὰ καὶ ἑκατὸν ἄνδρας L.—[וכבזה - ירם] καὶ οὐδὲν διήρπασαν (א ᶜ·ᵃ ᵐᵍ, 93*b* under * = 𝕳): om. L A: Haupt deletes.

292 ESTHER

17-19. om. L 𝕷.— [בימם־בו] om. 71.— [ביום] om. יום 𝕾 𝕲.— [שלושה
τέσσαρες A.— [לחדש] ב for ל 𝕾: om. 𝕲.— [אדר] + *primus apud omnes interfectionis fuit* 𝕵: om. א *.— [ונוח] ܘܢܬܬܠܒ 𝕾: om. A: inf. abs. as in the
preceding v. So the Vrss. in general. 𝕿¹ takes as a noun and translates וניחה היה לישראל. Haupt deletes this and the following word.—
[בו ܣܡ ܒܚܡܝܢ 𝕾: τοῦ αὐτοῦ μηνός 𝕲.— [ועשו] Q in some codd. G,
𝕵 𝕾 𝕲.— [משתה] ἀναπαύσεως μετὰ χαρᾶς 𝕲: ἀναπαύσεως 71.— [ושמחה]
om. 71.

18. om. K 76, 107, 111, 𝕾 L 𝕷 106.— [והיהודיים] והיהודים Q: *hi* 𝕵.—
[נקהלו] *in cæde versati sunt* 𝕵.— [בשלושה עשר בו] om. 𝕲 (exc. א ᶜ·ᵃ ᵐᵍ, 93b
under *): + μηνὸς Ἀδάρ 93b under ÷.— [ובארבעה] – end of v.] om. 71.—
בו ²] om. 𝕲 (exc. א ᶜ·ᵃ ᵐᵍ, 93b under *): τοῦ Ἀδάρ 74, 76.— [ונוח] καὶ οὐκ
ἀνεπαύσαντο B 55, 74, 76: ἀνεπαύσαντο א * ᶜ·ᵇ A N 93b C: καὶ ἀνεπαύσαντο
other codd.— בו ³] om. 𝕲.— [ועשו] וְעָשֹׂה K 176, Q: *et idcirco constituerunt*
𝕵: ἦγον δὲ 𝕲.— [אתו יום] om. 𝕲: + *solemnem* 𝕵.— [משתה] μετὰ χαρᾶς 𝕲.

19. om. L 𝕷.— [על כן] *hi vero* 𝕵.— [הפרוזים] הפרזים Q: om. 𝕵: the K
is to be read הַפְּרוּזִים or הַפְּרוֹזִים, 'the separated'; the Q, הַפְּרָזִים, 'the
villagers.' The next clause הישבים בערי הפרזות is an exact translation
of הפרזים and is probably, therefore, an early explanatory gloss.— [הישבים
ܡܥܡܪܝܢ ܒܩܘܪܝܐ 𝕾: om. 𝕲 (exc. א ᶜ·ᵃ, 93b under *).— [בערי הפרזות]
𝕾: *in oppidis non muratis ac villis* 𝕵: ἐν πάσῃ χώρᾳ τῇ ἔξω 𝕲: towns of the
remote regions, *i.e.*, of the country, in contrast to עָרִים בְּצָרֹת 'walled
towns' (Dt. 3⁵).— [את יום] ב 𝕾: om. 𝕲 (exc. 93b under *).— [לחדש] om.
חדש 𝕾 𝕲 (exc. 93b under *).— [ומשתה] om. 𝕲 (exc. א ᶜ·ᵃ, 93b under *).—
[ומשלוח] ומשלח some codd. N¹.— [לרעהו] + οἱ δὲ κατοικοῦντες ἐν ταῖς μητροπόλεσιν καὶ τὴν πεντεκαιδεκάτην τοῦ Ἀδάρ (+ ἡμέραν א A) εὐφροσύνην
(-ης א A) ἀγαθὴν ἄγουσιν ἐξαποστέλλοντες μερίδας καὶ τοῖς πλησίον B א A N
52, 55, 64, 74, 76, 108a, 236, 248, C, Ald. (with slight variations in the
different codd.).

INSTITUTION OF THE FEAST OF PURIM (9²⁰⁻³²).

The section 9²⁰⁻³² bears evidences of having been derived from a
different source from the rest of the book; but it must have been
excerpted by the author himself, since all that goes before leads up
to it. The author probably found 9²⁰⁻³² in a Jewish history entitled
"the Book of the Chronicles of the Kings of Media and Persia"
(10²), and wrote 1¹–9¹⁹ to serve as a new introduction to this section. It thus became the vehicle of his own thought, although
borrowed from another writer, and may practically be treated as
an integral part of the book (see *Introduction*, § 24).

MORDECAI COMMANDS TO KEEP BOTH THE FOURTEENTH AND THE FIFTEENTH OF ADAR (9^{20-22}).

20. *And Mordecai wrote the following words*]. This is not an assertion that he wrote the Book of Est., or even the foregoing section 1^1–9^{19}, as the early critics commonly assume. The added clause, *and sent letters*, shows that the things written were the contents of these letters, as given in vv. $^{21-22}$. *Cf.* v. ^{29}, where this *second message* can only refer to what follows (see p. 61).—*And he sent letters unto all the Jews that were in all the provinces of King Xerxes, those near and those far*]. *Cf.* 8^9.

21. *To establish for them* [𝔍 + with solemn honour] [𝔊 L + these good days] [L + for hymns and joy instead of pain and grief,] *that they should continue to keep the fourteenth day of the month of Adar and its fifteenth day in every single year*]. This v. and the next give the contents of the letters. According to v. ^{19} the Jews of the author's region kept partly the fourteenth and partly the fifteenth of Adar in memory of their escape; but according to this passage, Mordecai enjoined upon all the Jews to keep both days. This points to a different author who reflects the custom of another region. V. ^{19} shows perhaps the custom of the Palestinian Jews; this v., the custom of the Eastern Jews. The editor intends the celebration of the two days to be understood in the light of v. ^{19}, but this does not lie naturally in the language.

22. *Like the days on which the Jews rested from their enemies*], *i.e.*, in each successive year they are to celebrate these days as they did at first at the time of their deliverance (vv. $^{17\,f.}$). The translation *as the days* of AV. and RV. is ambiguous.—*And the month* [𝔊 + that is Adar] *that was changed for them from sorrow to joy and from mourning to a holiday*]. Before *the month*, *like* is to be supplied from the preceding clause (*cf.* 8^{17} 9^1).—*To keep them as days of banqueting and joy and of sending dainties to one another*]. The construction begun in v. ^{21} is resumed after the long parenthetical clause in v. ^{22a}. The language is almost identical with that of v. ^{19}. The similarity of this v. to 8^{17} $9^{1.\,17-19}$ does not prove identity of authorship. The editor who excerpted it from the Chronicle of Media and Persia was familiar with its language and imitated it in the earlier part of the book, which he meant to serve as an introduction to it.—[𝕌¹ + and alms] *and gifts to the poor.*] This feature does not appear in the account of the first celebration of the day 9$^{17-19}$, although, according to v. ^{22a}, the feast was to be celebrated every year just as at the time of its institution.

20. [וישלח ספרים] *et litteris comprehensa misit* 𝕁: εἰς βιβλίον καὶ ἐξαπέστειλε(ν) L 𝕲 𝕃.—[את כל הדברים] K 244, R 486, 𝕁.—[כל] om. 𝕁 𝕲 𝕃 L.—[בכל] om. 𝕲 𝕃 L.—[מדינות המלך] τῇ βασιλείᾳ 𝕲 L 𝕃.—[אחשורוש] om. 𝕁: 'Ἀρταξέρξου 𝕲 𝕃: Ξέρξου 19, 108b: Haupt deletes.—[הקרובים וגו'] not found in 1¹–9¹⁹ (cf. Dn. 9⁷).—[לְקַיֵּם] *Pi.* inf. of קום. Found also in vv. $^{27. 29. 31. 32}$, but not in 1¹–9¹⁹ (cf. Ru. 4⁷ Ez. 13⁶ Ps. 119$^{28. 106}$). A late word.

21. [עליהם] om. 𝕲 L: *pro festis* 𝕁.—[להיות עשים] om. L: the periphrastic form expresses the continuity of the action.—[את יום] om. L 𝕃 𝕲 (exc. 93b under *): ב 𝕾.—[לחדש] om. 𝕾 L 𝕃 𝕲 (exc. א $^{c. a mg}$, 93b under *).—[אדר] om. 𝕾 A L: τοῦ 'Ἀγάρ א *.—[יום] om. 𝕾 𝕃 L 𝕲 (exc. 93b under *).—[בכל-ושנה] om. 𝕲 𝕃 L: ܘܐܙܠ 𝕾.—[בו] om. 𝕲 𝕃 L: ܘܫܒܥܐ 𝕾.—[חמשה עשר] ܡܢ ܗܕܐ ܡܠܐ 𝕾: *revertente semper anno* 𝕁.

22. [כימים-ושמחה] om. L.—[כימים] βιμεις K 158, R 378, 11: ἐν γὰρ ταύταις ταῖς ἡμέραις 𝕲: *in diebus* 𝕁.—[אשר] om. 𝕲 (exc. א $^{c. a}$ A).—[נהו] *erraverunt* 𝕃.—[בהם] om. 𝕲 (exc. א $^{c. a mg}$, 93b under *): *et servati sunt* 𝕃.—[והחדש] om. החדש 𝕁: om. ו 𝕾: *secundum mensem* 𝕃.—[אשר] om. 𝕁.—[נהפך] *scriptus est* 𝕃: ἐγράφη א A.—[להם] om. 𝕾: + ὃς ἦν 'Ἀδάρ 𝕲 (93b under ÷, A om.).—[מיגון] not found in 1¹–9¹⁹.—[מיגון - טוב] om. א 93b.—[ומאבל - טוב] om. 106, 249.—[אותם] ὅλον ἀγαθὰς 𝕲: αὑτας A: ὅλας ἀγαθὰς 44, 106: ὁ λαὸς ἀγαθὰς 76: ὅλον εἰς ἀγαθὰς 68, 243, C, Ald.—[משתה] γάμων 𝕲 𝕃.—[ושמחה] om. שמחה 106.—[ומשלח ומשלוח] var.—: ἐξαποστέλλοντας 𝕲: καὶ ἀπέστειλε L: *mittere* 𝕃.—[מנות] *dona et partes* 𝕃.—[איש] *sacerdotibus* 𝕃: om. L.—[לרעהו] τοῖς φίλοις 𝕲: *et amicis* 𝕃: om. L.—[ומתנות] om. L 𝕃 𝕲 (exc. 93b under *).—[לאבינים] + *et orphanis et viduis* 𝕃.

THE JEWS AGREE TO OBEY THE INJUNCTION OF MORDECAI (9$^{23-28}$).

23. *And* [𝕌¹ + all] *the Jews made customary* [𝕁 + as a solemn rite] [𝕌¹ + for themselves in equal measure] *that which they had begun to do*], i.e., they agreed to keep every year the days that they had just celebrated.—*And that which Mordecai had written unto them*], as just related in vv. $^{20-22}$. The editor does not notice that what the Jews have begun to do 9$^{17-19}$ does not correspond with what Mordecai commands in 9$^{20-22}$. The Jews have continued to keep these days down to the present time, and they have added a number of rites to those prescribed in 9[19-22]. The most important of these is the reading of the Roll of Est. on the feast days. To the discussion of the proper performance of this ceremony the Talmudic tractate *Mᵉghillā* is mainly devoted. The roll must be read in unwalled towns on the eleventh, twelfth, thirteenth, or fourteenth of Adar; in walled towns, on the fifteenth. All Israelites, including women, must listen to it. It may be read in any language that is known to the people, and in Heb. and Gr., even when these are not understood (*Meg.* 18a). According to *Meg.* 7b there is no difference between the observance of the day of Purim and the Sabbath, except that on the former the preparation of food is allowed. According to *Meg.* 6b, if the Roll has been read in the first Adar, and a second Adar is intercalated, the Roll must be read again in the intercalary month. For the further development of the feast in post-Talmudic times, see Malter, Art. "Purim," in *Jewish Encycl.*

Verses [24-25] contain a brief duplicate account of Haman's conspiracy that varies in some respects from the account given in the earlier part of the book. Here the King has no knowledge of Haman's plans; but when they are brought to his attention, he commands to punish Haman. There is also no mention of Esther's part in averting the mischief. These facts favour the view suggested above that vv. [20-32] are derived by the author from an independent document.

24. *For Haman, son of Hammᵉdāthā, the Agagite, the enemy of all the Jews*]. See on 3[1, 10].—*Had devised (plans) against the Jews to annihilate them*]. See on 8[3]. *To annihilate them*, which is not found in the parallel vv. 8[3] 9[25], may have been copied by mistake from the end of this v.; so Sieg.; Haupt deletes the word at the end of the v.—*And he cast pur, that is, the lot, to discomfit them and to destroy them.*] See on 3[7].

> [𝔗² + And when men saw Haman and his sons hanging many days upon the gallows, they said, Why does Esther transgress the command of Scripture not to leave a corpse on the gallows? Esther answered and said to them, Because King Saul killed the Gibeonite proselytes, his sons were hanged on the gallows from the beginning of barley-harvest until

[the rain fell upon them, that was six months; and when the Israelites went up to appear before the Sanctuary, the heathen said to them, Why are these hanging there? The Israelites answered and said to them, Because their father laid hands upon the Gibeonite proselytes and slew them. How much more then ought the wicked Haman and his sons to hang forever on the gallows, since he wished to destroy the Israelites at one time.]

25. *And when it came before the King*]. 𝔊 reads, *and when he came before the King*. The f. suffix translated *it* is understood by 𝖏 𝕾 𝕿¹ 𝕿² and many modern comm. of Esther, but this is unnatural, since she is not mentioned in the context (9¹³ is the last occurrence of her name). This suffix, accordingly, must be taken as neuter referring to the conspiracy of Haman just mentioned (so Bert., Keil, Oet., Wild., Sieg., Stre.). The nonmention of Esther in this passage is additional evidence of its literary independence.—*He said in connection with the writing* [𝕿² + *that they should blot out the memory of the house of Amalek from beneath the heavens*]. This is commonly supposed to mean, *he commanded in writing*, but the expression is peculiar and does not occur elsewhere. In 7⁹ no mention is made of an edict when Haman was sentenced. 𝔊 reads, *saying to hang Mordecai*. 𝖏, Meg. 17a, 𝕿², read *she said*, and 𝕿² refers the *writing* to the command in Ex. 17¹⁴⁻¹⁶. The text is apparently corrupt (see note). —*Let his wicked plan which he has devised against the Jews return upon his own head*]. Cf. 8³ 1 K. 2³³ Ob. ¹⁵ Ps. 7¹⁷ ⁽¹⁶⁾. A different account of the transaction and of the reason for the King's sentence is given in 7⁸ ᶠ. This is a further evidence of the literary independence of this section.—*And let them hang him and his sons upon the gallows*.] According to 7¹⁰, Haman was hanged alone; and according to 9¹⁴, his sons were not hanged until after the massacre of the 13th of Adar. Here the hanging of the father and the sons seems to take place at the same time.

26. *Therefore they called the days Purim because of the name of the pur*.] Here, for the first time, we find the reason for the insertion of the remark about *pur* meaning *the lot* in 3⁷ 9²⁴. It is to furnish an etymology for *Purim*, the well-known name of the feast. On the real origin of this name, see *Introduction*, § 28. *There-*

fore]. The predicate which belongs to this is found at the beginning of v. ²⁷. Between the two stands the long parenthetical clause ²⁶ᵇ. The Vrss. have not understood the construction and consequently have supplied various predicates after the conjunction (see note). *Because of all the words of this message,* [𝕵 + that is, the things that are written in this book,] [𝕿¹ + in order that they might be heard by all the people of the house of Israel and that they might know]. *This message* 𝕵 𝕿¹ 𝕿² and many comm. understand of the Book of Est., but it is evidently the same as the *letter* mentioned in v. ²⁰, which is certainly not this book (see on v. ²⁰).—*And because of what they had seen in this respect* [𝕿¹ + in regard to the observance of Purim]. *Seen* is used in the sense of *experienced,* as in Ex. 10⁶.—*And because of what* [𝕿¹ + was done among them that was wonderful for Mordecai and Esther, and that they might know the deliverance which] *had come unto them*]. The last two clauses are a duplicate to the narrative of 8¹–9¹⁸.

27. *The Jews established* [𝕿¹ + the statute] *and made it customary for themselves*]. A continuation of the sentence begun with *therefore* in v. ²⁶. The statement is a duplicate to 9¹⁹.—*And for their descendants and for all who should join themselves to them* [𝕿¹ + as proselytes]. The addition of 𝕿¹ gives the true sense. Those who *join themselves* are the same as those who *become Jews* in 8¹⁷. Here, as there, the allusion is an evidence of the late date of the book.—*That it might not be repealed*], like the unchangeable laws of the Medes and Persians (1¹⁹).—*To continue to keep these two days in accordance with the letter that prescribed them and in accordance with the time set for them*], lit. *according to their writing and according to their time.* The possessive pronouns refer to *days.* The *writing* is the same as the *letters* of v. ²⁰ and the *message* of v. ²⁶. The *time* is that set by Mordecai in v. ²¹.—[𝕿¹ + By reading the Roll in Hebrew characters in their synagogues upon the eleventh, twelfth, thirteenth, and fourteenth days in villages, and in towns of the provinces, and in cities] *in every single year*]. The language imitates that of the letter in v. ²¹.

28. *And that these days might be remembered and be kept* [𝕿¹ + as a feast] *in every single generation and every single family* [𝕿¹ + of the priests and Levites] *and* [𝕿¹ + of all the house of Israel that abode in] *every single province and* [𝔊¹ + that abode in] *every single city*]. The language is similar to that of 1²² 3¹² 8⁹, but *generation* and *family* have not been used before in the book. On *kept*, *cf.* v. ²¹.—*That these days of Purim might not be repealed by the Jewish community*], lit. *might not pass over from the midst of the Jews.* See on 1¹⁹ 8⁸.—*And that the memory of them might not cease among their descendants* [𝔍 + who are bound to keep these ceremonies] [Jos.²⁹⁴ + And, since they were about to be destroyed by Haman on these days, and on them escaped the danger and took vengeance on their enemies, that they might do well by celebrating them and giving thanks to God].

23–25. Haupt deletes as a gloss on the ground that Purim is derived from a Pers. word meaning 'portions,' and that, therefore, v. ²⁶, which describes the giving of this name, should follow immediately after v. ²², in which the sending of 'portions' is mentioned. Both the etymology of Purim and the proposed emendation are extremely doubtful (see p. 79). —וקבל[וקבלו 29 codd. K R, 𝔊¹ 𝔊² 𝔍 𝔖 𝔊 𝔏 L, Oort, Haupt: sg. because preceding the subject (Kau. § 145 *g*, *o*). Perf. with ְו instead of impf. with ו consec., in accordance with late usage (Driver, *Tenses*, § 133). There is no certain case of this construction in 1¹–9¹⁹ (*cf.* 3¹²), but it is common in 9²⁰⁻³² (*cf.* 9²⁴· ²⁵· ²⁷). It is an evidence, therefore, of the literary independence of this section. קבל in the late sense of 'make traditional' is found only in this section (*cf.* v. ²⁷). In 4⁴ it means 'receive.'—[היהודים] + ܒܚܟܡܬ 𝔖: + *in solemnem ritum* 𝔍.—[לעשות את׳] om. L 𝔊 (exc. 93*b* under *): *et posuerunt in commemoratione* 𝔏.—ואת – end of v. ²⁵] om. L.—[מרדכי] om. 𝔏.—[אליהם עליהם 19 codd. K, 26 codd. R: om. K 236, 𝔖.

24. om. L 𝔏.—[כי] πῶς 𝔊: ὅπως א A: περὶ 44, 106: ܡܚܓܠ 𝔖.—[המדתא ᾽Αμαδάθου 𝔊: ᾽Αμαγάθουν א *: ᾽Αμαθάδου A: + ὁ Ἐβουγαῖος א c. a mg: ܐܓܓܝ 𝔖ᴬᵁ: ܐܓܓܝ 𝔖ᴸ: om. 44, 71, 106.—[האגגי ܐܓܓܝ 𝔖: (ὁ) Μακεδῶν 𝔊: Γωγαῖος 93*b*: om. 44, 71, 108*a*.—[צרר כל היהודים] om. 𝔊.—[צרר + *et adversarius* 𝔍.—[כל] om. K 95, 170, R 266, 547, 𝔍.—[חשב] ἐπολέμει 𝔊: ὃς ἐπολέμει 44, 106: πολέμει 108*a*.—[על היהודים] αὐτούς 𝔊: αὐτοῖς 74, 76, 249, Ald.: τοὺς Ἰουδαίους A 93*b*: + *malum* 𝔍.—[לאבדם] om. 𝔊.—והפיל [והפל N¹ C: καθὼς ἔθετο 𝔊: καὶ ὡς ἔθετο א c. a A 93*b*: וְהִפֵּל is pf. with ו connective, as in 9²³.—והפל – v. ²⁵ [ראשו] om. 106.—[פור] *phur* 𝔍: ܦܘܪ 𝔖: ψήφισμα 𝔊: om. 71.—[הוא הגורל] *quod nostra lingua vertitur in sortem* 𝔍: καὶ κλῆρον 𝔊: καὶ ἔβαλε(ν) φοῦρ ὅ ἐστιν κλῆρος א c. a, 93*b* under *.—[להמם] om. 𝔍. *Qal* inf. with sf. 3 pl. Not used in 1¹–9¹⁹. A play in sound upon the name Haman (Cas., Schu.).—[ולאבדם] om. 𝔍 𝔊.

25. om. L 𝔏.—[הספר – ובבאה] om. 71.—[וּבְבֹאָהּ so Oc.: וּבְבֹאָה (*Raphe*)

THE FEAST OF PURIM 299

Or. (Ginsburg): *et postea ingressa est Esther* 𝔍: ܘܡܢ ܒܬܪܟܢ ܥܠܬ ܐܣܬܝܪ 𝔖: καὶ ὡς εἰσῆλθεν 𝔊.— [אמר עם הספר] *obsecrans ut conatus ejus litteris regis irriti fierent* 𝔍: ܫܐܠ ܗܘܐ ܐܓܪܬܐ 𝔖: λέγων κρεμάσαι τὸν Μαρδοχαῖον 𝔊 (93*b* under ÷): 𝔘¹ omits עם הספר: Haupt translates 'in spite of the letter,' and regards as a tertiary gloss.—[וישוב] ܘܢܬܗܦܟ 𝔖: ἐγένοντο 𝔊: ἐγένετο A.— [אשר חשב] 𝔖. ראשו tr. aft. [אשר–היהודים] 𝔊 𝔍. om. [מחשבתו] ܥܘܫܒܗ 𝔖: ὅσα δὲ ἐπεχείρησεν ἐπάξαι 𝔊 (πράξαι 71, ἐπάγαγεν 93*b*).—על [ראשו] ܥܠ ܪܫܗ 𝔖: καὶ ἐκρεμάσθη αὐτὸς 𝔊.— [ותלו אתו] ἐπ᾿ αὐτὸν 𝔊.—[על העץ] om. 𝔊 (exc. א ᶜ·ᵃ· ᶜ·ᵇ A N, 93*b* under *).

26. om. 𝔏 71.—[לימים האלה] om. A.—[פורים] *phurim* 𝔍: ܦܘܪܝܐ 𝔖: Φρουραὶ 𝔊: Φρουρὶμ א ᶜ·ᵃ·: Φουρδαῖα L (Φουρμαῖα 19, 108*b*, Φουρδία 93*a*): Φουρουρεὶμ 93*b*: Φρουρὶν 249: Φουρὶμ C: Φρουρέας (Φρουραίους) Jos. xi. § 295.—[על שם] *id est* 𝔍: διὰ 𝔊 L.—[הפור] *sortium* 𝔍: ܦܨܐ 𝔖: τοὺς κλήρους 𝔊 L: τοὺς καιροὺς N.—על כן— end of v.] Haupt deletes as a gloss.— [על כן] *eo quod* 𝔍: ὅτι 𝔊: τοὺς πεσόντας L: om. 𝔖 106: + *phur id est sors in urnam missa fuerint* 𝔍: + τῇ (+ ἰδίᾳ 249) διαλέκτῳ αὐτῶν καλοῦνται Φρουραὶ (Φοὺρ 93*b*: all under ÷ 93*b*) 𝔊.—על ³— end of v. 27] om. L.—[על] *et* 𝔍: διὰ 𝔊: καὶ διὰ 93*b*.—[כל] om. 𝔖 𝔊.—[דברי] *quæ gesta sunt* 𝔍: om. 108*a*. — [האגרת] *epistolæ* + *id est libri hujus volumine continentur* 𝔍: τῆς ἐπιστολῆς 𝔊: As. *egirtu*, Gr. ἄγγαρος, is a late loan-word synonymous with ספרים in v. ²⁰. See Nöldeke, *ZDMG*. xl. 733; Meyer, *Entstehung d. Judenthums*, p. 22.—[ומה] ܡܟܝܠ ܗܟܢܐ 𝔖: - end of v. om. 44, 106.—[ראו] *sustinuerunt* 𝔍: πεπόνθασιν 𝔊.—[על ככה] διὰ ταῦτα (ταύτην: αὐτήν) 𝔊: om. 𝔍 𝔖: lit. 'upon thus.' Here only a prp. is used before ככה. *Cf.* 8⁶.— [ומה] ²ܡܟܝܠ ܗܟܢܐ 𝔖.—[הגיע אליהם] *deinceps immutata sunt* 𝔍.

27. om. L 𝔏.—[קימו] καὶ ἔστησε(ν) 𝔊: ἔστησαν N: ἔστησε μνημόσυνον 74, 76, 236: om. 𝔖 𝔍: see 9²¹. Haupt reads וקימו in immediate connection with הפור.—[קימו–יעבור] om. 44, 71, 106.—[וקבל] וקבלו Q, K*thîbh in many codd. N¹ 𝔘¹ 𝔘² 𝔍 𝔖 𝔊. The Q*rê is meant to be read וְקַבֵּל. *Pi.* inf. abs., as so often in this book instead of the finite vb. The K*thîbh substitutes the finite vb. Haupt deletes as a gloss to the preceding vb.— [כל] om. 𝔊 (exc. 93*b* under *).—[הנלוים] sg. 𝔖.—[ולא] 𝔖.—[על] 𝔖.—[יעבור] ἄλλως χρήσονται 𝔊: the sg. is difficult, since it has no subject. Either with 𝔘¹ we must supply חק before it, or we must read יעברו, in which case the meaning will be, 'that they might not transgress.' Haupt reads לא יעברו and transposes to the end of the v. after וישנה.—[להיות]-end of v.] om. 𝔊 (exc. 93*b* under *).—[ככתבם] *cf.* 1²² 3¹². ¹⁴ 4⁸ 8⁸· ⁹· ¹³.—[וכזמנם] ܨܒܝܢܗܘܢ 𝔖.— [ושנה] om. 𝔖.

28. om. 44, 106.—[והימים] εἰς τὰς ἡμέρας L: *et diei* 𝔏.—[האלה] om. 𝔏.— [נזכרים] μνημόσυνον 𝔊: μνημοσύναι A: εἰς μνημόσυνον L: *mentionem fecit* 𝔏: the ptc. is dependent upon היות in the preceding v.—[ונעשים]-end of v. ³²] om. L.—[ונעשים] om. 𝔏: ἐπιτελούμενον 𝔊: ἐπιτελουμέναι A.—[בכל] om. כל 𝔊 𝔏.—[דור ודור] om. 𝔖: *progeniam* 𝔏.—[משפחה ומשפחה] om. 𝔍: ܘܫܪܒܬܐ 𝔖: καὶ πατριὰν 𝔊 𝔏.—[וכדינה] om. 𝔍 𝔖 𝔏.—[ועיר] om. 𝔍 𝔊 𝔏.

—28b Haupt deletes as a late explanatory gloss.—וימי] *indicens* 𝔏.—
הפורים] τῶν Φρουραί 𝔊: τῶν Φρουρῶν ℵ *: τοῦ Φρουραί A: τῶν Φουρουρείμ
93b: τῶν Φρουρίν 249: *vigilias* 𝔏: *phurim* 𝔍: ڡصڅا 𝔖.—האלה] *id est
sortium* 𝔍: om. 𝔏.—לא יעברו] *nec non observentur* 𝔍: ἀχθήσονται 𝔊: *quas
celebrareni* 𝔏.—מתוך היהורים] *a Judæis* 𝔍: εἰς τὸν ἅπαντα χρόνον 𝔊𝔏.—
וזרעם] .מן with construed only here [יסוף .𝔍 .om [וזכרם לא יסוף *ab
eorum progenie* 𝔍: ἐκ τῶν γενεῶν 𝔊: *de progenie* 𝔏.

ESTHER AND MORDECAI WRITE A SECOND LETTER CONCERNING PURIM (9$^{29-32}$).

On the origin of this section and its relation to 9$^{20-28}$, see *Introduction*, § 24.

29. [*Meg.* 7a + Esther sent to the wise, saying, Establish for the future a festival in my honour. They sent back word to her, Thou wilt arouse hatred against us among the heathen (similarly JT. *Meg.* 1^1).] *Then wrote Esther the Queen, the daughter of 'Ăbîḥayil, and Mordecai the Jew* [𝔗^1 + all this Roll] *with all power*]. *Wrote* is f. sg., so that the following words *and Mordecai the Jew* are possibly a gloss derived from v. ^{31} (see note). According to v. ^{31}, Esther writes to confirm the words of Mordecai; it is not natural, therefore, that he should take part in this letter. Esther's purpose is to add the weight of her authority to that of the grand vizier in securing the observance of Purim. On *'Ăbîḥayil*, see 2^{15}. *With all power*, Keil and Sieg. understand to mean *with all emphasis*. Others think that it means *with all the authority of her position.*—*To establish the following second message concerning Purim,* [𝔗^2 + that if there were a year with an intercalated month, they should not read the Roll in the first Adar, but should read it in the second Adar.] The expression *this message*, like *these words*, in v. ^{20}, does not refer to the foregoing, but to the following narrative. Just as the substance of Mordecai's letter is given in vv. $^{21\,f.}$, so that of Esther's letter is given in v. ^{31}. On Purim, see *Introduction*, § 28.

30. *And* [*she*] *sent letters unto all the Jews*]. As remarked above, probably Esther alone writes to confirm Mordecai's previous letter; consequently, instead of the m. sg. *he sent* at the beginning of this v., we must read *she sent*, or else with 𝔍𝔖 read the pl. Possibly the accidental insertion of the m. form at this point has induced the interpolation of the words *and Mordecai the Jew* in the preceding v.—*Unto 127 provinces, the kingdom of Xerxes*]. See on $1^1 8^9$. —(*Containing*) *friendly and faithful words*], lit. *words of peace and truth;* in apposition with *letters* in the preceding clause. These letters began with the usual Oriental expressions of good will, and added the assurance that Esther would remain a faithful Jewess.

31. *To establish these days of Purim* [𝕌¹ + in the second Adar] *at their appointed time* [𝕌¹ + of intercalation]. Here we get the contents of the *second letter* mentioned in v. ²⁹. 𝕌¹ rightly feels that it is superfluous after 9^{20-28}, and therefore makes the above interpolations to give Esther something new to write about (*cf.* 𝕌² on v. ²⁹).—*As Mordecai the Jew had established for them and Esther the Queen*]. The allusion is evidently to the previous letter of Mordecai vv. ²⁰⁻²². Esther's purpose in writing is solely to back up Mordecai's letter with her authority, and to keep the Jews from forgetting the feast of Purim. The vb. is sg., although two subjects follow, and in v. ²⁰ Mordecai alone writes. It looks, therefore, as if the words *and Esther the Queen* were an interpolation from v. ²⁹.—*And as they* [𝕌¹ + the Jews] *had established for themselves and for their descendants*], as narrated in vv. ²³⁻²⁸.—[𝕌¹ + to remember] *the matters of the fastings and of their cry of distress.*] These have been mentioned in 4^3 as occurring at the time when Haman's edict went out; but Mordecai's letter 9^{20-22} contains no express mention of them, nor do the Jews agree to do so in 9^{23-28}. Probably the author's idea is, that the words of Mordecai's letter 9^{22}, "like the days on which the Jews rested from their enemies, and the month that was changed for them from sorrow to joy, and from mourning to a holiday," mean to say that the Jews are to keep the days of Purim every year just as they did the first year, that is both with fasting and with feasting. This the Jews agree to do in 9^{27}. From this passage it does not appear which day of Adar was to be kept as a fast. The later Jews fixed it on the 13th, the day that Haman appointed for their destruction, under the name of "Esther's Fast."

32. *So the command of Esther established these matters of Purim and it was committed to writing* [𝕌¹ + by the hand of Mordecai in the Roll.] 𝔍𝔗[1], *Meg.*, Jewish comm. in general, and many Christian comm. understand the phrase *it was committed to writing* of the writing of the Book of Est. Pisc., Jun. and Trem., Grot., Raw., *al.* understand it of the Persian annals (*cf.* 2[23] 6[1] 10[2]); Mal., Osi., Vat., of the Jewish annals; Bert., Keil, Oet., Wild., Sieg., Stre., of a special document used by the author of Est. All of these views labour under two difficulties, (1) that *write in the book* in Heb. idiom means no more than *commit to writing* (*cf.* Ex. 17[14] Nu. 5[23] Jb. 19[23]). There is no need, therefore, to see in the expression *the book* any reference to a well-known work. (2) The abandonment of the construction with *Waw* consec. shows that the establishing of the matters of Purim and the writing are not subsequent to the events just narrated, but are coincident with them. This v. is merely a summing up of what has just been told in vv. [29-30]. The statement that *the commandment of Esther established these matters of Purim* is not something new, but is a reference to the enactment recorded in v. [31] (note the identity of phraseology). The committing to writing is the same that is recorded in v. [29]. The same word *book* is used of Esther's letter in v. [30].

29-32. Haupt deletes as a gloss.

29. om. L.— [ויכתב] so 𝔐 (with large ר); some codd. with ordinary ת. The large initial letter possibly suggests that the text is suspicious. The f. sg. agreeing with the nearest subject is possible, even if another subject follows, but is less usual than the pl. and suggests that ומרדכי היהודי may be a gloss. Haupt reads ותכתב אסתר המלכה את כל תקף מרדכי היהודי. — [אביחיל] 'Ἀμιναδάβ 𝔊: 'Ἀμιναδάν א: om. 𝔏.— [היהודי] om. 71, 74, 76, 106, 236, 𝔏.— [את כל תקף] τό τε στερέωμα 𝔊: τότε εἰς μνημόσυνον 44, 106: ܚܝܠܐ ܣܓܝܐܐ 𝔖: *omni studio* 𝔍: *firmamentum* 𝔏: הִקֶף is an Aram. word that occurs only here and 10[2] and Dn. 11[17]. את in the sense of 'with' is unnatural in this connection, we should expect ב. This leads Haupt to make the transposition indicated above.— [לקים] *ut sanciretur* 𝔍.— ܘܠܡܫܕܪ 𝔖: ὅσα ἐποίησαν 𝔊: *fecit* 𝔏: *cf.* 9[21. 27. 32].— [אגרת] *cf.* 9[26].— [הפרים] *dies solemnis* 𝔍: ܦܘܨܕܝܐ 𝔖: τῶν Φρουραί 𝔊 (Φρουρῶν א *: Φρουρίμ א c. b: Φρουραία A: Φουρουρείμ 93*b*): *custodientium* 𝔏.— [הזאת השנית] om. 𝔊𝔏: om. השנית 𝔖: + *in posterum* 𝔍.

30. om. L 𝔏 𝔊.— [וישלח] pl. 𝔍𝔖.— [הספרים] om. 𝔍.— [מלכות] *regis* 𝔍: ܘܥܒܕܬ ܡܠܟܘܬܐ 𝔖: Haupt reads במלכות.— [שלום ואמת] tr. 𝔖.

31. om. L 𝔏 106.— [לקים] some late editions לקיים.— [לקים - בזמניהם] om. 𝔊.— [הפרים] *sortium* 𝔍.— [האלה] *cum gaudio* 𝔍.— [קים] pl. 𝔍 𝔖: καὶ ἔστησαν 𝔊 (93*b* under ÷: om. to קימו 71).— [עליהם] ἑαυτοῖς καθ' ἑαυτῶν 𝔊 (ἑαυτούς 74, 76, 236: 93*b* under ÷): not to be referred to זמניהם (Wild.), but to the Jews (*cf.* v. ²¹).—[היהודי om. 𝔊.—[וכאשר קימו om. ו 𝔖: καὶ τότε στήσαντες 𝔊 (93*b* under ÷): om. 74, 76, 236: καὶ τότε ἔστησαν 249.—על נפשם] κατὰ τῆς ὑγ(ι)είας (τὴν νηστείαν C) (ἐ)αυτῶν 𝔊 (93*b* under ÷): τὰ περὶ τῆς βουλῆς 71: τὰ περὶ τῆς ὑγ(ι)είας 74, 76, 236.—[ועל זרעם] καὶ τὴν βουλὴν (ἑ)αυτῶν 𝔊: καὶ ὑγείας αὐτῶν 71: καὶ τῆς βουλῆς αὐτῶν 74, 76, 236: om. 93*b*.—[דברי] ܒܢܝܡܝܢ 𝔖: om. 𝔍 𝔊.—[הצומות] ܣܘܡܐ ܗ̈ܢܘܢ 𝔖: om. 𝔊.—[וזעקתם] + *et sortium dies* 𝔍: om. 𝔊.

32. om. L 𝕷 71, 106.—[ומאמר] καὶ λόγῳ: λόγῳ א * A: *qui vocatur* 𝔍.—[קים – האלה] קים + ܠܗ 𝔖: *et omnia quæ libri hujus* 𝔍: ἔστησεν (+ αὐτά 74, 76) εἰς τὸν αἰῶνα 𝔊.—[ונכתב בספר] *historia continentur* 𝔍: καὶ ἐγράφη εἰς μνημόσυνον 𝔊: + literal version of v. 30 אמת to end of v. 32, 93*b* under *.

APPENDIX TO THE BOOK

THE SUBSEQUENT HISTORY OF MORDECAI (10¹⁻³).

1. *Then King Xerxes imposed tribute upon the mainland and upon the islands of the sea.* [𝔘² + But when King Xerxes knew Esther's race and her descent, he treated them like free men in the world, and made the peoples of all races and kingdoms serve them.] The object of this *tribute* is not stated. Raw. and others conjecture that it was to recoup himself for his unsuccessful war with Greece. The wide extent of his kingdom, including the *islands* (or *coastlands*) of the Mediterranean, is evidence that this monarch is Xerxes the Great (see *Introduction*, § 22). From 9²⁰ to 9³² the author has been quoting an older document. He continues here, as though he were about to give an extended account of Xerxes' reign, but stops abruptly at the end of this v. and contents himself with a reference to the Book of the Chronicles, from which he has derived these items.

2. *But all his powerful activity and his might*], lit. *all the work of his power and his might.* The *might* of a king is the record of his famous deeds (1 K. 15²³ and often).—*And the exact account of the greatness of Mordecai with which the King magnified him* [𝕷 + in his kingdom]. The same expression is used of the glorification of Haman 3¹ 5¹¹. Mordecai was so great that his deeds, as well as those of the King, were recorded in the Chronicle.—*Are they not written in the Book of the Chronicles of the Kings of Media and*

Persia?] This is the regular formula with which the authors of Kings and Chronicles refer to their authorities (1 K. 11^{41} 14$^{19, 29}$, *etc.*; 2 Ch. 25^{26} 28^{26} 32^{32}, *etc.*). This is supposed by many to be the same as the royal diary mentioned in 2^{23} 6^1. In that case the citation is a fraud on the part of the author of Est. designed to imitate the ancient histories and to give authority to his work, since it is inconceivable that the royal annals of Persia were accessible to him, or that they contained an account of the greatness of Mordecai. It is not clear, however, that these Chronicles are the same as the royal diaries. In 2^{23} we read of "the book of the acts of the days before the King," and in 6^1 of "the book of the memorable things of the acts of the days." This is evidently the private diary of King Xerxes; but here we read of "the book of the acts of the days of the kings of Media and Persia," which seems to be a history of the Medo-Persian Kings. The Books of the Chronicles, to which the authors of Kings and Chronicles refer, are not royal annals, but are late historical compilations, accessible to everybody, in which fuller information might be found concerning the kings. So here the author is probably thinking of some Jewish history, like the Book of the Chronicles of the Kings of Judah and Israel used by the Chronicler, that gave from the Jewish point of view the traditional history of the kings of Media and Persia. From this work apparently the passage 9^{20}–10^1 has been extracted (see *Introduction*, § 24). Media is here placed first because the Median monarchy preceded the Persian. In 1$^{3, 14, 19}$ Persia is placed first, because in the time of Xerxes it held the hegemony in the dual kingdom.

3. *For Mordecai the Jew was next in rank to King Xerxes*]. This is the reason why so much is said about him in the Book of the Chronicles. He was grand vizier, the real ruler of the Persian empire (*cf.* 8$^{2, 9, 15}$ 9$^{3 f.}$ 2 Ch. 28^7 Tob. 1^{22}).—[𝕿^1 𝕿^2 + Treasurer and elder of the Jews, chief over all the peoples; and from one end of the world to the other there was obedience to him and honour. And all kings feared before him, and they trembled before him as before the King. Mordecai himself was like the morning-star among the stars, and like the dawn going forth in the morning.] *And he was great in the esteem of the Jews and liked by the multi-*

APPENDIX TO THE BOOK

tude of his brethren, [*Meg.* 16*b* + but not by all his brethren, for a part of the Sanhedrin turned away from him (RaShI + because, when he became great, he neglected the study of the Law).] The expression does not mean, as *Meg.*, Ramb., think, that there was a minority that was not pleased with Mordecai. *The multitude of his brethren* is parallel to *the Jews* in the last clause and means all his fellow Israelites (*cf.* 5[11]). In spite of his exaltation Mordecai was envied by no one.—*Seeking the welfare of his people, and caring for the peace of all his race* [Jos. [296] + Enjoying at the same time the fellowship of the Queen, so that by means of them the affairs of the Jews were prosperous beyond all expectation. This, then, was the way in which things happened to them in the reign of Artaxerxes.] This gives the reason why Mordecai was so beloved by all the Jews. In his high position he did not forget his kinsmen, but constantly laboured for their good. Thus the book closes with a pleasant picture of the happiness and prosperity of the Jews under the beneficent rule of their coreligionist.

1. om. 𝔏: Haupt regards as a misplaced gloss to 2[18].— וייזם] ἔγραψεν δὲ 𝔊: ἔγραψεν γὰρ A: καὶ ἔγραψεν L: *fecit* 𝔍.— אחשרש] so Oc.: אחשורוש Q Oc.: אחשורוש K*ethîbh* Or. N[1] S C: om. 𝔊 L (exc. א [c. a mg inf], 93*b* under *): see Ba. This spelling, which occurs here only in the book, is nearer to the original Pers. *Khshayarsha* than the usual spelling.— םס] a word of unknown origin, meaning in early Heb. 'forced labour.' Here, as in New Heb., it means 'tribute': *tributarias* 𝔍: τέλη א A 93*b* (under *): τὰ τέλη L: om. 𝔊. — על] *omnem* 𝔍: + ܟܠܗ̇ 𝔖: ἐπὶ τὴν βασιλείαν 𝔊 (τὴν βασιλείαν under ÷ 93*b*): ἐπὶ τὴν βασιλείαν αὐτοῦ 44: om. L.— ואיי] + *cunctas* 𝔍: om. איי 𝔊 L.

2. וכל-וגבורתו] om. 𝔏: Haupt transposes after the following clause.— כל מעשה] pl. 𝔖: om. 𝔊 L.— תקפו] τὴν ἰσχὺν αὐτοῦ 𝔊 L: *cf.* 9[29].— ופרשת גדלת] ܘܡܚܘܐ καὶ (τὴν) ἀνδραγαθίαν (+ αὐτοῦ 44, 106) 𝔊: om. L.— ܕܨܒܘܬܗ 𝔖: πλοῦτόν τε καὶ δόξαν L 𝔊 (93*b* under ÷): *et annuntiata est gloria* 𝔏.— מרדכי] τῆς βασιλείας αὐτοῦ 𝔊: καὶ Μαρδοχαῖος L: *Mardochæi* 𝔏.— אשר-המלך] om. 𝔊 (exc. 93*b* under *): ἐδόξασε L: Haupt deletes as a scribal expansion.— הלוא הם] om. 𝔍: καὶ L: הם 𝔖: ἰδοὺ (+ ταῦτα * 93*b*) 𝔊: *sicut* 𝔏.— כתובים] ܟܬܒ 𝔖: γέγραπται 𝔊: ἔγραψεν L.— ספר] *libris* 𝔍: τοῖς βιβλίοις L.— דברי הימים] om. L 𝔏 𝔍 𝔊 (exc. 93*b* under *).— למלכי] *regis* 𝔏: om. 𝔍 L 64, 71, 74, 76, 93*a*, 106, 236, 243, 248, 249, C, Ald. — ופרס] + εἰς μνημόσυνον 𝔊 L (93*b* under ÷): om. 𝔏.

3. היהודי] om. 𝔊 L 𝔏 (exc. א [c. a mg], 93*b* under *).— משנה] + ܗܘ 𝔖: διεδέχετο 𝔊 L: *suscipiebat* 𝔏.— למלך] τὸν βασιλέα 𝔊 𝔏 L: the usual expression is Haupt deletes.— אחשורוש] Ἀρταξέρξην 𝔊: Ξέρξην L: + *in die illa* 𝔏: ונדול] + סה 𝔖: + ἦν 𝔊 𝔏 L.— ליהודים] ἐν τῇ βασιλείᾳ 𝔊 L 𝔏: ܠ for ל 𝔖: Haupt reads ביהודים.— אחיו – ורצוי] om. 𝔖.— ורצוי] καὶ δεδοξασμένος 𝔊: καὶ φιλούμενος L: *et magnificatus* 𝔏.— לרב אחיו] ὑπὸ τῶν Ἰουδαίων (Βασιλέων 71) καὶ φ.λούμενος 𝔊 (om. καὶ φιλ. 44, 106, 249): ὑπὸ πάντων τῶν Ἰουδαίων L: *a Judæis et ex ducatu* 𝔏.— דרש] (δι)ηγεῖτο 𝔊: καὶ ἡγεῖτο L: *præerat* 𝔏.— טוב] τὴν ἀγωγὴν 𝔊: om. L 𝔏.— לעמו – שלום] om. 𝔊 𝔏: αὐτῶν καὶ δόξαν περιετίθει L.— דבר שלום] 'care for the welfare' (*cf.* Zc. 9¹⁰ Ps. 85⁹).— וזרעו] τῷ ἔθνει αὐτοῦ 𝔊 L 𝔏: not 'his posterity,' but parallel to לעמו, as Is. 61⁹.

ADDITION F.

THE INTERPRETATION OF MORDECAI'S DREAM AND CLOSING SUBSCRIPTION.

After 10³ 𝔊 𝔏 L append the following passage, F¹⁻¹¹ (= Vulg. and Eng. Ad. Est. 10⁴–11¹). On the origin and antiquity of the passage, see *Introduction*, §§ 13, 20. For the Gr. text and variants, see Paton in *HM*. ii. pp. 50–51.

¹Then Mordecai said, These things have come from God. ²For I remember the dream which I saw concerning these matters, for nothing of them has failed. ³As for the little fountain that became a river, and there was light, and the sun, and much water, the river is Esther, whom the King married, and made Queen: ⁴and the two dragons are I and Haman: ⁵and the nations are those that were assembled to destroy the name of the Jews: ⁶and my nation, this is Israel, which cried to God and were saved: and the Lord saved his people, and the Lord delivered us from all these evils, and God wrought signs and great wonders, which have not been done among the nations. ⁷Therefore he made two lots, one for the people of God, and another for all the nations. ⁸And these two lots came at the hour, and time, and day of judgment before God (for his people) and against all the nations. ⁹So God remembered his people, and justified his inheritance. ¹⁰Therefore these days shall be kept by them in the month of Adar, on the fourteenth and fifteenth days of the month, with an assembly, and joy, and with gladness before God, throughout the generations for ever among his people Israel.

¹¹In the fourth year of the reign of Ptolemy and Cleopatra, Dositheus, who said that he was a priest and Levite, and Ptolemy his son, brought the foregoing letter concerning Purim (Phrourai), which they said was genuine, and that Lysimachus, son of Ptolemy, one of the people in Jerusalem, had interpreted it.

INDEXES.

INDEXES.

I. INDEX OF HEBREW WORDS.

אֲבַגְתָא, 67.
אָבַד, 59.
אַבֵּד, 207.
אִבְרָן, 62, 272.
אֲבִיחַיִל, 185, 302.
אֶבְיֹנִים, 59.
אֵבֶל, 59.
אֲנִי, 69.
אִגֶּרֶת, 59, 299.
אֲדַלְיָא, 70.
אַדְסָתָא, 68.
אָדָר, 59.
אהב, 59.
אוֹרָה, 62, 281.
אָח, 59.
אחד, 59.
אָחוּז, 144.
אֲחַשְׁדַּרְפְּנִים, 65, 212, 277.
אֲחַשְׁוֵרוֹשׁ, 131, 305.
אֲחַשְׁרֵשׁ, 305.
אֲחַשְׁתְּרָנִים, 65, 273, 277.
אֹיֵב, 59.
אִיִּים, 59.
אֵל, 166, 223.
אִלּוּ, 62, 261.
אִם טוֹב, 59.
אָמַר, 181.
אָמַר לְ, 59, 62.
אֱמֶת, 59.

אָנַס, 62, 147.
אַסְפְּתָא, 70.
אֶסְתֵּר, 69.
אֶפְרֶן, 144.
אַרְגְּמָן, 144.
אֲרִידַי, 71.
אֲרִידָתָא, 71.
אֲרִיסַי, 71.
אֲשֶׁר = 'so that,' 285; = 'that,' 278; = 'when,' 284.
אֲשֶׁר הִגִּיעַ, 284.
אֵת with undefined noun, 166; = 'with,' 302.
אֵת כֹּל, 181.

בְּ of instrument, 251; of essence, 260.
בָּאָה, 181.
בְּאָמְרָם, 159, 199.
בִּנְתָא, 67.
בִּגְתָן, 69.
בהט, 145.
בָּהַל, 62, 177.
בְּהֵרָאֹתוֹ, 135.
בּוּץ, 62, 144.
בִּזָּה, 59, 62.
בַּז, 59.
בִּזָּיוֹן, 62, 159.

בִּזְתָא, 67.
בִּירָה, 59, 62, 134.
בֵּית הַמֶּלֶךְ, 224.
בִּיתָן, 62, 144.
בָּכֵן, 229.
בעת, 62.
בַּקָּשָׁה, 59, 62.
בִּקֵּשׁ עַל, 62, 219.

גָּדוֹל, 285.
גְּדוּלָה, 59.
גְּדוּלָתוֹ, 135.
גָּדַל, 195.
גּוֹרָל, 59.
גָּלִיל, 62, 145.
גְּלוּי, 213.
גְּנָזִים, 63, 65, 207.

דָּבָר טוֹב עַל, 267.
דְּבַר שָׁלוֹם, 306.
דּוֹר, 59.
דָּחַף, 63, 256.
דְּחוּפִים, 213.
דִּין, 154.
דַּלְפוֹן, 70.
דָּר, 145.
דָּרַשׁ, 59.
דָּת, 65, 146, 154.
דָּתוֹ, 233.

INDEX

הַבָּזוֹת, 62.
הֲגָא, 69.
הֱגֵי, 69.
הָגִיד, 199.
הִגִּיעַ, 225, 260.
הֹדוּ, 132.
הַמְדְּתָא, 69.
הַמֶּלֶךְ, 132.
הָמַס, 60.
הָמָן, 69.
הֲנָחָה, 63, 186.
הֶעֱבִיר, 268.
הָעֲשׂוּת, 289.
הִפִּיל פּוּר, 59.
הָפַךְ, 59.
הַצָּלָה, 63.
הֵצֶר, 262.
הָרַג, 59.
הַשְׁקוֹת, 146.
הַשְׁתִיָּה, 146.
הָתַךְ, 70.

וּבְבֹאָהּ, 299.
וּבְזֹה, 180.
וְהִפֵּל, 298.
וְהַקָּרֵב, 154.
וַיְהִי, 120, 131.
וַיִּזְעַק, 71.
וָנוֹחַ, 291, 292.
וְשָׁתִי, 66.
וְהִכָּתֵב, 302.
וְהֵעָשׂ, 237.

זֶה, 224.
זוּעַ, 63, 242.
זָכַר, 60.
זְמָן, 60.
זֶרַע, 59, 306.
חֶרֶשׁ, 243.
יֶתֶר, 68.

חוּל, 63.
חוּר, 63, 144.
חלל, 59.
חֵמָה, 59.
חָפוּ, 267.
חָפֵץ, 59.
חֲצִי הַמַּלְכוּת, 59.
חָצֵר, 223.
חַרְבוֹנָא, 67.
חָרַשׁ, 59.
חָשַׁב, 59.
חָתַם, 59.

טַבַּעַת, 59.
טוּף, 59.

יָגוֹן, 60, 294.
יָד, 59.
יָרַע, 59.
יַחַד, 63.
יוֹם טוֹב, 59, 63, 281.
יוֹשִׁיט, 223.
יֵ... מִן, 63, 253.
יֶטַב בְּעֵינֵי, 59, 177.
יַיִן, 59.
יָכֹל, 59.
יְמִינִי, 172.
יִסַּד עַל, 147.
יַעֲבוֹר, 159, 299.
יָצָא, 59.
יָעַץ, 216.
יָקָר, 59, 63, 135.
יָשַׁב, 192.
יָשַׁט, 63.
יִשְׁנוֹ, 207.

כְּ with inf., 242.
כָּבַשׁ, 266.
כְּרִי, 159.
כָּטוֹב, 151.

כִּי, concessive, 160.
כָּנַס, 63.
כִּסֵּא מַלְכוּת, 63.
כִּסֵּא מַמְלַכְתּוֹ, 63.
פַּרְפַּס, 65, 68, 144.
פַּרְשָׁנָא, 68.
כֶּשֶׁבֶת, 133.
כָּשֵׁר, 63, 271.
כָּתַב, 59.
כֶּתֶר, 63, 151.

לְ, with inf., 59, 159, 162, 177, 219, 246, 251; emphatic, 266; with passive, 243.
לֵב, 59.
לְבַד, 223.
לָבִיא, 181.
לָבַת, 171.
לְהָבִיא, 159.
לְהַנִּיחָם, 207.
לָוָה, 60.
לְעֵת, 224.
לָקַח, 59.
לָרַבִּים, 215.
לָשׁוֹן, 59.
לָתֵת לָהּ, 177.

מַאֲמַר, 59, 63.
מַגֶּרֶת, 192.
מַגִּיעַ, 215.
מְדִינָה, 59, 63, 133.
מָה, 235.
מָה רָאוּ, 60, 63.
מָהוּפָן, 67.
מָהַר, 235, 252.
מוֹלֶדֶת, 59.
מְחֻשֶּׁבֶת, 59.
מִי יוֹדֵעַ, 224.

INDEX

מְלָא, 59.
מִלְאוּ, 262.
מְלָאכָה, 60.
מְלֵה, 59.
מַלְקָה, 59.
מַלְכוּת, 59, 63, 143, 146, 159, 233.
קְמוֹכָן, 69.
מָן, 224.
מָנוֹת, 59.
מַס, 60, 186, 305.
מַעֲשֶׂה, 60.
מָצָא, 59, 271.
מָצָא חֵן, 63, 177.
מָצָא חֶסֶד, 177.
מָקוֹם, 59, 215.
מֶקֶץ, 180.
מָרְדֳּכַי, 172.
מָרוּק, 180.
מֶרֶס, 68.
מַרְסְנָא, 68.
מַשְׂאֵת, 186.
מִשְׁלוֹחַ, 59.
מִשְׁנֶה לַמֶּלֶךְ, 60, 306.
מִשְׁפָּחָה, 60.
מִשְׁתֶּה, 59.
מִתְיַהֲדִים, 282.
מַתָּנָה, 60.

נְבוּכַדְנֶאצַּר, 172.
נִבְעַת, 262.
נֶגֶד, 59.
נִגְזַר, 166.
נָגַע, 59.
נוּחַ, 59, 63.
נֶזֶק, 63, 261.
נֶחְתּוֹם, 272.
נֶחְתָּם, 212.
נָכֹה כ', 285.

נִמְצָאִים, 143.
נָפַל, 59.
נָפַל, 266.
נֶפֶשׁ, 59.
נָשָׂא חֵן, 63, 177.
נָשָׂא חֶסֶד, 177.
נִשְׂאֵת, 185.
נִשְׁלוֹחַ, 212.
נָתוּן, 251.
נָתַן, 59.
נִתַּן, 251.

סוּס, 59.
סוּף, 60, 300.
סוּר, 59.
סֹחֶרֶת, 146.
סִינָן, 277.
סֵפֶר, 59, 162.
סָרִיס, 59.

עָבַר, 59.
עוֹבֵר אֶת מִצְוֹת, 199.
עֶבֶר, 59.
עוֹנָה, 158.
עֹמֶרֶת, 281.
עִיר, 59.
עַל, 159, 207, 219, 272.
עַל כָּכָה, 60, 63, 299.
עַל כִּסֵּא מַלְכוּתוֹ, 133.
עַם, 59.
עַם הָאָרֶץ, 281.
עַם מָרְדֳּכַי, 202.
עָמַד, 63, 224.
עָמַד עַל, 63.
עִם הַסֵּפֶר, 299.
עֵץ, 59.
עָשָׂה, 59.
עֹשֵׂי הַמְּלָאכָה, 207.
עֵת, 243.

פּוּר, 77-93, 202.
פּוּרָה, 78, 83.
פּוּרִים, 60, 299 f., 302.
פּוּרְתָא, 70.
פָּתָה, 59.
פַּחוֹת, 212.
פִּילַנְשִׁים, 181.
פָּרוּזִים, 292.
פַּרְמַשְׁתָּא, 71.
פָּרָס, 159.
פַּרְשֶׁגֶן, 65, 212.
פָּרָשָׁה, 63.
פַּרְשַׁנְדָּתָא, 70.
פַּרְתְּמִים, 65, 135.
פִּתְגָם, 65, 160.
פִּתְשֶׁגֶן, 65, 212.

צָהַל, 281.
צָוָה, 59.
צוֹם, 59, 63.
צַר, 261.
צָרִים, 278.
צָרַר, 59.

קִבֵּל, 59, 218, 298.
קָבַץ, 59.
קָם, 60, 294.
קָם עַל, 147.
קָם, 242.
קָרָא, 59.
קָרָה, 271.
קְרוּבִים, 294.

רָאָה, 59.
רָאָה בְּ, 271.
רָאוּיוֹת, 63, 177.
רְאִיָּה, 185.
רְאִיוֹת, 177.
רֹאשׁ, 59.
רִאשֹׁנָה, 154.

312   INDEX

רַב, 59.	שַׂק וָאֵפֶר, 63, 215.	שַׁעַר, 59.
רֹב, 59.	שַׂר, 59.	שַׁעֲשֻׁעַי, 69.
רֹב בָּנָיו, 243.	שָׂרַר, 162.	שַׁרְבִיט, 63, 223, 271.
רֶוַח, 224.		שֵׁשׁ, 62 f., 145.
רָכַב, 59.	שְׁאֵלָה, 59.	שְׂחִיָּה, 63.
רֶגֶשׁ, 277.	שֵׂיָה, 63, 163, 261.	שָׁתַר, 68.
רַקִּים, 278.	שֶׁכָּךְ, 165.	
רַע, 59.	שְׁכֵכָה, 267.	תַּאֲמַרְנָה, 159.
רָצִים, 59.	שָׁלַח יָד, 272.	תָּכְלֵת, 144.
רִצְפַת, 145.	שֶׁלֶט, 63, 285.	תַּכְרִיךְ, 63, 281.
	שָׁמַר, 59.	תַּמְרוּק, 166.
שָׂבָר, 63, 284.	שֶׁמֶן הַמֹּר, 180.	תִּפְאָרֶת, 135.
שִׂים, 59.	שֵׁמַע, 285.	הֵקֶף, 60, 63, 302.
שִׂמְחָה, 281.	שָׁנָה, 63, 177.	חֶרֶשׂ, 69.
שִׂחָה, 59.	שֵׁנִי, 181.	תַּרְשִׁישׁ, 68.
שִׂגָּא, 59.	שֵׁנִית, 192.	תִּהְחַלְחֵל, 218.

II. INDEX OF AUTHORS AND BOOKS.

AARON IBN SARGADO, 105.
Abayob, 110.
Aben Ezra, see Ibn Ezra.
Abenmelech, 110.
'*Abhoda Zara*, 287.
Abulwalid ibn Ganaḥ, 105.
Ackermann, 113.
Adamus, 110.
Adeney, xiii, 117.
'*Ādhath Dᵉbhārîm*, 2.
Aeschimann, 113.
Aeschylus, 64, 129, 196.
Ahikar, Story of, 75.
Alber, 117.
Albrecht, 158, 223.
Aldine edition, xi, 33.
Alexander-Romance, 67.
Alḳabeẓ, 18, 20, 24, 41, 101, 110.
Almosnino, 110.
Alsheikh, 110.
Amama, 109.
American Journal of Semitic Languages, xiii.
Anan b. David, 104.
Ananikian, viii.
André, xiii, 43, 46, 104.
Andreae, 212.

Antoninus, 35.
Antwerp Polyglot, 19.
Apocrypha, vii, 33.
Apostolic Canons, 5.
Aquila, 29, 34.
Aquine, d', 105.
Arabian Nights, 65, 76, 180.
Arama, 110.
Arnaud, 117.
Arrian, 52, 123.
Asher, 139.
Ashkenazi, 110, 118, 164.
Asolanus, 33.
Assemani, 4, 6, 8.
Aster, 52.
Athanasius, 4, 101.
Athenæus, 92, 129, 140, 142.
Athias, 12.
Aucher, 112.
Augusti, 113, 116.
Augustine, 5, 60, 101.
Authorized Version, xi.
Avesta, 72, 165.

BABA BATHRA, 119.
Babylonian Talmud, xi, 2, 20, 98 f., 101, see *Mᵉghillā*.

INDEX

Bacher, 104.
Baer, xi, 9, 12, 135, 143, 172, 181, 284.
Ball, 46.
Bamberger, 106.
Barnes, 17.
Barrett, xiii, 116, 187.
Basel Polyglot, 18.
Basila, 7.
Baudissin, xiii, 115.
Bauer, xiii, 113.
Baumgarten, xiii, 53, 113, 125, 128-130, 134, 161, 183, 195, 201, 220.
Bawli, 118.
Beck, 114.
Bede, 53.
Bellamy, 116.
Bellarmin, xiii, 53.
Benary, 71.
Ben Asher, 9, 12-15, 145, 195, 219, 233.
Ben Bezalel, 110.
Ben David, 104.
Benfey, 69-71.
Ben Hayyim, 11-13.
Ben Hayyim Gaon, 14.
Benjamin of Tudela, 139.
Ben Naphtali, 9, 14 *f.*, 145, 195, 219, 233.
Benson, 116.
Benter, 108.
Ben Uphran, 232.
Berger, 40.
Berliner, 106.
Bernstein, 116.
Berossus, 92 *f.*
Bertheau, xiii, 43, 57, 116, 120, 127, 132, 150, 156, 162, 169, 176 *f.*, 181, 183, 185 *f.*, 196, 202, 206, 209, 213, 223 *f.*, 233, 243, 256, 260-262, 291, 296, 302.
Bertholdt, 113.
Bevan, 54.
Bezold, 54, 137.
Biblia Magna Commentariorum, 109.
Biblia Maxima, 109.
Biblia Sacra Vulgata cum plur. interp., 111.
Biblical World, xiii.
Billerbeck, 134.
Birch, 126.
Bissell, xiii, 8, 43, 46.
Blau, 273.
Bleek, 77, 113.
Bloch, 57, 63, 113 *f.*

Blunt, 116.
Böttcher, xiii, 162.
Bohlen, von, 123.
Bomberg, 11.
Bomberg Bible, 1516-17, xi.
Bomberg Bible, 1526, xi, 18, 22.
Bonart, xiii, 53, 109, 130, 164, 174, 176, 183, 186, 196 *f.*, 226, 262, 274.
Boothroyd, 116.
Boysen, 116.
Breithaupt, 103, 105.
Brent, 108.
Brescia Edition, xi, 10.
Brisson, 124, 148, 150, 195.
Brockelmann, 207.
Brown, Driver, Briggs, *Heb.-Eng. Lexicon*, xiii, 144 *f.*, 159 *f.*, 181, 207, 212, 224, 251, 266, 284.
Brugsch, 145.
Bruns, 112.
Buber, 103 *f.*
Buchholz, 124.
Buckley, 116.
Buhl, 127, 135, 145, 162, 181, 202, 224, 261, 291.
Bullinger, 95, 235.
Bunsen, 57.
Burder, 116.
Burmann, 110.
Buxtorf, xiii, 13, 284.

CAHEN, 118.
Cajetan, xiii, 53, 108 *f.*, 186, 197, 248.
Calmberg, 116.
Calmet, xiii, 111.
Calovius, xiii, 110.
Calvin, xiii, 108.
Canney, 145 *f.*
Canons of Carthage, 5, 42.
Canons of Laodicea, 4.
Canons of Trent, 42.
Capellus, 53.
Carpzov, xiii, 53, 112.
Carthusianus, 108.
Caspi, 107.
Cassel, xiii, 22 *f.*, 116, 125, 133, 158, 176, 188, 298.
Cassiodorus, 4.
Castalio, 108 *f.*
Celædeiis, 56, 109.
Ceriani, 17.
Chais, 111.
Chandler, 112.
Chavannes, 115.

Cheyne, xiii, 67, 77, 113 *f.*, 133, 144.
Chipiez, 121.
Chrysostom, 37.
Clarke, 110, 116.
Clay, 89.
Clement of Alexandria, 60, 101.
Clericus, xiii, 53, 111, 128, 130, 133, 142, 161, 164, 167 *f.*, 178, 187, 190, 209, 248, 261.
Codex Alexandrinus, xi, 5, 32.
Codex Ambrosianus, xi, 16.
Codex Basiliano-Vaticanus, xi, 4, 32.
Codex Claromontanus, 4.
Codex Complutensis, 40.
Codex Corbeiensis, 40 *f.*
Codex Frederico-Augustanus, 32.
Codex Oratorius, 40 *f.*
Codex Pechianus, xi, 40 *f.*
Codex Petropolitanus, 6.
Codex Sinaiticus, xi, 5, 31 *f.*
Codex Vallicellanus, 40.
Codex Vaticanus, xi, 4, 31.
Complutensian Polyglot, xi, 10; its Greek text, 33.
Condamin, 267.
Cooper, 108.
Cordthwaite, 116.
Cornelius Nepos, 220.
Cornely, 114, 117.
Cornill, xiii, 17, 92.
Corrodi, 112.
Coste, 121.
Couzio, 109.
Cramer, 113.
Critici Sacri, xiii, 109.
Crommius, 109.
Crusius, 112.
Ctesias, 69, 71, 190, 136.
Cumming, 95, 117, 235.
Curtius, 129, 138, 196, 255, 264.
Curzon, 134.
Cyril of Jerusalem, 4.

DALMAN, 8.
Damasius, 24.
Dathe, 116, 187.
David, 22, 24.
Davidson, xiii, 113, 116.
Deane, 46.
Delitzsch, xiii, 91, 134 *f.*, 144, 146.
Derenbourg, 6, 80.
Deutsch, 6.
Dialogue of Timothy and Aquilla, 4.
Diestel, xiii.
Dieu, de, 108 *f.*

Dieulafoy, 65, 126, 134, 136 *f.*, 161, 165, 173, 188, 231, 248, 261.
Dijserinck, 45.
Dillmann, xiii.
Dio Chrysostom, 92.
Diodati, 108.
Diodorus Siculus, 77, 190, 192.
Dodd, 116.
D'Oyley, 116.
Dozy, 145.
Driver, xiii, 38, 115, 281, 298.
Drusius, xiii, 53, 108 *f.*, 125, 136, 150, 152, 164, 185 *f.*, 190, 196, 261 *f.*
Dukes, 15.
Duncker, 123.
Duran, 110.
Dutch Annotations, 108.

EBEDJESU, 4.
Eckard, 112.
Ehrenpreis, 118.
Eichhorn, xiii, 53, 112, 130.
Eliezer b. Hyrcanus, 102.
Eliezer b. Judah of Worms, 106.
Eliezer, Rabbi, 232.
Elijah hag-Gaon, 118.
Ellicott, 114.
Encyclopædia Biblica, xiii, 136, 206.
Encyclopædia Britannica, xiii.
Epiphanius, 4, 101.
Erbt, 52, 60, 75 *f.*, 78, 80–82, 88, 193.
Erman, 126.
Escobar et Mendoza, 109.
Estius, xiii, 109, 168 *f.*, 284.
Eusebius, 4, 34 *f.*, 52, 98, 101.
Ewald, xiii, 113, 181, 202.
Expositor, xiii.
Expository Times, xiii.
Eybeschütz, 118.

FERNS, 109.
Ferrand, 51.
Feuardentius, 109.
Field, 32, 35, 37.
Fihrist, 76.
Fillion, 117.
Firdausí, 76, 136.
First Targum, xi, 18–21, 101.
Fiske, 114.
Flandin, 121.
Fränkel, 43.
Frankfurter, 107.
Frazer, 87, 92.
Frensdorff, 13.

INDEX

Fritzsche, xiii, 8, 37 f., 43, 45, 276.
Fryar, 131.
Fürst, 45, 85, 118.
Fuller, 8, 43, 46.

GALLIKO, 110.
Gaster, 104.
Geiger, 113, 124.
Geiger-Kuhn, 121, 148.
Gelbhaus, 23.
Gemara, xiii, 99 f., see *Talmud, Babylonian Talmud*.
Genebrard, 52, 161, 100.
Geneva Version, 109.
Gersonides, 107.
Gesenius, xiii, 70 f., 132, 261, 277.
Gildemeister, 212.
Gill, 116.
Ginsburg, 3, 6, 9, 11 f., 13, 138, 172, 219, 272, 299.
Gladden, 114 f.
Goeje, de, 76.
Göttingsche Gelehrte Anzeigen, xiii.
Göttingsche Gelehrte Nachrichten, xiii.
Goldschmidt, 100.
Gordon, 53.
Grabe, 32.
Grätz, 63, 83, 113.
Gray, 116.
Greek Version, xi, 24, 29-47.
Grotius, 108 f., 155 f., 161, 169, 176, 182, 187, 197, 284, 302.
Grüneisen, 87.
Grünthal, 17.
Gunkel, 87, 90.
Gute, 112.

HÄVERNICK, xiii, 113, 128, 183.
Halévy, 78, 115.
Haley, 116, 196.
Hall, 116.
Hamburger, 113.
Hamel, du, 111.
Hammer, von, 85.
Haræus, 109.
Harkavy, 6.
Harper, vi, xiii, 117.
Hastings' Dictionary of the Bible, xiii, 145, 188, 206
Haug, 277.
Haupt, 46 f., 54, 68, 70, 79, 81 f., 86, 88, 92, 94, 115, 127, 135, 144 f., 147, 153 f., 156, 158-163, 166, 171, 176 f., 179-181, 185-188, 191-195, 199, 202, 207, 212 f., 215, 219, 224, 242 f., 246, 251, 260-262, 266 f., 272, 274, 277 f., 282, 291, 295, 298 f., 302, 305.
Hause, 114.
Haweis, 116.
Haye, de la, 109.
Heidenheim, 13.
Heilbronn, 110.
Helmolt, 134.
Hengstenberg, 45.
Henry, xiii, 110.
Herbst, 52, 113.
Herodotus, xiii, 54, 64.
—— i, 99, 220.
—— i, 106, 200.
—— i, 126, 142.
—— i, 133, 128, 236.
—— i, 134, 195.
—— i, 136, 238.
—— i, 192, 206.
—— iii, 31, 153, 158.
—— iii, 67, 185.
—— iii, 69, 178, 221.
—— iii, 72, 20.
—— iii, 77, 220.
—— iii, 79, 200.
—— iii, 84, 72, 153, 165, 220.
—— iii, 89, 72, 123.
—— iii, 94-106, 123.
—— iii, 95 f., 129, 205.
—— iii, 97, 123.
—— iii, 118, 153, 220.
—— iii, 125, 287.
—— iii, 128, 201.
—— iii, 129, 267.
—— iii, 138, 245.
—— iii, 140, 220, 245.
—— iv, 44, 123.
—— v, 11, 245.
—— v, 14, 160.
—— v, 18, 150.
—— v, 53 f., 137.
—— vi, 30, 287.
—— vii-ix, 121.
—— vii, 4, 126.
—— vii, 8, 128.
—— vii, 9, 123.
—— vii, 27, 129.
—— vii, 28, 206.
—— vii, 65, 69 f., 123.
—— vii, 70, 123.
—— vii, 100, 192.
—— vii, 114, 71.
—— vii, 136, 197.
—— vii, 151, 137.
—— vii, 187, 121.

INDEX

Herodotus, vii, 238, 287.
—— viii, 85, 192, 245.
—— viii, 90, 192.
—— viii, 98, 160.
—— viii, 99, 214.
—— viii, 105, 148.
—— ix, 24, 214.
—— ix, 32, 69.
—— ix, 80 f., 129, 140.
—— ix, 82, 139 f.
—— ix, 107, 245.
—— ix, 109, 233.
—— ix, 110, 150, 240.
—— ix, 112, 71.
Herxheimer, 117.
Herzfeld, 113.
Hess, 112.
Hesychius, xi, 31, 36.
Heumann, 112.
Hewlett, xiii, 116.
Hexapla, 34.
Heyse, 24.
Hezelius, 186.
Hilary, 4, 101.
Hillesum, 118.
Hilprecht, 133.
Hirsch, 115.
Hitzig, 84, 113, 162 f., 243.
Hoffmann, 93.
Holmes and Parsons, xiii, 35–37.
Holzmann, 113.
Hommel, 87, 91, 114.
Hooght, van der, vi, 12.
Horace, 142.
Horowitz, 104, 114.
Horsley, 111.
Houbigant, 111.
Hübsch, 106, 118.
Hughes, 116.
Hugo of St. Victor, 56, 107.
Hummelauer, 117.
Hunter, 114.
Huntley, 53.
Hurwitz, 14.

Ibn Ezra, xiii, 11, 20, 52, 106 f., 128, 161, 164, 169, 196, 248, 261, 284, 286.
Ibn Ganaḥ, 105.
Ibn Melech, xiii, 110, 261.
Ibn Sargado, 105.
Ibn Yaḥya, 110.
Immanuel b. Solomon b. Jukuthiel, 106.
Isaac ben Eleazar, 15.
Isaiah b. Elijah di Trani, 107.

Isiodorus, 5.
Isserles, 56, 118.

Jablonski, 12.
Jackson, 108.
Jacob, 30, 40, 133.
Jahn, 46 f., 113, 134, 146, 187, 262.
Jahrbücher für protestantische Theologie, xiii.
Jamieson, 116.
Jampel, 115, 134.
Jastrow, 137.
Jehring, 95, 235.
Jekuthiel the Punctuator, 13.
Jellinek, 8, 43, 103, 106.
Jensen, 67, 69 f., 75, 87, 89, 91–93, 215.
Jeremiah, Rabbi, 232.
Jerome, xiii, 5, 10, 24–28, 33 f., 36 f., 41 f., 53.
Jerusalem Talmud, xi, 99, 101.
Jewish Encyclopædia, xiii.
Jewish Quarterly Review, xiii.
Johanan, 174.
John of Damascus, 4.
Johns, 78, 88, 93.
Joseph b. Goryon, 102.
Josephus, xi, xiii, 8, 37, 39, 42, 44, 53, 60, 61, 78, 80, 83, 98, 100, 102, 124, 134, 150, 153, 164.
Josephus Gorionides, 102.
Journal Asiatique, xiii.
Journal of the American Oriental Society, xiii.
Journal of Biblical Literature, xiii.
Journal of the Roy. Asiat. Soc., 137.
Judah Löw b. Bezalel, 110.
Judah the Prince, 99.
Jüdisches Litteraturblatt, xiii.
Junilius, 5.
Junius and Tremellius, xiv, 53, 64, 101, 108 f., 127 f., 136, 141, 161, 181, 196 f., 248, 256, 261, 302.
Justi, 53, 66–70, 121, 124.

Kahle, 16.
Kamphausen, xiv, 57, 116, 127, 169, 196.
Ḳara, 106.
Kaulen, 42, 114.
Kautzsch, xiv, 8, 46, 114, 143, 156, 159, 166, 177, 181, 192, 212, 215, 216, 219, 224, 242 f., 251, 257, 260–262, 266, 272, 291.
Keerl, 45.
Keil, 113, 116, 120, 128, 131, 139,

INDEX

150, 156, 161, 169, 176 f., 182 f., 186 f., 196, 200, 206, 209, 213, 221, 224, 260 f., 282, 296, 300, 302.
Keilinschriften u. das A. T., xiv, 145.
Keilinschriftliche Bibliothek, xiv.
Kelle, 113.
Kennicott, xi, 6 f., 9, 111.
Kerner, 108.
Ḳimḥi, 135.
Kirkpatrick, 114.
Kittel, 12.
Kleinert, 113.
Kleist, von, 82.
Knabenbauer, 117.
Knudtson, 132.
Köhler, 113, 116.
König, ixv, 46, 82, 114, 181, 207.
Kohlreif, 52.
Kohn, 118.
Kohut, 104.
Kosters, 115.
Kraft, 6.
Krauss, 224.
Kuenen, xiv, 30, 76, 82, 197.
Kuhn, 124.

LAGARDE, xiv, 4, 8, 18, 21, 32, 35, 37, 65, 85, 91, 135, 144, 147, 151, 212.
Langen, 38, 42, 45.
Lapide, à, xiv, 52, 108 f., 128, 186, 190, 196, 223, 256, 284.
Lassen, 123.
Lavater, 108.
Lawson, 116.
Layard, 249.
Ledrain, 114, 117.
Lee, 16.
Leimdörfer, 115.
Leitner, 100.
Le Long, 6.
Leo Hebræus, 107.
Leon de Bagnols, 107.
Levi ben Gershom, xiv, 107.
Levita, 9, 13.
Levy, xiv, 170, 178.
Lightfoot, 53, 169.
Lilienthal, 112.
Lion, 136.
Littmann, 36.
Livy, 264.
Löwe, 117.
Loftus, 134.
London Polyglot, xi, 16, 18, 20.
Lucian, 150.
Lucian the Martyr, 31, 37.

Lucian's recension, xi, 37–38, 44, 52, 85 f., 100.
Luther, 96, 108.
Lyra, 52, 107, 109, 131, 174, 221, 262.

M'CLYMONT, 115.
Macrae, 116.
M'Crie, 116.
Macrobius, 150.
Magazin für die Geschichte u. Wissenschaft des Judenthums, xiv.
Maḥzor Vitry, 14.
Maimonides, 9, 14, 97.
Malbin, 118.
Mally, 114.
Malter, 94.
Malvenda, xiv, 53, 109, 128, 133, 136, 174, 182, 186, 196, 256, 295, 302.
Mant, 116.
Marchant, 111.
Mariana, xiv, 109, 133, 169, 187, 256, 261.
Marquart, 67 ff., 114.
Marsham, 51.
Marti, 147, 151, 160, 212.
Martianay, 111.
Mason, 116.
Massora, xi, 11–16, 248.
Mas'údí, 76.
Mathna, 139.
Maurer, xiv, 116, 162, 186, 251.
Mayer, xiv, 110, 169.
Megasthenes, 52.
M^eghillā, xiv, 20, 28 f., 93, 98–100, 119, 290 f., 295, 305.
Megillath Ta'anith, 78, 80.
Meier, 84, 113.
Meijboom, 63, 85, 113.
Meir b. Ḥayyim, 111.
Meissner, 87, 90, 92, 110.
Melammed, 110.
Melito, 97.
Menahem b. Ḥelbo, 105.
Mendelssohn, 117.
Menochius, xiv, 53, 109, 164, 169, 174, 190, 196, 256, 262, 284.
Mercator, 52.
Merkel, 110.
Merx, 8.
Meyer, xiv, 53, 100, 121, 124, 212, 299.
Mez, 39.
Michaelis, xi, xiv, 7, 57, 78, 83, 111 f., 116, 166, 226.

Midrash Abba Goryon, xiv, 103, 199, 240, 245.
Midrash Esther Rabba, xiv, 103.
Midrash from Yemen, 104.
Midrash Megillath Esther, xiv, 103.
Midrash Leqaḥ Ṭob, xiv, 103.
Midrash Ponim Aherim, xiv, 104.
Midrash published by M. Gaster, 104.
Midrash Shoḥer Ṭob, xiv, 104.
Millman, 113.
Mishna, xiv, 95, 98 f., 119.
Mitteilungen der Vorderasiatischen Gesellschaft, xiv.
Moʻed, 99.
Moldenhauer, 112.
Molder, 108.
Mommsen, 5.
Montanus, 12, 20, 109, 141.
Moor, de, 115.
Moore, vi, 145.
Morgan, 116.
Morgan, de, 126, 134.
Moses the Punctuator, 13.
Mosul edition, Syriac, xi, 16.
Movers, 113.
Müller, 76, 133, 153, 201.
Münster, xiv, 108 f., 181 248.
Munk, 22, 24.
Muss-Arnolt, 87.

Naḥmias, 106.
Naples editions of Bible, xi, 10.
Nathan ben Jehiel, 20.
Nathan of Soncino, 10.
Nehemiah, Rabbi, 88.
Nestorideo, 111.
Neteler, xiv, 117, 136, 196.
Neubauer, 6, 134.
New Testament, xi.
Nicephorus, 4.
Nickes, 51, 113.
Niebuhr, 121.
Niemeyer, 112.
Niese, 39.
Nöldeke, xiv, 30, 43, 46, 113, 115, 205, 299.
Norzi, 7, 166, 172.
Nowack, xiv, 87.

Oeder, 112.
Oettli, xiv, 69, 117, 120, 156, 169, 177, 186, 190, 197, 206, 262, 296, 302.
Old Latin Version, 24, 40 f., 100.
Old Testament, xi.

Olshausen, xiv, 185, 207, 272, 298.
Oppert, xiv, 66–71, 113 f., 137.
Orelli, 114.
Orientalistiche Litteratur-Zeitung, xiv.
Origen, xi, 4, 31 f., 34 f., 97, 101.
Osgood, 137.
Osiander, xiv, 108 f., 152, 186, 197, 261, 302.
Ostervald, 116.

Pagninus, xiv, 108 f., 141, 152, 161, 248.
Pamphilus, 34 f.
Pape, 118.
Pareus, xiv, 108, 150, 158.
Paris Polyglot, 19.
Paton, 115, 182, 210, 227, 230, 275, 306.
Patrick, xiv, 110, 152, 168.
Paulus Burgensis, xiv, 107.
Payne-Smith, 178.
Pellican, xiv, 108.
Pereles, 118.
Perles, 267.
Perreau, 106.
Perrot, 121.
Peshitto, 16 f.
Petavius, 53.
Petrie, 126.
Petronius, 148.
Petrus Comestor, 107.
Pfeiffer, 53.
Pförtner, 46.
Philippsohn, 117.
Philo, 31, 61, 98.
Pirqe Rabbi Eliezer, xiv, 20, 24, 102, 196.
Piscator, xiv, 108 f., 127, 136, 141, 152, 161, 164, 181, 248, 261, 302.
Pliny, 145.
Plutarch, 139, 141, 150, 196, 240, 248.
Polybius, 126, 137.
Poole, 109.
Pope, 115.
Posner, 18, 20, 23.
Pott, 69, 277.
Poznansky, 105.
Prayer-book of Yemen, 105.
Preuschen, 5.
Priestly, 116.
Prince, 115.
Proceedings of the Society of Biblical Archæology, xiv.
Pseudo-Athanasius, 4.

INDEX

Ptolemaic Canon, 126.
Purver, 116.
Pyle, 110.

RAB, 132, 136, 144, 174, 226.
Raba, 162.
Rabba b. Abuhu, 234.
Rahlfs, 16.
RaLBaG, 107.
Raleigh, 116.
Rambach, xiv, 110, 152, 167 *f.*, 181, 187, 248, 261, 305.
RaShBaM, 106.
RaShI, 11, 24, 52, 105, 107, 118, 132, 135, 161, 164, 196, 277, 284, 305.
Ratner, 100.
Raven, 115.
Rawicz, 100.
Rawlinson, xiv, 68–71, 116, 130, 162, 167 *f.*, 171, 176, 183, 186 *f.*, 196, 200, 206, 209, 302 *f.*
Real-Encyclopädie für protestantische Theologie u. Kirche, xiv.
Records of the Past, 137.
Reggio, 117.
Renan, 86.
Reusch, 113.
Reuss, xiv, 46, 78, 80, 113 *f.*, 117, 224, 291.
Revised Version, xi.
Revue des Etudes Juives, xiv.
Rhabanus Maurus, 53, 107.
Richardson, 108.
Riehm, 113 *f.*
Rinck, 116.
Robertson, 114.
Robiou, 114.
Rodkinson, 100.
Roediger, 69, 132, 277.
Rosenthal, 249, 270.
Rossi, de, xi, 6–9, 42, 60, 110 *f.*
Ruffinus, 5.
Rupertus Abbatis Tuitiensis, 107.
Rupprecht, 115.
Ryle, 3.
Ryssel, xiv, 8, 31, 43, 46, 57, 116, 117, 125, 127, 138 *f.*, 156, 162, 181, 188, 200, 202, 213, 233, 243, 260, 276, 282, 291.

SÀ, 109.
Sa'adia, 14, 104.
Saba, 56.
Sabatier, 40.
Sachau, 86, 161.
Sacy, de, 117.

Salianus, xiv, 53, 130.
Samuel ben Meïr, xiv, 106.
Samuel, Rabbi, 132, 135, 144, 174, 226.
Sanctius, xiv, 53, 108 *f.*, 125, 128, 133, 176, 183, 196.
Sanday, 5.
Sartorius, 112.
Sayce, 72, 114.
Scaliger, 52, 71.
Schanz, 114.
Scheftelowitz, 67–71, 115, 132.
Scheil, 134.
Schenkel, xiv.
Schiller-Szinessy, 6.
Schirmer, 116.
Schlatter, 114.
Schlottmann, 114.
Schmidt, 78, 116.
Schnurrer, 111.
Schoene, 52, 101.
Scholtz, 37, 95.
Scholz, 42, 46, 56, 113 *f.*, 120, 124, 128, 130, 132, 138, 162, 168, 196.
Schott, 116.
Schrader, xiv, 113, 138.
Schudt, 93.
Schürer, xiv, 43, 46, 115.
Schultz, xv, 53, 114, 116, 127, 147, 156, 158, 161, 169, 177, 186–188, 196, 200, 209, 221, 225, 261 *f.*, 270, 298.
Schulze, 112, 116.
Schwally, 86, 88.
Scott, 116, 130.
Second Targum, xi, 21–23.
Seder 'Olam, 53, 100.
Seisenberger, 42, 117.
Seligsohn, 170, 194.
Semler, 13, 112.
Serarius, xv, 53, 109, 128, 131, 133, 174, 196, 221.
Shahin, 104.
Siegfried, xv, 86, 117, 138 *f.*, 143, 154, 156, 158, 162, 166, 169, 177, 181, 185, 187, 200, 202, 206, 213, 222–224, 239, 243, 251, 256, 260, 262, 267, 274, 282, 290, 295 *f.*, 300, 302.
Simeon, 116.
Simeon b. Lakish, 97.
Sirach, 61.
Smith, H. P., 78, 115.
Smith, W. R., 114.
Smith's Dictionary of the Bible, xv.
Smend, 88, 114.

INDEX

Solomon ben Isaac, xiv, 105.
Solomon ibn Melech, xiii, 110, 261.
Soncino Edition, xi, 10.
Spiegel, xv, 121, 123 *f.*, 135, 137, 146, 273.
Spiegelberg, 126, 212.
Spinoza, 111.
Stade, xv, 143 *f.*, 146, 186, 195, 207, 218, 224, 267, 272, 282, 285.
Stähelin, 113.
Stanley, 113.
Stebbins, 114.
Steinschneider, 6, 107.
Steinthal 95, 114.
Stenco, 108.
Stier, 45.
Stolze, 121.
Strabo, 88, 92 *f.*, 126, 129, 137, 140.
Strack, xv, 6, 14, 99, 114, 224, 284.
Strassmaier, 54.
Streane, xv, 117, 130, 169, 186, 188, 256, 262, 296, 302.
Strigel, xv, 108.
Strong, 116.
Sutcliffe, 116.
Swete, 5, 31 *ff.*, 35.
Symmachus, 29, 34.
Synopsis Criticorum, 109.
Syriac Version, xi, 16.

Tabarí, 76.
Taiṭazak, 110.
Talmud, 28, 42, 60, 102, 162, 287, 273, 290 *f.*, 295; see M^{e}ghillā, Babylonian Talmud, Jerusalem Talmud.
Tanḥuma, 130.
Targums, vi, 42, 101; see *First Targum, Second Targum.*
Targum Rabbathi, 41.
Tayler, 18
Tedeschi, 118.
Terence, 148.
Terry, 116.
Thayer, viii.
Theodoret of Antioch, 37.
Theodotion, 34, 29.
Theologische Literaturzeitung, xv.
Theologische Studien u. Kritiken, xv.
Theologisch Tijdschrift, xv.
Thucydides, 245.
Tiele, 115.
Tigurina, xv, 109, 141, 181, 248.
Tintori, de, of Bologna, 10.
Tirinus, xv, 52, 109, 186, 190, 196, 206, 284.

Tischendorf, 24, 31.
Tobiah b. Eliezer, 103.
Tommasi, 40.
Toy, 87.
Transactions of the Society of Biblical Archæology, xv.
Trapp, 108.
Tremellius, 108 *f.*, 127, 141, 302.

Unger, 112.
Uri, 6.
Urumia edition of Syriac, xi, 16.
Ussher, 35, 37 *f.*

Valerio, 110.
Vatable, xv, 52, 108 *f.*, 141, 181 *f.*, 187, 248, 261, 302.
Vatke, 114.
Vernes, 114.
Vignoles, des, 52.
Vigouroux, 114.
Villiers, de, 114.
Vitringa, xv, 151, 164.
Vos, 112.
Vulgate, see Jerome.
Vullers, 65, 70.

Wace, 8.
Wachsmuth, 126.
Wade, 115.
Wahl, 123.
Wallafridus Strabus, 107.
Walther, 52, 108.
Watson, 115.
Weber, 113 *f.*
Weisslovits, 87.
Wellhausen, 174.
Wells, 110.
Welte, 42, 52.
Wendel, 145.
Wesley, 116.
Westminster Assembly's Annotations, 108, 130, 168.
Wette, de, 113, 138.
Wetzer, 42.
Whiton, 114.
Wiener Zeitschrift für die Kunde des Morgenlandes, xv.
Wildeboer, xv, 57, 86–89, 114, 117, 120, 162, 169, 176 *f.*, 181, 186, 188, 196, 202, 206, 233, 251, 256, 260, 262, 291, 296, 302.
Willrich, xv, 42, 63, 77, 115, 125, 261.
Wilson, 108.
Winckler, xv, 52, 87, 90, 131–134, 144, 186, 193, 207, 212 *f.*, 215, 235.

Winer, 113.
Wisdom of Jesus son of Sirach, 30.
Wokenius, 52, 110.
Wolder, 108.
Wolf, 6.
Wolfsohn, 117.
Wordsworth, 116.
Wright, 115.
Wünsche, 101, 103, 125.

XENOPHON, *Anabasis*, 153, 185.
Xenophon, *Cyropædia*, 129, 134, 136, 140, 160, 185, 201.
Xenophon *Hellenica*, 245.
Ximenes, 10.

Yalqut Shim'oni, xv, 88, 104.
Yeçîra, 15.
Yonge, 116.

Yosippon, xv, 8, 20, 42, 102, 227.

ẒAHALON, 110.
Zahn, 5.
Zechariah, 118.
Zechariah b. Seruk, 110.
Zedner, 106.
Zeitschrift des deutschen Palästina Vereins, xv.
Zeitschrift für Ägyptologie, xiii.
Zeitschrift für die Alttestamentliche Wissenschaft, xv.
Zeitschrift für Assyriologie, xv.
Zeller, 108.
Zimmern, 87, 90–93, 144, 215.
Zinck, 116.
Zöckler, 46.
Zschokke, 113.
Zunz, 8, 23, 85, 113.

III. INDEX OF SUBJECTS.

AARON, 255.
Ab, 93, 201.
'Ābhaghthā, 67, 148.
Abib, 200.
Abiel, 168, 259.
Abigail, 149, 171.
'Ăbîḥayil, 171, 181, 300.
Abimelech, 241, 255.
'Ăbînādāb, 182.
Abishai, 167.
Ab-Kharkha, 227.
Abraham, 169, 242, 255, 259, 284.
Accad, 132.
Achæmenes, 126.
Achæmenian inscriptions, 72, 128.
Achmetha, 134.
Acropolis of Susa, 126, 137, 227; see Fortress, Susa.
Acrostics, 8.
'Ădā, 231.
'Ādalyā, 70, 284, 287.
Adam, 75.
Adar, 49 f., 55, 61, 78, 84, 86, 92, 94, 98, 202 f., 209 f., 275 f., 282, 287–291, 293, 295, 300, 306.
Adar, the Second, 300 f.
Adasa, 78 f.
Additions of the versions, vi, vii; in Aramaic, 8, 42; in Greek, 8, 25, 33, 41; regarded as canonical, 42; supposed Heb. originals are translations of Josephus, 42; contradict the Heb. text, 43; not a part of the original Greek version, 44; added to supply a religious element, 44; literature on the additions, 45; the short additions, 46; Addition A, 44, 90, 119; Addition B, 210; Addition C, 227; Addition D, 230; Addition E, 44, 275; Addition F, 90, 306; in Josephus, 39; in Lucian, 38; in Old Latin, 40; additions in Talmud, 28; in Targums, 19, 22.
Adhmāthā, 68, 152.
Africa, 152, 230, 250.
Agag, 70, 73, 194, 231, 256, 265.
Agagite, 43, 49, 69, 72, 90, 120, 194, 269, 284, 295.
Age of Est., v; ancient theories, 60; makes no claim for itself, 61; LXX version earliest witness, 61; historical standpoint shows late Greek period, 61; intellectual standpoint, 62; language, 62.
'Ăhasht'rānîm, 273.
'Ăhashwērôsh, 48, 51, 53 f., 121 f., 124, 128, 133.
Ahasuerus, 43, 47 f., 51, 56, 60, 64, 71, 77, 95, 108, 121, 169; identified with Cyaxares, 51; with Astyages, 52; with Cambyses, 52; with

INDEX

Darius, I, 52; with Xerxes, 52; with Artaxerxes I, 53; with Artaxerxes II, 53; with Artaxerxes III, 53; monuments prove that he was Xerxes, 53; statements of Est. agree, 54.
Ahasuerus, the father of Darius the Mede, 51.
Ahura-Mazda, 137, 148, 153.
Akra, 134.
Alabaster, 145.
Alexander Balas, 81 f.
Alexandria, 125.
Alexandrian Jews, 96.
Allegorical interpretation, 56, 138, 162, 168.
Alms, 294.
Amalek, 194, 222, 231, 256, 265, 283, 286, 288 f., 290, 296.
Amalekites, 73, 194, 200.
Amesha-Spentas, 148, 153.
Amestris, 71, 150, 240.
'Ammihud, 168, 259.
'Ammînādāb, 170, 182.
Ammon, 152.
Amorin, 99.
Anadatos, 88, 92.
Anagrams, 95.
Anahita, 137.
Anaitis, 88, 93.
Angaroi, 184, 208.
Angel, 147, 221, 232, 242, 255, 259, 262 f., 286.
Annals of Persia, 49 f., 74, 192, 302; see Chronicles, Book.
Annunaki, 91.
Antimeros, 194.
Antiochan text, 37.
Antiochus Epiphanes, 61 f., 63, 78.
Antonia, 134.
Apadāna, 137, 139, 144.
Aphiah, 168, 259.
Aphliṭus, 231.
Apocrypha, vii, 33.
Apocryphal additions, 96.
Appendix, 303.
Approaching the king, 43, 72, 220, 269.
Arabic, 161.
Arabic learning, 104.
Arabic version, 105.
Aramaic, 62, 72, 160 f., 273.
Aramaic original of Greek additions 8.
'Ăriday, 70, 284, 288.
'Ărîdhāthā, 70, 284, 288.

'Ărişay, 71, 284, 288.
Armour, 249.
Artaxerxes, 52 f., 119 f., 137, 150, 210, 275, 305.
Artaxerxes I., Longimanus, 52 f., 60, 76, 124, 133.
Artaxerxes II., Mnemon, 53, 65, 136 f.
Artaxerxes III., Ochus, 53, 190.
Artaynte, 233.
Ashes, 214, 227 f., 230, 254.
Ashurbanipal, 133.
Aspathā, 70, 284, 287.
Assembly, 306.
Assembly of the gods, 91.
Assueros, 52.
Assyria, 132 f., 160, 190, 192.
Assyrian, 160.
Astrakhan, 146.
Astrologers, 151, 201, 255.
Astyages, 52, 127.
Atniṣomus, 231.
Atossa, 121.
Aufklärung, 111.
Authorship of Esther, 63.
Azariah, 154, 239, 255.

Ba'al, 155.
Baanah, 168, 259.
Babylon, 125, 128, 130, 132, 134, 137, 149, 167, 176, 255.
Babylonia, 90, 132 f., 192.
Babylonian, 160.
Babylonians, 202.
Babylonian creation story, 90.
Babylonian Election Day, 94.
Babylonian holy days, 83.
Babylonian legends, 125.
Babylonian months, 200, 272.
Babylonian New Year's festival, 79, 91.
Babylonian origin of Purim, 87, 91.
Babylonian scribes, 14.
Babylonian tablets, 54.
Babylonian Talmud, xi, 2, 20, 98 f., 101; see M^eghillā.
Bagoas, 161.
Bahman Ardashir, 76.
Bal'aqan, 194.
Balder, 79.
Banquet, 48 f., 65, 91, 126, 128, 135, 150, 184, 234 f., 238, 240, 257, 280, 290, 293; see Feast.
Banquet-hall, 263.
Barber, 253.
Baris, 134.

INDEX

Barnabazos, 39, 190.
Baths, 165, 253.
Bazaars, 204.
Beautiful women, 147, 149, 171.
Bechorath, 168, 259.
Bed-chamber, 247, 259.
Beds, 139
Behar, 84.
Bekhorath, 168, 259.
Bela, 168.
Bells, 249.
Belshazzar, 75, 128.
Benefactors of the King, 65, 245.
Benjamin, Tribe of, 48, 119, 168, 198, 255, 259.
Beryl, 279.
Beth essentiae, 229.
Bibliography, vii.
Bighthā, 67, 148.
Bighthān, 69, 189, **244.**
Bilshan, 169.
Bird of paradise, 279.
Birds, 279, 288.
Bīthān, 137, 143.
Biurists, 117.
Biznai, 231.
Bizzᵉthā, 67, 148.
Bomberg Bible, 18, 22.
Book, 302.
Book of Moses, see Law.
Book of the acts of the days, 304.
Book of the memorable things, 304.
Bowing before superiors, 62, 195; see Prostration.
Boys, 279.
Bridle, 252.
Broad place, 217.
Bulis, 197.

CABALA, 106.
Cæsarea, 34.
Caiaphas, 256.
Calah, 132.
Calneh, 132.
Cambyses, 52, 123, 128, 158.
Canaanites, 281.
Canonicity, vii, 63 *f.*, 94, 101.
Cappadocian, 161.
Captivity, see Exile.
Carian, 161.
Carmeli, 78.
Carnival, 92.
Carpenters, 240.
Casting of lots, see Lot.
Catholic Commentators, 108.
Cattle, 227.

Cedar, 266.
Chain, 249 *f.*, 252.
Chalybonian wine, 141.
Chamber of Fate, 91.
Chapter division, 12.
Chariot, 248.
Chedorlaʻomer, 133.
Children, 274.
Chislev, 202.
Choaspes, 126, 227.
Christ, does not quote Est., 97.
Christian attitude toward Est., 97, 101.
Chronicler, 52.
Chronicles of the Kings of Judah and Israel, 58.
Chronicles of the Kings of Media and Persia, 42, 57 *f.*, 120, 191 *f.*, 244, 292 *f.*, 303 *f.*; see Annals, Book.
Circumcise, 204, 280.
Circumstantial clause, 281, 285.
Cities, 291, 297 *f.*
City of Susa, 126, 211, 280.
City-square, 249.
Cleopatra, 30, 77, 81 *f.*, 306.
Codices, Hebrew, 2, 6, 8; Greek, 4 *f.*, 31 *f.*; Latin, 40 *f.*; Syriac, 16.
Colours, 279.
Columns, 137.
Commentators, Catholic, 107–109, 111, 117; Jewish, 13, 97, 101–107, 109, 111, 117, 161; Protestant, 107, 110, 115.
Commercialism, 62.
Commissioners, 164, 173.
Complutensian Polyglot, 10, 33.
Composition, Erbt's theory, 81; see Unity.
Compulsion to drink, 141.
Concubines, 180, 187.
Conspiracy, 190, 295; see Plot.
Contradictory statements in Est., 58.
Coptic versions, 36.
Copy, 211, 217.
Cords, 138.
Corpse, 295.
Cosmetics, 165, 174, 178.
Cotton, 138, 144.
Cotton cloth, 138, 144.
Couch, 263.
Council of princes, 73, 128, 154, **238.**
Counsellors, 151, 255.
Country Jews, 288, 290.
Couriers, 49, 65, 208, 273, 276.
Coursers, 273, 276.

INDEX

Court, 136.
Courtiers, 127, 184, 195, 197, 220.
Cousin, 170 f.
Covering the head, 254, 264.
Creation story, 91.
Crier, 249.
Critical period of exegesis, 111.
Crown, 148, 230, 244, 248 f., 259, 279.
Crucifixion, 44, 191.
Crying, 59, 214, 301.
Crystal, 140.
Cup, 148, 254.
Cup-bearer, 141.
Curtains, 138.
Custom, 152.
Cyaxares, 51 f., 127, 169.
Cyreneans, 77.
Cyrus, 52, 75, 121–123, 125, 127, 130, 134, 169.

Daghesh forte conjunctivum, 257.
Dainties, 174, 290, 293.
Dalphôn, 70, 284, 287.
Damascus, 190.
Daniel, 75, 121, 128, 148, 154, 169, 174, 216, 239.
Darius, 52 f., 75, 121–124, 129, 137, 169, 258.
Darius the Mede, 52, 122–124.
Date of the book, 281; see Age.
Date of the Greek version, 31.
Daughter of Haman, 254.
Daughter-voice, 240.
David, 164, 166 f., 239, 248.
Day of Atonement, 74, 202.
Day of Mordecai, 61, 80, 91.
Day of Nicanor, see Nicanor's Day.
Days of the Week, 201.
Dead, 214; cult of, 86.
Decree, 49, 72, 248, 269; see Edict, Dispatches.
Dedication of Feast, 202.
Deioṣoṣ, 231.
Delay in bringing girls to the King, 183.
Descendants, 297.
Diary, 58, 304; see Annals, Chronicles.
Diaspora, 61, 63, 203.
Dínázád, 76.
Dioces, 220.
Dionysius, 131.
Dios, 194.
Dioses, 194.
Dispatches, 160, 208, 269, 272; see Decree, Edict.

Divine honours, 196.
Dizful, 126.
Dogs, 239.
Doorkeepers, 189.
Dositheus, 30, 77, 306.
Dragons, 120, 306.
Dravidian, 160.
Dream of Mordecai, 8, 39, 42, 102, 104, 119, 306.
Drink, 140 f., 147, 211.
Drinking-cups, 140 f.
Drunkenness of Persians, 129, 150, 163.
Dung, 228.
Duplicate accounts, 58, 295, 297.
Dust, 230.
Dustros, 282.

EASTERNS, 15.
Ecbatana, 125, 134.
Edict, 43, 50, 157, 210, 276, 282, 287; see Decree, Dispatch.
Edom, 78, 152.
Egypt, 128, 152, 161, 169, 211.
Egyptian, 161.
Egyptians, 241.
Elah, 168, 259.
Elam, 54, 89, 90, 125, 127, 133 f., 160.
Elder, 304.
Elephantine, 161.
Eleventh of Adar, 295, 297.
Eliel, 168, 259.
Elijah, 86, 234.
Elijah the high priest, 213.
Eliphael, 168.
Eliphalot, 194.
Elíphaz, 194, 231.
Elpa'al, 259.
Elul, 201.
Emerald, 145, 279.
Enameled tiles, 137.
Enemy, 260, 267, 276, 282–284, 287, 289, 291, 293, 295.
En-Mashti, 89.
Ephraim, 255.
Ephrath, 78.
Eponymy, 93.
Erech, 89, 132 f.
Esarhaddon, 132.
Esau, 194, 197 f., 220, 231, 265.
Escorting guests, 257.
Esther, the queen, 43, 45, 48, 55, 65–67, 71–73, 77 f., 81, 88, 90 f., 93; etymology of name, 69, 85;= Ishtar, 69, 78 f., 170; not identical

INDEX

with Amestris, 71; analogue of Judith, 75; of Shahrazád, 76; moral character, 96, 108; origin and bringing up, 170-171; taken to the palace, 173; gains favour of Hēgai, 174; conceals her race, 175; visited by Mordecai, 176; brought to the King, 182; made Queen, 184; conceals her origin, 188; communicates with Mordecai, 216; resolves to go to the King, 225; her prayer, 228; goes to the King, 230; prayer in court, 231; received by the King, 232; her request, 234; second request, 236; gives thanks for Mordecai's honour, 254; denounces Haman, 257; entreated by Haman, 263; seeks to counteract Haman's edict, 268; sees Mordecai's honour, 280; asks for second slaughter, 286; writes to confirm Mordecai's letter, 300; the fountain in Mordecai's dream, 306.
Esther's Fast, 301.
Ethiopia, 54, 73, 122 *f.*, 133, 208, 210, 275.
Ethiopic, 36.
Euergetes II, 77.
Eunuchs, 43, 49 *f.*, 120, 148-150, 153, 165, 171, 176, 179, 189, 216, 244, 257, 264.
Euphrates, 130.
Eustochium, 25.
Evil-Merodach, 121 *f.*, 130, 149.
Exegesis, Christian, no commentaries for seven centuries, 101; mediæval commentators, 107; Protestant commentators of the Reformation period, 107; Catholic commentators of this period, 108; compendia of commentators, 109; post-Reformation period, Protestant commentators, 110; Catholic commentators, 111; modern critical period, 111; introductory works, 112; modern Protestant commentaries, 115; Catholic commentaries, 117.
Exegesis, Jewish, 13; *haggada*, 97; *halakha*, 98; collection of *halakhoth* into *Mishna*, 98; the *Talmuds*, 99; collection of *haggadhoth* into *midrashim*, 100; *midrash* in the *Gemara*, 100; *First Targum*, 101; *Second Targum*, 102; *Midrash*

Esther Rabba, 103; *Midrash Leqaḥ Tob*, 103; *Midrash Abba Goryon*, 103; *Midrash Megillath Esther*, 103; other *midrashim*, 104; Sa'adia and the literal method of interpretation, 104; the Spanish school, 105; RaShI, 105; his followers, 106; rise of the allegorical method, 106; commentators of the Reformation period, 109; post-Reformation period, 111; modern period, 118.
Exile, 135, 168, 239.
Extraordinary letters, 6, 284, 302.
Ezra, 53, 60, 202.

FARVARDÎGÂN, 85-87, 91.
Fast, 49, 59, 95, 189, 215, 225, 227, 250, 280, 301.
Fates of men, 91, 94.
Father, 101, 276.
Father to the king, 283.
Feast, 48, 49, 142, 240, 276, 280 *f.*; see Banquet.
Fiction, 247.
Fiery furnace, 255.
Fifteenth of Adar, 288, 290 *f.*, 293, 306.
First Targum, editions, 18; relation to Heb., 18; its insertions, 19; short recension in Antwerp and Paris Polyglot, 20; age, 20; sources 20; oral origin, 21; text-critical value, 21; its exegesis, 101.
Five Mᵉgillôth, 2 *f.*, 103.
Food, 140, 174; of heathen unclean, 43, 175, 189, 229, 271.
Fortress, 126, 136, 165-167, 169, 172, 176, 211, 279 *f.*, 283, 286, 290; see Acropolis, Susa.
Fortune of the city, 279.
Fountain, 120.
Fourteenth of Adar, 288, 290, 293, 295, 297, 306.
Friends, 255.

GABATHA, 120.
Gabriel 149, 221, 225, 245, 263.
Gallows, 50 *f.*, 74, 89, 163, 191, 240, 246, 257, 264, 266, 270, 284, 287, 295.
Garden, 136, 262.
Garments, 216, 230, 242, 249.
Garments of King, 244, 248, 252 *f.*, 259, 279.
Gate of the King, see King's gate.

Gates, 188.
Gemara, xiii, 99 *f*.; see *Talmud, Babylonian Talmud*.
Gentiles, hatred of, 45, 62, 229.
Genuineness of subscription, 30.
Genûnîtha, 174.
Gera, 259.
Geresh, 89.
Geshem, 234, 236, 258.
Gezah, 168.
Gibeonite, 295.
Gifts, 79, 294; of food, 185; to the poor, 59.
Gilgamesh, 82, 89 *f*.
Gilgamesh Epic, 89, 90.
Girdle, 279.
Girisha, 89.
Girls, 164 *f*., 172, 178, 186, see Maidens, Virgins.
Gladness, 306.
God, 275 *f*., 298, 306; name intentionally omitted, 44, 94; theory of anagrams, 95; not due to skepticism, 95; nor to residence in Persia, 95; nor to reverence, 95; due to the revels at Purim, 95; see also 222, 232, 244, 282.
Gog, 56.
Gogite, 70, 191, 194.
Gold, 139 *f*., 230, 279.
Goliath, 239.
Governors, 208, 272, 283.
Grand vizier, 268, 304.
Graves whitewashed, 86.
Great Synagogue, 60, 169, 190, 202.
Greece, 121, 128, 183, 206, 303.
Greek, 161, 295.
Greek historians, 71.
Greek origin of Purim, 83.
Greek period, 281.
Greek Version, xi, 24, 29; subscription to Esther, 30; its genuineness, 30; date of version, 31; recension of the uncials, 31; *Codex Sinaiticus*, 32; *Codex Alexandrinus*, 32; *Codex Basiliano-Vaticanus*, 32; other similar codices, 32; additions of text of uncials to Heb., 33; omissions from the text, 33; recension of Origen, 34; the *Hexapla*, 34; the Origenic text, 35; recension of Hesychius, 36; codices, 36; secondary versions, 36; recension of Lucian, 37; its codices, 37; editions, 37; additions to Heb., 38; omissions from Heb., 38; differences from Heb., 38; text of Josephus, 39; Old Latin secondary version, 40; long additions in Greek, 41; regarded as canonical, 42; supposed Heb. or Aram. originals are translations of Josephus, 42; no internal evidence of Heb. originals, 43; contradict the Heb. text, 43; not a part of the original Greek version, 44; added to supply a religious element, 44; literature on the additions, 45; the short additions in Greek, 46; text-critical value of Greek, 46; omissions in Greek, 47; also 100, 102.
Guza, 259.

HABISHA, 126.
Hadassah, 78, 85, 88 *f*., 170.
Hadros, 194.
Haggada, 97, 100, 104.
Haggai, 208.
Haircloth, 214, 216, 227; see Sackcloth.
Hair cut, 253.
Halakha, 97, 104, 252.
Half of the Kingdom, 233, 236.
Hamadan, 134.
Haman, 43–45, 47–50, 55, 62, 65, 72 *ff*., 77 *ff*, 81, 86, 88, 92 *f*., 120; etymology of name, 69, 85;= Humman, 69, 79, 88–91, analogies in Jewish literature, 75; the King's favourite, 120; same as M mûkhân, 154; plots against the King, 190; his origin, 194, 196; promoted by the King, 195; defied by Mordecai, 195; an Amalekite, 194, 197, 200; angry with Mordecai, 199; plans to destroy the Jews, 200; casts lots, 201; goes to the King, 203; promises 10,000 talents for the Jews, 205; sends out edict against the Jews, 208; his daughter, 231; wishes to slay Esther, 232; comes to Esther's banquet, 235; plans to hang Mordecai, 237; wears an idol, 242; accused by angel, 244; commanded by King to honour Mordecai, 246; executes command, 252; narrates his disgrace at home, 255; denounced by Esther, 257; meaning of his name, 259; sentenced to death, 262;

begs Mordecai for mercy, 265; a Macedonian, 275; duplicate account of his plot, 295; left hanging on gallows, 295; is dragon in the dream, 306.
Hamdān, 231.
Hamlets, 290 *f.*
Hammᵉdhāthā, 69, 78, 88, 92, 120, 194, 231, 240, 269, 275, 284, 295.
Ḥammurabi, 133.
Hananiah, 154, 239, 255, 259.
Handful of meal, 252.
Hanging as death-penalty, 44, 65, 163, 168, 191, 246, 270, 284, 287, 295.
Ḥarbônā, 67, 148, 264.
Harem, 137, 165, 176, 179; see House of the women.
Harness, 252.
Harṣum, 231.
Hartford Theological Seminary, viii.
Harum, 231.
Harvard Divinity School, viii.
Ḥashom, 259.
Hathakh, 49, 70, 217, 221.
Heathen, 280, 296, 300.
Heathen feast borrowed, 83.
Heaven, 282.
Heavenly voice, 259.
Hebrew, 295.
Hebrew consonantal text, xi.
Hēghai, or Hēghē, 48, 69, 165, 172–174, 182, 226.
Helix Ianthina, 138.
Helmet, 279.
Heman, 78.
Hemdan, 78.
Heminæ, 141.
Herod, 134, 233.
Hesychius' recension of the Greek, xi, 31, 36; its codices, 36; secondary Coptic and Ethiopic versions, 36.
Hexapla, 34.
Hezekiah, 125, 194.
Higher Criticism, 47, 111.
Historical character of Est., vii, wishes to be regarded as history, 64; so regarded by the Jews, 64; some of its statements confirmed, 64; correct idea of Persian customs, 65; Persian words, 65; most of its statements unconfirmed, 66; proper names unknown elsewhere, 66; proposed Persian etymologies, 67–71; statements of Est. contradicted by Greek historians, 71; contrary to Persian custom, 72; inner inconsistencies, 73; statements historically improbable, 73; analogues in apocryphal literature, 75; analogues in the Arabian Nights, 76; conclusion, cannot be regarded as historical, 77; see also 79, 111.
Hŏddû, 132.
Hokhma, 106.
Holiday, 280, 286, 290, 293.
Holophernes, 75.
Hôlta, 174.
Holy House, 198; see Temple, Sanctuary.
Holy Spirit, 191, 230.
Homái, 76.
Honours, 50, 248 *f.*, 254, 280.
Horses, 209, 244, 248 *ff.*, 252 *f.*, 259, 277.
House of the concubines, 179.
House of father, 223.
House of Haman, 270.
House of the King, 143, 173, 179; see Palace, Royal house.
House of the Kingdom, 143.
House of the women, 137, 143, 165, 173, 176, 179; see Harem.
Hrungner, 79.
Humbaba, 82, 89.
Humban, 69, 89.
Humman, 67, 69, 89 *f.*
Ḥûrpîthā, 174.
Husband, 155, 158, 161.
Hushim, 168.
Hymns, 293.

Idol, 195, 199, 217, 228, 231, 242.
Igigi, 91.
Impaling, 191.
Imperfect with *Waw* consec., 60.
Improbabilities in Est., 73, 240, 244 *f.*, 256, 287, 289, 304; see Historical character.
India, 52, 54, 73, 122 *f.*, 132, 152, 160, 208, 210, 272, 275.
Indus, 123.
Infinitive absolute, 285, 291, 299.
Inner court, 220 *f.*, 230.
Inscriptions, 160.
Inspiration of the Book of Esther, 182, 247.
Intercalated month, 300 *f.*
Interpreter, 258.
Introductions to Book of Est., 112.

INDEX

Irene, 81 f.
Irnina, 89.
Isaac, 240, 242, 255, 259.
Ishtar, 67, 69, 78 f., 88–93, 170.
Ishtar-feast, 93.
Islam, 104.
Islands of the Mediterranean, 54, 303.
Israel, 168, 281.
Issachar, sons of, 151 f.
Iṣtahar, 170.
Ištar, 78 f.; see Ishtar.
Ithaca, 81.
Iyar, 201.

JACOB, 168 f., 197 f., 200, 220, 242, 255, 259.
Jair, 119, 167, 259.
Jamnia, Synod of, 97.
Jeconiah, 51, 120, 168.
Jehoiachin, 51, 53, 73, 121, 168.
Jehoiakim b. Joshua, 60.
Jehoram, 168.
Jemshîd, 79.
Jerahmeel, 67, 78.
Jerahmeeli, 78.
Jerome's Latin Version, 5, 10, 24; prologue, 24; aim to give a literal version, 25; additions to Massoretic text, 26; omissions from text, 27; differences from Massoretic text, 27; general similarity to Massoretic text, 28.
Jerubba'al, 168, 259.
Jeruḥam, 259.
Jerusalem, 140, 169, 194, 208, 279, 306.
Jerusalem Talmud, xi, 99, 101.
Jewish commentators, 13, 97, 101–107, 109, 111, 117, 161.
Jewish Theological Seminary, viii.
Jews, 49, 73, 136, 167, 175, 198, 200, 203, 206, 209–211, 217, 225, 234, 255, 270, 273, 275 f., 280, 282 f., 286, 290, 293 f., 297, 305.
Job, 82.
Jötunheim, 79.
John Hyrcanus, 79.
Jonathan, 79, 82, 168, 259.
Joseph, 95, 169, 239, 248.
Joseph, the tax-gatherer, 83.
Josephus' recension of the Greek, additions, omissions, and variations, 39.
Joshua, 169.
Joy, 280, 290, 293, 306.
Judæan, 166, 255.

Judah, 166.
Judaism, 97.
Judas Maccabæus, 61, 78 f., 81.
Judith, 75, 79, 97.

Kallatu, 89.
Karaites, 104.
Ḳarçum, 196, 253.
Ḳarkaṣ, 68, 148.
Karshᵉnā, 68, 152.
Kašše, 132.
Kassite, 161.
Kefer Qarçum, 196, 253.
Kᵉthîbh, 13.
Khorsabad, 137.
Khshayarsha, 53, 305.
Khshatřa, 273.
King of Persia, 94.
King's business, 283.
King's gate, 137, 188 f., 197, 214, 217, 237, 239, 250, 254, 268, 279.
King's house, 230, 246, 283, 288; see Palace.
King, not approached without summons, 43, 49, 72, 220, 269.
Kirisha, 70, 89.
Kish, 119, 168, 194, 259.
Kurigalzu II, 133.
Kush, 123, 132 f., 250, 272.
Kûšu, 132.
Kutir Laḫgamar, 133.
Kutirnaḫunte, 133.
Kuza, 194.

LAMENTATION, 215.
Lamentations, Book of, 82.
Language, 59, 62, 160, 208, 273.
Latin version; see Old Latin.
Latin version of Jerome; see Jerome.
Law of Moses, 142, 167, 189, 203, 211, 217, 227, 229, 280, 282.
Laws of the Medes and Persians, 72, 141, 146, 149, 152 f., 157, 178, 217, 220, 276, 279, 282, 286 f.; were unchangeable, 43, 75, 150, 157, 270, 297.
Lebanon, 122.
Leprous, 149.
Letters, 51, 210, 293, 297, 300, 306; of the King, 44 f.; of Mordecai, 44, 274 f.; see Message.
Levi, 169.
Levites, 298, 306.
Light, 280.
Linen, 144 f., 279.
Longest verse, 273.

INDEX

Loos, 93.
Lots, 49, 55, 74, 77, 79, 84, 86, 91, 93, 200 f., 276, 295, 306.
Lower criticism, 111.
Lucian's recension of the Greek, xi, 37; its codices, 37; editions, 37; additions to Heb., 38; omissions from Heb., 38; differences from Heb., 38; see also 44, 52, 85f., 100.
Lucky and unlucky days, 65.
Lydian, 161.
Lyre, 240.
Lysimachus, 30, 306.

MA'ADAN, 194.
Macedonian, 43, 53, 194, 275 f., 279.
Magi, 200.
Magic, 177.
Maidens, 73; see Girls, Virgins.
Maids, 174, 216, 226, 230, 232, 258.
Mainland, 303.
Malachi, 169, 208.
Malachite, 145.
Manasseh, 239, 255.
Manôth, 79.
Mantle, 279.
Manuscripts, 5; of the Babylonian family, their origin, 14; statements concerning them, 14; their characteristics, 15; best MS. for Esther, 16.
Manuscripts, of the Tiberian family, their number, 5; catalogues, 6; characteristics, 6; consonantal variants, 7; Aramaic additions in some, 8; acrostics of YHWH, 8; variants in vocalization and accentuation, 9; descended from a single prototype, 9.
Marble, 139 f., 145.
Marchesvan, 202.
Mardochaios, 88.
Mardonius, 68.
Marduk, 67, 77, 79, 82, 88–91, 93.
Marduk, Feast of, 91.
Mares, 278.
Market-place, 217.
Marsᵉna, 68, 152,
Mashti, 88.
Masistes, 240.
Massacre, 201, 209, 287; see Slaughter.
Massora, xi, 6, 12–14, 16, 248.
Massora Magna, 11.
Massora Parva, 11.
Massoretic Hebrew text, xi, 27, 47.

Massoretic summaries, 12.
Massorites, 6.
Maul-clubs, 283.
Media, 52, 54, 127, 134, 153, 156, 304.
Median, 279.
Medieval Christian interpretation, 107.
Medieval Jewish Commentaries, 104.
Mediterranean, 303.
Medo-Persian migration, 134.
M*ᵉghillā*, presupposes consonantal text, 28; additions to the text, 29.
Mᵉhûmān, 67, 148.
Meloch, 168, 259.
Memnonium, 136.
Mᵉmûkhān, 48, 69, 152, 154–160, 168, 194.
Mephibosheth, 259.
Mereṣ, 68, 152.
Merimoth, 168.
Merrymaking of Purim, 95.
Mesopotamia, 161.
Message, 297, 300; see Letter.
Messianic hope, 62.
Method of recording variant readings, v.
Micha, 168, 259.
Michael, 168, 221, 225, 242, 244, 259.
Midrashim, 13, 43, 100–109.
Miriam, 86.
Mishael, 154, 239, 255.
Mishna, 98 f.
Mithra, 137.
Moab, 152.
Mock-king, 92.
Money-changer, 188.
Months, 201.
Moors, 105.
Moral teaching of Est., 96; estimate of Alexandrian Jews, 96; of N. T. writers, 97; of Church Fathers, 97; of later Judaism, 97; also 108, 173.
Mordecai, 43–45, 48–50, 52 f., 60, 62, 66 f., 72–74, 81, 93, 102, 108, 120; analogies in Jewish literature, 75;=Marduk, 77, 79, 88–91; etymology of name, 85; moral character, 96; his dream, 119; not present at Xerxes' feast, 138; his personal history, 166–172; bids Esther conceal her origin, 175; visits Esther, 176; sits in the

King's gate, 188, 189; bids Esther conceal her origin, 188; discovers the plot of the eunuchs, 190; refuses to bow to Haman, 195, 237; address to the courtiers, 197; denounced to Haman, 200; hears of Haman's edict, 213; communicates with Esther, 216; proclaims a fast, 226; his prayer, 227; answers reproaches of Jews, 242; remembered by the King, 244; honoured by King, 252; ordered to execute Haman, 265; put in place of Haman, 267; sends out dispatches, 272; his royal attire, 279; his power, 283; not author of Est., 293, 300; commands to keep Purim, 293; subsequent history, 303; is dragon in the dream, 306.
Mordecai of Ezr. 2², Ne. 7¹, 169.
Morning-star, 305.
Mosaic, 140.
Moses, 86, 98, 203, 255.
Mother-of-pearl, 140, 145.
Mourning, 65, 214 f., 228, 254, 293.
Murex Brandaris, 145.
Murex Trunculus, 145.
Myrrh, 178, 180, 279.

NABOPOLASSAR, 127.
Nadab, 75.
Nana, 133 f.
Napkin, 262.
Nations, 306.
Naurôz, 79.
Nebuchadnezzar, 51, 75, 120, 122, 125, 130, 139 f., 142, 148 f., 164, 168 f., 255.
Nebuchadrezzar, 168.
Negar, 194, 231.
Nehardea, 14.
Nehemiah, 53, 170.
Nehôrîtha, 174.
Nestorians, 97.
Neuruz, 84.
New Year feast, 93.
Nicanor, 61, 78–82.
Nicanor's day, 61, 79, 80, 92.
Night, 241.
Nineveh, 127, 132 f.
NIN-IB, 89.
Nisan, 91–93, 119, 183, 200 f.
Nubia, 123, 133.

OBEISANCE, 65.
Occidental MSS. xi,

Occidentals, 9.
Officials, 126, 155 f., 163, 184, 208, 249, 272, 283.
Ointments, 228, 230.
Old Latin version, 24, 100; codices, 40; relation to Greek version, 40; additions not found in Greek, 40; their origin, 41; omissions, 41; differences in the codices, 41.
Omanos, 88, 92.
Omissions in Greek, 33, 47; in Lucian, 38; in Old Latin, 41; in Jerome, 27.
Omphacinum, 180.
Ophir, 122, 230, 279.
Oral tradition, 98, 100, 101.
Oriental MSS. xi.
Orientals, 9.
Origen's recension of the Greek, xi, 32, 34; the Hexapla, 34; the separate Origenic text, 35.
Origin of Purim, 74.
Orosangai, 245.
Outer Court, 221, 246.
Outline of the book, 47.

PAGES, 164, 245, 247.
Palace of Xerxes, 65, 126, 136 f., 143, 165, 173, 188, 214, 262, 279, 283, 286; see House of the King, Royal House.
Palestine, 161.
Panbabylonisten, vii.
Parar, 78.
Park, 136.
Parmashta, 7, 70, 194, 231, 284, 288.
Parshandatha, 7, 70, 284, 287.
Parthian, 85, 279.
Passover, 92, 204, 226, 230, 252.
Paula, 25.
Pearl, 145, 230, 250, 279.
Penuel, 259.
People of the land, 281.
Peoples of the earth, 280.
Perfect with *Waw* connective, 60, 147, 212, 298.
Perfumes, 73, 178.
Periphrastic form of verb, 294.
Peroṣ, 194, 231.
Persepolis, 125, 160.
Persia, 52, 65, 95, 127, 134, 153, 156, 160, 192, 205, 304.
Persians, 129, 131, 140 f., 195, 201, 255, 264, 276.
Persian customs, 64 f., 72, 84, 125, 143, 149, 220.

INDEX

Persian king, 54.
Persian language, 63, 65 f., 84, Old Persian, 160.
Persian monuments, 53.
Persian New Year's festival, 79.
Persian origin of Purim, 84.
Persian source of story of Esther, 76.
Persian spring festival, 85.
Persian year, 84, 87.
Peshaṭ, 104–106.
Peshiṭto, editions, 16; groups of texts, 17; relation to Heb. in Est., 17.
Pethahiah, 169.
Pethuel, 168.
Petition, 233, 236, 257, 286.
Phædyma, 221.
Pharaoh, 241, 255.
Pharaoh the Lame, 125.
Phœnician, 161, 273.
Phourdaia, 85 f.
Phraortes, 51, 127.
Phrourai, 85 f., 306.
Phylactery, 279 f.
Pillars, 139.
Pirqe Rabbi Eliezer, 102.
Pitcher, 148, 254.
Pithaḥ, 259.
Pithoigia, 84.
Pithon, 168.
Pithqa, 141.
Place of Est. in Greek Bible, 3; arrangements in codices and in Fathers, 4–5.
Place of Est. in Heb. Bible, 1; various arrangements of the codices and editions, 2.
Platæa, 183.
Pleiades, 198.
Plot, 49, 102, 190; see Conspiracy.
Plunder, 209, 274, 284, 288 f.
Poison, 190.
Pomegranates, 249.
Poor, 294.
Pôrātha, 70, 284, 287.
Porphyry, 140.
Portions, 79, 174, 298.
Post-reformation period, 110.
Prayers, 280, 291.
Prayer after fasting, 225.
Prayer-mantle, 253.
Prayer of Jews, 241.
Prayers of Esther, 44, 102, 173, 228, 231.
Prayers of Mordecai, 8, 42, 44, 102, 227.
Precious stones, 230, 279.

Priestly Code, 74, 83.
Priests, 227, 279, 298, 306.
Princeton Theological Seminary, viii.
Printed editions, 3; based on Tiberian MSS., 10; edition Naples (1486–1487), 10; Naples (1491–1493), 10; Brescia (1492), 10; Complutensian Polyglot, 10; Bomberg (1516), 11; Bomberg (1525), 11; Montanus (1571), 12; other editions, 12.
Prison, 239.
Proclamation before one, 249, 254.
Proper names, 66.
Property, 267 f.
Prophets, 204, 241.
Proselyting, 61, 95, 226, 281 f., 295, 297.
Prostration before high officials, 195; see Bowing.
Provinces, 122–124, 128, 132, 155, 173, 184, 203, 208, 220, 269, 272, 274 f., 280, 282 f., 286, 289, 293, 298, 301.
Pseudo-Smerdis, 52.
Ptolemy, 30, 306.
Ptolemy IV Philopator, 83.
Ptolemy V (Epiphanes), 30.
Ptolemy VI (Philometor), 30, 77.
Ptolemy VII (Physcon), 30, 77, 81.
Ptolemy VIII (Lathuros), 30.
Puhrā, 86, 91.
Puḳru, 91 f.
Pur, 55, 74, 84, 86, 200 f., 295.
Pûrā, 78, 83.
Purdeghan, 85.
Purim, viii, 33, 44, 48, 51, 54 f., 56, 57, 59, 61, 64; theories of Jewish origin, 77; Willrich's theory, 77; Cheyne's theory, 77; Michaelis holds equals Nicanor's Day, 78; Haupt's theory, 79; difficulties, Purim does not fall on Nicanor's Day, 80; Esther has nothing to do with the victory over Nicanor, 81; no connection between the feast and its legend, 81; does not explain the name Purim, 82; theories of Greek origin, 83; theories of Persian origin, 84; Meier's theory, 84; Hitzig's theory, 84; Fürst's theory, 85; Meijboom's theory, 85; von Hammer's theory, 85; Lagarde's theory, 85; Schwally's theory, 86; difficulties with Persian theory, 86; theories

of Babylonian origin, 87; Babylonian counterparts to personages of the book, 88; Jensen's theory, 89; Gunkel's theory, 90; Zimmern's theory, 90; Winckler's theory, 90; Babylonian counterparts to the feast of Purim, Zimmern's theory, 91; Meissner's theory, 92; Frazer's theory, 92; Jensen's theory, 93; Johns' theory, 93; summing up, 94; Purim an annual merrymaking, 93, 95, 99, 276, 289; origin of two days, 292; commanded by Mordecai, 293; adopted by Jews, 294; manner of keeping, 295; name derived from *pur*, 296; made unchangeable by Jews, 297; confirmed by Esther, 300; connected with Mordecai's dream, 306.
Purple, 138, 145, 249, 252, 254, 279.
Purpose of Est., to justify feast of Purim, 54; unity of plan, 55; no allegorical purpose, 56; no purpose to justify Hellenizing party, 57.
Pûrti, 79.
Pûru, 93 f.
Pythius, 129, 206.

Q⁽ᵉ⁾rê, 13.
Queen of Persia, 72, 165, 184.
Queen of Sheba, 125.

RABBIS, 252.
Races, 155, 276, 283.
Rahab, 149, 171.
Rationalists, 111.
Reading before the King, 74, 244.
Reading the Roll of Esther, 6, 98 f., 273, 290, 295, 297.
Reclining at table, 140.
Red Sea, 255.
Reformation Period, 107.
Regoʻîtha, 174.
Rehoboth-Ir, 132.
Release, 142, 184.
Religion, absent from Est., supplied by Greek additions, 44, 62, 214 f.
Remuth, 259.
Rending garments, 213, 227.
Resen, 132.
Rest of Jews, 293.
Revenue, 205.
Revival of learning, 107.
Rewarding of benefactors, 245, 250.

Riches, 267; see **Wealth.**
Ring, 268, 273.
Robes, 231; see **Garments.**
Rods, 138, 145.
Rôhashîtha, 174.
Roll of Esther, 119, 295.
Rome, 223.
Rôqʻîtha, 174.
Roses, 140, 146.
Royal garment, 259; see Garments of King.
Royal house, 142, 182, 231; see House of the King, Palace.

SABBATH, 147, 189, 201, 204, 280, 295.
Sabouchadas, 39, 257.
Sackcloth and ashes, 49, 72, 252, 254; see Haircloth.
Ṣadda, 194.
Saddle, 252.
Sakæa, 88, 92 f.
Salome, 233.
Samson, 240.
Samuel, 222.
Sanballat, 234, 236, 258.
Sanctuary, 122, 140, 152, 169, 194, 234, 236, 241, 258, 296; see Temple.
Sandals, 230.
Sanhedrin, 189, 250, 254, 305.
Sanskrit, 160.
Sarah, 122, 149, 170 f., 202, 241.
Sarchedonus, 75.
Sargon, 70.
Sason, 259.
Sassanian rule, 134.
Satrapies, 72, 124.
Satraps, 208, 272, 283.
Saturnalia, 92.
Saul, 73, 167 f., 194, 222, 259, 295.
Sceptre, 189, 220, 232, 269.
Scissors, 253.
Scribes, 208, 244, 272, 288.
Script, 208, 273.
Scriptures, 204, 295.
Scythians, 133, 200.
Sea, 303.
Seal, 206, 208, 270, 273.
S⁽ᵉ⁾bhîrîn, 13.
Second gathering, 186.
Second Targum, editions, 21; relation to Heb. 22; additions to the text, 22; age, 23; sources, 24; see also 101 f.
Secretary, 244 f., 272.

INDEX

Sĕdhārîm, 6.
Segar, 194.
Seleucia, 186.
Seleucus Nicator, 85.
Self-defense, 274, 283.
Sennacherib, 75, 125, 241.
Separation of women, 189.
Septuagint; see Greek version.
Serpentine, 145.
Seven, 148.
Seven counsellors, 152.
Seven eunuchs, 91, 149.
Seven princes, 65.
Seven viziers, 91, 153, 163.
Seventy years of exile, 128.
Sha'ashgaz, 69, 179.
Shahrazád, 76.
Shalmaneser II, 134.
Shebaṭ, 202.
Shecarith, 168.
Shechorah, 168.
Sheep, 227.
Shegar, 231.
Sheḥarim, 259.
Sheḥorah, 259.
Shehriyar, 180.
Shema, 204.
Shemida, 168, 259.
Shephaṭiah, 168, 259.
Shēthar, 68, 152.
Shifregaz, 250.
Shimei, 119, 167, 259.
Shimmeshe, 288.
Shimri, 168, 259.
Shinar, 132.
Shishak, 125, 168.
Shush, 126.
Shushan, 48; see Susa.
Shushinak, 133.
Shutruk-Naḫunte, 133.
Sibyl, 256.
Signet-ring, 206, 268, 270, 273.
Signs, 306.
Silk, 230, 249.
Silver, 49, 139 *f.*, 205, 217.
Simon, 134.
Single prototype of Heb. MSS., 9.
Siris, 70, 89.
Sitting as an official posture, 125, 188 *f.*
Sivan, 201, 272.
Skeptic, 95.
Slaughter, 283, 287; see Massacre.
Slaves, 258.
Sleeplessness, 241, 244.
Smerdis, 52, 178, 221.

Smiths, 240.
Socks, 279.
Solar-heroes, 90.
Solomon, 167, 248.
Sons of Haman, 238, 240, 262, 265 *f.*, 270, 279, 284, 286 *f.*, 295.
Soothsayers, 201; see Astrologers.
Sorrow, 293.
Source of Esther, 292.
Spain, 105.
Spartans, 129.
Sperthies, 197.
Spring festival, 84.
Square, 217.
Stable, 250, 252.
Stacte, 180.
Stall, 252.
Stallions, 278.
Standard Codex of O. T., 9, 29.
Stateira, 150.
Statue, 184.
Steeds, 273, 276.
Steward, 283.
Stirrups, 252.
Stud, 273, 278.
Subscription to Greek Esther, 30, 306.
Sumerian, 161.
Summons to go to King, 43, 49, 72, 220, 269.
Sûmqar, 231.
Suppliants, 263.
Sura, 14, 99, 104.
Susa, 44, 48–51, 54, 65, 73 *f.*, 80, 84, 92, 120, 125 *f.*, 131, 133 *f.*, 136, 137, 139, 165 *f.*, 167, 169, 172, 176, 183, 188, 194, 208, 211, 217, 270, 275 *f.*, 276, 279 *f.*, 283, 286–290; history of the city, 133 *f.*
Susa the fortress; see Fortress.
Susian, 160.
Sword, 190, 249, 265, 279, 283, 288.
Synagogue, 204, 297.
Syria, 161.
Syriac Version, 16, 42; see Peshiṭto.
Syrian Christians, 97.

TABERNACLE, 138.
Tabernacles, 202.
Tablets of fate, 91.
Tail, 149.
Talents of silver, 49, 74, 205, 217, 253, 279.
Talmud, 28, 42, 60, 102, 162, 273, 287, 290; see *Babylonian Talmud, Jerusalem Talmud, Mᵉghillā*.

INDEX

Talyon, 231.
Tammuz, 201.
Tammuz-Ishtar myth, 90.
Targums, vi, 42, 101; see *First Targum, Second Targum*.
Tarsee, 190.
Tarshîsh, 68, 152.
Tatnai, 238.
Tĕbhēth, 182, 202.
Tell-el-Amarna Letters, 162.
Temple, 126, 128, 130, 134, 139, 145, 208, 253.
Tendenz, 44.
Teresh, 69, 189, 244.
Text of Esther, v, 5.
Text of O. T., 111.
Text of the Ṣopherim, 29.
Text of the uncials, 44.
Textus receptus, vi, 12.
Tharra, 120.
Thirteen as an unlucky number, 202.
Thirteenth of Adar, 79 $f.$, 202, 209, 275 $f.$, 282, 287, 289 $f.$, 295, 297, 301.
Threshold, 190.
Throne, 125, 153, 184, 189, 195, 231, 248.
Throne of Solomon, 125.
Tiâmat, 82.
Tiberian MSS., 5.
Tiberias, 6, 99.
Time of Purim, 297.
Tiribazos, 248.
Tishri, 201.
Title of book, 119.
Tobiah, 234, 236, 258.
Tobit, 75, 97.
Tôrā, 290.
Towns, 297.
Treasurer, 267, 304.
Treasury, 49, 205, 217, 249, 252.
Trees, 266.
Tribute, 303, 305.
Tritæchmes, 206.
Trumpets, 227, 279.
Trumpets, Feast of, 74, 201.
Tunic, 279.
Turban, 148, 184, 248, 279.
Twelfth of Adar, 295, 297.

UKNÛ, 126, 227.
Uncial codices, 31.
Uncircumcised, 229.
Union Theological Seminary, viii.
Unity of the book, v; unquestionable as far as 9^{19}, 57; independence of 9^{20}–10^3, 57; refers to an independent source, 57; duplicate to 3–7, 58; contradicts earlier narrative, 58; different language, 59.
Unrevised Greek text, 31.
Unwalled towns, 291, 295.
Uzza, 259.
Uzziah, 168, 259.

VALUE of Book of Est., 96.
Vanic, 161.
Variants in accentuation, 9.
Variants in the consonantal text, 7.
Variants of vocalization, 9.
Vashti, 48, 55, 65–67, 72 $f.$, 77, 79, 85, 88–91, 93, 108; prevents building of Temple, 122; her wedding, 136; makes a feast for the women, 142; form in the Vrss., 147; stripped Heb. maidens, 147; summoned by Xerxes, 148; one of the four beautiful women, 149, 171; refuses to come to the King, 150; tried by the council, 153; denounced by Daniel, 154; by M^{e}mûkhān, 155; remembered by King, 163; put to death, 163; a successor sought, 164; superseded by Esther, 184; reason for her death, 231.
Veiling of women, 72, 149.
Vengeance upon enemies, 276, 287.
Venus, 88, 170.
Verd-antique, 145.
Verse numbers, 12.
Versions of Esther, v, xi; see Greek, Hesychian, Jerome, Josephus, Lucian, Old Latin, Midrashes, Origen, Peshiṭto, Talmud, Targums.
Vessels, 140.
Villagers, 292.
Vinalia, 83.
Violet, 138, 144, 279.
Virgin Mary, 56, 108.
Virgins, 164 $f.$, 173, 186; see Girls, Maidens.
Visions, 241.
Viziers, 151–160, 163, 195.

WAILING, 95.
Walled cities, 291 $f.$, 295.
Wayzāthā, 7, 71, 194, 231, 284, 288.
Wealth, 268; of the Persian King, 129.
Wedding-feast, 184.

Wedding-gift, 179.
Weeping, 215, 269.
Westerns, 15.
White, 279.
Wife, 155, 161, 265 f.
Wife of Mordecai, 171, 176.
Wine, 122, 141, 143, 147, 149, 189, 211, 229, 236, 256, 262.
Wise men, 151, 255, 300.
Women, 142 f., 147, 155, 158, 189, 204, 274, 295.
Wonders, 306.
Wool, 279.
World to come, 226.
Writing, 270, 296 f., 302.

XERXES I, 52–55, 64 f., 71, 73, 96; personal history, 121; description of $⛛^2$, 122; extent of his empire, 123; beginning of his reign, 124, 126; legend of his throne, 125; his conquest of Egypt, 126; his first banquet, 126-131; his wealth, 129; his second banquet, 135; dispute with the kings, 147; takes counsel concerning Vashti, 151; follows the advice of his viziers, 160; remembers Vashti, 163; consults pages, 164; gathers maidens, 172; receives them in the palace, 178; makes Esther queen, 181–186; assassinated by servants, 190; gives Jews to Haman, 206; issues edict, 208; receives Esther, 232; grants her request, 235; offers a second petition, 236; is reminded of Mordecai, 244; commands Haman to reward Mordecai, 247; sentences Haman to death, 262; issues a new edict, 270; grants second slaughter, 286; imposes tribute, 303.
Xerxes II, 121, 124.

YAHWEH, 8, 95; anagram of name, 235.
Yale University, viii.
Yim, 79.

ZABDI, 168.
Zagmuk, 91–93.
Zebadiah, 168, 259.
Zechariah, 208.
Zeresh, 70, 89, 240, 238 f., 255, 265, 288.
Zeror, 168, 259.
Zerubbabel, 75, 169.
Zethar, 68, 148.
Zibdi, 259.
Zoganes, 93.

IV. INDEX OF BIBLICAL PASSAGES.

Genesis 2^{13}, 132; 2^{16}, 219; 4^3, 180; 8^1, 165; $10^{6\text{f.}}$, 132; $10^{8\text{-}12}$, 132; 11^7, 285; 12^{20}, 219; 13^{16}, 285; 14, 133; 14^1, 121; $14^{22\text{f.}}$, 284; 18^5, 226; 18^6, 235; 18^{11}, 178; 19^{13}, 148; 19^{27}, 148; 20^3, 155; 21^{16}, 271; 23^7, 196, 281; $23^{12\text{f.}}$, 281; 25^{24}, 180; 27^{29}, 196; 28^6, 219; 28^{12}, 215; 29^{21}, 180; 31^{35}, 178; 33^2, 154; 33^3, 196 f., 197, 198; 35^5, 280; 36^{26}, 78; 37^{22}, 190; 37^{29}, 214; 37^{34}, 214; 38^{28}, 154; 39^4, 267; $41^{38\text{-}44}$, 249; 41^{42}, 206; 41^{43}, 248; 43^{14}, 226; 44^1, 267; 44^4, 267; 44^{29}, 256; 44^{34}, 270; 45^7, 224; 46^{27}, 169; 50^3, 180; 50^{20}, 224.

Exodus 1^1, 131; 2^{16}, 132; 2^{21}, 132; 5^6, 281; 6^{13}, 223; 11^2, 157; 12, 226; 15^{16}, 280; 17^8, 73, 194; 17^{14}, 302; 17^{16}, 256; 20^{26}, 285; 26^{32}, 139; 26^{37}, 139; 27^{10}, 139; 27^{11}, 139; 27^{17}, 139; 28^2, 135; 28^{40}, 135; $30^{11\text{-}13}$, 205; 36^{36}, 139; 36^{38}, 139.

Leviticus 1^1, 131; 4^{27}, 281; 5^8, 154; 12^6, 143; 17^{14}, 219; 20^2, 281; 20^4, 281; $21^{13\text{f.}}$, 164; $23^{27\text{ff.}}$, 215.

Numbers 1^1, 131; 2^9, 154; 2^{32}, 205; 5^{23}, 302; 6^{21}, 223; 8^{22}, 219; 10^9, 278; 12^1, 132; 14^9, 281; 22^{26}, 226; 24^7, 72–73, 194; 24^{20}, 256; 26^{51}, 74.

Deuteronomy 3^5, 291, 292; $4^{5\text{-}8}$, 203; 4^{10}, 285; 4^{40}, 285; 6^3, 285; 11^{25}, 280; 22^{23}, 166; 24^4, 155; 25^{17}, 194; $25^{17\text{-}19}$, 256; 26^{13}, 199; 28^{10}, 282; 29^{14}, 207.

Joshua 1^1, 131; 4^{24}, 282; 5^6, 135; 6^{27}, 285; 9^9, 285; 10^8, 283; 10^{10}, 285; 10^{13}, 233; 10^{17}, 143; 15^{18}, 233; 21^{10}, 154; 21^{44}, 283; 21^{45}, 252; 23^9, 283.

Judges 1^1, 131; 2^{19}, 252; 7^4, 262; 9^{35}, 233; 11^{39}, 180; 16^5, 251; 21^{12}, 166.

INDEX

1 Samuel 1¹, 131; 1⁴ᶠ·, 174; 1⁷, 159; 2¹⁸, 148; 4¹², 214; 5¹⁰, 133; 9¹, 167, 172; 9⁴, 172; 14³⁹, 207; 14⁵¹, 167; 15, 70, 167, 256; 15⁷ᶠ·, 194; 15⁸, 72, 73; 15⁹, 194; 15²⁸, 157; 17¹², 121; 18⁴, 248; 18³⁰, 159; 20⁷, 263; 20⁹, 263; 23²³, 207; 24⁷, 190; 24⁹, 196; 24¹¹, 159, 190; 25⁸, 281; 25¹⁷, 263; 25²⁴, 263; 25³⁰, 267; 25³⁶, 237; 28¹⁷, 157; 31¹⁰, 287.

2 Samuel 1¹, 131; 1², 214; 1⁸ᶠᶠ·, 256; 12³, 171; 12¹⁶⁻²³, 225; 13¹⁹, 214; 14²⁴, 153; 14²⁶, 180; 14³², 153; 15³⁰, 255; 15³², 214; 16⁵ᶠᶠ·, 167; 20¹, 172; 21¹, 121; 23¹⁰, 285; 24⁴, 127; 24¹⁷, 285.

1 Kings 1¹, 131; 1², 164; 1²⁻⁴, 164; 1³³, 248; 2⁸, 167; 2³³, 296; 2³⁶⁻⁴⁰, 167; 2⁴³, 219; 5⁷, 154; 5⁸, 273, 277; 5¹⁵, 127; 7², 139; 7³, 139; 7⁵, 139; 7¹⁵, 139; 8⁵³, 282; 8⁶⁰, 282; 9⁵, 133; 10¹³, 141; 10²¹, 121; 11⁴¹, 304; 13⁸, 267; 13³³, 251; 14¹⁹, 192, 304; 14²⁸, 159; 14²⁹, 304; 15⁷, 192; 15²⁰, 127; 15²³, 303; 15²⁷, 190; 16⁹, 190; 18²⁵, 154; 20¹², 257; 20¹⁴, 133; 20¹⁵, 133; 20¹⁷, 133; 20¹⁹, 133; 20²³, 127; 20³¹ᶠ·, 214; 21⁶, 251; 21²⁷, 214; 21²⁷⁻²⁹, 225; 21²⁹, 121; 22³, 127; 22⁹, 235.

2 Kings 1¹, 131; 4⁶, 143; 4⁸, 159; 4²⁷, 263; 6³⁰, 214; 8¹⁵, 190; 9¹⁴, 190; 11¹, 207; 15¹⁰, 190; 15²⁵, 190; 19¹ᶠ·, 214; 19⁵, 127; 19⁹, 133; 19³⁷, 190; 21²², 190; 24⁶⁻¹⁷, 168; 24¹², 176; 25²², 127.

Isaiah 2¹⁶, 146; 3¹⁸, 135; 12⁶, 281; 18¹, 133; 20³, 132; 28¹⁹, 159; 29²², 144; 37³, 133; 44²⁵, 151; 45³, 130; 47¹⁰⁻¹⁵, 151; 52¹, 135; 53⁸, 62; 54¹, 281; 55¹³, 170; 61⁹, 306.

Jeremiah 4³⁰, 160; 6²⁴, 285; 14⁴, 255; 14¹², 160; 16¹⁸, 154; 22¹¹, 132; 24¹, 168; 25¹², 143; 27²⁰, 168; 28⁴, 168; 29², 168; 29¹⁰, 128; 31²⁰, 159; 32¹¹, 213; 32¹⁴, 213; 32⁴², 267; 36²⁴, 127; 40⁵, 185; 40⁷, 127; 40¹³, 127; 49¹⁹ᶠ·, 160; 49²⁸, 172; 49³⁴⁻³⁹, 134; 50¹¹, 160; 50³⁵, 151.

Ezekiel 1¹, 131; 5², 143; 5¹³, 263; 8²⁵, 136; 13⁶, 294; 16¹⁷, 135; 16³⁹, 135; 19⁸, 133; 23²⁶, 135; 27¹⁶, 62; 27¹⁸, 141; 27³⁰, 214; 29¹⁰, 133; 31¹³, 282; 37¹¹, 62; 38, 70; 38–39, 194; 40¹⁷ᶠ·, 145.

Hosea 2¹⁶, 155; 12⁵, 219; 13¹⁵, 160.

Joel 1¹⁴, 225.
Amos 5¹¹, 185; 6⁴, 139 ƒ·; 9⁷, 132.
Obadiah 1¹⁵, 296.
Jonah 1¹, 120; 3⁵⁻⁹, 226; 3⁶, 214.
Micah 1¹³, 273, 277.
Nahum 1¹⁰, 160; 2³, 160.
Habakkuk 3⁷, 132.
Zephaniah 1¹², 225; 3¹⁰, 133; 3²⁰, 282.
Zechariah 1¹⁰, 170; 7³⁻⁵, 215; 8⁶, 160; 8¹³, 281; 8¹⁹, 215; 9¹⁰, 306.
Psalms 7¹⁷ (¹⁶), 296; 22, 104; 33⁷, 63; 34⁶, 267; 37²⁴, 160; 49¹⁹ᶠ·, 160; 85⁹, 306; 88⁶, 62; 97¹¹, 280; 105³⁸, 280; 119²⁸, 294; 119¹⁰⁶, 294; 137³, 160; 139¹², 281.
Proverbs 12⁷, 198; 20²¹, 62.
Job 1⁴, 257; 6²⁰, 267; 8¹⁵, 267; 9¹⁵, 219; 19¹⁶, 219; 19²³, 302; 22²⁸, 280; 30²⁶, 280; 39²⁵, 159.
Canticles 5¹⁴, 63, 145; 5¹⁵, 63, 145; 6¹¹, 144.
Ruth 1¹, 131; 1⁵, 224; 3¹⁰, 243; 4⁷, 294.
Lamentations 1¹, 133; 3⁵⁴, 62.
Ecclesiastes 2⁸, 63, 133; 2¹⁵, 63; 2¹⁹, 63; 2²⁶, 63; 3¹, 63; 3¹¹, 166; 3¹⁵, 166; 3²², 223; 5¹, 62, 177; 5⁷, 133; 6⁶, 62, 261; 7⁷, 166; 7⁹, 62, 177; 7¹⁶, 63; 8⁹, 63; 8¹⁰, 63; 10¹⁰, 63; 10¹⁷, 146; 11⁶, 63, 271; 12², 63; 12⁹, 63; 12¹², 251.
Esther (except passages discussed in regular order in the commentary).
Esther 1¹, 7, 19, 22, 25, 27, 33, 38, 48, 52, 54, 59, 61, 63, 72 ƒ·, 119, 208, 240, 273; 1² 19, 22, 27, 54, 59, 62 ƒ·, 211, 231, 242, 283; 1³ᶠ·, 19, 25, 41, 59, 64 ƒ·, 208, 251, 278, 290, 304; 1⁴, 22, 27, 41, 59, 63, 128, 240, 243, 246, 280; 1⁵, 22, 25, 27, 38, 48, 59, 62, 126, 179, 225, 259; 1⁶, 6, 25, 27, 38, 62 ƒ·, 65, 279; 1⁷, 22, 25, 27, 159, 177, 192; 1⁸, 22, 26 ƒ·, 62 ƒ·, 212, 287; 1⁹, 38, 48, 66, 72, 159, 224 ƒ·, 231; 1¹⁰, 22, 26 ƒ·, 38, 48, 66–68, 165, 181, 237, 257, 264; 1¹¹, 19, 22, 26, 63, 66, 89, 184, 279, 281; 1¹², 22, 26, 38, 66, 73; 1¹³, 26 ƒ·, 38, 48, 66, 73, 238; 1¹⁴, 19, 22, 26 ƒ·, 52, 61, 65 ƒ·, 68, 194, 304; 1¹⁵, 27, 59, 63, 66, 192, 212, 247, 251, 258; 1¹⁶, 22, 38, 48, 54, 66, 73; 1¹⁷, 59, 62, 66, 159, 223; 1¹⁸, 22, 26 ƒ·, 62; 1¹⁹, 19, 26 ƒ·, 38, 43, 52, 59, 66, 72, 225, 236,

269, 271, 278, 286, 298, 304;
1^{20}, 8, 38, 135, 246; 1^{21}, 48, 177,
240, 265; 1^{22}, 26 f., 38, 59, 63, 72,
147, 208, 269, 273, 298; 2^1, 19, 22,
38, 48, 62, 66, 73, 266; 2^2, 45, 72,
245; 2^3, 26 f., 38, 66, 69, 126, 155,
171, 174, 180, 186, 251; 2^4, 26 f.,
38, 66, 72, 177, 240, 265; 2^5, 22,
48, 63, 66, 73, 104, 126, 147, 176,
188, 191, 195, 239, 255; 2$^{6f.}$, 19,
23, 27, 38, 51, 52; 2^7, 23, 26 f., 38,
69, 93, 224; 2^8, 23, 26 f., 38, 66,
72, 96, 126, 251, 283; 2^9, 19, 23,
26 f., 38, 45, 48, 59, 62 f., 148,
180, 226, 260, 278, 290; 2^{10}, 19,
26, 38, 72 f., 96, 147, 199, 218 f.,
269, 278; 2^{11}, 7, 26, 72 f., 165,
175, 188, 199, 214, 216, 239, 250;
2^{12}, 26 f., 48, 73, 165, 172, 180,
212, 240; 2^{13}, 26 f., 165, 174, 231;
2^{14}, 15, 26 f., 66, 69, 247, 251, 258;
2^{16}, 27, 43, 45, 65, 71, 73, 143, 159,
172, 186, 200, 225, 231, 271; 2^{17}, 19,
23, 59, 63, 66, 72, 151, 177, 233,
279, 281; 2^{18}, 26 f., 38, 45, 63, 136,
141; 2^{19}, 26, 38, 49, 167, 181, 195;
214, 217, 237, 239, 250, 254;
2^{20}, 19, 45, 59, 63, 73, 96, 216,
269; 2^{21}, 19, 23, 26 f., 43, 54, 66,
176, 188, 237, 239, 245, 250, 272,
282; 2^{22}, 264; 2^{23}, 58 f., 74, 162,
193, 245 f., 250, 302, 304; 3$^{1f.}$, 19,
23, 38, 43, 45, 48 f., 66, 69, 72 f.,
193, 197, 206, 238, 256, 260, 269,
295, 304; 3^2, 19, 26, 38, 49, 62,
65, 73, 96, 127, 167, 188, 193,
237–239, 250; 3^3, 23, 26 f., 38,
188, 197, 239; 3^4, 27, 41, 73, 175,
191, 196, 255, 278; 3^5, 7, 26, 43;
3^6, 26 f., 49, 73 f., 191, 199, 255,
272, 282; 3^7, 23, 26 f., 38, 55,
58 f., 64 f., 71, 73 f., 84, 86, 91 f.,
208, 243, 255; 3^8, 23, 26 f., 38, 49,
58 f., 61, 63, 74, 85, 155, 163, 175,
177, 192 212; 3^9, 19, 23, 38, 59
60, 62 f., 74, 157, 159, 209, 217,
219, 236, 238, 240, 251, 268, 271,
283; 3^{10}, 26, 59, 194, 260, 268, 295;
3^{11}, 23, 26, 73, 250, 265, 268;
3^{12}, 38, 54, 62, 64, 72, 124, 160,
226, 240, 269, 272, 273, 283, 298;
3^{13}, 33, 59, 65, 162, 201, 206 f.,
269, 272–275, 278, 282 f.; 3^{14}, 27,
38, 40, 219, 251, 276; 3^{15}, 23, 26 f.,
38, 59, 63, 74, 126, 208, 215, 256 f.,
273, 278, 280, 287; 4^1, 19, 23, 26,

38, 49, 63, 73, 147, 215, 280; 4^2, 23,
38, 65, 72, 176, 188; 4^3, 26 f., 38,
59, 63, 95, 215, 225 f., 243, 260,
280, 282, 284, 301; 4^4, 26, 38,
40 f., 49, 59, 63, 239, 298; 4^5, 19,
26, 38, 41, 66, 70, 216, 219, 223;
4^6, 41, 70, 188, 280; 4^7, 41, 52, 63,
213, 256, 271; 4^8, 27, 38, 41, 62,
258; 4^9, 41, 70, 258; 4^{10}, 38, 49, 70,
219; 4^{11}, 23, 26 f., 59, 61, 63, 72,
127, 189, 219, 231, 233, 247 f.,
269, 278; 4^{12}, 19, 27, 38; 4^{13}, 26 f.,
59, 62, 126, 223, 246; 4^{14}, 26 f., 38,
63, 94 f., 226, 260, 282 f.; 4^{15}, 26 f.,
38; 4^{16}, 7, 26 f., 40 f., 63, 73, 95 f.,
181, 282, 284; 4^{17}, 7, 23, 33, 40 f.;
5^1, 7, 19, 23, 26 f., 33, 49, 63, 143,
147, 159, 194, 223, 225 f., 263,
269, 283; 5^2, 27, 44, 63, 177, 223;
5^3, 19, 62, 257, 286; 5^4, 8, 38, 43,
74, 149, 157, 159, 236, 257 f., 269;
5^5, 27, 41, 50, 252, 265; 5^6, 27 f.,
62, 233, 257, 262, 286; 5^7, 6, 26 f.,
62, 74, 234, 248; 5^8, 23, 38, 62 f.,
157, 159, 257 f., 269; 5^9, 19, 26,
38, 41, 50, 63, 188, 239, 250;
5^{10}, 26, 38, 59, 66, 70, 88 f., 239,
255–257; 5^{11}, 7, 26 f., 38, 59, 127,
268, 304, 305; 5^{12}, 38, 257; 5^{13}, 8,
15, 163, 175, 188, 191, 237, 250,
255; 5^{14}, 19, 23, 28, 38, 59, 65, 70,
74, 88, 177, 191, 247, 255, 257,
264; 6^1, 19, 23, 26, 28, 38, 44, 48,
50, 58, 74, 76, 162, 192 f., 223,
250, 282, 302, 304; 6^2, 26, 27 f.,
38, 53, 264, 272, 278; 6^3, 26, 28,
38, 41, 43, 59, 135, 191, 250;
6^4, 26, 38, 43, 50, 74, 191, 219,
223; 6^5, 27; 6^6, 7, 26 f., 63, 135,
246, 252; 6^7, 27; 6^8, 26–28, 38, 63,
65, 75, 151, 159, 190 f., 225, 279,
281; 6^9, 27 f., 135, 270, 280, 285;
6^{10}, 23, 28, 73, 188, 191, 235, 237,
239, 254, 265; 6^{11}, 7, 23, 26 f., 38,
50, 126, 191, 279; 6^{12}, 63, 188,
213, 237, 239, 264; 6^{13}, 23, 26 f.,
59, 70, 73, 217, 238, 271; 7^1, 27,
50, 58, 211; 7^2, 27 f., 38, 62, 181,
233, 236 f., 262, 286; 7^3, 62 f., 73,
157, 159, 234, 236, 269; 7^4, 26, 28,
38, 62 f., 260, 269; 7^5, 27 f., 38,
265; 7^6, 19, 26, 59, 62, 73, 74;
7^7, 8, 26, 28, 50, 62, 137, 144, 219,
236, 283; 7^8, 26, 28, 38, 58, 62,
74, 93, 96, 126, 255, 269, 296;
7^9, 23, 27, 38, 59, 66, 157, 191,

268, 296; 7^{10}, 38, 44, 59, 191, 270, 287, 296; 7^{12}, 33; 8^1, 28, 50, 59, 260, 274, 279, 297; 8^2, 7, 28, 38, 73, 206, 304; 8^3, 26 $f.$, 38, 50, 59, 219, 263, 295, 296; 8^4, 26-28, 38, 63, 223; 8^5, 7, 26-28, 38, 59, 63, 157, 162, 236; 8^6, 7, 28, 38, 62, 299; 8^7, 26-28, 38, 44, 191, 239, 287; 8^8, 26, 28, 38, 43, 61, 72, 157, 206, 208, 269, 285, 298; 8^9, 7, 26-28, 54, 72, 96, 123 $f.$, 132, 160, 206, 208, 212, 223, 282, 298, 304; 8^{10}, 26-28, 54, 65, 162, 208 $f.$, 269; 8^{11}, 7, 26 $f.$, 59, 63, 74, 96, 206, 209, 276, 282 $f.$, 286, 289; 8^{12}, 23, 26 $f.$, 38, 44, 59; 8^{13}, 27, 38, 41, 162, 212, 274, 291; 8^{14}, 28, 26 $f.$, 62 $f.$, 126, 177, 208, 213, 256, 260, 273; 8^{15}, 19, 26-28, 50, 62 $f.$, 126, 138, 159, 196, 225, 248, 251, 254, 304; 8^{16}, 27, 62, 135; 8^{17}, 26, 28, 59, 61, 63, 95, 225, 260, 282-284, 289 $f.$, 293, 297; 9^1, 26, 28, 38, 50, 59, 63, 225, 260, 274, 293; 9^2, 7, 26 $f.$, 74, 96, 272, 280, 289; 9^3, 26, 28, 60, 124, 212, 283, 304; 9^4, 26-28, 38, 147; 9^5, 27 $f.$, 62, 289; 9^6, 26 $f.$, 126, 290; 9^7, 6, 66; 9^8, 70 $f.$; 9^9, 7, 71, 138; 9^{10}, 26, 59, 62, 238, 260, 268, 289; 9^{11}, 23, 27, 38, 51, 126; 9^{12}, 7, 26-28, 59, 62, 126, 233, 237; $9^{13f.}$, 74, 96, 157, 191; 9^{14}, 7, 19, 59, 62, 191, 223, 284, 296; 9^{15}, 27, 38, 41, 59, 62, 206, 225, 289; 9^{16}, 7, 26-28, 51, 59, 62 $f.$, 274, 283; 9^{17}, 26, 38, 55, 59, 80, 84, 290, 293; 9^{18}, 7, 26-28, 59, 290; 9^{19}, 27 $f.$, 58 $f.$, 63, 79, 95, 98, 174, 281, 297; 9^{20}, 7, 26-28, 44, 48, 51 $f.$, 55, 57-61, 74, 162, 269, 272, 292, 297, 300, 301; 9^{22}, 7, 59, 60, 63, 79, 95, 174, 215, 281, 290, 301; 9^{23}, 7, 26, 51, 59, 298, 301; 9^{24}, 8, 23, 26 $f.$, 38, 41, 58-60, 91, 260, 298; 9^{25}, 26-28, 58-60, 162, 191, 269, 295, 298; 9^{26}, 26, 28, 51, 55, 59, 60, 63, 74, 84, 225, 260, 302; 9^{27}, 8, 19, 27-32, 38, 59, 60 $f.$; 63, 74, 95, 147, 159, 199, 294, 298, 301; 9^{28}, 26-28, 59 $f.$; 9^{29}, 7, 26, 28, 38, 51, 59 $f.$, 63, 66, 138, 181; 9^{30}, 26 $f.$, 41, 54, 56, 59, 162, 269; 9^{31}, 27 $f.$, 59 $f.$, 63, 147, 215, 300; 9^{32}, 28, 57, 59-61, 63, 162, 192; 10^1, 28, 41, 48, 51, 54, 59 $f.$, 186; 10^2, 27,

42, 57-60, 63, 128, 162, 192, 217, 246, 292, 302; 10^3, 23, 52, 59 $f.$, 63, 66, 72.

Daniel 1^3, 135; 1^5, 174, 236; 1^8, 236; 2^{10}, 177; 2^{27}, 151; 2^{46}, 177; 2^{48}, 75; 3^1, 123; 5^2, 141; 5^{11}, 75; 5^{15}, 151; 5^{28}, 128; 5^{29}, 75; 5^{30}, 141; 6^2 (^{1}), 123; $6^{3f.}$, 75; 6^9 (^{8}), 72, 128, 157, 159; 6^{13} (^{12}), 128, 157; 6^{16} (^{15}), 128; 6^{24}, 177; 6^{29}, 75; 8^2, 126, 133, 134; 8^{17}, 62, 262; 8^{20}, 128; 8^{24}, 235; 8^{25}, 63; 9^1, 51, 52; 9^3, 63, 214, 225; 9^7, 294; 11^{14}, 63; 11^{17}, 63; 11^{24}, 62; 133; 11^{45}, 144; 12^1, 274.

Ezra 1^1, 131; 2^1, 124, 133; $2^{2ff.}$, 169; 2^{63}, 224; 3^3, 282; 4^1, 281; 4^{5-7}, 52; 4^6, 122; 4^{11}, 212; 4^{15}, 192; 4^{23}, 212; 4^{24}, 52; 5^6, 212; $6^{1f.}$, 134; 7^5, 62; 7^{11}, 212; 7^{14}, 153; 8^{23}, 62, 219; 8^{25}, 143; 8^{36}, 146; $9^{1f.}$, 282; 9^{11}, 282; 10^2, 282.

Nehemiah 1^1, 126, 134; 1^3, 133; 2^1, 62, 219; 2^5, 157; 2^6, 63, 149; 2^8, 134, 141; 3^{30}, 181; 5^5, 266; 5^{15}, 63; 7^2, 134; 7^5, 124; $7^{7ff.}$, 169; 7^{65}, 225; 8^1, 62, 131; 8^{10}, 174; 8^{12}, 174; 9^{15}, 62, 246; 9^{30}, 282; 10^{29}, 282; $10^{31f.}$, 282; 11^3, 124; 12^{44}, 63; $13^{22ff.}$, 161.

1 Chronicles $3^{16f.}$, 168; 4^{21}, 62; $4^{42f.}$, 194; 5^{25}, 282; 8^{33}, 167; 9^{22}, 147; 12^{32}, 151; 13^4, 62; 15^{16}, 62; 21^1, 63; 21^{18}, 62; 21^{30}, 62, 262; 22^1, 62, 63, 246; 22^{10}, 133; $22^{12f.}$, 219; 28^5, 133; 29^1, 134; 29^2, 139, 145; 29^6, 207; 29^{10}, 134; 29^{17}, 136.

2 Chronicles 1^1, 131; 1^{18}, 246; 2^{13}, 246; 3^{14}, 62; 5^{12}, 62; 6^{33}, 282; 7^{18}, 133; 12^{11}, 159; 12^{32}, 152; 15^9, 282; $14^{9ff.}$, 132; 14^{13}, 62; 17^{12}, 285; 18^8, 235; 20^{23}, 63; 21^{16}, 132; 24^{20}, 199; 25^{26}, 304; 26^{18}, 63; 26^{20}, 62, 63, 213; 26^{21}, 62; 28^7, 304; 28^{26}, 304; 29^{21}, 62; 29^{27}, 62; 29^{30}, 62; 31^4, 62; 31^{11}, 62; 32^{19}, 282; 32^{32}, 304; 33^{16}, 62; 34^{32}, 136; 35^{21}, 62, 177.

1 Esdras 3^2, 123.

Tobit $1^{21\,22}$, 75; $1^{2\cdot}$, 304; 2^{10}, 75; 11^{18}, 75; $1^{21f.}$, 75; 14^{10}, 75.

Rest of Esther, A^{1-17}, 119; A^1, 92, 172; A^{2-12}, 43; $A^{11f.}$, 192; A^{12}, 192; A^{12-17}, 41; A^{13}, 43, 193; A^{14}, 193; A^{15}, 193; A^{16}, 43, 191, 193; A^{17}, 43, 195; B^1, 123; C^{1-30}, 227; $C^{4f.}$, 175; C^{5-7}, 45; C^7, 196; C^{12-30}, 173; C^{23}, 43; C^{26-27}, 43; C^{27-29}, 45;

D, 33; D$^{1-16}$, 230; E, 33; E^1, 123; E^{10}, 43; E^{12}, 44; E^{14}, 53; E^{17}, 43; E^{18}, 191; E^{22}, 44; F$^{1-11}$, 33, 306; F^{11}, 30; 10, 90; 10^4–11^5, 33, 306; 11, 90; 11^1, 30; 11^2, 33, 90, 119; 11^3, 43; 12^1, 43; 12^2, 43; 12^5, 43; 12^7, 43; 13$^{1-7}$, 33; 13^{8}–14^{19}, 33, 227; 13$^{12-14}$, 45; 13^{14}, 196; 14^{15}, 43; 14^{16}, 43, 45; 14^{17}, 43; 15$^{4-19}$, 33; 16$^{1-24}$, 33; 16^{10}, 43; 16^{14}, 53; 16^{17}, 43; 16^{18}, 44; 16^{22}, 44.

Ecclesiasticus 44–49, 61, 66.

1 Maccabees 134; 6^{15}, 206; 7$^{39-50}$, 78; 7^{40}, 78; 7^{45}, 78; 7^{49}, 61, 78, 80; 8^{17}, 223; 10^{38}, 185; 12^1, 223.

2 Maccabees 15$^{20-36}$, 78; 15^{36}, 61, 78, 80, 91.

Matthew 15^2, 98; 18^{10}, 153; 23^{15}, 61; 27^{15}, 185.

Mark 6^{23}, 233; 7^3, 98; 7^5, 98.

Luke 14^{17}, 239, 259.

John 7^{49}, 282; 11$^{49-42}$, 256.

Acts 5^3, 259.

Hebrews, 7$^{9f.}$, 169.